5 0 miles 5 10
10 5 0 kilometres 5 10 15
4 centimetres to 10 kilometres (one grid square)
1 kilometre = 0·6214 mile
1 mile = 1·61 kilometre
AYLESBURY
OXFORD
THAME
PRINCES RISBOROUGH
HIGH WYCOMBE
WENDOVER
TRING
BERKHAMSTED
HEMEL HEMPSTEAD
HARPENDEN
WATFORD
CHESHAM
AMERSHAM
RICKMANSWORTH
CHORLEYWOOD
BEACONSFIELD
GERRARDS CROSS
MARLOW
MAIDENHEAD
SLOUGH
WINDSOR
STAINES
EGHAM
HENLEY-ON-THAMES
READING
WALLINGFORD
ABINGDON
CHILTERN HILLS
CHILTERN HUNDREDS
THE THREE HUNDREDS OF AYLESBURY

Jim D.

COUNTY
STREET ATLAS

BUCKS

Ordnance Survey

COUNTY STREET ATLAS

PHILIP'S

BUCKS

3½ INCHES TO 1 MILE

2nd edition

COUNTY STREET ATLAS
BUCKINGHAMSHIRE

First Edition published 1990
Second Edition published 1991 by

Ordnance Survey
Romsey Road
Maybush
Southampton SO9 4DH

and

George Philip Ltd
59 Grosvenor Street
London W1X 9DA

ISBN 0 540 05660 X (George Philip)
ISBN 0 319 00275 6 (Ordnance Survey)

To the best of the Publishers' knowledge, the information in this atlas was correct at the time of going to press. No responsibility can be accepted for any errors or their consequences.

The representation in this atlas of a road, track or path is no evidence of the existence of a right of way.

Printed in Great Britain by
Butler & Tanner Ltd, Frome and London

CONTENTS

Key to map pages	vi-vii
Administrative boundaries	viii
Street maps	1-213
Index explanation and abbreviations	214
Index of towns, villages and rural localities	215
Index of street names	216-237

KEY TO MAP SYMBOLS

British Rail Station

London Transport Station

Private Railway Station

Bus or Coach Station

Heliport

Police Station
(may not be open 24hrs)

Hospital with Casualty Facilities
(may not be open 24hrs)

Post Office

Place of Worship

Important Building

P Parking

Motorway and Dual Carriageway

Main or through road

A27(T) Road numbers (Dept of Transport)

Gate and obstruction to traffic
(restrictions may not apply at all times and to all vehicles)

Footpath
Bridleway
The representation in this atlas of a road, track or path is no evidence of the existence of a right of way.

120 Adjoining Page Indicator

Amb Sta	Ambulance Station	Liby	Library
Coll	College	Mus	Museum
FB	Foot Bridge	Sch	School
F Sta	Fire Station	TH	Town Hall
LC	Level Crossing		

The large letters and numbers around the edge of the maps form the referencing system.
An explanation of how to use the system for locating the position of street names appears on page **214**.

The small numbers identify the 1 kilometre National Grid lines.

Scale of Maps is 3½ inches to 1 mile (1 : 18103)

0 ¼ ½ ¾ 1 Mile

0 250m 500m 750m 1 Kilometre

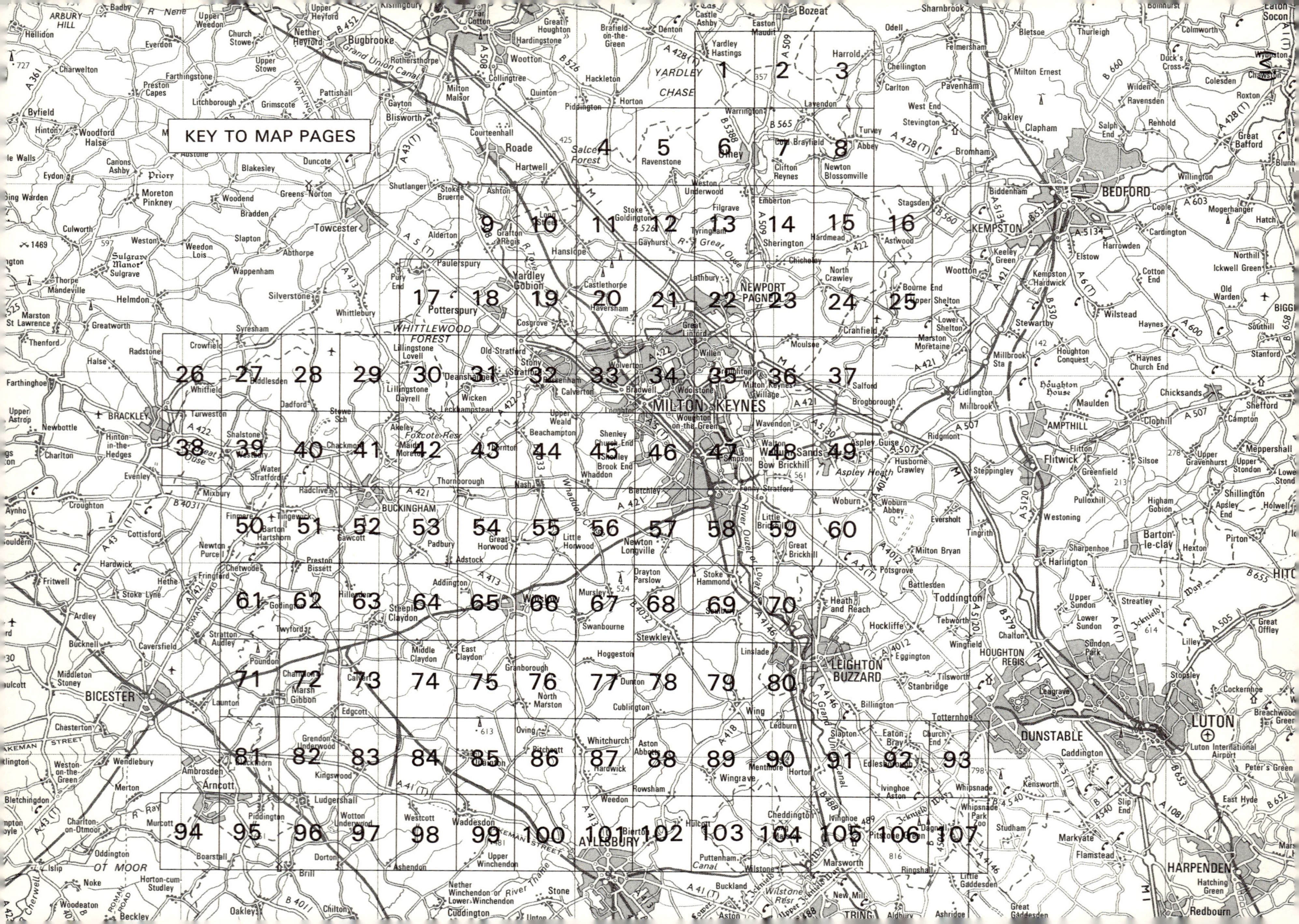
KEY TO MAP PAGES
1 2 3 4 5 6 7 8 9 10 11 12 13 14 15 16 17 18 19 20 21 22 23 24 25 26 27 28 29 30 31 32 33 34 35 36 37 38 39 40 41 42 43 44 45 46 47 48 49 50 51 52 53 54 55 56 57 58 59 60 61 62 63 64 65 66 67 68 69 70 71 72 73 74 75 76 77 78 79 80 81 82 83 84 85 86 87 88 89 90 91 92 93 94 95 96 97 98 99 100 101 102 103 104 105 106 107
BEDFORD
KEMPSTON
MILTON KEYNES
NEWPORT PAGNELL
BUCKINGHAM
BRACKLEY
BICESTER
AYLESBURY
LEIGHTON BUZZARD
DUNSTABLE
HOUGHTON REGIS
LUTON
HARPENDEN
AMPTHILL
TRING
Towcester
Olney
Woburn
Flitwick
Toddington
WHITTLEWOOD FOREST
YARDLEY CHASE
Grand Union Canal
River Ouzel or Lovat
R. Great Ouse
R. Tove
R. Thame
R. Nene
R. Ray
Luton International Airport

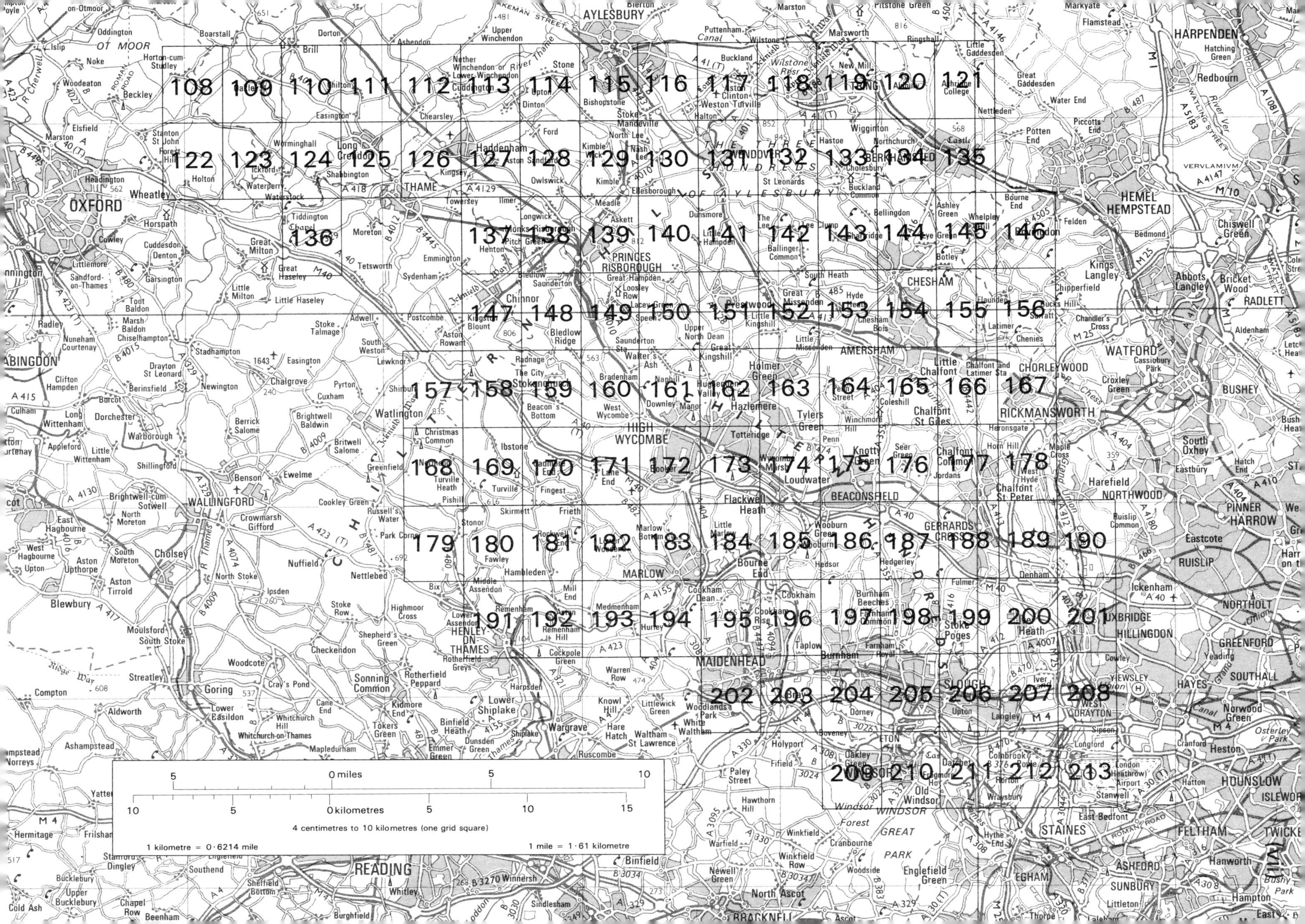
108 109 110 111 112 113 114 115 116 117 118 119 120 121
122 123 124 125 126 127 128 129 130 131 132 133 134 135
136 137 138 139 140 141 142 143 144 145 146
147 148 149 150 151 152 153 154 155 156
157 158 159 160 161 162 163 164 165 166 167
168 169 170 171 172 173 174 175 176 177 178
179 180 181 182 183 184 185 186 187 188 189 190
191 192 193 194 195 196 197 198 199 200 201
202 203 204 205 206 207 208
209 210 211 212 213
AYLESBURY
HARPENDEN
OXFORD
THAME
HEMEL HEMPSTEAD
PRINCES RISBOROUGH
CHESHAM
AMERSHAM
WATFORD
CHORLEYWOOD
RICKMANSWORTH
HIGH WYCOMBE
BEACONSFIELD
NORTHWOOD
WALLINGFORD
MARLOW
GERRARDS CROSS
UXBRIDGE
HILLINGDON
HENLEY-ON-THAMES
MAIDENHEAD
SLOUGH
WEST DRAYTON
READING
STAINES
EGHAM
HOUNSLOW
FELTHAM
BRACKNELL
ABINGDON
RUISLIP
BUSHEY
RADLETT
0 miles 5 10
10 5 0 kilometres 5 10 15
4 centimetres to 10 kilometres (one grid square)
1 kilometre = 0·6214 mile
1 mile = 1·61 kilometre

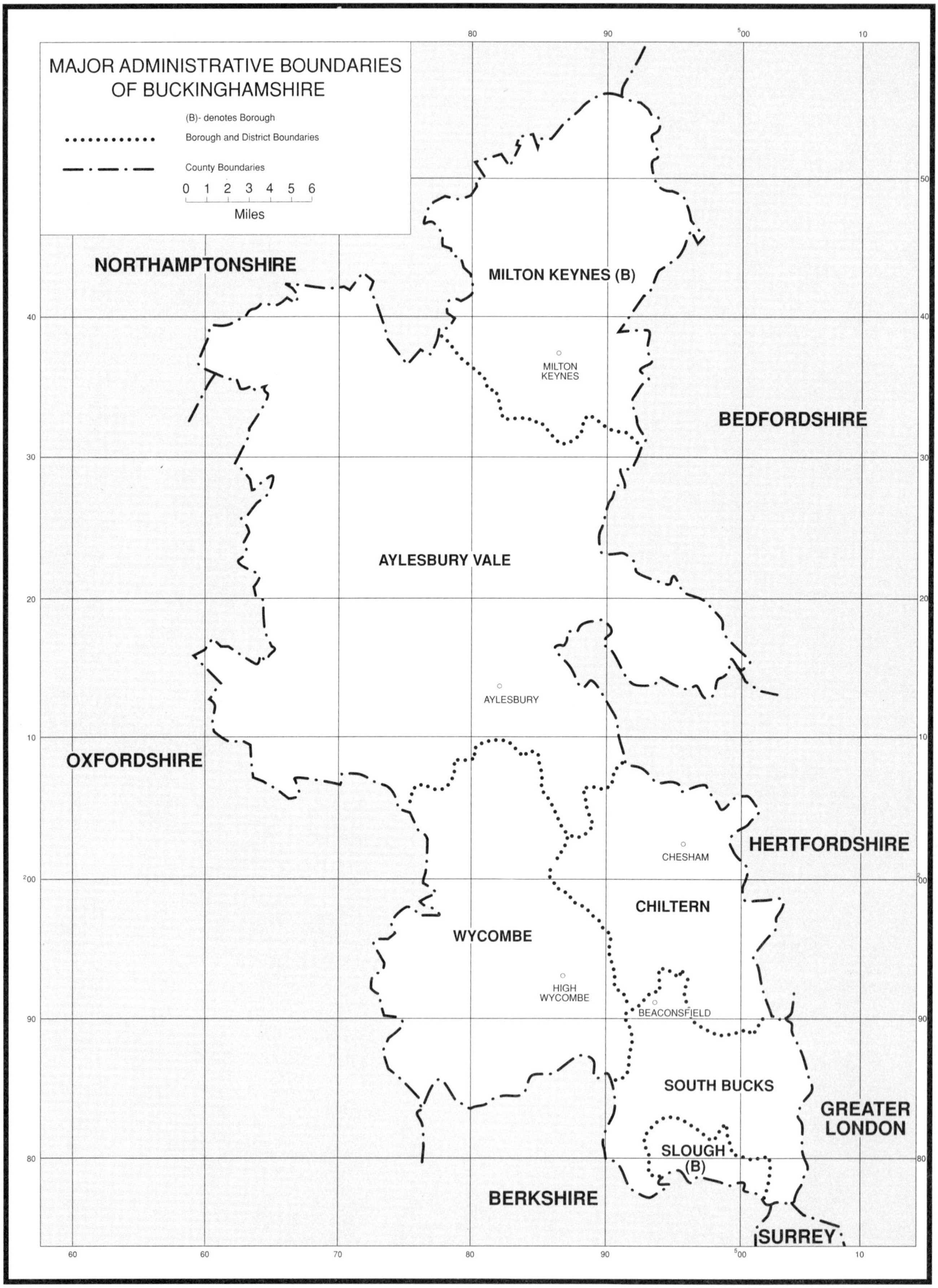
MAJOR ADMINISTRATIVE BOUNDARIES
OF BUCKINGHAMSHIRE
(B)- denotes Borough
Borough and District Boundaries
County Boundaries
0 1 2 3 4 5 6
Miles
NORTHAMPTONSHIRE
MILTON KEYNES (B)
MILTON KEYNES
BEDFORDSHIRE
AYLESBURY VALE
AYLESBURY
OXFORDSHIRE
HERTFORDSHIRE
CHESHAM
CHILTERN
WYCOMBE
HIGH WYCOMBE
BEACONSFIELD
SOUTH BUCKS
GREATER LONDON
SLOUGH (B)
BERKSHIRE
SURREY
80
90
500
10
50
40
30
20
200
60
70

not continued, see key diagram

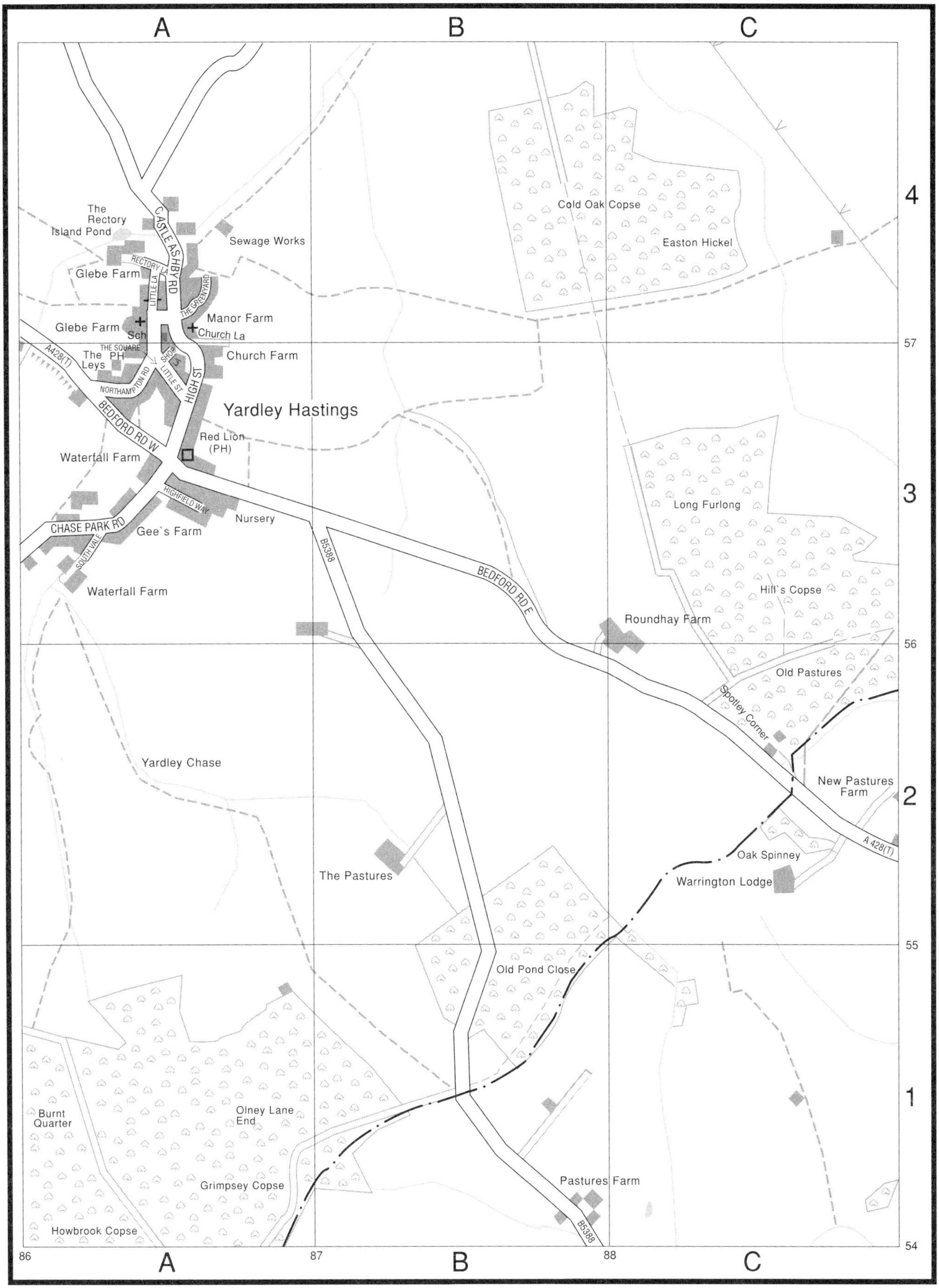

not continued, see key diagram

2

6

not continued, see key diagram

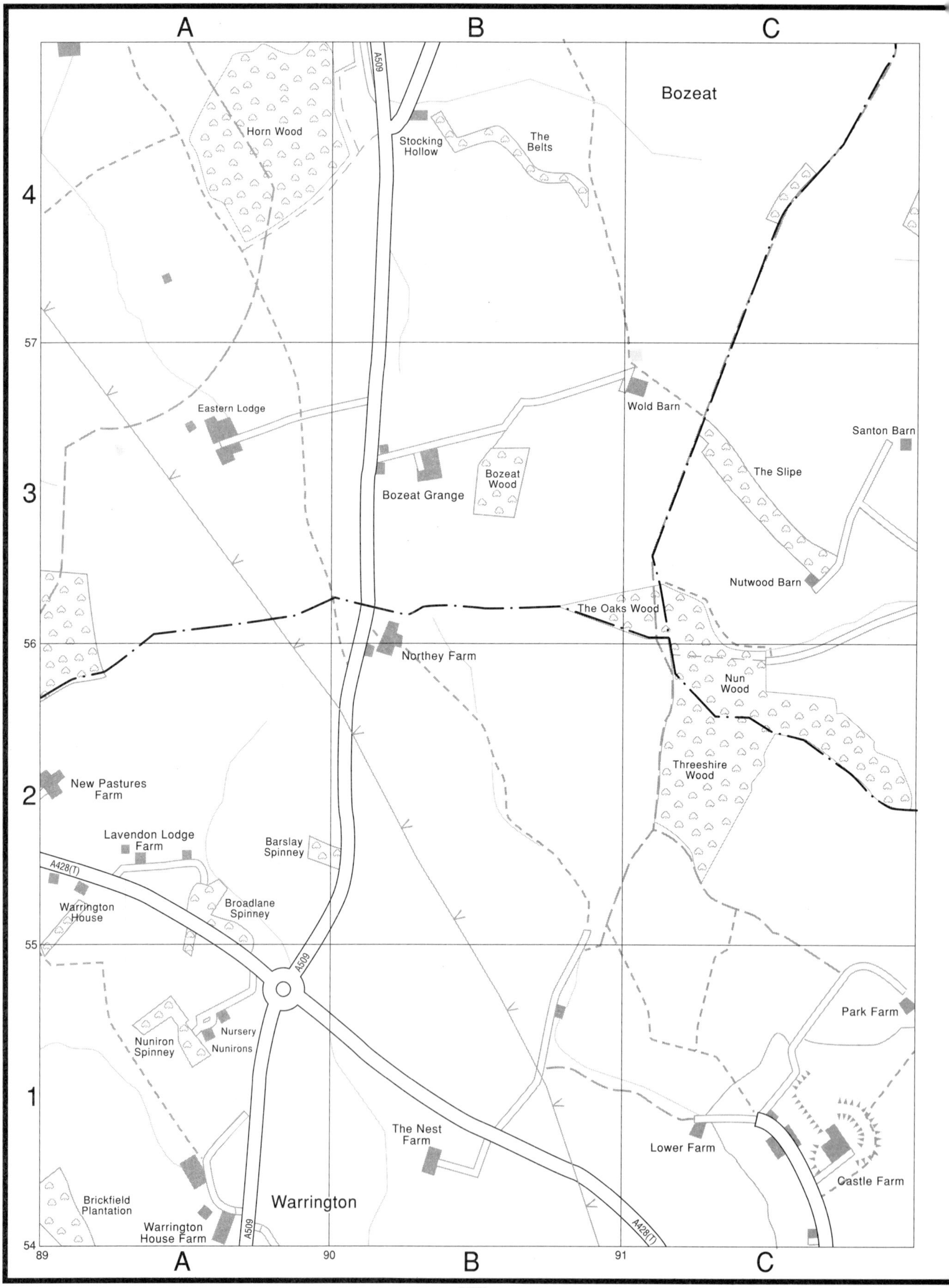

1

7

not continued, see key diagram

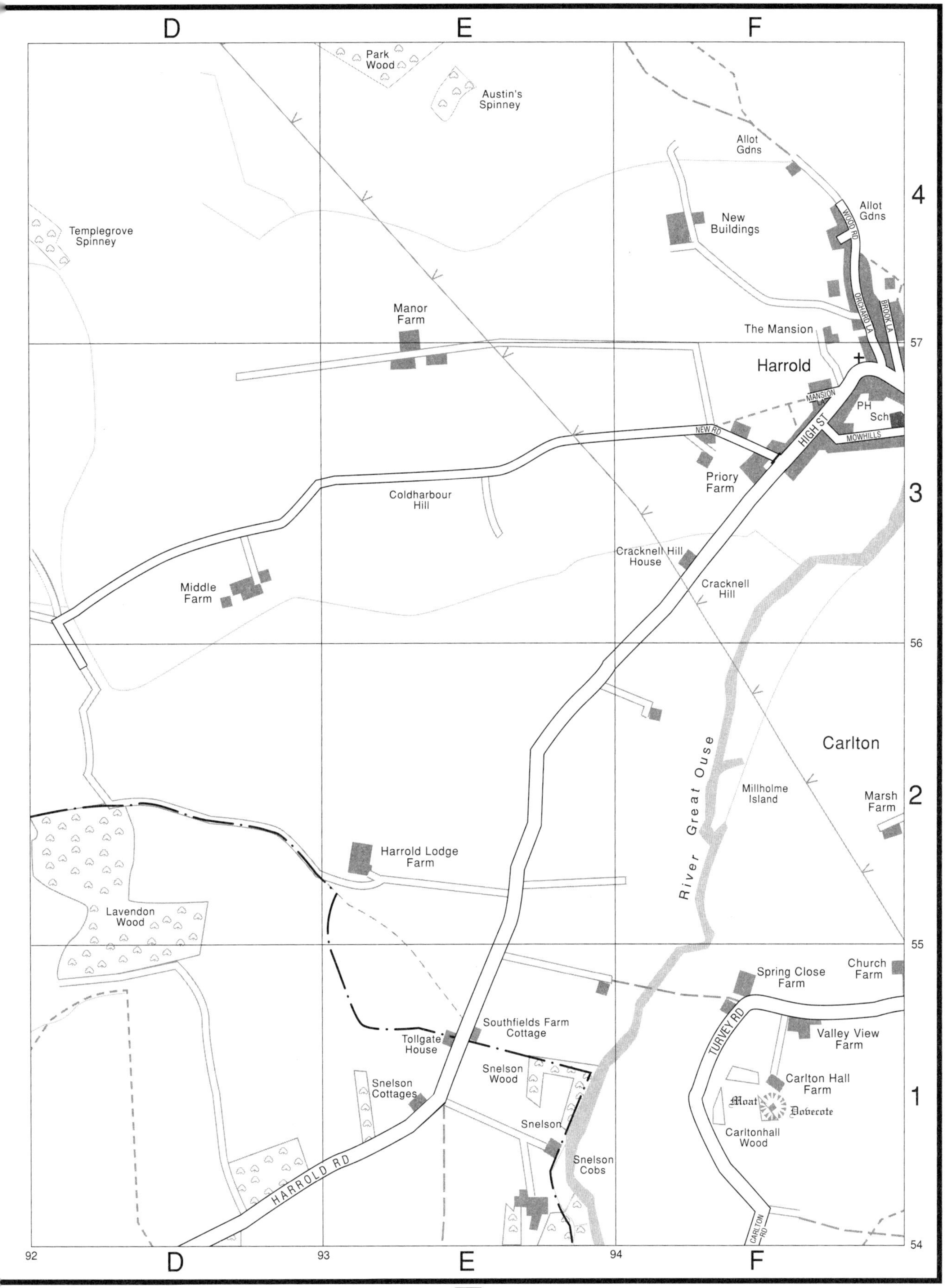

not continued, see key diagram

8

not continued, see key diagram

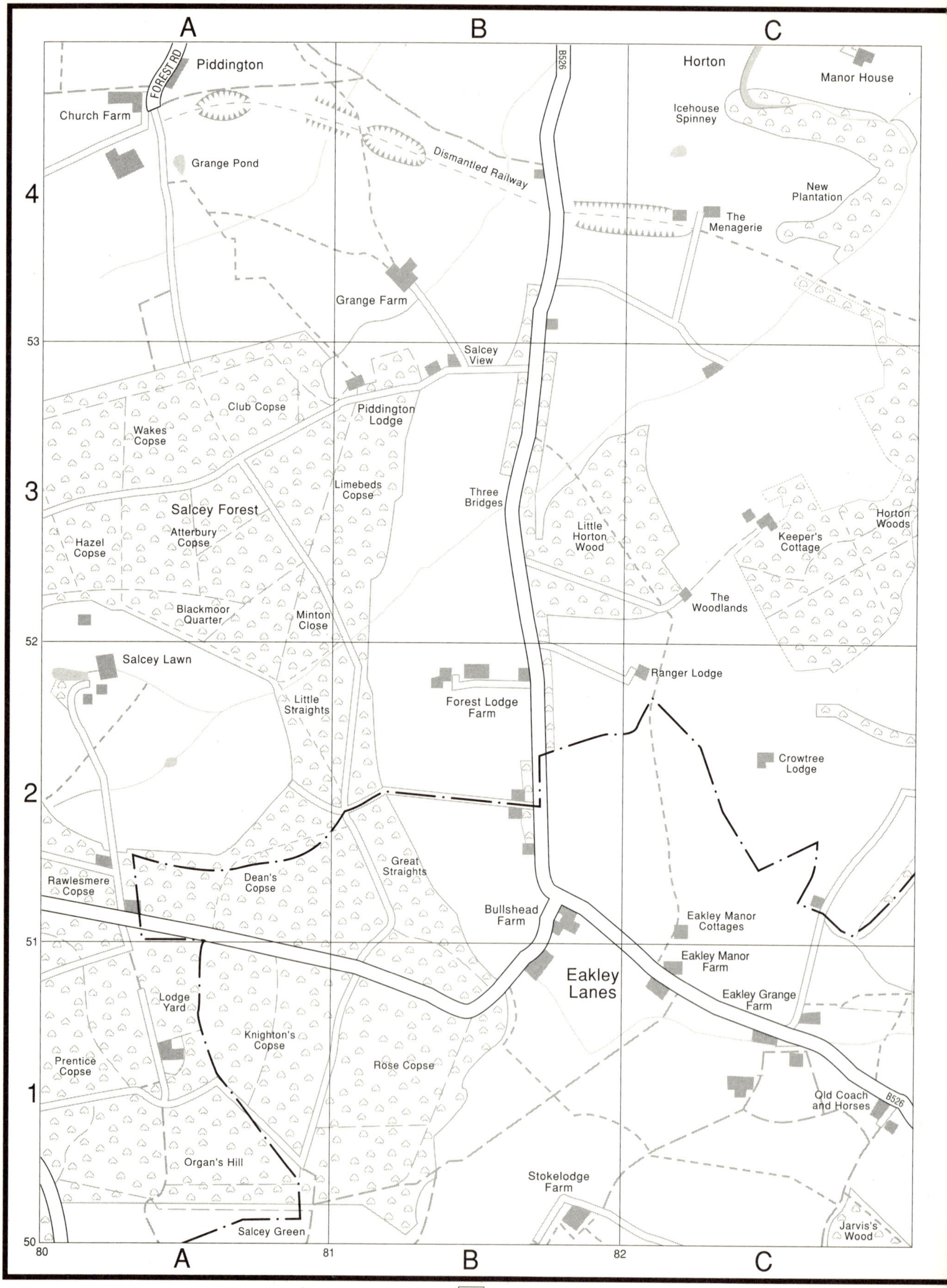

not continued, see key diagram

11

not continued, see key diagram

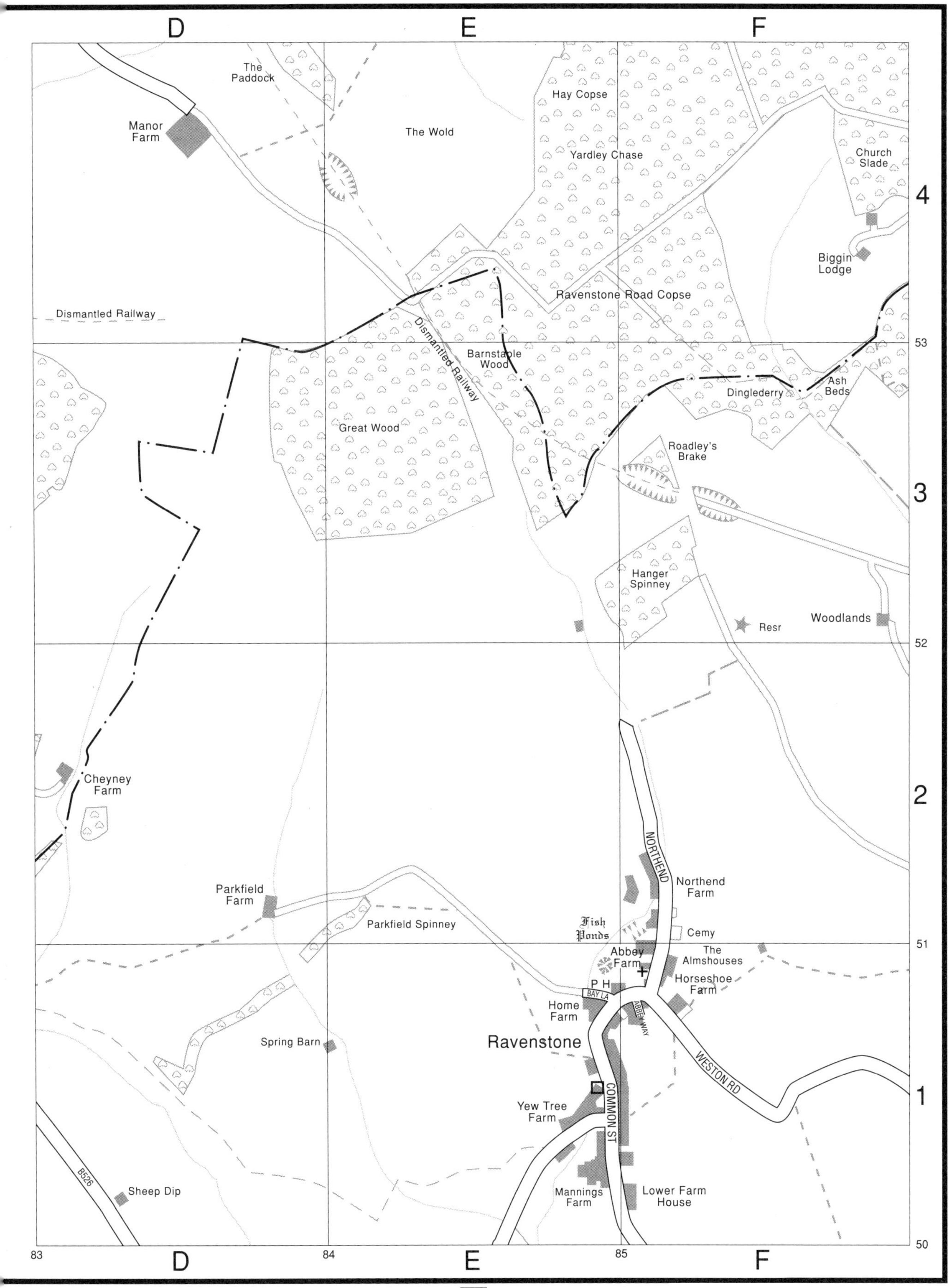

9

12

1

5

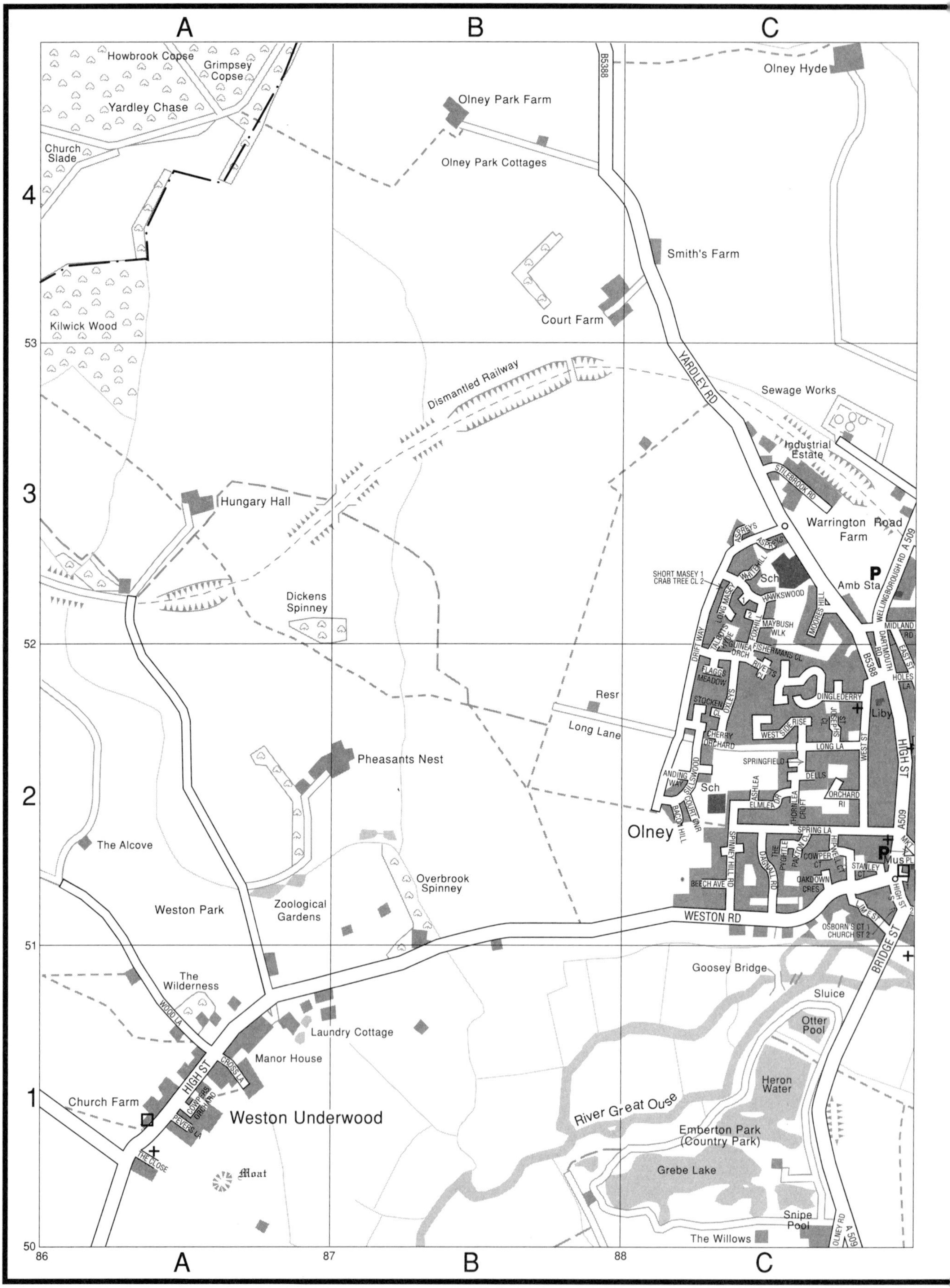

A
B
C
Howbrook Copse
Grimpsey Copse
Yardley Chase
Church Slade
Olney Park Farm
Olney Park Cottages
Olney Hyde
B5388
Smith's Farm
Court Farm
Kilwick Wood
Dismantled Railway
YARDLEY RD
Sewage Works
Industrial Estate
STILEBROOK RD
Warrington Road Farm
Hungary Hall
Dickens Spinney
Sch
Amb Sta
P
WELLINGBOROUGH RD A509
SHORT MASEY 1
CRAB TREE CL 2
HAWKSWOOD
MAYBUSH WLK
MOORES HILL
MIDLAND RD
DARTMOUTH RD
EAST ST
HOLES LA
DRIFT WAY
FLAGGS MEADOW
FISHERMANS CL
GUINEA ORCH
STOCKEN CL
OXLEYS
DINGLEDERRY
Liby
Resr
Long Lane
WEST SIDE RISE
CHERRY ORCHARD
LONG LA
WEST ST
HIGH ST
SPRINGFIELD
DELLS
ORCHARD RI
Pheasants Nest
Sch
ASHLEA
ELMLEA
THORNLEA CROFT
BACON HILL
COURT CNR
Olney
SPRING LA
SPINNEY HILL RD
DAGNALL RD
THE PYGHTLE
PAXTON CL
COWPER CT
STANLEY CT
OAKDOWN CRES
BEECH AVE
Mus
A509
The Alcove
Overbrook Spinney
Weston Park
Zoological Gardens
WESTON RD
LIME ST
OSBORN'S CT 1
CHURCH ST 2
BRIDGE ST
The Wilderness
Goosey Bridge
Sluice
Otter Pool
WOOD LA
Laundry Cottage
Manor House
CROSS LA
HIGH ST
Heron Water
Church Farm
COWPERS ORCHARD
Weston Underwood
River Great Ouse
Emberton Park (Country Park)
PEVERS LA
THE CLOSE
Moat
Grebe Lake
Snipe Pool
The Willows
OLNEY RD
A 509
4
53
3
52
2
51
1
50
86
87
88

13

2

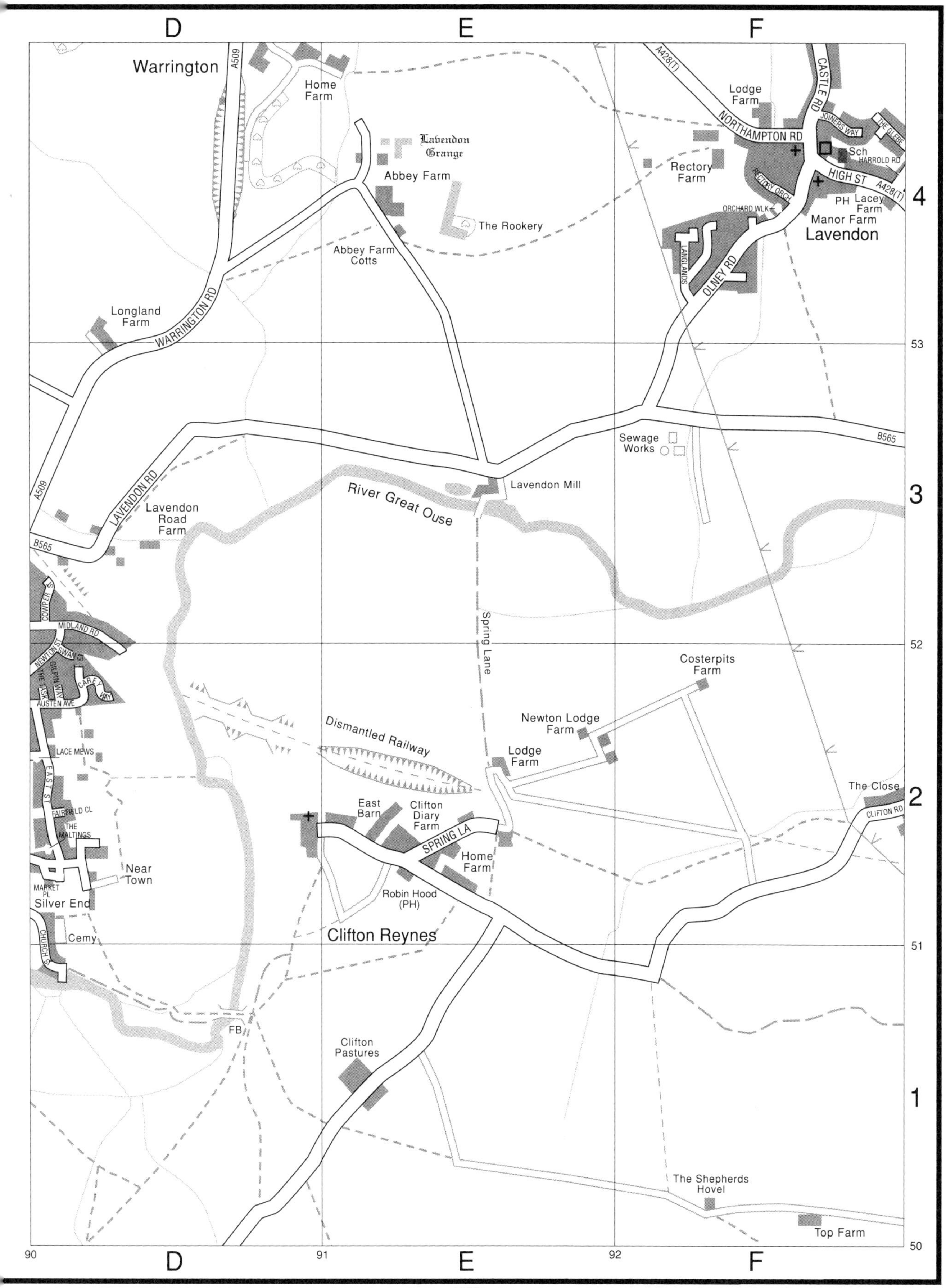

D
E
F
Warrington
A509
Home Farm
Lavendon Grange
Abbey Farm
The Rookery
Abbey Farm Cotts
Longland Farm
WARRINGTON RD
A428(T)
Lodge Farm
CASTLE RD
NORTHAMPTON RD
JOINERS WAY
THE GLEBE
Sch
HARROLD RD
Rectory Farm
HIGH ST
A428(T)
RECTORY ORCH
ORCHARD WLK
PH
Lacey Farm
Manor Farm
Lavendon
LANGLANDS
OLNEY RD
4
53
B565
Sewage Works
Lavendon Mill
River Great Ouse
3
A509
LAVENDON RD
Lavendon Road Farm
B565
COWPER ST
MIDLAND RD
NEWTON ST
SWAN CT
GILPIN WAY
THE TASK
CAREY WAY
AUSTEN AVE
Spring Lane
52
Costerpits Farm
Newton Lodge Farm
Dismantled Railway
Lodge Farm
LACE MEWS
EAST ST
FAIRFIELD CL
THE MALTINGS
The Close
2
CLIFTON RD
East Barn
Clifton Diary Farm
SPRING LA
Home Farm
Near Town
MARKET PL
Silver End
Robin Hood (PH)
Cemy
CHURCH ST
Clifton Reynes
51
FB
Clifton Pastures
1
The Shepherds Hovel
Top Farm
50
90
91
92
D
E
F

8

14

3

A
B
C
4
3
2
1
53
52
51
50
92
93
94
HARROLD RD
THE GLEBE
Moat
Uphoe Manor Farm
Snip Wood
Cemy
A428(T)
New Barn
Copymoor
CARLTON RD
New Park
Cricket Ground
Cemy
Turvey House
Chantry Farm
Sch
New Gains Farm
B565
BEDFORD RD
Cold Brayfield
Waterfield Farm
Brayfield Farm
Brayfield House
Turvey Bridge
Ye Three Fyshes Inn (PH)
BRIDGE ST
Turvey
Sch
Turvey Abbey
Ford
JACK'S LA
TANDYS CL
NEWTON RD
Long Belt
Abbey Farm
Lodge
Top Lodge
Newton Blossomville
Old Mill (PH)
Sch
BROOK LA
HARDMEAD RD
Home Farm
River Great Ouse
Turvey Cottage
Woodside Cottage
Mossy Bank Wood
New Wood
Keepers Cottage
Westfields Barn
Dismantled Railway
Turvey Hall Farm
Newton Park
Gullet Wood
Two Chimneys
Clifton Spinney
Newton Wood
Sheepwalks Spinney
Turvey Lodge Farm

7

15

not continued, see key diagram

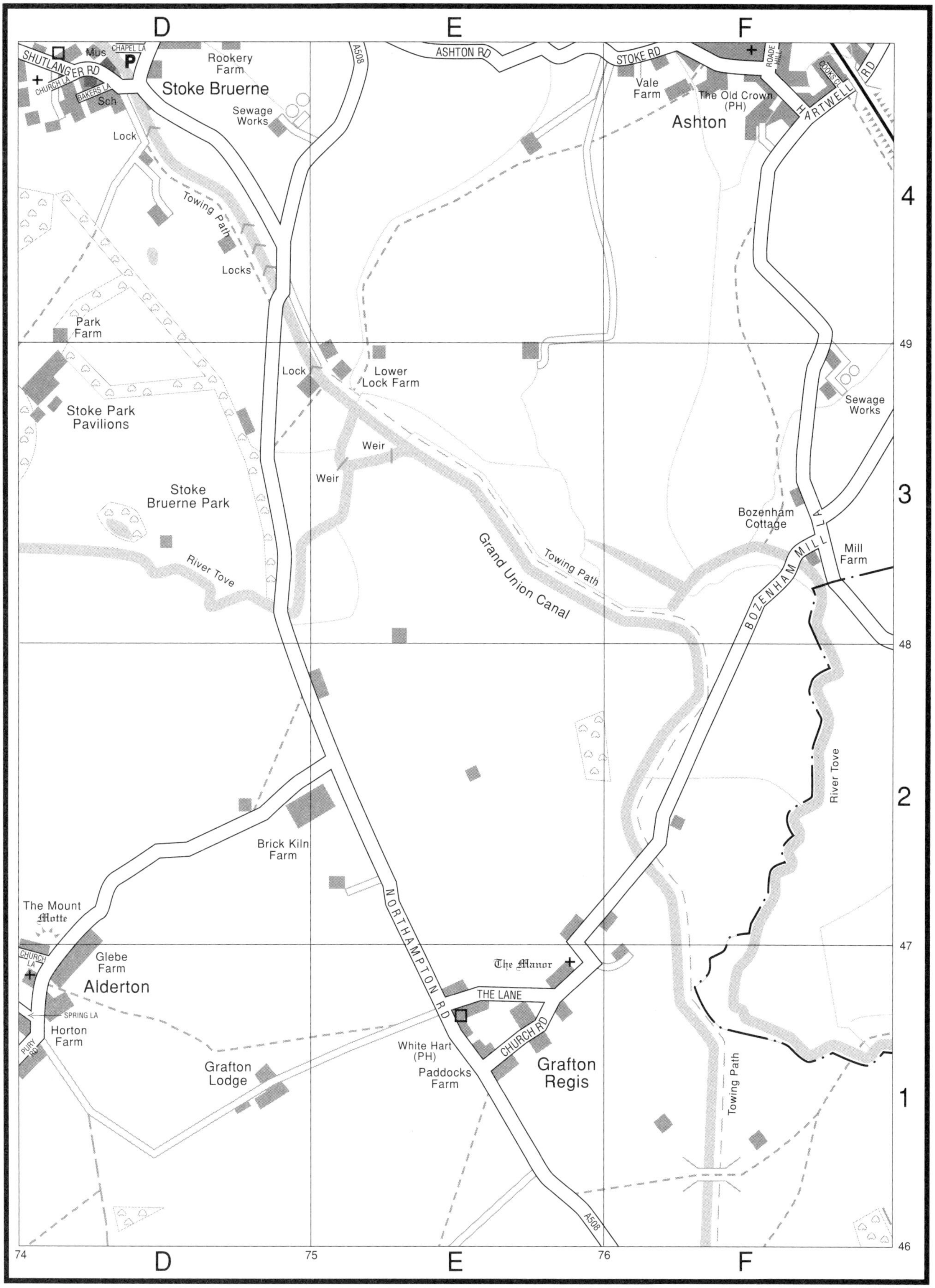

10

18

not continued, see key diagram

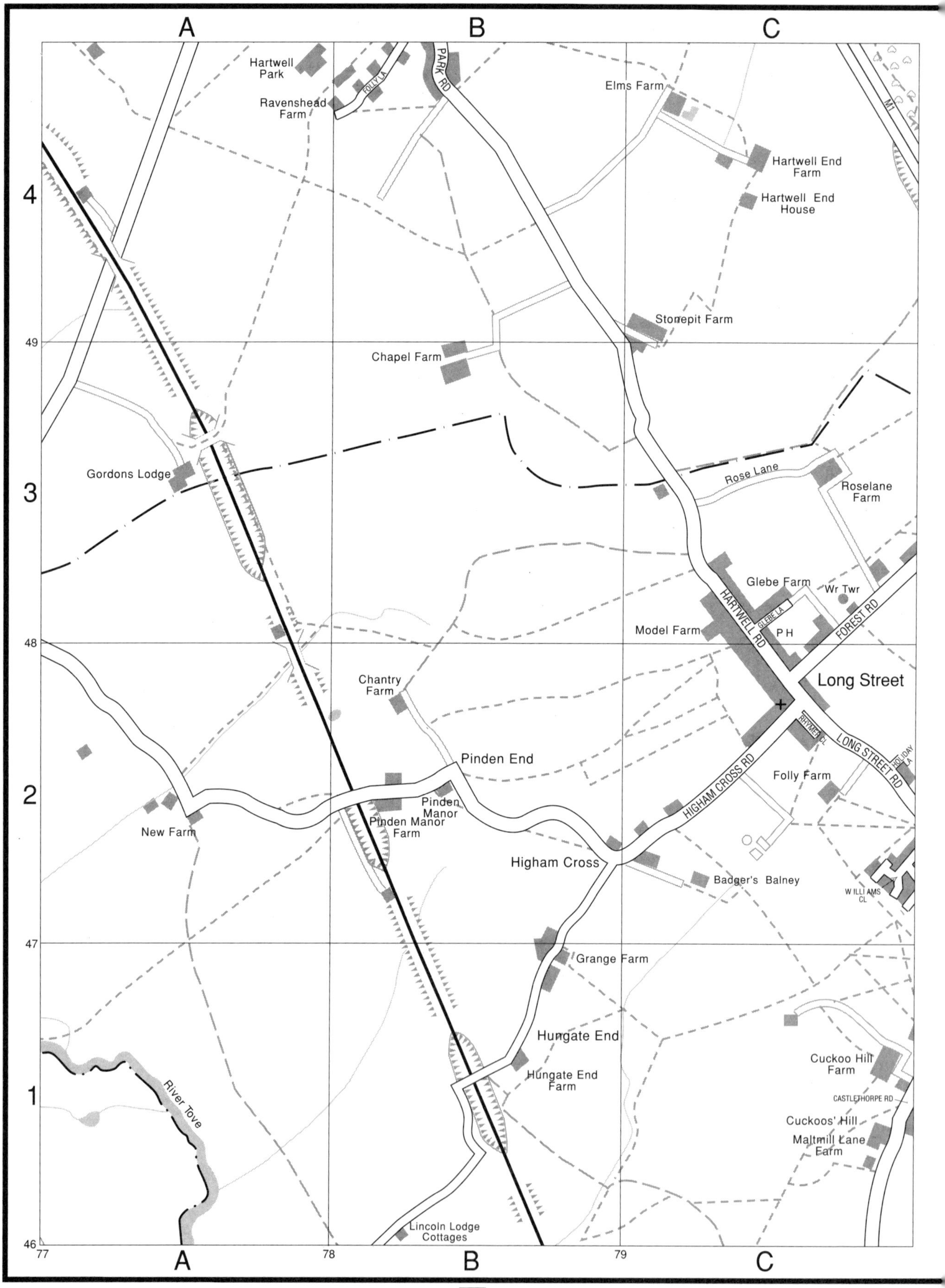

9

19

4

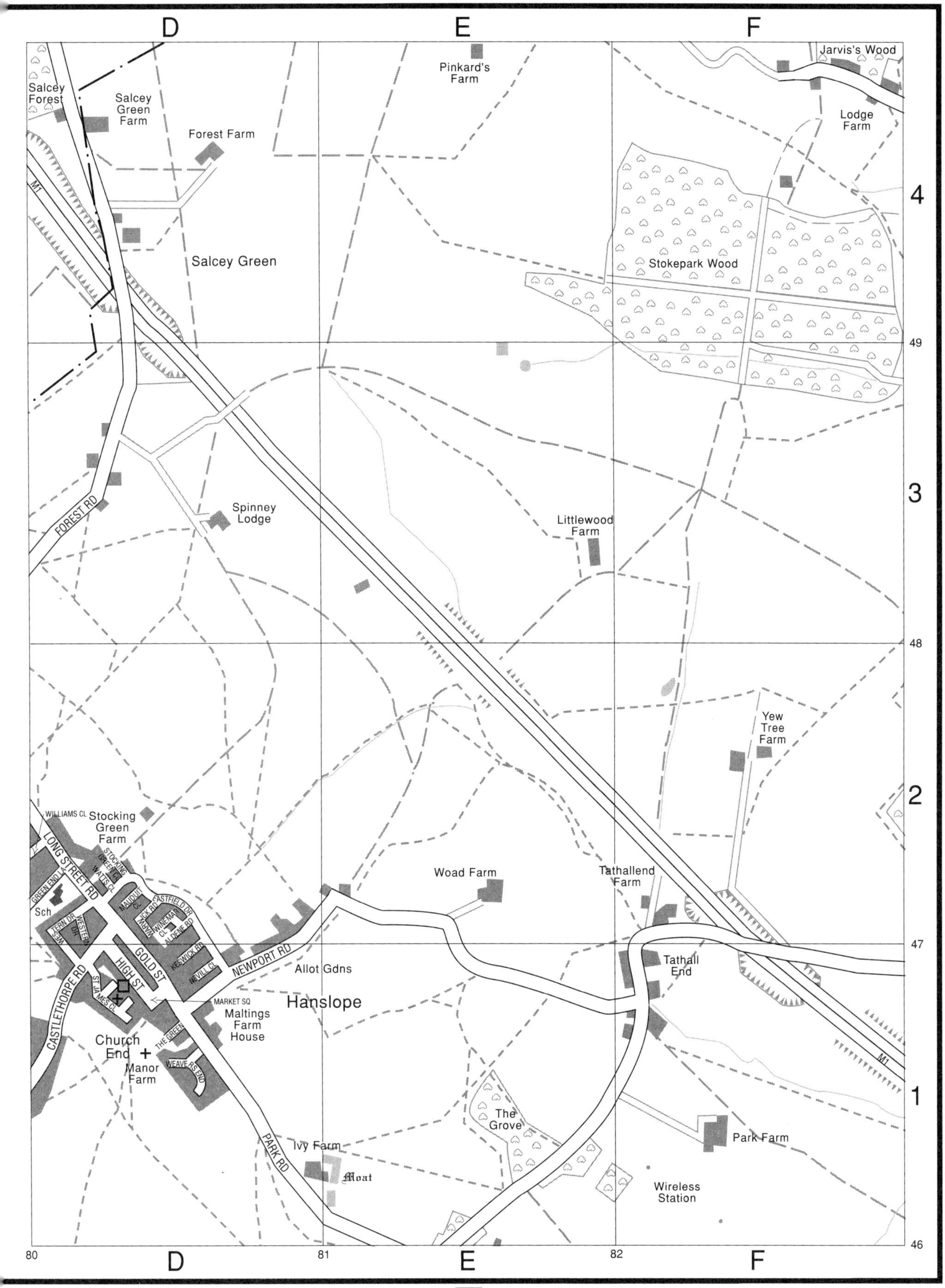
D
E
F
Jarvis's Wood
Pinkard's Farm
Salcey Forest
Salcey Green Farm
Forest Farm
Lodge Farm
M1
4
Salcey Green
Stokepark Wood
49
Spinney Lodge
FOREST RD
3
Littlewood Farm
48
Yew Tree Farm
2
WILLIAMS CL
Stocking Green Farm
LONG STREET RD
STOCKING GREEN CL
WATTS CL
GREEN END
Sch
Woad Farm
Tathallend Farm
MAUDUIT CL
EASTFIELD DR
ALDENE RD
KESWICK RD
NEVILL CL
NEWPORT RD
HIGH ST
GOLD ST
CASTLETHORPE RD
MARKET SQ
Allot Gdns
Tathall End
47
Hanslope
Maltings Farm House
Church End
Manor Farm
THE GREEN
WEAVERS END
1
The Grove
Park Farm
PARK RD
Ivy Farm
Moat
Wireless Station
80
81
82
46

12

20

5

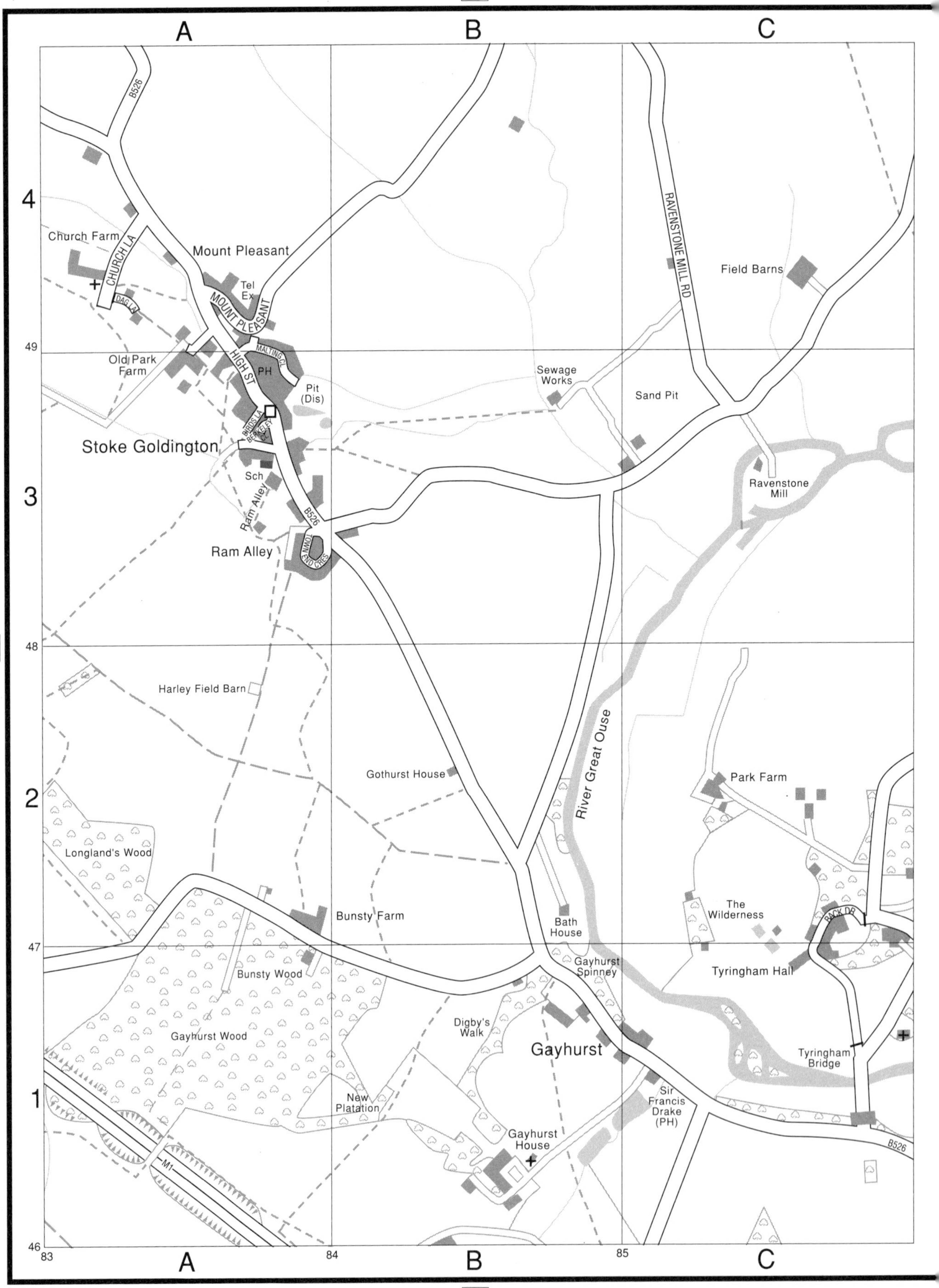
A
B
C
4
3
2
1
49
48
47
46
83
84
85
B526
Church Farm
CHURCH LA
DAG LA
Mount Pleasant
Tel Ex
MOUNT PLEASANT
MALTING CL
HIGH ST
PH
Pit (Dis)
Old Park Farm
BIRDS LA
BERKELEY CL
Stoke Goldington
Sch
Ram Alley
TOWN END CRES
Sewage Works
Sand Pit
RAVENSTONE MILL RD
Field Barns
Ravenstone Mill
Harley Field Barn
Gothurst House
River Great Ouse
Park Farm
Longland's Wood
The Wilderness
BACK DR
Bunsty Farm
Bath House
Gayhurst Spinney
Tyringham Hall
Bunsty Wood
Digby's Walk
Gayhurst Wood
Gayhurst
Tyringham Bridge
New Platation
Sir Francis Drake (PH)
Gayhurst House
M1

11

21

6

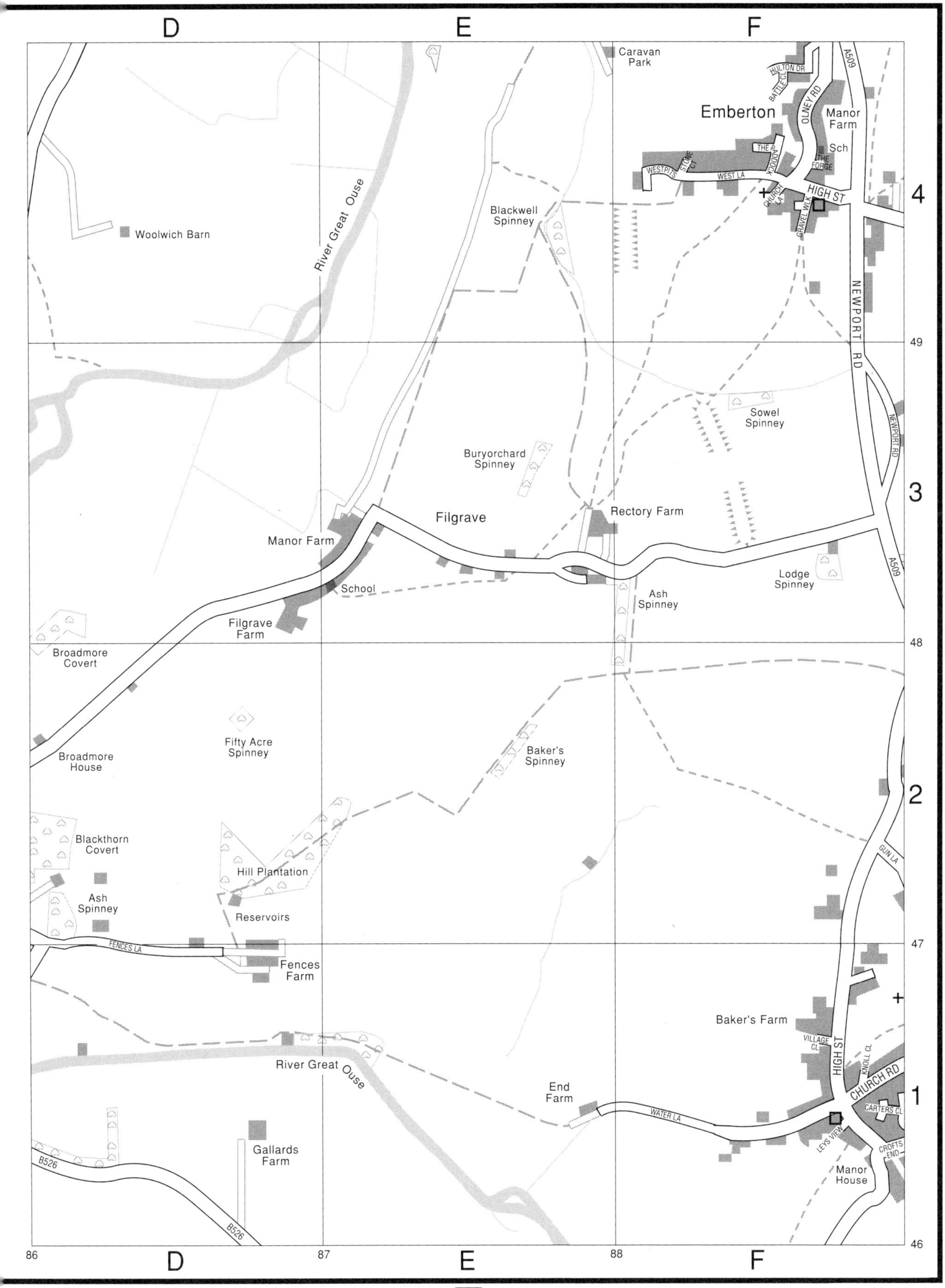
D
E
F
Caravan Park
Emberton
HULTON DR
BATTLE CL
OLNEY RD
A509
Manor Farm
THE PADDOCK
Sch
THE FORGE
WESTPITS
STOWE CT
WEST LA
CHURCH LA
HIGH ST
GRAVEL WLK
4
Blackwell Spinney
Woolwich Barn
River Great Ouse
NEWPORT RD
49
Sowel Spinney
NEWPORT RD
Buryorchard Spinney
3
Filgrave
Rectory Farm
Manor Farm
Lodge Spinney
A509
School
Ash Spinney
Filgrave Farm
Broadmore Covert
48
Fifty Acre Spinney
Baker's Spinney
Broadmore House
2
Blackthorn Covert
GUN LA
Hill Plantation
Ash Spinney
Reservoirs
FENCES LA
47
Fences Farm
Baker's Farm
VILLAGE CL
HIGH ST
KNOLL CL
River Great Ouse
CHURCH RD
End Farm
1
WATER LA
CARTERS CL
LEYS VIEW
CROFTS END
Gallards Farm
Manor House
B526
B526
86
87
88
46
D
E
F

14

22

7

13

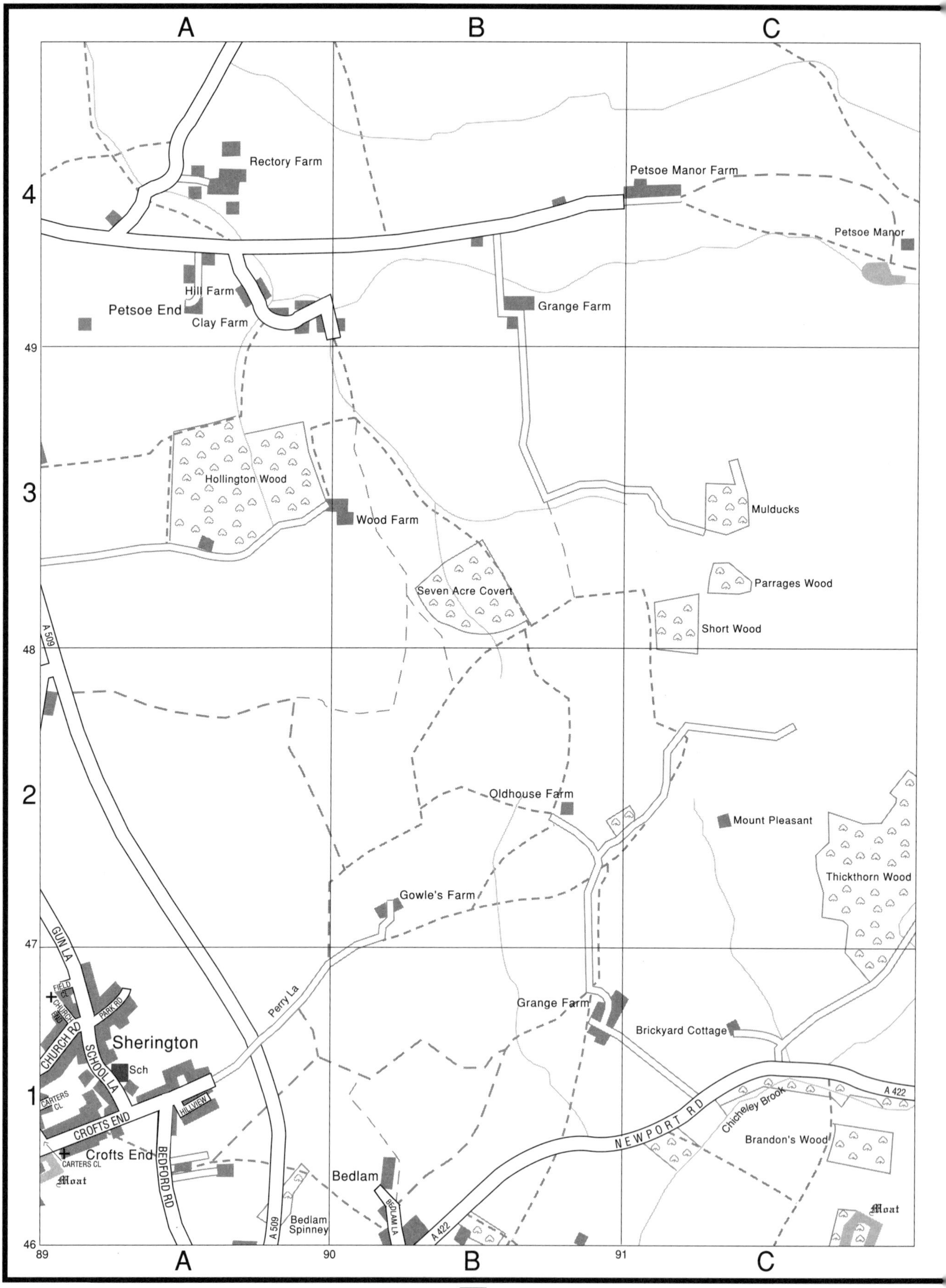
A
B
C
4
3
2
1
49
48
47
46
89
90
91
Rectory Farm
Petsoe Manor Farm
Petsoe Manor
Hill Farm
Petsoe End
Clay Farm
Grange Farm
Hollington Wood
Wood Farm
Mulducks
Seven Acre Covert
Parrages Wood
Short Wood
A 509
Oldhouse Farm
Mount Pleasant
Thickthorn Wood
Gowle's Farm
GUN LA
FIELD CL
CHURCH END
PARK RD
CHURCH RD
SCHOOL LA
Sherington
Sch
Perry La
Grange Farm
Brickyard Cottage
CARTERS CL
CROFTS END
HILLVIEW
Crofts End
CARTERS CL
Moat
BEDFORD RD
Bedlam
BEDLAM LA
Bedlam Spinney
A 422
NEWPORT RD
Chicheley Brook
Brandon's Wood
A 422
Moat

23

8

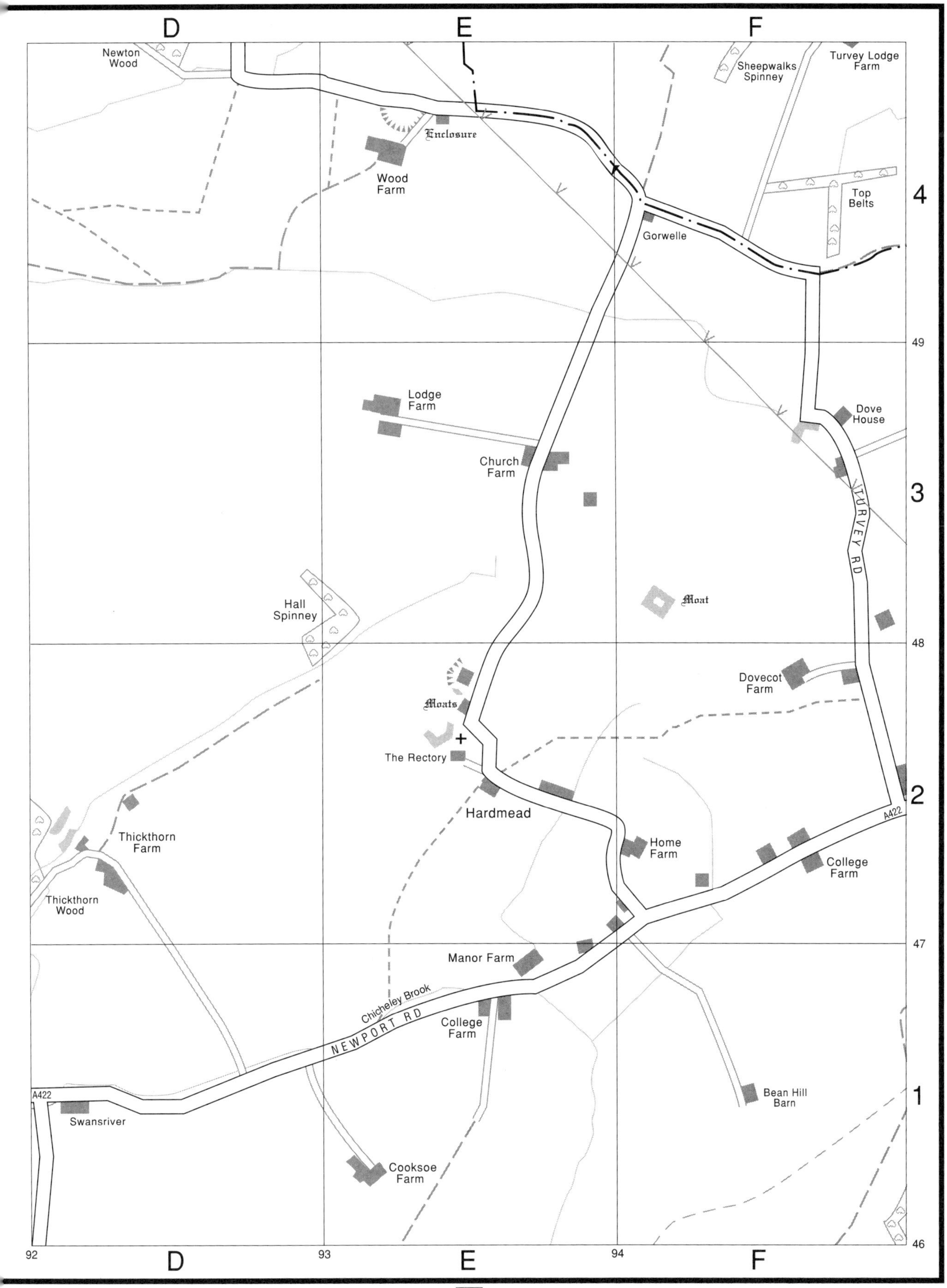
D
E
F
Newton Wood
Sheepwalks Spinney
Turvey Lodge Farm
Enclosure
Wood Farm
Top Belts
4
Gorwelle
49
Lodge Farm
Dove House
Church Farm
3
TURVEY RD
Hall Spinney
Moat
48
Dovecot Farm
Moats
The Rectory
2
Hardmead
A422
Thickthorn Farm
Home Farm
College Farm
Thickthorn Wood
47
Manor Farm
Chicheley Brook
NEWPORT RD
College Farm
1
A422
Swansriver
Bean Hill Barn
Cooksoe Farm
46
92
93
94
D
E
F

16

24

not continued, see key diagram

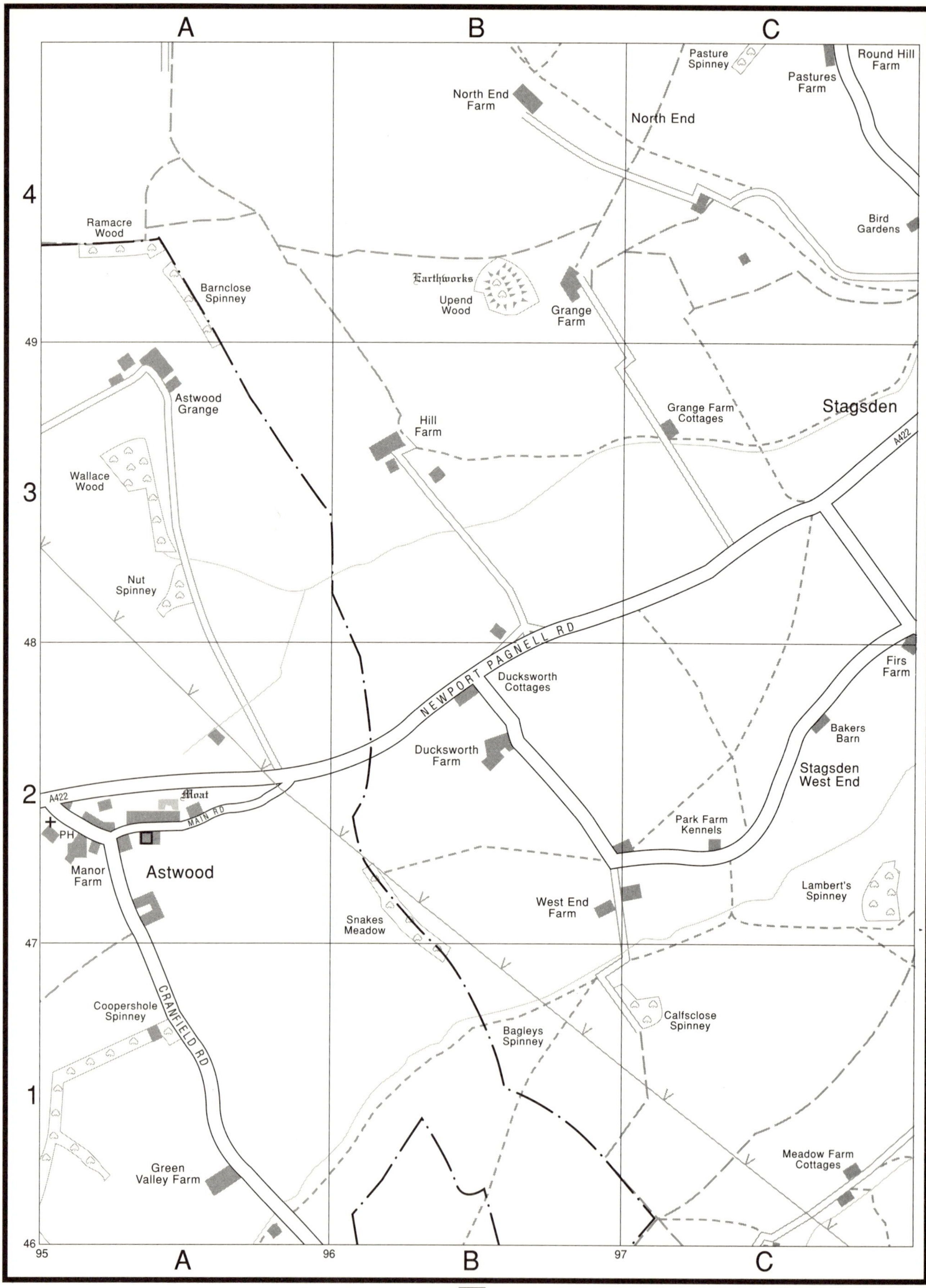

15

25

not continued, see key diagram

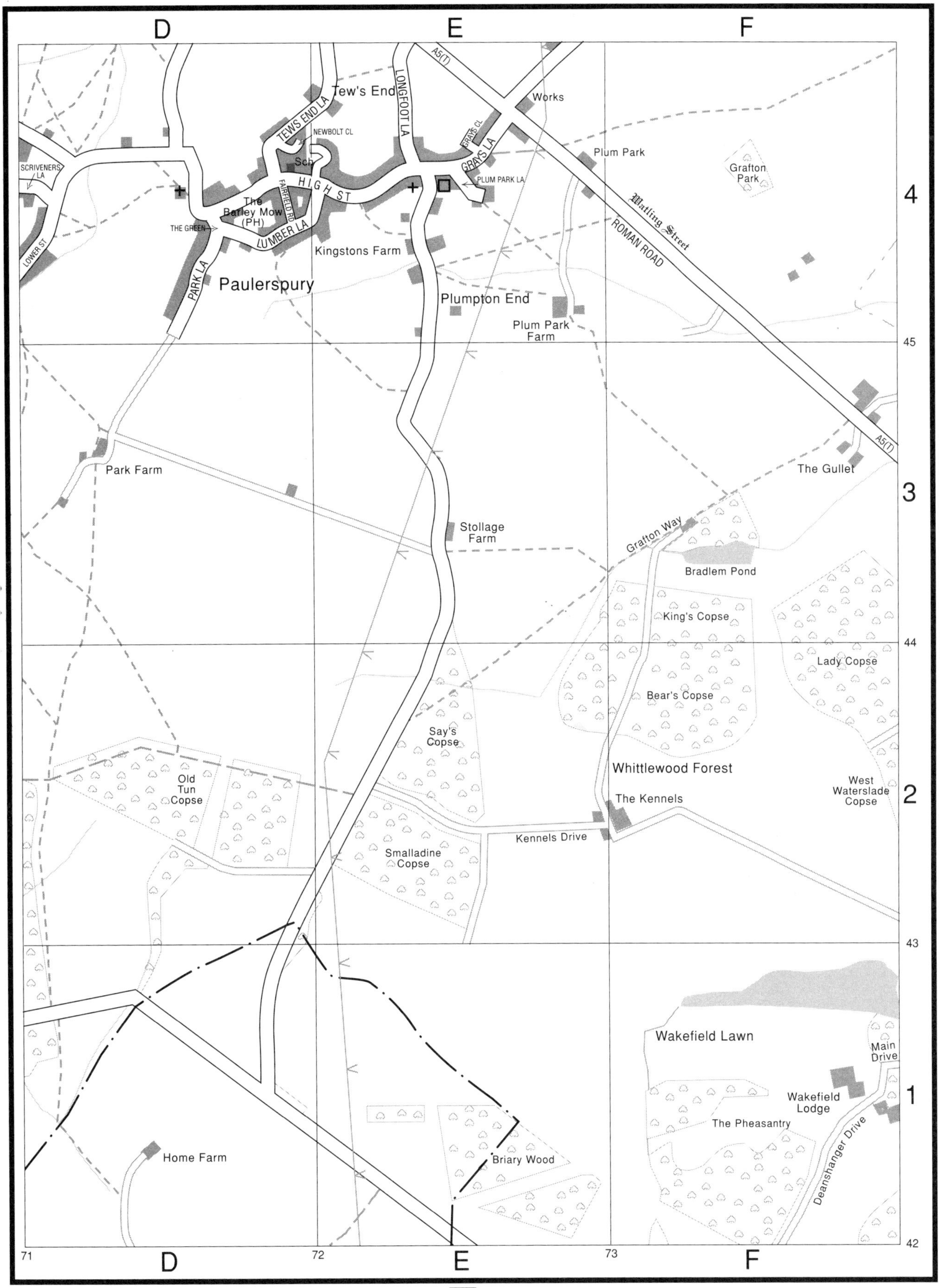

18

30

9

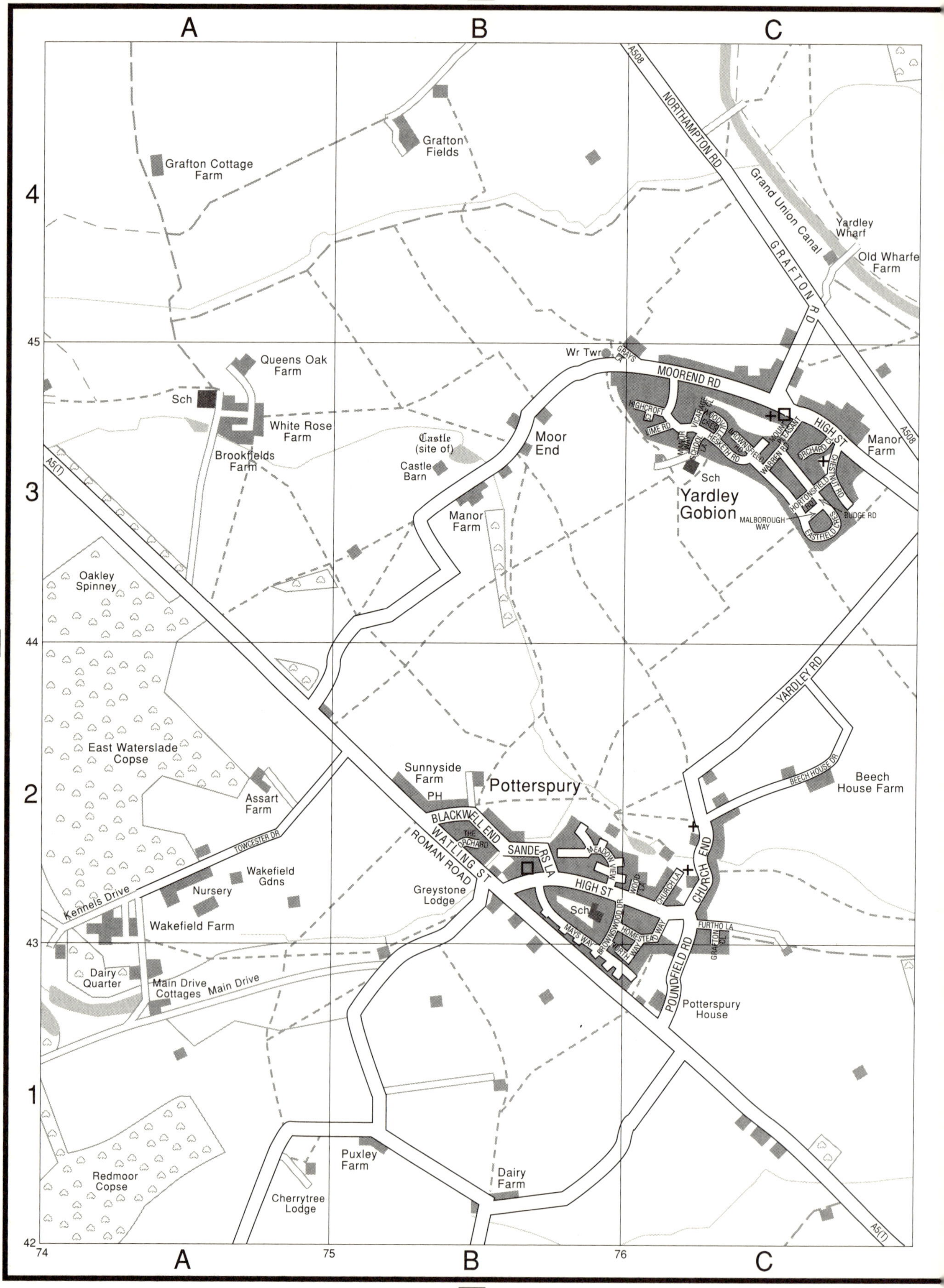
A
B
C
4
3
2
1
45
44
43
42
74
75
76
A508
NORTHAMPTON RD
Grand Union Canal
GRAFTON RD
Yardley Wharf
Old Wharfe Farm
Grafton Fields
Grafton Cottage Farm
Queens Oak Farm
Sch
White Rose Farm
Brookfields Farm
Castle (site of)
Castle Barn
Moor End
Manor Farm
Wr Twr
GRAYS LA
MOOREND RD
HIGHCROFT CL
LIME RD
VICARAGE CL
HESKETH RD
BROWNSFIELD RD
WARREN RD
HIGH ST
ORCHARD CL
CHESTNUT RD
HORTONSFIELD RD
MALBOROUGH WAY
BUDGE RD
EASTFIELD CRES
Sch
Yardley Gobion
Manor Farm
A5(T)
Oakley Spinney
East Waterslade Copse
Assart Farm
TOWCESTER DR
Kennels Drive
Nursery
Wakefield Gdns
Wakefield Farm
Dairy Quarter
Main Drive Cottages
Main Drive
Sunnyside Farm
PH
Potterspury
BLACKWELL END
THE ORCHARD
WATLING ST
ROMAN ROAD
SANDERS LA
MEADOW VIEW
HIGH ST
WOOD LA
CHURCH LA
CHURCH END
Sch
MAYS WAY
BROWNSWOOD DR
HOMESTEAD WAY
NORTH WAY
FURTHO LA
GRAFTON CL
POUNDFIELD RD
Greystone Lodge
YARDLEY RD
BEECH HOUSE DR
Beech House Farm
Potterspury House
Redmoor Copse
Puxley Farm
Cherrytree Lodge
Dairy Farm
A5(T)

17

31

10

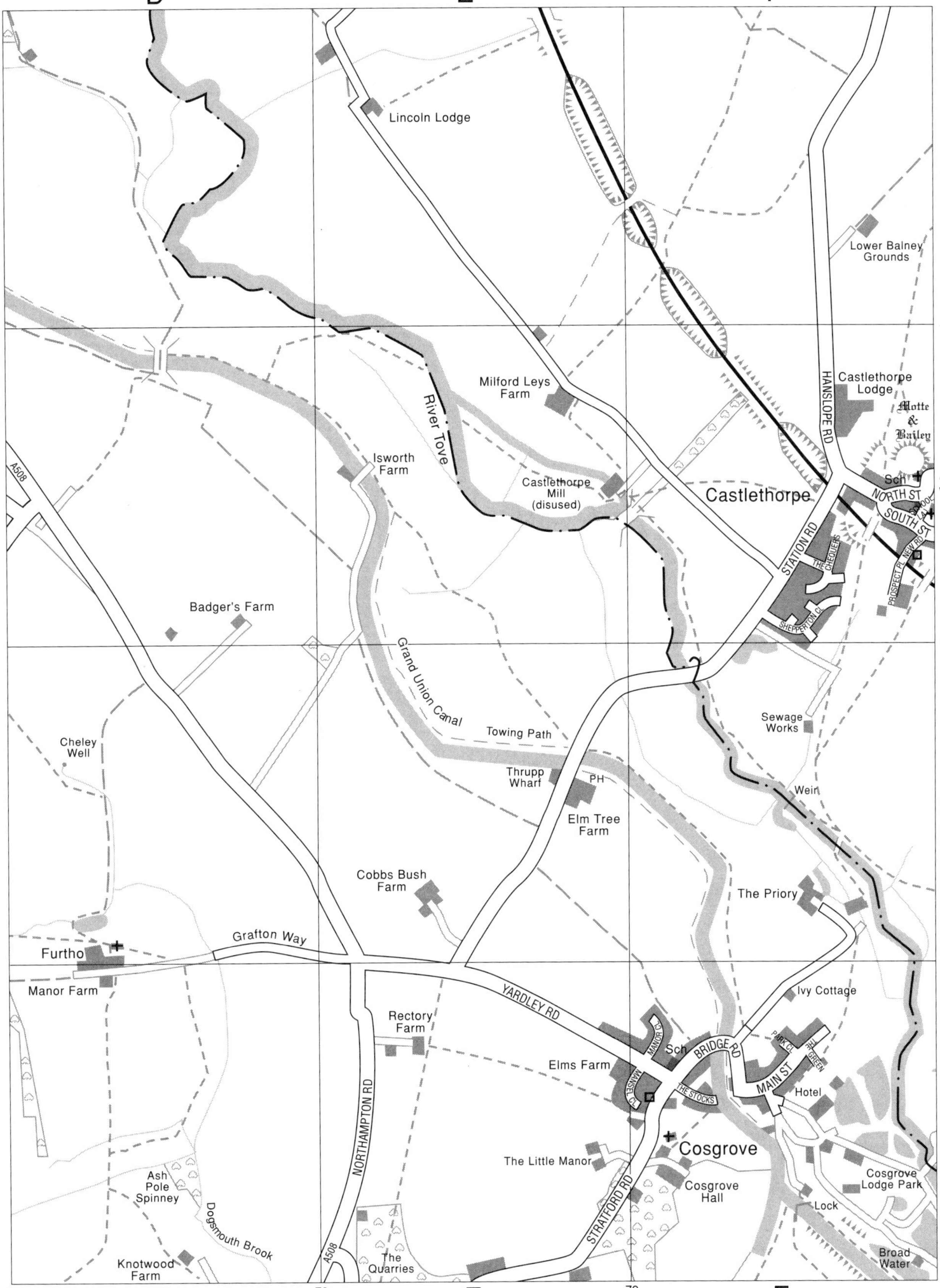
D
E
F
4
3
2
1
45
44
43
42
77
78
79
Lincoln Lodge
Lower Balney Grounds
Castlethorpe Lodge
Motte & Bailey
HANSLOPE RD
Milford Leys Farm
River Tove
Isworth Farm
Castlethorpe Mill (disused)
Castlethorpe
Sch
NORTH ST
SOUTH ST
SCHOOL LA
STATION RD
THE CHEQUERS
SHEPPERTON CL
PROSPECT PL
NEW RD
A508
Badger's Farm
Grand Union Canal
Towing Path
Sewage Works
Cheley Well
Thrupp Wharf
PH
Elm Tree Farm
Weir
Cobbs Bush Farm
The Priory
Grafton Way
Furtho
Manor Farm
Ivy Cottage
YARDLEY RD
Rectory Farm
MANOR CL
Sch
BRIDGE RD
PARK CL
THE GREEN
MAIN ST
Elms Farm
MANSEL CL
THE STOCKS
Hotel
NORTHAMPTON RD
The Little Manor
Cosgrove
Cosgrove Hall
Cosgrove Lodge Park
Ash Pole Spinney
Dogsmouth Brook
STRATFORD RD
Lock
Knotwood Farm
The Quarries
Broad Water

20

32

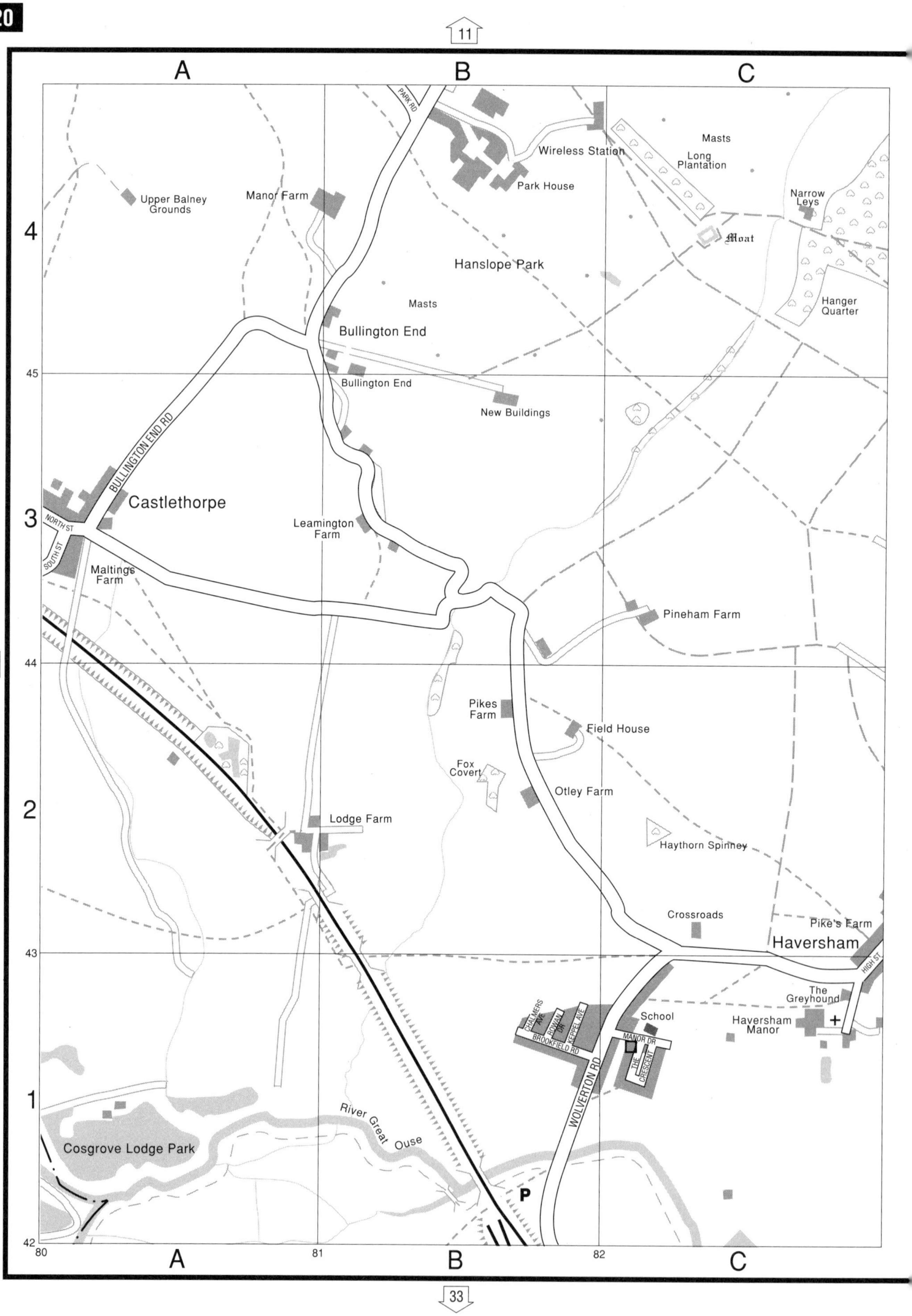
11
A
B
C
4
3
2
1
45
44
43
42
80
81
82
19
33
PARK RD
Wireless Station
Masts
Long Plantation
Upper Balney Grounds
Manor Farm
Park House
Narrow Leys
Moat
Hanslope Park
Masts
Hanger Quarter
Bullington End
Bullington End
New Buildings
BULLINGTON END RD
Castlethorpe
NORTH ST
SOUTH ST
Leamington Farm
Maltings Farm
Pineham Farm
Pikes Farm
Field House
Fox Covert
Otley Farm
Lodge Farm
Haythorn Spinney
Crossroads
Pike's Farm
Haversham
HIGH ST
The Greyhound
CHALMERS AVE
ROWAN DR
KEPPEL AVE
BROOKFIELD RD
School
MANOR DR
THE CRESCENT
Haversham Manor
WOLVERTON RD
River Great Ouse
Cosgrove Lodge Park
P

12

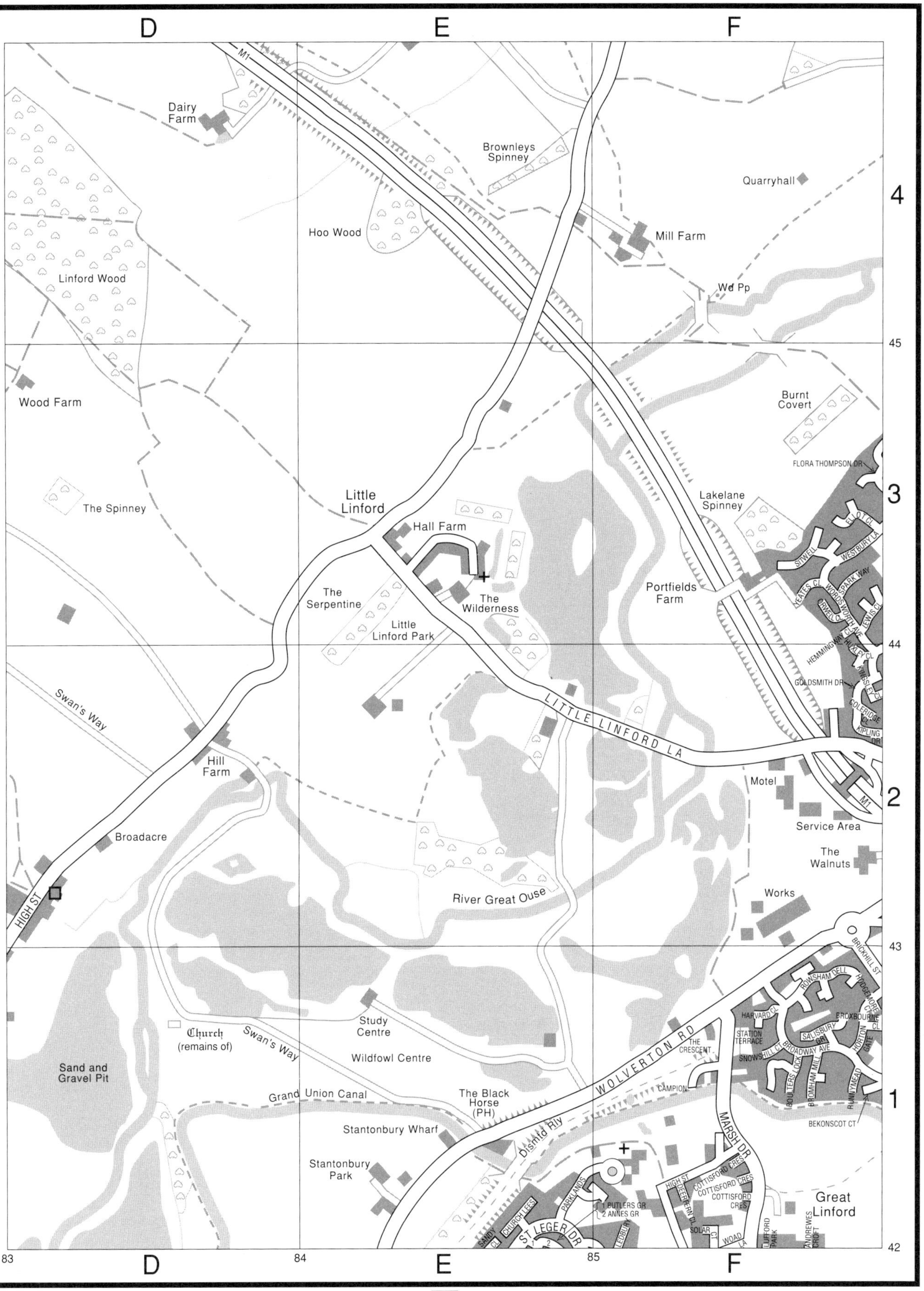
D
E
F
M1
Dairy Farm
Brownleys Spinney
Quarryhall
4
Hoo Wood
Mill Farm
Linford Wood
Wd Pp
45
Wood Farm
Burnt Covert
FLORA THOMPSON DR
3
The Spinney
Little Linford
Lakelane Spinney
Hall Farm
ELLIOT CL
SITWELL
WESTBURY LA
SPARK WAY
The Serpentine
The Wilderness
Portfields Farm
YEATES CL
WORDSWORTH AVE
LEWIS CL
Little Linford Park
44
HEMMINGWAY
HUXLEY CL
GOLDSMITH DR
Swan's Way
LITTLE LINFORD LA
COLERIDGE CL
KIPLING DR
Hill Farm
Motel
M1
2
Service Area
Broadacre
The Walnuts
Works
HIGH ST
River Great Ouse
43
BRICKHILL ST
ROWSHAM DELL
HODGEMORE CT
HARVARD CL
BROXBOURNE CL
STATION TERRACE
SALISBURY GR
HORTON GATE
Study Centre
Church
(remains of)
Swan's Way
WOLVERTON RD
THE CRESCENT
SNOWSHILL CT
BROADWAY AVE
Sand and Gravel Pit
Wildfowl Centre
BOULTERS LOCK
BROMHAM MILL
RUNNYMEDE
CAMPION
1
Grand Union Canal
The Black Horse (PH)
BEKONSCOT CT
Dismtd Rly
Stantonbury Wharf
MARSH DR
Stantonbury Park
HIGH ST
COTTISFORD CRES
Great Linford
PARKLANDS
1 BUTLERS GR
2 ANNES GR
CHURCH LEES
SANDY CL
ST LEGER DR
LEDBURN
SOLAR CT
WOAD LA
LUFFORD PARK
ANDREWES CROFT
42
83
84
85

22

34

13

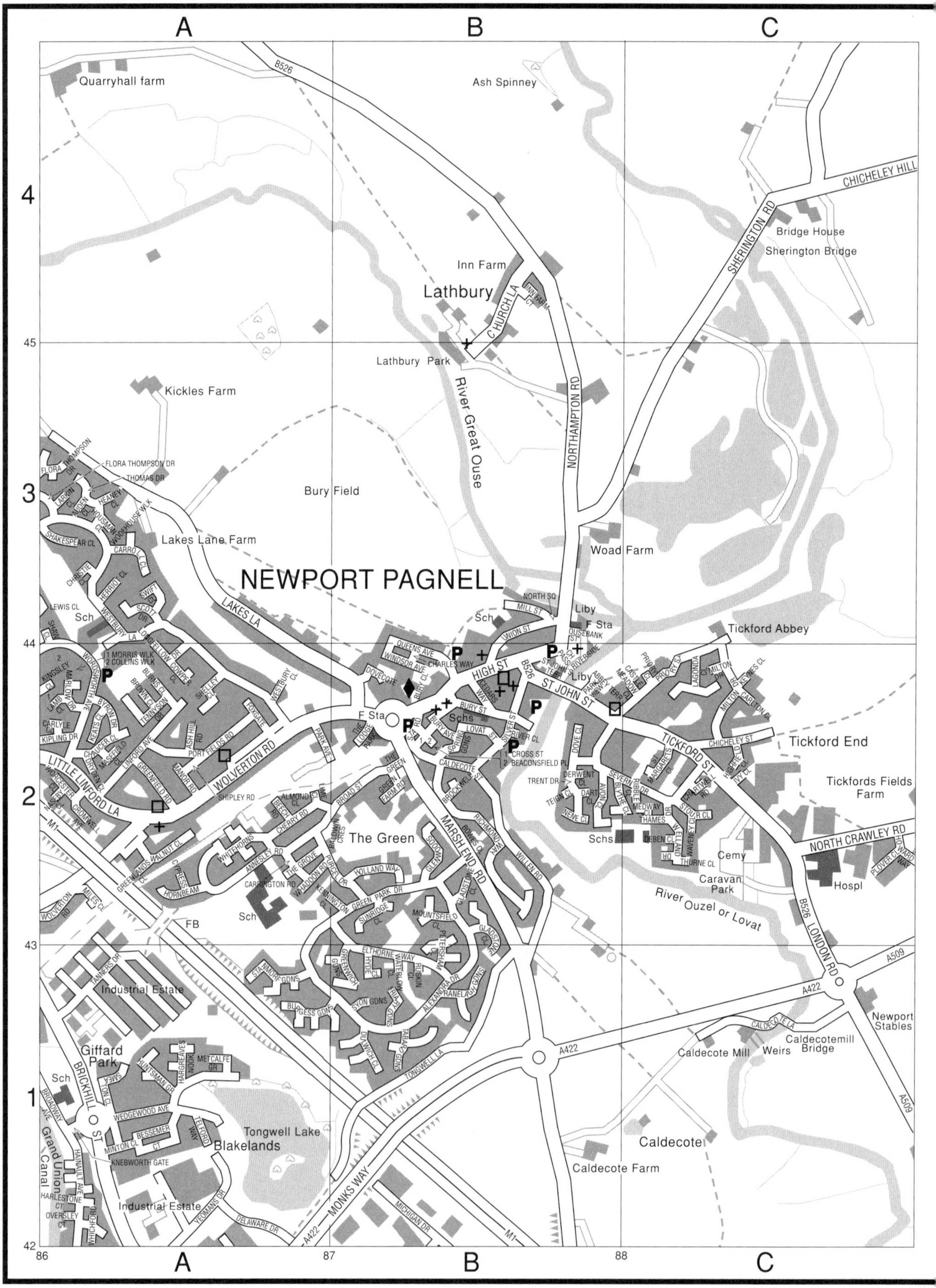
A
B
C
4
3
2
1
45
44
43
42
86
87
88
Quarryhall farm
Ash Spinney
B526
CHICHELEY HILL
Bridge House
Sherington Bridge
SHERINGTON RD
Inn Farm
Lathbury
CHURCH LA
Lathbury Park
River Great Ouse
NORTHAMPTON RD
Kickles Farm
Bury Field
Lakes Lane Farm
Woad Farm
NEWPORT PAGNELL
FLORA THOMPSON DR
THOMAS DR
SHAKESPEAR CL
LAKES LA
Sch
Liby
F Sta
Tickford Abbey
HIGH ST
ST JOHN ST
TICKFORD ST
Tickford End
Tickfords Fields Farm
NORTH CRAWLEY RD
Hospl
Cemy
Caravan Park
River Ouzel or Lovat
WOLVERTON RD
LITTLE LINFORD LA
MARSH END RD
The Green
Schs
Sch
FB
M1
Industrial Estate
Giffard Park
BRICKHILL ST
Grand Union Canal
Tongwell Lake
Blakelands
Industrial Estate
MONKS WAY
A422
A509
LONDON RD
Newport Stables
Caldecotemill Bridge
Caldecote Mill
Weirs
Caldecote
Caldecote Farm
TONGWELL LA

21

35

14

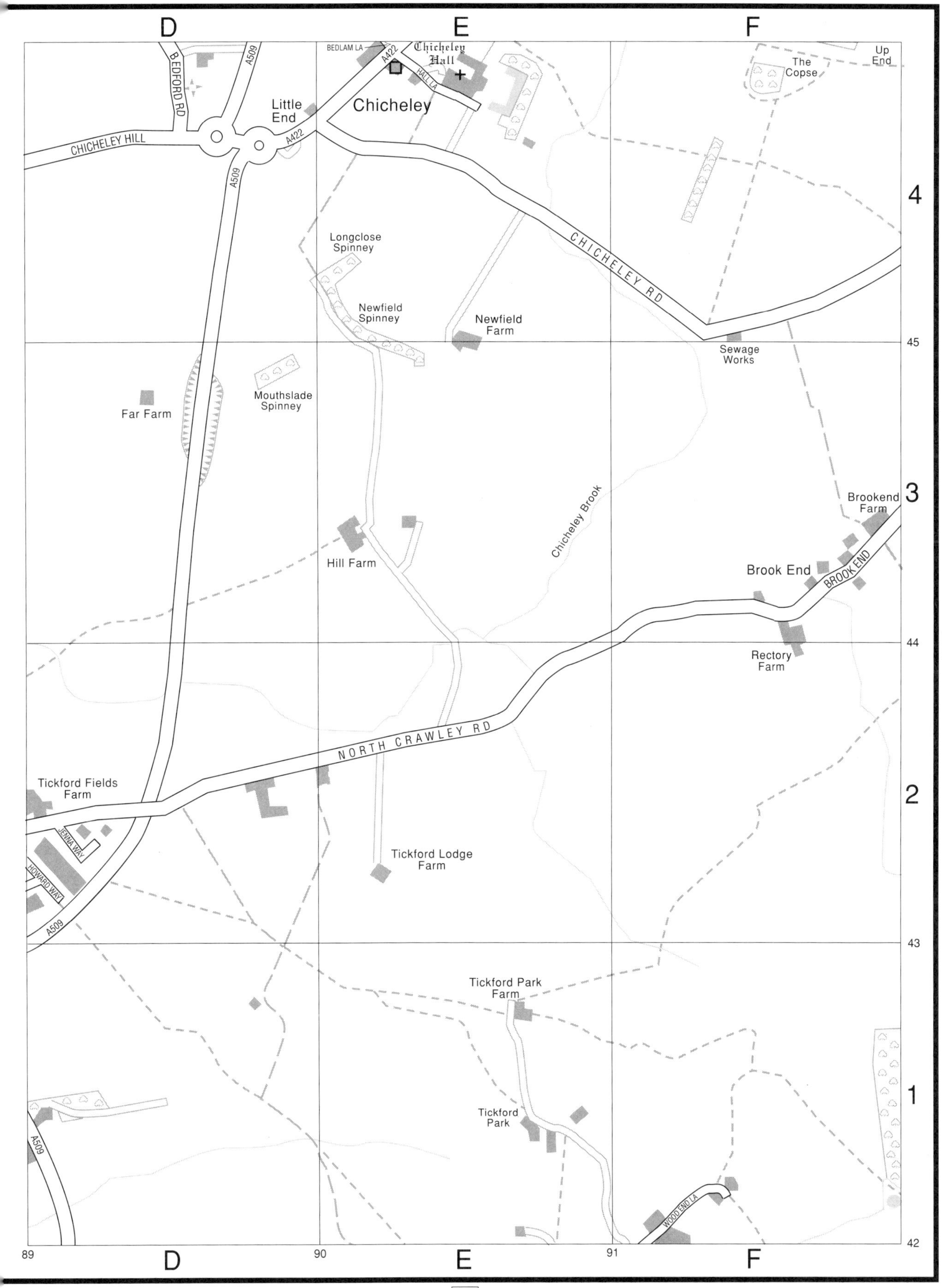
D
E
F
BEDFORD RD
A509
BEDLAM LA
A422
Chicheley Hall
HALL LA
Little End
Chicheley
CHICHELEY HILL
The Copse
Up End
4
Longclose Spinney
Newfield Spinney
Newfield Farm
CHICHELEY RD
45
Sewage Works
Far Farm
Mouthslade Spinney
Chicheley Brook
Brookend Farm
3
Hill Farm
Brook End
BROOK END
44
Rectory Farm
NORTH CRAWLEY RD
Tickford Fields Farm
2
JENNA WAY
HOWARD WAY
Tickford Lodge Farm
43
Tickford Park Farm
1
Tickford Park
WOOD END LA
42
89
90
91

24

36

15

23

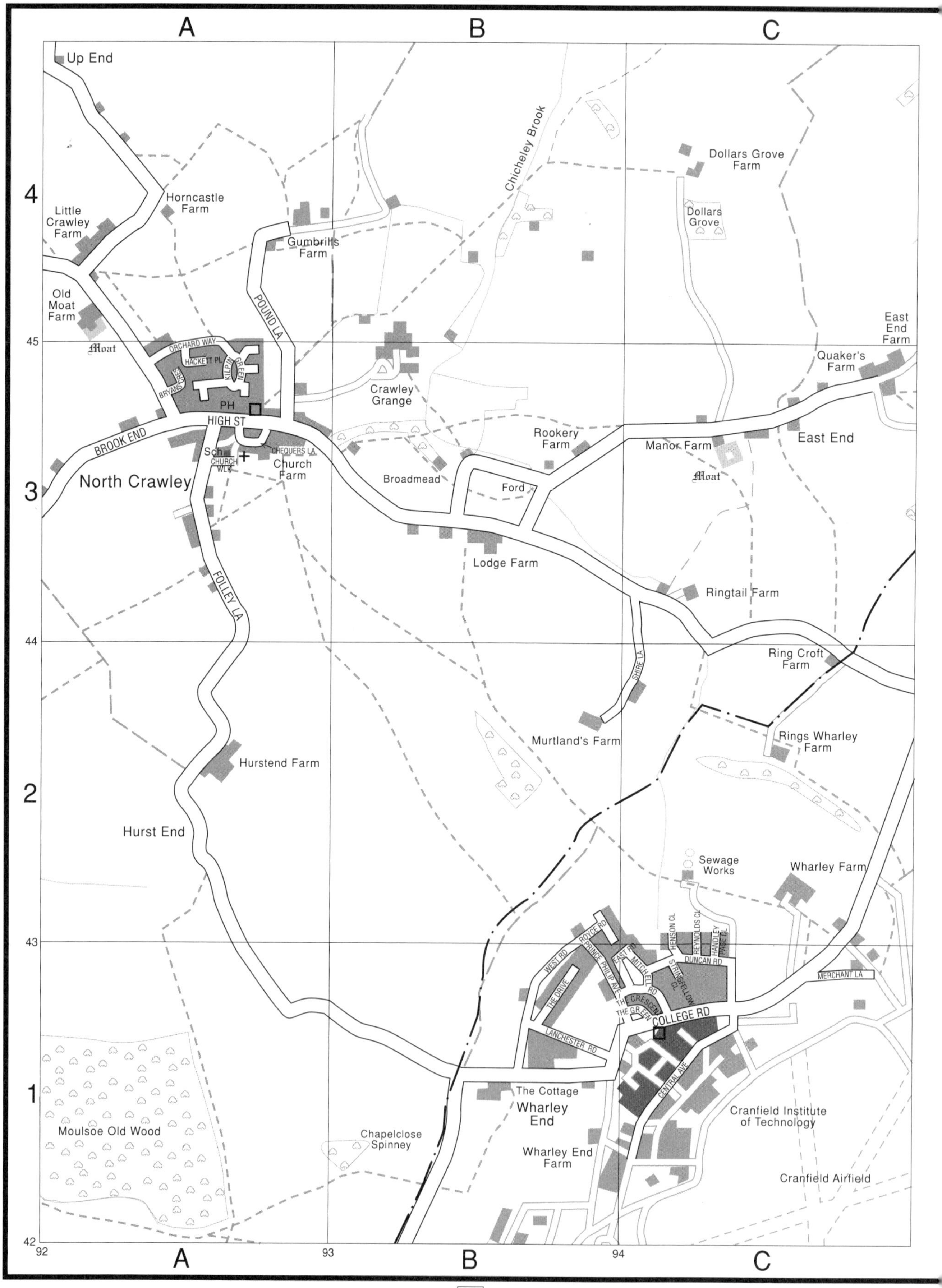

A
B
C
Up End
Little Crawley Farm
Horncastle Farm
Gumbrills Farm
Chicheley Brook
Dollars Grove Farm
Dollars Grove
Old Moat Farm
Moat
POUND LA
ORCHARD WAY
HACKETT PL
KILPIN GREEN
BRYANS CRES
PH
HIGH ST
BROOK END
Sch
CHURCH WLK
CHEQUERS LA
Church Farm
North Crawley
Crawley Grange
Broadmead
Rookery Farm
Ford
Manor Farm
Moat
East End
Quaker's Farm
East End Farm
Lodge Farm
Ringtail Farm
FOLLEY LA
SHIRE LA
Ring Croft Farm
Murtland's Farm
Rings Wharley Farm
Hurstend Farm
Hurst End
Sewage Works
Wharley Farm
ROYCE RD
WEST RD
PRINCE PHILIP AVE
EAST RD
MITCHELL RD
HENSON CL
REYNOLDS CL
HANDLEY
PAGE CL
DUNCAN RD
STRINGFELLOW CL
THE DRIVE
THE CRESCENT
THE GREEN
COLLEGE RD
MERCHANT LA
LANCHESTER RD
CENTRAL AVE
The Cottage
Wharley End
Wharley End Farm
Moulsoe Old Wood
Chapelclose Spinney
Cranfield Institute of Technology
Cranfield Airfield
4
45
3
44
2
43
1
42
92
93
94

37

16

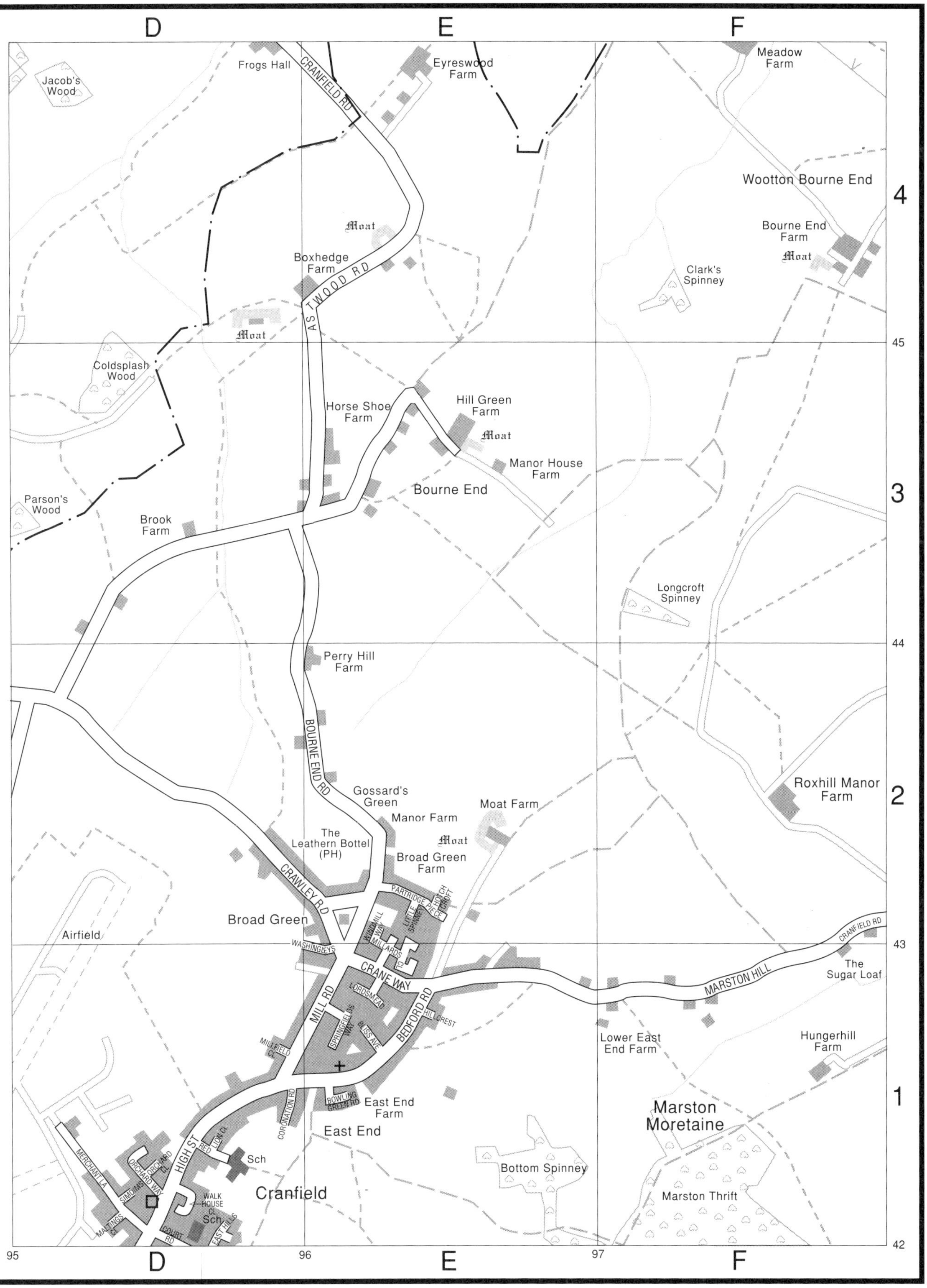

not continued, see key diagram

not continued, see key diagram

not continued, see key diagram

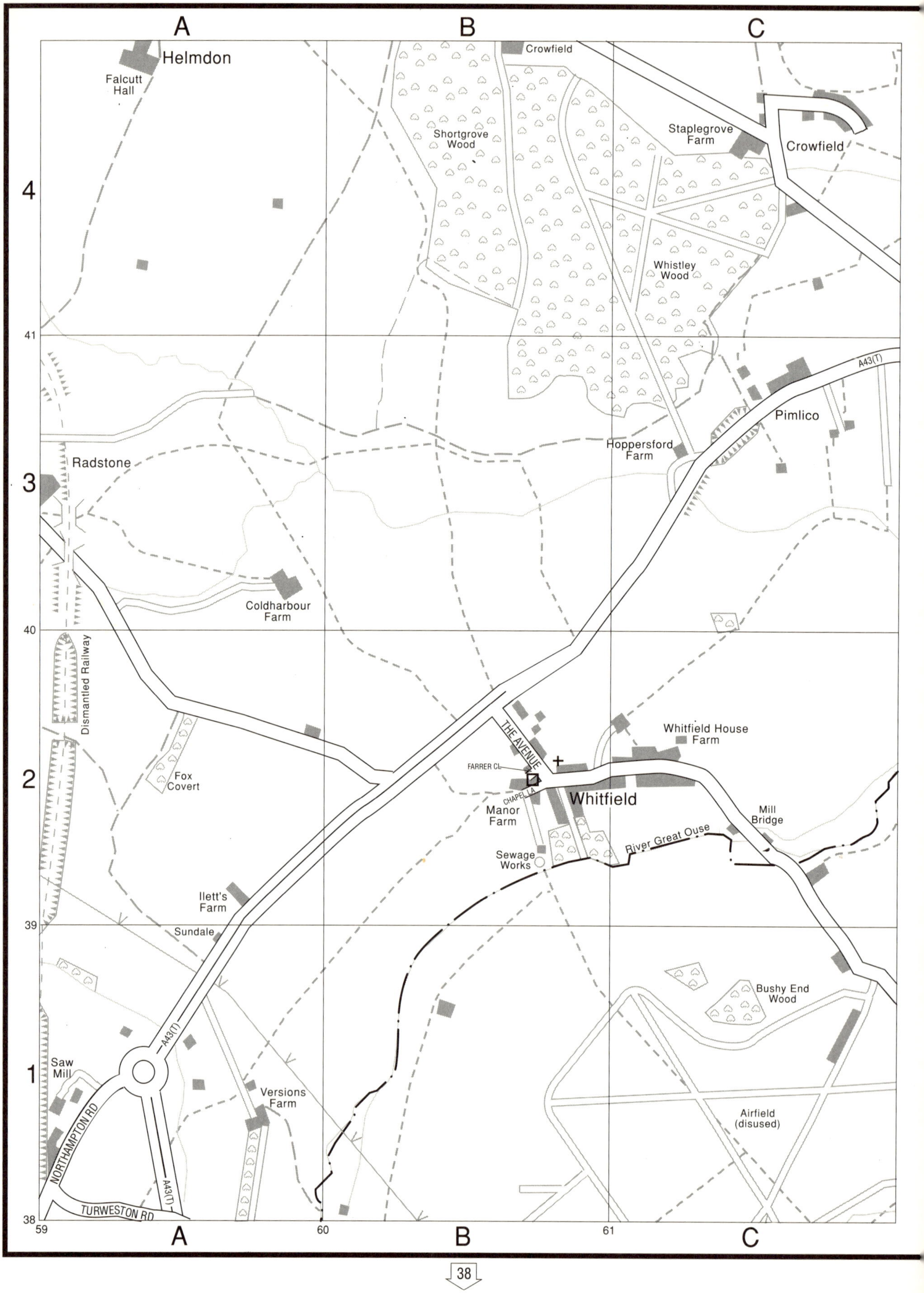

not continued, see key diagram

not continued, see key diagram

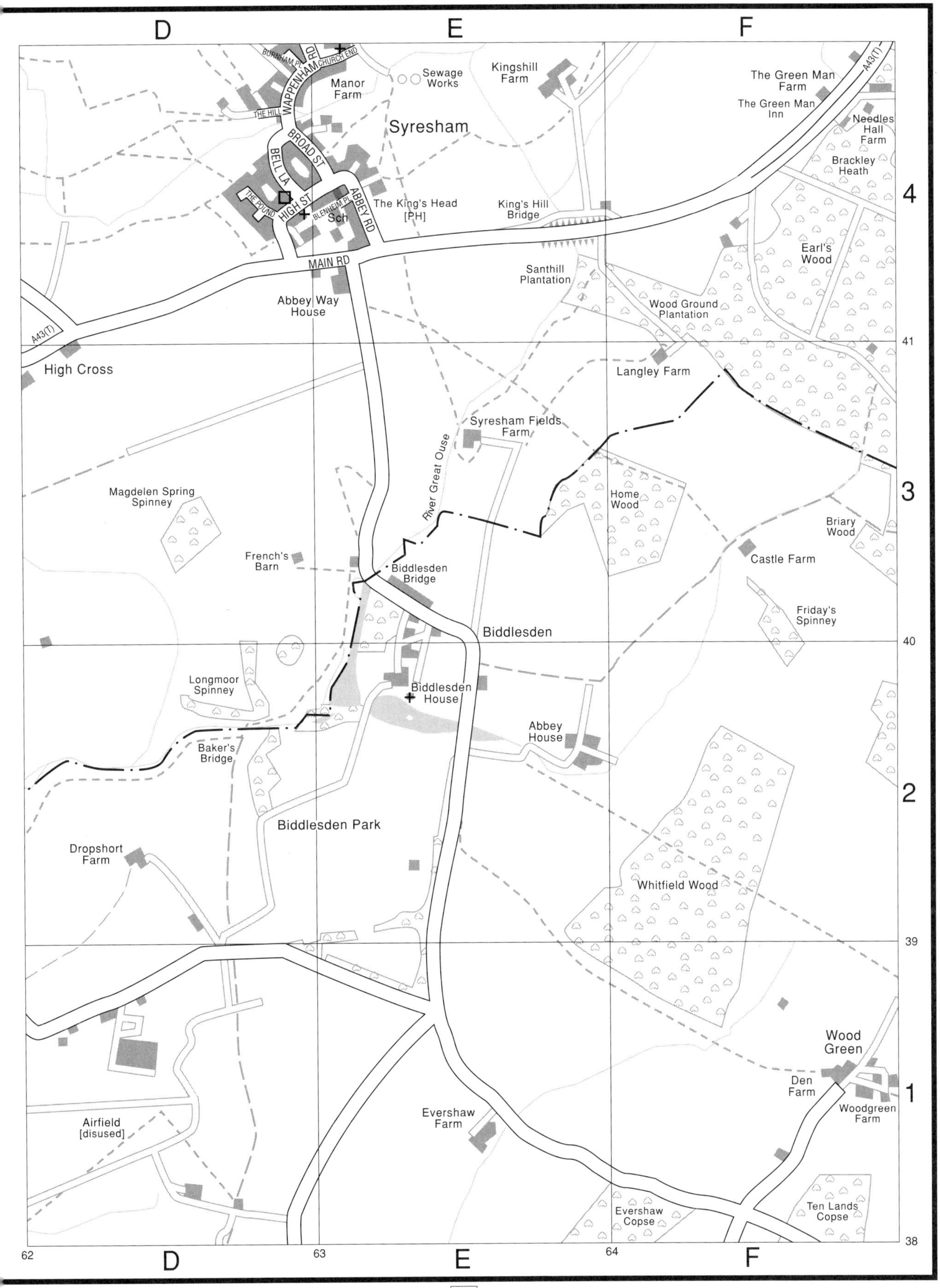

39

27

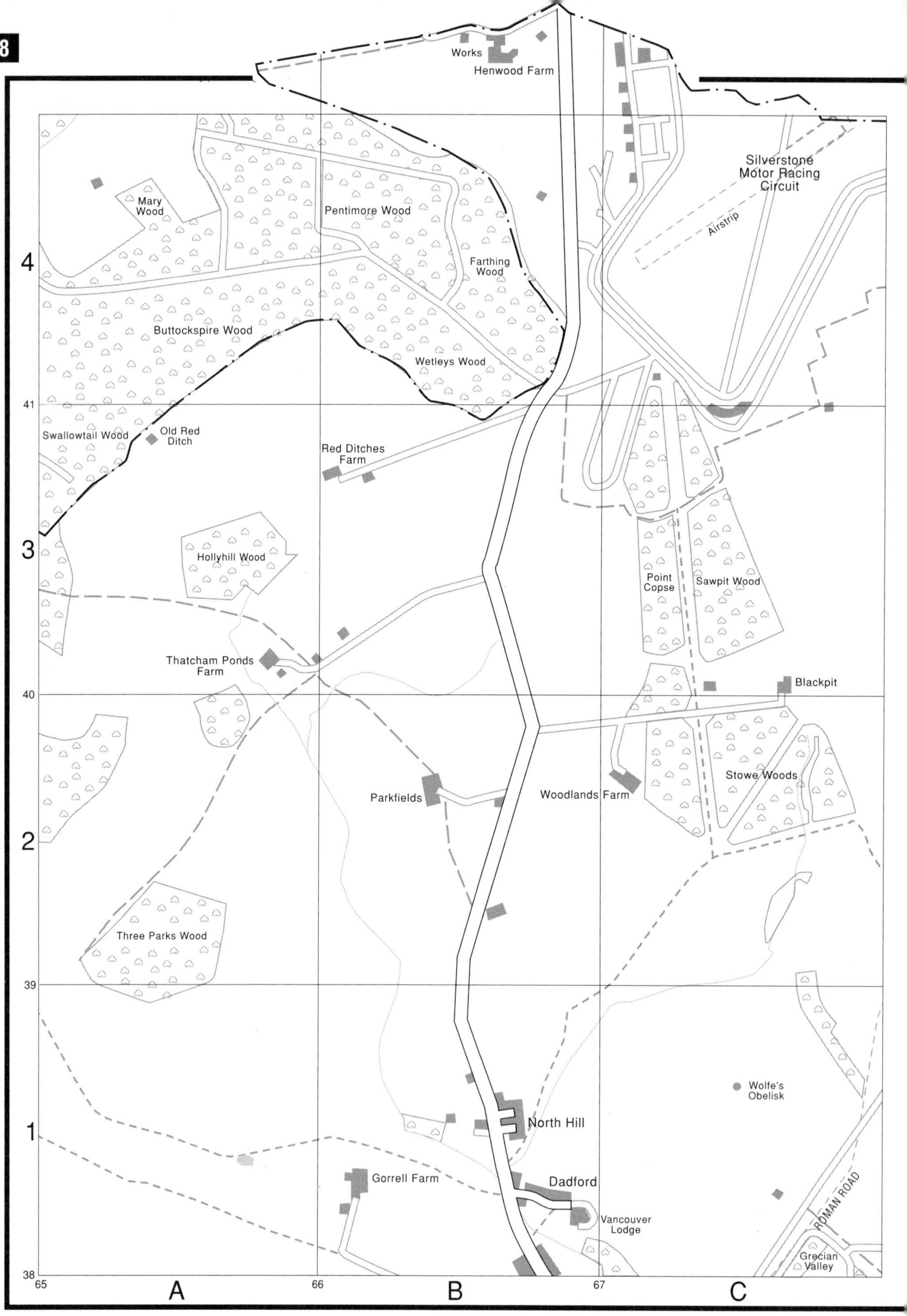
Works
Henwood Farm
Silverstone Motor Racing Circuit
Airstrip
Mary Wood
Pentimore Wood
Farthing Wood
Buttockspire Wood
Wetleys Wood
Swallowtail Wood
Old Red Ditch
Red Ditches Farm
Hollyhill Wood
Point Copse
Sawpit Wood
Thatcham Ponds Farm
Blackpit
Stowe Woods
Parkfields
Woodlands Farm
Three Parks Wood
Wolfe's Obelisk
North Hill
Gorrell Farm
Dadford
Vancouver Lodge
ROMAN ROAD
Grecian Valley
4
41
3
40
2
39
1
38
65
A
66
B
67
C

40

not continued, see key diagram

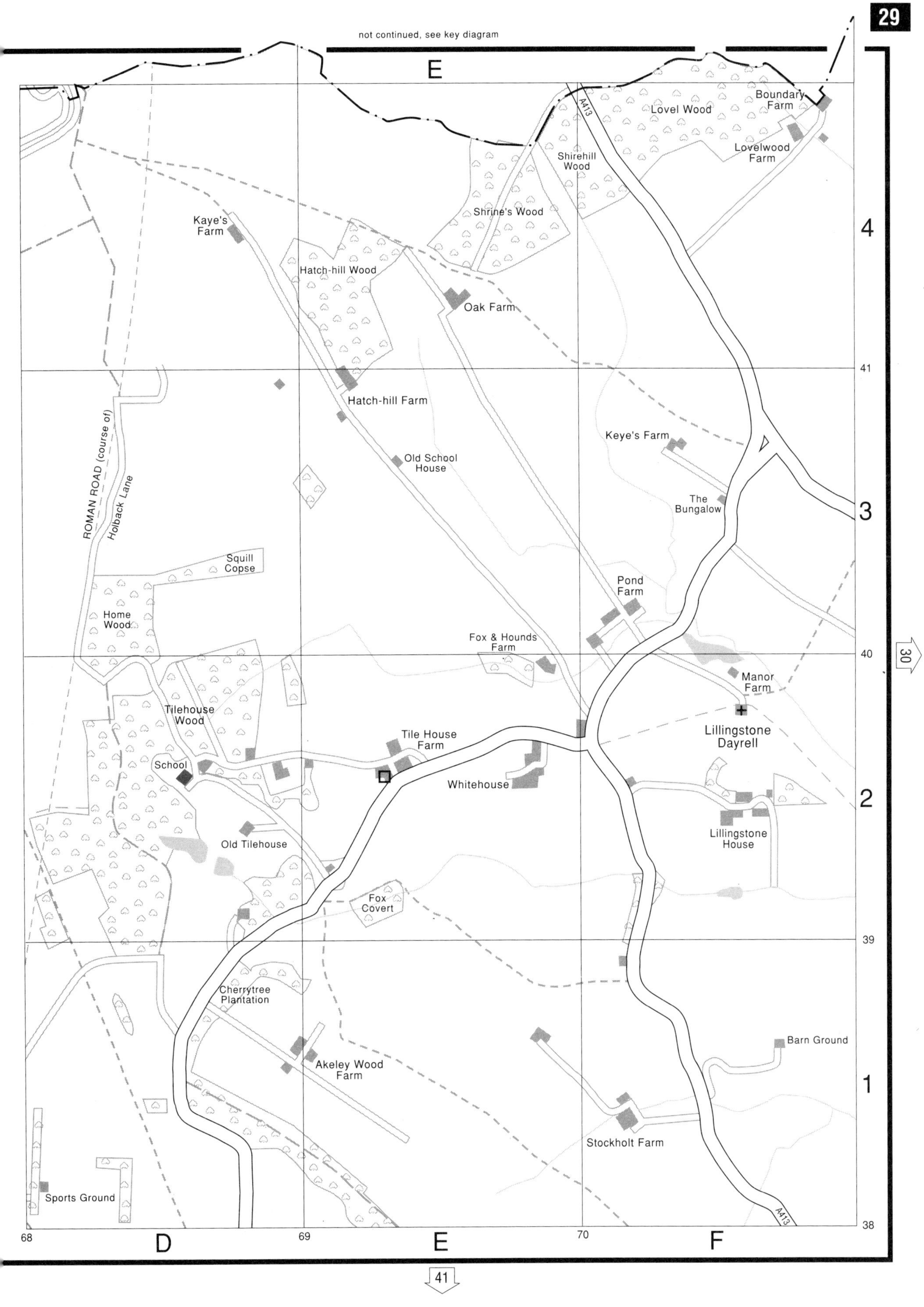

41

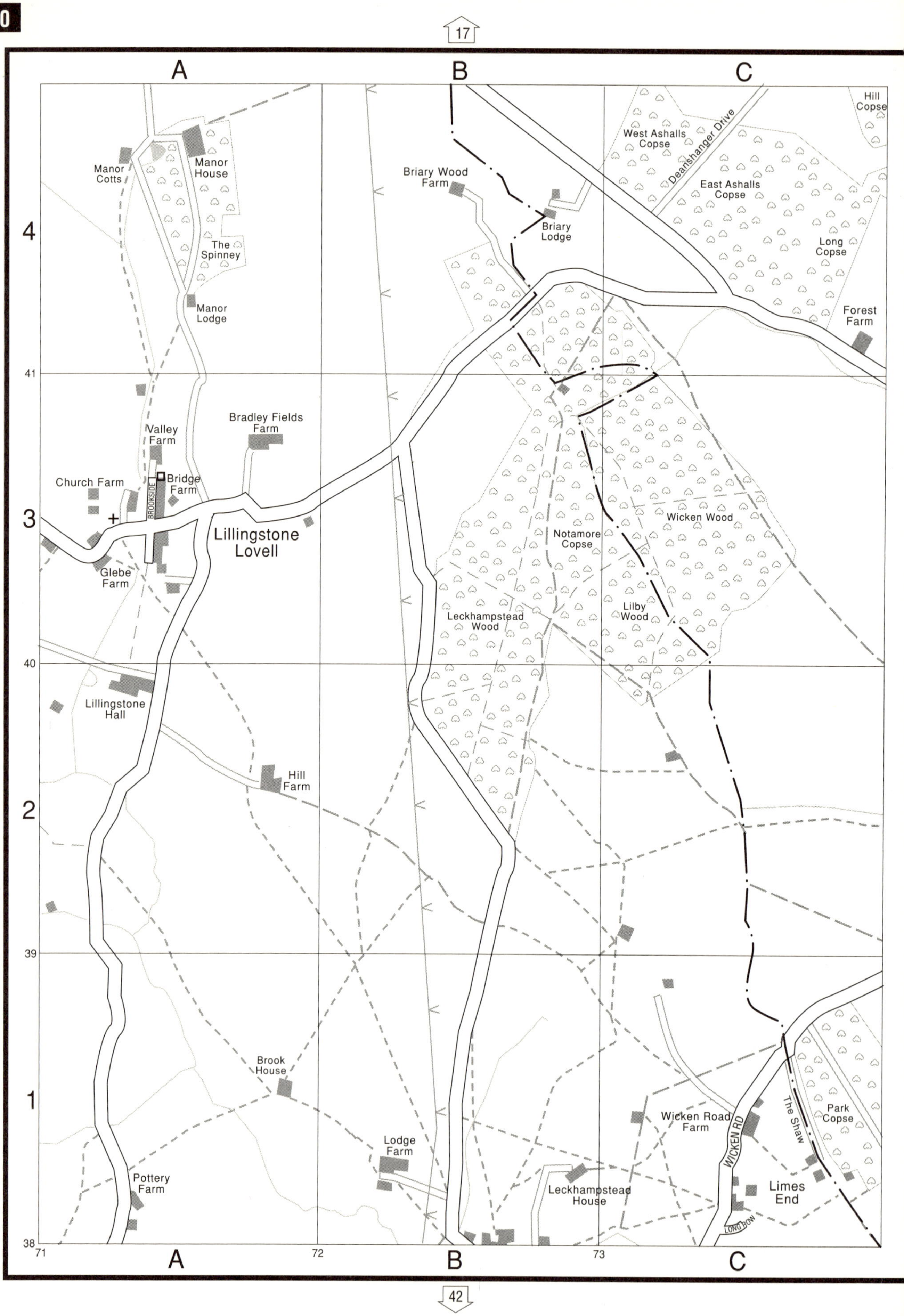
17
29
42
A
B
C
4
3
2
1
41
40
39
38
71
72
73
Hill Copse
West Ashalls Copse
Deanshanger Drive
East Ashalls Copse
Long Copse
Forest Farm
Manor Cotts
Manor House
The Spinney
Manor Lodge
Briary Wood Farm
Briary Lodge
Valley Farm
Bradley Fields Farm
Church Farm
BROOKSIDE
Bridge Farm
Lillingstone Lovell
Glebe Farm
Notamore Copse
Wicken Wood
Leckhampstead Wood
Lilby Wood
Lillingstone Hall
Hill Farm
Brook House
Lodge Farm
Pottery Farm
Leckhampstead House
Wicken Road Farm
WICKEN RD
The Shaw
Park Copse
Limes End
LONG ROW

18

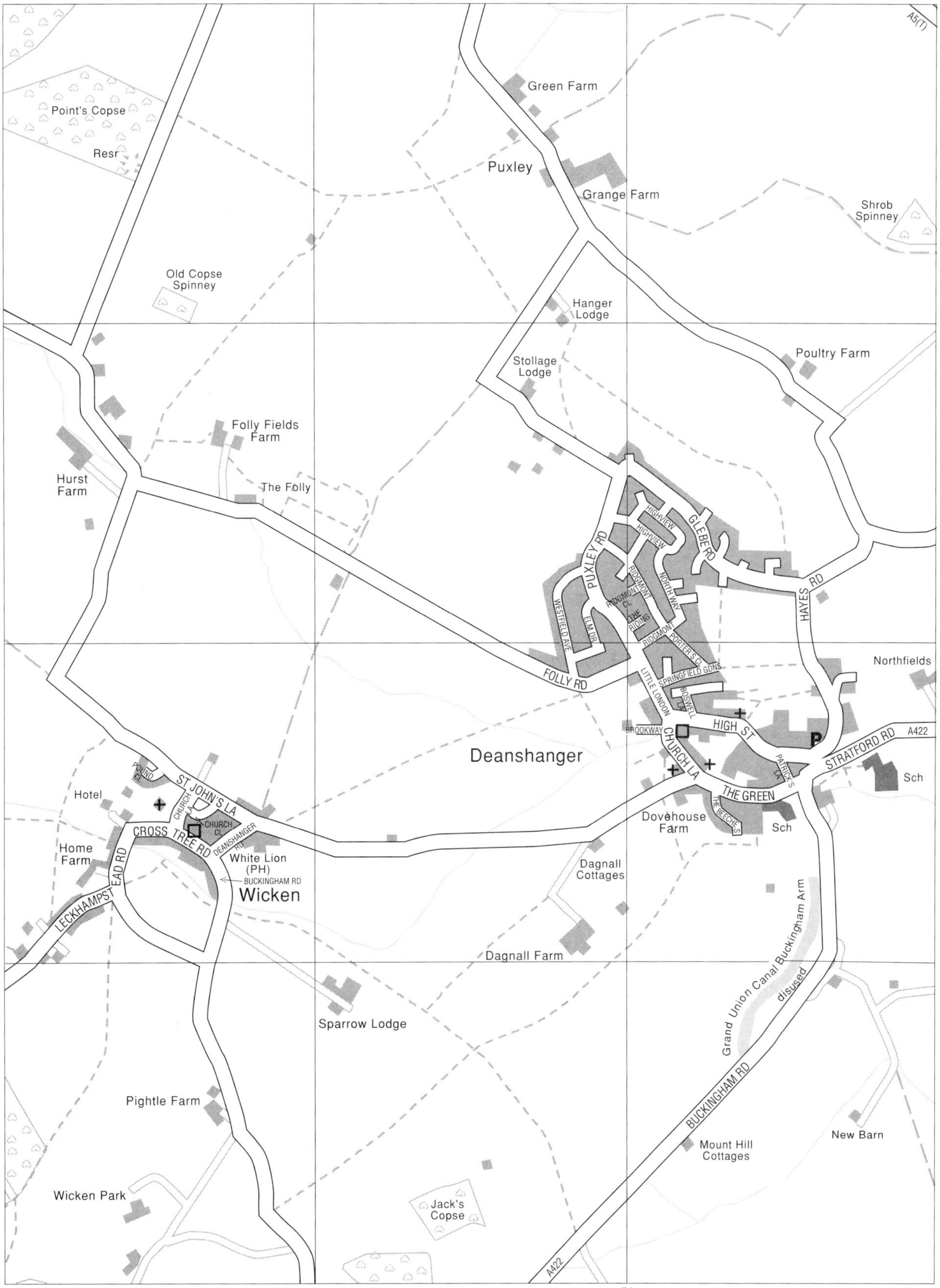
D
E
F
A5(T)
Green Farm
Point's Copse
Resr
Puxley
Grange Farm
Shrob Spinney
4
Old Copse Spinney
Hanger Lodge
41
Poultry Farm
Stollage Lodge
Folly Fields Farm
Hurst Farm
The Folly
3
HIGHVIEW
GLEBE RD
PUXLEY RD
RIDGMONT CL
NORTH WAY
WESTFIELD AVE
ELM DR
THE RIDING
RIDGMONT
PORTER'S CL
HAYES RD
40
SPRINGFIELD GDNS
LITTLE LONDON
BOSWELL LA
FOLLY RD
Northfields
HIGH ST
BROOKWAY
CHURCH LA
STRATFORD RD
A422
Deanshanger
PATRICK'S LA
Sch
POUND CL
ST JOHN'S LA
Hotel
CHURCH
CHURCH CL
CROSS TREE RD
DEANSHANGER RD
THE GREEN
2
THE BEECHES
Dovehouse Farm
Home Farm
LECKHAMPSTEAD RD
White Lion (PH)
BUCKINGHAM RD
Wicken
Dagnall Cottages
Grand Union Canal Buckingham Arm disused
Dagnall Farm
39
Sparrow Lodge
BUCKINGHAM RD
Pightle Farm
1
New Barn
Mount Hill Cottages
Wicken Park
Jack's Copse
A422
74
75
76
38
D
E
F

32

43

19

31

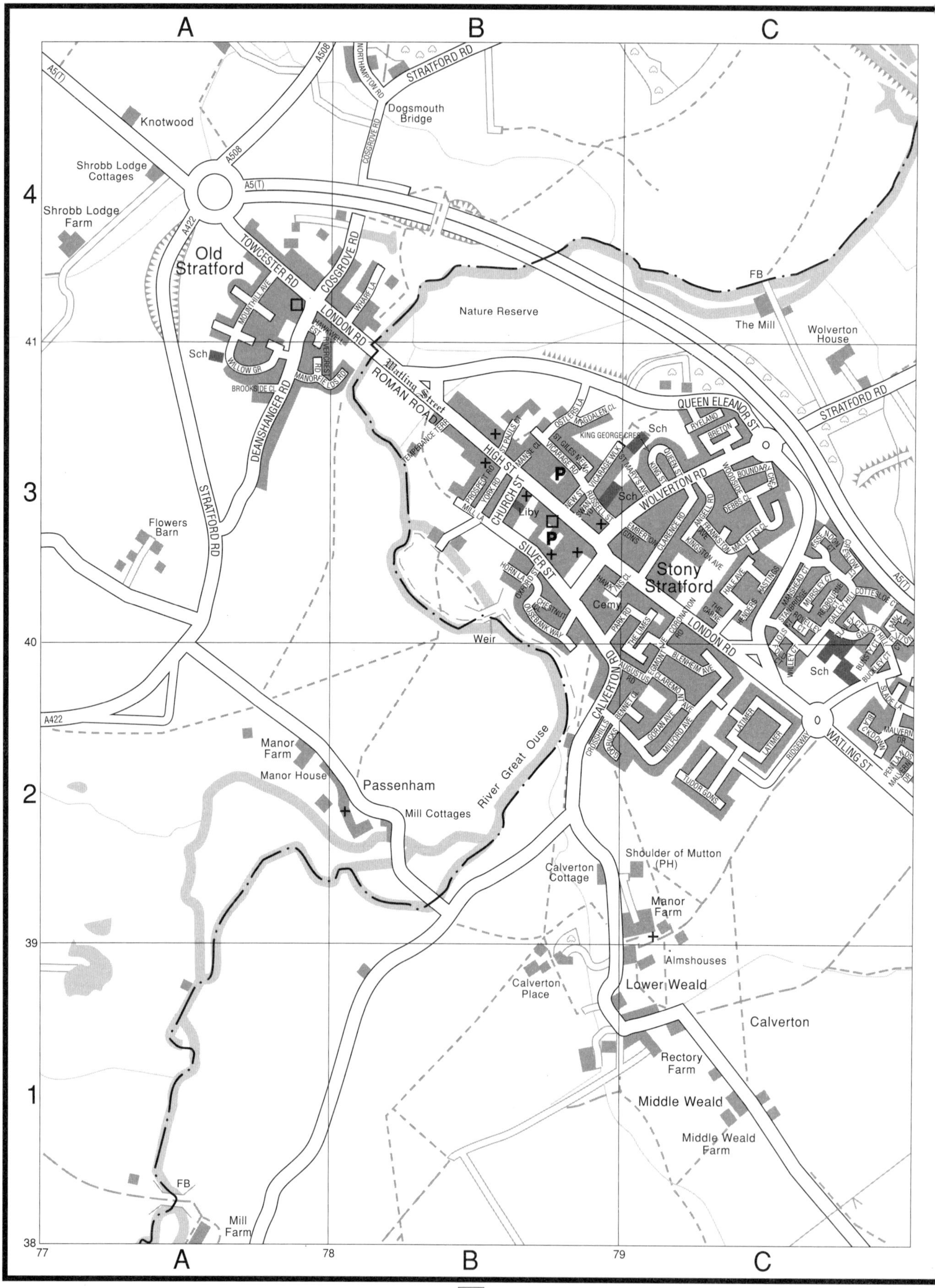
A
B
C
4
3
2
1
41
40
39
38
77
78
79
A5(T)
A508
STRATFORD RD
NORTHAMPTON RD
COSGROVE RD
Dogsmouth Bridge
Knotwood
Shrobb Lodge Cottages
Shrobb Lodge Farm
A422
Old Stratford
TOWCESTER RD
COSGROVE RD
WHARF LA
MOUNTHILL AVE
LONDON RD
HAWKWELL EST
RIVERCREST
MANORFIELDS RD
WILLOW GR
BROOKSIDE CL
Sch
DEANSHANGER RD
STRATFORD RD
Nature Reserve
FB
The Mill
Wolverton House
Watling Street
ROMAN ROAD
TEMPERANCE TERR
HIGH ST
ST PAULS CT
PROSPECT RD
YORK RD
MILL LA
CHURCH ST
MANSE CL
OSTLERS LA
MAGDALEN CL
ST GILES MEWS
VICARAGE RD
KING GEORGE CRES
VICARAGE WLK
ST MARY'S AVE
RUSSELL ST
NEW ST
SWAN TER
Sch
QUEEN ELEANOR ST
RYELAND
BRETON
KING ST
QUEENS CT
WOLVERTON RD
WOODSIDE
BOUNDARY CRES
DEBBS CL
STRATFORD RD
P
Liby
EMBERTON GDNS
CLARENCE RD
ANGELL RD
FRANKSTON AVE
KINGSTON AVE
MALLETTS CL
SILVER ST
HORN LA
OXFORD ST
CHESTNUTS
OUSEBANK WAY
HAWKINS CL
Cemy
Stony Stratford
HALE AVE
HASTINGS
THE CARNE
HENDERS
PARK RD
THE LIMES
CORONATION RD
LONDON RD
Weir
CALVERTON RD
AUGUSTUS RD
EGMONT AVE
CLAREMONT AVE
BLENHEIM AVE
BENNETT CL
GORAN AVE
MILFORD AVE
LATIMER
RIDGEWAY
TUDOR GDNS
CROSSHILLS
GOLDCREST
WATLING ST
Sch
A5(T)
River Great Ouse
Manor Farm
Manor House
Passenham
Mill Cottages
Flowers Barn
Calverton Cottage
Shoulder of Mutton (PH)
Manor Farm
Almshouses
Calverton Place
Lower Weald
Calverton
Rectory Farm
Middle Weald
Middle Weald Farm
FB
Mill Farm

44

20

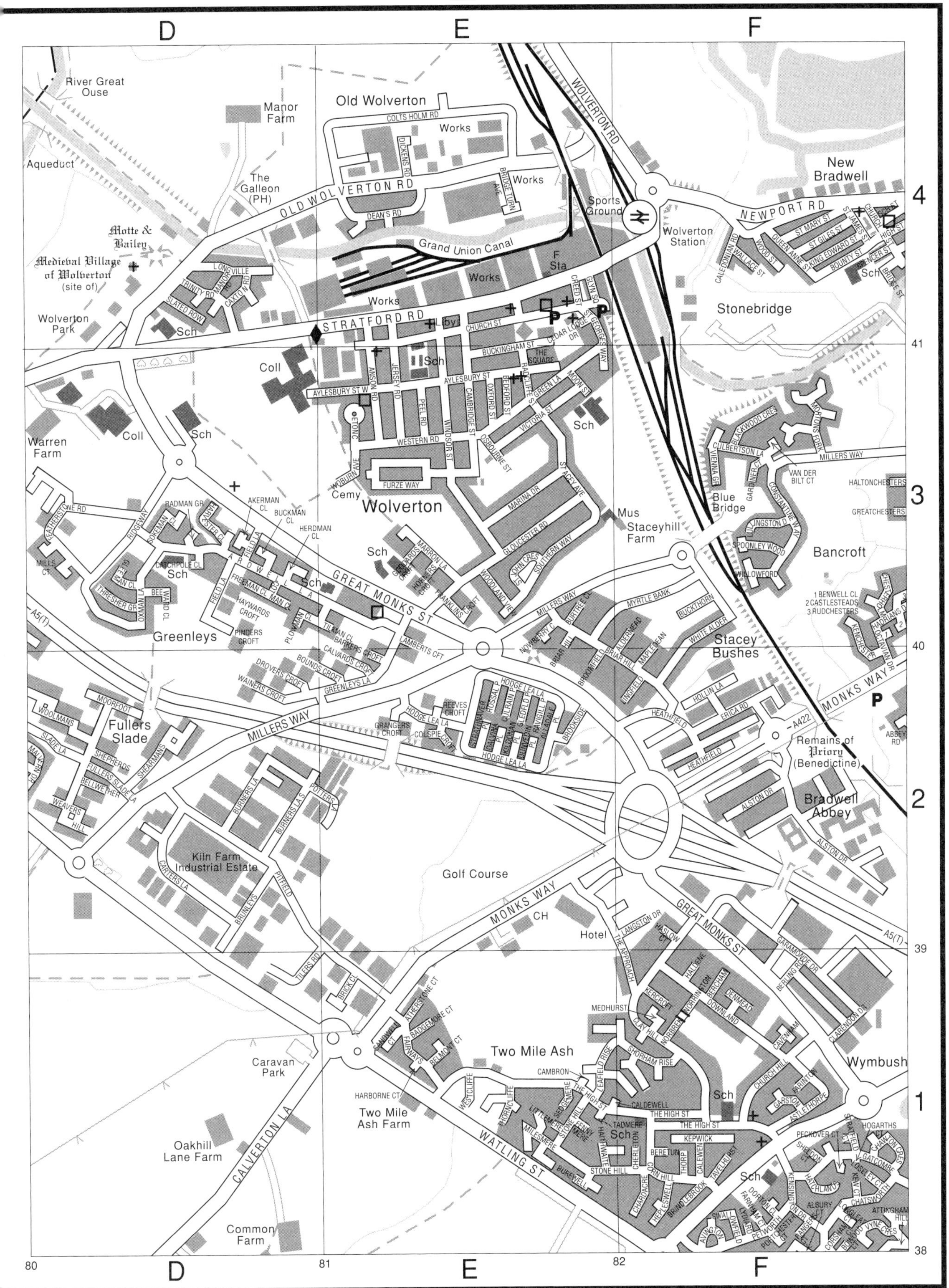
D
E
F
River Great Ouse
Manor Farm
Old Wolverton
COLTS HOLM RD
Works
DICKENS RD
Aqueduct
The Galleon (PH)
OLD WOLVERTON RD
DEAN'S RD
BRIDGE TURN AVE
Works
WOLVERTON RD
New Bradwell
Sports Ground
Wolverton Station
NEWPORT RD
Motte & Bailey
Medieval Village of Wolverton (site of)
Grand Union Canal
F Sta
Works
CALEDONIAN RD
WALLACE ST
WOOD ST
QUEEN ANNE'S ST
ST MARY ST
ST GILES ST
KING EDWARD ST
BOUNTY ST
ST JAMES ST
CHURCH ST
HIGH ST
SPENCER ST
BRIDGE ST
Sch
LONGVILLE
MANOR RD
CAXTON RD
TRINITY RD
SLATED ROW
Works
STRATFORD RD
Lby
CHURCH ST
CREED ST
GLYN SQ
ST GEORGES WAY
CEDAR LODGE DR
Stonebridge
Wolverton Park
Sch
BUCKINGHAM ST
THE SQUARE
Coll
Sch
AYLESBURY ST
AYLESBURY ST W
ANSON RD
JERSEY RD
PEEL RD
CAMBRIDGE ST
OXFORD ST
BEDFORD ST
RADCLIFFE ST
GREEN LA
MOON ST
ETON CR
WINDSOR ST
VICTORIA ST
WESTERN RD
OSBOURNE ST
Sch
Warren Farm
Coll
Sch
MORTONS FORK
BLACKWOOD CRES
CULBERTSON LA
VIENNA GR
MILLERS WAY
VAN DER BILT CT
WOBURN AVE
FURZE WAY
Cemy
Wolverton
STACEY AVE
MARINA DR
GARDINER CT
CONSTANTINE WAY
HALTONCHESTERS
GREATCHESTERS
Blue Bridge
Mus
Staceyhill Farm
LIVINGSTON DR
SPOONLEY WOOD
WILLOWFORD
Bancroft
RADMAN GR
AKERMAN CL
BUCKMAN CL
HERDMAN CL
RIDGEWAY
SOKEMAN CL
HARVESTER CL
FEATHERSTONE RD
MILLS CT
GLEEMAN CL
CATCHPOLE CL
Sch
ARDWELL LA
Sch
GREAT MONKS ST
MARRON LA
GLOUCESTER RD
SOUTHERN WAY
ST JOHN CRES
WOODLAND VIEW
MILLERS WAY
BURTREE CL
MYRTLE BANK
BUCKTHORN
1 BENWELL CL
2 CASTLESTEADS
3 RUDCHESTERS
THRESHER GR
OXMAN LA
BEEWARD CL
FIELD LA
FREEMAN CL
HAYWARDS CROFT
PINDERS CROFT
PLOWMAN CL
TILLMAN CL
BARKERS CROFT
FRANKLINS CROFT
Greenleys
LAMBERTS CFT
NORBURY CL
BRIAR HILL
ALDERMEAD
MAPLE DEAN
WHITE ALDER
Stacey Bushes
CALVARDS CROFT
BOUNDS CROFT
DROVERS CROFT
WAINERS CROFT
GREENLEYS LA
BROOMFIELD
HOLLIN LA
KENCHESTER
HADRIANS DR
OCTAVIAN DR
MONKS WAY
P
A5(T)
MOORFOOT
WOOLMANS
SLADE LA
Fullers Slade
SHEARMANS
SHEPHERDS
FULLERS SLADE
BELLWETHER
WEAVERS HILL
HODGE LEA LA
REEVES CROFT
GRANGERS CROFT
COLSPIE
STRATHNAVER PL
DALVINA PL
KILDONAN PL
RUSSELL
CULRAIN
LEDFIELD PL
TOWNSON PL
BAWGILL PL
ALLAHDALE PL
BROOKSIDE
LINGFIELD
HEATHFIELD
ERICA RD
A422
Remains of Priory (Benedictine)
ABBEY RD
MILLERS WAY
BURNERS LA
BURNERS LA S
POTTERS LA
ALSTON DR
Bradwell Abbey
Kiln Farm Industrial Estate
CARTERS LA
PITFIELD
BRUNLEYS
Golf Course
MONKS WAY
CH
Hotel
LANGSTON DR
HASLOW CT
THE APPROACH
GREAT MONKS ST
GARAMONDE DR
BERLINGE RD
A5(T)
TILERS RD
BRICK CL
ATHERSTONE CT
BADGEMORE CT
FAIRWAYS
BELMONT CT
SANDWELL CT
MEDHURST
KERCROFT
HALDENE
NORTHSTOW
BERCHAM
DENMEAD
DOWNLAND
CLAY HILL
NORBREK
SHORHAM RISE
CAVENHAM
CLARENDON DR
Caravan Park
Two Mile Ash
CAMBRON
LEAFIELD RISE
THE HIGH ST
Sch
CHURCH HILL
ABINGTON
GARSTON
ASTLETHORPE
Wymbush
HARBORNE CT
Two Mile Ash Farm
WESTCLIFFE
THORNCLIFFE
SEDGEMERE
LITTLEMERE
MILESMERE
FENNY MERE
STONE HILL
CALDEWELL
THE HIGH ST
THE HIGH ST
TADMERE
KEPWICK
Sch
BERETUN
HAITHWAITE
CHERLETON
THORP
CALEWEN
TAVELHURST
HOGARTHS CT
PECKOVER CT
SHELDON CT
STRATFIELD CT
GATCOMBE
HAWTON CRES
CALVERTON LA
Oakhill Lane Farm
WATLING ST
BUREWELL
STONE HILL
CHARNACRE
HEPLESWELL
BRINDLEBROOK
Sch
HATCHLANDS
KEW CT
CHATSWORTH
ALBURY CT
LOSELEY CT
ATTINGHAM HILL
AVINGTON
SWALL CT
DORTON CL
FARNHAM CT
LYDIARD
PETWORTH
PORTCHESTER CT
KENSINGTON DR
LANGLEY CT
CORSHAM CT
BOWOOD CT
VYNE CRES
Common Farm
80
81
82
D
E
F
38
39
40
41
1
2
3
4

34

45

21

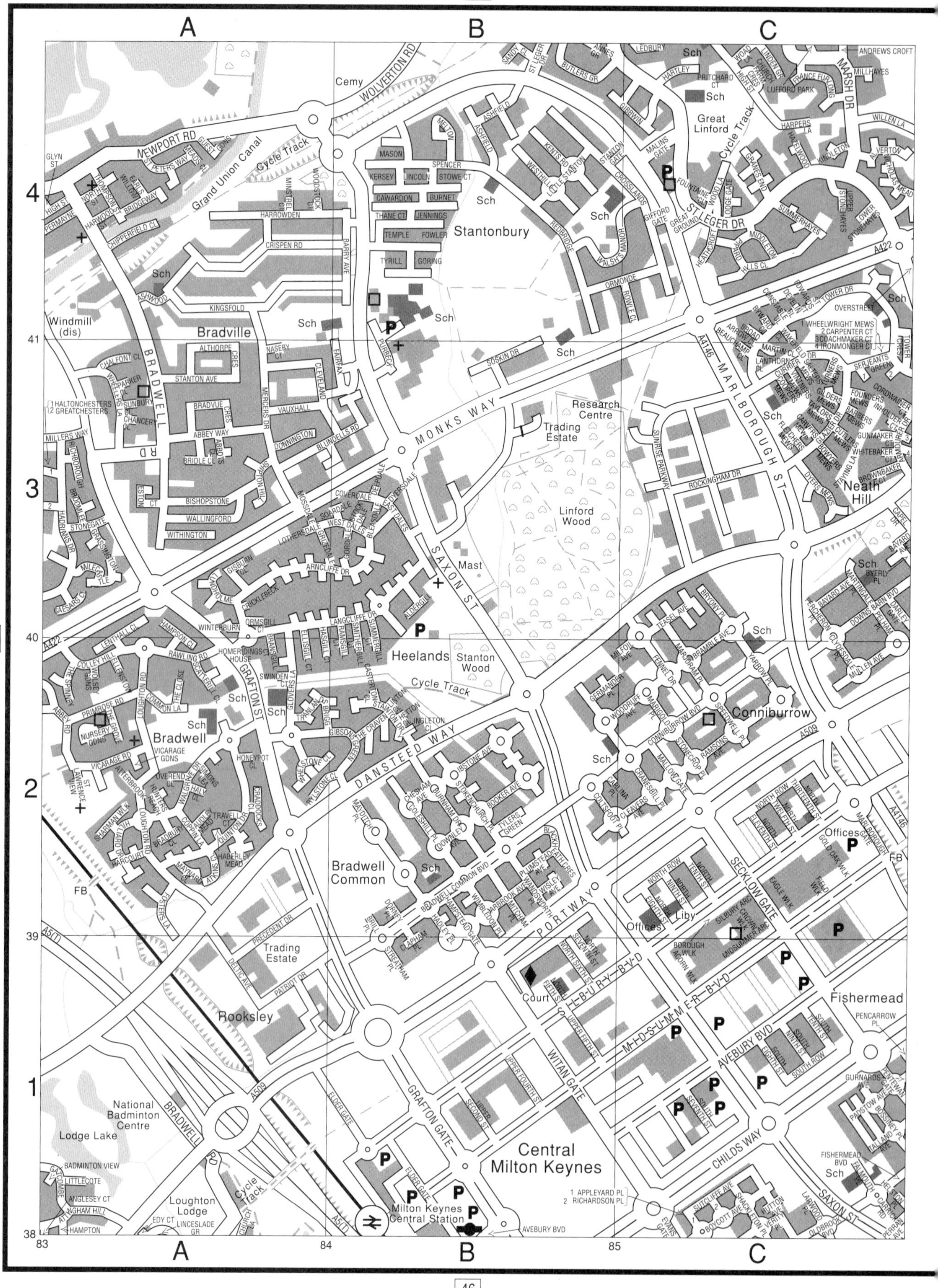

A
B
C
4
3
2
1
41
40
39
38
83
84
85
Cemy
WOLVERTON RD
NEWPORT RD
Grand Union Canal
Cycle Track
GLYN ST
HIGH ST
PERMAYNE
HARWOOD ST
BRIDGEWAY
CHIPPERFIELD CL
ST PETERS WAY
HARROWDEN
CRISPEN RD
KINGSFOLD
ASHWOOD
MINSTREL CT
WOODSTOCK CT
BARRY AVE
MASON
SPENCER
KERSEY
LINCOLN
STOWE CT
CAWARDON
BURNET
THANE CT
JENNINGS
TEMPLE
FOWLER
TYRILL
GORING
MELTON
ASHFIELD
Stantonbury
Sch
LITTLE STANTON
KENTS RD
WESTHILL
STANTON GATE
CROSSLANDS
REDBRIDGE
WALSH'S MANOR
ORMONDE
ROWLE CL
GIFFORD GATE
MALINS GATE
GIBBWIN
BUTLERS GR
ST LEGER CT
SANDY CL
LEDBURY
HARTLEY
PRITCHARD CT
Great Linford
Cycle Track
FOUNTAINE CL
WOOD LA
LODGE GATE
GREAT GROUND
ST LEGER DR
HEATHCROFT
MIDDLETON
HILLS CL
SUMMERHAYES
UPPER STONEHAYES
LOWER STONEHAYES
HARPERS LA
HAZELWOOD
KINDLETON
ALVERTON
LUFFORD PARK
FRANCE FURLONG
MARSH DR
MILLHAYES
ANDREWS CROFT
WILLEN LA
A422
TOWER DR
OVERSTREET
1 WHEELWRIGHT MEWS
2 CARPENTER CT
3 COACHMAKER CT
4 IRONMONGER CT
TOWER CRES
SERJEANTS GREEN
CORDWAINER CT
FOUNDERS MEWS
BARBERS MEWS
GUNMAKER CT
WHITEBAKER CT
BROWNBAKER CT
Neath Hill
DYERS MEWS
STAVING LA
A4146
MARLBOROUGH ST
Windmill (dis)
Bradville
CHALFONT CL
STANTON AVE
ALTHORPE CRES
NASEBY CT
FAIRFAX
CLEVELAND
PURBECK
1 HALTONCHESTERS
2 GREATCHESTERS
MILLERS WAY
SUNBURY CL
CHANCERY CL
BRADWELL RD
BRADVUE CRES
ABBEY WAY
ABBOTS CL
BRIDLE CL
BISHOPSTONE
WALLINGFORD
WITHINGTON
ESTON CT
MERCERS DR
VAUXHALL
DONNINGTON
BLUNDELLS RD
SHIPTON HILL
RICHBOROUGH
BROOMLEE
STONEGATE
HADRIANS DR
CAESARS CL
MONKS WAY
SOSKIN DR
Research Centre
Trading Estate
SUNRISE PARKWAY
ROCKINGHAM DR
Linford Wood
Mast
SAXON ST
COVERDALE
DEEPDALE
WHARFEDALE
WEST DALES
ARNCLIFFE DR
GISBURN CL
CRICKLEBECK
WINTERBURN
ORMSGILL CT
LANGCLIFFE DR
ELLISGILL CT
HASGILL CT
RAMSGILL CT
ALDERGILL
Heelands
Stanton Wood
A422
LENTHALL CL
HAMPSON CL
RAWLING RD
COLLEY HILL
THE SPINNEY
PRIMROSE RD
NURSERY GDNS
COMMON LA
THE CLOSE
LOUGHTON RD
GRAFTON ST
HOMER HOUSE
SWINDEN CT
GLOVERS LA
Bradwell
VICARAGE RD
VICARAGE GDNS
ST LAWRENCE VIEW
HONEYPOT CL
DANSTEED WAY
INGLETON CL
Cycle Track
KILNSTONE CL
GIBSONS GREEN
MAYDITCH PL
CHESHAM AVE
BURNHAM DR
COLESHILL PL
STOKENCHURCH PL
IBSTONE AVE
BOOKER AVE
TYLERS GREEN
Bradwell Common
BRADWELL COMMON BVD
HADLEY PL
CLAPHAM PL
STREATHAM PL
BRILL PL
DORNEY PL
FB
FOSTERS LA
HABERLEY MEAD
TRAVELL CT
A5(T)
PRECEDENT DR
Trading Estate
DELTIC AVE
PATRIOT DR
Rooksley
A509
BRADWELL
National Badminton Centre
Lodge Lake
BADMINTON VIEW
LITTLECOTE
ANGLESEY CT
HAMPTON
Loughton Lodge
LINCESLADE GR
EDY CT
Cycle Track
CHURCH LA
A5(T)
Milton Keynes Central Station
P
ELDER GATE
GRAFTON GATE
Central Milton Keynes
AVEBURY BVD
1 APPLEYARD PL
2 RICHARDSON PL
MILFOIL AVE
TEASEL AVE
BRYONY PL
MARJORAM PL
BRAMBLE AVE
Sch
Conniburrow
CONNIBURROW BVD
SPEEDWELL PL
YARROW PL
GERMANDER PL
WOODRUFF AVE
MARIGOLD PL
STONECROP PL
RAMSONS AVE
MALLOW GATE
CARLINA PL
COLTSFOOT PL
CLEAVERS AVE
A509
NORTH ROW
NORTH ELEVENTH ST
NORTH TWELFTH ST
NORTH THIRTEENTH ST
PORTWAY
NORTH TENTH ST
NORTH NINTH ST
NORTH EIGHTH ST
SECKLOW GATE
SILBURY ARC
CROWN WLK
MIDSUMMER ARC
BOROUGH WLK
ACORN WLK
Liby
Offices
Offices
MARLBOROUGH GATE
A4146
GOLD OAK WLK
EAGLE WLK
FIELD WLK
FB
Court
NORTH SIXTH ST
NORTH SEVENTH ST
SILBURY BVD
MIDSUMMER BVD
AVEBURY BVD
WITAN GATE
UPPER FIFTH ST
UPPER FOURTH ST
UPPER SECOND ST
SOUTH ROW
SOUTH NINTH ST
SOUTH TENTH ST
SOUTH EIGHTH ST
SOUTH SEVENTH ST
Fishermead
PENCARROW PL
GURNARDS AVE
PADSTOW AVE
BOSSINEY PL
FALMOUTH PL
CHILDS WAY
SAXON ST
FISHERMEAD BVD
Sch
SUTCLIFFE AVE
BOYCOTT AVE
SHACKLETON PL
HUTTON AVE
LARWOOD PL
OLDBROOK BVD
VERITY PL
EVANS GATE

33

46

22

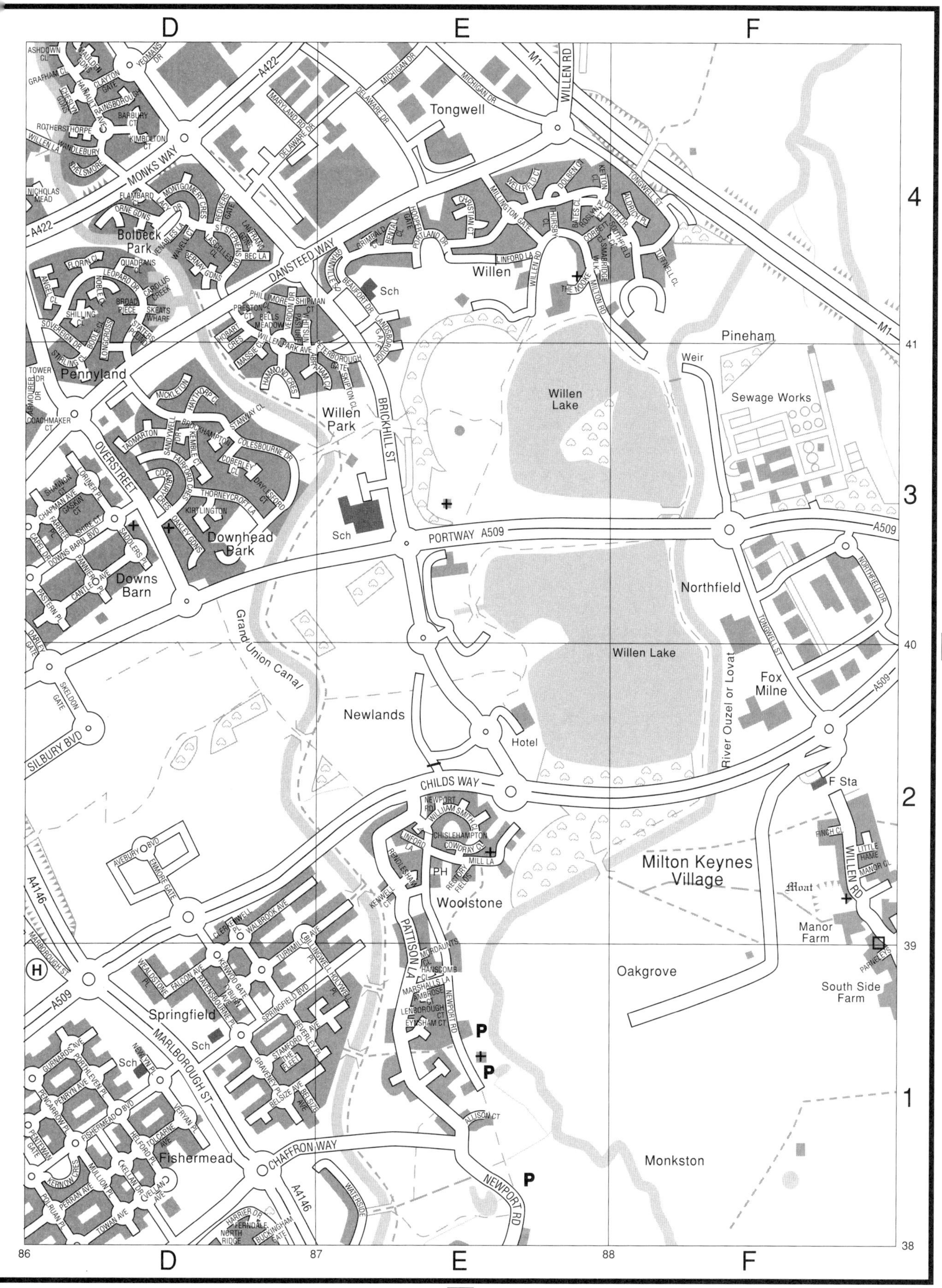
D
E
F
4
3
2
1
41
40
39
38
86
87
88
Tongwell
Willen
Bolbeck Park
Pennyland
Willen Park
Willen Lake
Pineham
Weir
Sewage Works
Downhead Park
Downs Barn
Northfield
Fox Milne
Newlands
Hotel
Grand Union Canal
River Ouzel or Lovat
F Sta
Milton Keynes Village
Moat
Manor Farm
South Side Farm
Woolstone
PH
Oakgrove
Springfield
Fishermead
Monkston
Sch
P
H
M1
A422
A509
A4146
MONKS WAY
DANSTEED WAY
PORTWAY A509
CHILDS WAY
CHAFFRON WAY
SILBURY BVD
MARLBOROUGH ST
OVERSTREET
BRICKHILL ST
WILLEN RD
NEWPORT RD
PATTISON LA
TONGWELL ST
NORTHFIELD DR
MICHIGAN DR
DELAWARE DR
MARYLAND RD
TONGWELL ST
LINFORD LA
MILTON RD
THE WOOKE
AVEBURY BVD
ENMORE GATE
WALBROOK AVE
TURNMILL AVE
HOLYWELL PL
SPRINGFIELD BVD
MILL LA
ALLISON CT
WATERSIDE
HARRIER DR
FERNDALE
NORTH RIDGE
BUCKINGHAM GATE
TOWAN AVE
PERRAN AVE
FISHERMEAD BVD
VERYAN PL
KERNOW CRES
SKELDON GATE
DARLEY GATE
TOWER DR
COACHMAKER CT
NICHOLAS MEAD
ASHDOWN CL
YEOMANS DR
KIMBOLTON CT
BARBURY CT
FLAMBARD CL
ORNE GDNS
MONTGOMERY CRES
QUADRANS CL
LEOPARD DR
CAROLUS CREEK
SKEATS WHARF
BROAD PIECE
SHILLING CL
SOVEREIGN DR
LONGCROSS
STIRLING CL
MICKLETON
TADMARTON
STANWAY CL
COLESBOURNE DR
THORNEYCROFT LA
KIRTLINGTON
DAYLESFORD CT
GRANVILLE SQ
BEAUFORT DR
LANDSBOROUGH GATE
STAPLETON CL
KETTON CL
TUFFNELL CL
WILLIAM SMITH CL
CHISLEHAMPTON
COWDRAY CL
RECTORY FIELDS
KENWELL CT
MORDAUNTS CT
HANSCOMB CL
MARSHALLS LA
AMBROSE CT
LENBOROUGH CT
EYNSHAM CT
PARNELL CL
FINCH CL
LITTLE HAME
MANOR CL

36

47

23

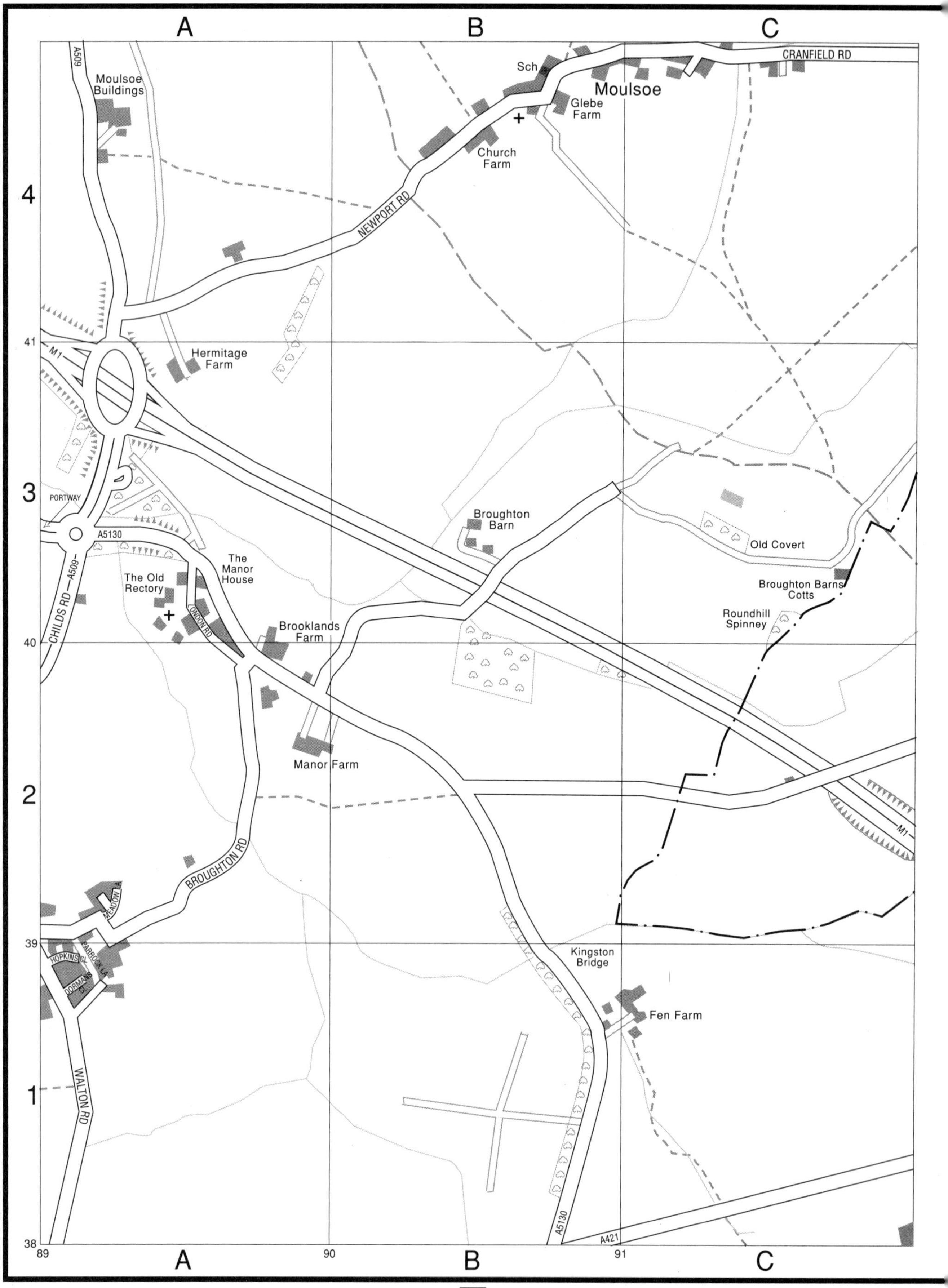
A
B
C
4
3
2
1
41
40
39
38
89
90
91
A509
Moulsoe Buildings
Sch
Moulsoe
Glebe Farm
Church Farm
CRANFIELD RD
NEWPORT RD
M1
Hermitage Farm
PORTWAY
A5130
CHILDS RD—A509
Broughton Barn
Old Covert
The Manor House
The Old Rectory
LONDON RD
Brooklands Farm
Broughton Barns Cotts
Roundhill Spinney
Manor Farm
BROUGHTON RD
MEADOW LA
HOPKINS CL
PARROCK LA
DORMANS CL
Kingston Bridge
Fen Farm
WALTON RD
A5130
A421

35

48

24

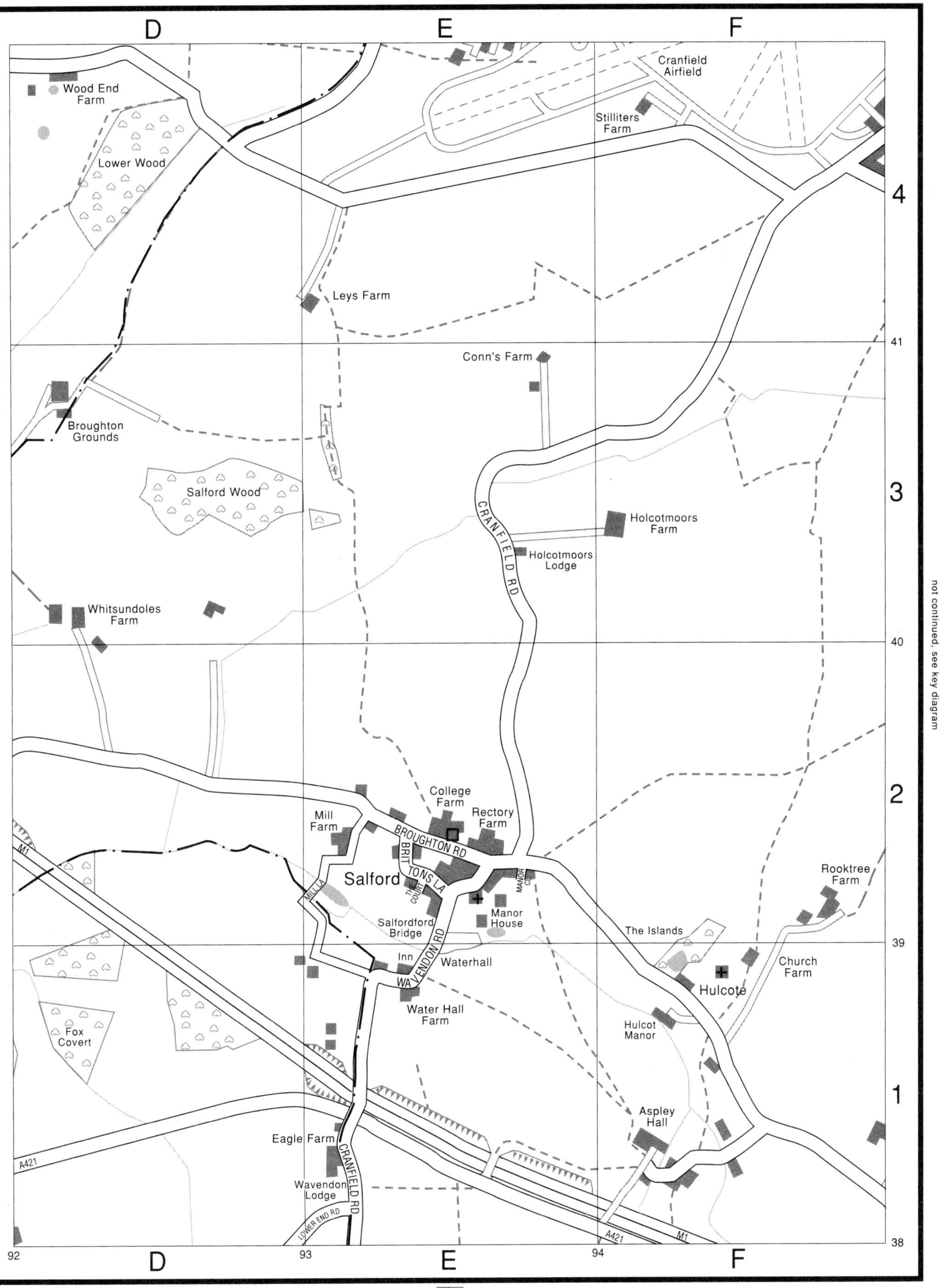
D
E
F
Cranfield Airfield
Wood End Farm
Stilliters Farm
Lower Wood
4
Leys Farm
41
Conn's Farm
Broughton Grounds
3
Salford Wood
CRANFIELD RD
Holcotmoors Farm
Holcotmoors Lodge
Whitsundoles Farm
40
2
College Farm
Rectory Farm
Mill Farm
BROUGHTON RD
BRITTONS LA
M1
Salford
MILL LA
THE COURT
MANOR CL
Rooktree Farm
Manor House
Salfordford Bridge
WAVENDON RD
The Islands
39
Inn
Waterhall
Church Farm
Hulcote
Fox Covert
Water Hall Farm
Hulcot Manor
1
Aspley Hall
Eagle Farm
CRANFIELD RD
A421
Wavendon Lodge
LOWER END RD
A421
M1
38
92
93
94
D
E
F
not continued, see key diagram

49

26

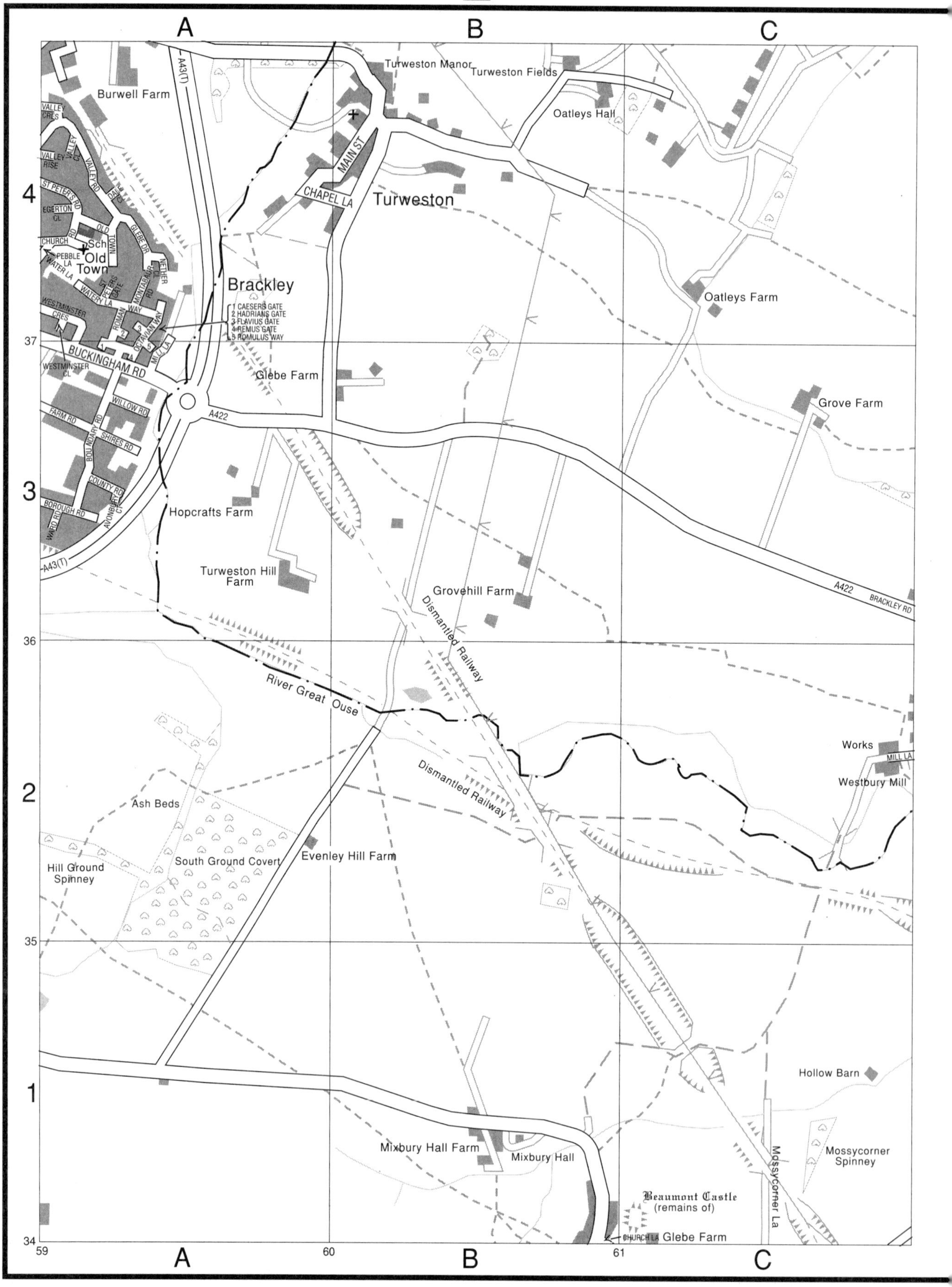

not continued, see key diagram

not continued, see key diagram

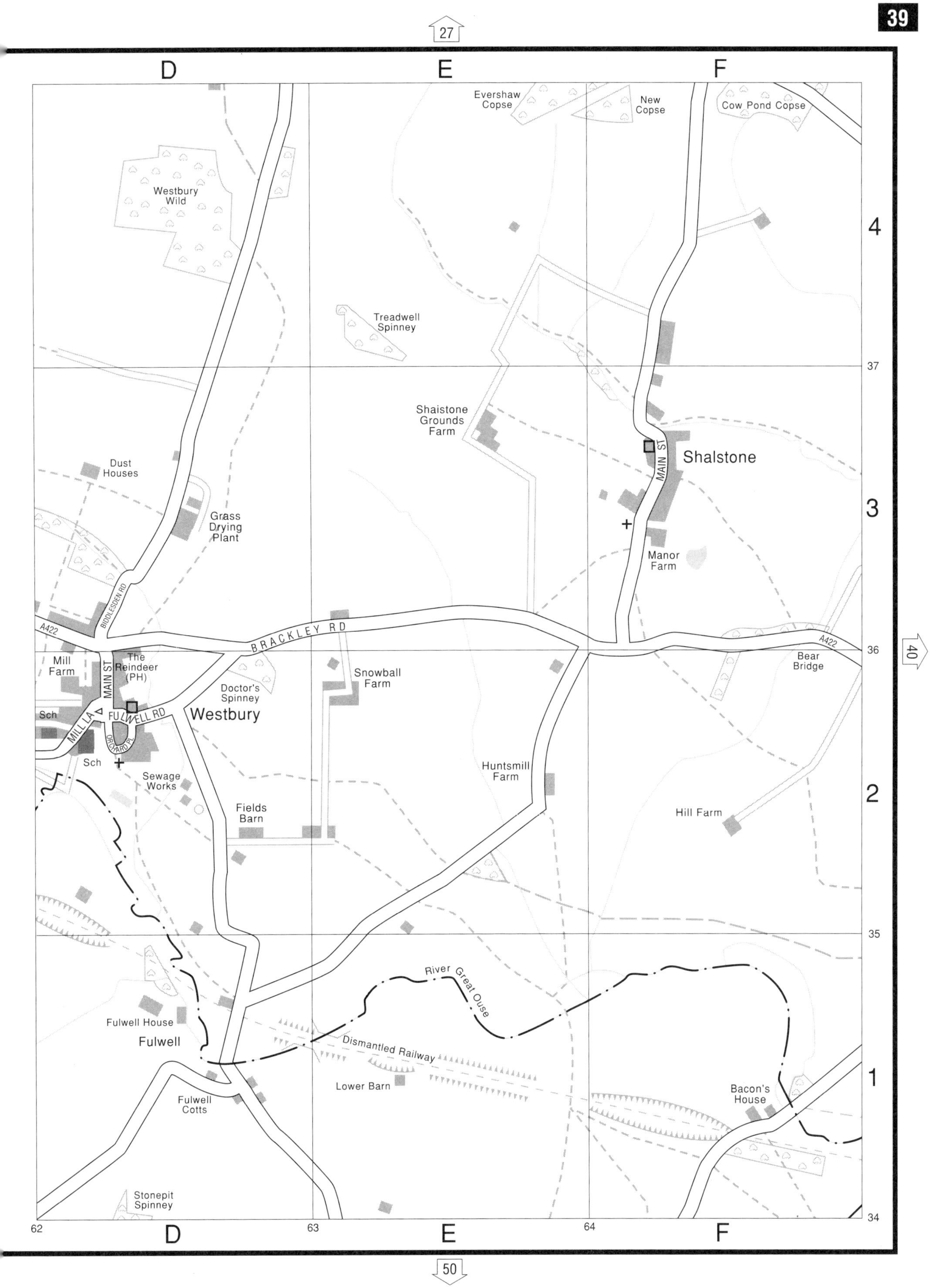
27
D
E
F
Evershaw Copse
New Copse
Cow Pond Copse
Westbury Wild
4
Treadwell Spinney
37
Shaistone Grounds Farm
MAIN ST
Shalstone
Dust Houses
Grass Drying Plant
3
Manor Farm
BIDDLESDEN RD
A422
BRACKLEY RD
A422
36
Bear Bridge
40
Mill Farm
MAIN ST
The Reindeer (PH)
Snowball Farm
Doctor's Spinney
Sch
MILL LA
FULWELL RD
ORCHARD PL
Westbury
Sch
Sewage Works
Huntsmill Farm
2
Fields Barn
Hill Farm
35
River Great Ouse
Fulwell House
Fulwell
Dismantled Railway
1
Lower Barn
Fulwell Cotts
Bacon's House
Stonepit Spinney
34
62
63
64
D
E
F
50

28

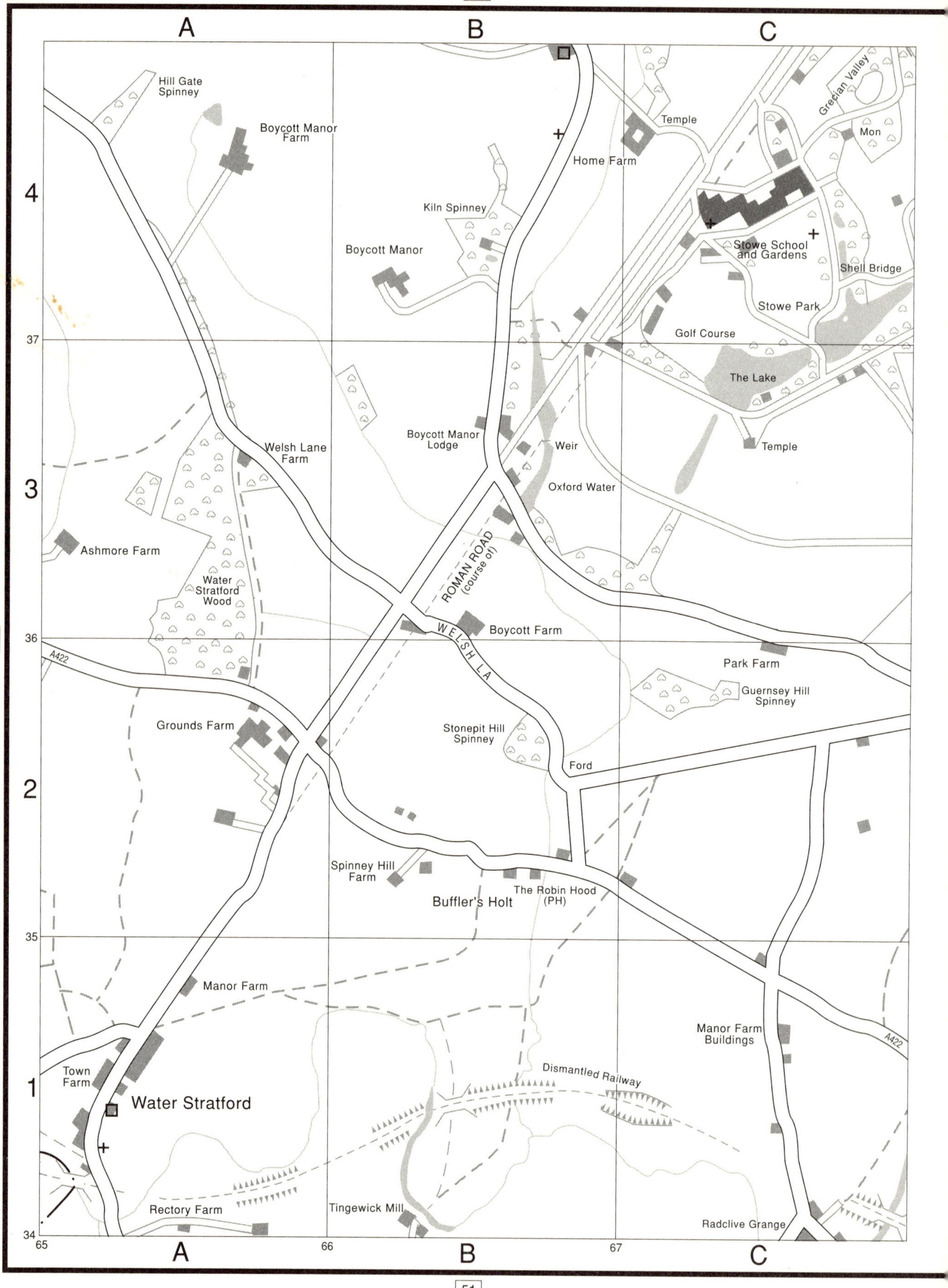
A
B
C
4
3
2
1
37
36
35
34
65
66
67
Hill Gate Spinney
Boycott Manor Farm
Home Farm
Temple
Grecian Valley
Mon
Kiln Spinney
Boycott Manor
Stowe School and Gardens
Shell Bridge
Stowe Park
Golf Course
The Lake
Temple
Boycott Manor Lodge
Weir
Welsh Lane Farm
Oxford Water
Ashmore Farm
Water Stratford Wood
ROMAN ROAD (course of)
Boycott Farm
WELSH LA
A422
Park Farm
Guernsey Hill Spinney
Grounds Farm
Stonepit Hill Spinney
Ford
Spinney Hill Farm
The Robin Hood (PH)
Buffler's Holt
Manor Farm
Manor Farm Buildings
A422
Town Farm
Water Stratford
Dismantled Railway
Rectory Farm
Tingewick Mill
Radclive Grange

39

51

29

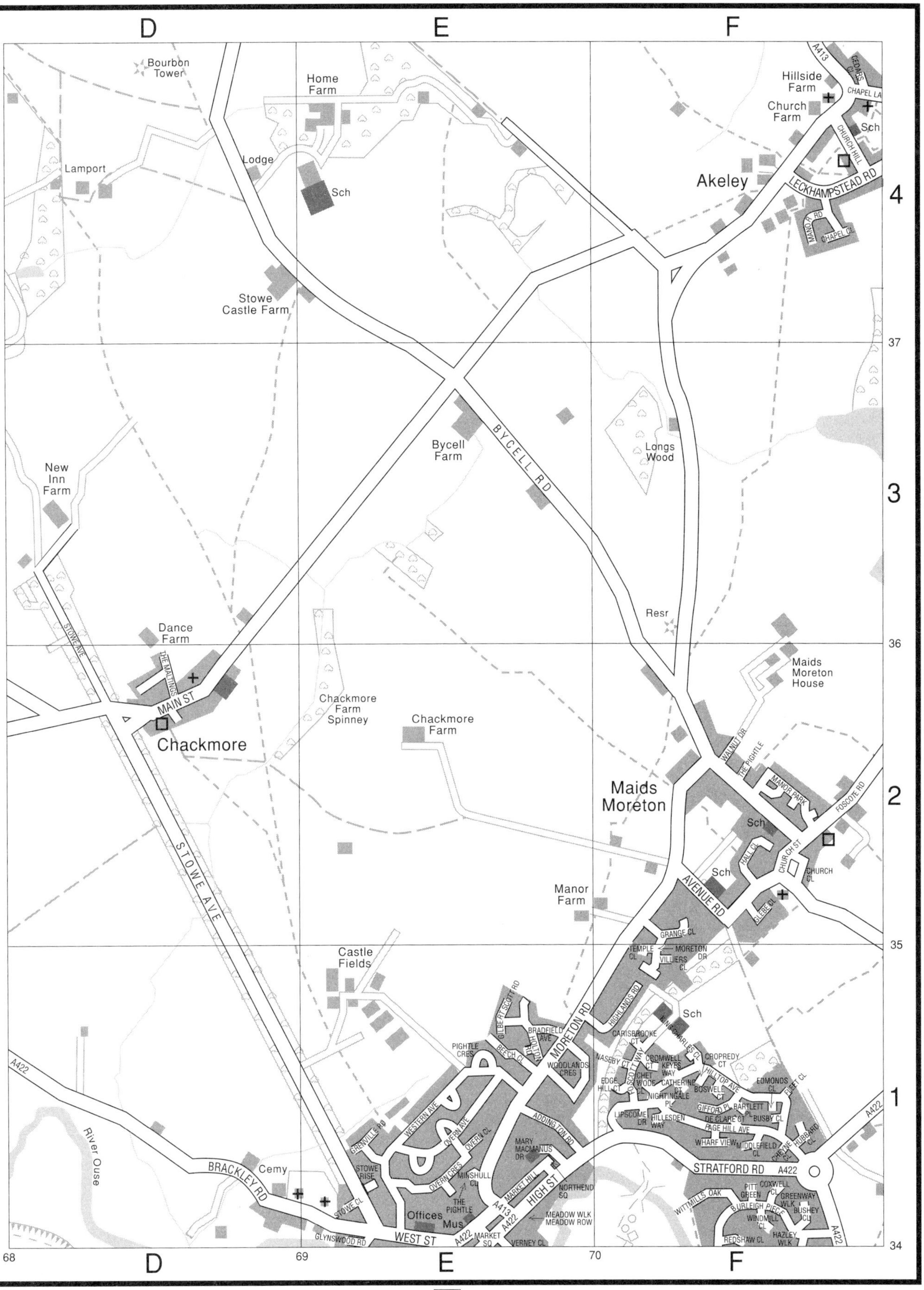
D
E
F
Bourbon Tower
Home Farm
Hillside Farm
Church Farm
Sch
Lamport
Lodge
Sch
Akeley
LECKHAMPSTEAD RD
CHAPEL CL
CHURCH HILL
4
Stowe Castle Farm
37
New Inn Farm
Bycell Farm
BYCELL RD
Longs Wood
3
Resr
Dance Farm
MAIN ST
Chackmore
36
Maids Moreton House
Chackmore Farm Spinney
Chackmore Farm
Maids Moreton
2
STOWE AVE
Sch
Sch
AVENUE RD
CHURCH ST
Manor Farm
35
Castle Fields
MORETON RD
Sch
1
River Ouse
BRACKLEY RD
Cemy
STRATFORD RD
A422
WEST ST
HIGH ST
Offices
Mus
34
68
69
70
D
E
F

42

52

30

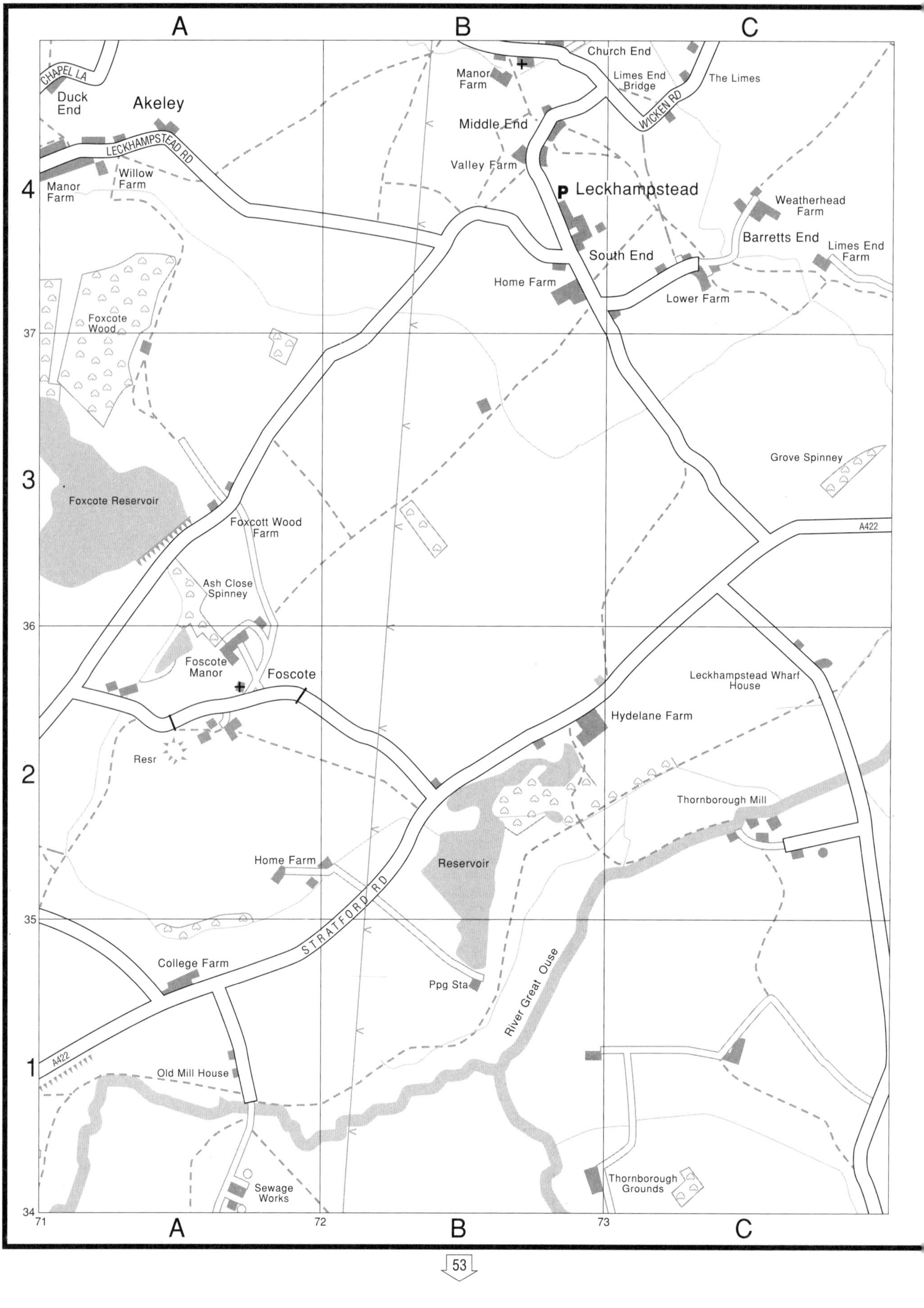
A
B
C
Chapel La
Duck End
Akeley
Leckhampstead Rd
Manor Farm
Willow Farm
Church End
Manor Farm
Limes End Bridge
The Limes
Wicken Rd
Middle End
Valley Farm
P Leckhampstead
Weatherhead Farm
Barretts End
Limes End Farm
South End
Home Farm
Lower Farm
Foxcote Wood
Grove Spinney
Foxcote Reservoir
Foxcott Wood Farm
A422
Ash Close Spinney
Foscote Manor
Foscote
Leckhampstead Wharf House
Hydelane Farm
Resr
Thornborough Mill
Home Farm
Reservoir
Stratford Rd
College Farm
Ppg Sta
River Great Ouse
A422
Old Mill House
Sewage Works
Thornborough Grounds
4
37
3
36
2
35
1
34
71
72
73
A
B
C

41

53

31

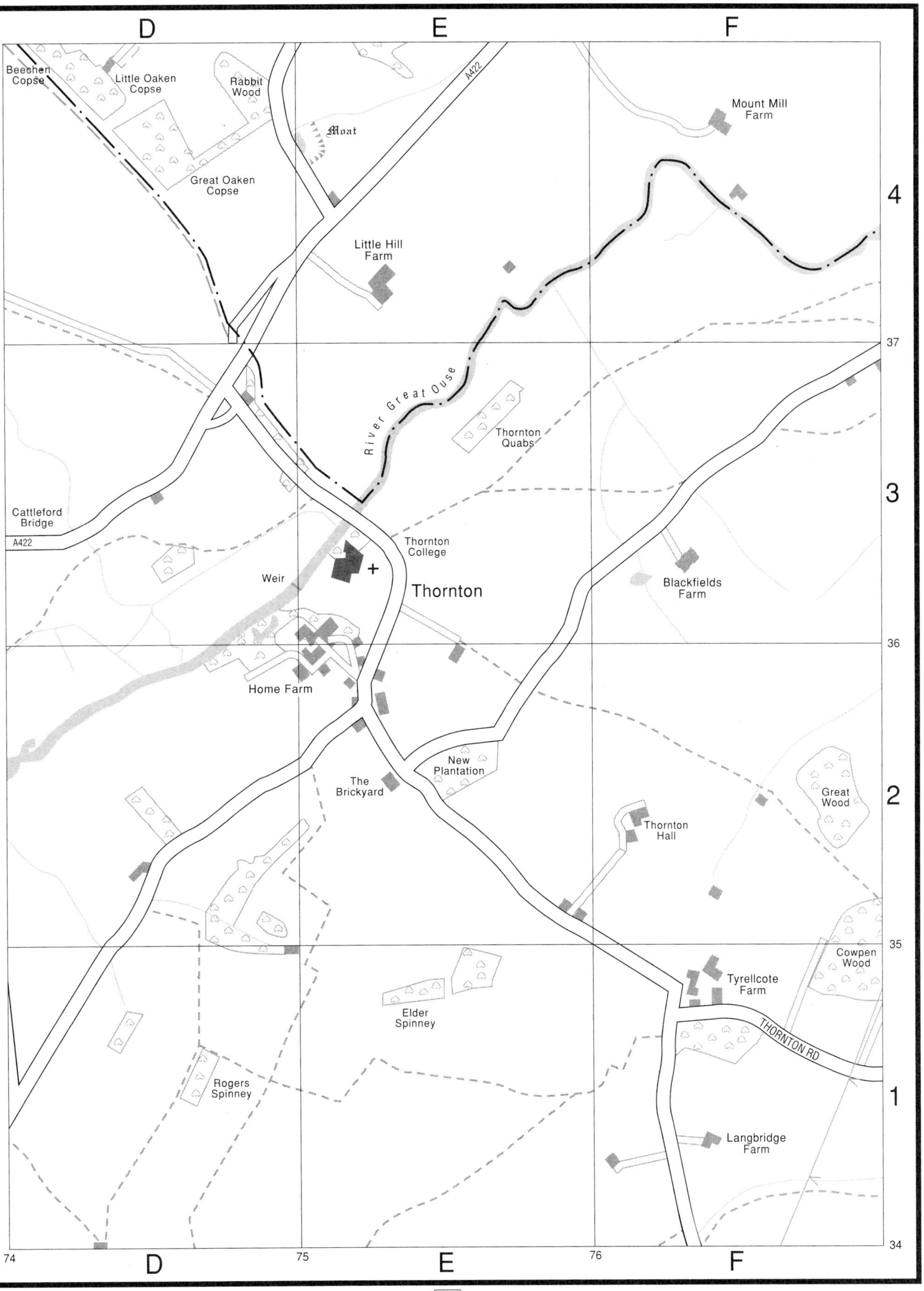
D
E
F
Beechen Copse
Little Oaken Copse
Rabbit Wood
Moat
A422
Mount Mill Farm
Great Oaken Copse
4
Little Hill Farm
37
River Great Ouse
Thornton Quabs
3
Cattleford Bridge
A422
Thornton College
Weir
Thornton
Blackfields Farm
36
Home Farm
New Plantation
The Brickyard
2
Great Wood
Thornton Hall
35
Cowpen Wood
Tyrellcote Farm
Elder Spinney
THORNTON RD
Rogers Spinney
1
Langbridge Farm
34
74
75
76
D
E
F

44

54

32

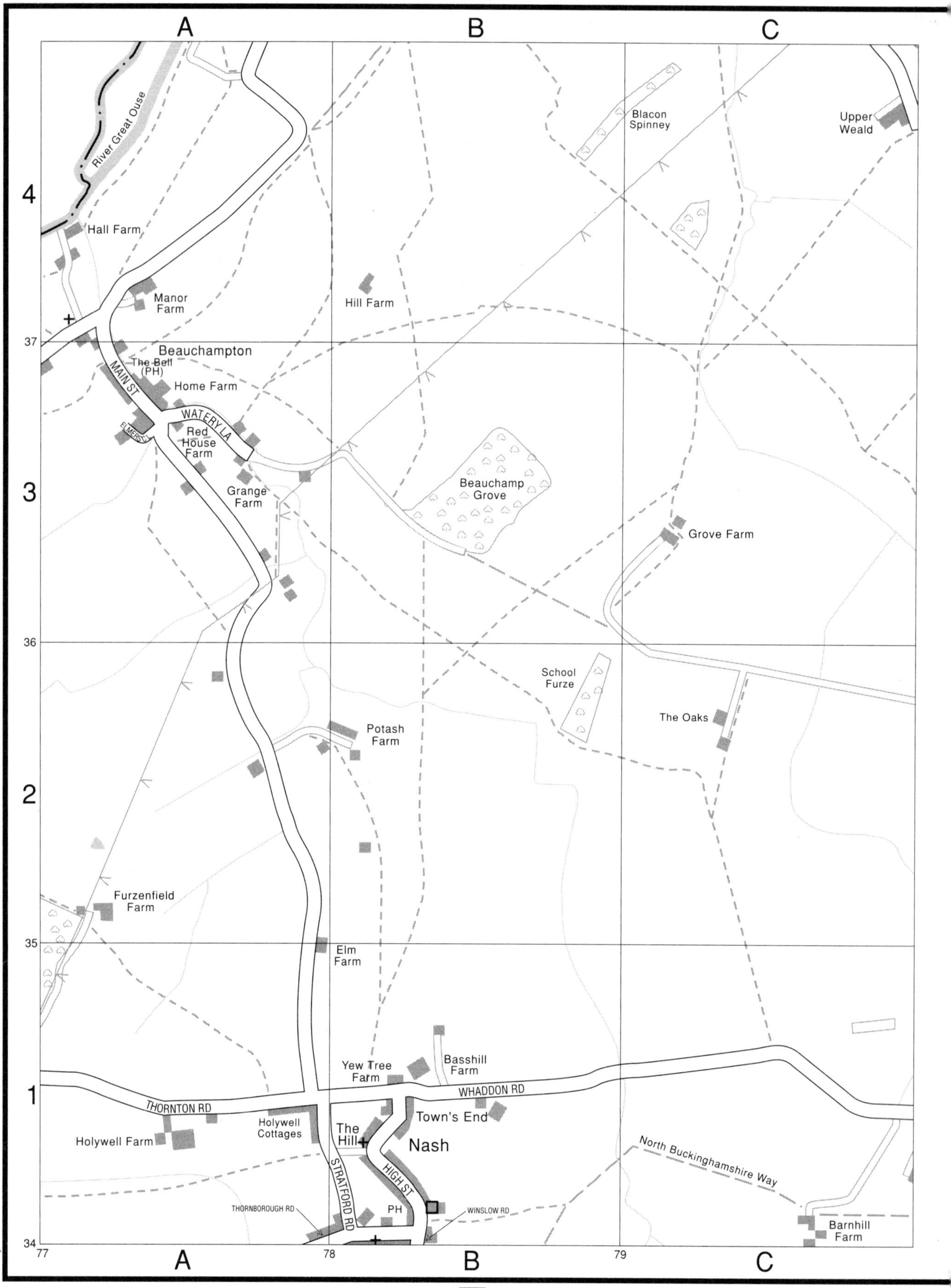
A
B
C
4
3
2
1
37
36
35
34
77
78
79
River Great Ouse
Hall Farm
Manor Farm
Hill Farm
Blacon Spinney
Upper Weald
Beauchampton
The Bell (PH)
Home Farm
MAIN ST
WATERY LA
ELMERS CL
Red House Farm
Grange Farm
Beauchamp Grove
Grove Farm
School Furze
The Oaks
Potash Farm
Furzenfield Farm
Elm Farm
Yew Tree Farm
Basshill Farm
WHADDON RD
THORNTON RD
Town's End
Holywell Farm
Holywell Cottages
The Hill
Nash
North Buckinghamshire Way
STRATFORD RD
HIGH ST
THORNBOROUGH RD
PH
WINSLOW RD
Barnhill Farm

43

55

33

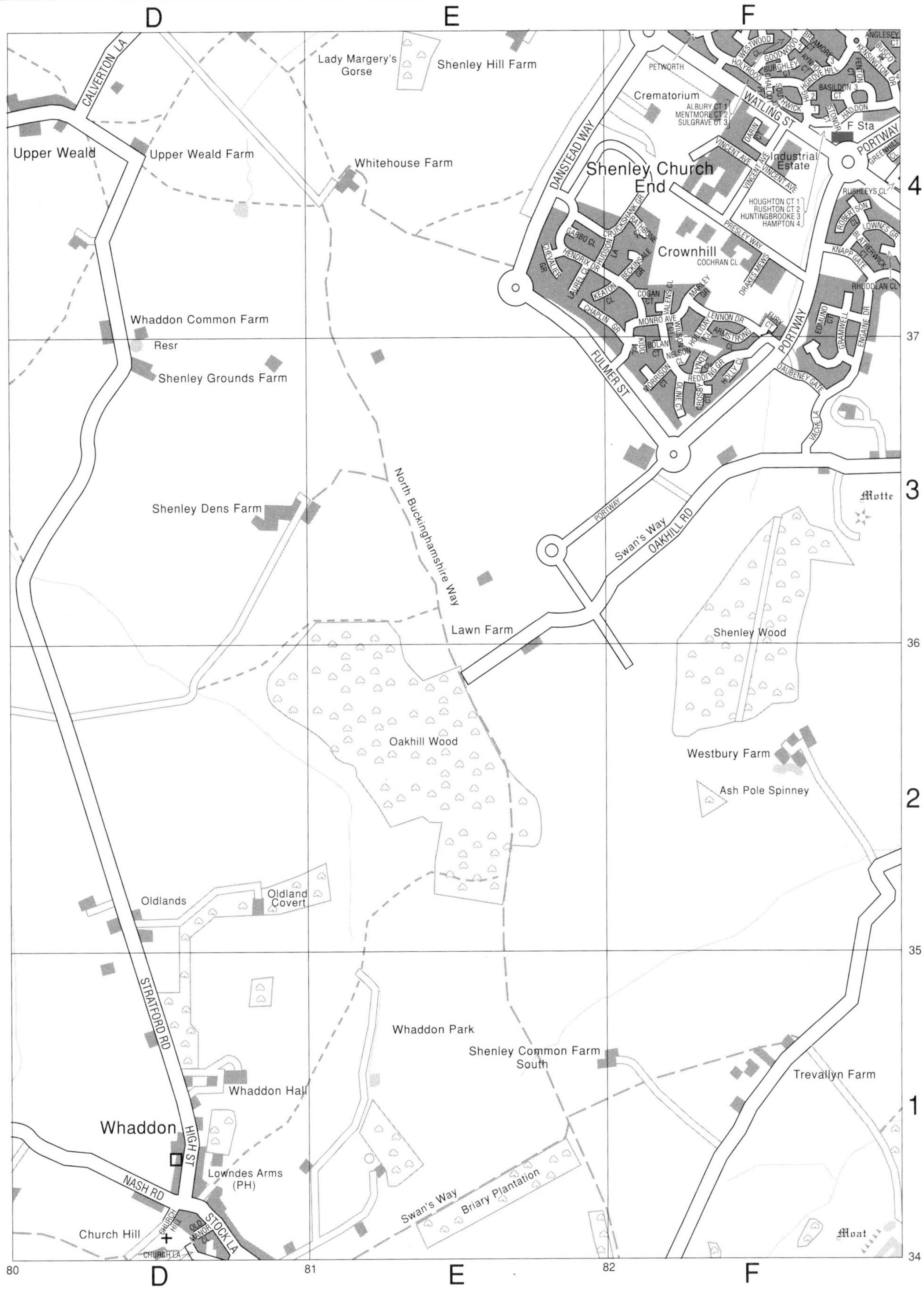
D
E
F
Calverton La
Lady Margery's Gorse
Shenley Hill Farm
Petworth
Crematorium
Albury Ct 1
Mentmore Ct 2
Sulgrave Ct 3
Watling St
Westwood
Holyrood
Goodwood
Burghley Ct
Southwick
Basildon
Haddon
Anglesey Ct
Kensington Dr
Fenton Ct
F Sta
Portway
Upper Weald
Upper Weald Farm
Whitehouse Farm
Danstead Way
Shenley Church End
Industrial Estate
Vincent Ave
Rushleys Cl
Houghton Ct 1
Rushton Ct 2
Huntingbrooke 3
Hampton 4
Presley Way
Crownhill
Cochran Cl
Drakes Mews
Garbo Cl
Chevalier Gr
Hendrix Dr
Laurel Cl
Keaton Cl
Chaplin Gr
Cogan Ct
Monro Ave
Lennon Dr
Armstrong Cl
Marley Gr
Bolan Ct
Kidd Cl
Nelson Cl
Morrison Ct
Redding Gr
Oline Ct
Crosby Ct
Holly Cl
Fulmer St
Roberson Cl
Lownes Gr
Knapp Gate
Rhuddlan Cl
Edmund Ct
Gramwell
Engaine Dr
Daubeney Gate
Vache La
Whaddon Common Farm
Resr
Shenley Grounds Farm
4
37
Motte
3
Shenley Dens Farm
North Buckinghamshire Way
Portway
Swan's Way
Oakhill Rd
Lawn Farm
Shenley Wood
36
Oakhill Wood
Westbury Farm
Ash Pole Spinney
2
Oldlands
Oldland Covert
35
Stratford Rd
Whaddon Park
Shenley Common Farm South
Trevallyn Farm
Whaddon Hall
1
Whaddon
High St
Lowndes Arms (PH)
Nash Rd
Swan's Way
Briary Plantation
Church Hill
Old Manor Cl
Stock La
Church La
Moat
34
80
81
82

46

56

34

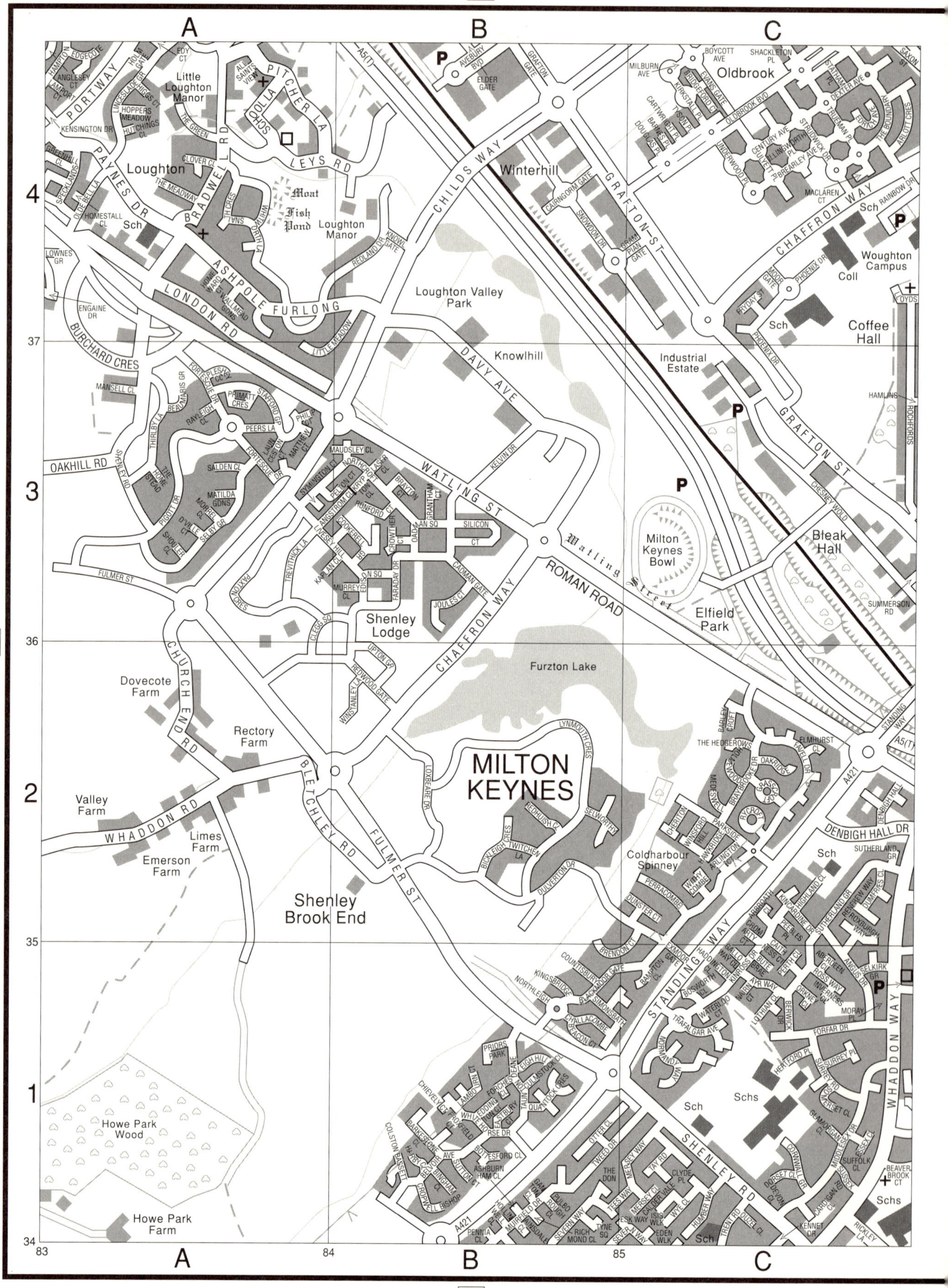
A
B
C
4
3
2
1
37
36
35
34
83
84
85
Little Loughton Manor
Loughton
Loughton Manor
Moat Fish Pond
Sch
Oldbrook
Winterhill
Woughton Campus
Coll
Coffee Hall
Loughton Valley Park
Knowlhill
Industrial Estate
Milton Keynes Bowl
Elfield Park
Bleak Hall
Shenley Lodge
Furzton Lake
Dovecote Farm
Rectory Farm
Valley Farm
Limes Farm
Emerson Farm
Shenley Brook End
MILTON KEYNES
Coldharbour Spinney
Schs
Howe Park Wood
Howe Park Farm
PORTWAY
PAYNES DR
KENSINGTON DR
BRADWELL RD
PITCHER LA
LEYS RD
ASHPOLE FURLONG
LONDON RD
BURCHARD CRES
OAKHILL RD
FULMER ST
CHILDS WAY
GRAFTON ST
GRAFTON GATE
CHAFFRON WAY
OLDBROOK BVD
DAVY AVE
WATLING ST
Watling Street
ROMAN ROAD
CHAFFRON WAY
CHURCH END RD
WHADDON RD
BLETCHLEY RD
FULMER ST
LYNMOUTH CRES
STANDING WAY
A421
A5(T)
DENBIGH HALL DR
SHENLEY RD
WHADDON WAY
TREVITHICK LA
PAXTON CRES
CLEGG SQ
UPTON GR
REDWOOD GATE
WINSTANLEY LA
LOXBEARE DR
REDHUISH CL
SELWORTHY
BICKLEIGH CRES
TWITCHEN LA
DULVERTON DR
DUNSTER CT
PERRACOMBE
BRENDON CT
COUNTISBURY
KINGSBRIDGE
NORTHLEIGH
TRAFALGAR AVE
WATERLOO CT
BOSWORTH CL
FORFAR DR
MORAY PL
SURREY PL
GLAMORGAN CL
MIDDLESEX DR
SUFFOLK CL
ESSEX CL
CORNWALL GR
DORSET CL
DEVON CL
KENNET DR
RICKLEY LA
TRENT RD
HUMBER WAY
SEVERN WAY
MERSEY WAY
TWEED DR
OTTER CL
BEAVERBROOK CT
HAMLINS
ROCHFORDS
SUMMERSON RD
CHESNEY WOLD
ELMHURST CL
THE HEDGEROWS
OAKRIDGE
MEDSWELL
PARKSIDE
RYCROFT
SUTHERLAND GR
KINCARDINE DR
PEEBLES PL
PERTH CL
SELKIRK GR
ARGYLL AVE
MACLAREN CT
RAINBOW DR
PHOENIX DR
FRYDAY ST
MOOR GATE
SILICON CT
GRANTHAM CT
CADMAN SQ
JOULES CT
FARADAY DR
EDISON SQ
MURREY CL
MAUDSLEY CL
SYMINGTON CT
NORTHCROFT
BRUNTON CT
CROWTHER CT
KELVIN DR
SALDEN CL
MATILDA GDNS
PIGOTT DR
SHOLLER CL
SELBY GR
THIRLBY LA
MANSELL CL
STAFFORD GR
FORTESCUE DR
RAYLEIGH CL
PEERS LA
PRIMATT CRES
SHENLEY RD
PRIORS PARK
CHIEVELY CT
BARKSTONE CT
COLSTON BASSET
BINGHAM CL
CRIPPELL BISHOP
ASHBURN HAM CL
PENNIA CL
GAMBLING

45

57

35

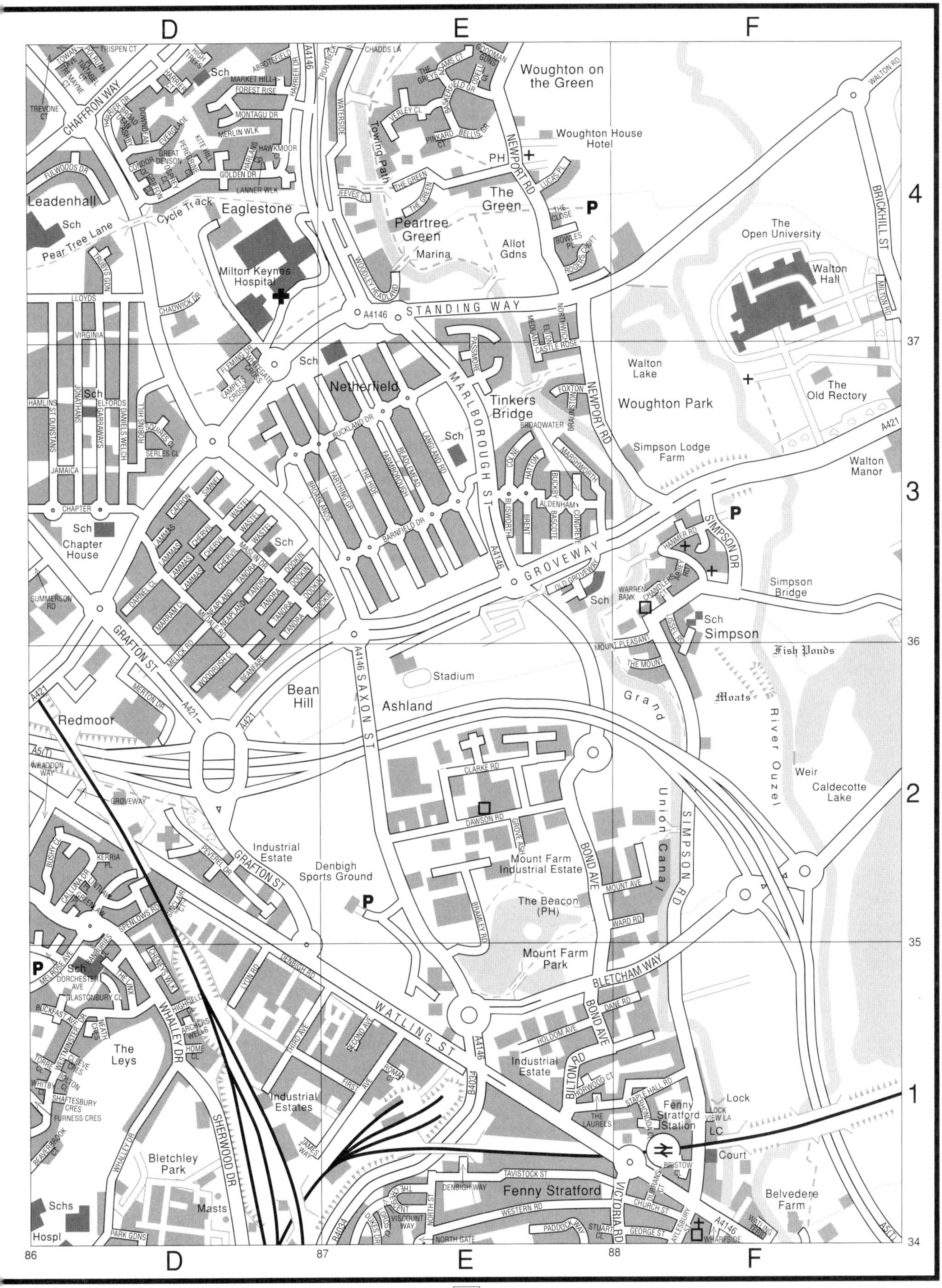
D
E
F
Woughton on the Green
Woughton House Hotel
PH
The Green
P
Leadenhall
Sch
Cycle Track
Eaglestone
Pear Tree Lane
Peartree Green
Marina
Allot Gdns
Towing Path
Milton Keynes Hospital
STANDING WAY
A4146
The Open University
Walton Hall
Walton Lake
Woughton Park
The Old Rectory
Netherfield
Tinkers Bridge
Simpson Lodge Farm
Walton Manor
Chapter House
GROVEWAY
MARLBOROUGH ST
Simpson Bridge
Simpson
Fish Ponds
Moats
Grand Union Canal
River Ouzel
Redmoor
Bean Hill
Ashland
Stadium
SAXON ST
GRAFTON ST
A421
A5(T)
Weir
Caldecotte Lake
Industrial Estate
Denbigh Sports Ground
Mount Farm Industrial Estate
The Beacon (PH)
Mount Farm Park
BLETCHAM WAY
BOND AVE
SIMPSON RD
WATLING ST
The Leys
Industrial Estate
Industrial Estates
Bletchley Park
Masts
Schs
Hospl
Fenny Stratford Station
Lock
LC
Court
Fenny Stratford
Belvedere Farm
VICTORIA RD
4
3
2
1
37
36
35
34
86
87
88

48

58

36

47

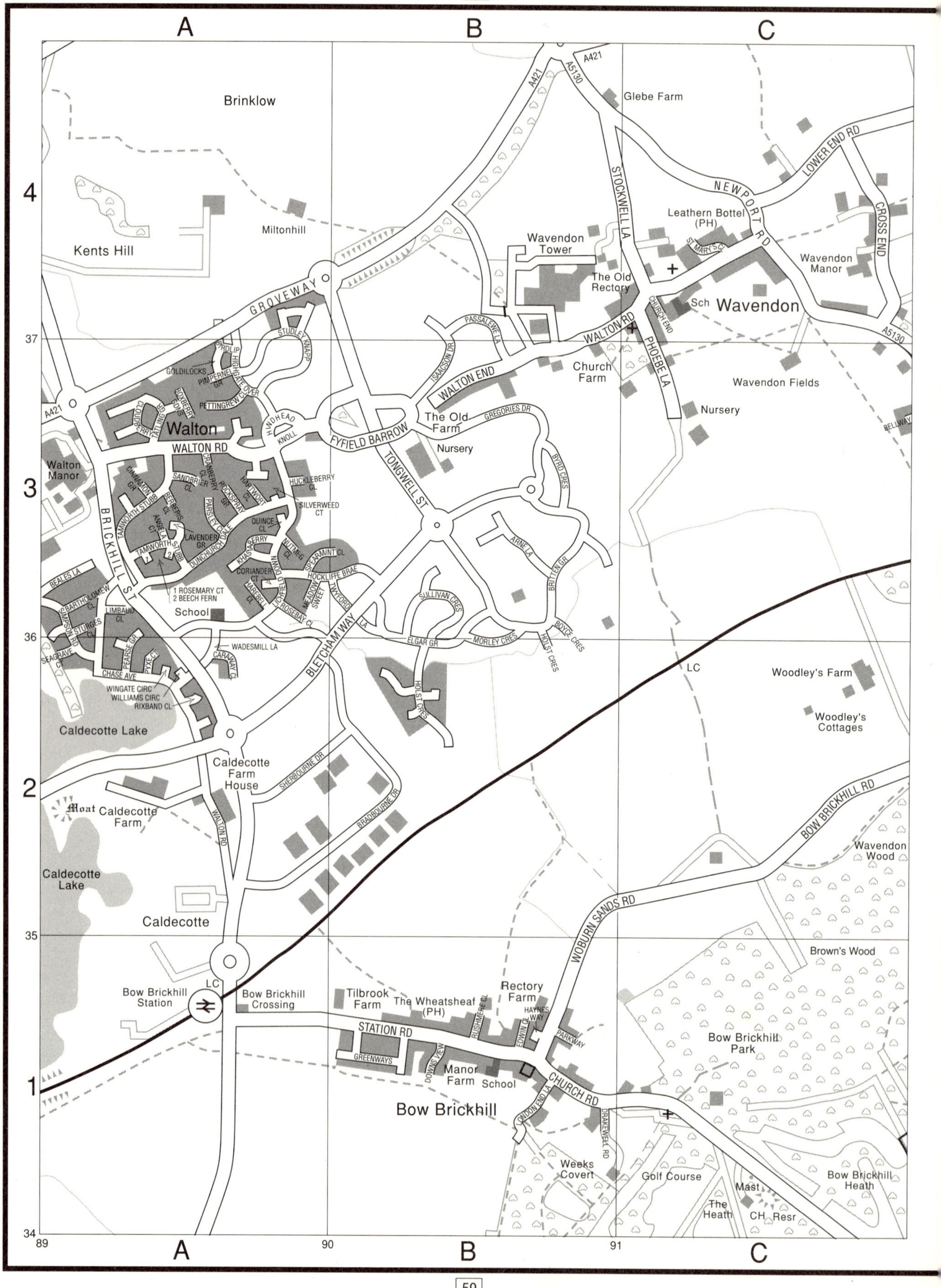
A
B
C
4
3
2
1
37
36
35
34
89
90
91
Brinklow
Kents Hill
Miltonhill
GROVEWAY
A421
A5130
Glebe Farm
STOCKWELL LA
LOWER END RD
NEWPORT RD
CROSS END
Leathern Bottel (PH)
ST MARY'S CL
Wavendon Tower
The Old Rectory
Wavendon Manor
Sch
Wavendon
CHURCH END
PHOEBE LA
WALTON RD
PASSALEWE LA
ISAACSON DR
WALTON END
Church Farm
Wavendon Fields
Nursery
BELLWAY
STUDLEY KNAPP
GOLDILOCKS
PIMPERNEL GR
HIGHGATE OVER
PETTINGREW CL
CLOUDBERRY
GOLDCREST
TATLING GR
Walton
WALTON RD
HINDHEAD KNOLL
FYFIELD BARROW
The Old Farm
GREGORIES DR
Nursery
TONGWELL ST
BYRD CRES
Walton Manor
CINNAMON GR
SANDBRIER CL
CRANBERRY CL
ROCKSPRAY GR
HAWTHORN CL
HUCKLEBERRY CL
SILVERWEED CT
BRICKHILL ST
TAMWORTH STUBB
BERBERIS CL
PARSLEY GR
ANISE CL
LAVENDER GR
QUINCE CL
DUNCHURCH DALE
TAMWORTH STUBB
KHASIBERRY
NUTMEG CL
SPEARMINT CL
ARNE LA
BRITTEN GR
CORIANDER CT
HOCKLIFFE BRAE
HAREBELL CL
LICHFIELD DOWN
MEADOW SWEET
TWYFORD LA
ROSEBAY CL
1 ROSEMARY CT
2 BEECH FERN
BEALES LA
BARTHOLOMEW CL
SIMPSON RD
STURGES CL
LIMBAUD CL
School
BLETCHAM WAY
SULLIVAN CRES
ELGAR GR
MORLEY CRES
BOYCE CRES
HOLST CRES
SEAGRAVE CT
PEARSE GR
PYKE CT
CHASE AVE
WADESMILL LA
CARAWAY CL
WINGATE CIRC
WILLIAMS CIRC
RIXBAND CL
HOLST CRES
LC
Woodley's Farm
Woodley's Cottages
Caldecotte Lake
Caldecotte Farm House
SHERBOURNE DR
BRADBOURNE DR
Moat
Caldecotte Farm
WALTON RD
BOW BRICKHILL RD
Wavendon Wood
Caldecotte Lake
WOBURN SANDS RD
Caldecotte
Brown's Wood
Bow Brickhill Station
LC
Bow Brickhill Crossing
Tilbrook Farm
The Wheatsheaf (PH)
RUSHMERE CL
Rectory Farm
HAYNES WAY
EDWIN CL
PARKWAY
STATION RD
GREENWAYS
DOWNS VIEW
Manor Farm
School
CHURCH RD
Bow Brickhill Park
Bow Brickhill
LONDON END LA
DRAKEWELL RD
Weeks Covert
Golf Course
Mast
The Heath
CH
Resr
Bow Brickhill Heath

59

37

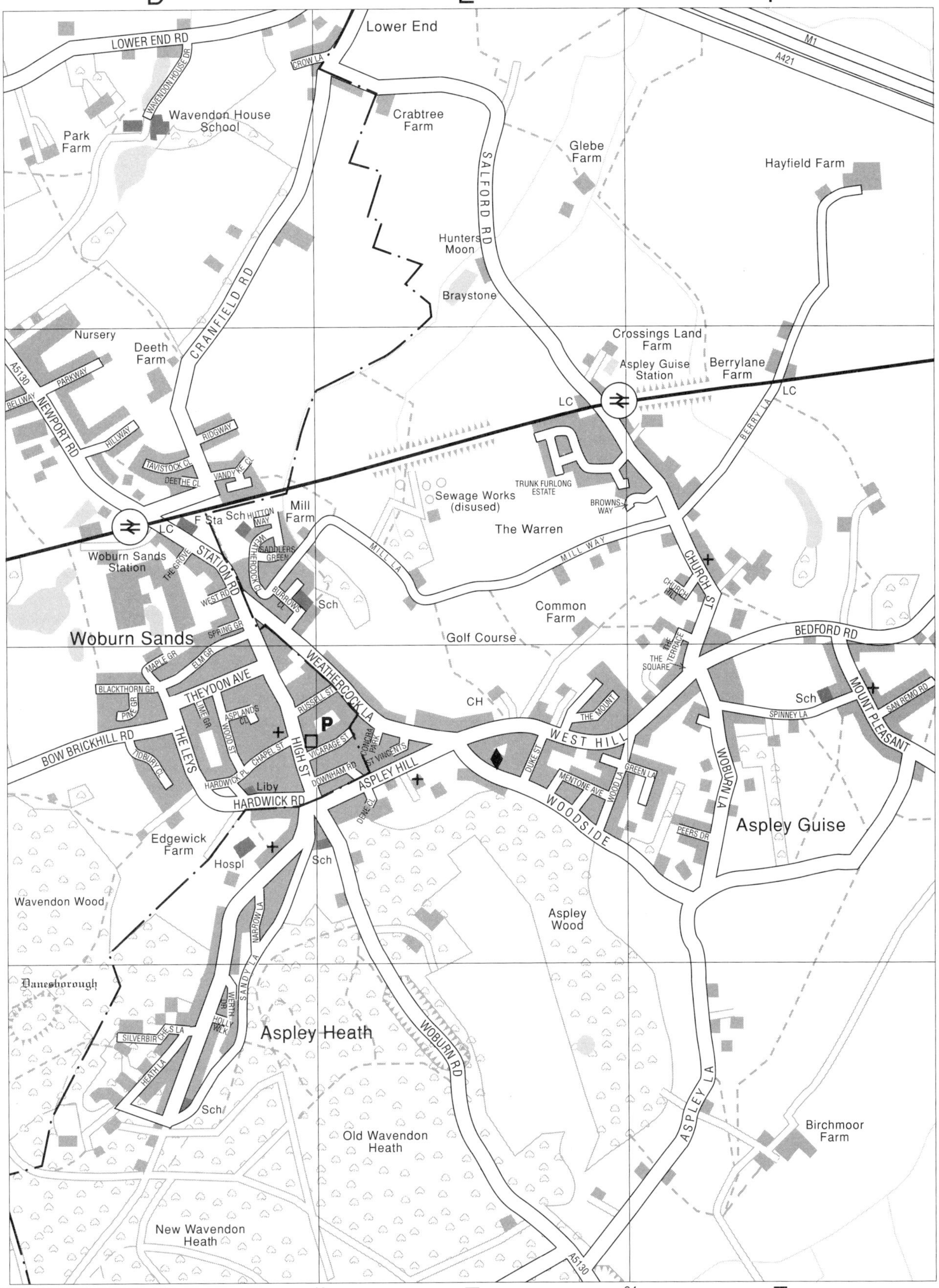
D
E
F
Lower End
LOWER END RD
CROW LA
WAVENDON HOUSE DR
Wavendon House School
Park Farm
Crabtree Farm
SALFORD RD
Glebe Farm
Hayfield Farm
M1
A421
Hunters Moon
Braystone
CRANFIELD RD
Nursery
Deeth Farm
A5130
PARKWAY
BELLWAY
NEWPORT RD
HILLWAY
RIDGWAY
TAVISTOCK CL
DEETHE CL
VANDYKE CL
Crossings Land Farm
Aspley Guise Station
Berrylane Farm
LC
BERRY LA
TRUNK FURLONG ESTATE
BROWNS WAY
Sewage Works (disused)
The Warren
Mill Farm
F Sta
Sch
HUTTON WAY
SADDLERS GREEN
WEATHERCOCK CL
BURROWS CL
Woburn Sands Station
THE GROVE
STATION RD
WEST RD
SPRING GR
MILL LA
MILL WAY
CHURCH ST
CHURCH HILL
Common Farm
Golf Course
Woburn Sands
BEDFORD RD
THE TERRACE
THE SQUARE
MAPLE GR
ELM GR
BLACKTHORN GR
THEYDON AVE
PINE GR
LIME GR
ASPLANDS CL
WOOD ST
RUSSELL ST
WEATHERCOCK LA
P
CH
THE MOUNT
WEST HILL
SPINNEY LA
MOUNT PLEASANT
SAN REMO RD
BOW BRICKHILL RD
TIDBURY CL
THE LEYS
CHAPEL ST
HIGH ST
VICARAGE ST
CONCRA PARK
ST VINCENTS
DOWNHAM RD
ASPLEY HILL
DIKE ST
MENTONE AVE
WOOD LA
GREEN LA
WOBURN LA
HARDWICK PL
Liby
HARDWICK RD
DENE CL
WOODSIDE
PEERS DR
Aspley Guise
Edgewick Farm
Hospl
Wavendon Wood
NARROW LA
Aspley Wood
Danesborough
SANDY LA
WERTH DR
HOLLY WLK
SILVERBIRCHES LA
Aspley Heath
WOBURN RD
HEATH LA
Sch
ASPLEY LA
Birchmoor Farm
Old Wavendon Heath
New Wavendon Heath
A5130
92
93
94
34
35
36
37
1
2
3
4
not continued, see key diagram

60

39

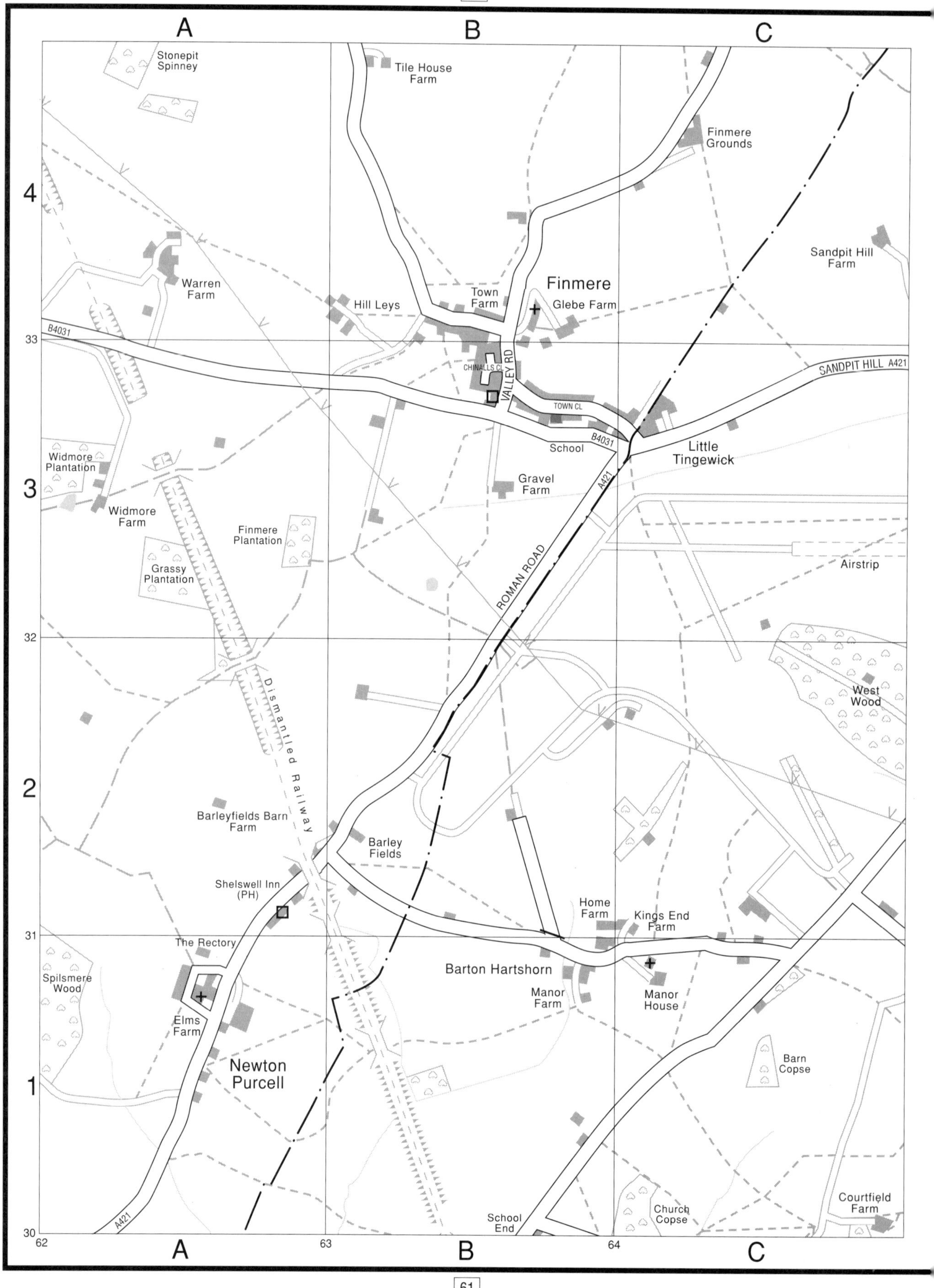

not continued, see key diagram

61

40

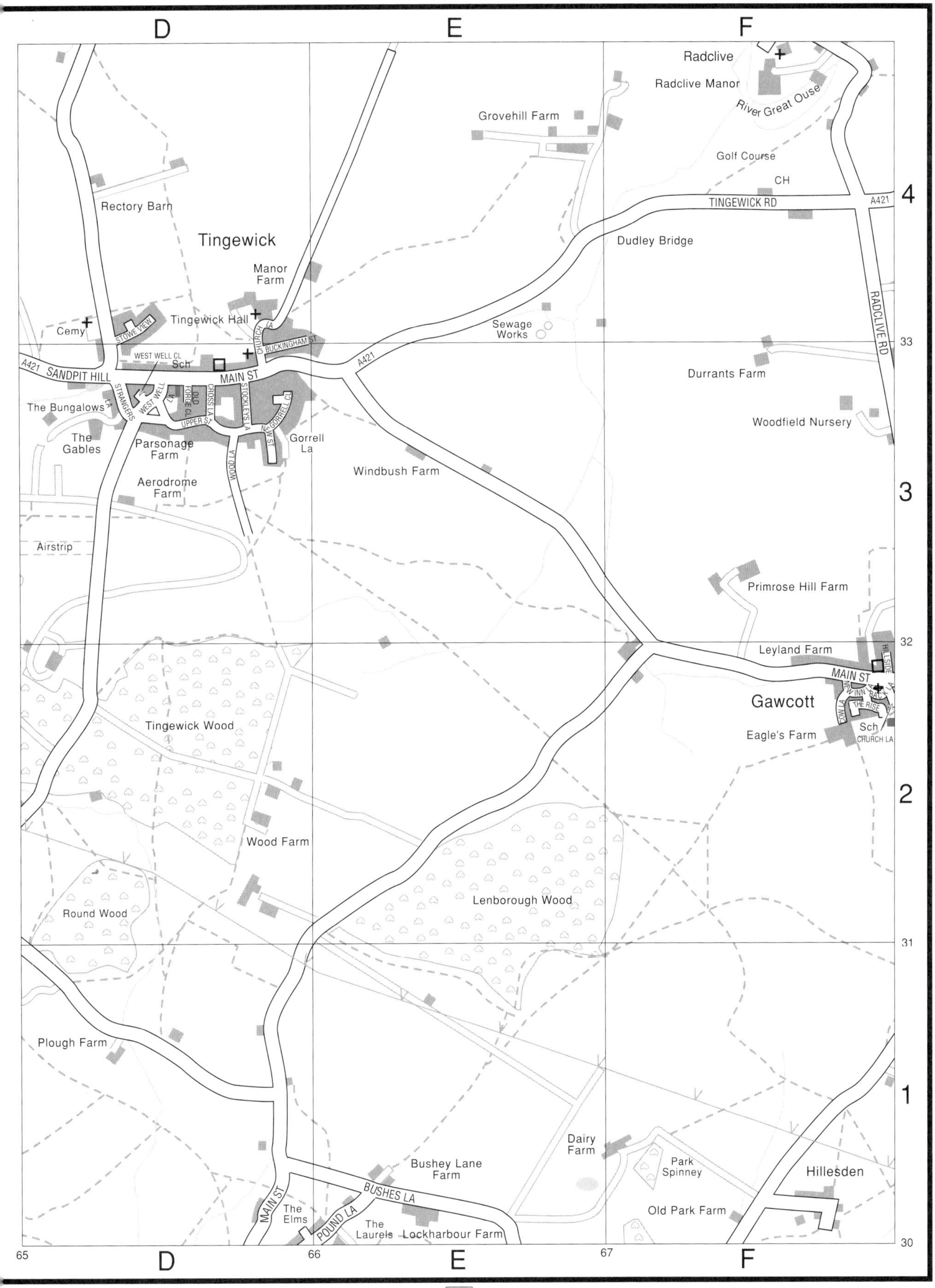

D
E
F
Radclive
Radclive Manor
River Great Ouse
Grovehill Farm
Golf Course
CH
TINGEWICK RD
A421
Rectory Barn
Tingewick
Dudley Bridge
Manor Farm
Sewage Works
Cemy
Tingewick Hall
STOWE VIEW
CHURCH LA
BUCKINGHAM ST
WEST WELL CL
Sch
A421
SANDPIT HILL
MAIN ST
STRANGERS LA
WEST WELL LA
OLD FORGE CL
CROSS LA
STOCKLEYS LA
NEW GORRELL CL
NEW ST
UPPER ST
The Bungalows
The Gables
Parsonage Farm
Gorrell La
WOOD LA
Aerodrome Farm
Windbush Farm
RADCLIVE RD
Durrants Farm
Woodfield Nursery
Airstrip
Primrose Hill Farm
Leyland Farm
HILLSIDE
MAIN ST
NEW INN
BACK LA
THE RISE
COW LA
Gawcott
Sch
Eagle's Farm
CHURCH LA
Tingewick Wood
Wood Farm
Lenborough Wood
Round Wood
Plough Farm
Dairy Farm
Park Spinney
Bushey Lane Farm
Hillesden
BUSHES LA
MAIN ST
The Elms
POUND LA
The Laurels
Lockharbour Farm
Old Park Farm
65
66
67
D
E
F
4
33
3
32
2
31
1
30

52

62

41

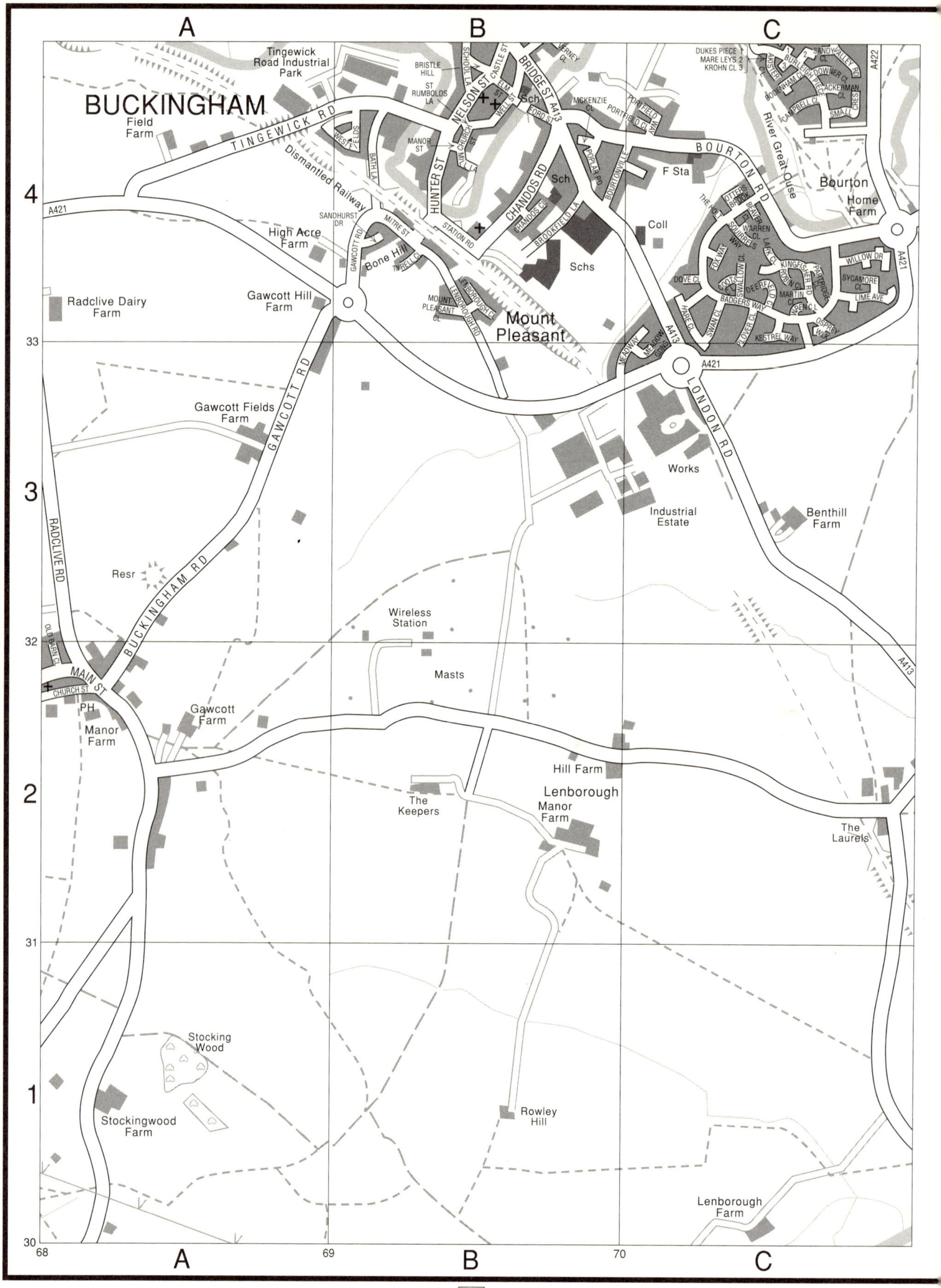

A
B
C
BUCKINGHAM
Tingewick Road Industrial Park
Field Farm
TINGEWICK RD
Dismantled Railway
BRISTLE HILL
SCHOOL LA
ST RUMBOLDS LA
NELSON ST
CASTLE ST
ELM ST
WELL ST
BRIDGE ST A413
FORD ST
MCKENZIE CL
PORTFIELD CL
PORTFIELD WAY
MANOR ST
CHURCH ST
MILL LA
HUNTER ST
BATH LA
WEST FIELDS
POPLAR RD
BOURTONVILLE
BOURTON RD
F Sta
Sch
CHANDOS RD
CHANDOS CL
BROOKFIELD LA
Schs
Coll
SANDHURST DR
MITRE ST
STATION RD
GAWCOTT RD
Bone Hill
TYRELL CL
High Acre Farm
LENBOROUGH CL
LENBOROUGH RD
MOUNT PLEASANT CL
Mount Pleasant
Gawcott Hill Farm
Radclive Dairy Farm
A421
A413
A422
DUKES PIECE 1
MARE LEYS 2
KROHN CL 3
AKISTER CL
BURLEIGH PIECE
SANDY CL
ALLEY RD
DOWNER CL
BODENHAM CL
ACKERMAN CL
CAMPBELL CL
SMALL CRES
River Great Ouse
Bourton
Home Farm
THE HOLT
OTTERS BROOK
BEAVER CL
WARREN CL
SQUIRRELS WAY
LARK CL
FOX WAY
KINGFISHER RD
PARTRIDGE CL
ROBIN CL
DOVE CL
COOTS CL
SWALLOW CL
DEERFIELD CL
MARTIN CL
WREN CL
BADGERS WAY
HARE CL
SWAN CL
PLOVER CL
KESTREL WAY
OSPREY WLK
WILLOW DR
SYCAMORE CL
LIME AVE
MEADOWAY
MEADOW GDNS
LONDON RD
Gawcott Fields Farm
GAWCOTT RD
Works
Industrial Estate
Benthill Farm
RADCLIVE RD
Resr
BUCKINGHAM RD
Wireless Station
Masts
OLD BARN CL
MAIN ST
CHURCH ST
PH
Manor Farm
Gawcott Farm
Hill Farm
Lenborough
Lenborough Manor Farm
The Keepers
The Laurels
Stocking Wood
Stockingwood Farm
Rowley Hill
Lenborough Farm
4
3
2
1
33
32
31
30
68
69
70

51

63

42

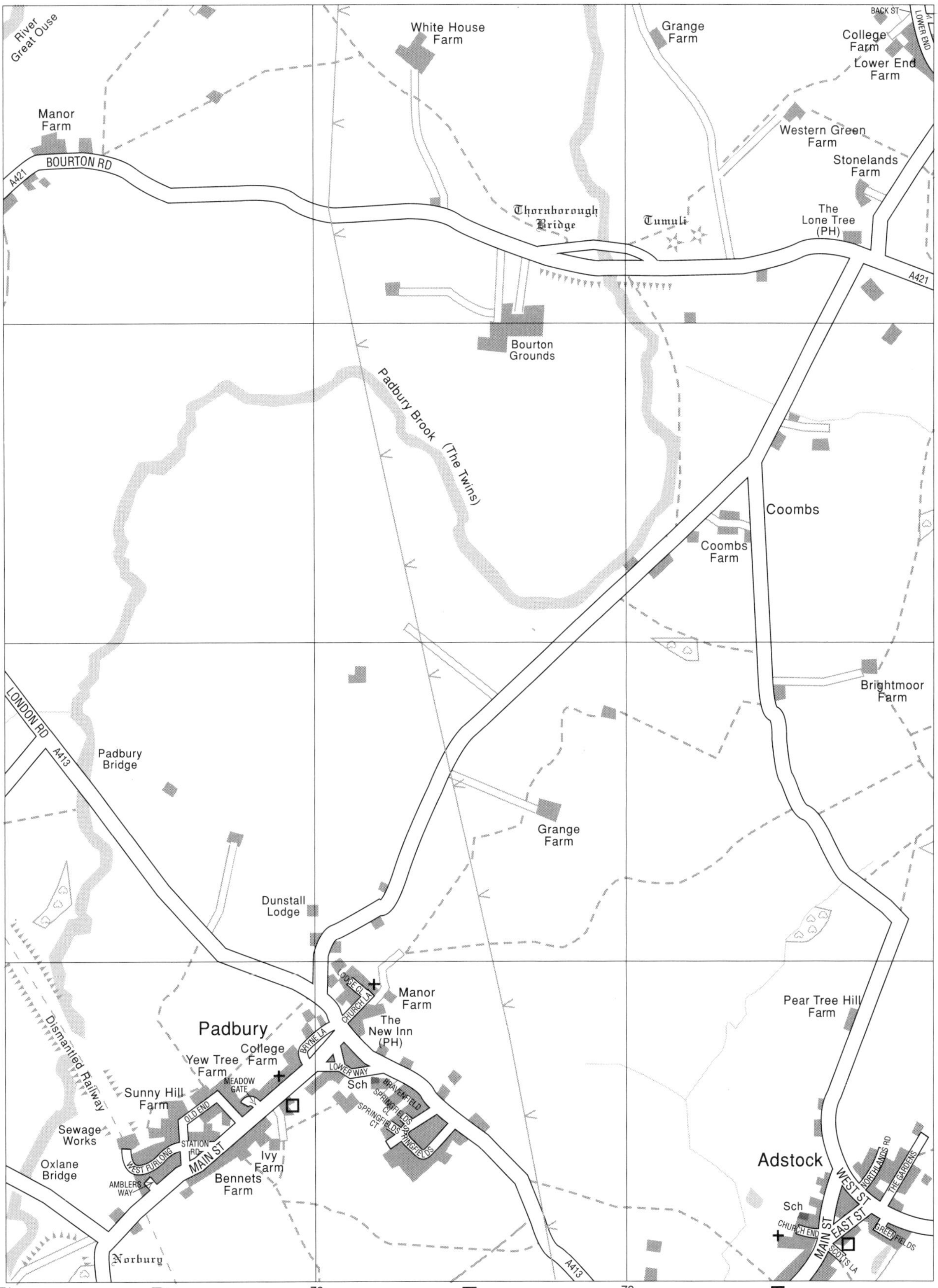

D
E
F
River Great Ouse
White House Farm
Grange Farm
BACK ST
LOWER END
College Farm
Lower End Farm
Manor Farm
Western Green Farm
Stonelands Farm
A421
BOURTON RD
Thornborough Bridge
Tumuli
The Lone Tree (PH)
A421
4
33
Bourton Grounds
Padbury Brook (The Twins)
3
Coombs
Coombs Farm
32
Brightmoor Farm
LONDON RD
A413
Padbury Bridge
2
Grange Farm
Dunstall Lodge
31
Manor Farm
The New Inn (PH)
Pear Tree Hill Farm
Padbury
College Farm
Yew Tree Farm
MEADOW GATE
BRYNE LA
LODGE CL
CHURCH LA
LOWER WAY
Sch
BRAVENFIELD
SPRINGFIELDS CL
SPRINGFIELDS CT
SPRINGFIELDS
Dismantled Railway
Sunny Hill Farm
OLD END
STATION RD
Sewage Works
WEST FURLONG
MAIN ST
Ivy Farm
Oxlane Bridge
AMBLERS WAY
Bennets Farm
1
Adstock
WEST ST
NORTHLANDS RD
THE GARDENS
Sch
CHURCH END
MAIN ST
EAST ST
GREENFIELDS
SCOTTS LA
Norbury
A413
30
71
72
73
D
E
F

54

64

43

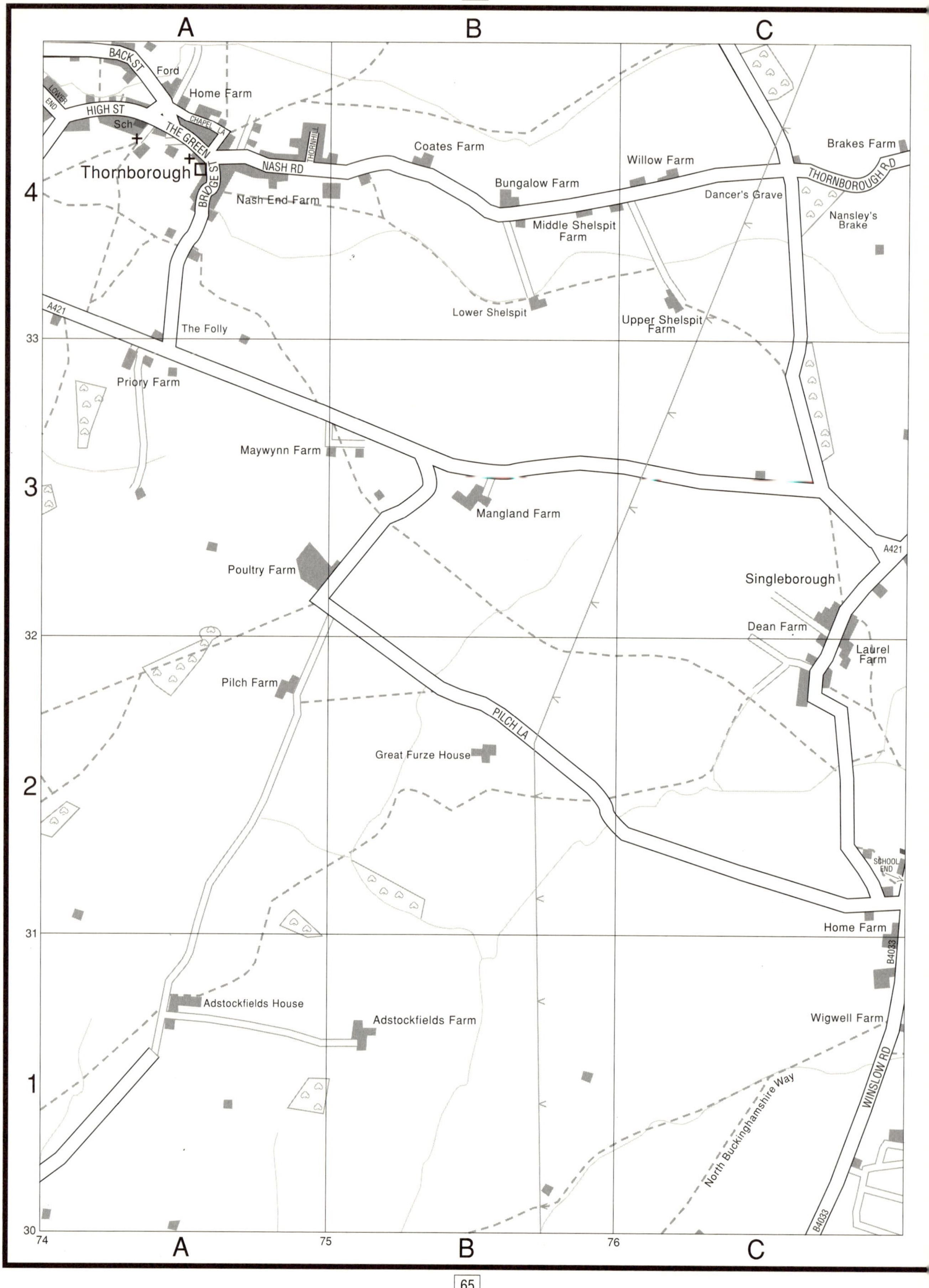
A
B
C
BACK ST
Ford
Home Farm
LOWER END
HIGH ST
CHAPEL LA
Sch
THE GREEN
THORNHILL
Thornborough
NASH RD
BRIDGE ST
Nash End Farm
Coates Farm
Bungalow Farm
Willow Farm
Brakes Farm
THORNBOROUGH RD
Dancer's Grave
Nansley's Brake
Middle Shelspit Farm
Lower Shelspit
Upper Shelspit Farm
A421
The Folly
Priory Farm
Maywynn Farm
Mangland Farm
Poultry Farm
Singleborough
Dean Farm
Laurel Farm
Pilch Farm
PILCH LA
Great Furze House
SCHOOL END
Home Farm
B4033
Adstockfields House
Adstockfields Farm
Wigwell Farm
WINSLOW RD
North Buckinghamshire Way
4
3
2
1
33
32
31
30
74
75
76

53

65

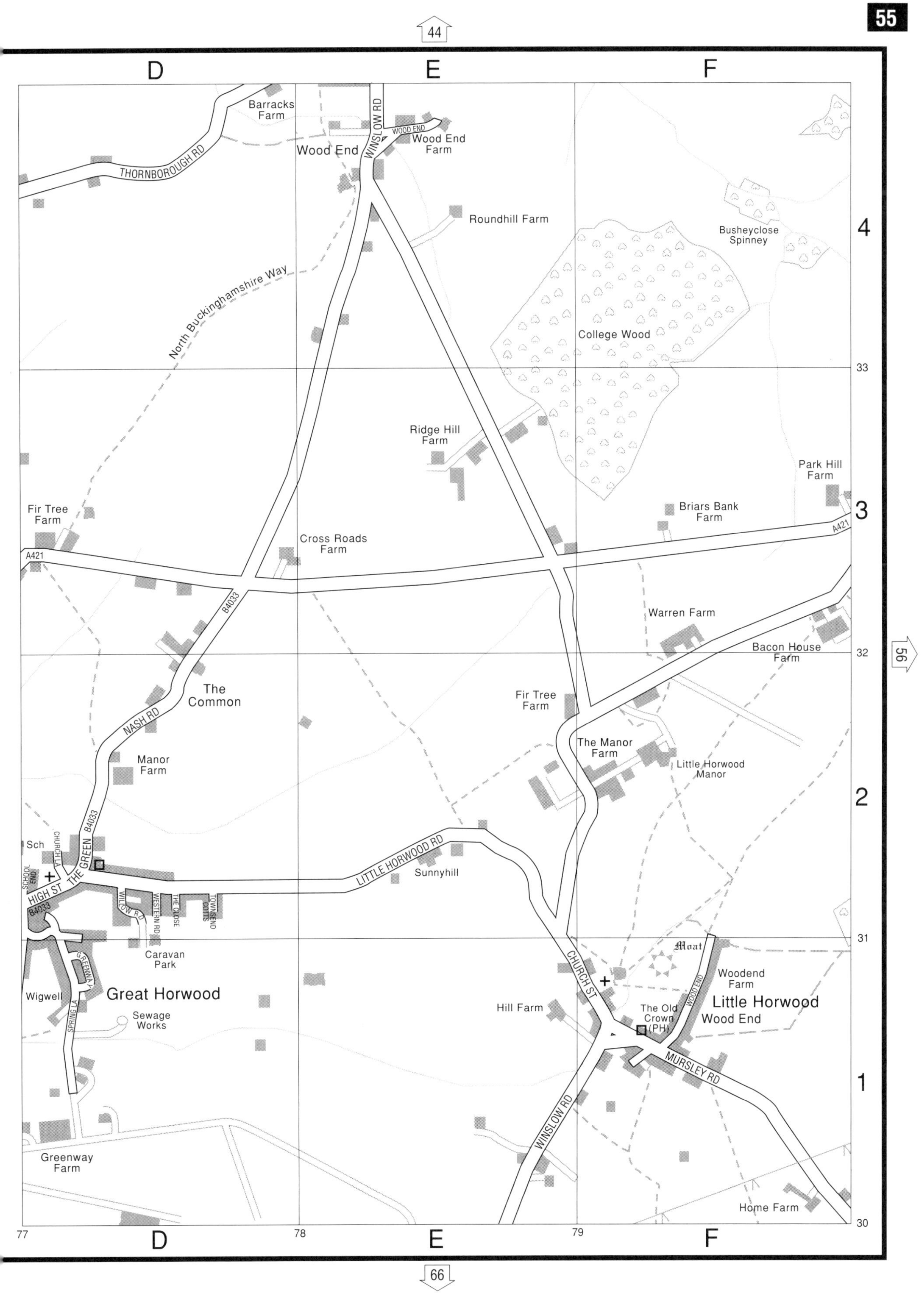

44
D
E
F
Barracks Farm
Wood End
WINSLOW RD
WOOD END
Wood End Farm
THORNBOROUGH RD
Roundhill Farm
Busheyclose Spinney
4
North Buckinghamshire Way
College Wood
33
Ridge Hill Farm
Park Hill Farm
Fir Tree Farm
Briars Bank Farm
3
A421
Cross Roads Farm
A421
B4033
Warren Farm
Bacon House Farm
32
56
The Common
Fir Tree Farm
NASH RD
The Manor Farm
Little Horwood Manor
Manor Farm
2
B4033
Sch
CHURCH LA
THE GREEN
LITTLE HORWOOD RD
Sunnyhill
SCHOOL END
HIGH ST
B4033
WILLOW RD
WESTERN RD
THE CLOSE
TOWNSEND COTTS
Caravan Park
31
CHURCH ST
Moat
Woodend Farm
GREENWAY
Wigwell
Great Horwood
WOOD END
Little Horwood
Hill Farm
The Old Crown (PH)
Wood End
SPRING LA
Sewage Works
MURSLEY RD
1
WINSLOW RD
Greenway Farm
Home Farm
30
77
78
79
D
E
F
66

45

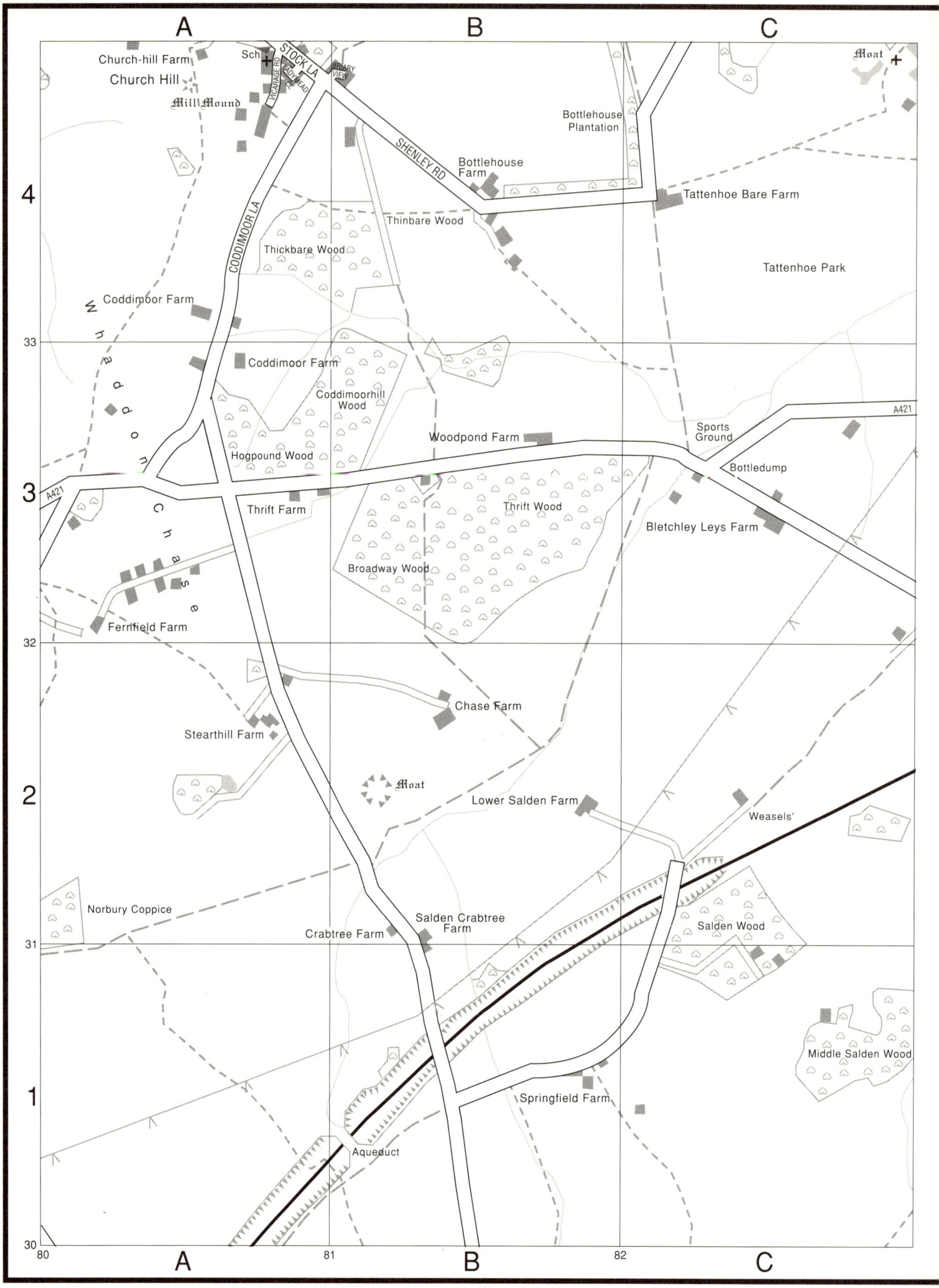
A
B
C
Church-hill Farm
Church Hill
Mill Mound
Sch
STOCK LA
VICARAGE RD
BRIARY VIEW
SHENLEY RD
Bottlehouse Plantation
Bottlehouse Farm
Moat
Tattenhoe Bare Farm
Thinbare Wood
Thickbare Wood
CODDIMOOR LA
Tattenhoe Park
Coddimoor Farm
W h a d d o n C h a s e
Coddimoor Farm
Coddimoorhill Wood
A421
Sports Ground
Woodpond Farm
Hogpound Wood
Bottledump
Thrift Farm
Thrift Wood
Bletchley Leys Farm
Broadway Wood
Fernfield Farm
Chase Farm
Stearthill Farm
Moat
Lower Salden Farm
Weasels'
Norbury Coppice
Salden Crabtree Farm
Crabtree Farm
Salden Wood
Middle Salden Wood
Springfield Farm
Aqueduct
4
33
3
32
2
31
1
30
80
81
82

55

67

46

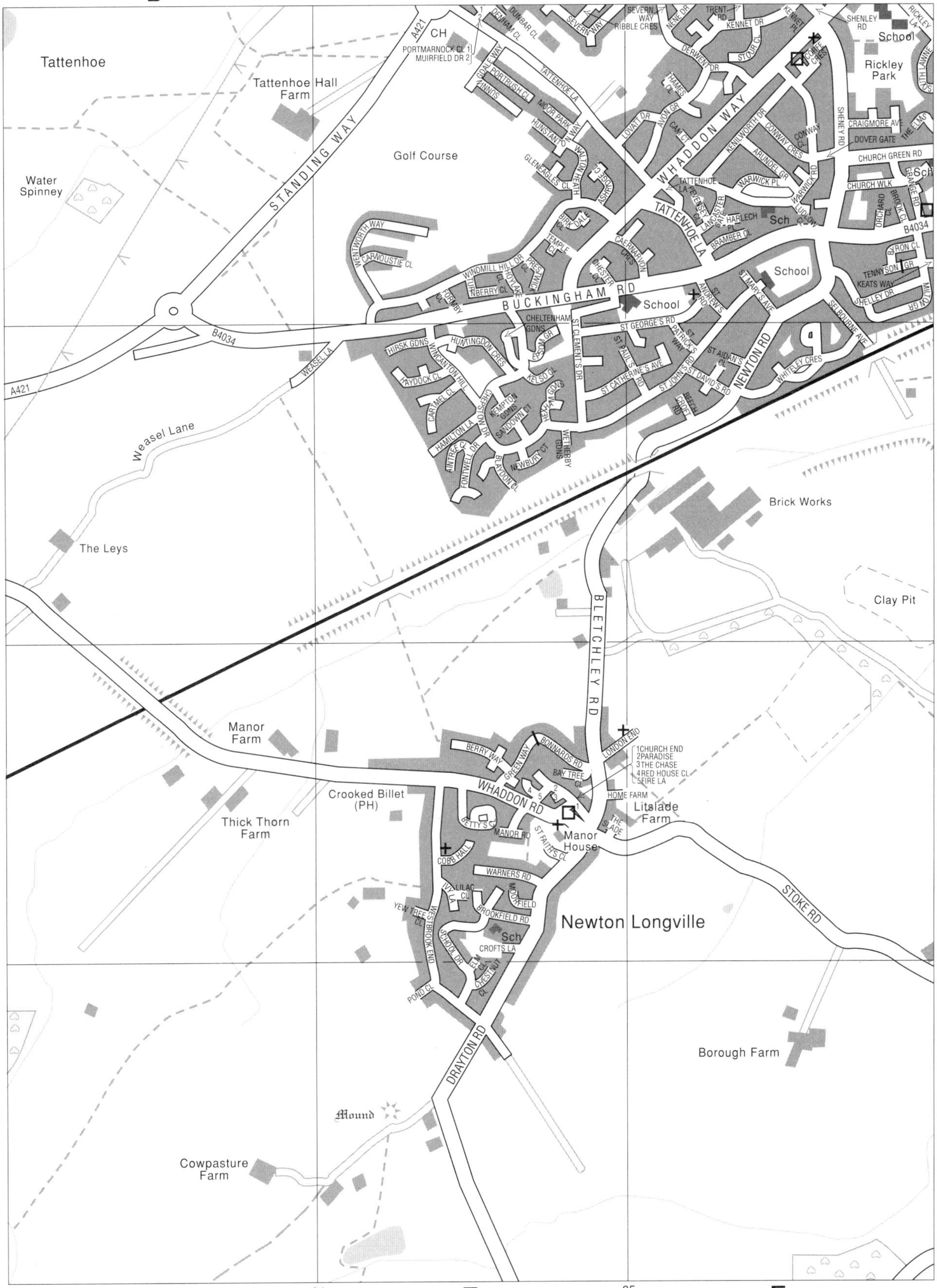
D
E
F
Tattenhoe
Tattenhoe Hall Farm
Golf Course
Water Spinney
STANDING WAY
A421
CH
PORTMARNOCK CL
MUIRFIELD DR
WHADDON WAY
TATTENHOE LA
BUCKINGHAM RD
B4034
School
Sch
Rickley Park
SHENLEY RD
CHURCH GREEN RD
CHURCH WLK
DOVER GATE
CRAIGMORE AVE
THE ELMS
TENNYSON GR
KEATS WAY
SHELLEY DR
NEWTON RD
ST GEORGE'S RD
ST CATHERINE'S AVE
ST CLEMENT'S DR
WEASEL LA
Weasel Lane
The Leys
Brick Works
Clay Pit
BLETCHLEY RD
Manor Farm
Thick Thorn Farm
Crooked Billet (PH)
WHADDON RD
Litslade Farm
Manor House
1 CHURCH END
2 PARADISE
3 THE CHASE
4 RED HOUSE CL
5 FIRE LA
HOME FARM
LONDON END
STOKE RD
Newton Longville
Sch
DRAYTON RD
Mound
Cowpasture Farm
Borough Farm
83
84
85
30
31
32
33
1
2
3
4

58

68

47

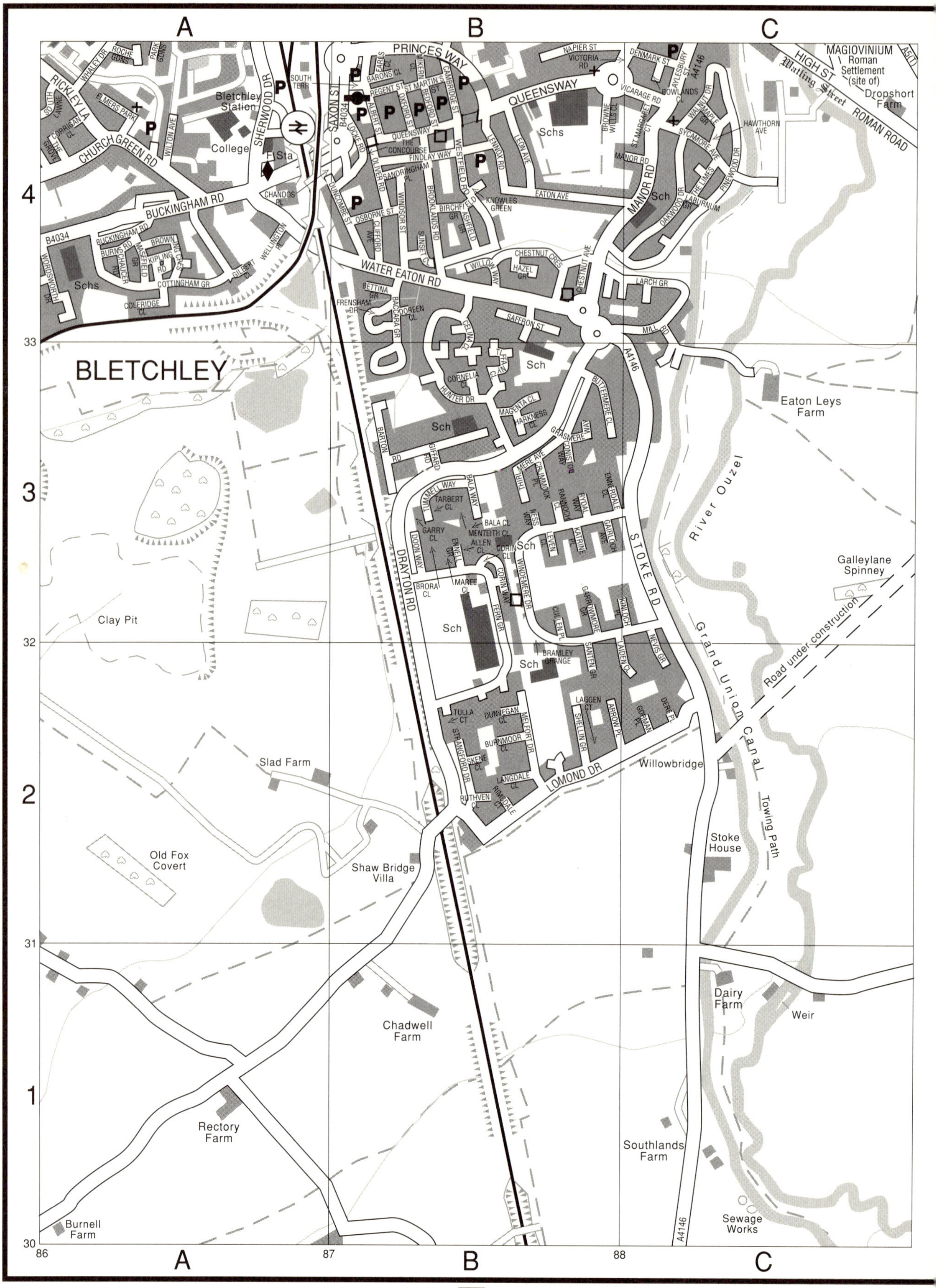
A
B
C
4
3
2
1
33
32
31
30
86
87
88
BLETCHLEY
PRINCES WAY
NAPIER ST
VICTORIA RD
DENMARK ST
AYLESBURY ST
A4146
MAGIOVINIUM
Roman Settlement (site of)
HIGH ST
Watling Street
ROMAN ROAD
Dropshort Farm
RICKLEY LA
WHALEY DR
ROCHE GDNS
PARK GDNS
ELMERS PARK
CHURCH GREEN RD
WILTON AVE
Bletchley Station
SHERWOOD DR
SOUTH TERR
College
F Sta
SAXON ST
B4034
QUEENSWAY
THE CONCOURSE
FINDLAY WAY
SANDRINGHAM PL
REGENT ST
ST MARTIN'S ST
BARONS CL
ALBERT ST
OXFORD ST
BEDFORD ST
CAMBRIDGE ST
WESTFIELD RD
LENNOX RD
LEON AVE
Schs
BROWNE WILLIS CL
VICARAGE RD
BOWLANDS CL
ST MARGARET CT
WALNUT DR
MAPLE GR
SYCAMORE AVE
HAWTHORN AVE
MANOR RD
Sch
THE LIMES
PINEWOOD DR
OAKWOOD DR
LABURNUM GR
EATON AVE
KNOWLES GREEN
BUCKINGHAM RD
CHANDOS CL
DUNCOMBE ST
OSBORNE ST
CLIFFORD AVE
WINDSOR ST
BROOKLANDS RD
BIRCHFIELD GR
ASHFIELD
B4034
BUCKINGHAM RD
BURNS RD
CHAUCER RD
MASEFIELD GR
BROWNING CRES
KIPLING RD
COTTINGHAM GR
GILBERT CL
WELLINGTON PL
WORDSWORTH DR
COLERIDGE CL
Schs
WATER EATON RD
WILLOW WAY
CHESTNUT CRES
HAZEL GR
CHESTNUT AVE
LARCH GR
MILL RD
BETTINA GR
FRENSHAM DR
BACCARA GR
DOREEN CL
SAFFRON ST
CELINA CL
TUFFA CL
CORNELIA CL
HUNTER DR
MAGENTA CL
HARKNESS CL
A4146
BUTTERMERE CL
Eaton Leys Farm
BARTON RD
GIFFARD RD
Sch
GRASMERE WAY
CONISTON WAY
THIRLMERE AVE
ELLESMERE...
RANNOCH CL
RYDAL WAY
ENNERDALE CL
LUMMELL WAY
BALA WAY
TARBERT CL
BALA CL
MENTEITH CL
GARRY CL
ALLEN CL
CORIN CL
DOON WAY
ENNELL GR
NESS WAY
LEVEN CL
KATRINE PL
GAIRLOCH AVE
STOKE RD
River Ouzel
Galleylane Spinney
DRAYTON RD
BRORA CL
MAREE CL
CORIN WAY
WINDERMERE DR
GARRY MORE...
KINLOCH PL
Clay Pit
Sch
FERN GR
CULLEN PL
BRAMLEY GRANGE
SANTEN GR
LAIDEN CL
NEVIS GR
Grand Union Canal
Road under construction
Sch
TULLA CT
DUNVEGAN CL
MELFORT DR
LAGGEN CT
SHELLIN GR
ARROW PL
GORMAN PL
DERE PL
BURNMOOR CL
STRANGFORD DR
SKENE CL
LANGDALE CL
RUTHVEN CL
RIMSDALE CT
LOMOND DR
Willowbridge
Slad Farm
Towing Path
Stoke House
Old Fox Covert
Shaw Bridge Villa
Dairy Farm
Weir
Chadwell Farm
Rectory Farm
Southlands Farm
Burnell Farm
Sewage Works
A4146

57

69

48

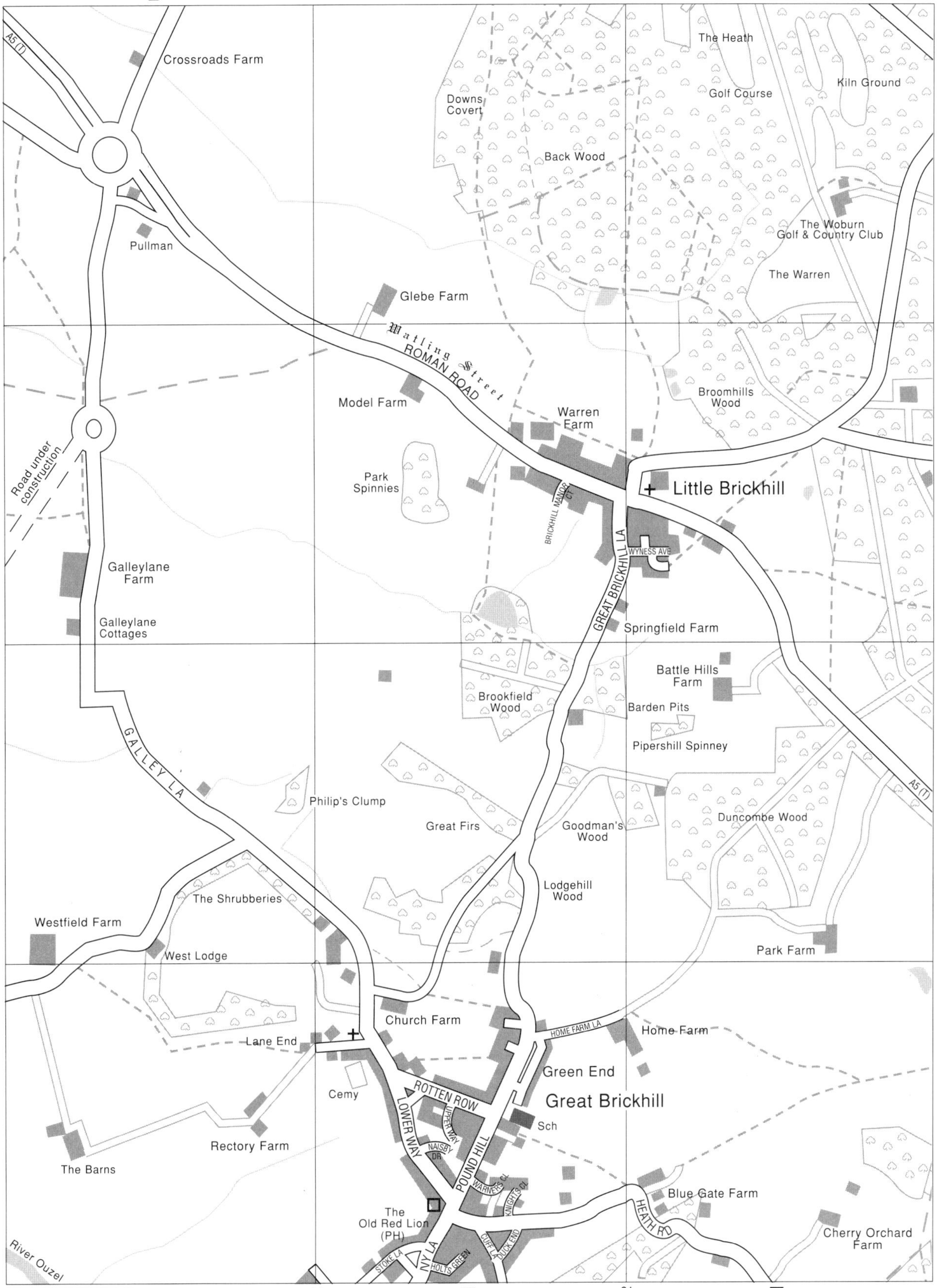
D
E
F
A5 (T)
Crossroads Farm
Downs Covert
The Heath
Golf Course
Kiln Ground
Back Wood
4
Pullman
The Woburn Golf & Country Club
The Warren
Glebe Farm
Watling Street
ROMAN ROAD
33
Model Farm
Warren Farm
Broomhills Wood
Road under construction
Park Spinnies
BRICKHILL MANOR CT
Little Brickhill
3
WYNESS AVE
Galleylane Farm
GREAT BRICKHILL LA
Galleylane Cottages
Springfield Farm
32
Battle Hills Farm
Brookfield Wood
Barden Pits
GALLEY LA
Pipershill Spinney
A5 (T)
Philip's Clump
2
Great Firs
Goodman's Wood
Duncombe Wood
Lodgehill Wood
The Shrubberies
Westfield Farm
West Lodge
Park Farm
31
Church Farm
HOME FARM LA
Home Farm
Lane End
Green End
Cemy
ROTTEN ROW
Great Brickhill
LOWER WAY
UPPER WAY
Sch
1
NAISBY DR
POUND HILL
Rectory Farm
The Barns
WARNERS CL
KNIGHTS CL
HEATH RD
Blue Gate Farm
The Old Red Lion (PH)
CUFF LA
DUCK END
STOKE LA
NY LA
HOLT GREEN
Cherry Orchard Farm
River Ouzel
30
89
90
91
D
E
F

60

70

49

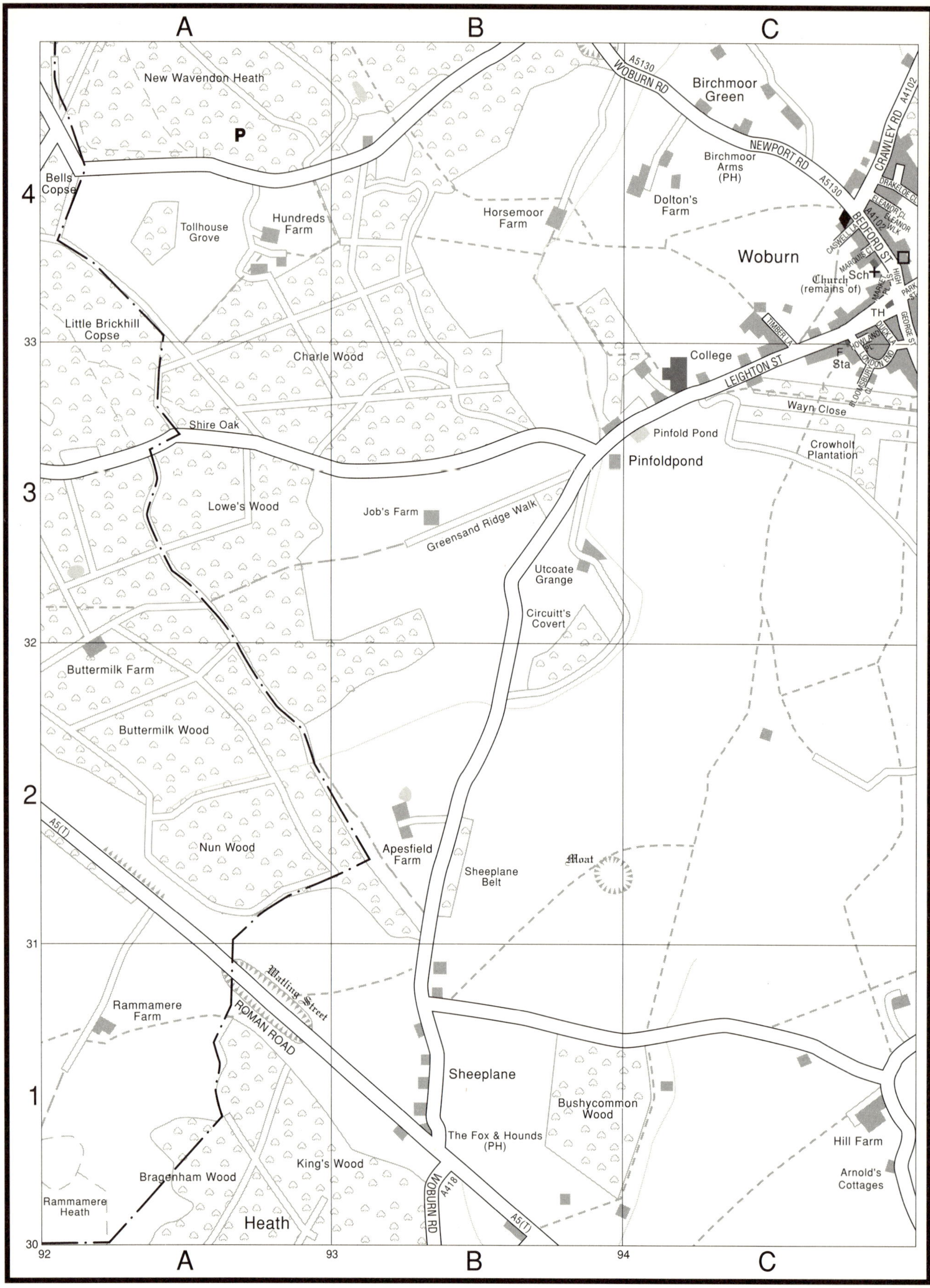
A
B
C
New Wavendon Heath
P
Bells Copse
Tollhouse Grove
Hundreds Farm
Horsemoor Farm
Birchmoor Green
Birchmoor Arms (PH)
Dolton's Farm
Woburn
WOBURN RD
A5130
NEWPORT RD
CRAWLEY RD
A4102
BEDFORD ST
Church (remains of)
Sch
TH
F
Sta
College
LEIGHTON ST
Little Brickhill Copse
Charle Wood
Shire Oak
Pinfold Pond
Pinfoldpond
Wayn Close
Crowholt Plantation
Lowe's Wood
Job's Farm
Greensand Ridge Walk
Utcoate Grange
Circuitt's Covert
Buttermilk Farm
Buttermilk Wood
Nun Wood
Apesfield Farm
Sheeplane Belt
Moat
A5(T)
Watling Street
ROMAN ROAD
Rammamere Farm
Sheeplane
Bushycommon Wood
The Fox & Hounds (PH)
Hill Farm
Arnold's Cottages
King's Wood
Bragenham Wood
Rammamere Heath
Heath
WOBURN RD
A418
4
3
2
1
33
32
31
30
92
93
94

59

50

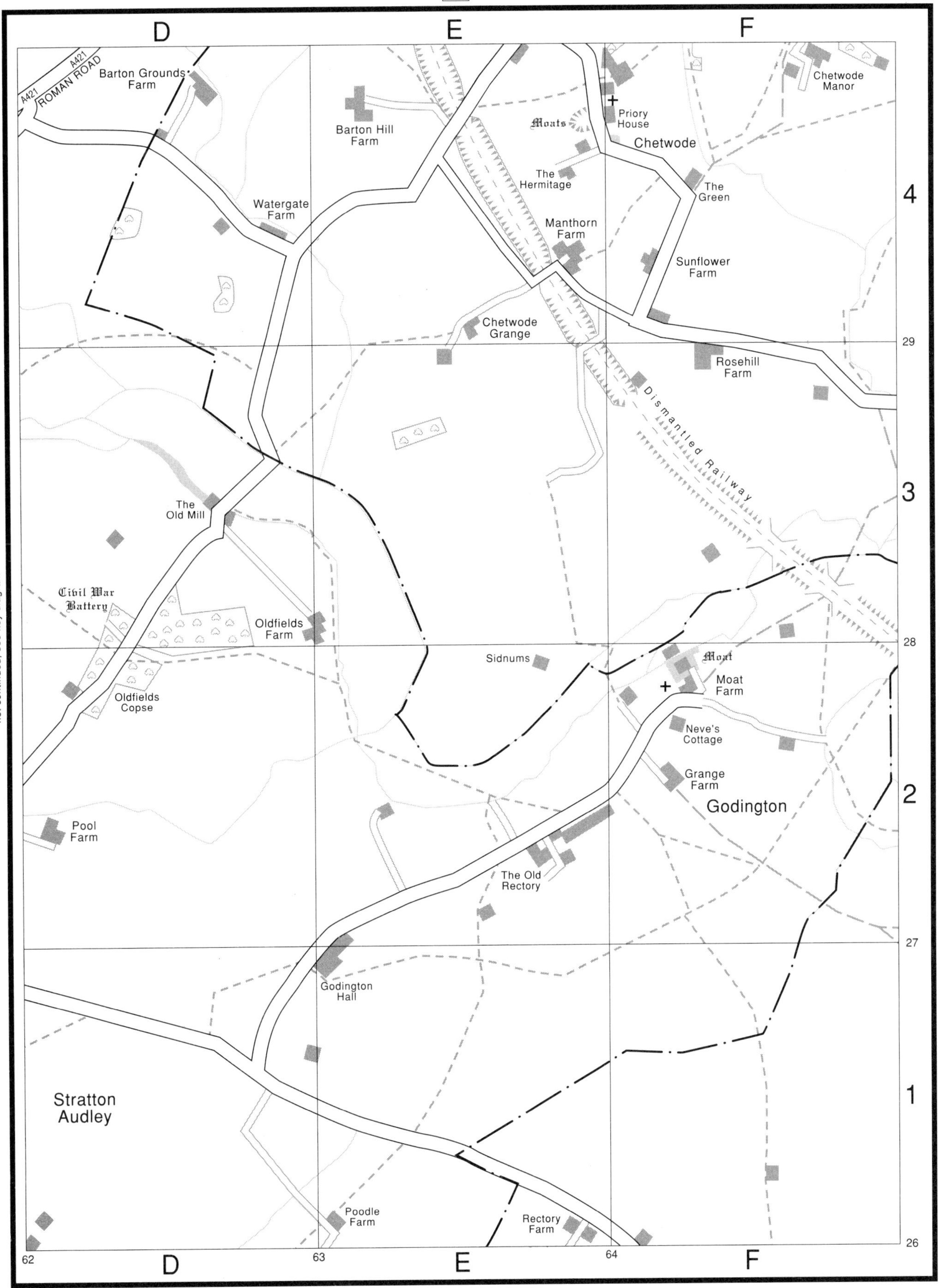
D
E
F
A421
A421
ROMAN ROAD
Barton Grounds Farm
Barton Hill Farm
Moats
Priory House
Chetwode
Chetwode Manor
The Hermitage
The Green
Watergate Farm
Manthorn Farm
Sunflower Farm
Chetwode Grange
Rosehill Farm
Dismantled Railway
The Old Mill
Civil War Battery
Oldfields Farm
Sidnums
Moat
Moat Farm
Oldfields Copse
Neve's Cottage
Grange Farm
Godington
Pool Farm
The Old Rectory
Godington Hall
Stratton Audley
Poodle Farm
Rectory Farm
4
3
2
1
29
28
27
26
62
63
64

62

71

51

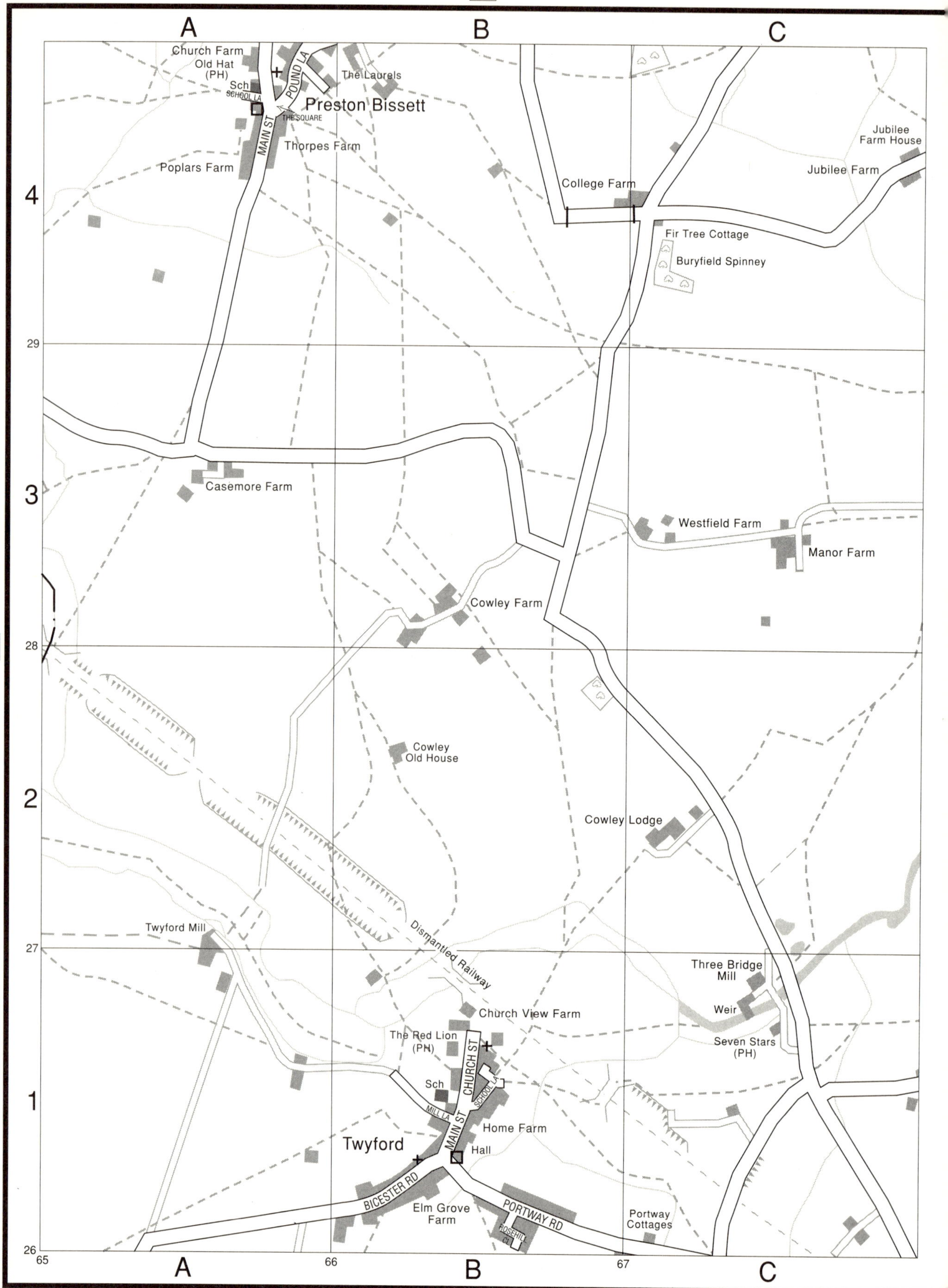

A
B
C
Church Farm
Old Hat (PH)
Sch
SCHOOL LA
POUND LA
The Laurels
Preston Bissett
THE SQUARE
MAIN ST
Thorpes Farm
Poplars Farm
Jubilee Farm House
Jubilee Farm
College Farm
Fir Tree Cottage
Buryfield Spinney
4
29
Casemore Farm
3
Westfield Farm
Manor Farm
Cowley Farm
28
Cowley Old House
2
Cowley Lodge
Dismantled Railway
Twyford Mill
27
Three Bridge Mill
Weir
Church View Farm
The Red Lion (PH)
CHURCH ST
Seven Stars (PH)
Sch
SCHOOL LA
1
MILL LA
MAIN ST
Home Farm
Twyford
Hall
BICESTER RD
Elm Grove Farm
PORTWAY RD
ROSEHILL CL
Portway Cottages
26
65
A
66
B
67
C

61

72

52

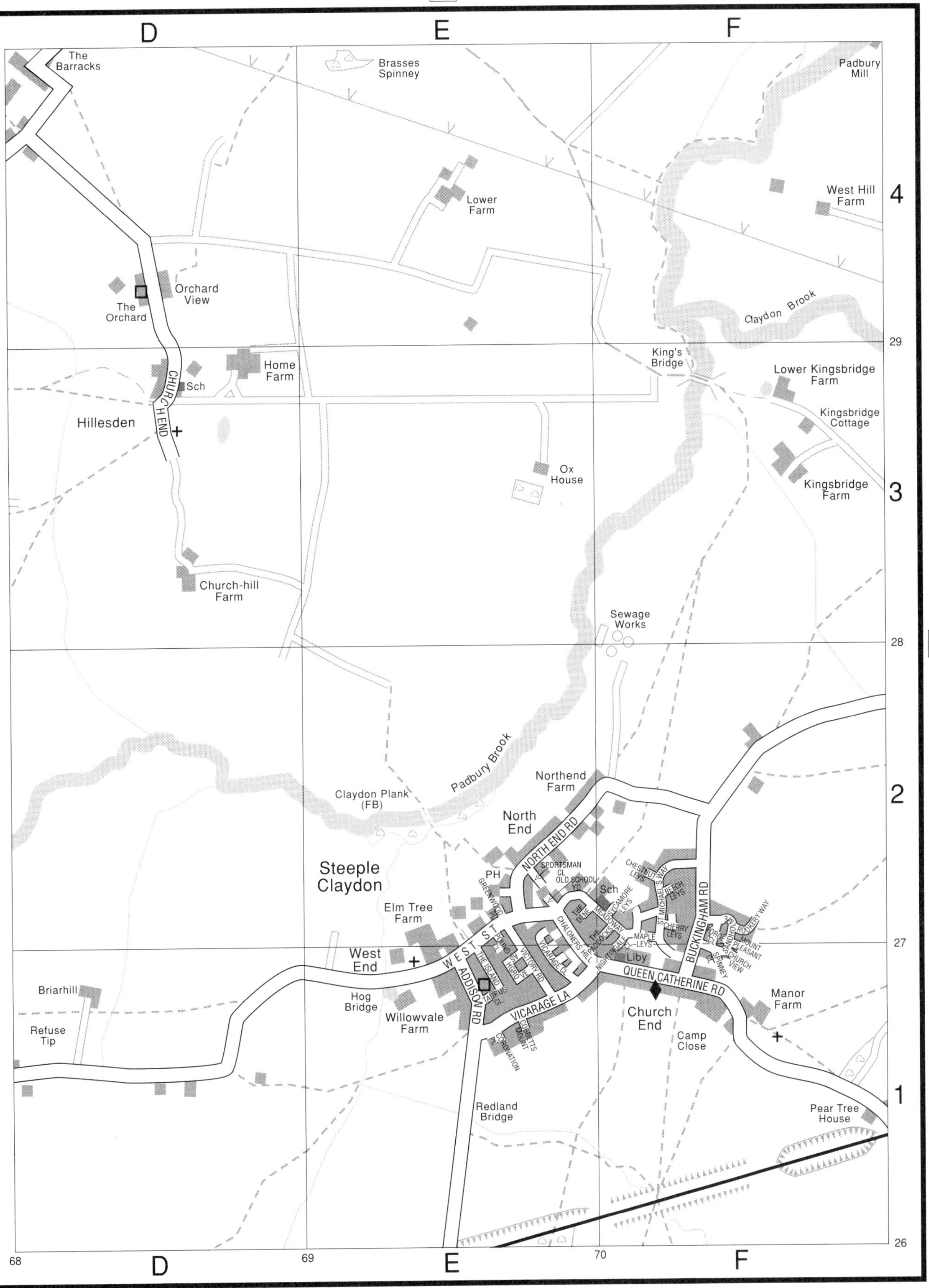
D
E
F
The Barracks
Brasses Spinney
Padbury Mill
Lower Farm
West Hill Farm
Orchard View
The Orchard
Claydon Brook
King's Bridge
Home Farm
Sch
CHURCH END
Hillesden
Lower Kingsbridge Farm
Kingsbridge Cottage
Ox House
Kingsbridge Farm
Church-hill Farm
Sewage Works
Padbury Brook
Northend Farm
Claydon Plank (FB)
North End
NORTH END RD
Steeple Claydon
PH
SPORTSMAN CL
OLD SCHOOL YD
CHESTNUT LEYS
ST MICHAEL'S WAY
BEECH LEYS
BUCKINGHAM RD
ROOKERY WAY
Elm Tree Farm
GREENWOOD
THE DENE
SYCAMORE LEYS
MEADOWAY
CHERRY LEYS
CHALONERS HILL
THE PADDOCKS
MAPLE LEYS
NIGHTINGALE CL
MOUNT PLEASANT
CHURCH VIEW
SPINNEY
Liby
West End
WEST ST
POUND CL
VICTORY RD
VICARAGE CL
THE ISLAND
TAURUS CL
QUEEN CATHERINE RD
Briarhill
Hog Bridge
ADDISON RD
VICARAGE LA
Church End
Manor Farm
Willowvale Farm
Camp Close
CORBETTS MOUNT
CORONATION PL
Refuse Tip
Redland Bridge
Pear Tree House
4
3
2
1
29
28
27
26
68
69
70

64

73

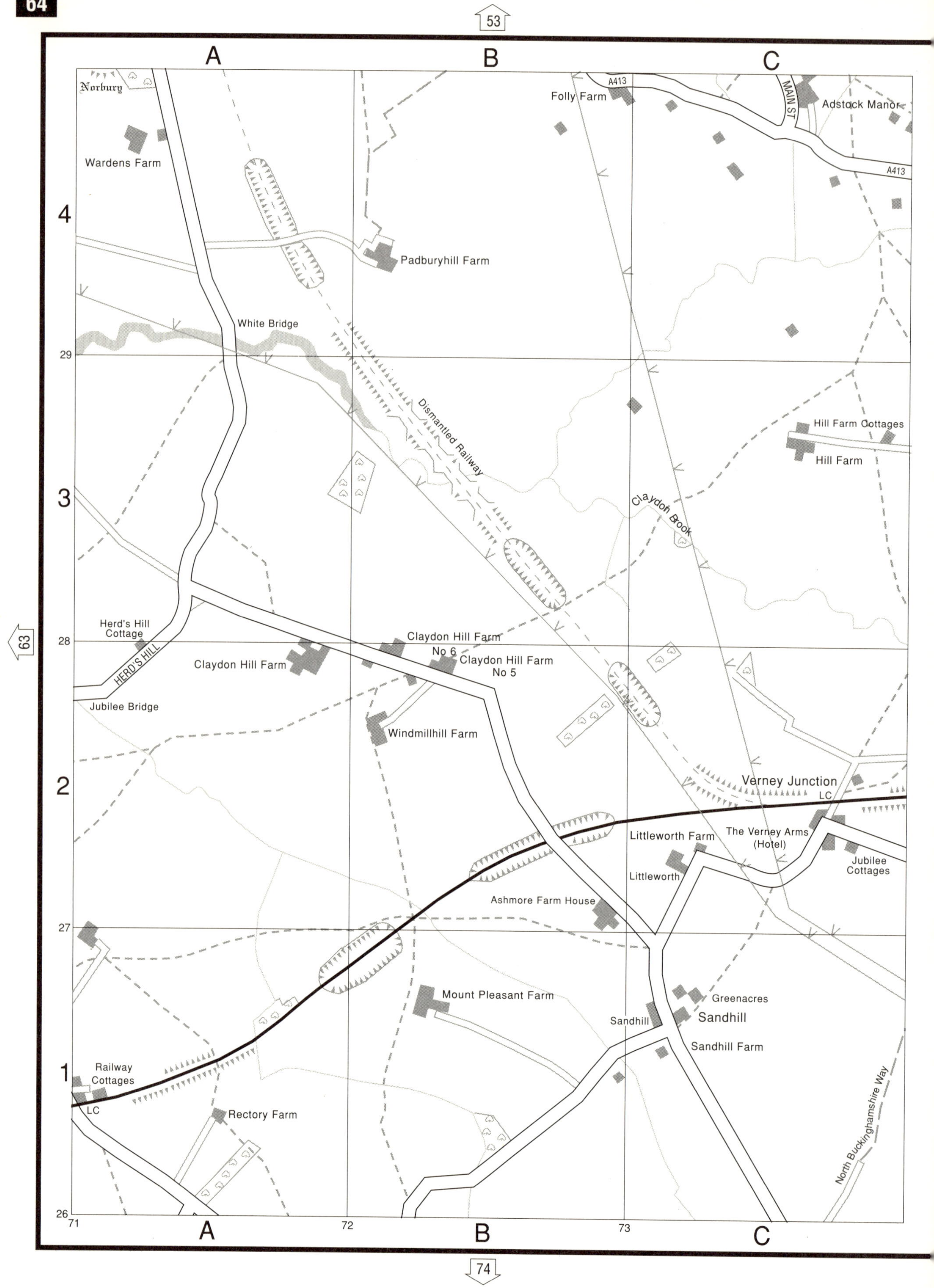
53
A
B
C
Norbury
Folly Farm
A413
MAIN ST
Adstock Manor
A413
Wardens Farm
4
Padburyhill Farm
White Bridge
29
Dismantled Railway
Hill Farm Cottages
Hill Farm
3
Claydon Brook
Herd's Hill
Cottage
28
63
Claydon Hill Farm
Claydon Hill Farm
No 6
Claydon Hill Farm
No 5
HERD'S HILL
Jubilee Bridge
Windmillhill Farm
2
Verney Junction
LC
Littleworth Farm
The Verney Arms
(Hotel)
Jubilee
Cottages
Littleworth
Ashmore Farm House
27
Mount Pleasant Farm
Greenacres
Sandhill
Sandhill
Sandhill Farm
1
Railway
Cottages
LC
Rectory Farm
North Buckinghamshire Way
26
71
A
72
B
73
C
74

54

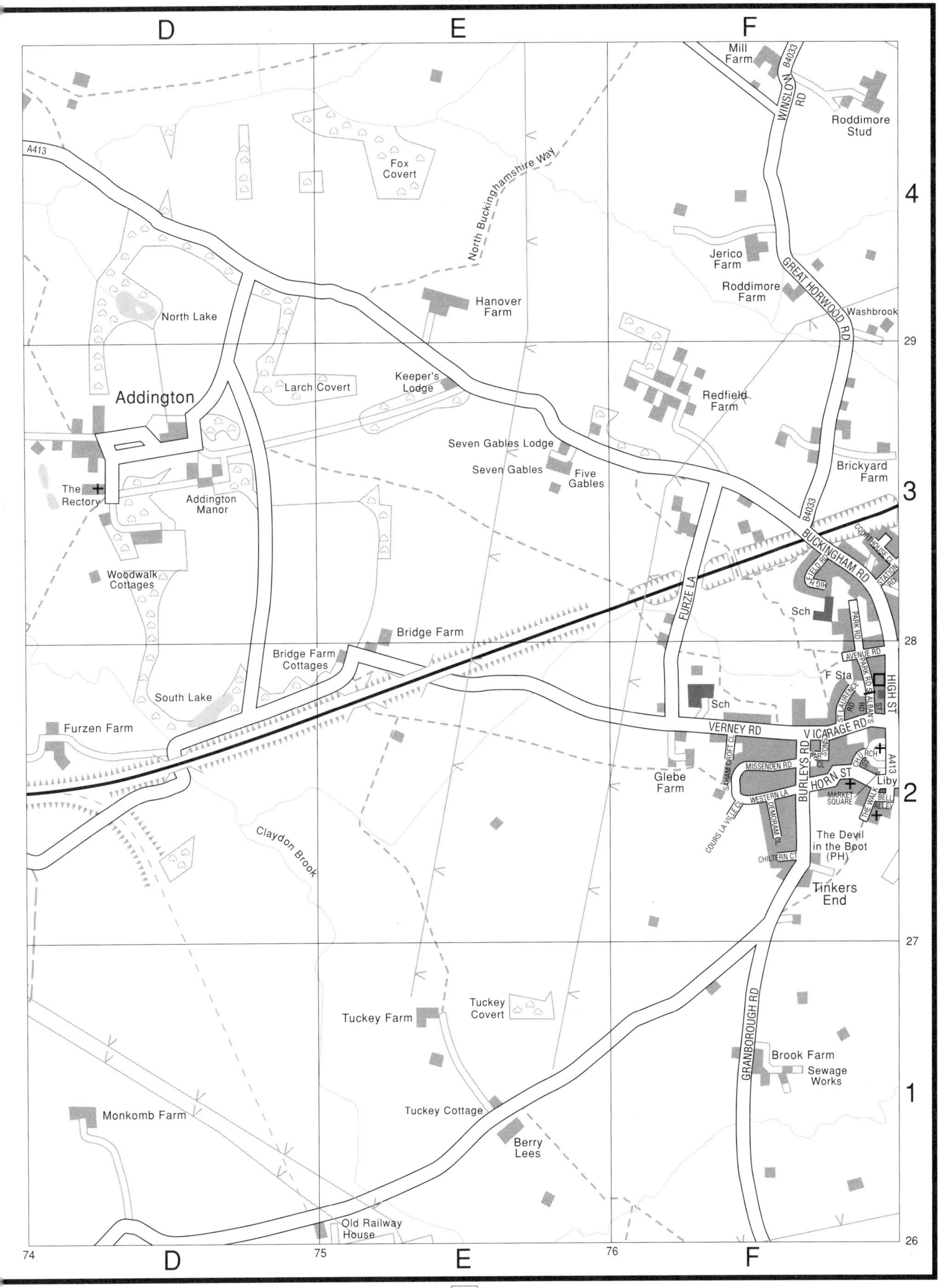

D
E
F
Mill Farm
B4033
WINSLOW RD
Roddimore Stud
A413
Fox Covert
North Buckinghamshire Way
4
Jerico Farm
Roddimore Farm
GREAT HORWOOD RD
Washbrook
Hanover Farm
North Lake
29
Larch Covert
Keeper's Lodge
Addington
Redfield Farm
Seven Gables Lodge
Brickyard Farm
Seven Gables
Five Gables
The Rectory
Addington Manor
3
B4033
BUCKINGHAM RD
COURT HOUSE CL
STATION RD
HIGH FIELD RD
Woodwalk Cottages
FURZE LA
Sch
PARK RD
Bridge Farm
28
AVENUE RD
Bridge Farm Cottages
F Sta
PARK RD
ST LAURENCE RD
ST ALBAN'S RD
HIGH ST
Sch
South Lake
Furzen Farm
VERNEY RD
VICARAGE RD
PARSONS CL
CHURCH ST
A413
SAHAM CROFT CL
MISSENDEN RD
BURLEYS RD
HORN ST
Liby
Glebe Farm
WESTERN LA
MARKET SQUARE
THE WALK
BELL ALLEY
2
COURS LA VILLE CL
DENNIRAM CL
Claydon Brook
The Devil in the Boot (PH)
CHILTERN CT
Tinkers End
27
GRANBOROUGH RD
Tuckey Covert
Tuckey Farm
Brook Farm
Sewage Works
1
Monkomb Farm
Tuckey Cottage
Berry Lees
Old Railway House
26
74
75
76

66

75

55

65

A
B
C
4
3
2
1
29
28
27
26
77
78
79
Greenway Farm
Mount Pleasant
The Hollows
Horwood House
Fishpond Spinney
Osierbed Spinney
Roddimore Covert
The White House
Moco Farm
Clare Farm
Canada
Foxhole Farm
Spring Corner
Redhall Farm
Dodley Hill Farm
Abovemead Farm
TANK HOUSE RD
THE SPINNEY
MAGPIE WAY
STATION RD
OLD MILL FURLONG
SCOTT EVANS CT
LOWNDES WAY
LONGLANDS CT
LONGLANDS WLK
KEACH CL
MEETING OAK LA
BEAMISH WAY
Sch
CRICKETERS ROW
DOVE HOUSE CL
NORTH CRES
FAIR MEADOW
ELMFIELDS GATE
ELMSIDE
COPSE GATE
Hall
Winslow
A413
SHEEP ST
HAYBUSHIN LA
Sch
Shipton Mead Farm
B4032
Rands Farm
Jubilee Cottages
Shipton
Shipton Farm
Ivy Farm
Duck End
FIELD END
SMITHFIELD
CHARLTON CL
B4032
WINSLOW RD
Swanbourne House School
Shipton Bridge
Claydon Brook
Haybush Farm
Bennett's Hill
North Hill Farm
A413
A
B
C

76

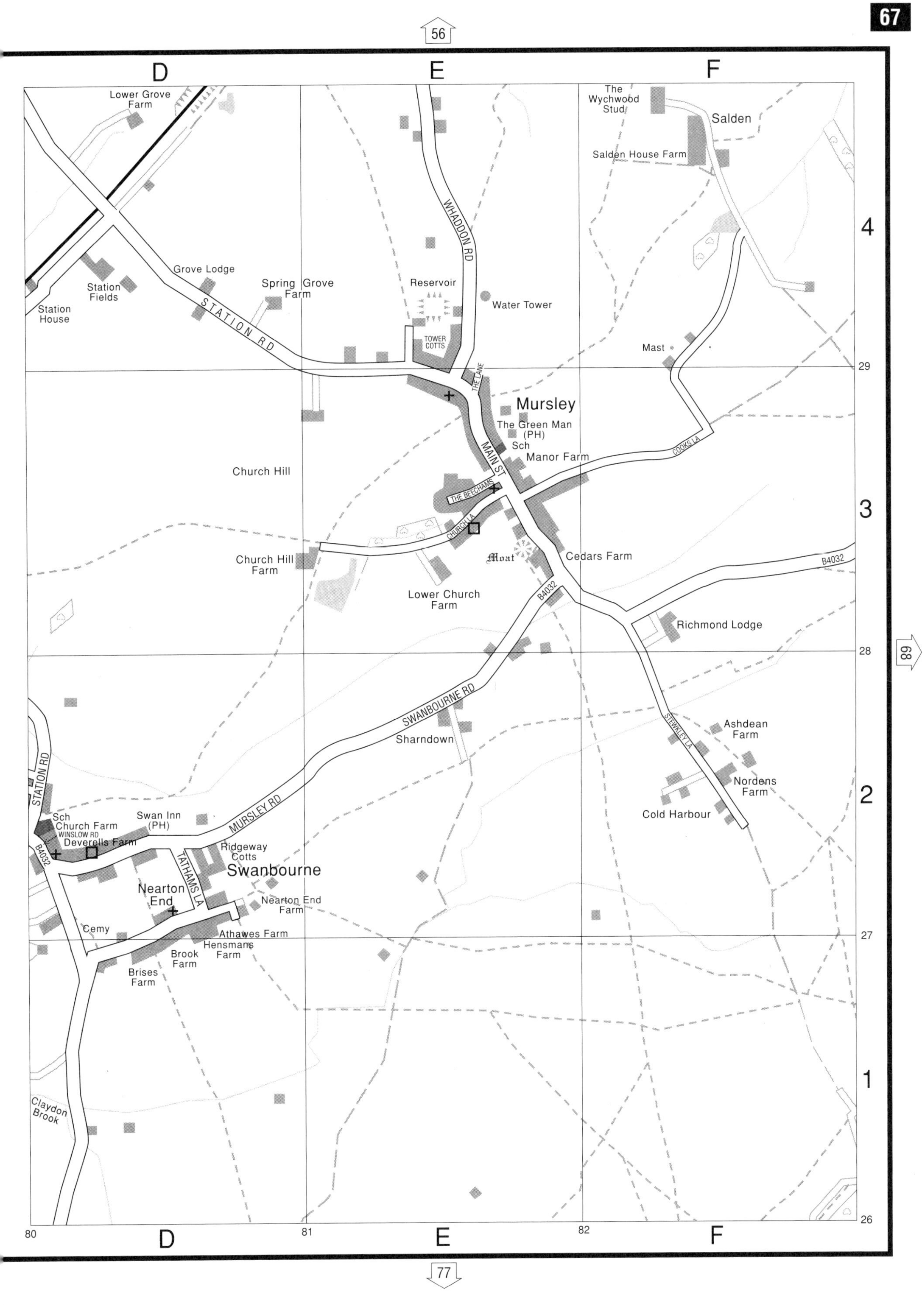
56
D
E
F
Lower Grove Farm
The Wychwood Stud
Salden
Salden House Farm
WHADDON RD
4
Grove Lodge
Spring Grove Farm
Reservoir
Water Tower
Station Fields
Station House
STATION RD
TOWER COTTS
Mast
29
THE LANE
Mursley
The Green Man (PH)
Sch
Manor Farm
MAIN ST
COOKS LA
Church Hill
THE BEECHAMS
3
CHURCH LA
Moat
Cedars Farm
Church Hill Farm
B4032
Lower Church Farm
B4032
Richmond Lodge
28
68
SWANBOURNE RD
Ashdean Farm
STEWKLEY LA
Sharndown
STATION RD
Nordens Farm
2
Cold Harbour
Sch
Church Farm
WINSLOW RD
Swan Inn (PH)
MURSLEY RD
Deverells Farm
B4032
Ridgeway Cotts
TATHAMS LA
Swanbourne
Nearton End
Nearton End Farm
Cemy
Athawes Farm
27
Hensmans Farm
Brook Farm
Brises Farm
1
Claydon Brook
26
80
D
81
E
82
F
77

57

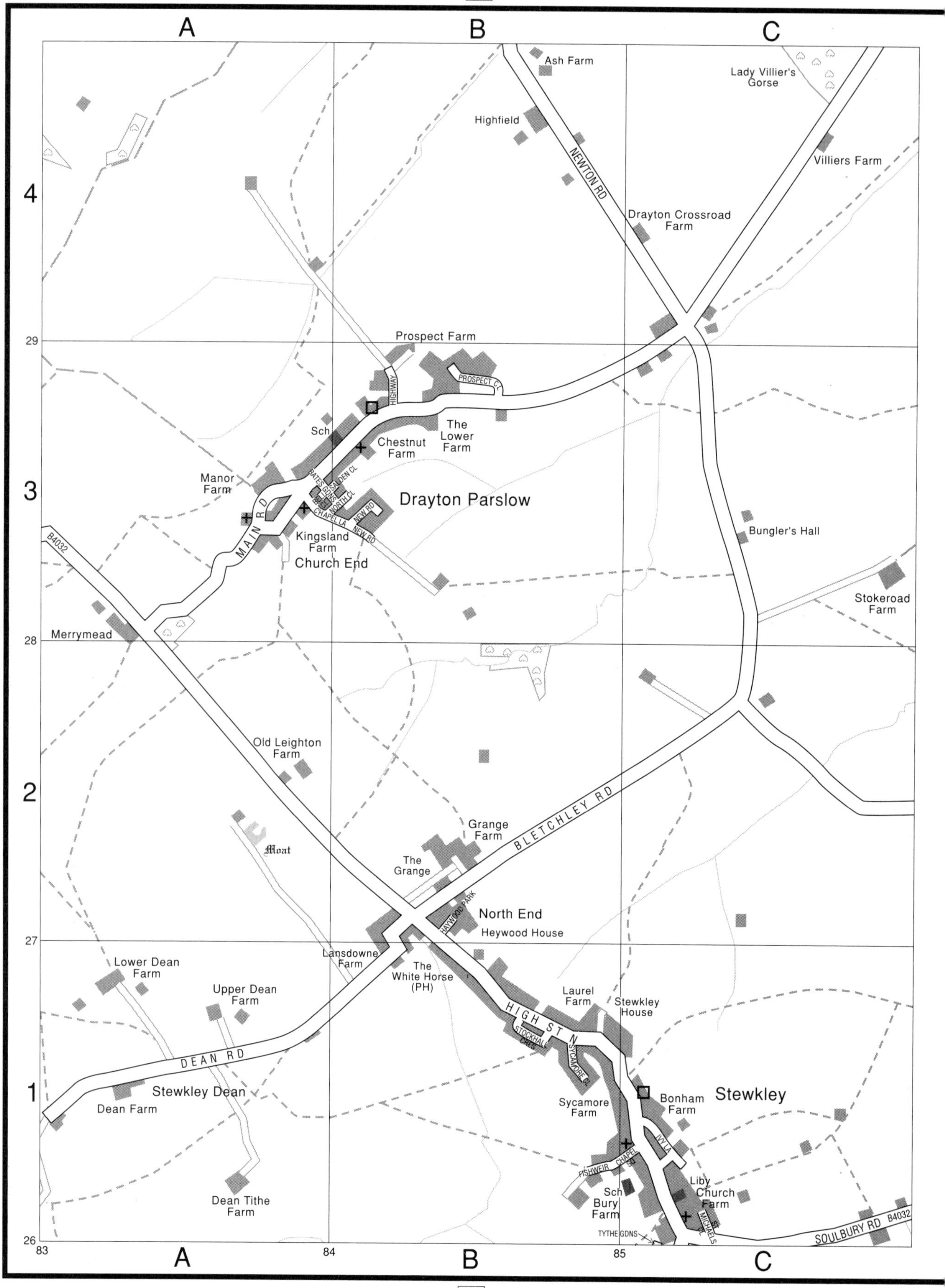
A
B
C
4
3
2
1
29
28
27
26
83
84
85
Ash Farm
Lady Villier's Gorse
Highfield
Villiers Farm
NEWTON RD
Drayton Crossroad Farm
Prospect Farm
PROSPECT CL
HIGHWAY
Sch
The Lower Farm
Chestnut Farm
Manor Farm
Drayton Parslow
BATES GDNS
SALDEN CL
NORTH CL
CHAPEL LA
NEW RD
MAIN RD
Kingsland Farm
Church End
B4032
Bungler's Hall
Stokeroad Farm
Merrymead
Old Leighton Farm
Moat
Grange Farm
BLETCHLEY RD
The Grange
HAYWOOD PARK
North End
Heywood House
Lansdowne Farm
The White Horse (PH)
Lower Dean Farm
Upper Dean Farm
HIGH ST
Laurel Farm
Stewkley House
STOCKHALL CRES
SYCAMORE CL
DEAN RD
Stewkley Dean
Dean Farm
Sycamore Farm
Bonham Farm
Stewkley
IVY LA
FISHWEIR
CHAPEL SQ
Sch
Bury Farm
Liby
Church Farm
ST MICHAELS CL
TYTHE GDNS
SOULBURY RD
B4032
Dean Tithe Farm

67

78

58

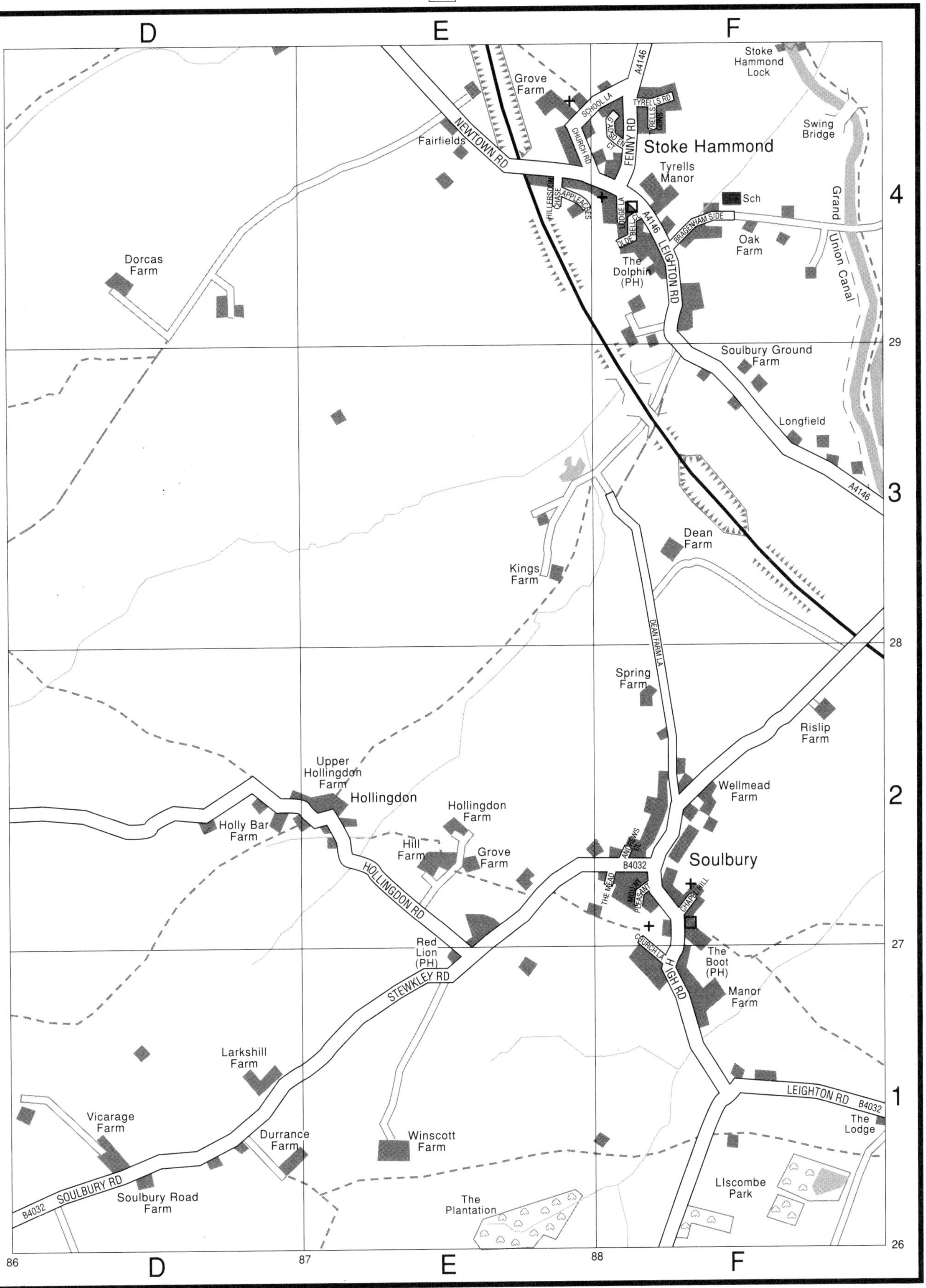
D
E
F
Stoke Hammond Lock
Grove Farm
Swing Bridge
Fairfields
NEWTOWN RD
SCHOOL LA
CHURCH RD
FENNY RD
TYRELLS RD
A4146
Stoke Hammond
Tyrells Manor
Sch
Grand Union Canal
HILLERSDON CHASE
APPLEACRES
LODGE LA
A4146
LEIGHTON RD
BRAGENHAM SIDE
Oak Farm
Dorcas Farm
The Dolphin (PH)
4
29
Soulbury Ground Farm
Longfield
A4146
3
Dean Farm
Kings Farm
DEAN FARM LA
28
Spring Farm
Rislip Farm
Upper Hollingdon Farm
Hollingdon
Wellmead Farm
2
Holly Bar Farm
Hollingdon Farm
Hill Farm
Grove Farm
ANDREWS CL
B4032
Soulbury
THE MEAD
MOUNT PLEASANT
CHAPEL HILL
HOLLINGDON RD
CHURCH LA
Red Lion (PH)
The Boot (PH)
27
STEWKLEY RD
HIGH RD
Manor Farm
Larkshill Farm
1
LEIGHTON RD
B4032
The Lodge
Vicarage Farm
Durrance Farm
Winscott Farm
Llscombe Park
B4032
SOULBURY RD
Soulbury Road Farm
The Plantation
26
86
87
88
D
E
F

70

79

59

69

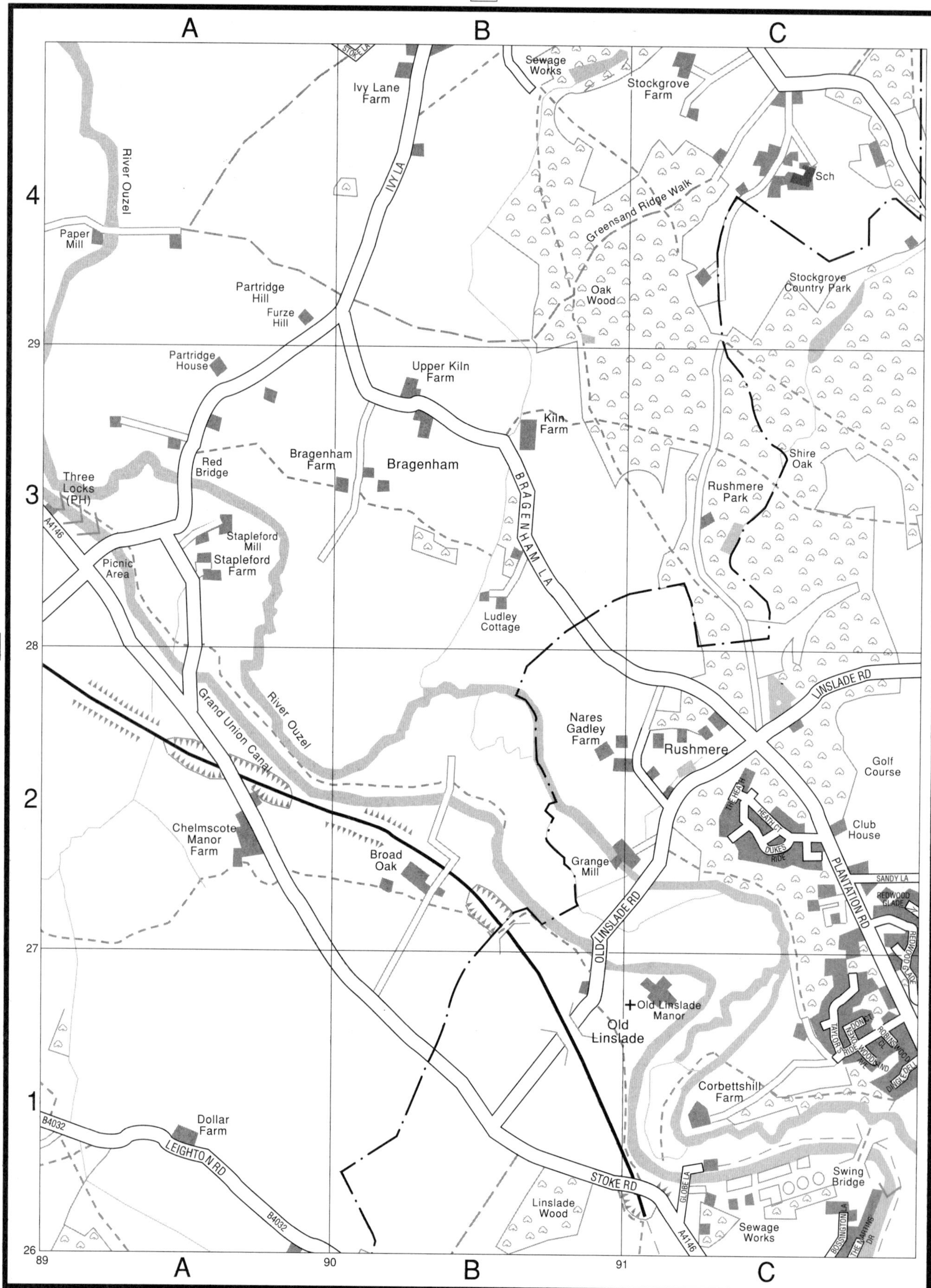

not continued, see key diagram

80

61

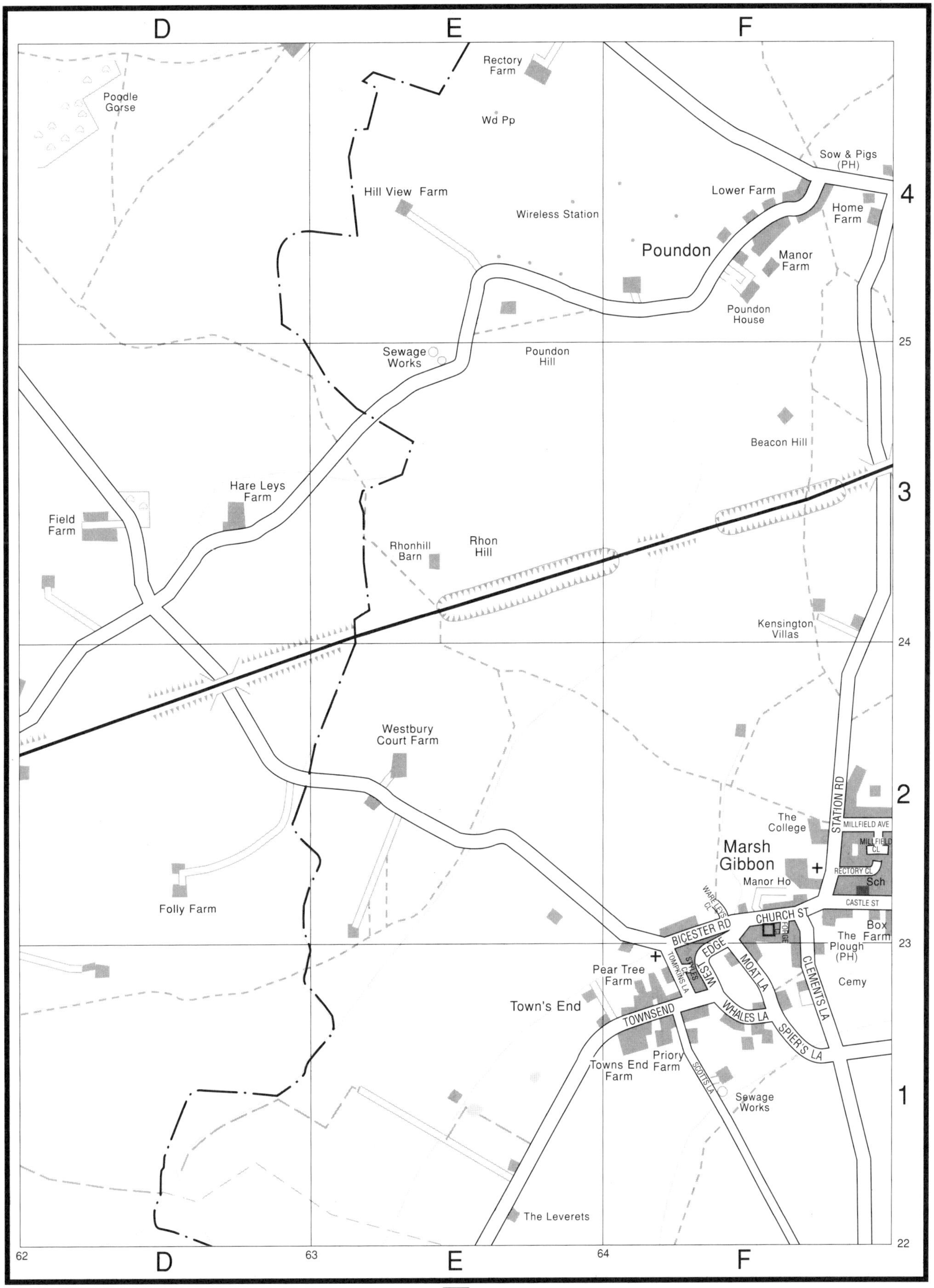
D
E
F
Rectory Farm
Poodle Gorse
Wd Pp
Sow & Pigs (PH)
Hill View Farm
Lower Farm
4
Wireless Station
Home Farm
Poundon
Manor Farm
Poundon House
Sewage Works
Poundon Hill
25
Beacon Hill
3
Hare Leys Farm
Field Farm
Rhonhill Barn
Rhon Hill
Kensington Villas
24
Westbury Court Farm
2
STATION RD
The College
MILLFIELD AVE
MILLFIELD CL
Marsh Gibbon
RECTORY CL
Sch
Manor Ho
WARE LEYS CL
CASTLE ST
Folly Farm
CHURCH ST
Box Farm
BICESTER RD
FORGE
The Plough (PH)
23
EDGE
WEST
STYLES CL
TOMPKINS LA
MOAT LA
CLEMENTS LA
Pear Tree Farm
Cemy
Town's End
TOWNSEND
WHALES LA
SPIER'S LA
Towns End Farm
Priory Farm
SCOTTS LA
Sewage Works
1
The Leverets
22
62
63
64
D
E
F

72

81

62

71

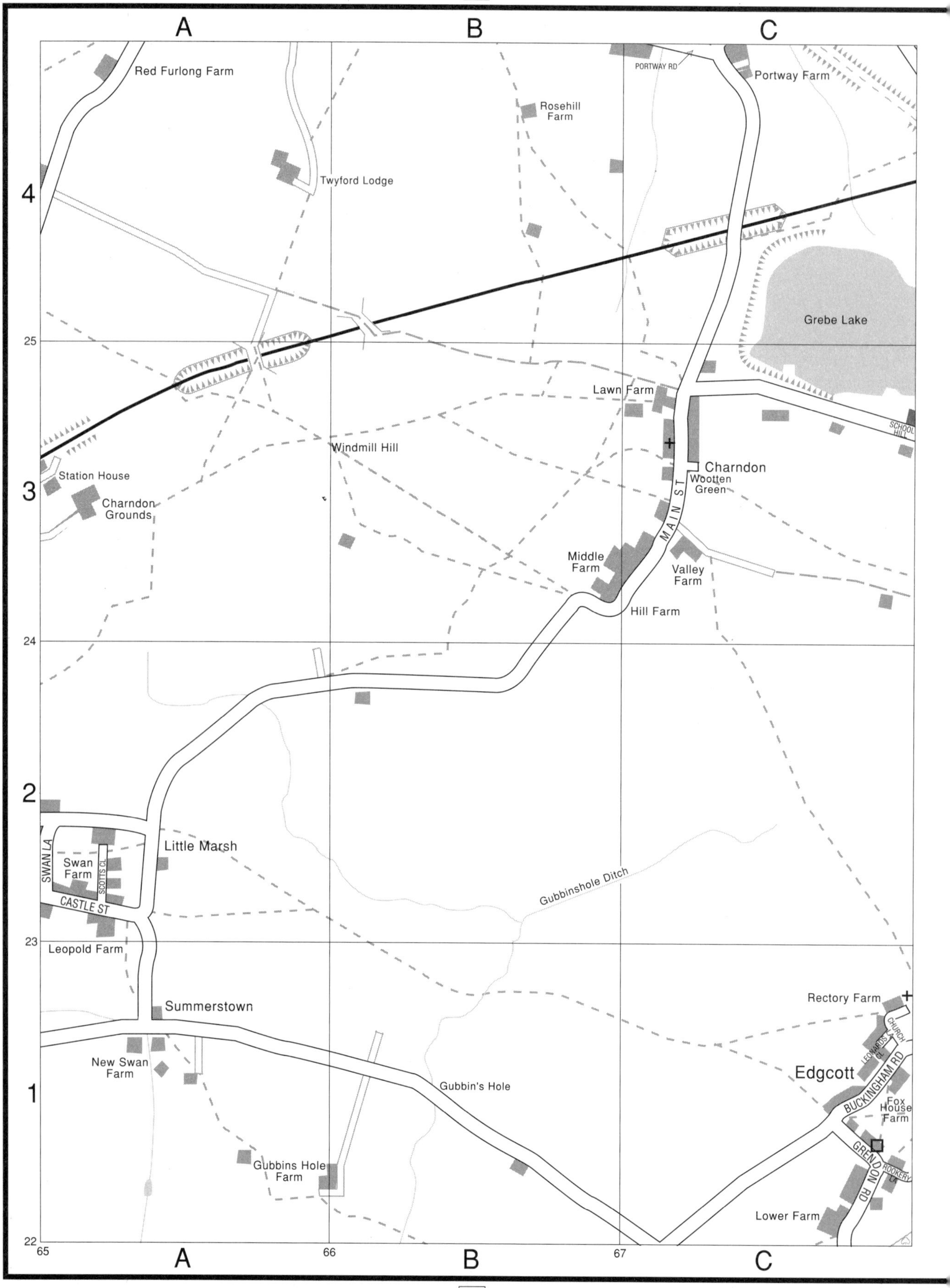
A
B
C
4
3
2
1
25
24
23
22
65
66
67
Red Furlong Farm
PORTWAY RD
Portway Farm
Rosehill Farm
Twyford Lodge
Grebe Lake
Lawn Farm
SCHOOL HILL
Windmill Hill
Station House
Charndon Grounds
Charndon
Wootten Green
MAIN ST
Middle Farm
Valley Farm
Hill Farm
Little Marsh
SWAN LA
Swan Farm
SCOTTS CL
CASTLE ST
Gubbinshole Ditch
Leopold Farm
Summerstown
Rectory Farm
New Swan Farm
Gubbin's Hole
Edgcott
CHURCH
LEONARDS
BUCKINGHAM RD
Fox House Farm
GRENDON RD
ROOKERY LA
Gubbins Hole Farm
Lower Farm

82

63

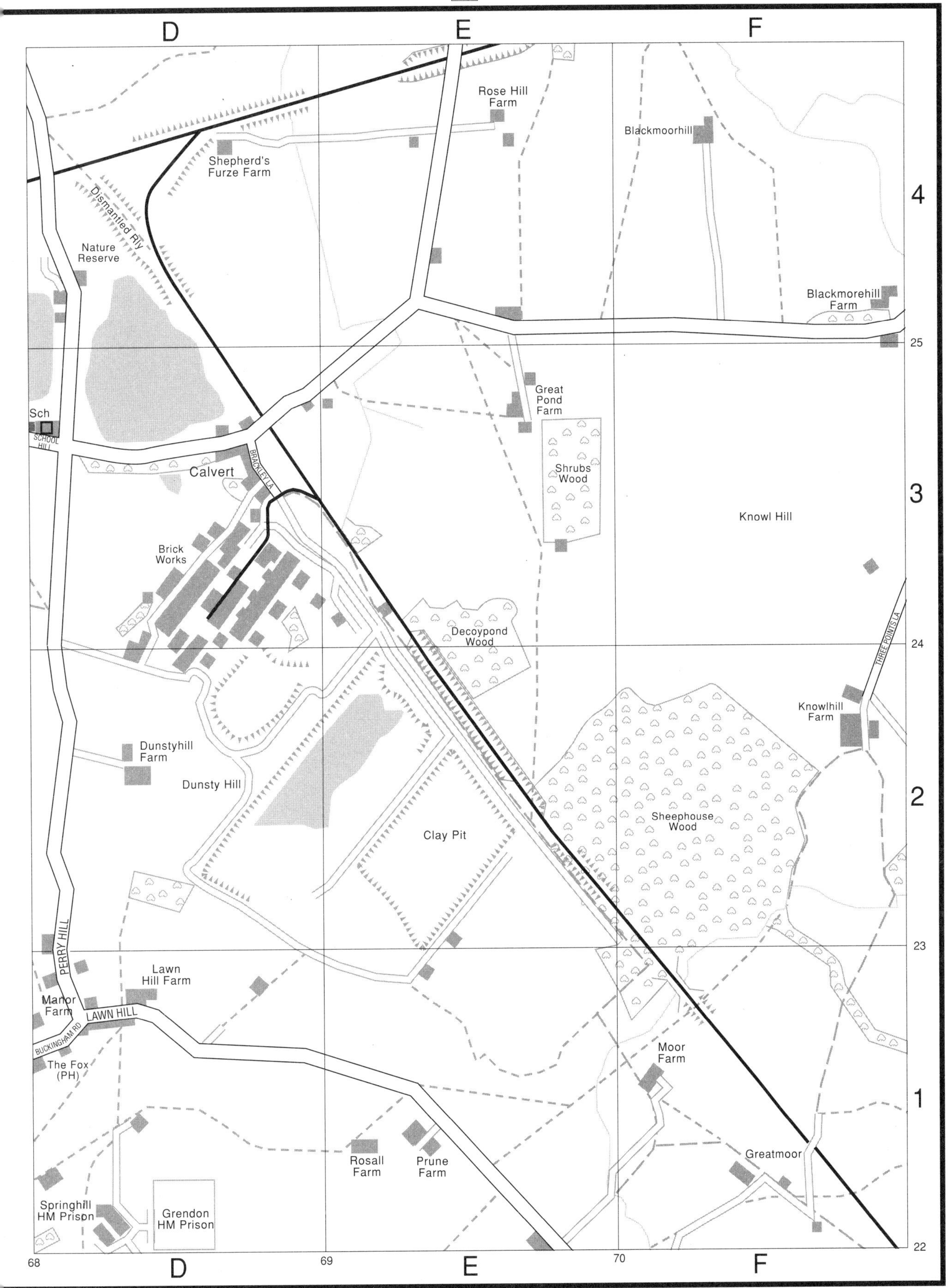

D
E
F
Rose Hill Farm
Blackmoorhill
Shepherd's Furze Farm
Dismantled Rly
4
Nature Reserve
Blackmorehill Farm
25
Great Pond Farm
Sch
SCHOOL HILL
Calvert
BRACKLEY LA
Shrubs Wood
3
Knowl Hill
Brick Works
Decoypond Wood
THREE POINTS LA
24
Knowlhill Farm
Dunstyhill Farm
Dunsty Hill
2
Sheephouse Wood
Clay Pit
PERRY HILL
23
Lawn Hill Farm
Manor Farm
LAWN HILL
BUCKINGHAM RD
The Fox (PH)
Moor Farm
1
Greatmoor
Rosall Farm
Prune Farm
Springhill HM Prison
Grendon HM Prison
22
68
69
70
D
E
F

74

83

64

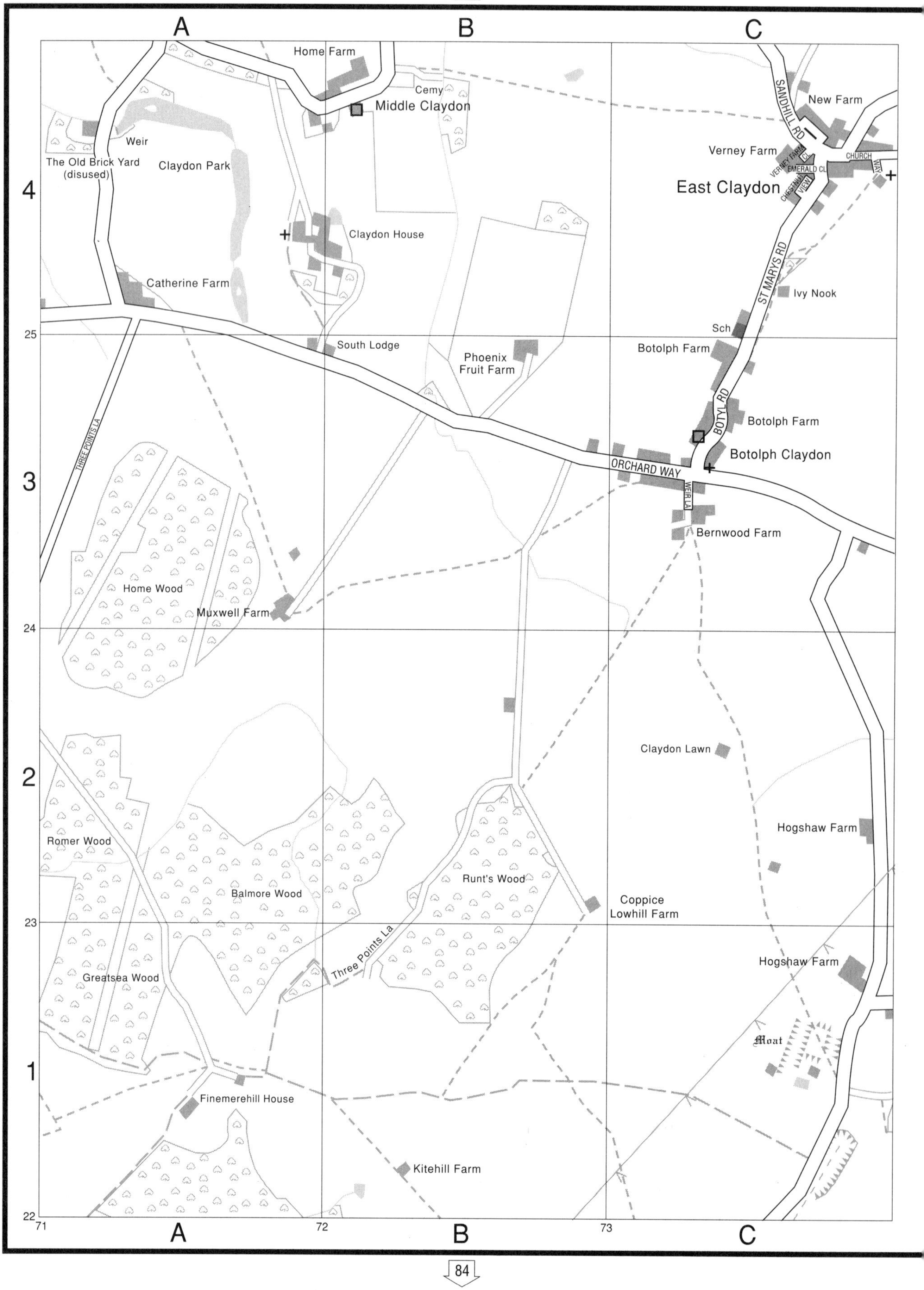
A
B
C
Home Farm
Cemy
Middle Claydon
New Farm
SANDHILL RD
Verney Farm
VERNEY FARM CL
EMERALD CL
CHURCH WAY
CHESTNUT VIEW
East Claydon
Weir
The Old Brick Yard (disused)
Claydon Park
4
Claydon House
Catherine Farm
ST MARYS RD
Ivy Nook
Sch
25
South Lodge
Phoenix Fruit Farm
Botolph Farm
BOTYL RD
Botolph Farm
Botolph Claydon
THREE POINTS LA
3
ORCHARD WAY
WEIR LA
Bernwood Farm
Home Wood
Muxwell Farm
24
Claydon Lawn
2
Romer Wood
Hogshaw Farm
Balmore Wood
Runt's Wood
Coppice Lowhill Farm
23
Three Points La
Greatsea Wood
Hogshaw Farm
Moat
1
Finemerehill House
Kitehill Farm
22
71
72
73
A
B
C

73

84

65

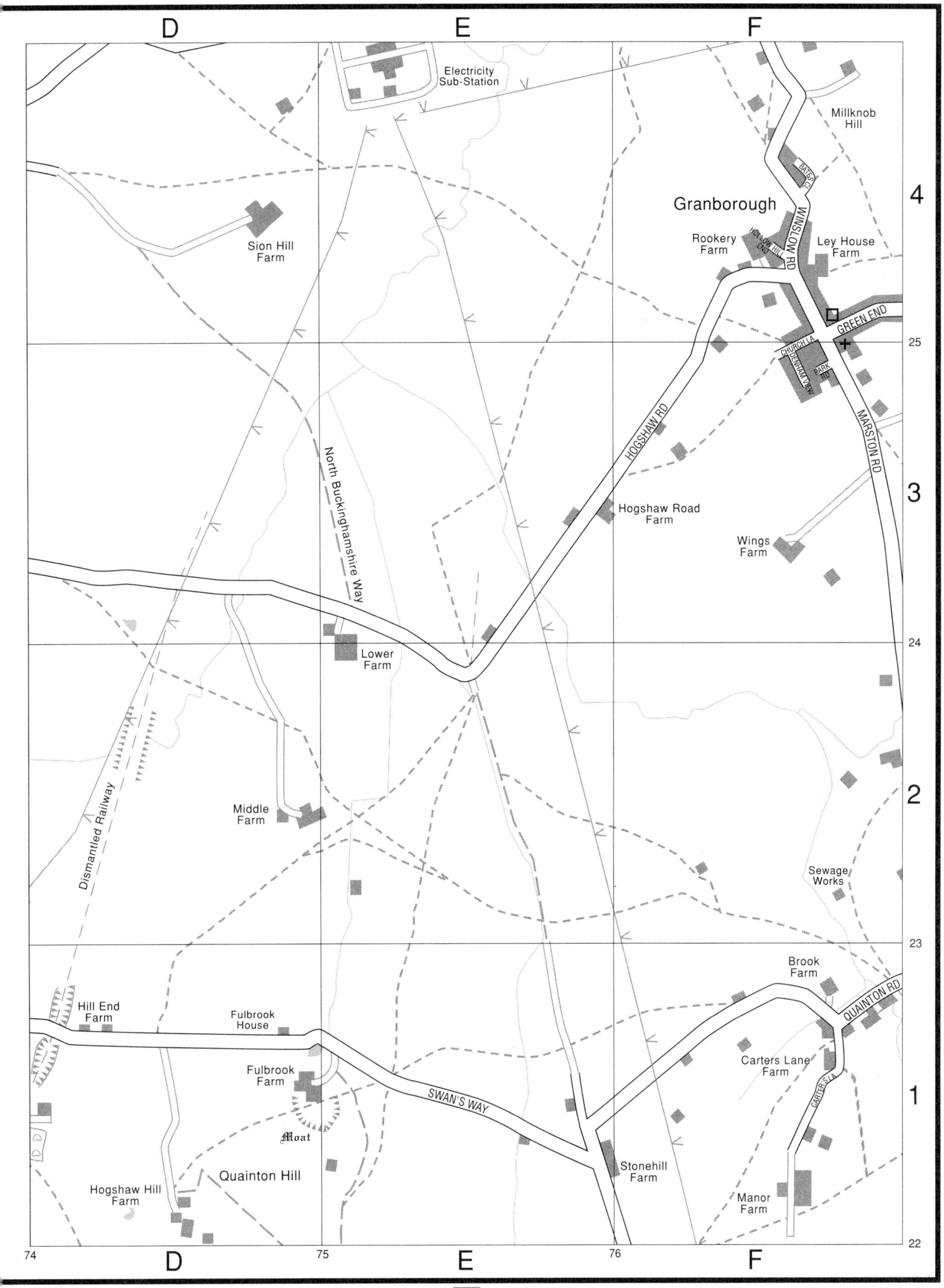
D
E
F
Electricity
Sub-Station
Millknob
Hill
Granborough
BATES CL
WINSLOW RD
HOLLOW HILL END
Rookery
Farm
Ley House
Farm
Sion Hill
Farm
GREEN END
CHURCH LA
DENHAM VIEW
PARK RD
MARSTON RD
HOGSHAW RD
North Buckinghamshire Way
Hogshaw Road
Farm
Wings
Farm
Lower
Farm
Dismantled Railway
Middle
Farm
Sewage
Works
Brook
Farm
QUAINTON RD
Hill End
Farm
Fulbrook
House
Carters Lane
Farm
CARTERS LA
Fulbrook
Farm
SWAN'S WAY
Moat
Quainton Hill
Stonehill
Farm
Hogshaw Hill
Farm
Manor
Farm
4
3
2
1
25
24
23
22
74
75
76
D
E
F

76

85

66

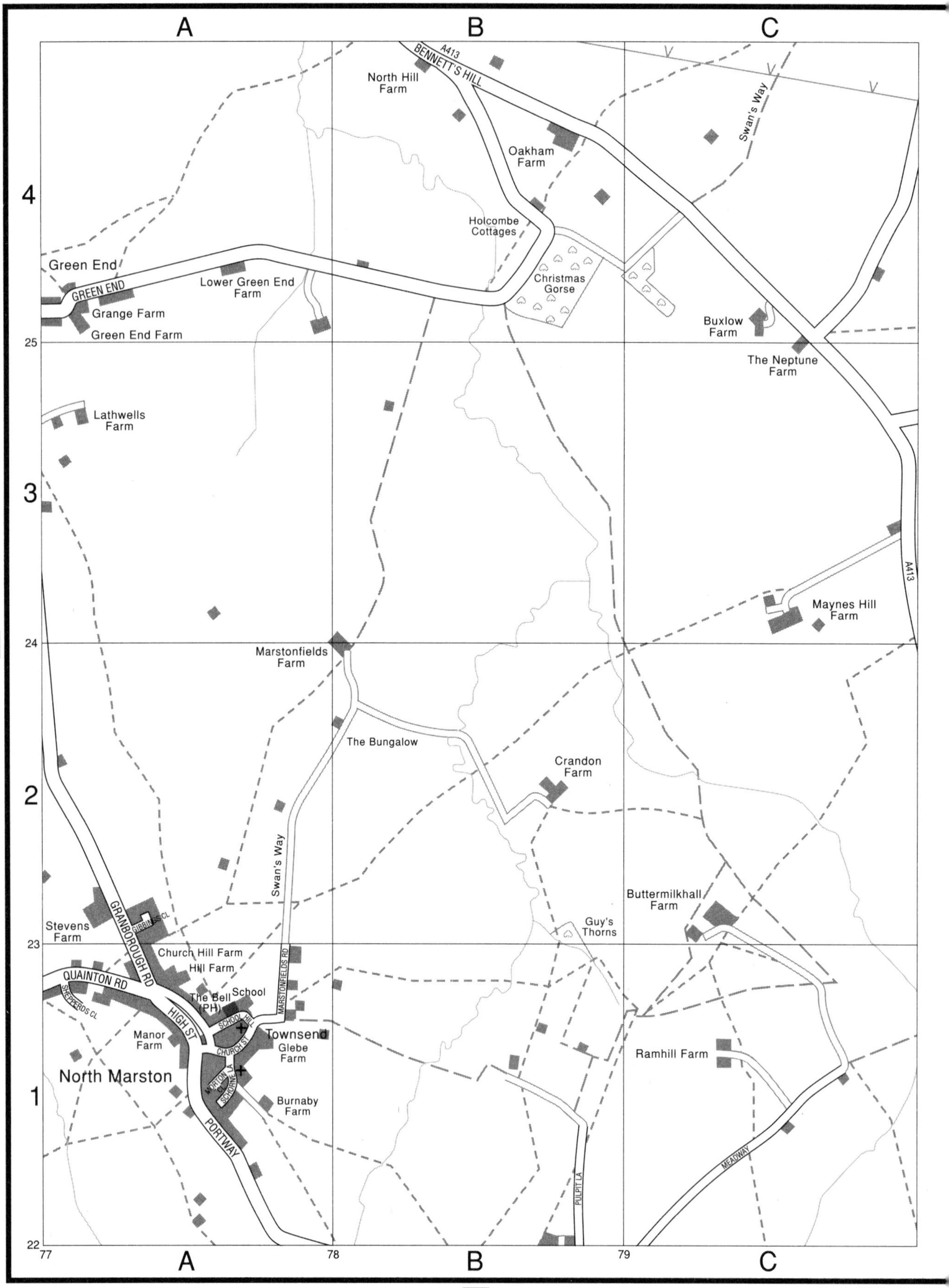
A
B
C
4
3
2
1
25
24
23
22
77
78
79
A413
BENNETT'S HILL
North Hill Farm
Swan's Way
Oakham Farm
Holcombe Cottages
Green End
GREEN END
Lower Green End Farm
Christmas Gorse
Grange Farm
Green End Farm
Buxlow Farm
The Neptune Farm
Lathwells Farm
A413
Maynes Hill Farm
Marstonfields Farm
The Bungalow
Crandon Farm
Swan's Way
Buttermilkhall Farm
Stevens Farm
GRANBOROUGH RD
GIBBINGS CL
Guy's Thorns
Church Hill Farm
Hill Farm
QUAINTON RD
SHEPPERDS CL
The Bell (PH)
School
MARSTONFIELDS RD
SCHOOL HILL
HIGH ST
Manor Farm
Townsend
CHURCH ST
Glebe Farm
Ramhill Farm
North Marston
SCHORNE LA
Burnaby Farm
PORTWAY
PULPIT LA
MEADWAY

75

86

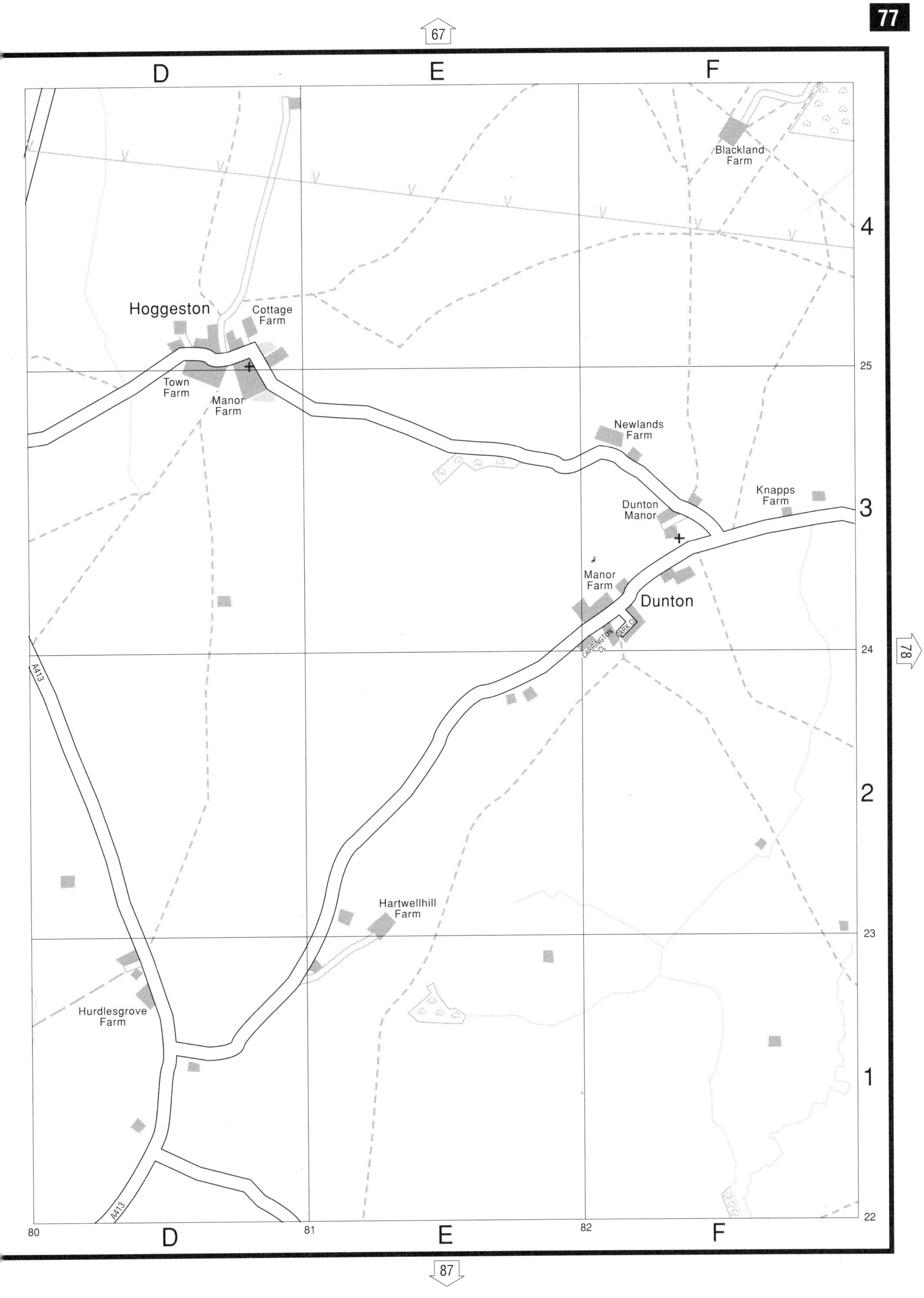
67
D
E
F
Blackland
Farm
4
Hoggeston
Cottage
Farm
25
Town
Farm
Manor
Farm
Newlands
Farm
Knapps
Farm
Dunton
Manor
3
Manor
Farm
Dunton
CARRINGTON CL
PARK CL
24
A413
78
2
Hartwellhill
Farm
23
Hurdlesgrove
Farm
1
A413
22
80
81
82
D
E
F
87

68

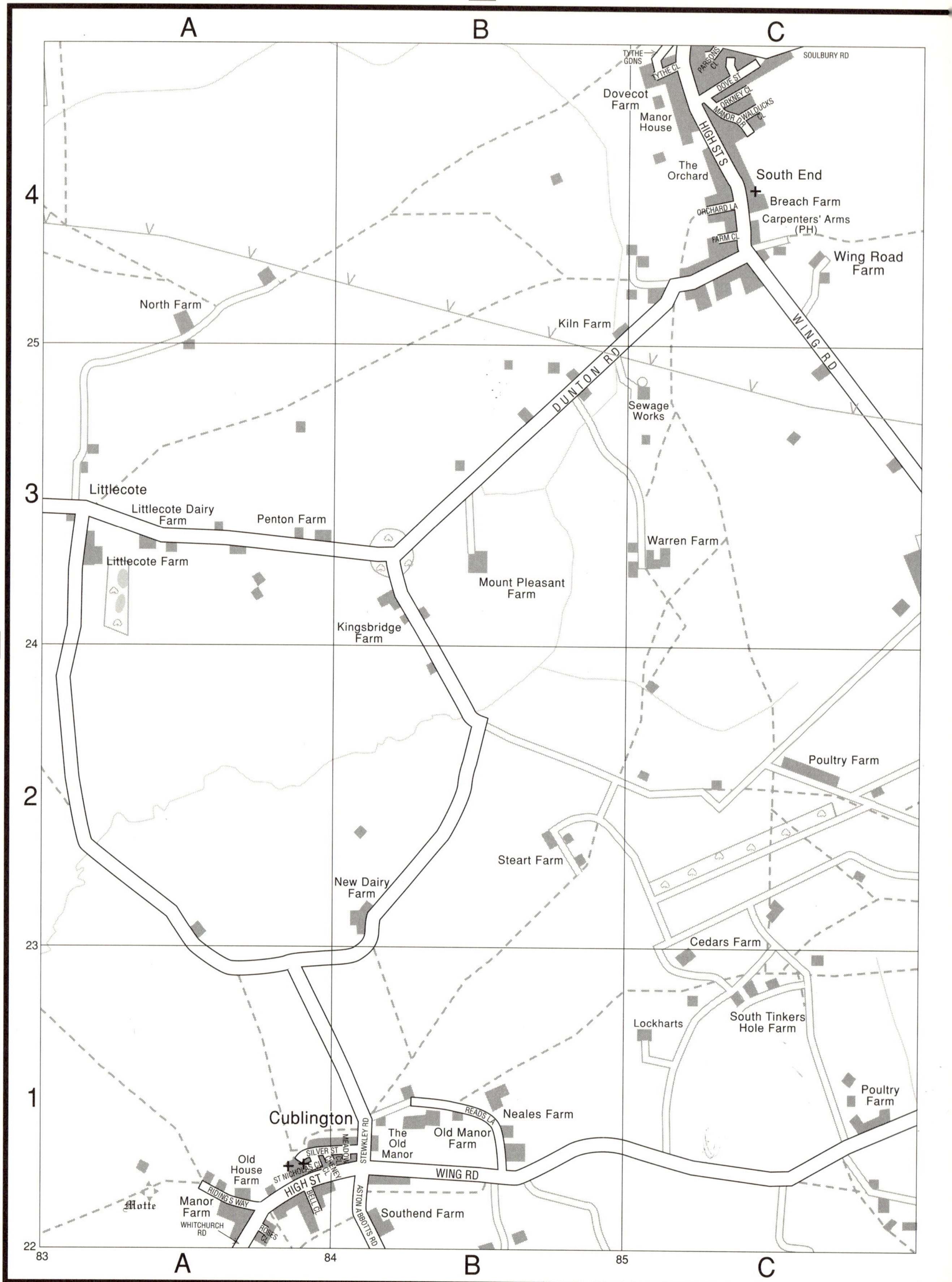
A
B
C
4
3
2
1
25
24
23
22
83
84
85
TYTHE GDNS
TYTHE CL
PARSONS CL
DOVE ST
ORKNEY CL
MANOR DR
WALDUCKS CL
SOULBURY RD
Dovecot Farm
Manor House
HIGH ST S
The Orchard
South End
Breach Farm
ORCHARD LA
Carpenters' Arms (PH)
FARM CL
Wing Road Farm
North Farm
Kiln Farm
WING RD
DUNTON RD
Sewage Works
Littlecote
Littlecote Dairy Farm
Penton Farm
Littlecote Farm
Warren Farm
Mount Pleasant Farm
Kingsbridge Farm
Poultry Farm
Steart Farm
New Dairy Farm
Cedars Farm
Lockharts
South Tinkers Hole Farm
Poultry Farm
Cublington
Neales Farm
READS LA
The Old Manor
Old Manor Farm
STEWKLEY RD
MEADOW
SILVER ST
ST NICHOLAS CL
CHENEY CL
Old House Farm
WING RD
HIGH ST
RIDING S WAY
BELL CL
ASTON ABBOTTS RD
Motte
Manor Farm
WHITCHURCH RD
ROSES CL
Southend Farm

77

88

69

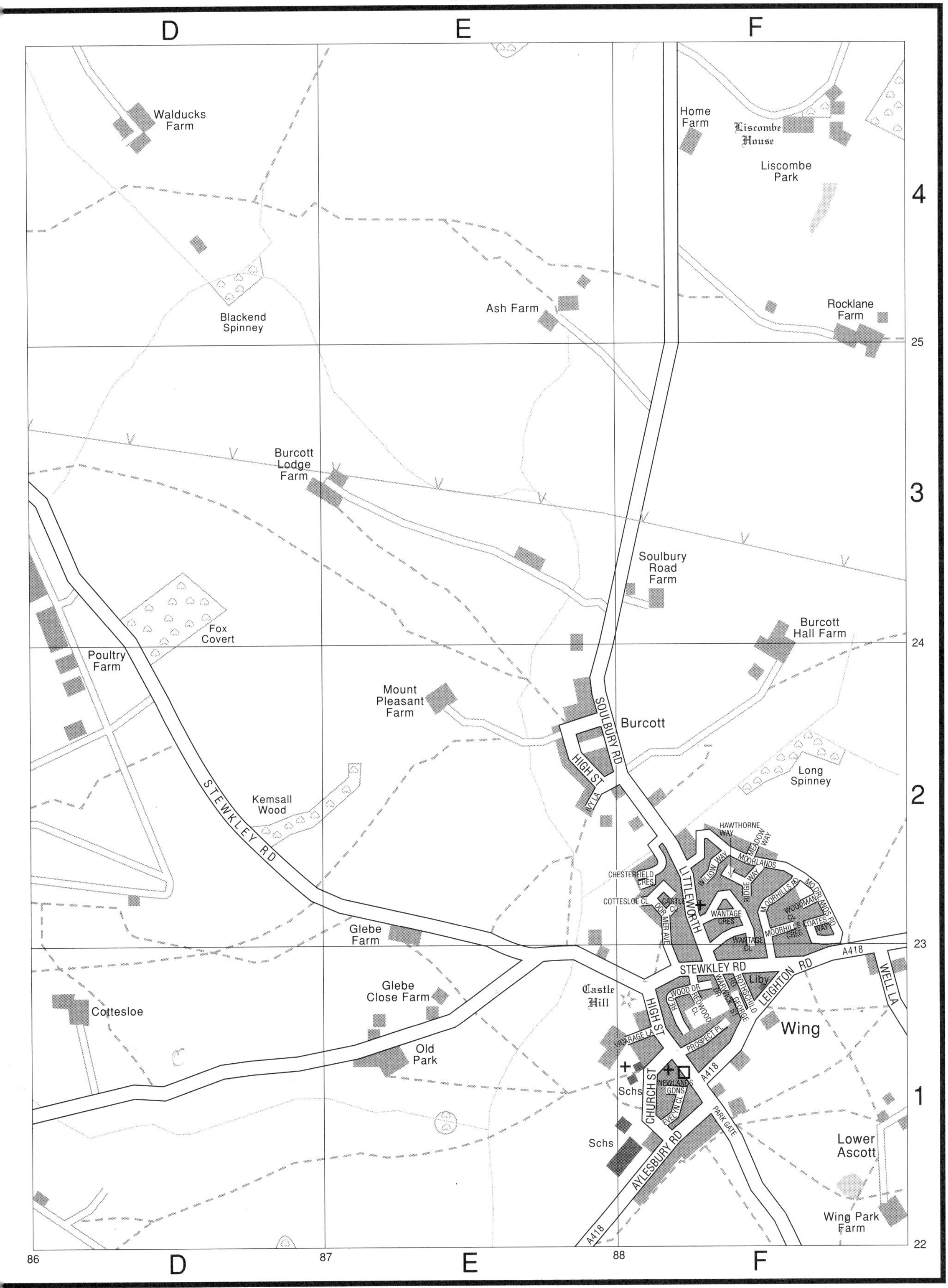

D
E
F
Walducks Farm
Home Farm
Liscombe House
Liscombe Park
4
Blackend Spinney
Ash Farm
Rocklane Farm
25
Burcott Lodge Farm
3
Soulbury Road Farm
Fox Covert
Poultry Farm
Burcott Hall Farm
24
Mount Pleasant Farm
Burcott
SOULBURY RD
HIGH ST
Long Spinney
2
Kemsall Wood
STEWKLEY RD
MYLA
HAWTHORNE WAY
MEADOW WAY
MOORLANDS
WILLOW WAY
RIDGE WAY
CHESTERFIELD CRES
COTTESLOE CL
CASTLE CL
LITTLEWORTH
DORMER AVE
WANTAGE CRES
MOORHILLS RD
WOODMAN CL
MOORLANDS RD
COATES WAY
MOORHILLS CRES
WANTAGE CL
Glebe Farm
23
A418
STEWKLEY RD
LEIGHTON RD
WELL LA
Liby
Castle Hill
WOOD DR
REDWOOD CL
WARWICK ST
ROTHSCHILD RD
GEORGE ST
Glebe Close Farm
Cottesloe
HIGH ST
VICARAGE LA
PROSPECT PL
Wing
Old Park
NEWLANDS GDNS
A418
Schs
CHURCH ST
1
EVELYN CL
PARK GATE
Schs
Lower Ascott
AYLESBURY RD
Wing Park Farm
A418
22
86
87
88

80

89

70

A
B
C
4
3
2
1
25
24
23
22
89
90
91
Hop Gardens
Milebush Farm
Valley Farm
Linslade
Sch
Leighton Buzzard Station
LEIGHTON BUZZARD
Grand Union Canal
River Ouzel
Amb Sta
Schs
Southcourt Stud Farm
Rock Lane
SOULBURY RD
HIMLEY GREEN
WING RD
LEIGHTON RD
STOKE RD
MENTMORE RD
CEDARS WAY
BUNKERS LA
DERWENT RD
A418
A4146
B4032
B488
Waterloo Farm
Ascott Kennels
Grimstone's Furze
Whitefields
Ascott Home Farm
Ascott
Round Spinney
Ascott House
Chelsea Clump
Hospl
Sand Pit
Grove Lock
WELL LA
Well Lane Dairy
Chucksell's Spinney
Hare & Hounds (PH)
Redborough Farm
Grove House Stud
not continued, see key diagram

79

90

71
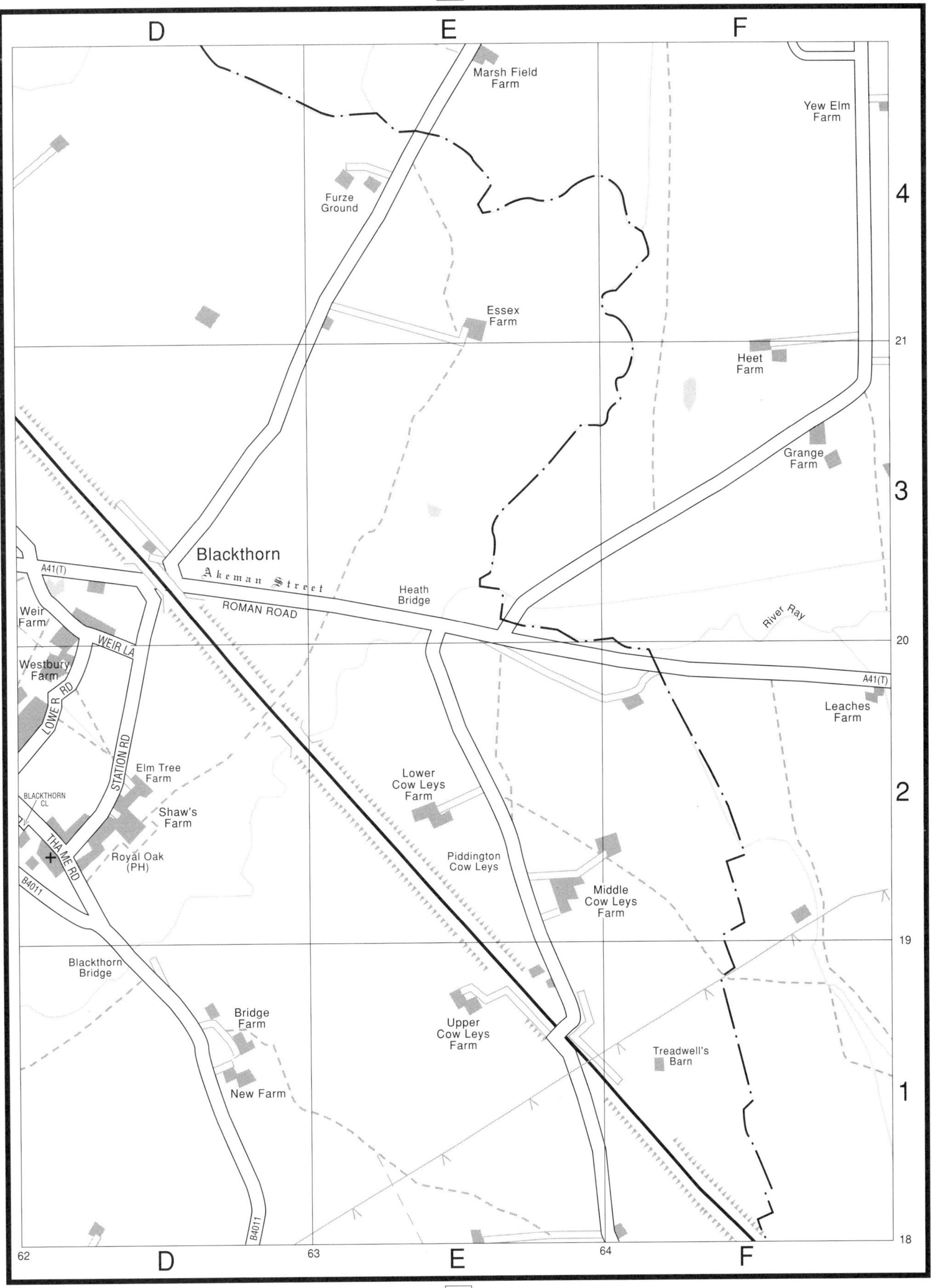
D
E
F
Marsh Field Farm
Yew Elm Farm
Furze Ground
4
Essex Farm
21
Heet Farm
Grange Farm
3
Blackthorn
A41(T)
Akeman Street
ROMAN ROAD
Heath Bridge
River Ray
Weir Farm
WEIR LA
20
A41(T)
Westbury Farm
LOWER RD
Leaches Farm
STATION RD
Elm Tree Farm
Lower Cow Leys Farm
2
BLACKTHORN CL
Shaw's Farm
THAME RD
Royal Oak (PH)
Piddington Cow Leys
B4011
Middle Cow Leys Farm
19
Blackthorn Bridge
Bridge Farm
Upper Cow Leys Farm
Treadwell's Barn
New Farm
1
B4011
18
62
63
64
D
E
F
82
95

72

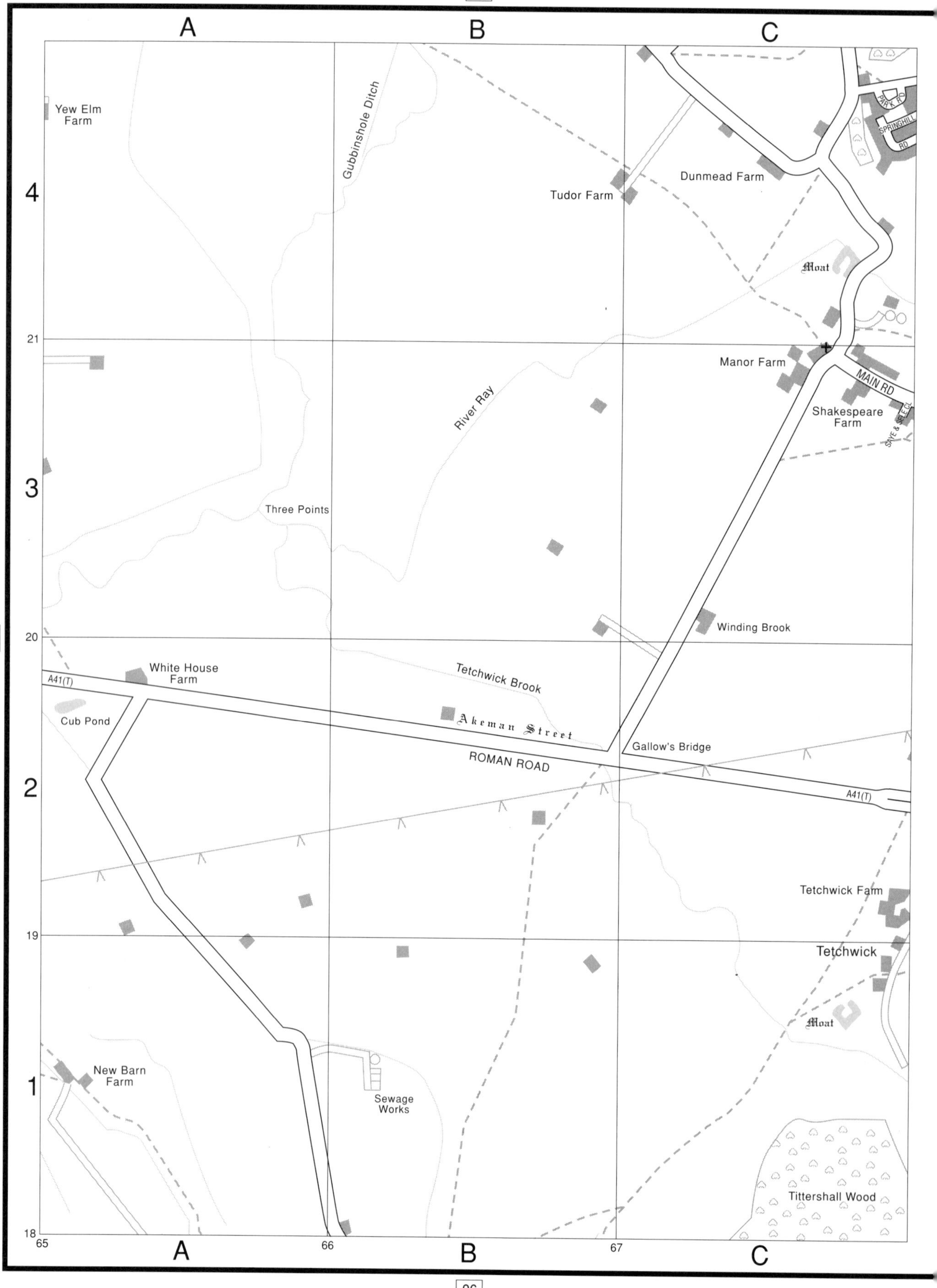
A
B
C
Yew Elm Farm
Gubbinshole Ditch
Tudor Farm
Dunmead Farm
PARK RD
SPRINGHILL RD
Moat
Manor Farm
MAIN RD
Shakespeare Farm
SAYE & SELE CL
River Ray
Three Points
Winding Brook
White House Farm
A41(T)
Tetchwick Brook
Cub Pond
Akeman Street
ROMAN ROAD
Gallow's Bridge
Tetchwick Farm
Tetchwick
Moat
New Barn Farm
Sewage Works
Tittershall Wood
4
21
3
20
2
19
1
18
65
66
67

81

96

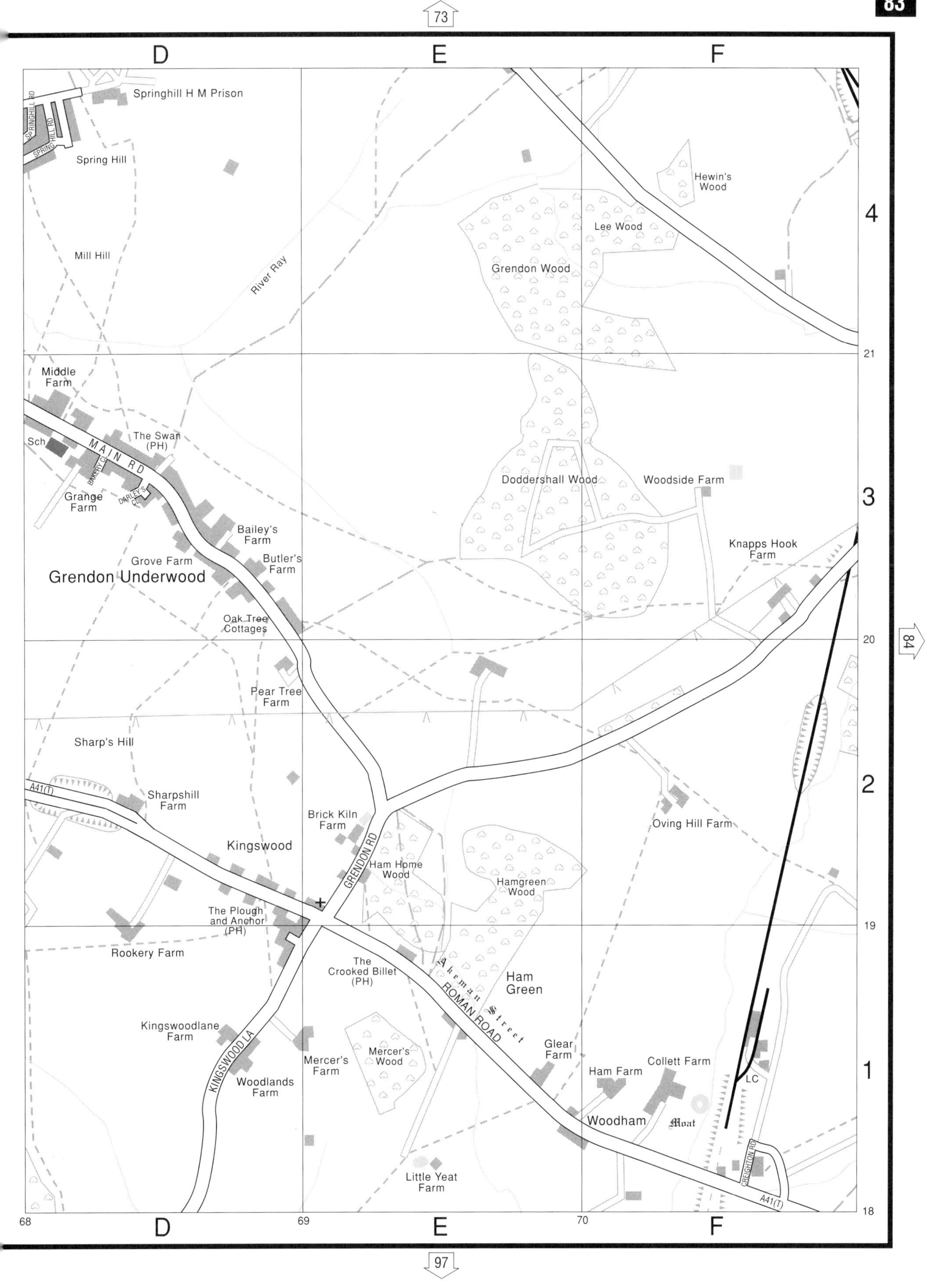
73
D
E
F
Springhill H M Prison
SPRINGHILL RD
SPRING HILL RD
Spring Hill
Hewin's Wood
Lee Wood
4
Mill Hill
River Ray
Grendon Wood
21
Middle Farm
Sch
The Swan (PH)
MAIN RD
BAKERY CL
DARLEY'S CL
Doddershall Wood
Woodside Farm
Grange Farm
3
Bailey's Farm
Knapps Hook Farm
Grove Farm
Butler's Farm
Grendon Underwood
Oak Tree Cottages
20
84
Pear Tree Farm
Sharp's Hill
A41(T)
Sharpshill Farm
2
Brick Kiln Farm
Oving Hill Farm
Kingswood
GRENDON RD
Ham Home Wood
Hamgreen Wood
The Plough and Anchor (PH)
19
Rookery Farm
The Crooked Billet (PH)
Akeman Street
ROMAN ROAD
Ham Green
Kingswoodlane Farm
Mercer's Farm
Mercer's Wood
Glear Farm
Collett Farm
1
Ham Farm
KINGSWOOD LA
Woodlands Farm
LC
Woodham
Moat
CREIGHTON RD
Little Yeat Farm
A41(T)
18
68
69
70
97

74

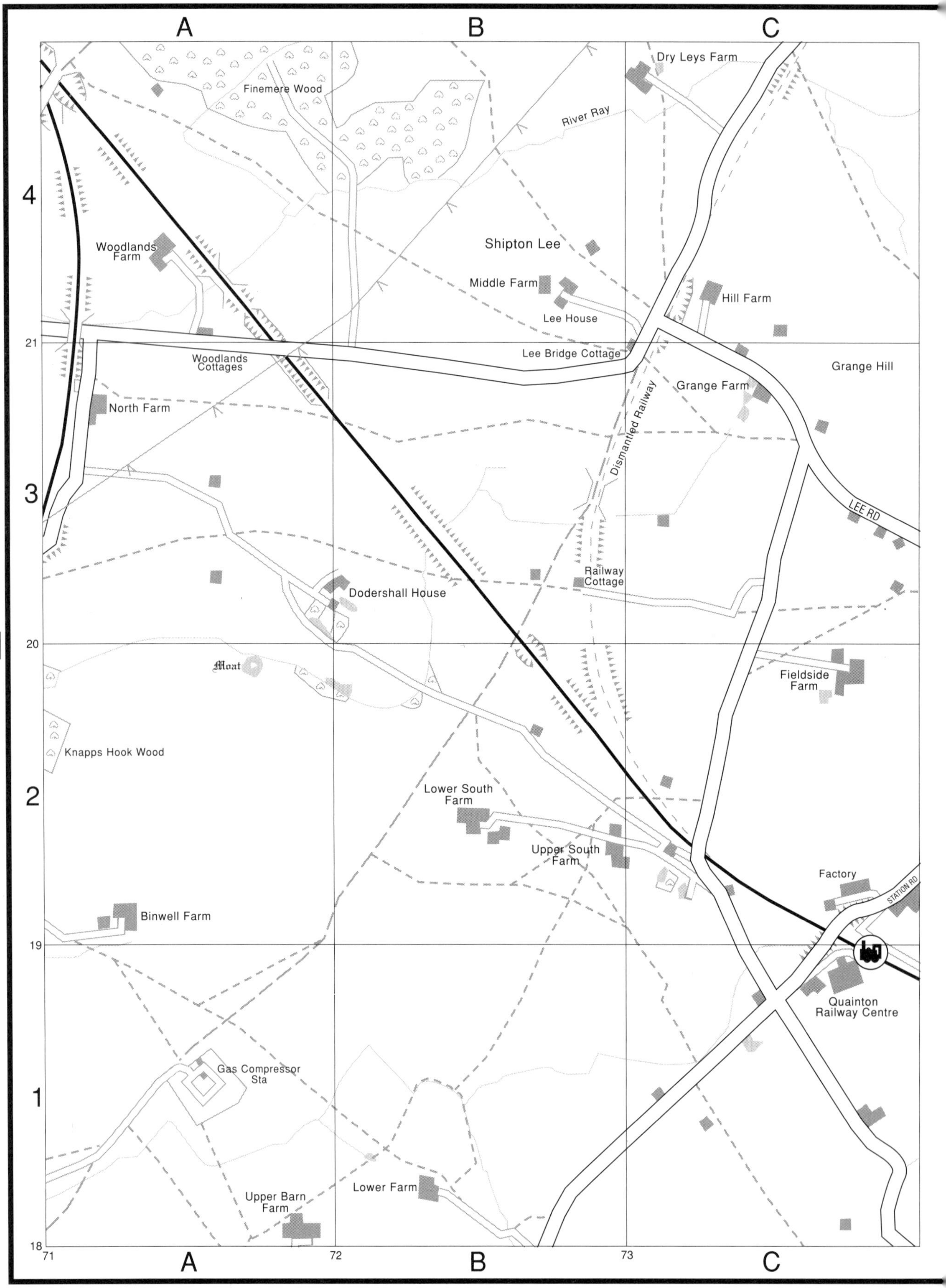
A
B
C
4
3
2
1
21
20
19
18
71
72
73
Finemere Wood
Dry Leys Farm
River Ray
Shipton Lee
Woodlands Farm
Middle Farm
Lee House
Hill Farm
Woodlands Cottages
Lee Bridge Cottage
Grange Hill
Grange Farm
North Farm
Dismantled Railway
LEE RD
Railway Cottage
Dodershall House
Moat
Fieldside Farm
Knapps Hook Wood
Lower South Farm
Upper South Farm
Factory
STATION RD
Binwell Farm
Quainton Railway Centre
Gas Compressor Sta
Upper Barn Farm
Lower Farm

83

98

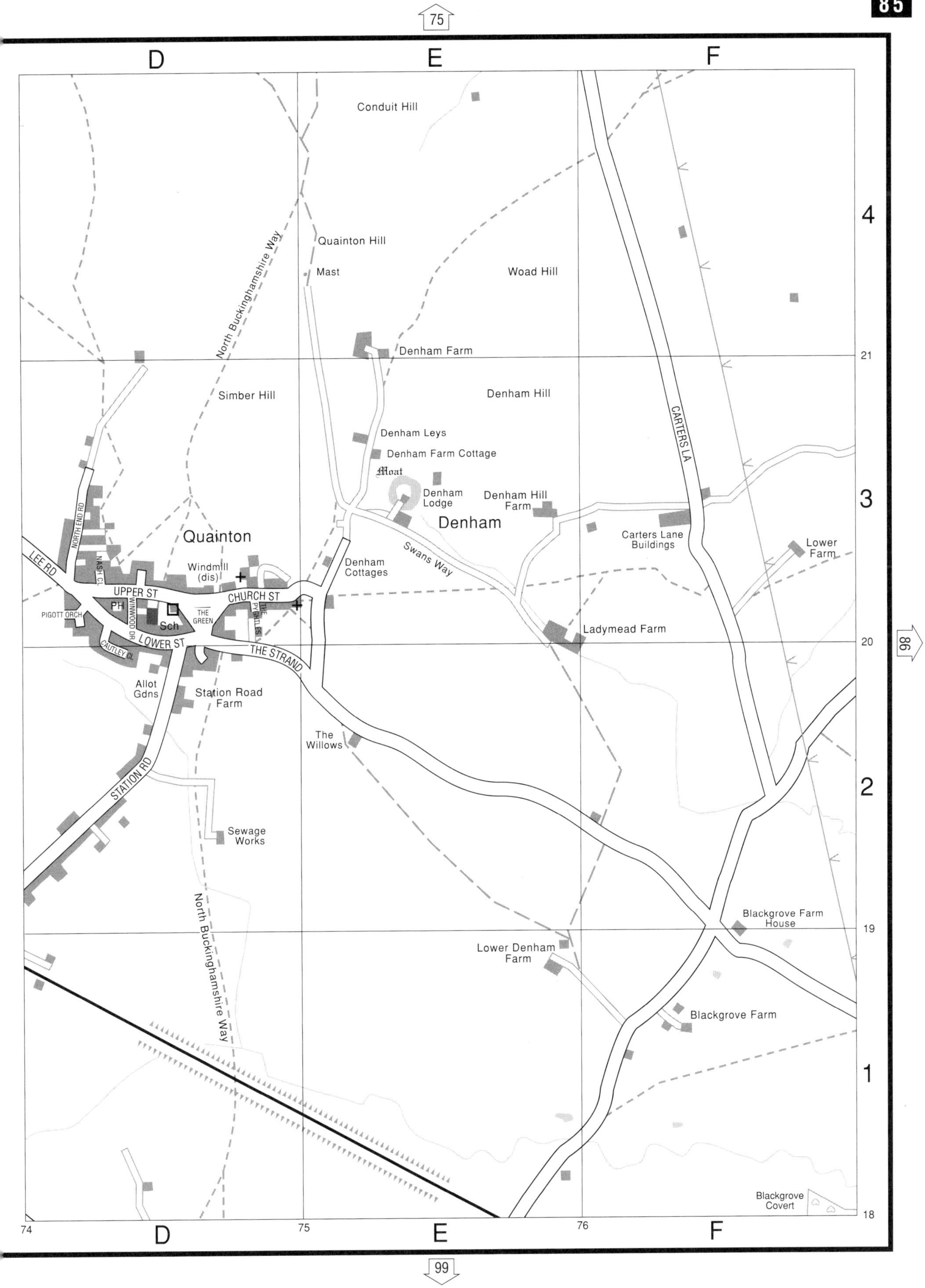
75
D
E
F
Conduit Hill
Quainton Hill
Mast
Woad Hill
North Buckinghamshire Way
Denham Farm
Simber Hill
Denham Hill
Denham Leys
Denham Farm Cottage
Moat
Denham Lodge
Denham Hill Farm
Denham
CARTERS LA
Carters Lane Buildings
Lower Farm
Quainton
NORTH END RD
LEE RD
NASH CL
Windmill (dis)
Denham Cottages
Swans Way
UPPER ST
CHURCH ST
PH
PIGOTT ORCH
WINWOOD DR
Sch
THE GREEN
THE PYGHTLES
LOWER ST
CAUTLEY CL
THE STRAND
Ladymead Farm
Allot Gdns
Station Road Farm
The Willows
STATION RD
Sewage Works
North Buckinghamshire Way
Blackgrove Farm House
Lower Denham Farm
Blackgrove Farm
Blackgrove Covert
4
3
2
1
21
20
19
18
74
75
76
D
E
F
96
99

76

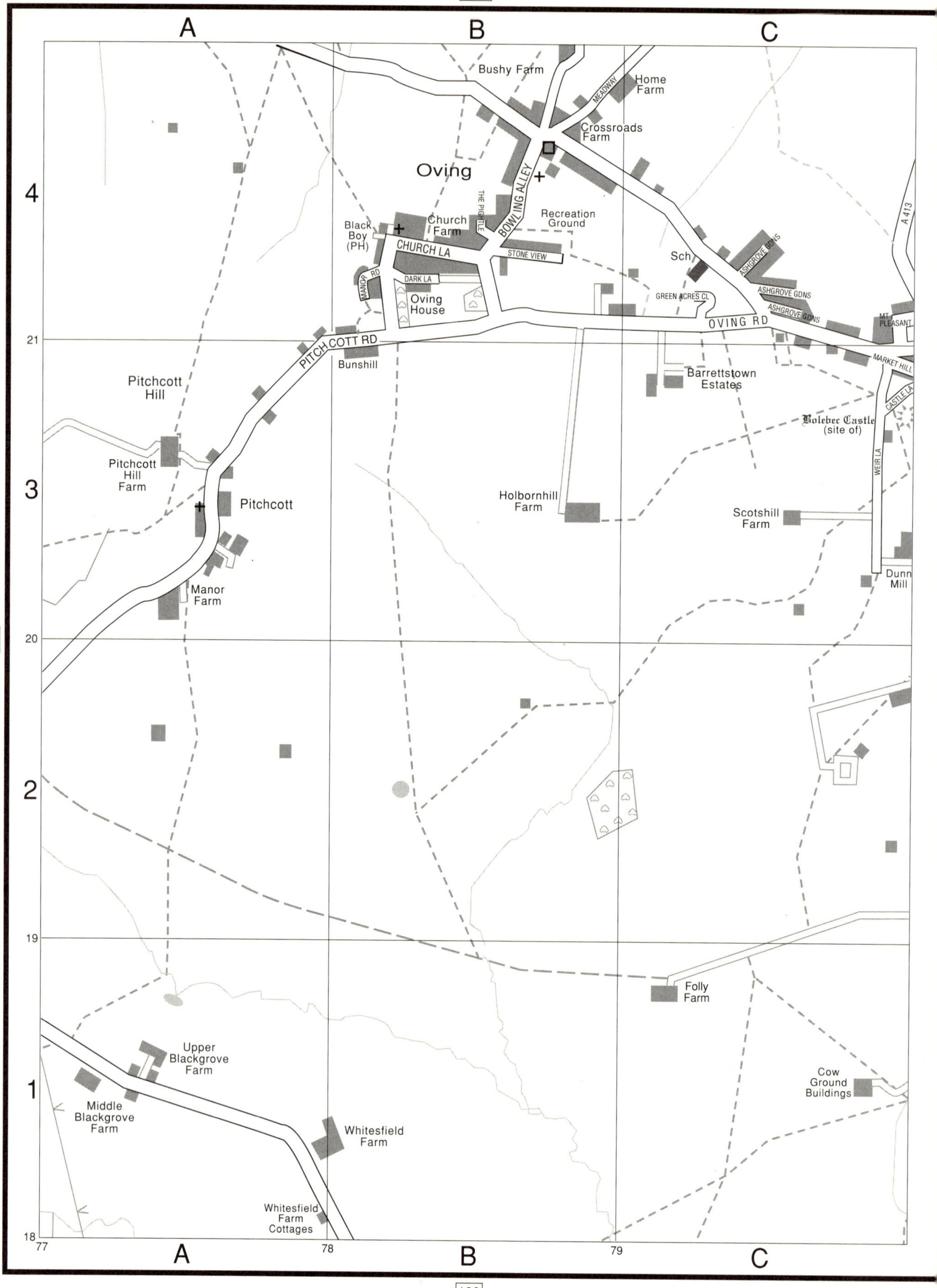
A
B
C
Bushy Farm
Home Farm
MEADWAY
Crossroads Farm
Oving
4
BOWLING ALLEY
THE PIGHTLE
Recreation Ground
Black Boy (PH)
Church Farm
CHURCH LA
STONE VIEW
A 413
Sch
ASHGROVE GDNS
MANOR RD
DARK LA
Oving House
GREEN ACRES CL
ASHGROVE GDNS
ASHGROVE GDNS
MT PLEASANT
21
PITCHCOTT RD
OVING RD
Bunshill
MARKET HILL
Barrettstown Estates
Pitchcott Hill
CASTLE LA
Bolebec Castle (site of)
Pitchcott Hill Farm
3
Pitchcott
WEIR LA
Holbornhill Farm
Scotshill Farm
Manor Farm
Dunn Mill
20
2
19
Folly Farm
Upper Blackgrove Farm
1
Cow Ground Buildings
Middle Blackgrove Farm
Whitesfield Farm
Whitesfield Farm Cottages
18
77
78
79
A
B
C

85

100

77

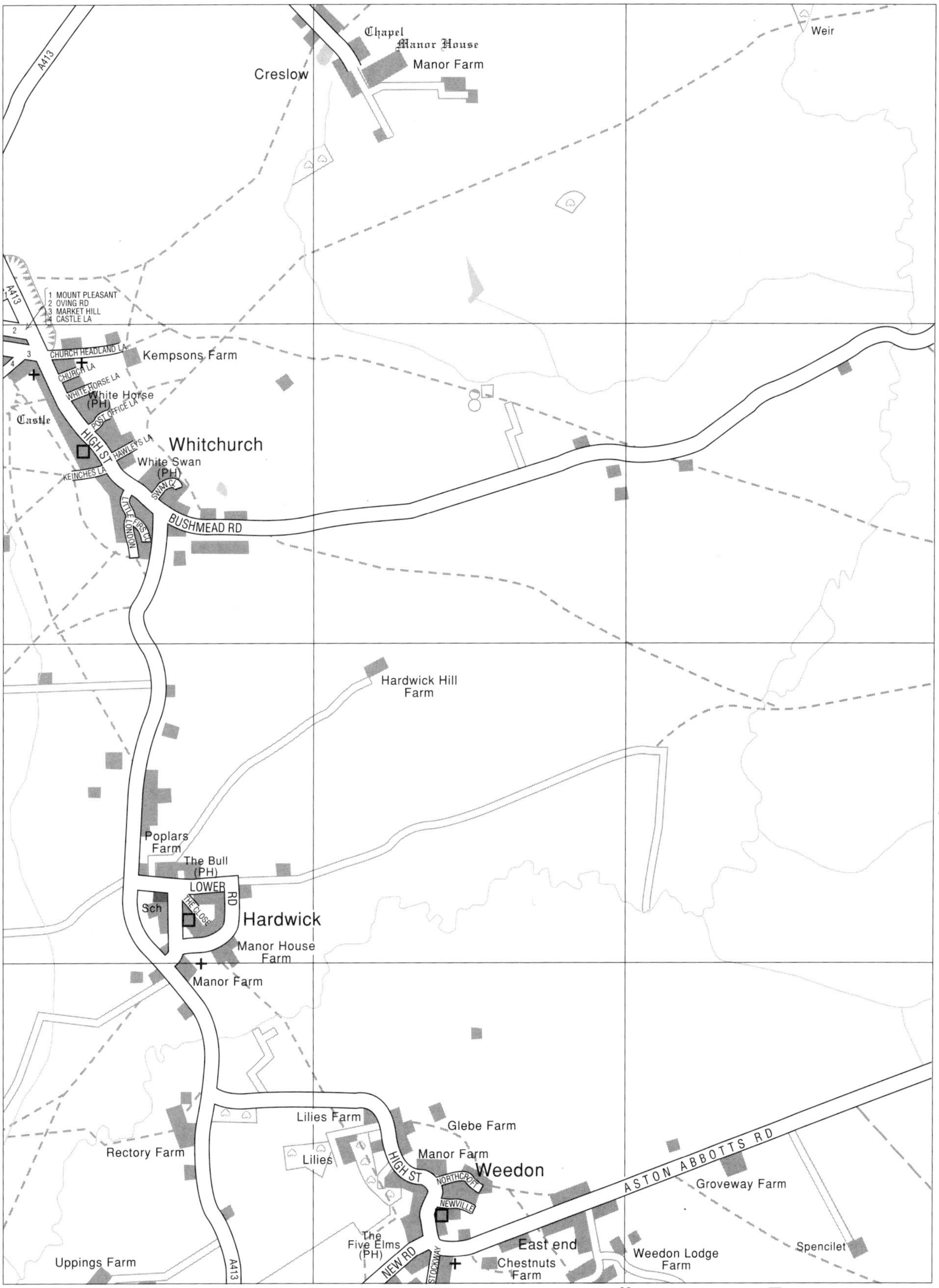
D
E
F
Chapel
Manor House
Manor Farm
Weir
Creslow
A413
1 MOUNT PLEASANT
2 OVING RD
3 MARKET HILL
4 CASTLE LA
CHURCH HEADLAND LA
CHURCH LA
WHITE HORSE LA
POST OFFICE LA
HAWLEYS LA
KEINCHES LA
Kempsons Farm
White Horse (PH)
Castle
Whitchurch
White Swan (PH)
SWAN CL
HIGH ST
LITTLE LONDON
FIRS CT
BUSHMEAD RD
Hardwick Hill Farm
Poplars Farm
The Bull (PH)
LOWER RD
Sch
THE CLOSE
Hardwick
Manor House Farm
Manor Farm
Lilies Farm
Glebe Farm
Rectory Farm
Lilies
Manor Farm
HIGH ST
NORTHCROFT
Weedon
NEWVILLE
ASTON ABBOTTS RD
Groveway Farm
The Five Elms (PH)
NEW RD
STOCKWAY
East end
Chestnuts Farm
Weedon Lodge Farm
Spencilet
Uppings Farm
A413
4
3
2
1
21
20
19
18
80
81
82
D
E
F

88

101

78

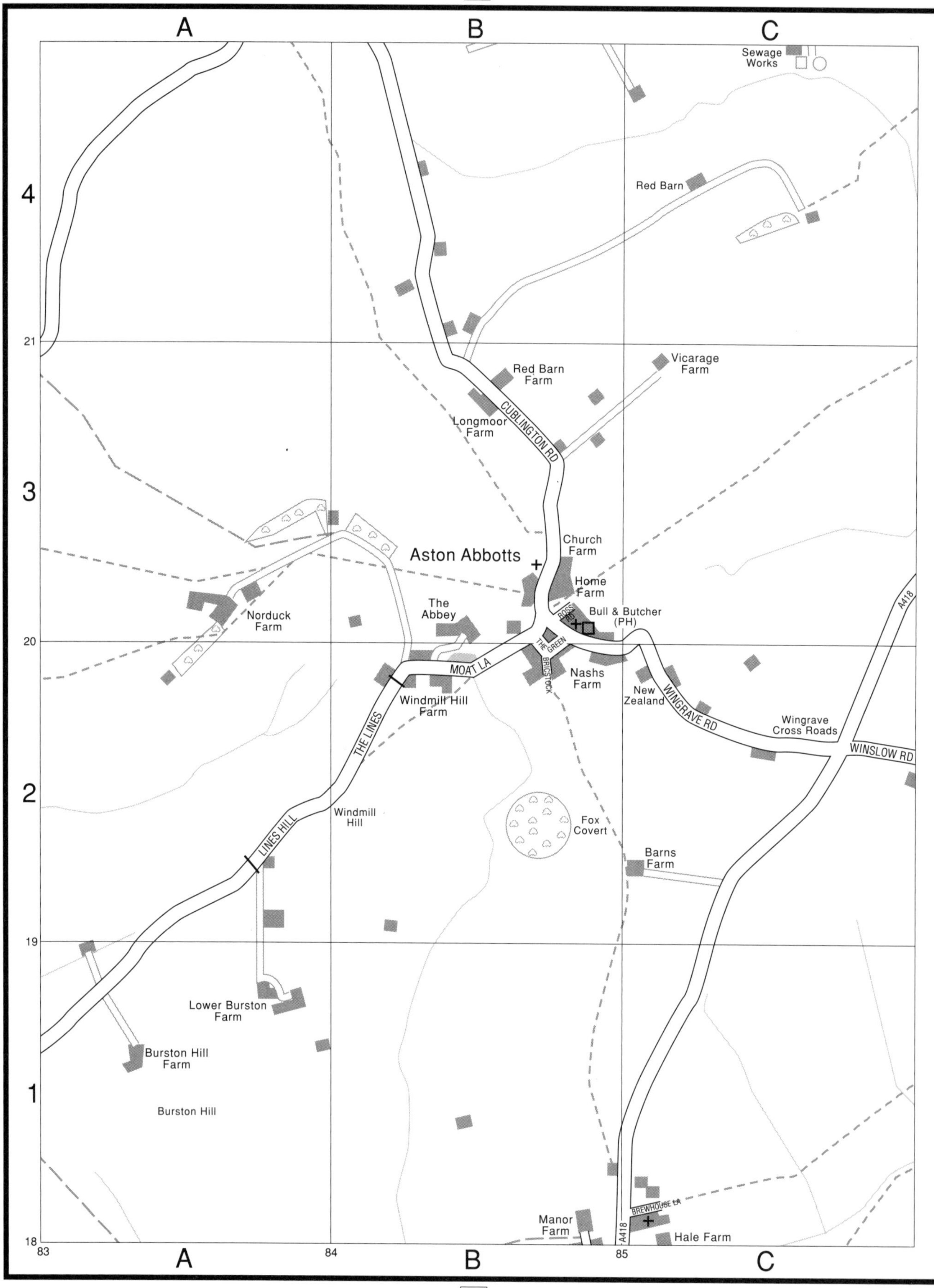
A
B
C
Sewage Works
Red Barn
4
21
Red Barn Farm
Vicarage Farm
Longmoor Farm
CUBLINGTON RD
3
Church Farm
Aston Abbotts
Home Farm
Norduck Farm
The Abbey
Bull & Butcher (PH)
ROSS RD
THE GREEN
THE BRICSTOCK
20
MOAT LA
Nashs Farm
New Zealand
WINGRAVE RD
A418
Windmill Hill Farm
Wingrave Cross Roads
WINSLOW RD
THE LINES
2
LINES HILL
Windmill Hill
Fox Covert
Barns Farm
19
Lower Burston Farm
Burston Hill Farm
1
Burston Hill
BREWHOUSE LA
Manor Farm
A418
Hale Farm
18
83
84
85
A
B
C

87

102

79

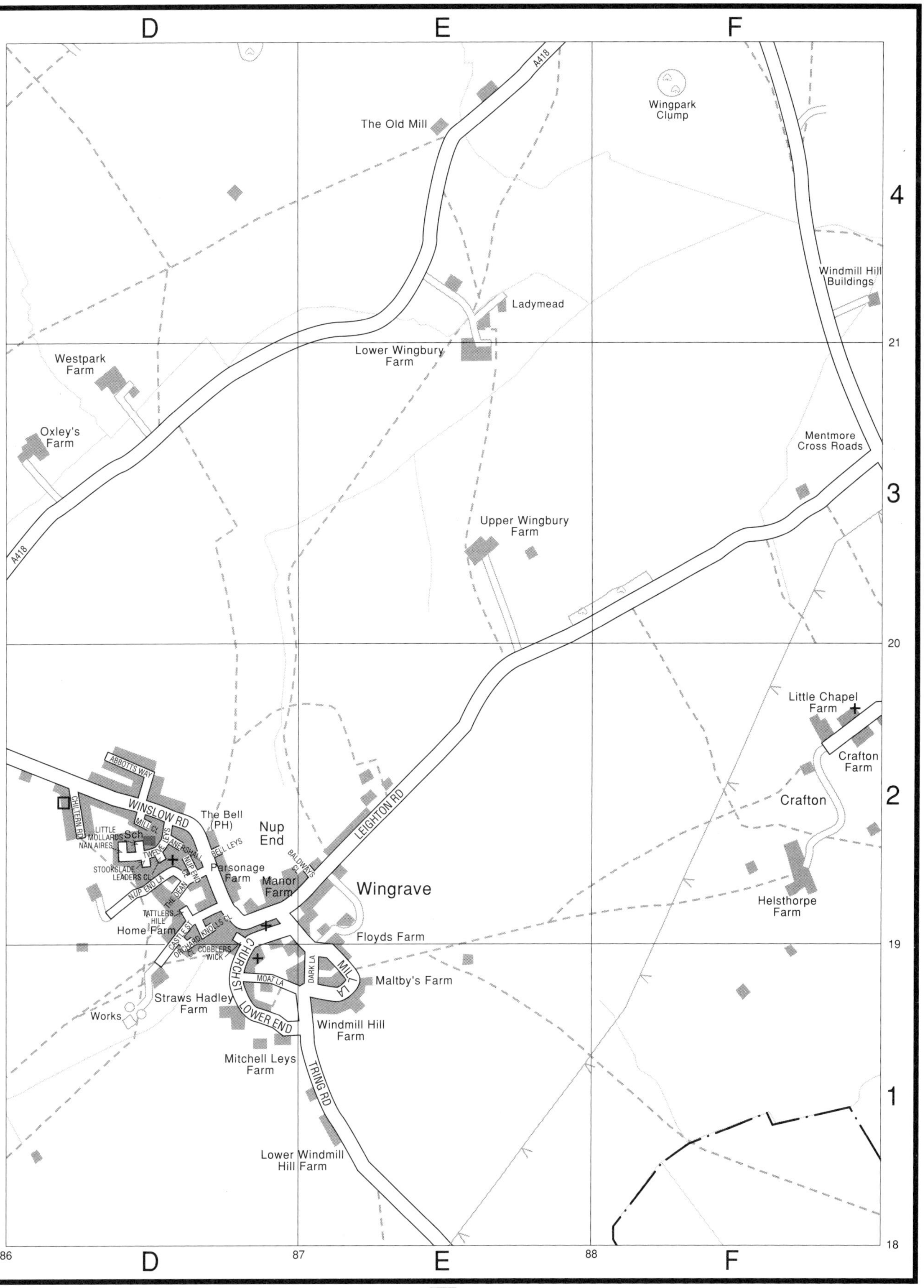
D
E
F
A418
The Old Mill
Wingpark Clump
4
Windmill Hill Buildings
Ladymead
Lower Wingbury Farm
21
Westpark Farm
Oxley's Farm
Mentmore Cross Roads
3
Upper Wingbury Farm
A418
20
Little Chapel Farm
Crafton Farm
Crafton
2
ABBOTTS WAY
CHILTERN RD
WINSLOW RD
MILL CL
LITTLE MOLLARDS
Sch
NAN AIRES
TWELVE LEYS
ANERSHALL
NUP END
BELL LEYS
The Bell (PH)
Nup End
BALDWAYS CL
LEIGHTON RD
STOOKSLADE
LEADERS CL
NUP END LA
THE DEAN
Parsonage Farm
Manor Farm
Wingrave
Helsthorpe Farm
TATTLERS HILL
Home Farm
CASTLE ST
ORCHARD CL
KNOLLS CL
COBBLERS WICK
CHURCH ST
Floyds Farm
19
MOAT LA
DARK LA
MILL LA
Maltby's Farm
Straws Hadley Farm
Works
LOWER END
Windmill Hill Farm
Mitchell Leys Farm
TRING RD
1
Lower Windmill Hill Farm
18
86
87
88
D
E
F

90

103

80

89

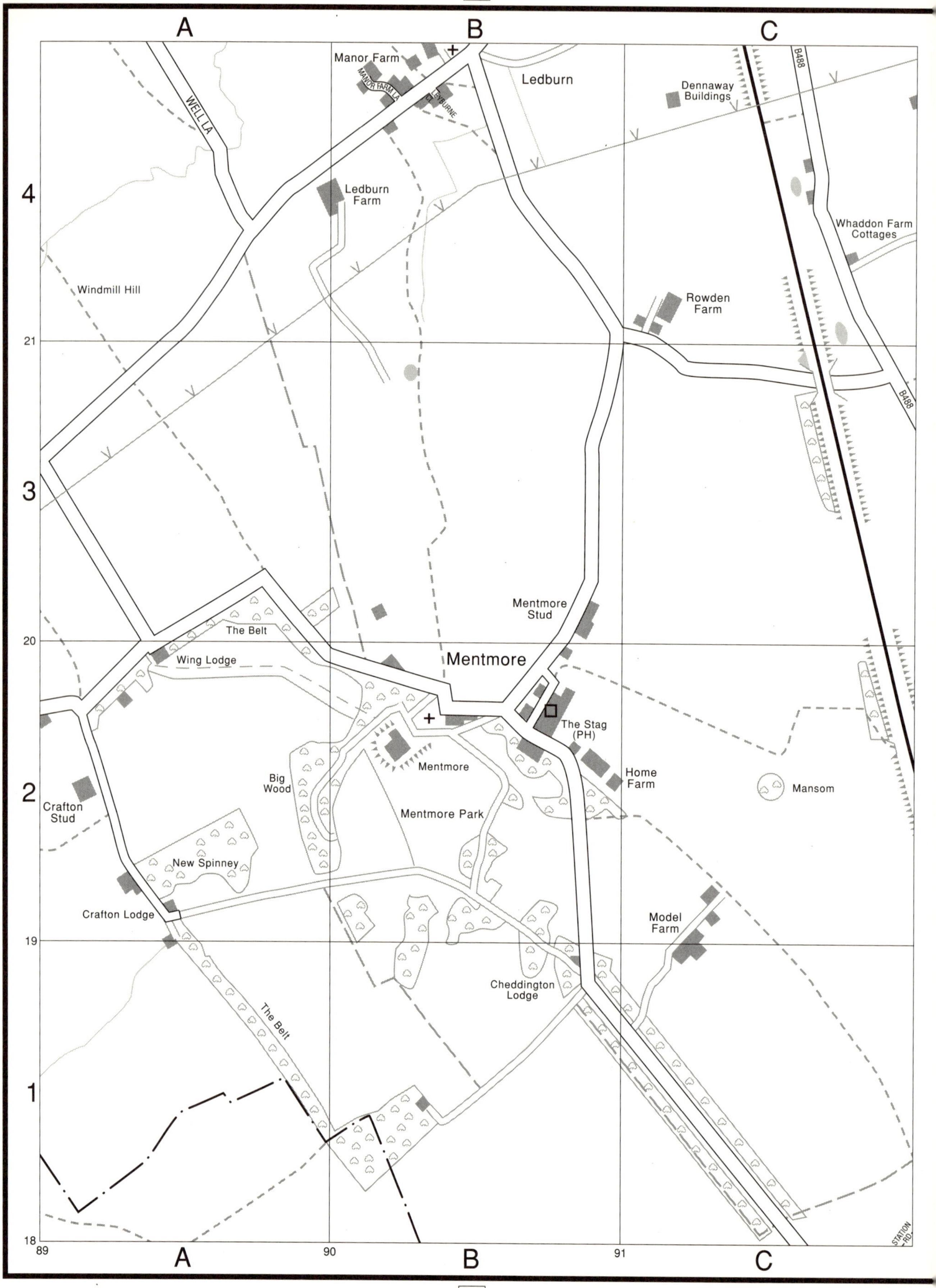
A
B
C
4
3
2
1
21
20
19
18
89
90
91
Manor Farm
MANOR FARM LA
LEDBURNE
Ledburn
Dennaway Buildings
B488
WELL LA
Ledburn Farm
Whaddon Farm Cottages
Windmill Hill
Rowden Farm
Mentmore Stud
The Belt
Wing Lodge
Mentmore
The Stag (PH)
Home Farm
Big Wood
Mentmore Park
Mansom
Crafton Stud
New Spinney
Crafton Lodge
Model Farm
Cheddington Lodge
STATION RD

104

not continued ,see key diagram

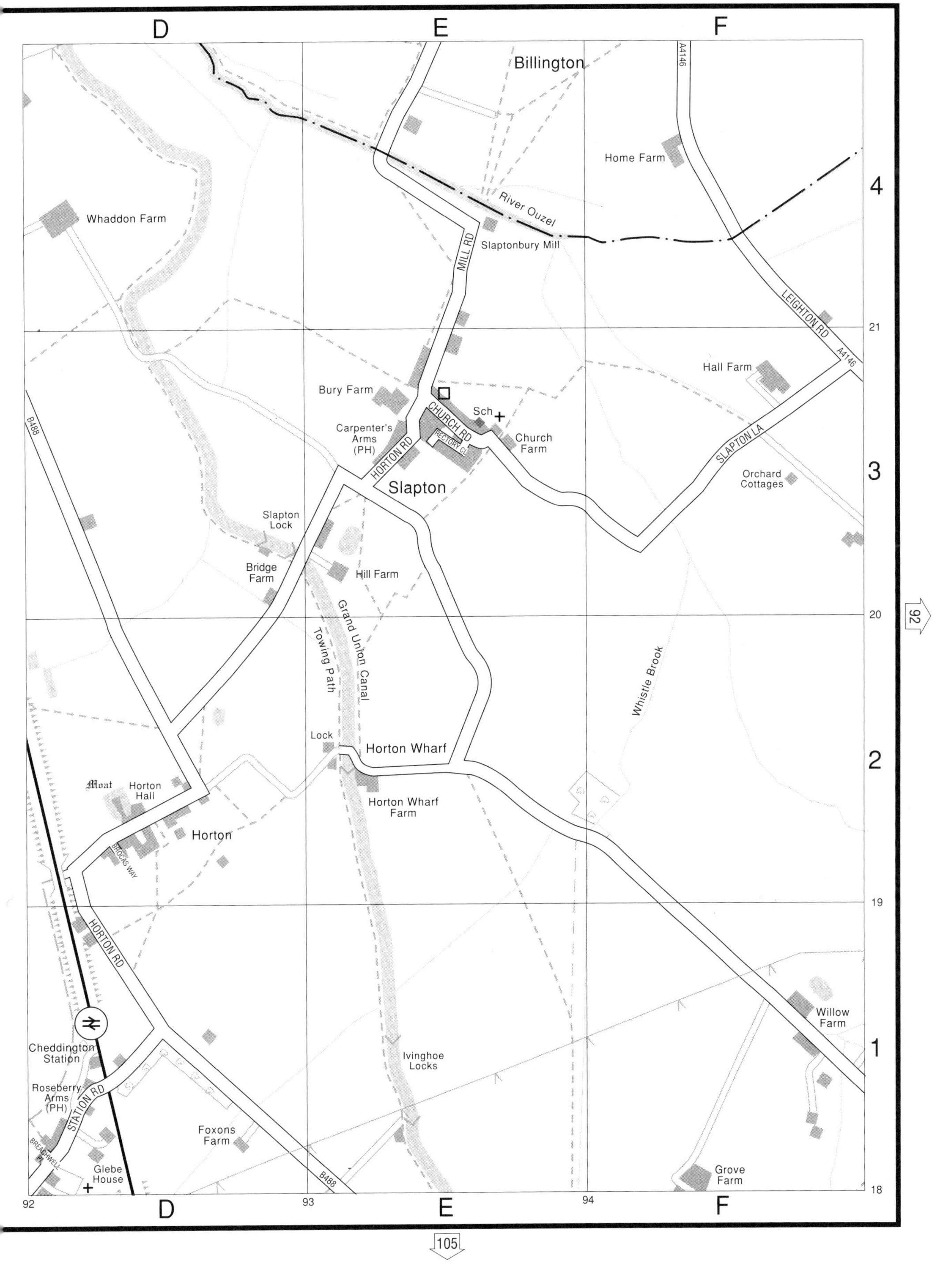

105

not continued,see key diagram

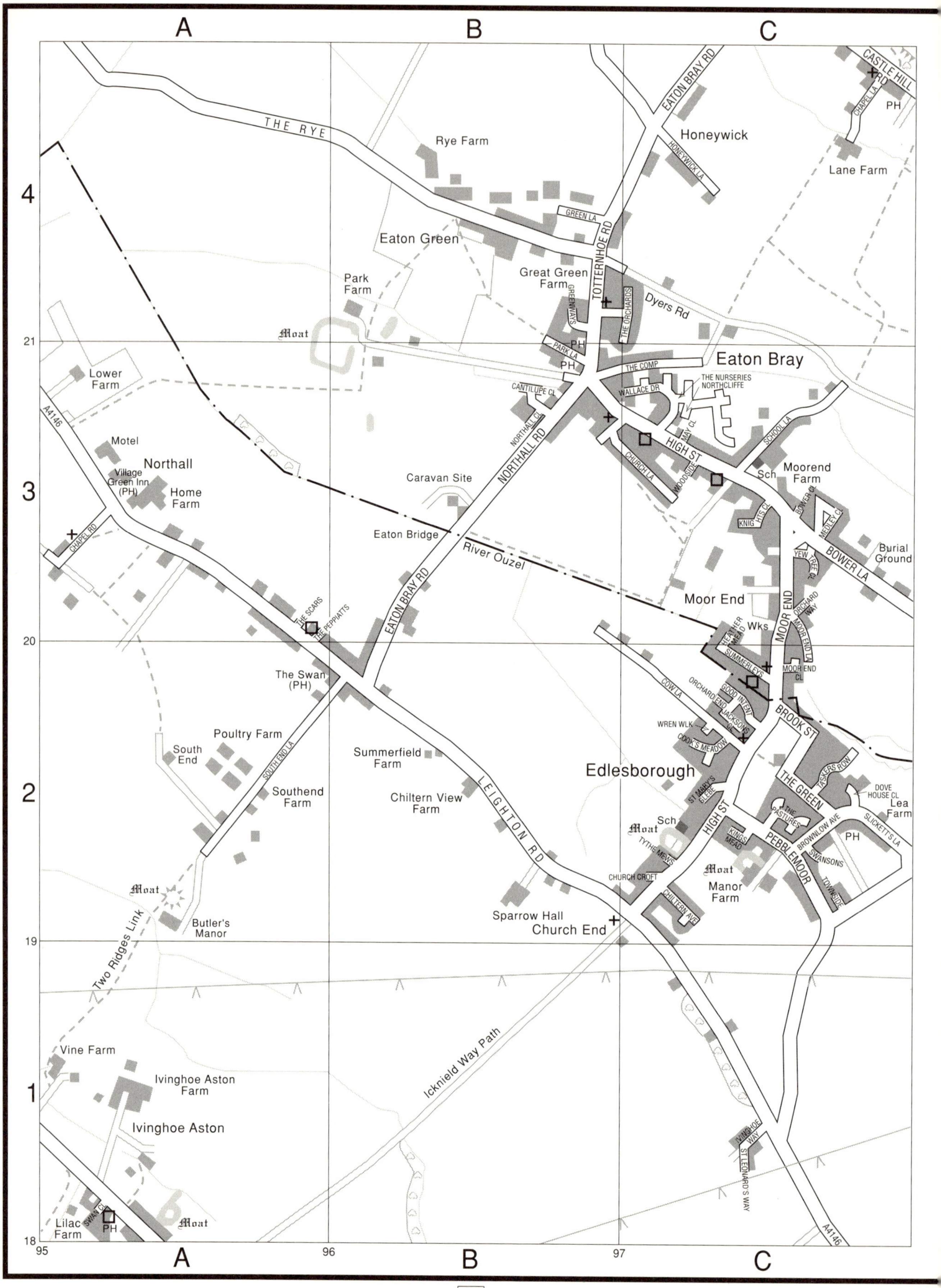

91

106

not continued, see key diagram

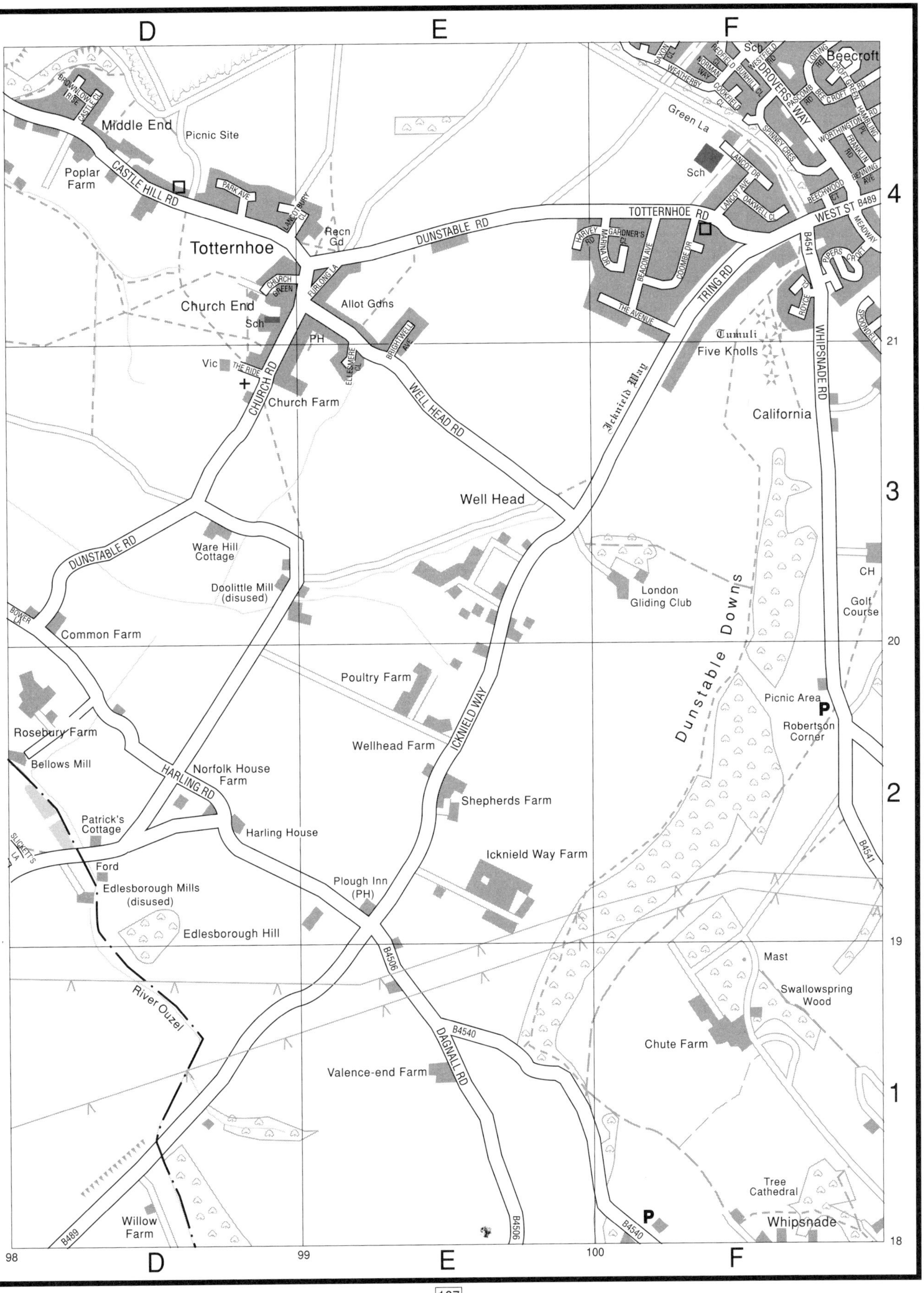

not continued, see key diagram

107

not continued, see key diagram

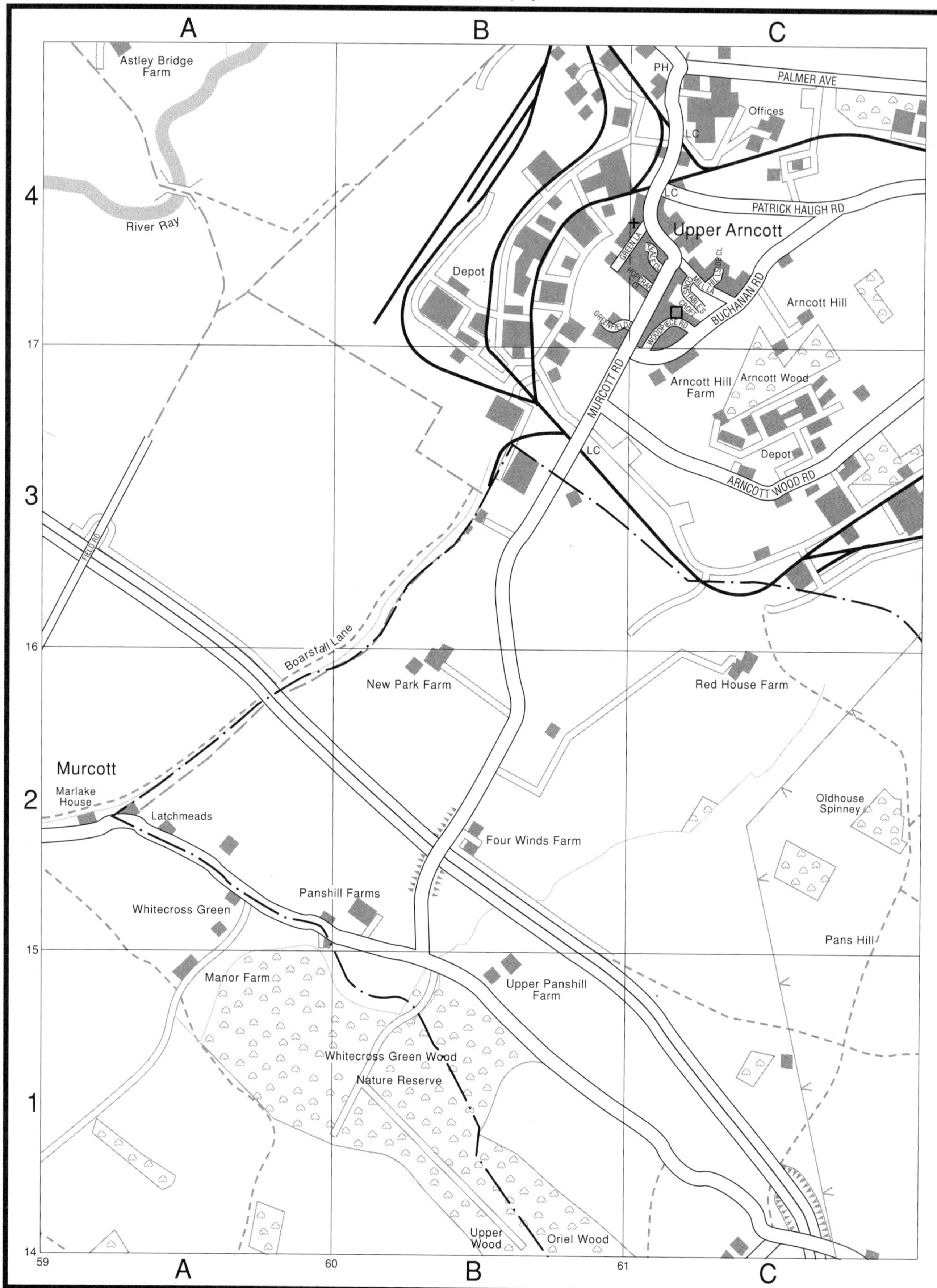

not continued, see key diagram

108

81

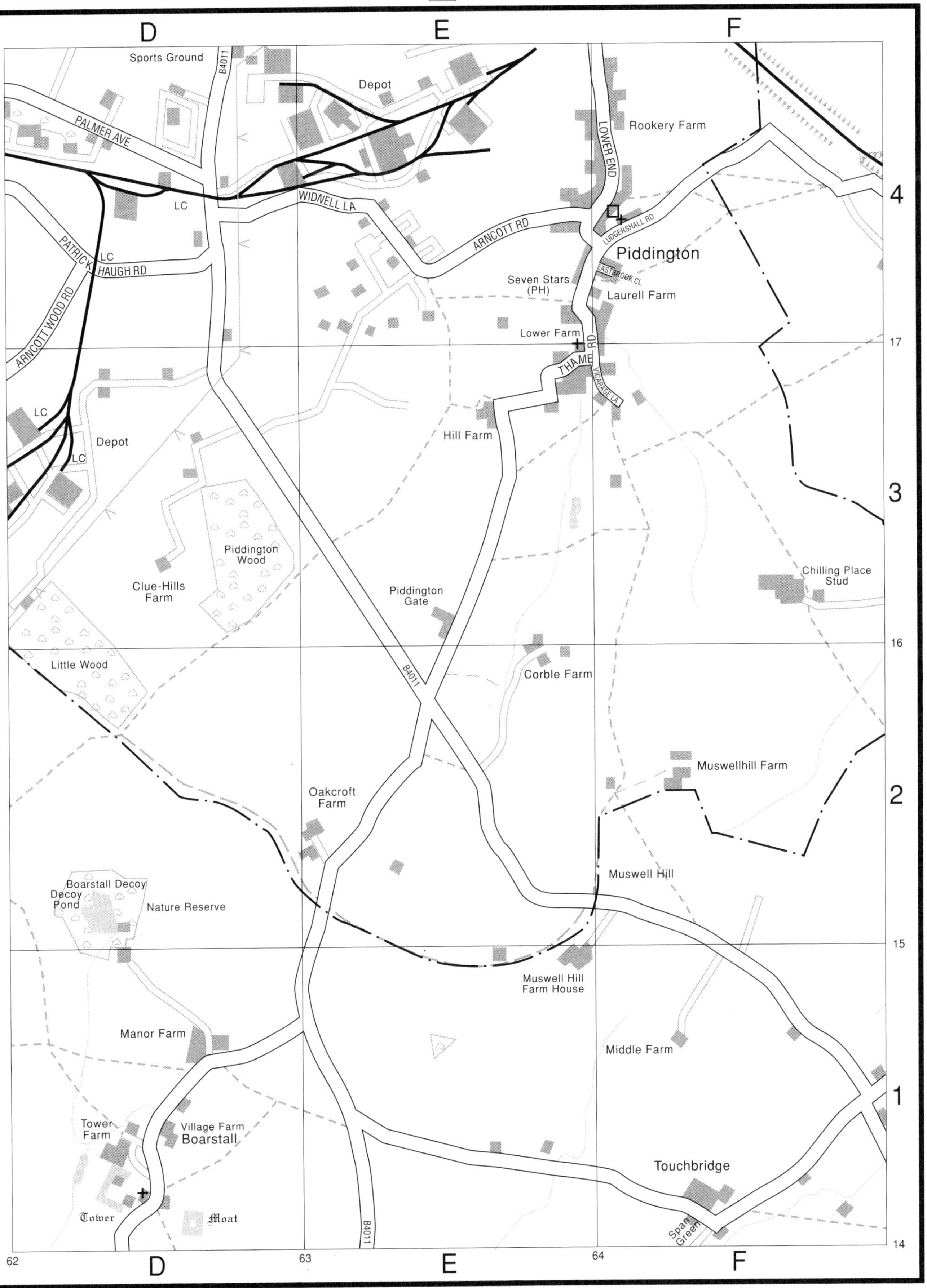
D
E
F
Sports Ground
B4011
Depot
PALMER AVE
Rookery Farm
LOWER END
LC
WIDNELL LA
ARNCOTT RD
LUDGERSHALL RD
Piddington
PATRICK HAUGH RD
LC
Seven Stars
(PH)
EASTBROOK CL
Laurell Farm
ARNCOTT WOOD RD
Lower Farm
THAME RD
VICARAGE LA
LC
Depot
LC
Hill Farm
Piddington
Wood
Clue-Hills
Farm
Piddington
Gate
Chilling Place
Stud
Little Wood
B4011
Corble Farm
Muswellhill Farm
Oakcroft
Farm
Muswell Hill
Boarstall Decoy
Decoy
Pond
Nature Reserve
Muswell Hill
Farm House
Manor Farm
Middle Farm
Tower
Farm
Village Farm
Boarstall
Touchbridge
Tower
Moat
B4011
Span
Green
62
63
64
14
15
16
17
1
2
3
4

96

109

82

95

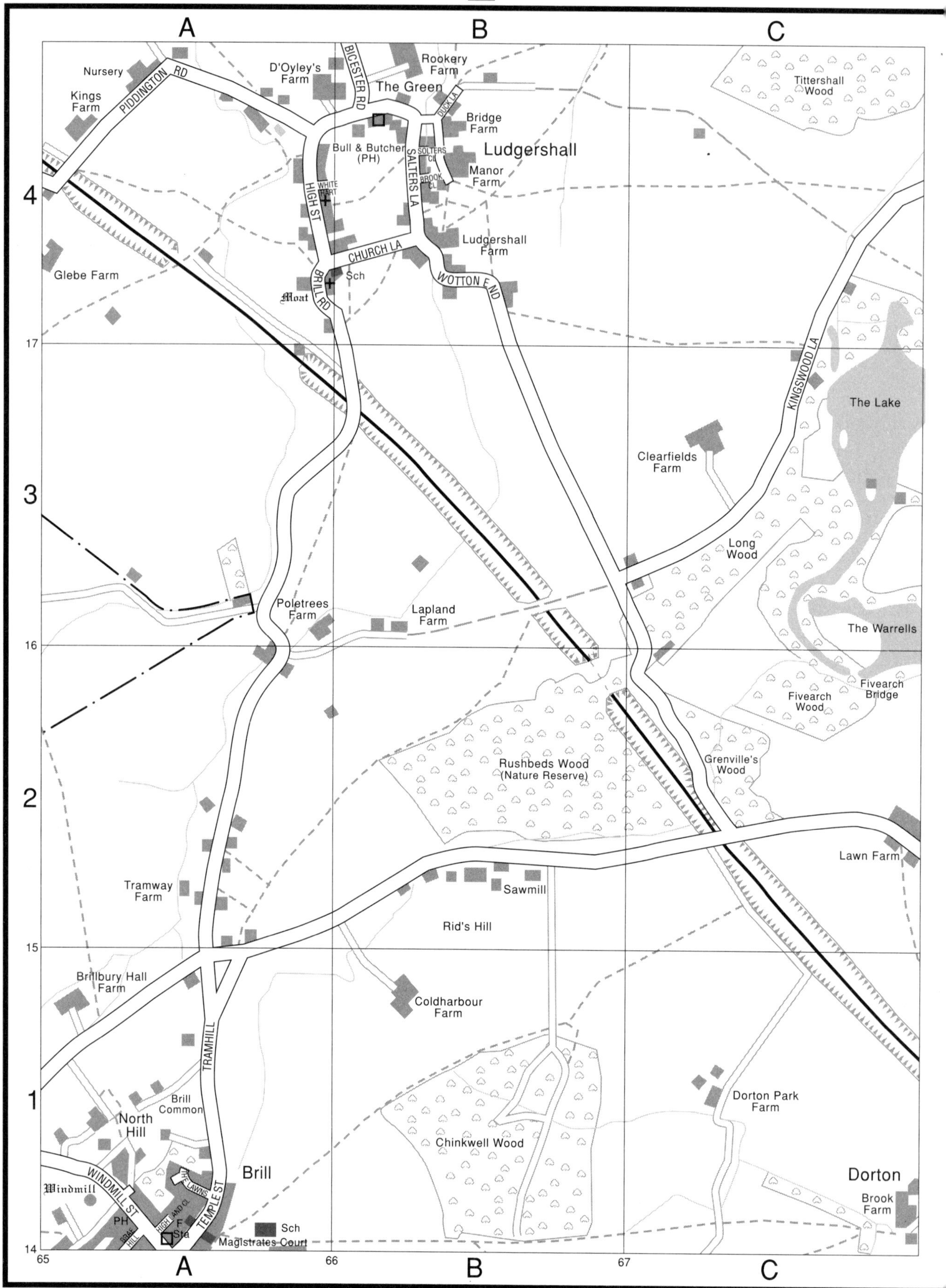

A
B
C
Nursery
Kings Farm
PIDDINGTON RD
D'Oyley's Farm
BICESTER RD
Rookery Farm
The Green
DUCK LA
Bridge Farm
Ludgershall
Bull & Butcher (PH)
SALTERS LA
SOLTERS CL
BROOK CL
Manor Farm
HIGH ST
WHITE HART
Tittershall Wood
4
Glebe Farm
CHURCH LA
Ludgershall Farm
Sch
WOTTON END
BRILL RD
Moat
17
KINGSWOOD LA
The Lake
Clearfields Farm
3
Long Wood
Poletrees Farm
Lapland Farm
The Warrells
16
Fivearch Bridge
Fivearch Wood
Rushbeds Wood (Nature Reserve)
Grenville's Wood
2
Lawn Farm
Tramway Farm
Sawmill
Rid's Hill
15
Brillbury Hall Farm
Coldharbour Farm
TRAMHILL
1
Brill Common
North Hill
Dorton Park Farm
Chinkwell Wood
Brill
Dorton
WINDMILL ST
THE LAWNS
TEMPLE ST
Windmill
Brook Farm
PH
HIGH LAND CL
F Sta
Sch
Magistrates Court
14
65
66
67

110

83

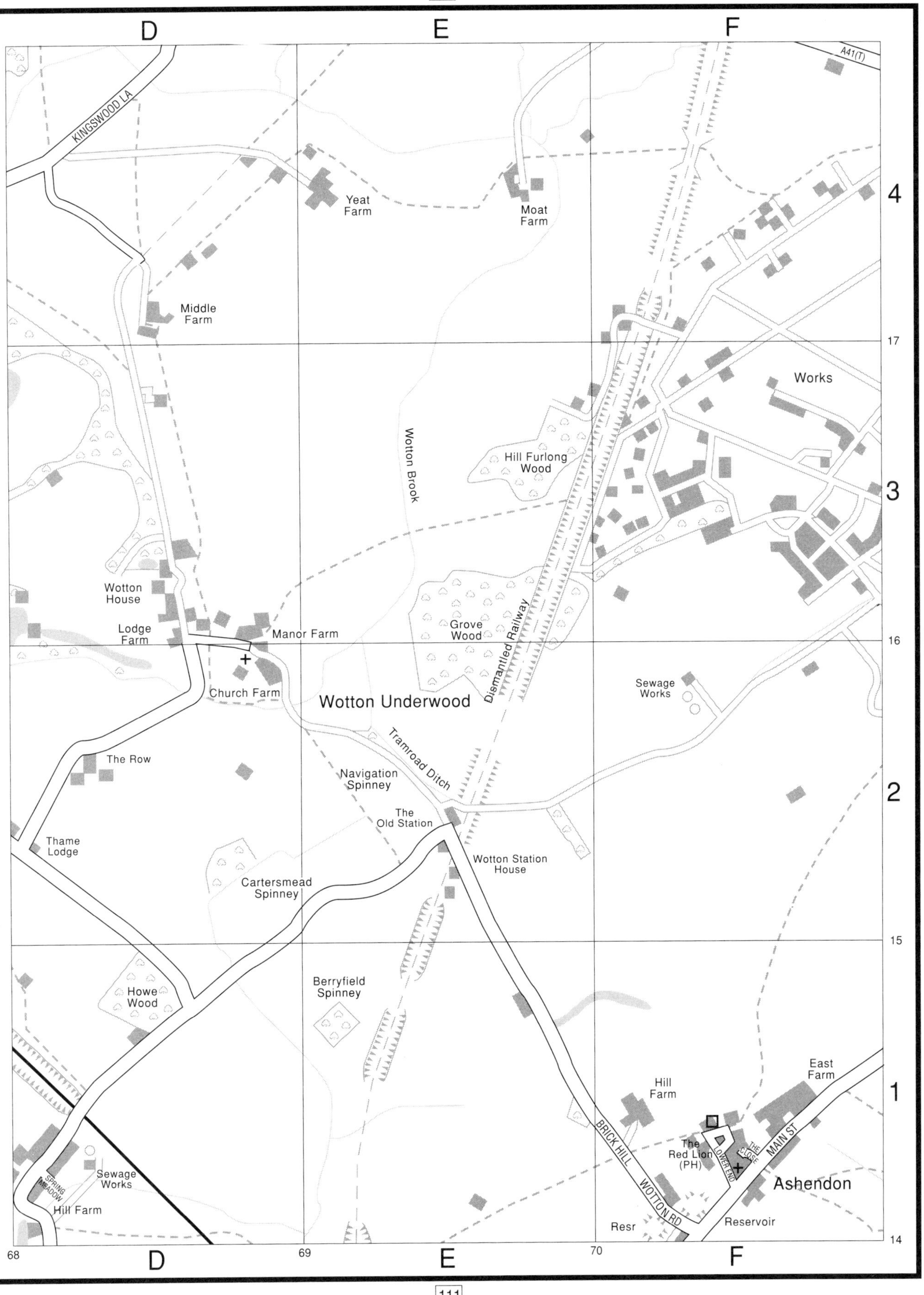

D
E
F
A41(T)
KINGSWOOD LA
Yeat Farm
Moat Farm
4
Middle Farm
17
Works
Wotton Brook
Hill Furlong Wood
3
Wotton House
Grove Wood
Lodge Farm
Manor Farm
Dismantled Railway
16
Church Farm
Wotton Underwood
Sewage Works
The Row
Tramroad Ditch
Navigation Spinney
2
The Old Station
Thame Lodge
Wotton Station House
Cartersmead Spinney
15
Howe Wood
Berryfield Spinney
East Farm
1
Hill Farm
BRICK HILL
The Red Lion (PH)
LOWER END
THE CLOSE
MAIN ST
Ashendon
SPRING MEADOW
Sewage Works
Hill Farm
WOTTON RD
Resr
Reservoir
14
68
69
70
D
E
F

98

111

84

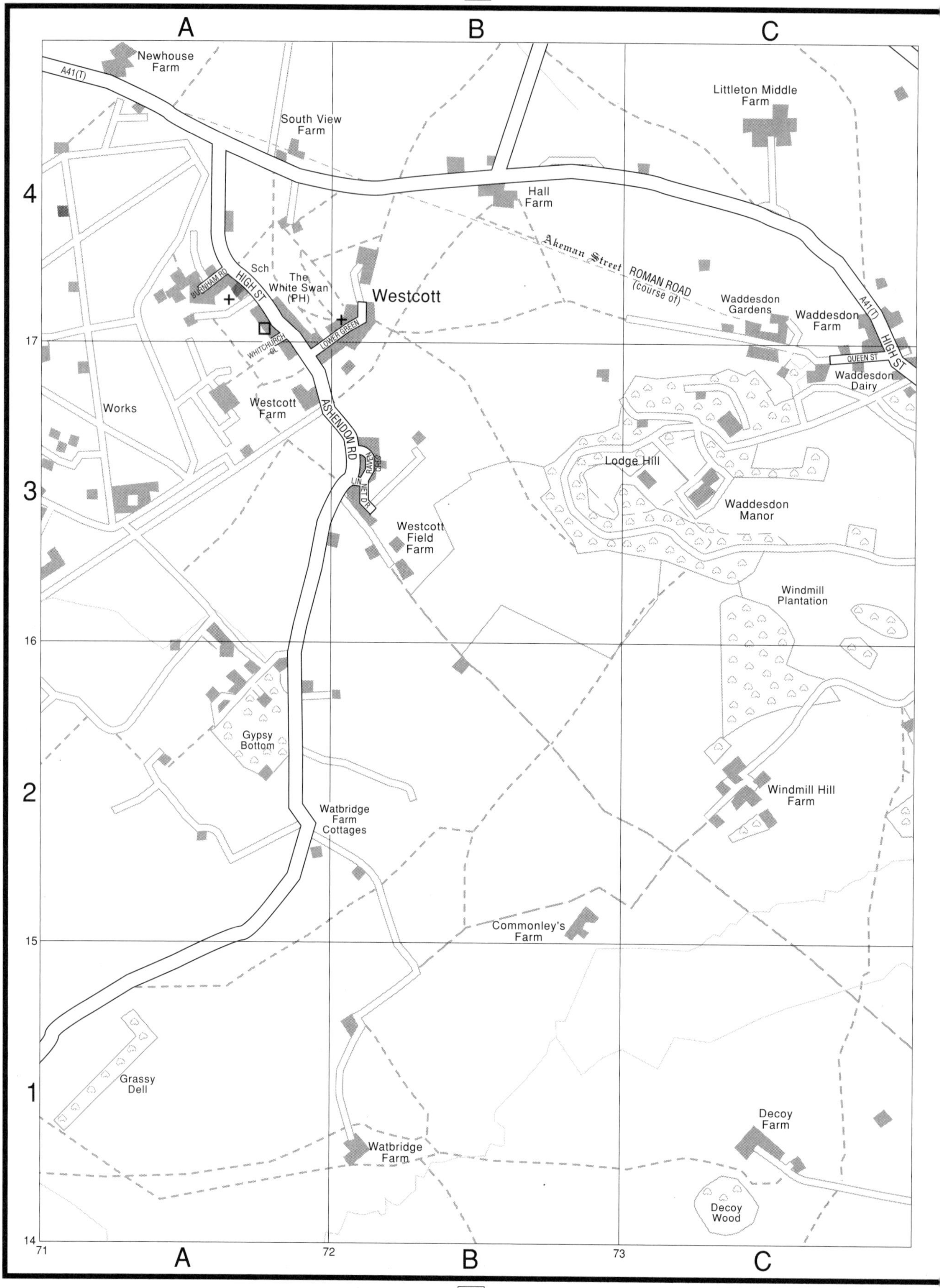
A
B
C
4
3
2
1
17
16
15
14
71
72
73
A41(T)
Newhouse Farm
South View Farm
Littleton Middle Farm
Hall Farm
Akeman Street ROMAN ROAD (course of)
Sch
The White Swan (PH)
Westcott
BURNHAM RD
HIGH ST
WHITCHURCH PL
LOWER GREEN
Waddesdon Gardens
Waddesdon Farm
HIGH ST
QUEEN ST
Waddesdon Dairy
Works
Westcott Farm
ASHENDON RD
RAVEN CRES
LINNET DR
Lodge Hill
Waddesdon Manor
Westcott Field Farm
Windmill Plantation
Gypsy Bottom
Windmill Hill Farm
Watbridge Farm Cottages
Commonley's Farm
Grassy Dell
Decoy Farm
Watbridge Farm
Decoy Wood

97

112

85
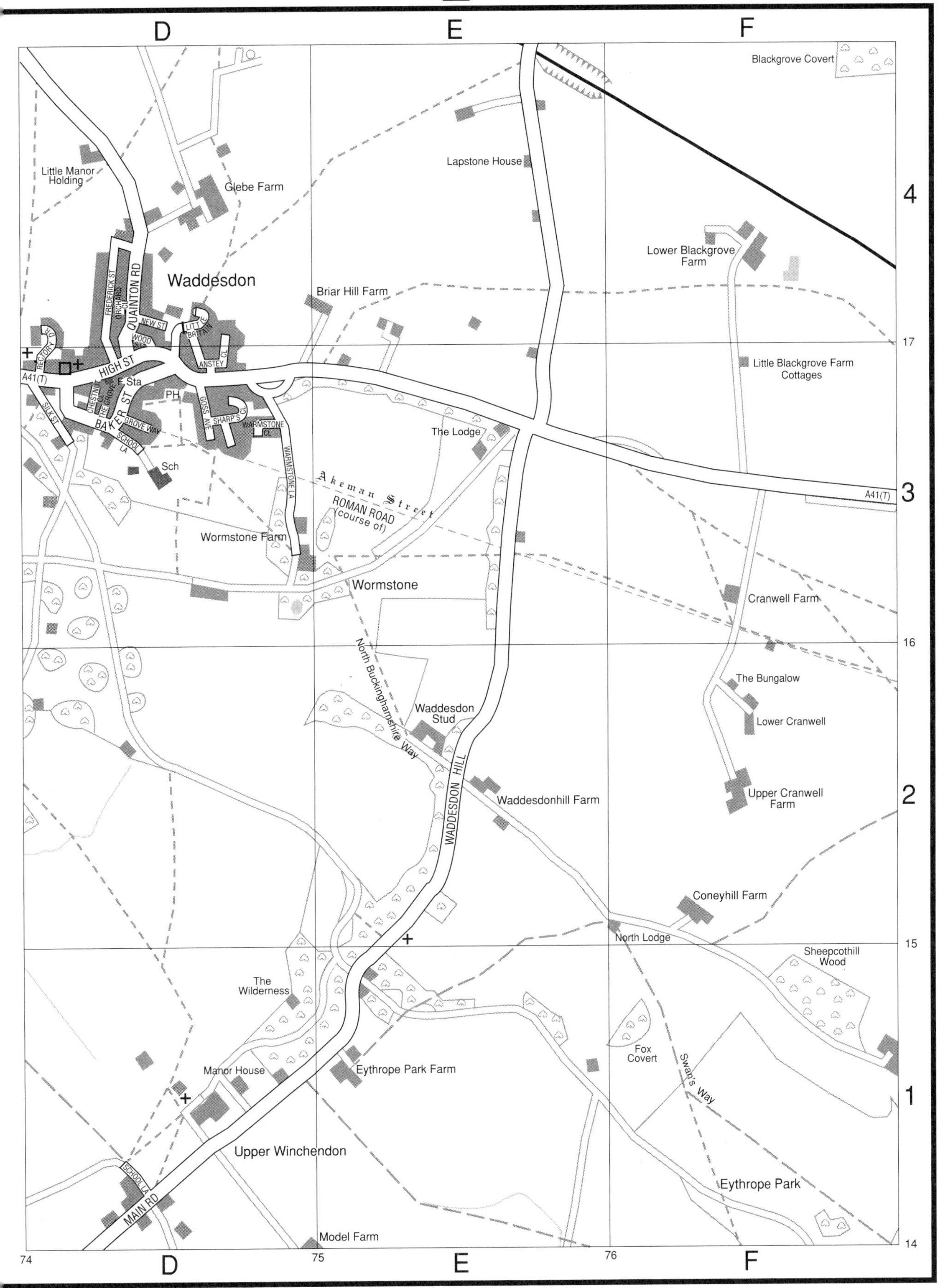
D
E
F
Blackgrove Covert
Lapstone House
Little Manor Holding
Glebe Farm
Waddesdon
Lower Blackgrove Farm
Briar Hill Farm
Little Blackgrove Farm Cottages
HIGH ST
A41(T)
F Sta
PH
Sch
The Lodge
Akeman Street
ROMAN ROAD (course of)
Wormstone Farm
Wormstone
Cranwell Farm
North Buckinghamshire Way
The Bungalow
Waddesdon Stud
Lower Cranwell
WADDESDON HILL
Waddesdonhill Farm
Upper Cranwell Farm
Coneyhill Farm
North Lodge
Sheepcothill Wood
The Wilderness
Fox Covert
Swan's Way
Manor House
Eythrope Park Farm
Upper Winchendon
Eythrope Park
SCHOOL LA
MAIN RD
Model Farm
4
3
2
1
17
16
15
14
74
75
76
100
113

86

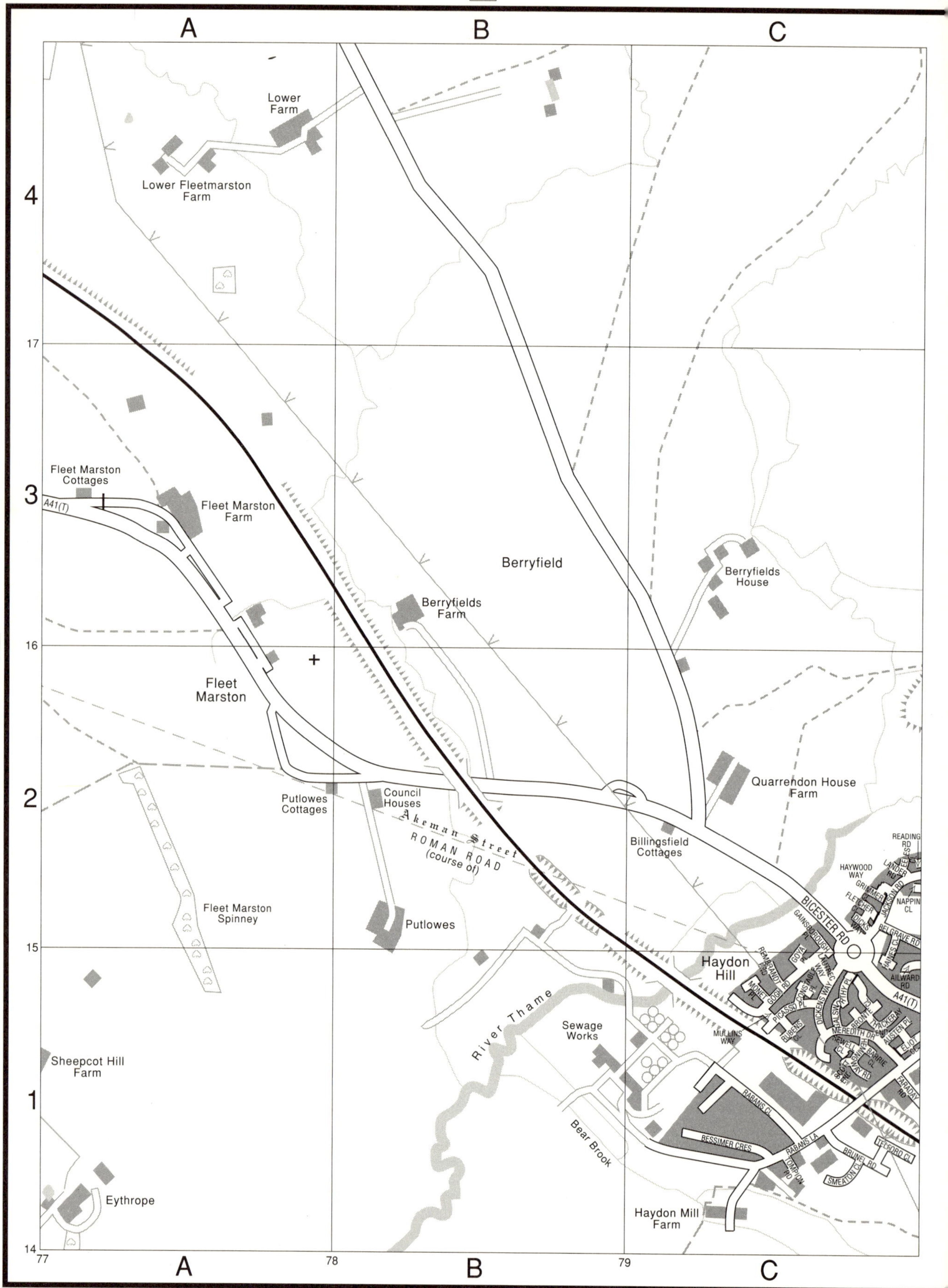
A
B
C
4
3
2
1
17
16
15
14
77
78
79
Lower Farm
Lower Fleetmarston Farm
Fleet Marston Cottages
A41(T)
Fleet Marston Farm
Berryfield
Berryfields House
Berryfields Farm
Fleet Marston
Quarrendon House Farm
Putlowes Cottages
Council Houses
Akeman Street
ROMAN ROAD (course of)
Billingsfield Cottages
READING RD
EELES CL
LANDER RD
HAYWOOD WAY
GRIMMER CL
FLETCHER CL
DICKS WAY
JACKSON RD
NAPPIN CL
BICESTER RD
BELGRAVE RD
HAINES CL
AILWARD RD
GAINSBOROUGH PL
GOYA PL
LAUTREC WAY
REMBRANDT END
Haydon Hill
MONET PL
GOGH RD
CONSTABLE PL
DICKENS WAY
GALSWORTHY PL
BRONTE CL
THACKERAY END
AUSTEN PL
ELIOT CL
PICASSO PL
RUBENS CL
MEREDITH DR
SEWELL CL
HEMINGWAY RD
BARRIE CL
SCOTT END
FARADAY RD
Fleet Marston Spinney
Putlowes
River Thame
Sewage Works
MULLINS WAY
Sheepcot Hill Farm
RABANS CL
BESSIMER CRES
RABANS LA
TOMPION RD
BRUNEL RD
SMEATON CL
TELFORD CL
Bear Brook
Eythrope
Haydon Mill Farm

99

114

87

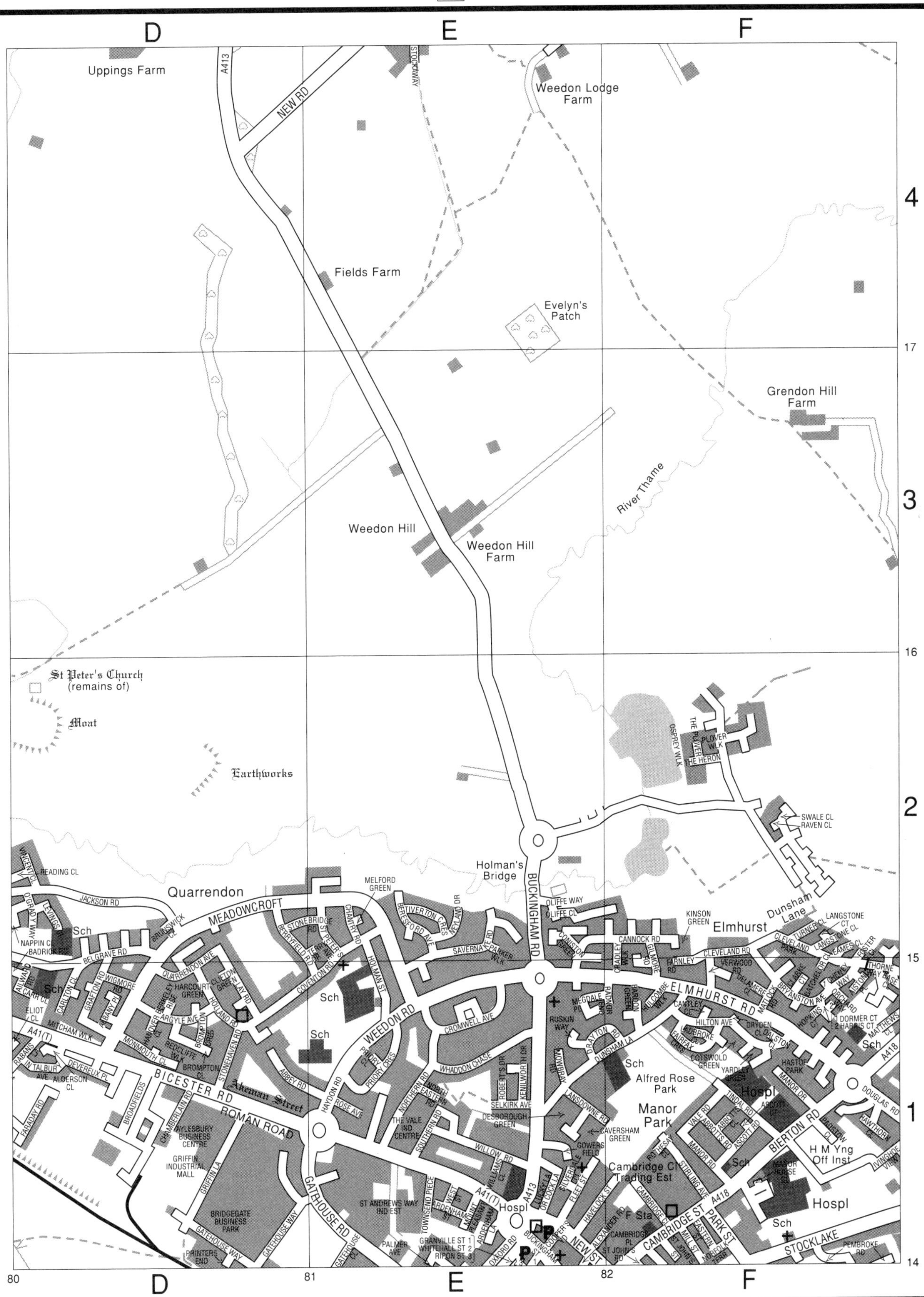

D
E
F
4
3
2
1
17
16
15
14
80
81
82
Uppings Farm
A413
NEW RD
STOCKWAY
Weedon Lodge Farm
Fields Farm
Evelyn's Patch
Grendon Hill Farm
River Thame
Weedon Hill
Weedon Hill Farm
St Peter's Church (remains of)
Moat
Earthworks
OSPREY WLK
THE PLOVER
PLOVER WLK
THE HERON
SWALE CL
RAVEN CL
Holman's Bridge
BUCKINGHAM RD
Quarrendon
READING CL
JACKSON RD
MEADOWCROFT
MELFORD GREEN
OLIFFE WAY
OLIFFE CL
KINSON GREEN
Elmhurst
Dunsham Lane
LANGSTONE CT
Sch
BELGRAVE RD
NAPPIN CL
BADRICK RD
BRUNSWICK CL
STONEBRIDGE RD
CHANTRY RD
TIVERTON CRES
WEYLAND DR
SAVERNAKE RD
PARKER WLK
CONISTON GREEN
CANNOCK RD
CRADLEY WLK
GILMORE RD
FARNLEY RD
CLEVELAND RD
VERWOOD RD
CLEVELAND PARK
TURNER CL
LANGSTONE CL
QUARRENDON AVE
HARCOURT GREEN
CLIFTON GREEN
COVENTON RD
HOLMAN ST
GRAFTON RD
WIGMORE RD
CARLTON CL
ELIOT CL
ALBANY PL
ARGYLE AVE
HOLLAND RD
ELMHURST RD
MEGDALE PL
BARLOW GREEN
HULCOMBE WLK
CANTLEY CL
HILTON AVE
DRYDEN CL
RUSKIN WAY
WEEDON RD
CROMWELL AVE
A41(T)
MITCHAM WLK
MONMOUTH CL
REDCLIFFE WLK
BROMPTON CL
STONEHAVEN RD
DEVEREUX PL
ALDERSON CL
IN TALBUR AVE
WHADDON CHASE
ROBERTS DR
KENILWORTH DR
DRAYTON RD
DUNSHAM LA
MOWBRAY DR
LADBROKE CL
COTSWOLD GREEN
YARDLEY GREEN
HASTOE PARK
MANOR DR
Alfred Rose Park
Hospl
BICESTER RD
Akeman Street
ROMAN ROAD
ABBEY RD
HAYDON RD
ROSE AVE
PRIORY CRES
NORTHERN RD
NORTH EASTERN RD
SELKIRK AVE
DESBOROUGH GREEN
LANSDOWNE RD
Manor Park
CAVERSHAM GREEN
GOWERS FIELD
VALE RD
ABBOTTS RD
SCOTT RD
ASCOTT CT
BIERTON RD
DOUGLAS RD
HAWTHORN CL
H M Yng Off Inst
FARADAY RD
BROADFIELDS
CHAMBERLAIN RD
AYLESBURY BUSINESS CENTRE
GRIFFIN INDUSTRIAL MALL
GRIFFIN LA
THE VALE IND CENTRE
SOUTHERN RD
WILLOW RD
WILLIAMS CL
A413
Cambridge Cl Trading Est
MANOR RD
STIRLING AVE
MANOR HOUSE CL
BRIDGEGATE BUSINESS PARK
GATEHOUSE WAY
GATEHOUSE RD
ST ANDREWS WAY IND EST
TOWNSEND PIECE
Hospl
HAVELOCK ST
ALEXANDER RD
F Sta
CAMBRIDGE ST
PARK ST
A418
Sch
STOCKLAKE
PEMBROKE RD
PRINTERS END
PALMER AVE
GRANVILLE ST 1
WHITEHALL ST 2
RIPON ST 3
OXFORD RD
NEW ST
CAMBRIDGE PL
ST JOHNS RD
DORMER CT
HARRIS CT
MATTHEWS CL

102

115

88

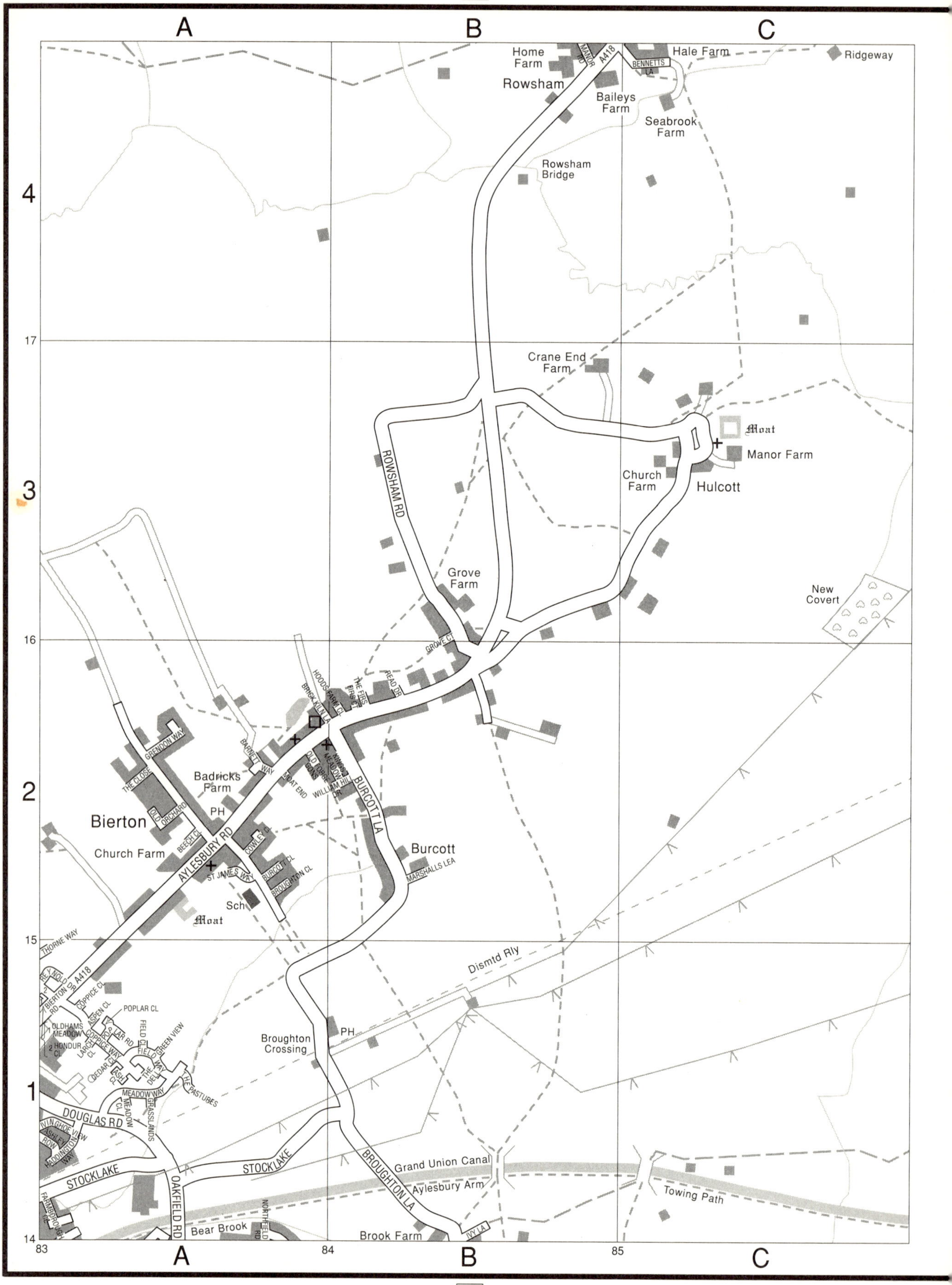

A
B
C
4
17
3
16
2
15
1
14
83
84
85
Home Farm
MANOR RD
A418
Hale Farm
BENNETTS LA
Ridgeway
Rowsham
Baileys Farm
Seabrook Farm
Rowsham Bridge
Crane End Farm
Moat
Manor Farm
Church Farm
Hulcott
ROWSHAM RD
Grove Farm
New Covert
GROVE CT
READ DR
THE FIRS
FIRS CT
HOODS FARM CL
BRICK KILN LA
BARNETT WAY
GRENDON WAY
THE CLOSE
Badricks Farm
OLD ORCHARD
PH
Bierton
BEECH CL
AYLESBURY RD
Church Farm
ST JAMES WAY
COWLEY CL
BURCOTT CL
BROUGHTON CL
Sch
Moat
MOAT END
OLD FORGE GDNS
MEADOW CL
KINGSLEY CL
WILLIAM HILL DR
BURCOTT LA
Burcott
MARSHALLS LEA
THORNE WAY
Dismtd Rly
A418
BIERTON RD
COPPICE CL
ASPEN CL
POPLAR CL
OLDHAMS MEADOW
HONDUR CL
LARCH CL
COPPICE WAY
POPLAR RD
FIELD CL
FIELD WAY
GREEN VIEW
CEDAR CL
ASH CL
THE DELL
THE PASTURES
MEADOW WAY
MEADOW CL
GRASSLANDS
DOUGLAS RD
IVINGHOE VIEW
ASHLEY ROW
HADDINGTON WAY
Broughton Crossing
PH
STOCKLAKE
STOCKLAKE
OAKFIELD RD
BROUGHTON LA
Grand Union Canal
Aylesbury Arm
Towing Path
FARNBOROUGH
Bear Brook
NORTHFIELD RD
Brook Farm
IVY LA

101

116

89

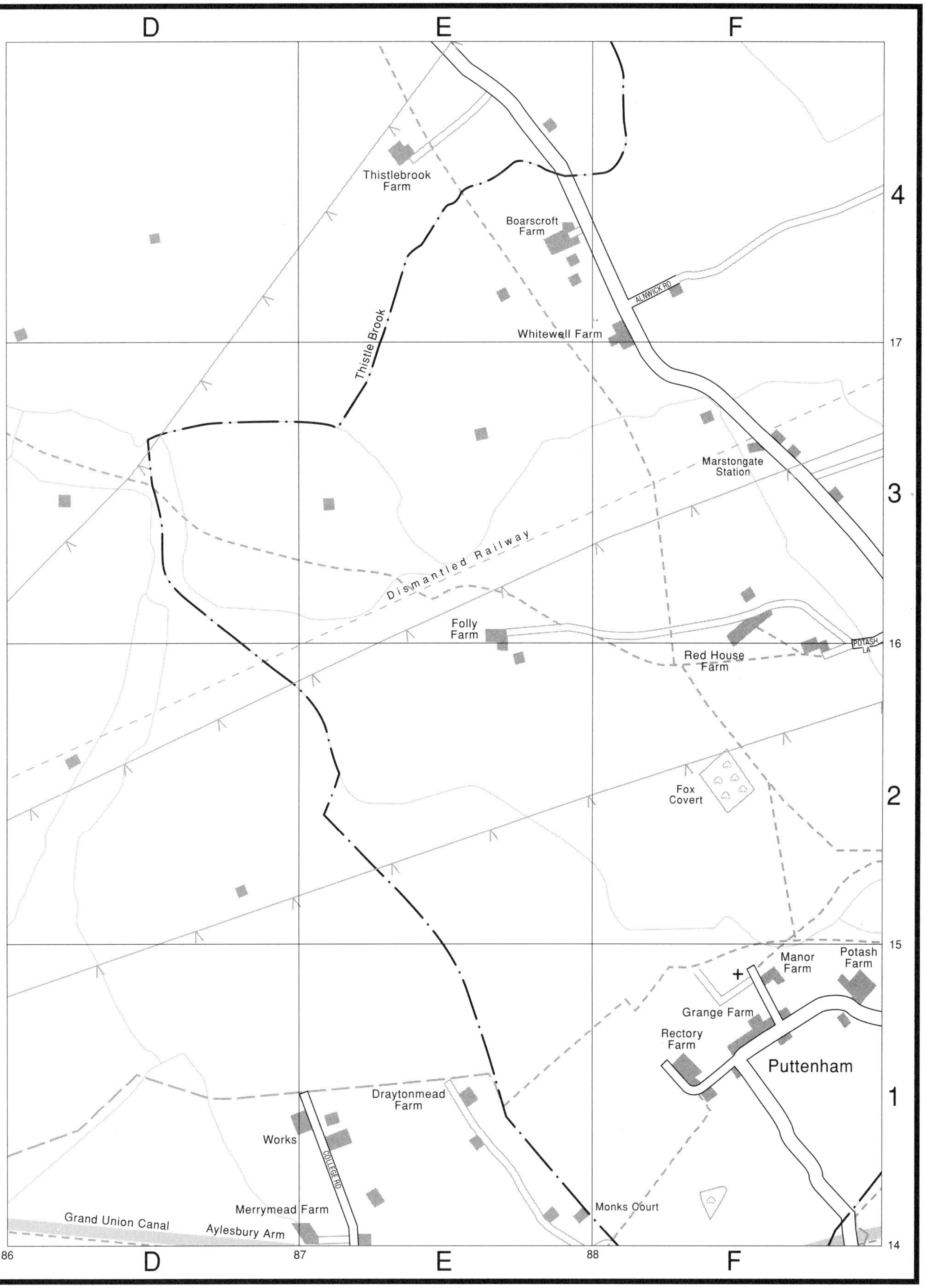
D
E
F
Thistlebrook Farm
Boarscroft Farm
ALNWICK RD
Whitewell Farm
Thistle Brook
Marstongate Station
Dismantled Railway
Folly Farm
Red House Farm
POTASH LA
Fox Covert
Manor Farm
Potash Farm
Grange Farm
Rectory Farm
Puttenham
Draytonmead Farm
Works
COLLEGE RD
Merrymead Farm
Grand Union Canal
Aylesbury Arm
Monks Court
4
3
2
1
17
16
15
14
86
87
88

104

117

90

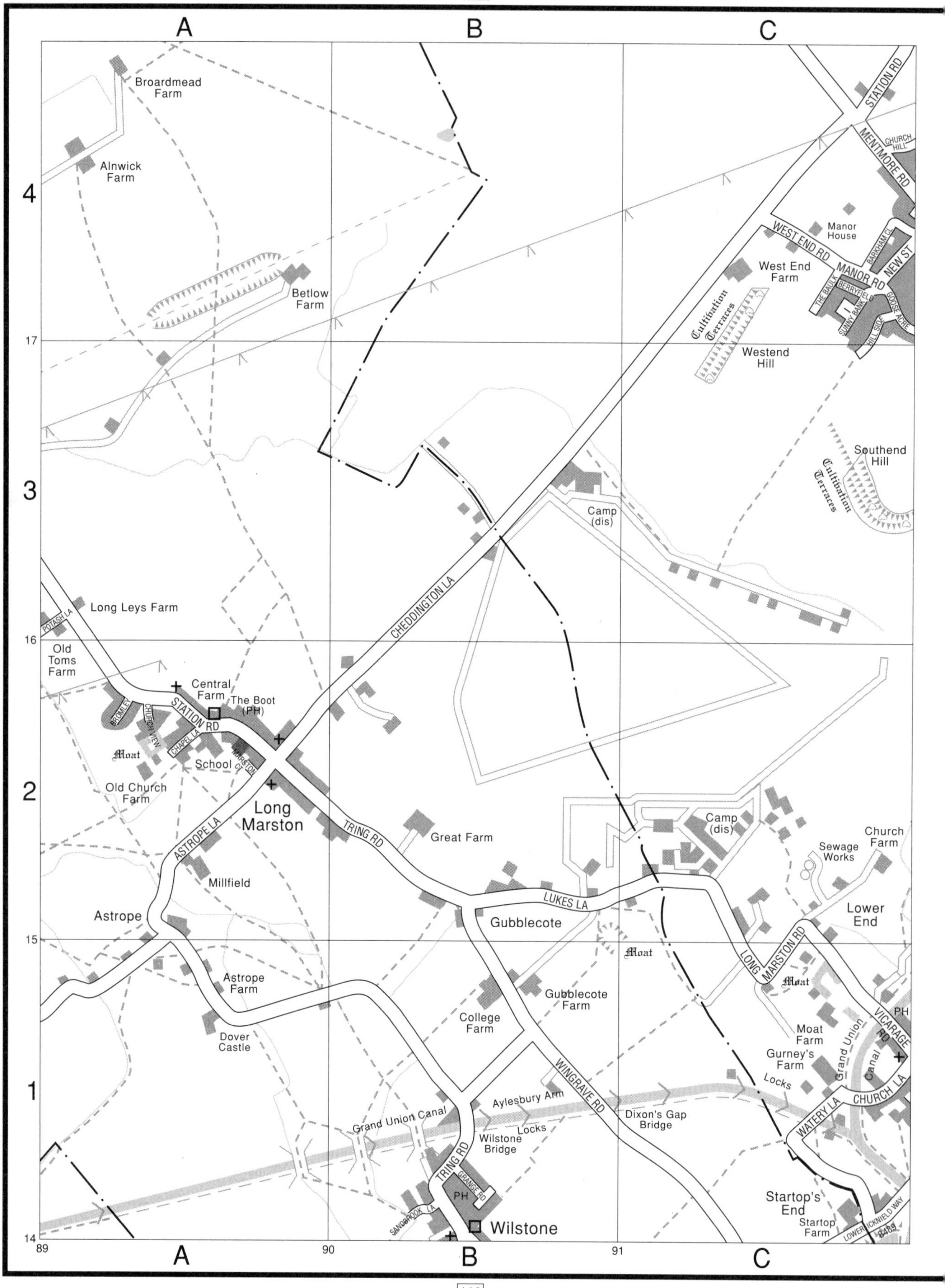

A
B
C
4
3
2
1
17
16
15
14
89
90
91
Broadmead Farm
Alnwick Farm
Betlow Farm
STATION RD
CHURCH HILL
MENTMORE RD
Manor House
WEST END RD
BARKHAM CL
NEW ST
MANOR RD
West End Farm
THE BAULK
BERRYFIELD
SUNNY BANK
GOOSE ACRE
HILL SIDE
Cultivation Terraces
Westend Hill
Southend Hill
Camp (dis)
CHEDDINGTON LA
Long Leys Farm
POTASH LA
Old Toms Farm
Central Farm
The Boot (PH)
BROMLEY
CHURCH VIEW
STATION RD
CHAPEL LA
MARSTON CL
Moat
School
Old Church Farm
Long Marston
ASTROPE LA
TRING RD
Great Farm
Church Farm
Sewage Works
Millfield
LUKES LA
Lower End
Astrope
Gubblecote
LONG MARSTON RD
Astrope Farm
Gubblecote Farm
College Farm
Dover Castle
Moat Farm
Gurney's Farm
VICARAGE RD
PH
Grand Union Canal
Locks
CHURCH LA
WINGRAVE RD
Aylesbury Arm
Grand Union Canal
Locks
Wilstone Bridge
Dixon's Gap Bridge
WATERY LA
TRING RD
GRANGE RD
PH
SANDBROOK LA
Wilstone
Startop's End
Startop Farm
LOWER ICKNIELD WAY
B489

103

118

91

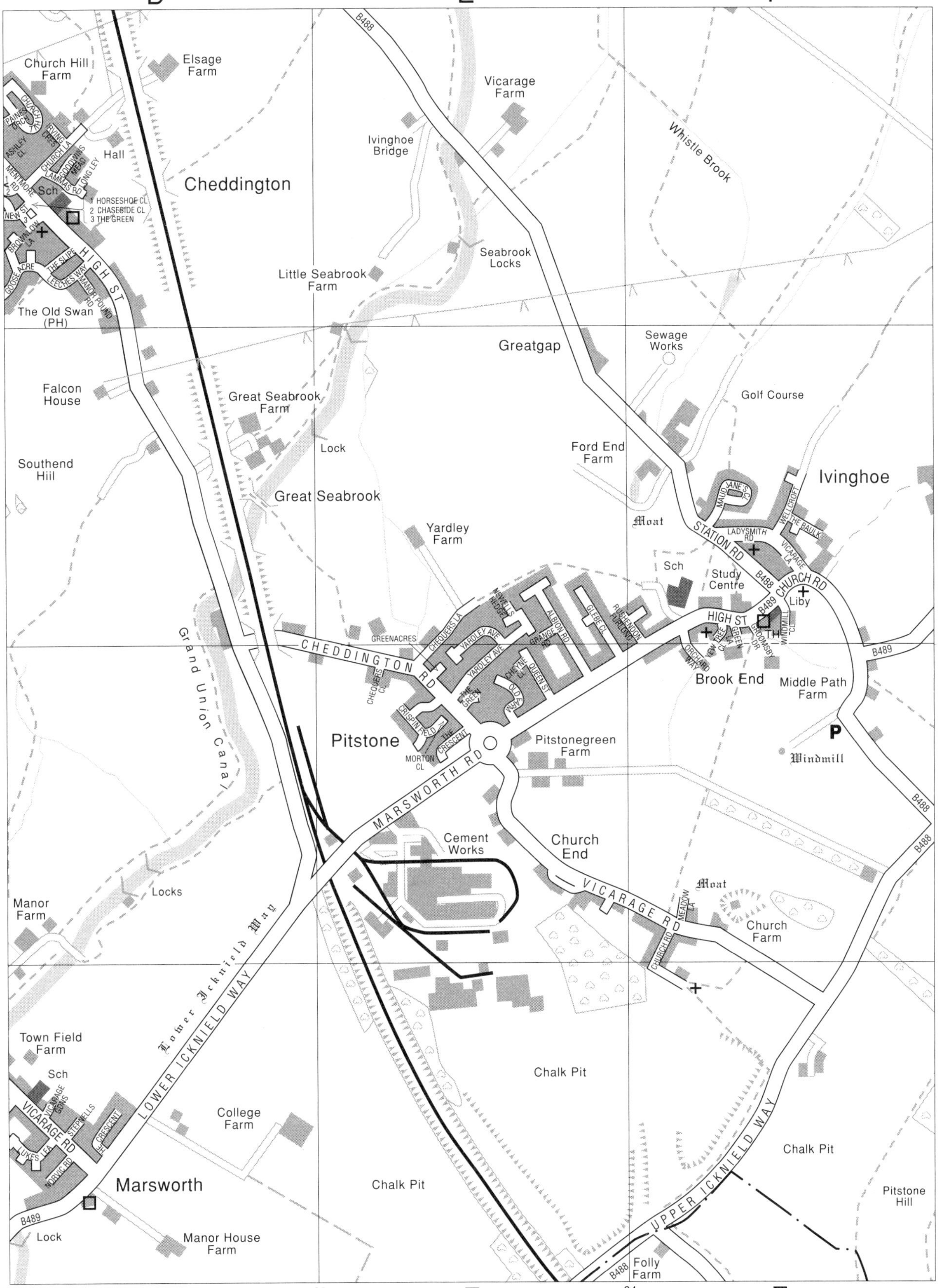
D
E
F
Church Hill Farm
Elsage Farm
Vicarage Farm
Ivinghoe Bridge
Hall
Cheddington
Whistle Brook
4
Sch
1 HORSESHOE CL
2 CHASESIDE CL
3 THE GREEN
HIGH ST
Seabrook Locks
Little Seabrook Farm
The Old Swan (PH)
17
Greatgap
Sewage Works
Falcon House
Great Seabrook Farm
Golf Course
Lock
Southend Hill
Ford End Farm
Ivinghoe
3
Great Seabrook
Moat
Yardley Farm
STATION RD
LADYSMITH RD
VICARAGE LA
Sch
Study Centre
CHURCH RD
Grand Union Canal
HIGH ST
Liby
GREENACRES
CHEDDINGTON RD
16
B489
Brook End
Middle Path Farm
Pitstone
Pitstonegreen Farm
Windmill
MARSWORTH RD
B488
2
Cement Works
Church End
Lower Icknield Way
Locks
Moat
VICARAGE RD
Manor Farm
Church Farm
15
LOWER ICKNIELD WAY
Town Field Farm
Chalk Pit
Sch
1
College Farm
UPPER ICKNIELD WAY
Chalk Pit
Marsworth
Chalk Pit
Pitstone Hill
B489
Lock
Manor House Farm
Folly Farm
B488
14
92
93
94
D
E
F

106

119

92

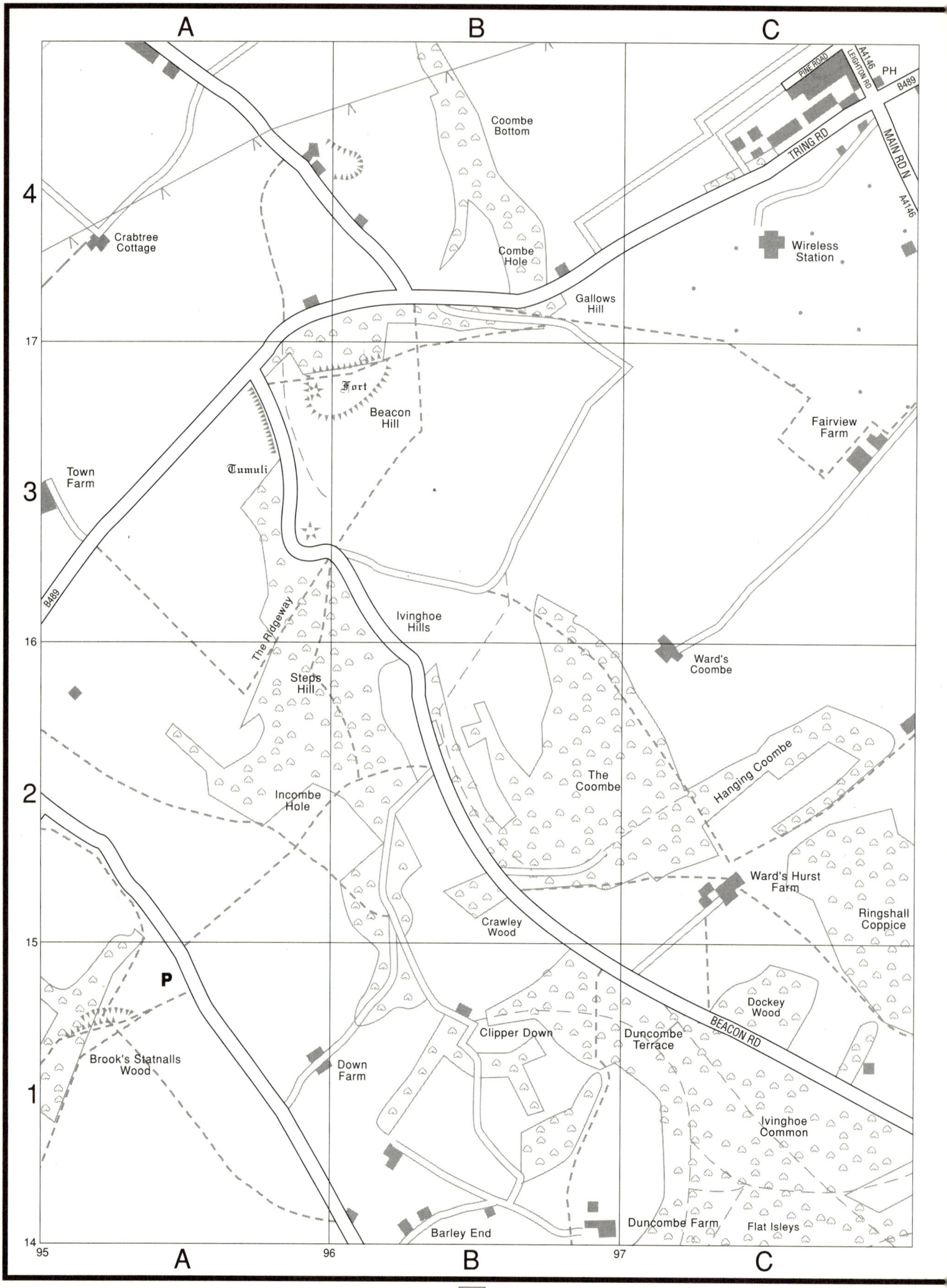
A
B
C
4
3
2
1
17
16
15
14
95
96
97
PINE ROAD
LEIGHTON RD
A4146
PH
B489
TRING RD
MAIN RD N
A4146
Coombe Bottom
Crabtree Cottage
Combe Hole
Wireless Station
Gallows Hill
Fort
Beacon Hill
Fairview Farm
Town Farm
Tumuli
3
B489
The Ridgeway
Ivinghoe Hills
Ward's Coombe
Steps Hill
Hanging Coombe
The Coombe
Incombe Hole
Ward's Hurst Farm
Crawley Wood
Ringshall Coppice
P
Dockey Wood
Clipper Down
Duncombe Terrace
BEACON RD
Brook's Statnalls Wood
Down Farm
Ivinghoe Common
Barley End
Duncombe Farm
Flat Isleys

105

120

93

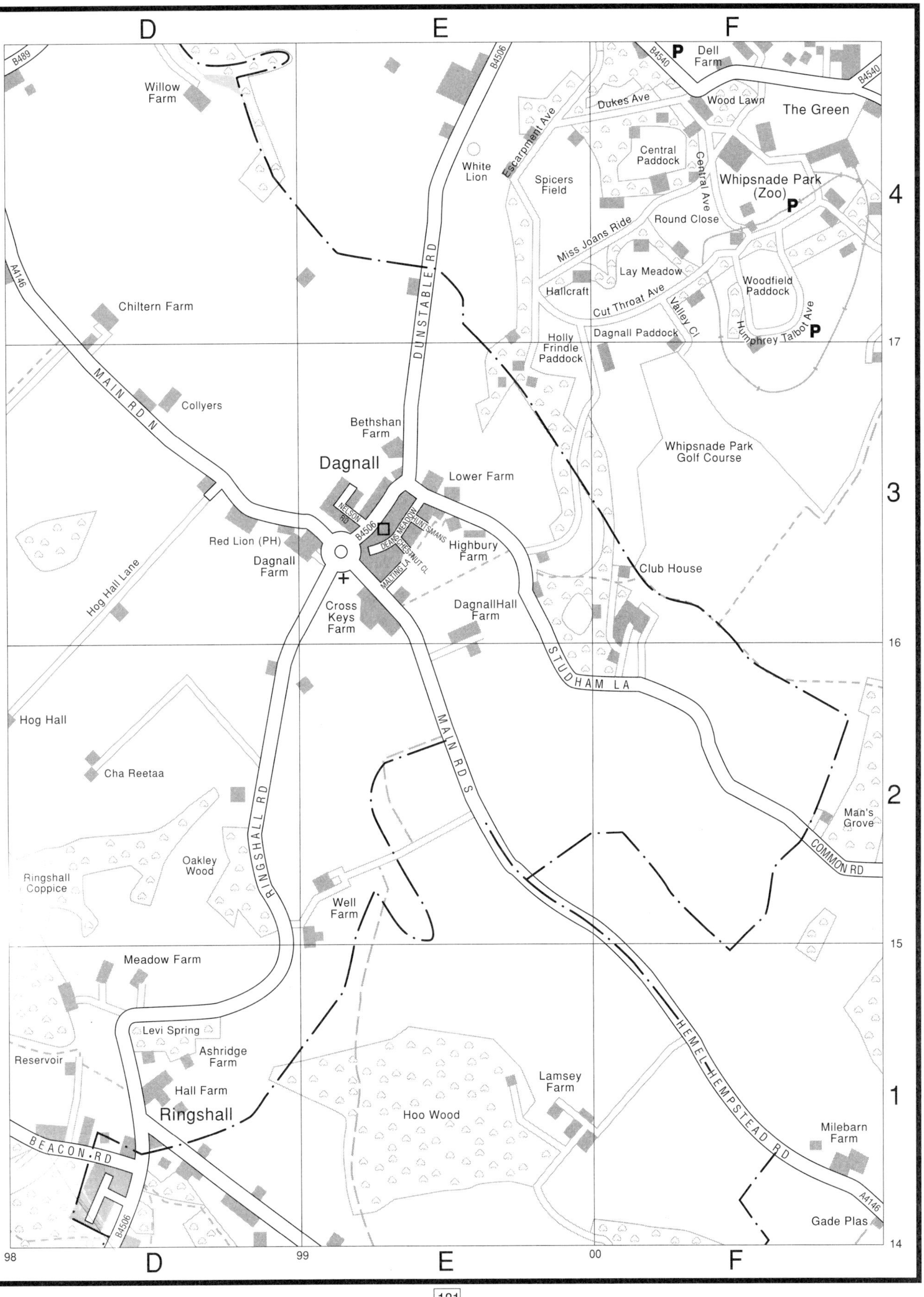
D
E
F
Willow Farm
Dell Farm
Wood Lawn
The Green
Dukes Ave
Escarpment Ave
Central Paddock
Central Ave
White Lion
Spicers Field
Whipsnade Park (Zoo)
Round Close
Miss Joans Ride
Lay Meadow
Hallcraft
Cut Throat Ave
Valley Cl
Woodfield Paddock
Humphrey Talbot Ave
Dagnall Paddock
Holly Frindle Paddock
Chiltern Farm
DUNSTABLE RD
MAIN RD N
Collyers
Bethshan Farm
Whipsnade Park Golf Course
Dagnall
Lower Farm
NELSON RD
DEANS MEADOW
HUNTSMANS
CHESTNUT CL
MALTING LA
Red Lion (PH)
Highbury Farm
Dagnall Farm
Club House
Hog Hall Lane
Cross Keys Farm
DagnallHall Farm
STUDHAM LA
Hog Hall
Cha Reetaa
MAIN RD S
Man's Grove
COMMON RD
RINGSHALL RD
Oakley Wood
Ringshall Coppice
Well Farm
Meadow Farm
Levi Spring
Ashridge Farm
Reservoir
HEMEL HEMPSTEAD RD
Lamsey Farm
Hall Farm
Ringshall
Hoo Wood
Milebarn Farm
BEACON RD
Gade Plas
B489
B4506
B4540
A4146
4
3
2
1
17
16
15
14
98
99
00
not continued, see key diagram

121

94

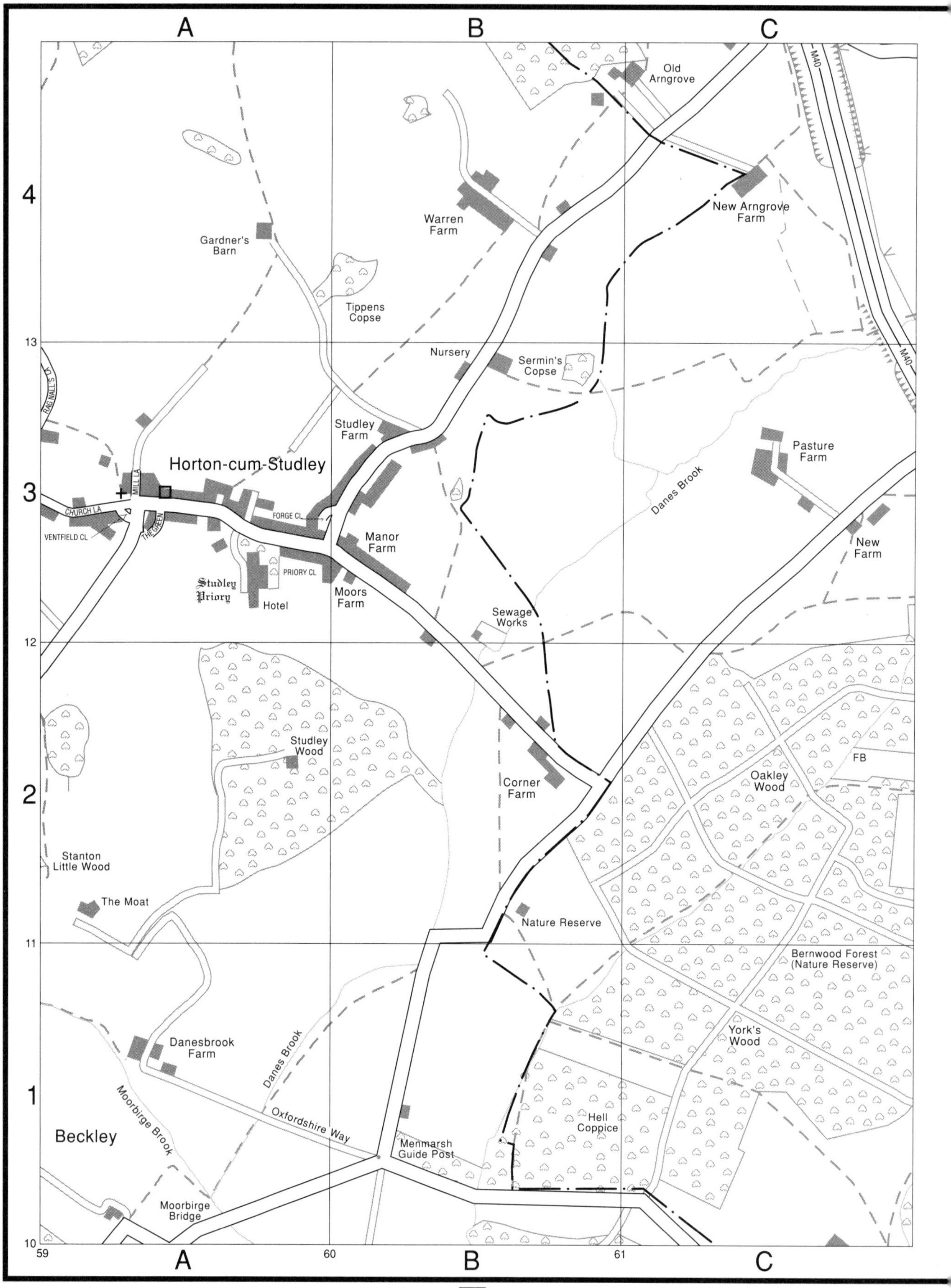

not continued, see key diagram

122

95

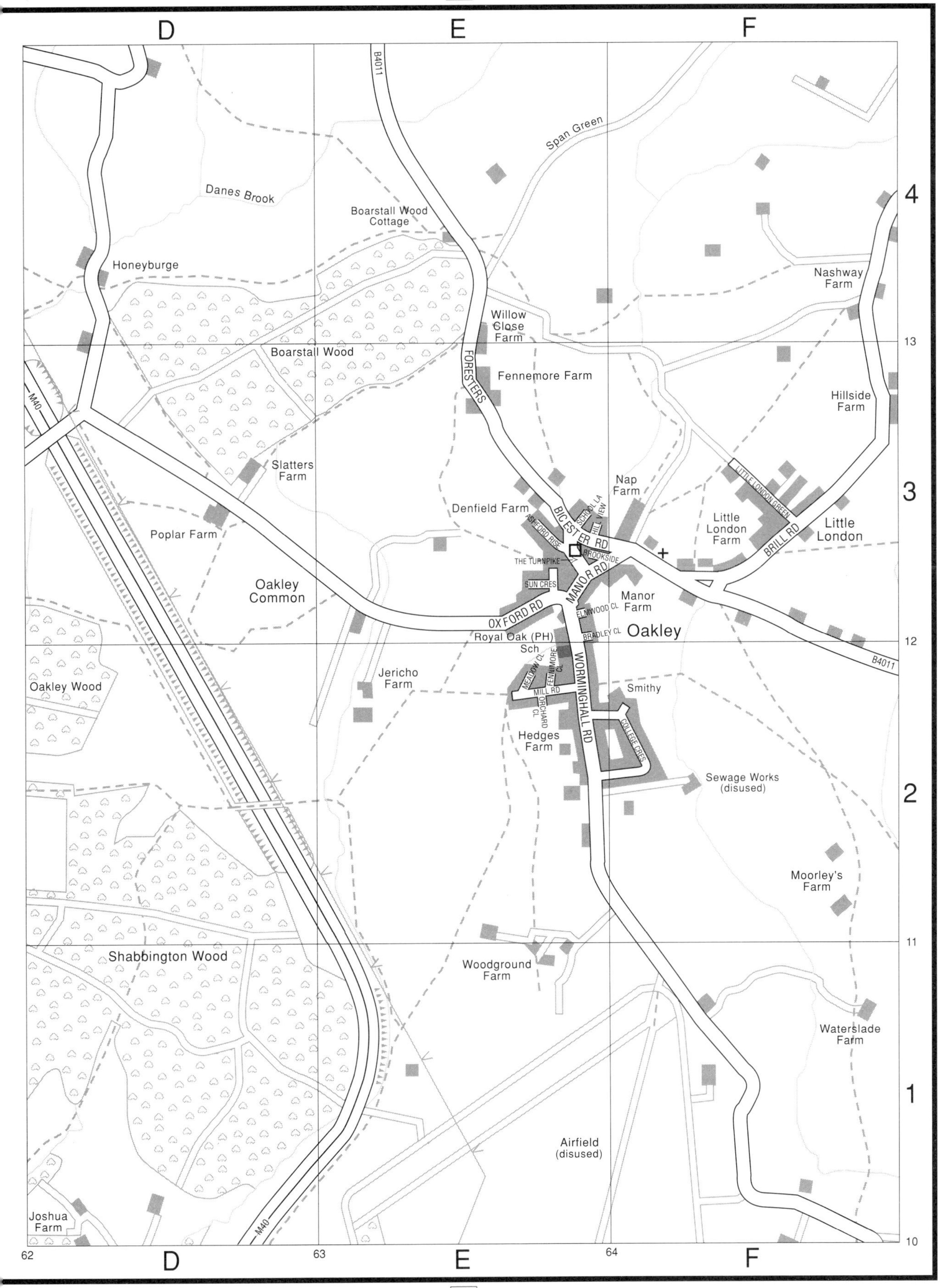
D
E
F
B4011
Span Green
Danes Brook
Boarstall Wood Cottage
Honeyburge
Nashway Farm
Willow Close Farm
Boarstall Wood
FORESTERS
Fennemore Farm
Hillside Farm
M40
Slatters Farm
Nap Farm
LITTLE LONDON GREEN
Denfield Farm
SCHOOL LA
HILL VIEW
BICESTER RD
ASHFORD RISE
Little London Farm
Little London
BRILL RD
Poplar Farm
THE TURNPIKE
BROOKSIDE
MANOR RD
SUN CRES
Oakley Common
OXFORD RD
ELMWOOD CL
Manor Farm
BRADLEY CL
Oakley
Royal Oak (PH)
Sch
Oakley Wood
Jericho Farm
MEADOW CL
FENNIMORE CL
WORMINGHALL RD
Smithy
MILL RD
ORCHARD CL
COLLEGE CRES
Hedges Farm
Sewage Works (disused)
Moorley's Farm
Shabbington Wood
Woodground Farm
Waterslade Farm
Airfield (disused)
Joshua Farm
4
3
2
1
13
12
11
10
62
63
64

110

123

96

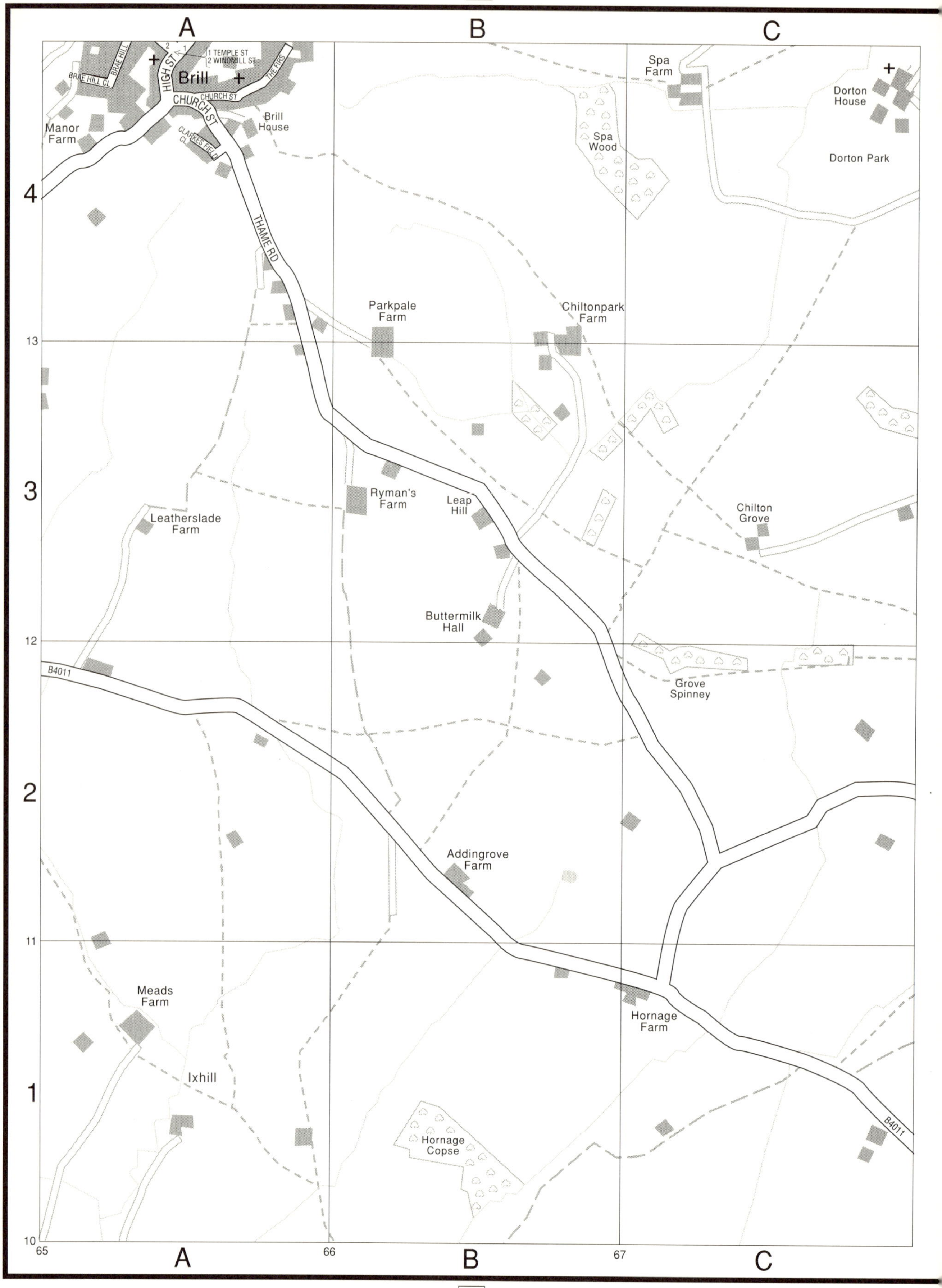
A
B
C
Spa Farm
Dorton House
Dorton Park
1 TEMPLE ST
2 WINDMILL ST
BRAE HILL
BRAE HILL CL
HIGH ST
Brill
THE FIRS
CHURCH ST
CHURCH ST
CLARKES FIELD CL
Brill House
Manor Farm
Spa Wood
4
THAME RD
Parkpale Farm
Chiltonpark Farm
13
3
Ryman's Farm
Leap Hill
Leatherslade Farm
Chilton Grove
Buttermilk Hall
12
B4011
Grove Spinney
2
Addingrove Farm
11
Meads Farm
Hornage Farm
Ixhill
1
Hornage Copse
B4011
10
65
66
67
A
B
C

109

124

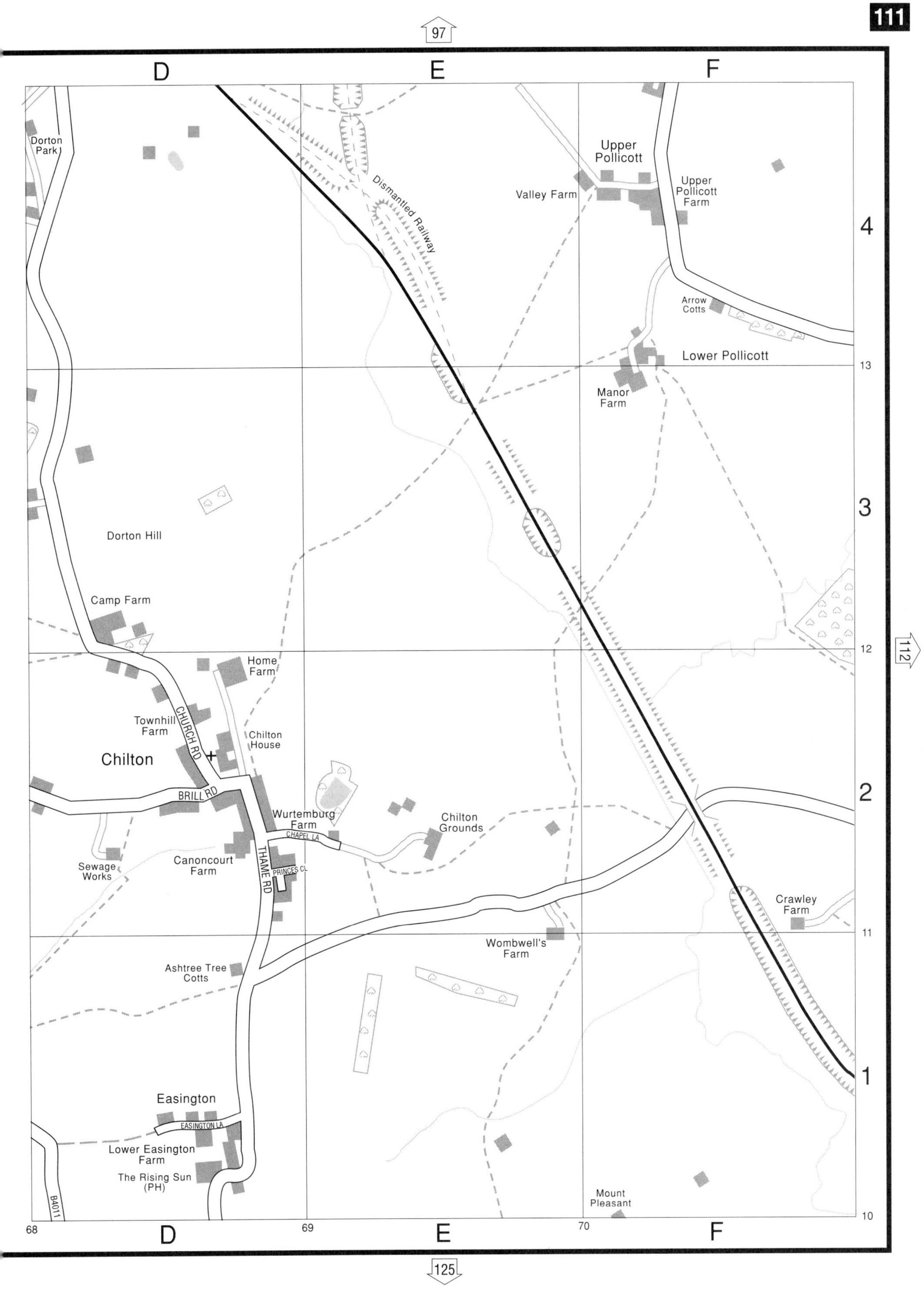
97
D
E
F
Dorton Park
Upper Pollicott
Valley Farm
Upper Pollicott Farm
Dismantled Railway
4
Arrow Cotts
Lower Pollicott
13
Manor Farm
3
Dorton Hill
Camp Farm
12
112
Home Farm
Townhill Farm
CHURCH RD
Chilton House
Chilton
BRILL RD
2
Wurtemburg Farm
Chilton Grounds
CHAPEL LA
Sewage Works
Canoncourt Farm
THAME RD
PRINCES CL
Crawley Farm
11
Wombwell's Farm
Ashtree Tree Cotts
1
Easington
EASINGTON LA
Lower Easington Farm
The Rising Sun (PH)
B4011
Mount Pleasant
10
68
69
70
125

98

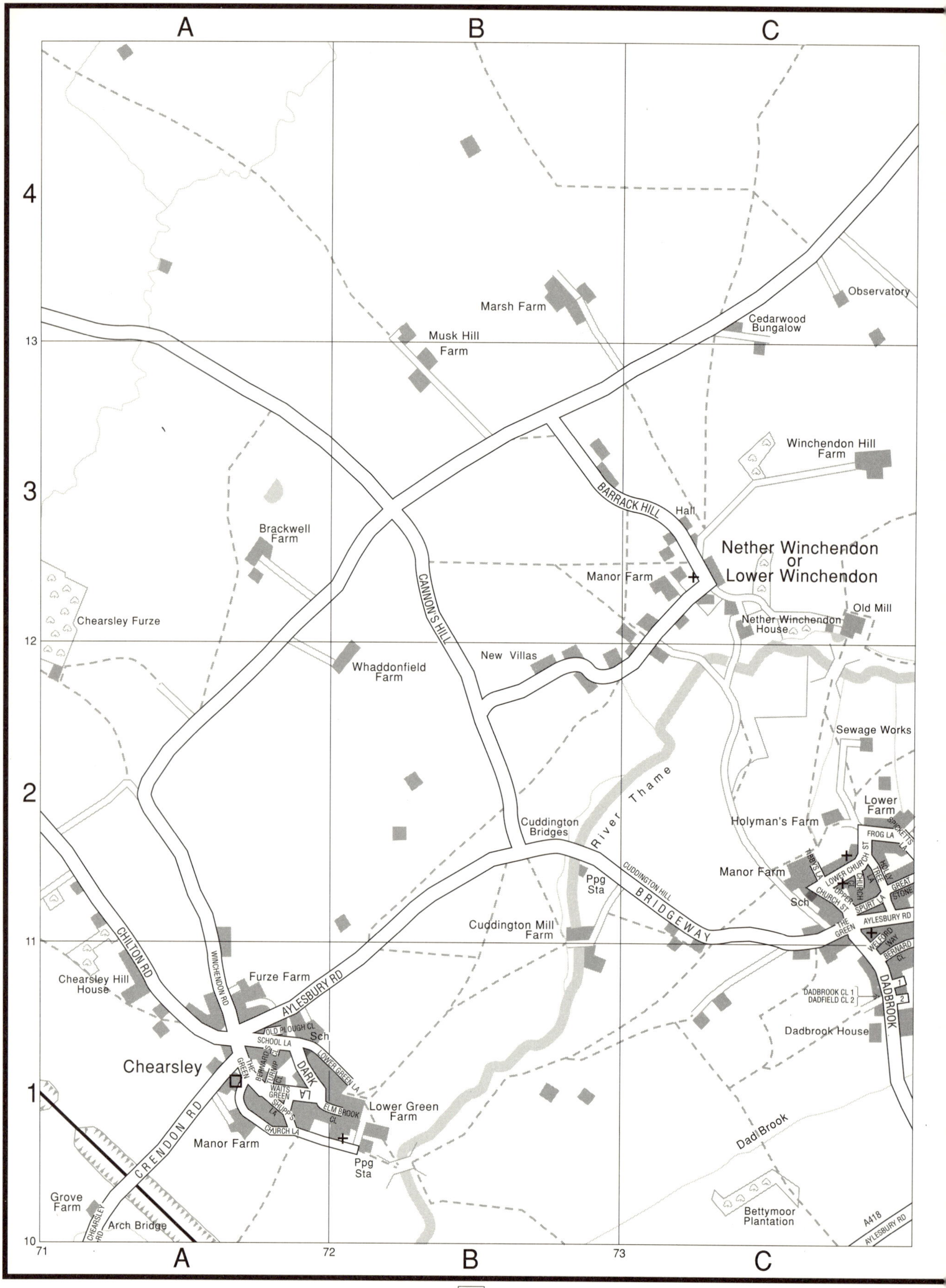
A
B
C
4
3
2
1
13
12
11
10
71
72
73
Marsh Farm
Musk Hill
Farm
Observatory
Cedarwood
Bungalow
Winchendon Hill
Farm
BARRACK HILL
Hall
Nether Winchendon
or
Lower Winchendon
Manor Farm
Old Mill
Nether Winchendon
House
Brackwell
Farm
Chearsley Furze
CANNON'S HILL
Whaddonfield
Farm
New Villas
Sewage Works
River Thame
Lower
Farm
Holyman's Farm
Cuddington
Bridges
FROG LA
SPICKETTS LA
LOWER CHURCH ST
CHURCH ST
UPPER CHURCH ST
HOLLY TREE LA
SPURT LA
GREAT STONE
Manor Farm
Ppg
Sta
CUDDINGTON HILL
BRIDGEWAY
Sch
THE GREEN
AYLESBURY RD
WELFORD WAY
BERNARD CL
Cuddington Mill
Farm
CHILTON RD
WINCHENDON RD
Furze Farm
AYLESBURY RD
Chearsley Hill
House
DADBROOK CL 1
DADFIELD CL 2
DADBROOK
Dadbrook House
OLD PLOUGH CL
SCHOOL LA
Sch
Chearsley
THE GREEN
BERNARD'S CL
TURNIP
WAITS GREEN
DARK LA
LOWER GREEN LA
SHUPP'S LA
ELM BROOK CL
CHURCH LA
Lower Green
Farm
Manor Farm
CRENDON RD
Ppg
Sta
Dad Brook
Grove
Farm
CHEARSLEY RD
Arch Bridge
Bettymoor
Plantation
A418
AYLESBURY RD
A
B
C

111

126

99

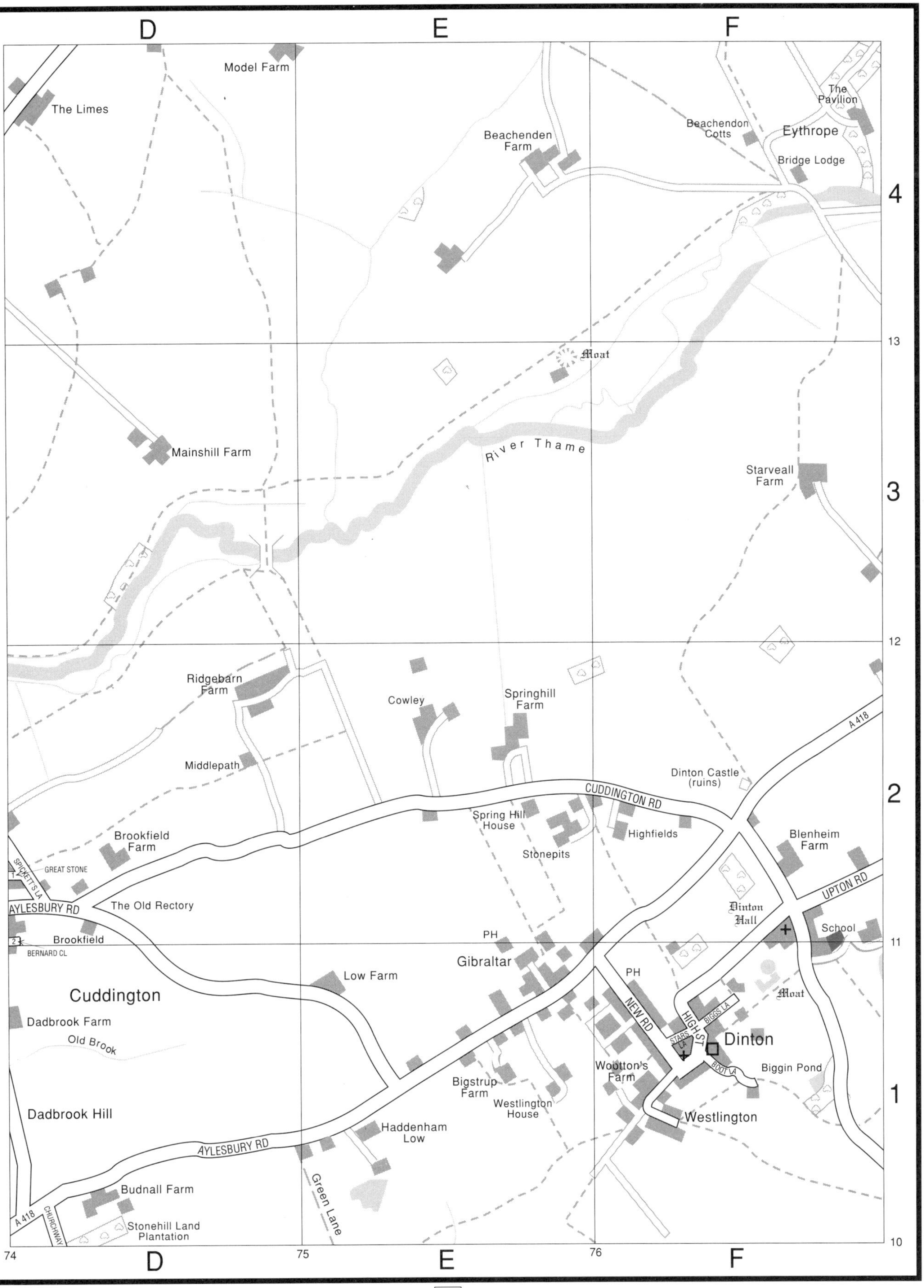
D
E
F
Model Farm
The Limes
Beachenden Farm
Beachendon Cotts
The Pavilion
Eythrope
Bridge Lodge
4
13
Moat
Mainshill Farm
River Thame
Starveall Farm
3
12
Ridgebarn Farm
Cowley
Springhill Farm
Middlepath
Dinton Castle (ruins)
A 418
CUDDINGTON RD
2
Brookfield Farm
Spring Hill House
Highfields
Blenheim Farm
Stonepits
SPICKETT'S LA
GREAT STONE
UPTON RD
AYLESBURY RD
The Old Rectory
Dinton Hall
School
Brookfield
PH
11
BERNARD CL
Gibraltar
PH
Low Farm
Moat
Cuddington
NEW RD
HIGH ST
BIGGS LA
STARS LA
Dadbrook Farm
Dinton
Old Brook
Wootton's Farm
BOOT LA
Biggin Pond
Bigstrup Farm
1
Westlington House
Dadbrook Hill
Westlington
Haddenham Low
AYLESBURY RD
Green Lane
Budnall Farm
A 418
CHURCHWAY
Stonehill Land Plantation
10
74
D
75
E
76
F

114

127

100

A
B
C
Bear Brook
Coldharbour Farm
Eythrope Park
River Thame
Weir Lodge
Weir
North Buckinghamshire Way
Littleworth Farm
Whaddon Hill Farm
Tumulus
Arthur's Gorse
Burn Hill
Lower Hartwell
Lower Hartwell Farm
The Nursery
Botts Furlong Farm
Cemy
Upper Hartwell
Barnet's Close
Hartwell House
Park Hill
EYETHROPE RD
BELLE VUE
COTTAGE GROUNDS
CROMHAMSTONE
THE SPIERT
OXFORD RD
STONE CROFT
MANOR FARM CL
Sch
DARNILL RD
LONG FURLONG
THE GLEBE
CHURCH WAY
ROUND HILL
LEE CRES
CHILTERN CL
CHILTERN AVE
Beech Walk
A418
MEADOWAY
MAYFLOWER CL
Stone
BISHOPSTONE RD
PH
WILLOWMEAD
Hospital
Colley Farm
Stone House
PORTWAY
SEDRUP LA
BITTENHAM CL
Peveral Court
Upton
UPTON RD
HOMESTEAD FARM
Lower Farm
LOWER FARM GATE
Alwyn Lawn
Sedrup
BISHOPSTONE
Wallace Farm
Sewage Works
Meadow Cottages
Pasture Farm
Chilboro Hill Farm
4
3
2
1
13
12
11
10
77
78
79

113

128

101

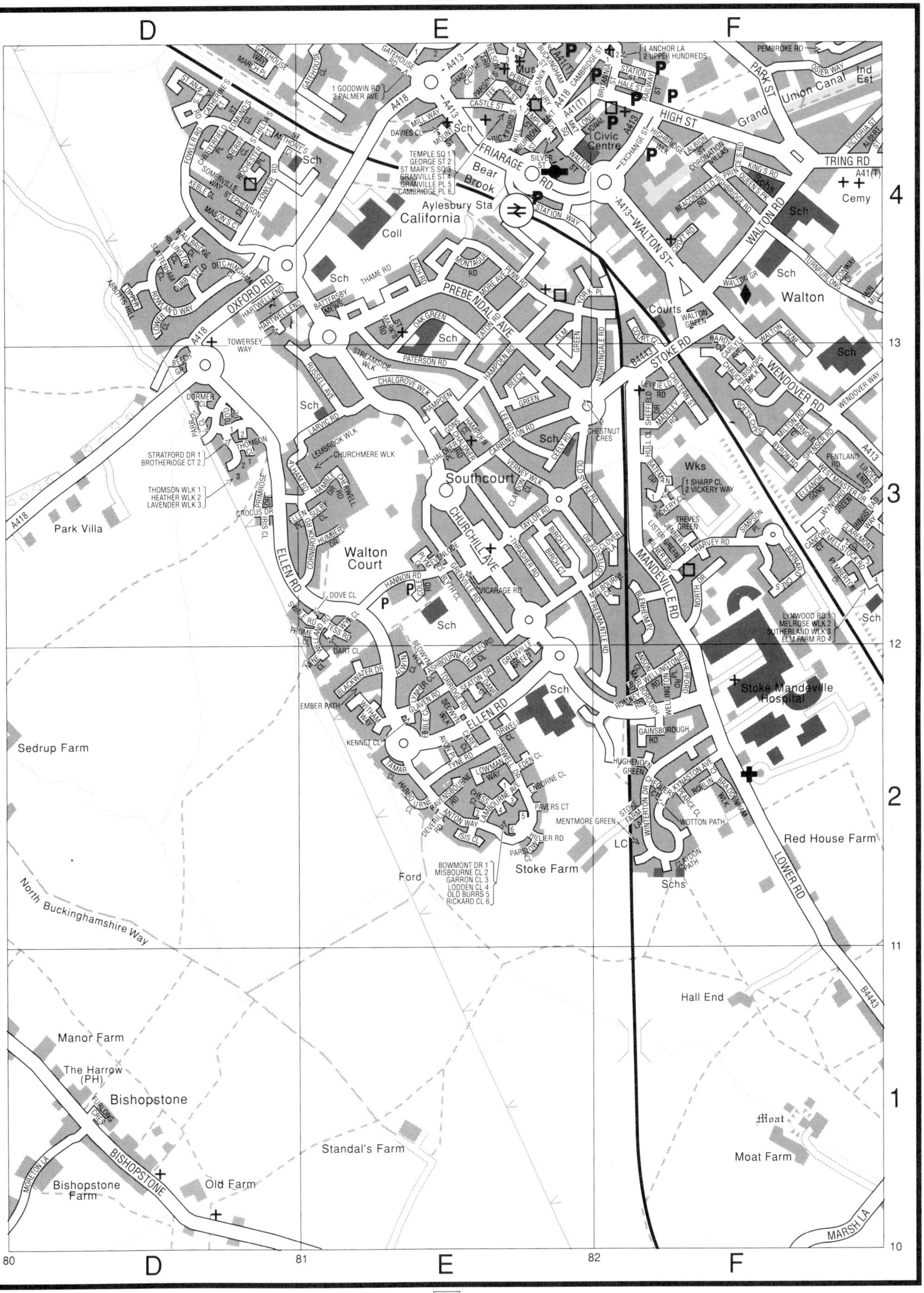

D
E
F
California
Coll
Aylesbury Sta
Civic Centre
Mus
Bear Brook
Grand Union Canal
Ind Est
HIGH ST
TRING RD
FRIARAGE RD
WALTON ST
WALTON RD
STOKE RD
Walton
Courts
Cemy
Southcourt
Walton Court
OXFORD RD
ELLEN RD
CHURCHILL AVE
PREBENDAL AVE
MANDEVILLE RD
WENDOVER RD
Wks
Stoke Mandeville Hospital
Red House Farm
Stoke Farm
Ford
Park Villa
Sedrup Farm
North Buckinghamshire Way
Hall End
Manor Farm
The Harrow (PH)
Bishopstone
BISHOPSTONE
Bishopstone Farm
Old Farm
Standal's Farm
Moat
Moat Farm
MARSH LA
LOWER RD
B4443
A418
A413
A41(T)
Sch
Schs
80
81
82
10
11
12
13
1
2
3
4

116

129

102

A
B
C
1
2
3
4
10
11
12
13
83
84
85
AYLESBURY
Oak Farm
Broughton
Manor Farm
Moat
Moat
Schs
Victoria Park
TRING RD
BROUGHTON LA
RICHMOND RD
A41(T)
NORTHFIELD RD
1 SOUTHFIELD RD
2 EASTFIELD RD
NARBERTH DR
COMO RD
HENRY RD
BARNSBURY AVE
OAKFIELD RD
CAMPION RD
MALVERN RD
BRAMCOTE CL
BROUGHTON CL
PARTON RD
LUDLOW PL
CONNAUGHT RD
HERON CL
CLINTON CRES
WALTON WAY
KING EDWARD AVE
HAZEL AVE
WINDSOR RD
BUTTERMERE
ALLONBY WAY
PENRITH WAY
WELTON RD
CUMBERLAND CL
REGENT RD
MIDDLE RD
LIMES AVE
CRAIGWELL AVE
THE PADDOCK
QUEENS MEAD
DOVER HEDGE
GRASS HAYS
NEW MEADOW
BEAUFORT CL
Akeman Street
ROMAN ROAD
ASTON CLINTON RD
BURNHAM FIELD
Broughton Farm
Weston Mead Farm
Sch
Sch
Sch
1 ASH GR
2 TURNFURLONG
WENDOVER WAY
WINDERMERE CL
NORTHUMBERLAND AVE
HOWARD AVE
LANCASTER RD
BEDGROVE
APLIN RD
GOOSEN GREEN
GREETHAN RD
WELBECK AVE
WYMERING RD
STAVELEY CL
LONG MEADOW
STRATTON GREEN
TINTERN WAY
CHADWELL PATH
WOODSTOCK CL
WESTMORLAND AVE
KENDAL CL
TURNFURLONG LA
JARVIS CL
1 RINGSTEAD WAY
2 LYNWOOD RD
A413
SOUTHWOLD CL
BRADEN CL
ORMESBY WAY
OULTON CL
EARLSWOOD CL
CRESWICK MEADOW
CROSLAND RD
DARLEY CL
CAMBORNE AVE
CALDICOT CL
EDGECOMBE RD
PEVENSEY CL
HEATH CL
AMBLESIDE
MIDHURST CL
Schs
PIKE CORNER
INGRAM AVE
FINMERE CRES
HULBERT END
DORSET PL
Westend Ditch
A41(T)
Bedgrove
Bedgrove Park
PEVERIL RD
BALLARD CL
LANGDON AVE
STUDLAND
HAMBLEDON
GRASMERE
HERSTON CL
DEHAM CL
1 COPPIDWELL DR
2 HAVEN SHAW CL
CHARMFIELD RD
ASHFORD
ELM FARM RD
DEAN CL
Sch
WAIVERS WAY
WEILL RD
KINGSLAND RD
JASMINE
EASTCOTE RD
HOLLIS CROFT
WYCOMBE
PATRICK WAY
EDWARD CL
EDWARD WALK
1 MARSHAM CL
2 THORPE CL
1 LOWBROOK CL
2 LYDIARD CL
3 ELIZABETH CL
CHARLES CL
JANE CL
HANSON WAY
WENDOVER RD
Hampden Hall
NEW RD
Rectory Farm
Club House
Golf Course
Weston Turville
Sch
WALTON PL
MIDDLE FIELD
PH
QUAKERS MEAD
BROOK END
B4544
THE HYDE
HOME CL
WATERMILL WAY
BAKERS WLK
BATES LA
PENFOLD
MAIN ST
WEST END
West End
Moat
Manor Farm
MANOR CL
BARLEY CL
ELM CL
GLEBE
BRIDLEWAY
SCHOOL LA
WILLIAM BURT CL
CHURCH LA
CHURCH WLK
Motte & Bailey
WORLD'S END LA
West End Farm
MARROWAY
B4544
A413
Stoke Mandeville
Malthouse Farm
Manor Farm
B4443
LOWER RD
MARSH LA
ESKDALE RD
IRVINE DR
SWALLOW LA
DORCHESTER CL
WALNUT CL
A4010
STATION RD
LINCOLN
COOMBE
MEADOW BANK
LIGO AVE
Stoke Mandeville Station
HAMPDEN PL
ORCHARD CL
HALLGROVE END
BRUDENELL DR
Wool Pack (PH)
CHESTNUT WAY
YEW TREE CL
CHAPEL LA
RISBOROUGH RD
A4010
Alberta Farm
Sch

115

130

103

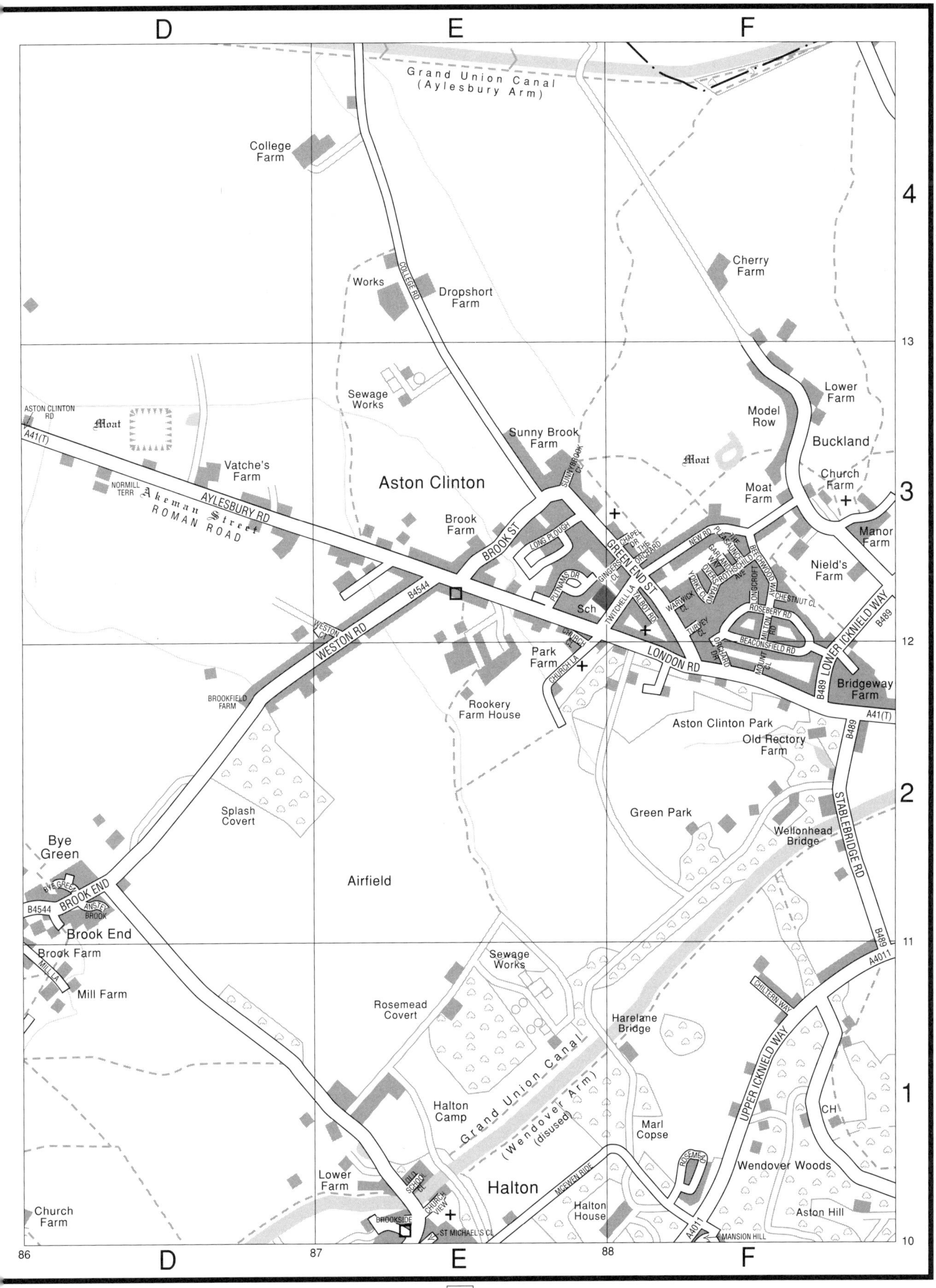
D
E
F
Grand Union Canal
(Aylesbury Arm)
College Farm
4
Cherry Farm
Works
Dropshort Farm
13
Sewage Works
Lower Farm
Model Row
ASTON CLINTON RD
Moat
A41(T)
Sunny Brook Farm
Buckland
Moat
Vatche's Farm
Aston Clinton
Moat Farm
Church Farm
NORMILL TERR
Akeman Street
ROMAN ROAD
AYLESBURY RD
3
Brook Farm
BROOK ST
LONG PLOUGH
GREEN END ST
Manor Farm
Nield's Farm
PUTNAMS DR
B4544
Sch
TWITCHELL LA
TALBOT RD
CHESTNUT CL
ROSEBERY RD
LOWER ICKNIELD WAY
B489
WESTON CL
WESTON RD
Park Farm
CHURCH LA
LONDON RD
BEACONSFIELD RD
12
BROOKFIELD FARM
Rookery Farm House
Bridgeway Farm
A41(T)
Aston Clinton Park
Old Rectory Farm
B489
2
Splash Covert
Green Park
Wellonhead Bridge
STABLEBRIDGE RD
Bye Green
Airfield
BROOK END
B4544
Brook End
B489
11
Brook Farm
Sewage Works
A4011
MILL LA
Mill Farm
Rosemead Covert
CHILTERN WAY
Harelane Bridge
Grand Union Canal
(Wendover Arm)
(disused)
1
Halton Camp
UPPER ICKNIELD WAY
CH
Marl Copse
Lower Farm
Wendover Woods
OLD SCHOOL CL
Halton
MCEWEN RIDE
ROSEMEAD
Church Farm
CHURCH VIEW
Halton House
Aston Hill
BROOKSIDE
ST MICHAEL'S CL
A4011
MANSION HILL
10
86
87
88
D
E
F

118

131

104

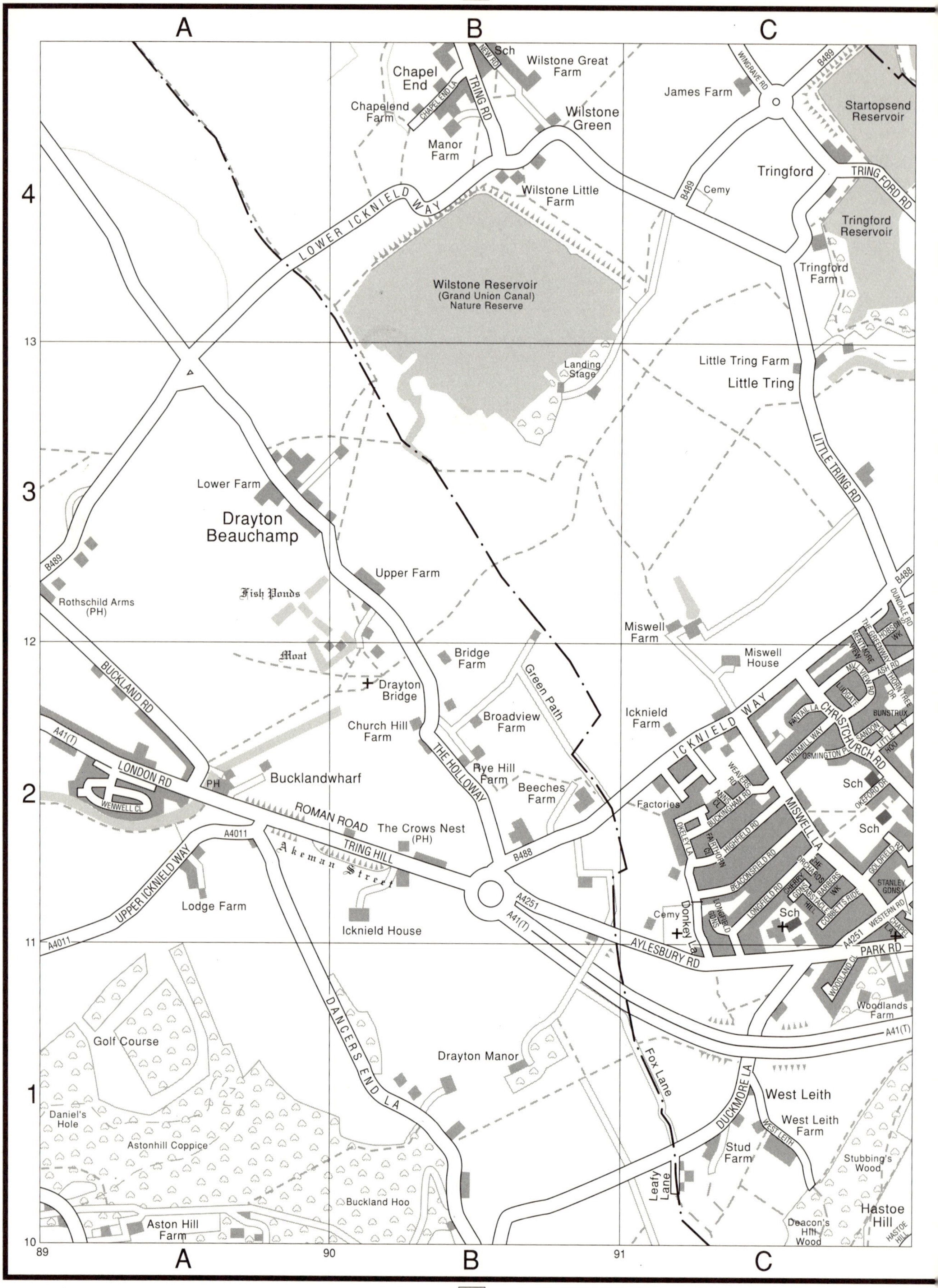

A
B
C
4
3
2
1
13
12
11
10
89
90
91
Chapel End
Chapelend Farm
Manor Farm
Sch
Wilstone Great Farm
Wilstone Green
James Farm
Startopsend Reservoir
Tringford
Cemy
Wilstone Little Farm
LOWER ICKNIELD WAY
Tringford Reservoir
Tringford Farm
Wilstone Reservoir
(Grand Union Canal)
Nature Reserve
Little Tring Farm
Little Tring
Landing Stage
LITTLE TRING RD
Lower Farm
Drayton Beauchamp
Upper Farm
Rothschild Arms (PH)
Fish Ponds
Moat
Miswell Farm
Miswell House
Bridge Farm
Drayton Bridge
Green Path
Icknield Farm
ICKNIELD WAY
BUCKLAND RD
Broadview Farm
Church Hill Farm
Rye Hill Farm
Beeches Farm
LONDON RD
Bucklandwharf
THE HOLLOWAY
PH
ROMAN ROAD
The Crows Nest (PH)
TRING HILL
Akeman Street
Factories
MISWELL LA
Sch
Sch
UPPER ICKNIELD WAY
Lodge Farm
Icknield House
Cemy
Donkey La
AYLESBURY RD
PARK RD
Woodlands Farm
Golf Course
DANCERS END LA
Drayton Manor
Fox Lane
DUCKMORE LA
West Leith
West Leith Farm
Daniel's Hole
Astonhill Coppice
Stud Farm
Stubbing's Wood
Leafy Lane
Buckland Hoo
Aston Hill Farm
Deacon's Hill Wood
Hastoe Hill
B489
B488
A41(T)
A4011
A4251
TRING RD
NEW RD
WINGRAVE RD
TRING FORD RD
CHRISTCHURCH RD
WENWELL CL

117

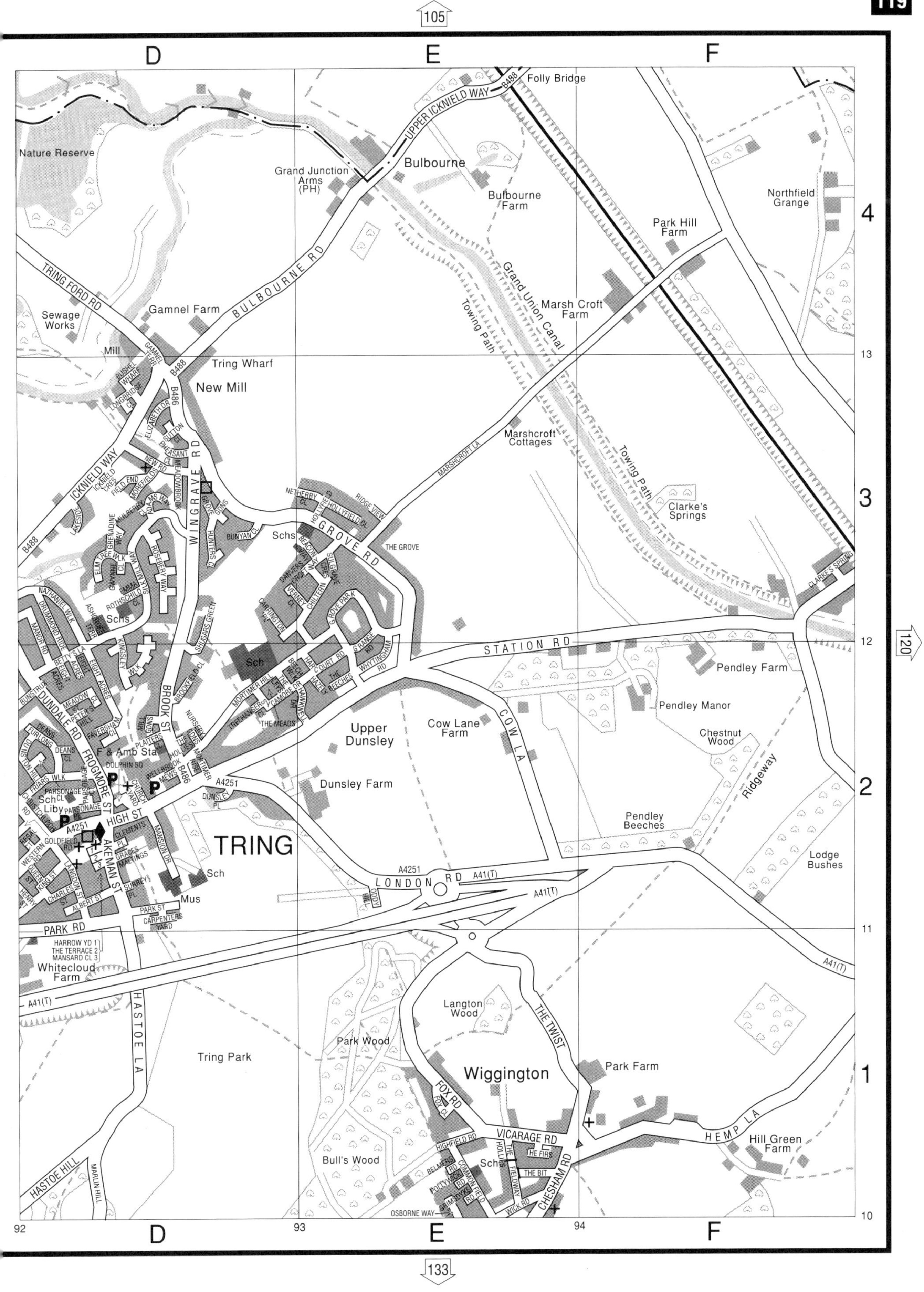
105
D
E
F
Folly Bridge
UPPER ICKNIELD WAY
B488
Nature Reserve
Grand Junction Arms (PH)
Bulbourne
Bulbourne Farm
Northfield Grange
Park Hill Farm
4
TRING FORD RD
BULBOURNE RD
Grand Union Canal
Towing Path
Marsh Croft Farm
Sewage Works
Gamnel Farm
Mill
13
Tring Wharf
New Mill
Marshcroft Cottages
MARSHCROFT LA
ICKNIELD WAY
WINGRAVE RD
Towing Path
Clarke's Springs
3
GROVE RD
Schs
THE GROVE
CLARKE'S SPRING
Schs
Sch
STATION RD
12
120
Pendley Farm
Pendley Manor
Chestnut Wood
Upper Dunsley
Cow Lane Farm
COW LA
BROOK ST
F & Amb Sta
Dunsley Farm
Ridgeway
2
FROGMORE ST
HIGH ST
A4251
Sch
Liby
Pendley Beeches
Lodge Bushes
TRING
Sch
AKEMAN ST
LONDON RD
A41(T)
Mus
PARK RD
11
HARROW YD 1
THE TERRACE 2
MANSARD CL 3
Whitecloud Farm
A41(T)
HASTOE LA
Langton Wood
THE TWIST
Tring Park
Park Wood
Wiggington
Park Farm
1
FOX RD
VICARAGE RD
HEMP LA
Hill Green Farm
Bull's Wood
Schs
CHESHAM RD
HASTOE HILL
MARLIN HILL
OSBORNE WAY
10
92
D
93
E
94
F
133

106

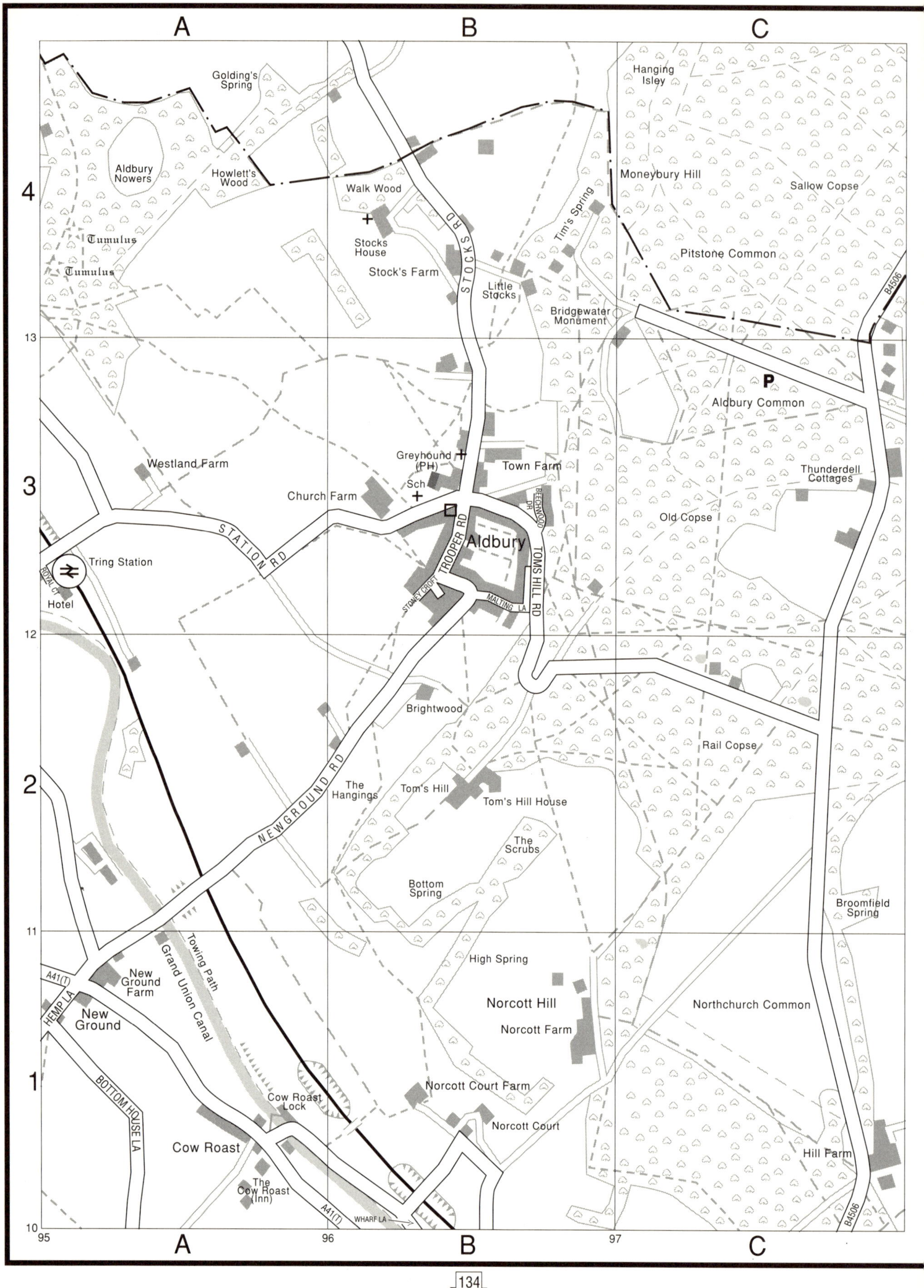
A
B
C
Golding's Spring
Hanging Isley
Aldbury Nowers
Howlett's Wood
Walk Wood
Moneybury Hill
Sallow Copse
Tim's Spring
Tumulus
Tumulus
Stocks House
Stock's Farm
STOCKS RD
Pitstone Common
Little Stocks
Bridgewater Monument
B4506
P
Aldbury Common
Greyhound (PH)
Westland Farm
Town Farm
Thunderdell Cottages
Sch
Church Farm
BEECHWOOD DR
Old Copse
STATION RD
TROOPER RD
Aldbury
TOMS HILL RD
Tring Station
ROYAL CT
STONEY CROFT
MALTING LA
Hotel
Brightwood
Rail Copse
NEWGROUND RD
The Hangings
Tom's Hill
Tom's Hill House
The Scrubs
Bottom Spring
Broomfield Spring
Towing Path
Grand Union Canal
High Spring
A41(T)
New Ground Farm
Norcott Hill
Northchurch Common
HEMP LA
New Ground
Norcott Farm
BOTTOM HOUSE LA
Cow Roast Lock
Norcott Court Farm
Norcott Court
Cow Roast
Hill Farm
The Cow Roast (Inn)
A41(T)
WHARF LA
B4506
4
13
3
12
2
11
1
10
95
96
97
119

134

107

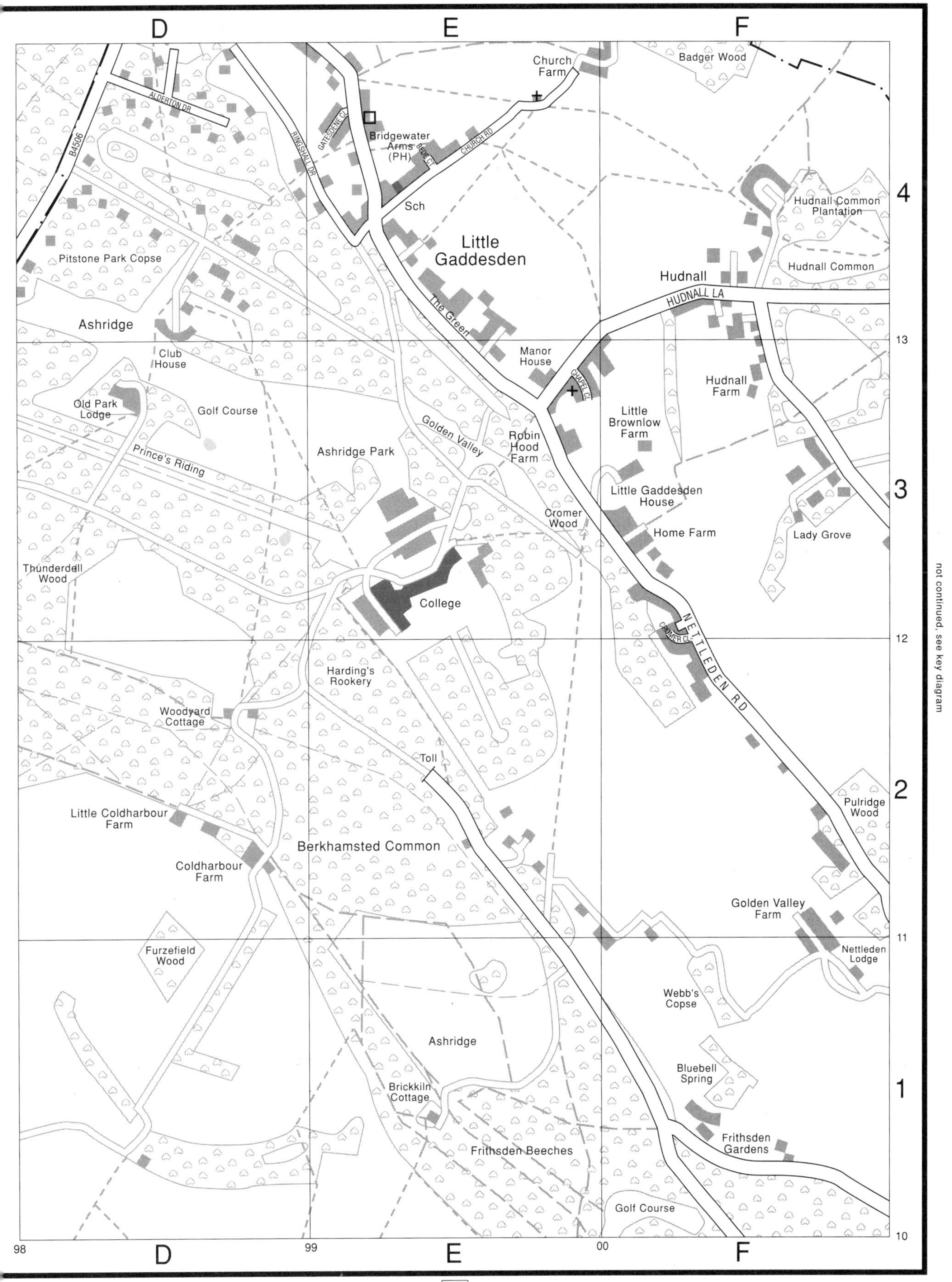
D
E
F
Church Farm
Badger Wood
Bridgewater Arms (PH)
ALDERTON DR
B4506
RINGSHALL DR
GATESDENE CL
BEDE CL
CHURCH RD
Sch
Little Gaddesden
Hudnall Common Plantation
Hudnall Common
Hudnall
HUDNALL LA
Pitstone Park Copse
Ashridge
The Green
Manor House
CHAPEL CL
Club House
Old Park Lodge
Golf Course
Hudnall Farm
Little Brownlow Farm
Golden Valley
Robin Hood Farm
Prince's Riding
Ashridge Park
Little Gaddesden House
Cromer Wood
Home Farm
Lady Grove
Thunderdell Wood
College
CROMER CL
NETTLEDEN RD
Harding's Rookery
Woodyard Cottage
Toll
Pulridge Wood
Little Coldharbour Farm
Berkhamsted Common
Coldharbour Farm
Golden Valley Farm
Furzefield Wood
Nettleden Lodge
Webb's Copse
Ashridge
Bluebell Spring
Brickkiln Cottage
Frithsden Gardens
Frithsden Beeches
Golf Course
4
13
3
12
2
11
1
10
98
99
00
not continued, see key diagram

135

108

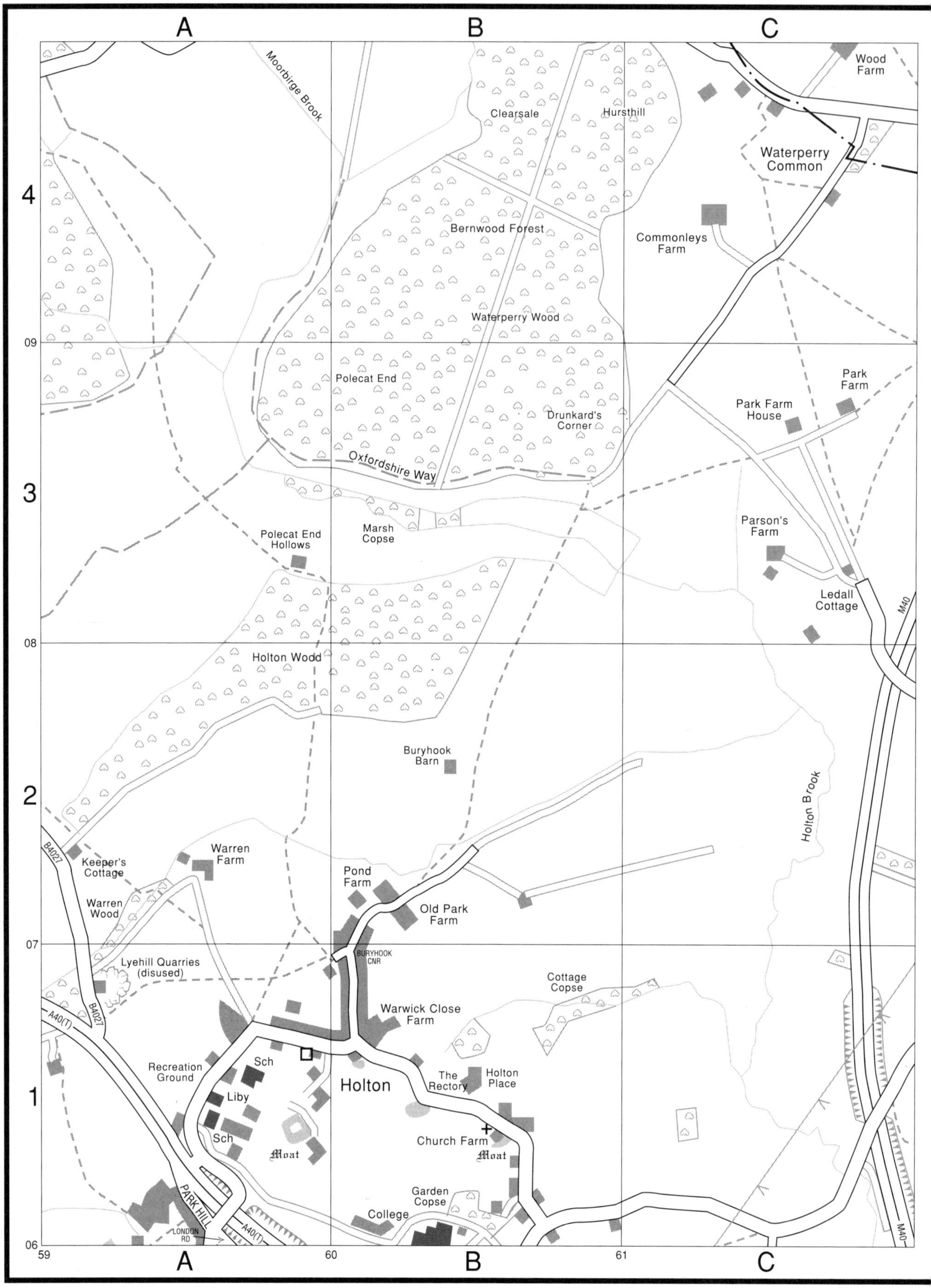

not continued, see key diagram

not continued, see key diagram

109

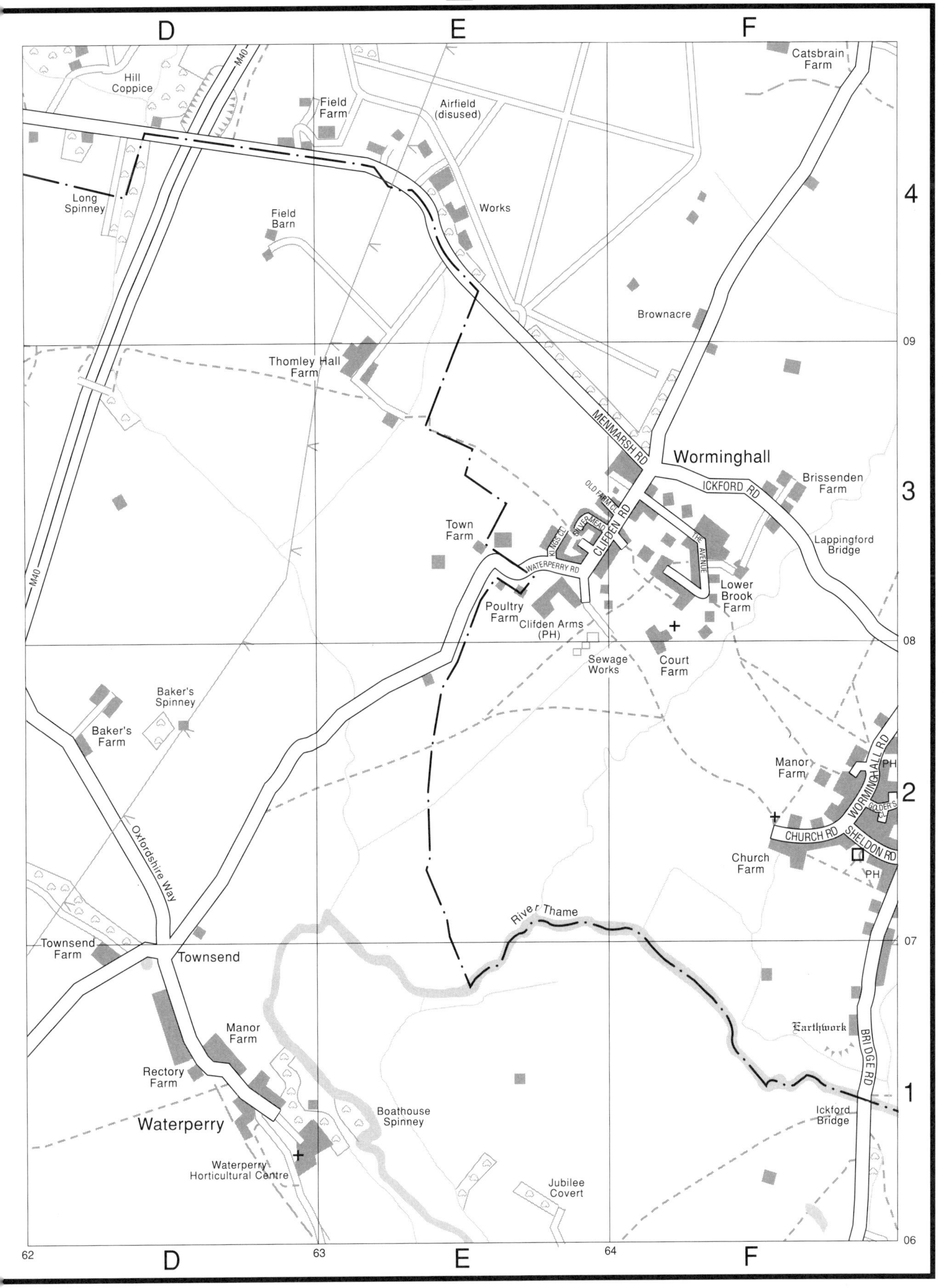
D
E
F
Hill
Coppice
M40
Field
Farm
Airfield
(disused)
Catsbrain
Farm
Long
Spinney
Field
Barn
Works
4
Brownacre
09
Thomley Hall
Farm
MENMARSH RD
Worminghall
ICKFORD RD
Brissenden
Farm
3
OLD FARM CL
SILVER MEAD
KINGS CL
CLIFDEN RD
THE AVENUE
Town
Farm
WATERPERRY RD
Lappingford
Bridge
Lower
Brook
Farm
Poultry
Farm
Clifden Arms
(PH)
Sewage
Works
Court
Farm
08
M40
Baker's
Spinney
Baker's
Farm
Manor
Farm
WORMINGHALL RD
PH
GOLDER'S CL
2
CHURCH RD
SHELDON RD
Church
Farm
PH
Oxfordshire Way
River Thame
Townsend
Farm
Townsend
07
Earthwork
BRIDGE RD
Manor
Farm
Rectory
Farm
1
Waterperry
Boathouse
Spinney
Ickford
Bridge
Waterperry
Horticultural Centre
Jubilee
Covert
06
62
63
64
D
E
F

124

110

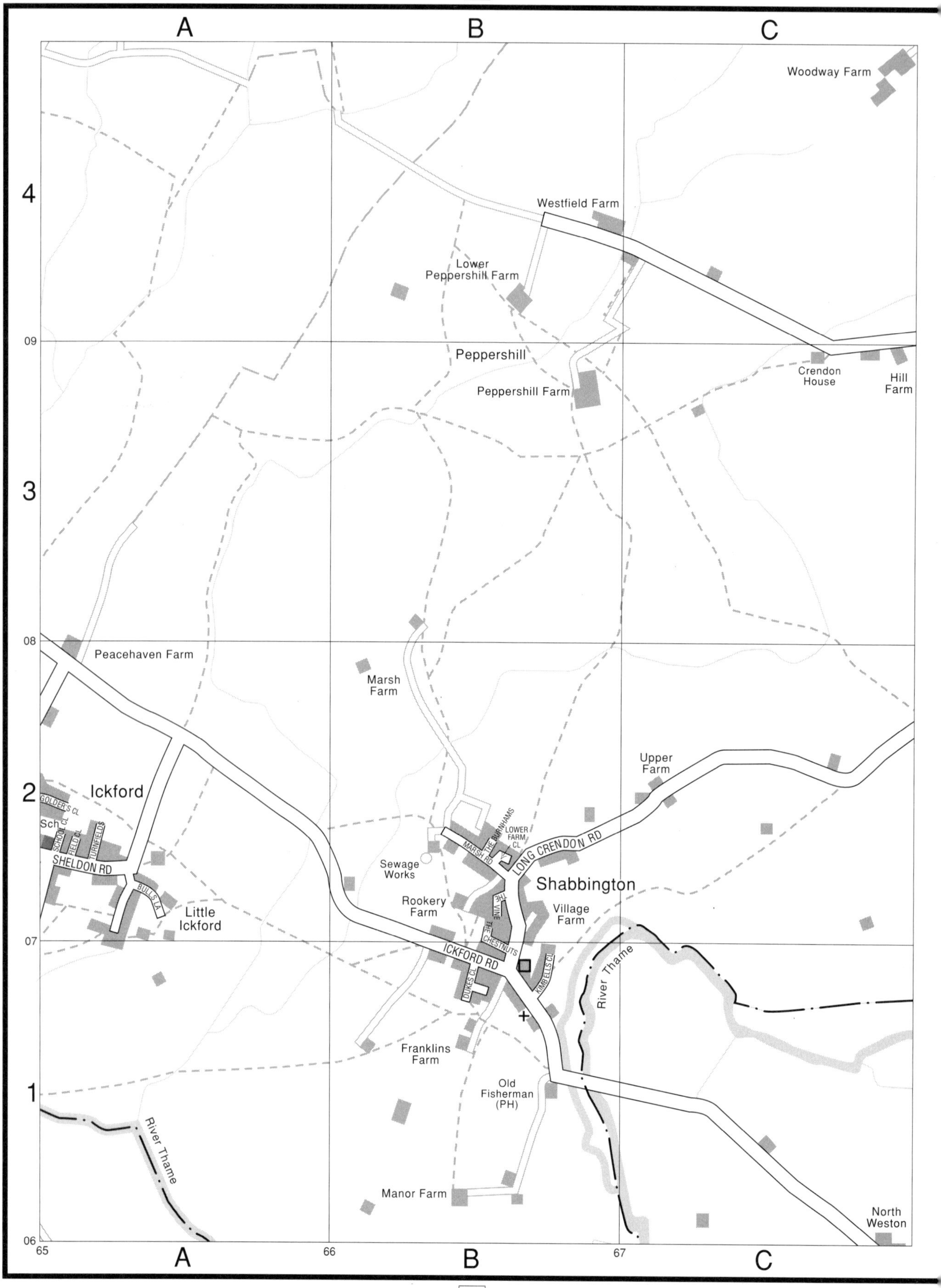
A
B
C
4
3
2
1
09
08
07
06
65
66
67
Woodway Farm
Westfield Farm
Lower Peppershill Farm
Peppershill
Peppershill Farm
Crendon House
Hill Farm
Peacehaven Farm
Marsh Farm
Upper Farm
Ickford
GOLDER'S CL
Sch
SCHOOL CL
FIELD CL
TURNFIELDS
SHELDON RD
BULLS LA
Little Ickford
Sewage Works
MARSH RD
THE BURNHAMS
LOWER FARM CL
LONG CRENDON RD
Shabbington
Rookery Farm
THE VINE
THE CHESTNUTS
Village Farm
ICKFORD RD
DUKES CL
KIMBELLS CL
River Thame
Franklins Farm
Old Fisherman (PH)
Manor Farm
North Weston

123

136

111

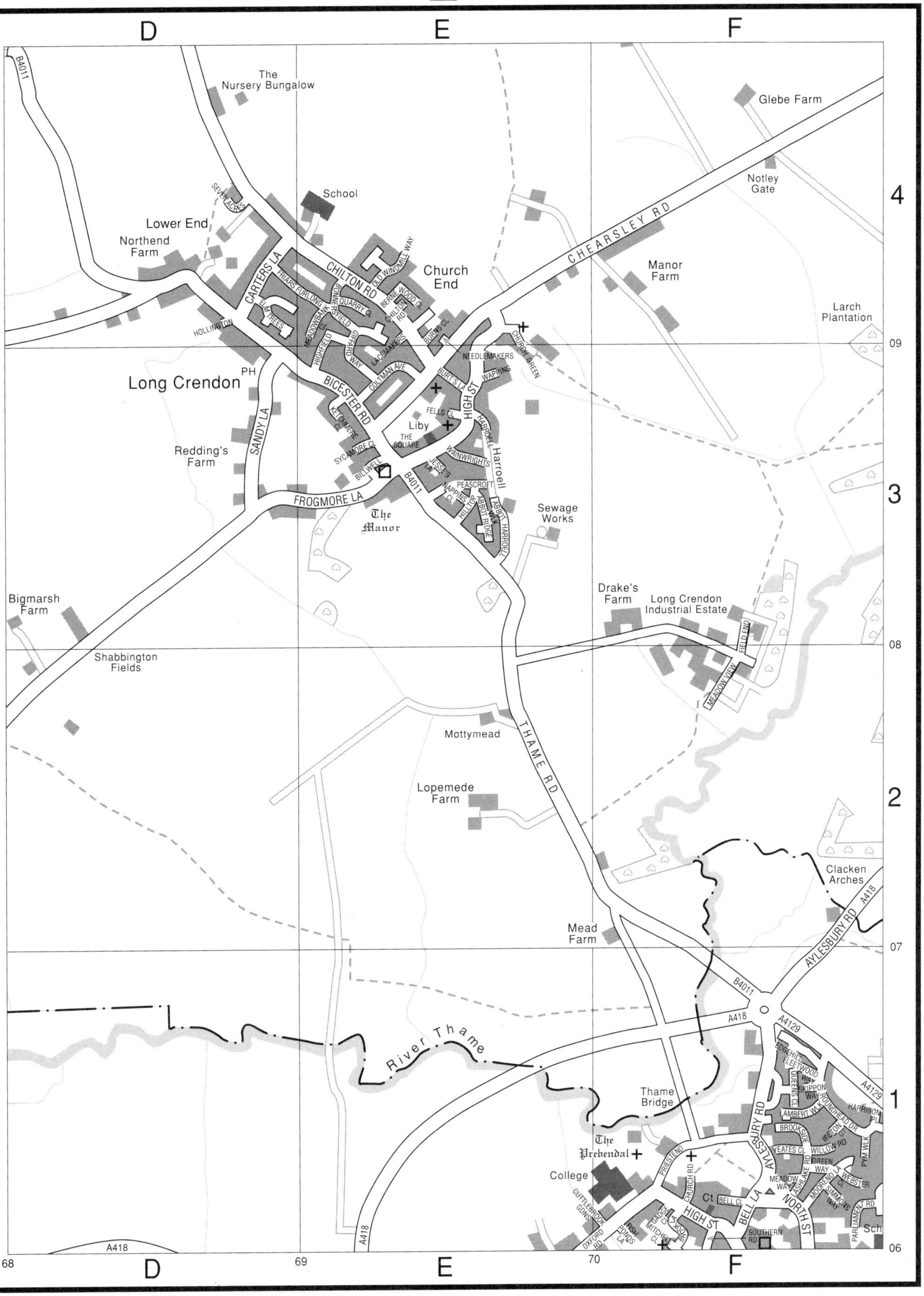

126

not continued, see key diagram

112

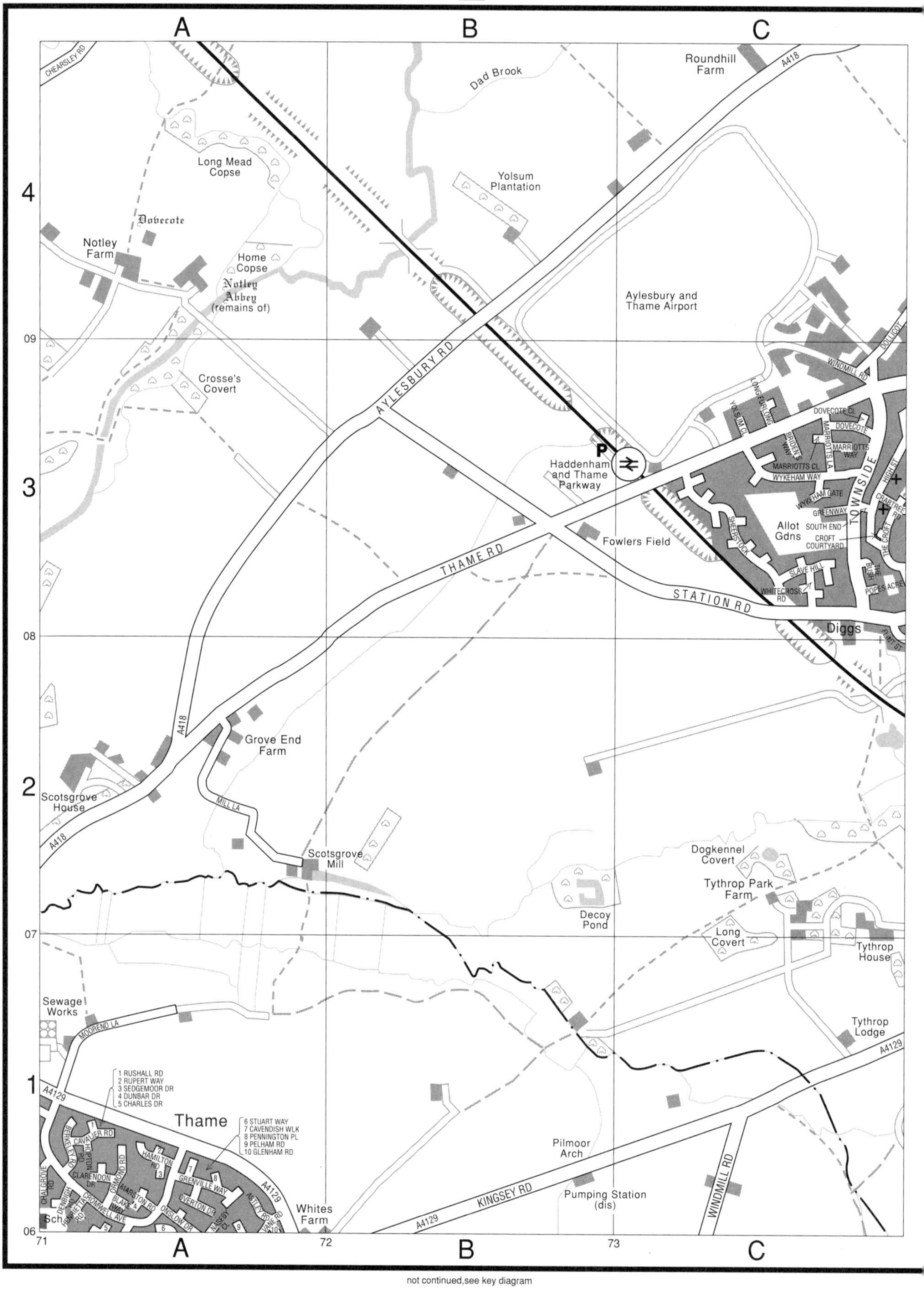

125

not continued,see key diagram

113

D
E
F
4
3
2
1
09
08
07
06
74
75
76
Townsend
Green Lane
THE CLAYS
ROSEMARY LA
WILLOW RISE
RUDD'S LA
DOLLICOTT
STOKES END
STOKES CROFT
THE CLOSES
FERN LA
STOKES LA
FRANKLIN CL
FRANKLIN RD
TANBRIDGE C
COTTLAND CLAY
RUN FURROW
BUTTFURLONG
STOKES CROFT
QUAKER'S MEDE
BANKS RD
Bradmoor Farm
Sch
F Sta
WOODWAYS
Liby
Sch
CHURCHWAY
Stockwell
STOCKWELL FURLONG
OLD MILL CL
ROBERTS RD
HARTS RD
WILLIS RD
CRABTREE RD
WYRE CL
Haddenham
THE GABLES
WHITE HART LA
Dragon Tail
GIBSON LA
THE PADDOCKS
Church End
STATION RD
Sch
FLINT ST
ASTON RD
Church Farm
Church Farm
Manor Farm
STANBRIDGE RD
Fairfields Farm
Folly Farm
Hewdon Farm
Moat
Mushroom Farm
Aston Mullins
The Manor
Aston Sandford
Stan Bridge
Wks
Aston Leys Farm
Old Farm
Kingsey
A4129
Manor Farm
Dove House Farm
Foxhill
Foxhill Covert
Shrove Furlong Farm
Whirlbush Farm
Blackbarn Farm
A4129

128

137

114

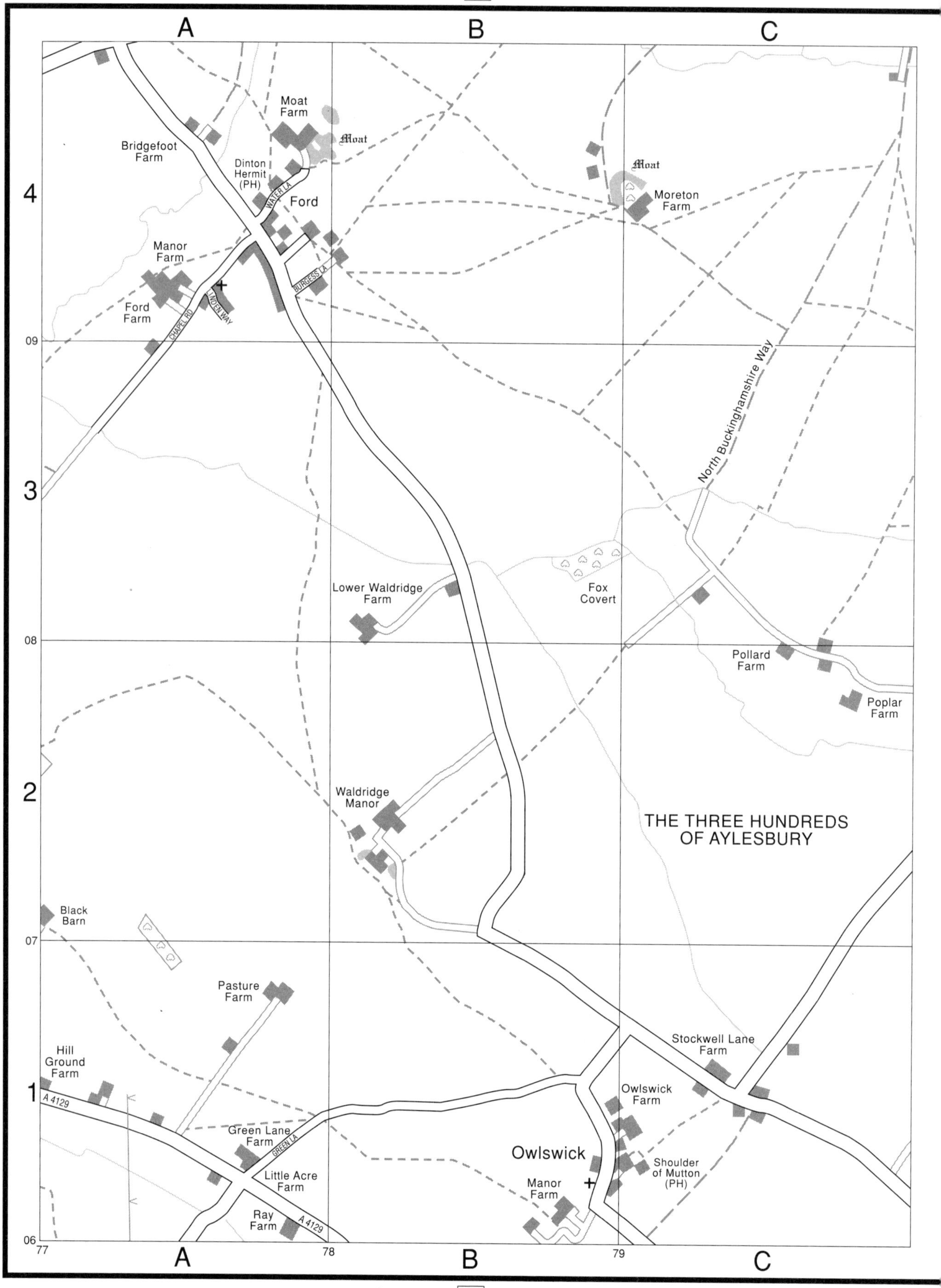

A
B
C
4
3
2
1
09
08
07
06
77
78
79
Moat Farm
Moat
Bridgefoot Farm
Dinton Hermit (PH)
WATER LA
Ford
Manor Farm
Ford Farm
BURGESS LA
CHAPEL RD
LINDEN WAY
Moreton Farm
North Buckinghamshire Way
Lower Waldridge Farm
Fox Covert
Pollard Farm
Poplar Farm
Waldridge Manor
THE THREE HUNDREDS OF AYLESBURY
Black Barn
Pasture Farm
Hill Ground Farm
A 4129
Green Lane Farm
GREEN LA
Little Acre Farm
Ray Farm
Stockwell Lane Farm
Owlswick Farm
Owlswick
Shoulder of Mutton (PH)

127

138

115

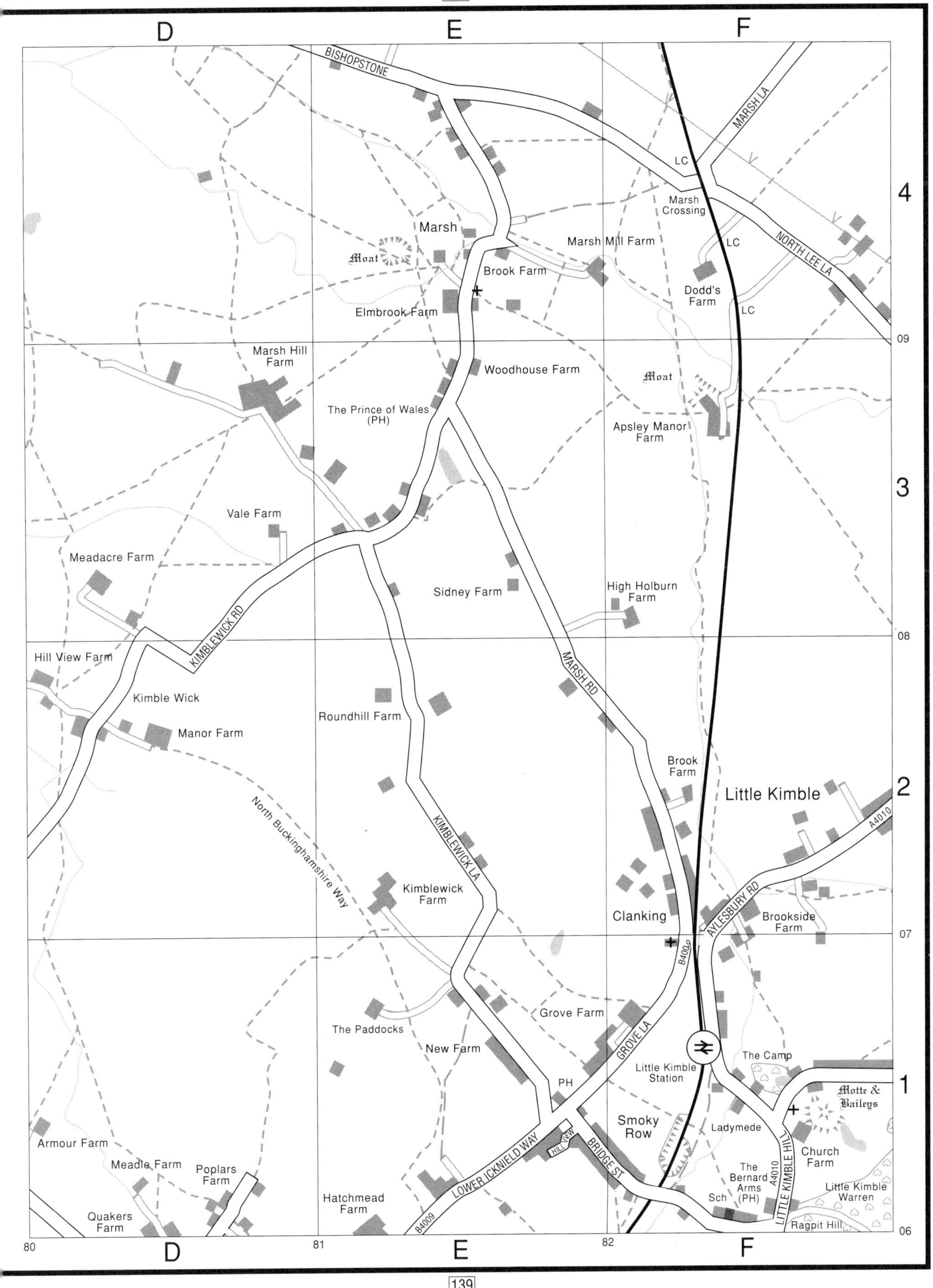
D
E
F
BISHOPSTONE
MARSH LA
LC
Marsh Crossing
NORTH LEE LA
Marsh
Moat
Marsh Mill Farm
Brook Farm
Dodd's Farm
Elmbrook Farm
Marsh Hill Farm
Woodhouse Farm
Moat
The Prince of Wales (PH)
Apsley Manor Farm
Vale Farm
Meadacre Farm
Sidney Farm
High Holburn Farm
KIMBLEWICK RD
Hill View Farm
MARSH RD
Kimble Wick
Roundhill Farm
Manor Farm
Brook Farm
Little Kimble
A4010
North Buckinghamshire Way
KIMBLEWICK LA
Kimblewick Farm
Clanking
AYLESBURY RD
Brookside Farm
B4009
Grove Farm
The Paddocks
New Farm
GROVE LA
Little Kimble Station
The Camp
PH
Motte & Baileys
Smoky Row
Ladymede
LOWER ICKNIELD WAY
HILL VIEW
BRIDGE ST
Church Farm
Armour Farm
Meadle Farm
Poplars Farm
The Bernard Arms (PH)
LITTLE KIMBLE HILL
A4010
Little Kimble Warren
Quakers Farm
Hatchmead Farm
Sch
B4009
Ragpit Hill
4
3
2
1
09
08
07
06
80
81
82

130

139

116

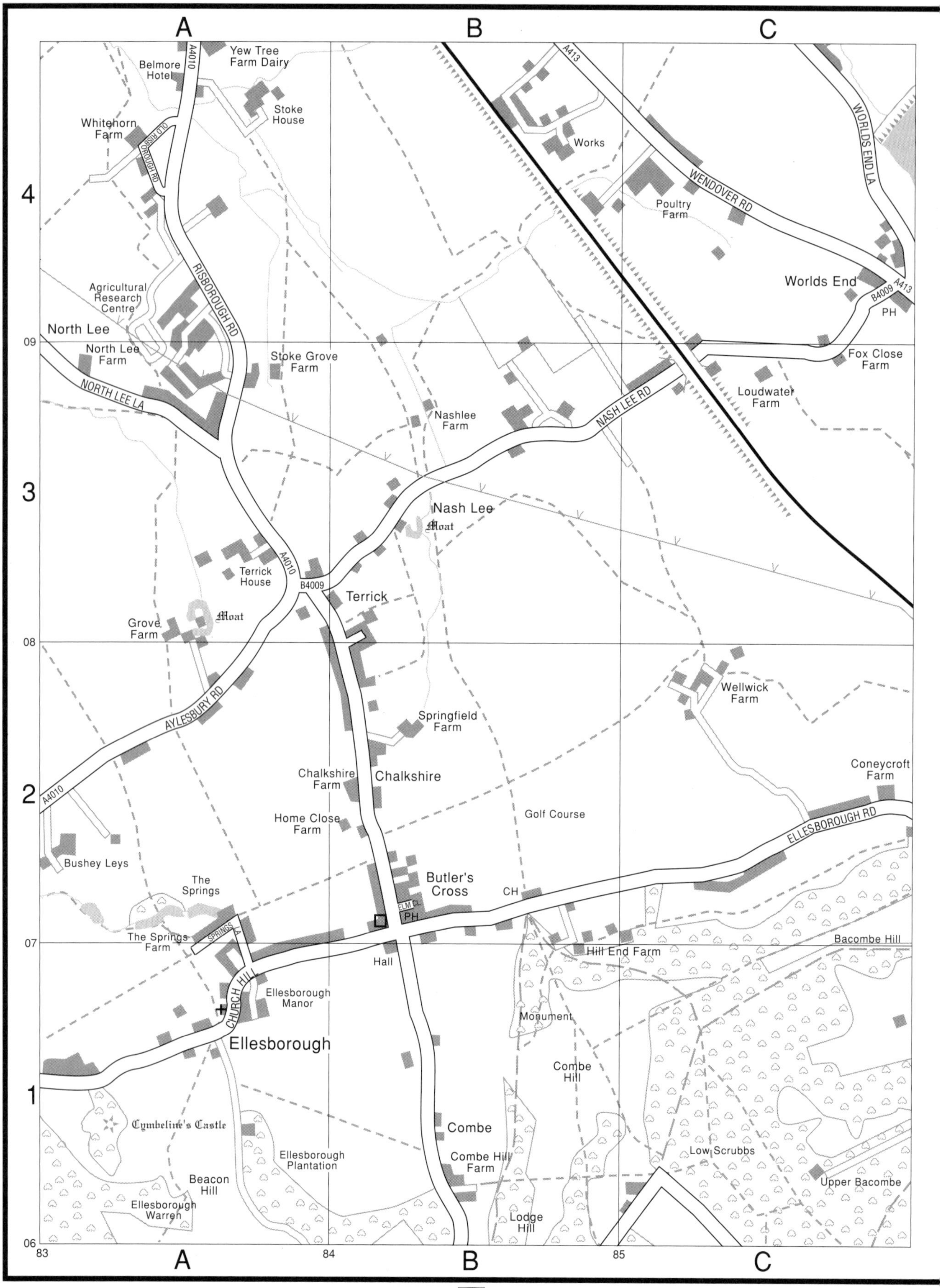
A
B
C
4
3
2
1
09
08
07
06
83
84
85
Yew Tree Farm Dairy
Belmore Hotel
Stoke House
Whitehorn Farm
OLD RISBOROUGH RD
A4010
Works
Poultry Farm
WENDOVER RD
WORLDS END LA
A413
Worlds End
B4009
PH
Agricultural Research Centre
RISBOROUGH RD
North Lee
North Lee Farm
NORTH LEE LA
Stoke Grove Farm
Fox Close Farm
Loudwater Farm
Nashlee Farm
NASH LEE RD
Nash Lee
Moat
Terrick House
Terrick
Grove Farm
Wellwick Farm
AYLESBURY RD
Springfield Farm
Chalkshire Farm
Chalkshire
Coneycroft Farm
Home Close Farm
Golf Course
ELLESBOROUGH RD
Bushey Leys
The Springs
Butler's Cross
CH
ELM CL
The Springs Farm
SPRINGS LA
Hall
Hill End Farm
Bacombe Hill
CHURCH HILL
Ellesborough Manor
Monument
Ellesborough
Combe Hill
Cymbeline's Castle
Combe
Ellesborough Plantation
Combe Hill Farm
Low Scrubbs
Beacon Hill
Upper Bacombe
Ellesborough Warren
Lodge Hill

129

140

117

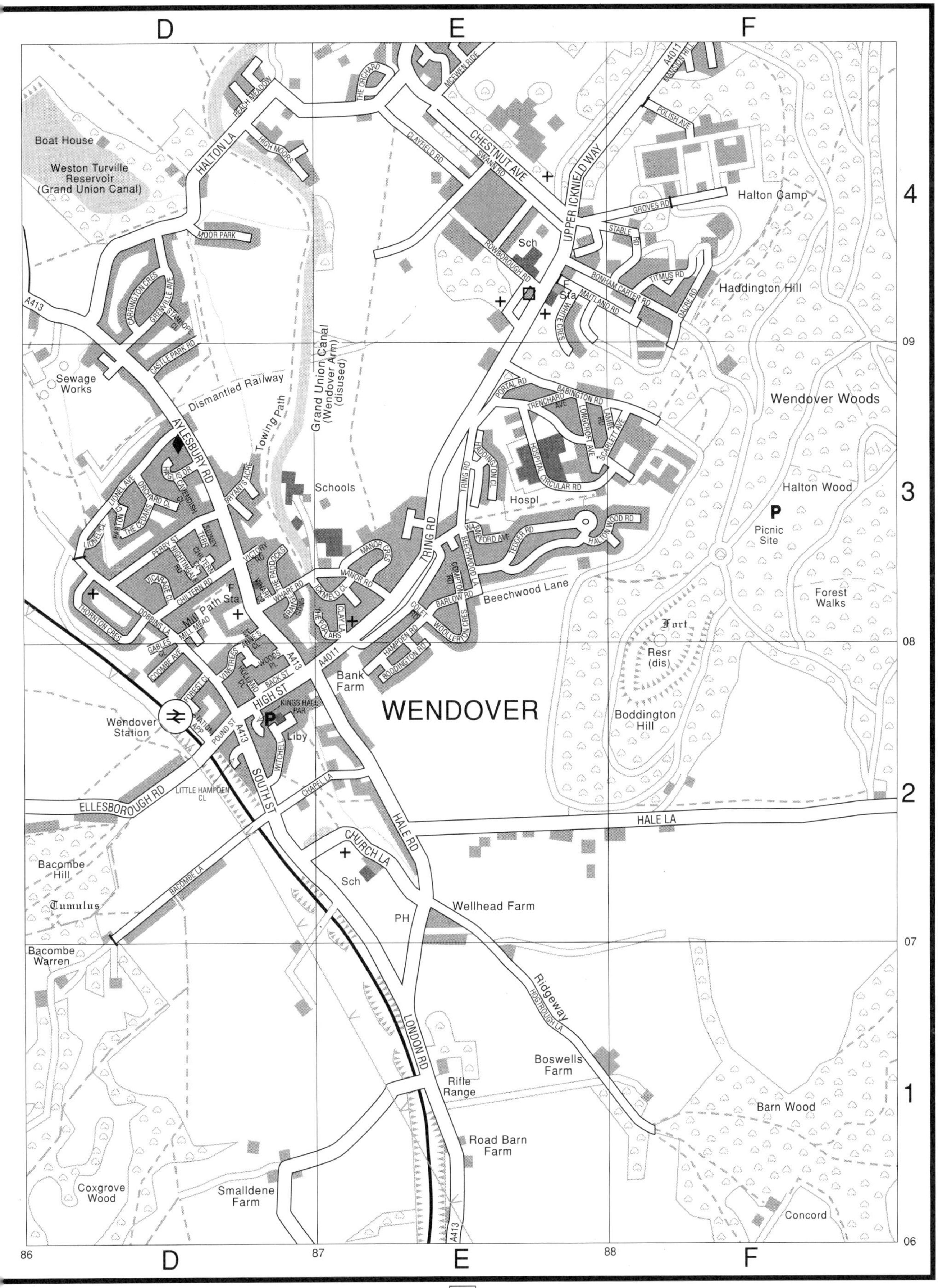
D
E
F
4
09
3
08
2
07
1
06
86
87
88
Boat House
Weston Turville
Reservoir
(Grand Union Canal)
HALTON LA
PEACH MEADOW
HIGH MOORS
THE ORCHARD
MCEWEN RIDE
CLAYFIELD RD
SWANN RD
CHESTNUT AVE
UPPER ICKNIELD WAY
A4011
MANSION HILL
POLISH AVE
GROVES RD
Halton Camp
STABLE RD
MOOR PARK
ROWBOROUGH RD
Sch
BONHAM CARTER RD
TITMUS RD
F Sta
MAITLAND RD
WHITE CRES
DACRE RD
Haddington Hill
A413
CARRINGTON CRES
GRENVILLE AVE
STANHOPE CL
CASTLE PARK RD
Sewage
Works
Dismantled Railway
Towing Path
Grand Union Canal
(Wendover Arm)
(disused)
PORTAL RD
BABINGTON RD
TRENCHARD AVE
LONGCROFT AVE
LAMBE RD
SCARLETT AVE
Wendover Woods
HADDINGTON CL
HOSPITAL CIRCULAR RD
Hospl
TRING RD
Halton Wood
AYLESBURY RD
Schools
BRYANTS ACRE
HALTON WOOD RD
TEDDER RD
WARDS FORD AVE
P
Picnic
Site
LIONEL AVE
PARTON CL
THE CEDARS
ORCHARD CL
HAGLIS DR
CAVENDISH CL
LIONEL CL
PERRY ST
NIGHTINGALE RD
SIDNEY TERR
CHILTERN CL
VICTORY RD
THE PADDOCKS
MANOR CRES
MANOR RD
ICKNIELD CL
CLAY LA
COMPTON RD
BEECHWOOD LA
Beechwood Lane
Forest
Walks
VICARAGE CL
CHILTERN RD
WHARF RD
GRANGE GDNS
BARLOW RD
COLET RD
F
Sta
THORNTON CRES
DOBBINS LA
Mill Path
MILL MEAD
THE POPLARS
HAMPDEN RD
WOOLLERTON CRES
Fort
Resr
(dis)
GABLES CL
COOMBE AVE
VINETREES
HOLLAND CL
WOODS PL
BACK ST
A413
A4011
BODDINGTON RD
Bank
Farm
FOREST CL
HIGH ST
KINGS HALL PAR
WENDOVER
Wendover
Station
STATION APP
POUND ST
A413
P
Liby
WITCHELL
Boddington
Hill
SOUTH ST
ELLESBOROUGH RD
LITTLE HAMPDEN CL
CHAPEL LA
HALE RD
HALE LA
CHURCH LA
Bacombe
Hill
Sch
Tumulus
BACOMBE LA
Wellhead Farm
PH
Bacombe
Warren
Ridgeway
HOGTROUGH LA
LONDON RD
Boswells
Farm
Rifle
Range
Barn Wood
Road Barn
Farm
Coxgrove
Wood
Smalldene
Farm
A413
Concord
D
E
F

132

141

118

131

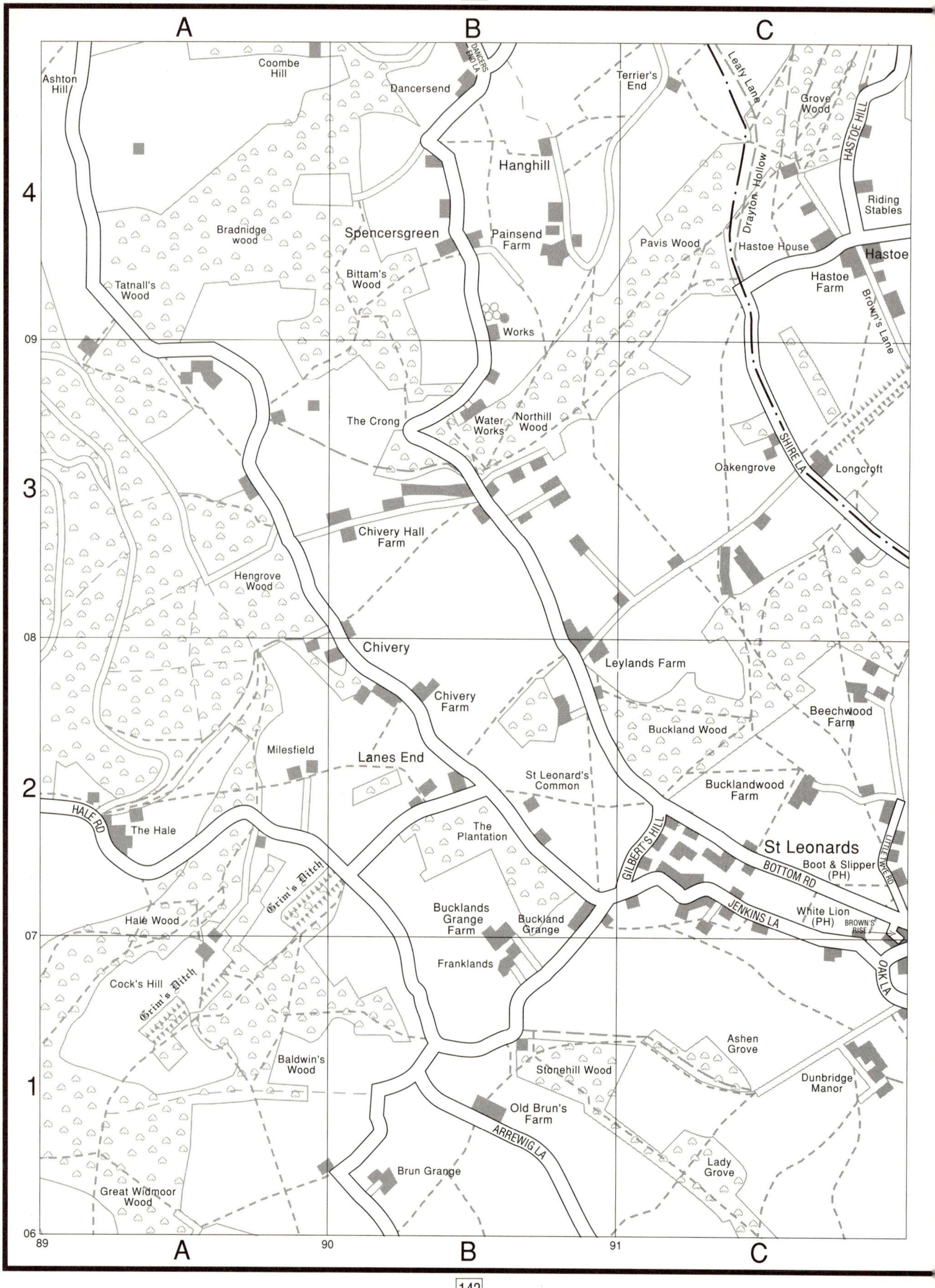
A
B
C
4
3
2
1
09
08
07
06
89
90
91
Ashton Hill
Coombe Hill
Dancersend
DANCERS END LA
Terrier's End
Leafy Lane
Grove Wood
HASTOE HILL
Hanghill
Drayton Hollow
Riding Stables
Bradnidge wood
Spencersgreen
Painsend Farm
Pavis Wood
Hastoe House
Hastoe
Tatnall's Wood
Bittam's Wood
Hastoe Farm
Brown's Lane
Works
The Crong
Water Works
Northill Wood
SHIRE LA
Oakengrove
Longcroft
Chivery Hall Farm
Hengrove Wood
Chivery
Leylands Farm
Chivery Farm
Beechwood Farm
Buckland Wood
Milesfield
Lanes End
St Leonard's Common
Bucklandwood Farm
HALE RD
The Hale
The Plantation
GILBERT'S HILL
St Leonards
LITTLE TWIST RD
Boot & Slipper (PH)
BOTTOM RD
Grim's Ditch
Hale Wood
Bucklands Grange Farm
Buckland Grange
JENKINS LA
White Lion (PH)
BROWN'S RISE
Franklands
OAK LA
Cock's Hill
Grim's Ditch
Ashen Grove
Baldwin's Wood
Stonehill Wood
Dunbridge Manor
Old Brun's Farm
ARREWIG LA
Lady Grove
Brun Grange
Great Widmoor Wood

142

119

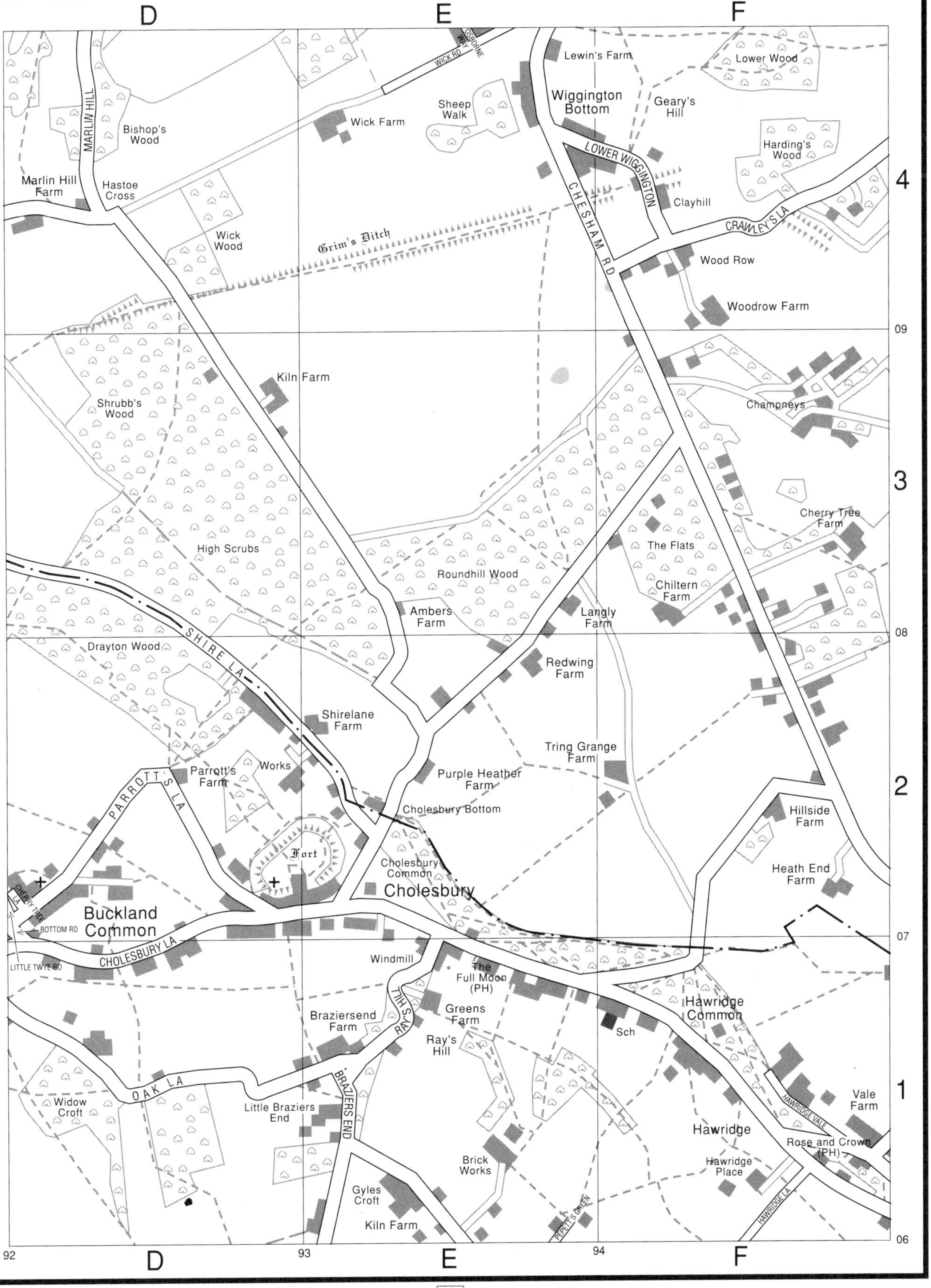
D
E
F
WICK RD
OSBORNE WAY
Lewin's Farm
Lower Wood
Wiggington Bottom
Geary's Hill
Sheep Walk
Wick Farm
MARLIN HILL
Bishop's Wood
Harding's Wood
LOWER WIGGINGTON
Marlin Hill Farm
Hastoe Cross
CHESHAM RD
Clayhill
CRAWLEY'S LA
Wick Wood
Grim's Ditch
Wood Row
Woodrow Farm
Kiln Farm
Shrubb's Wood
Champneys
Cherry Tree Farm
The Flats
High Scrubs
Roundhill Wood
Chiltern Farm
Ambers Farm
Langly Farm
Drayton Wood
SHIRE LA
Redwing Farm
Shirelane Farm
Tring Grange Farm
Parrott's Farm
Works
PARROTT'S LA
Purple Heather Farm
Cholesbury Bottom
Hillside Farm
Fort
Cholesbury Common
Cholesbury
Heath End Farm
CHERRY TREE LA
Buckland Common
BOTTOM RD
CHOLESBURY LA
LITTLE TWYE RD
Windmill
The Full Moon (PH)
RAY'S HILL
Braziersend Farm
Greens Farm
Hawridge Common
Ray's Hill
Sch
OAK LA
BRAZIERS END
HAWRIDGE VALE
Vale Farm
Widow Croft
Little Braziers End
Hawridge
Rose and Crown (PH)
Brick Works
Hawridge Place
Gyles Croft
PEPETT'S GREEN
HAWRIDGE LA
Kiln Farm
4
09
3
08
2
07
1
06
92
93
94
D
E
F
134

143

120

133

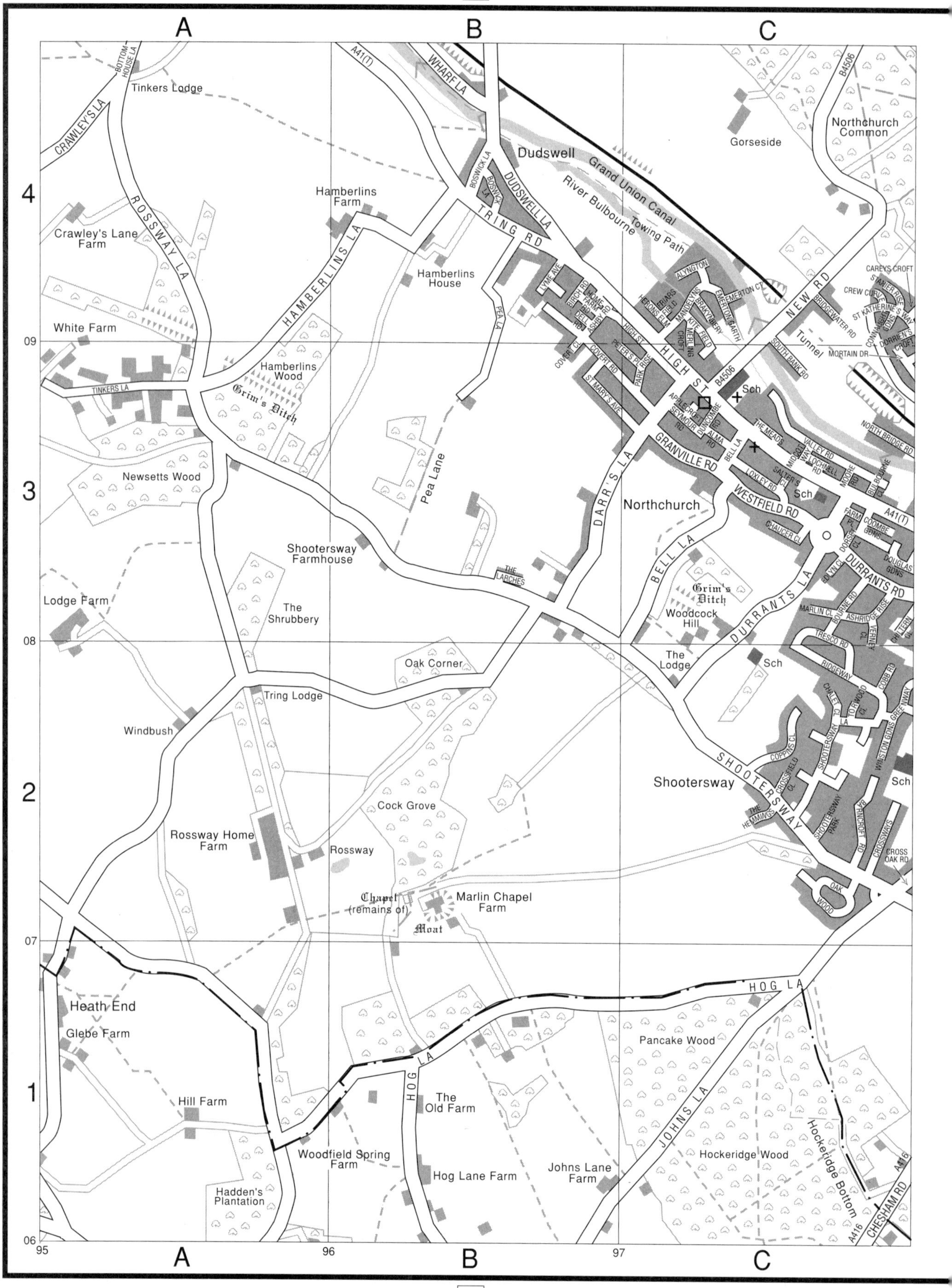
A
B
C
4
3
2
1
09
08
07
06
95
96
97
Tinkers Lodge
CRAWLEY'S LA
BOTTOM HOUSE LA
ROSSWAY LA
Crawley's Lane Farm
White Farm
TINKERS LA
Newsetts Wood
Lodge Farm
Windbush
Hamberlins Farm
HAMBERLINS LA
Hamberlins Wood
Grim's Ditch
Hamberlins House
PEA LA
Pea Lane
A41(T)
WHARF LA
BOSWICK LA
DUDSWELL LA
TRING RD
Dudswell
Grand Union Canal
River Bulbourne
Towing Path
Gorseside
Northchurch Common
B4506
NEW RD
HIGH ST
Sch
DARR'S LA
GRANVILLE RD
Northchurch
WESTFIELD RD
BELL LA
DURRANTS LA
DURRANTS RD
Woodcock Hill
The Lodge
Tunnel
MORTAIN DR
Shootersway Farmhouse
THE LARCHES
The Shrubbery
Oak Corner
Tring Lodge
Cock Grove
Rossway Home Farm
Rossway
Chapel (remains of)
Marlin Chapel Farm
Moat
SHOOTERSWAY
Shootersway
CROSS OAK RD
Heath End
Glebe Farm
Hill Farm
Hadden's Plantation
Woodfield Spring Farm
HOG LA
The Old Farm
Hog Lane Farm
Johns Lane Farm
JOHNS LA
Pancake Wood
Hockeridge Wood
Hockeridge Bottom
A416
CHESHAM RD

144

121

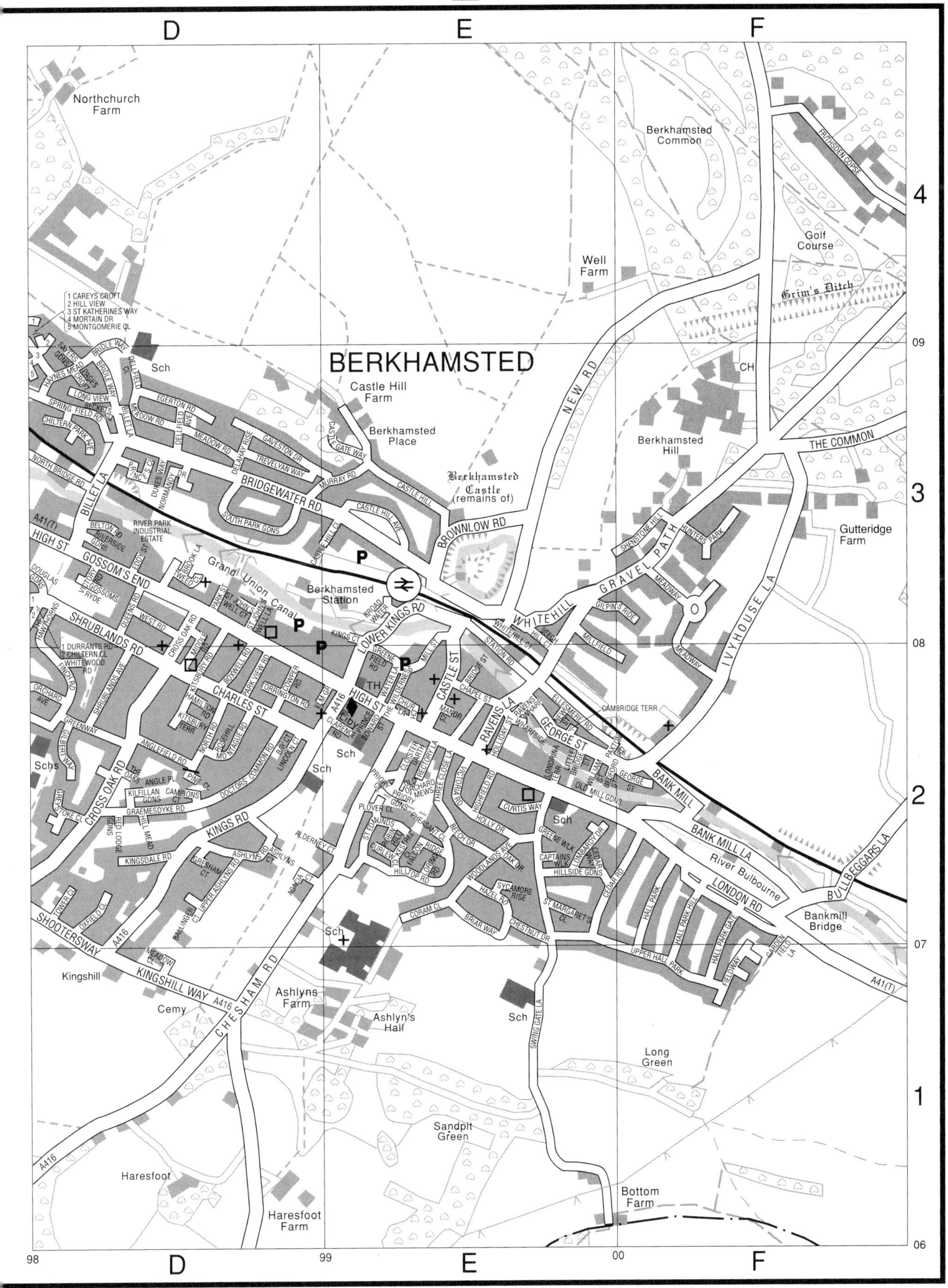

not continued, see key diagram

145

124

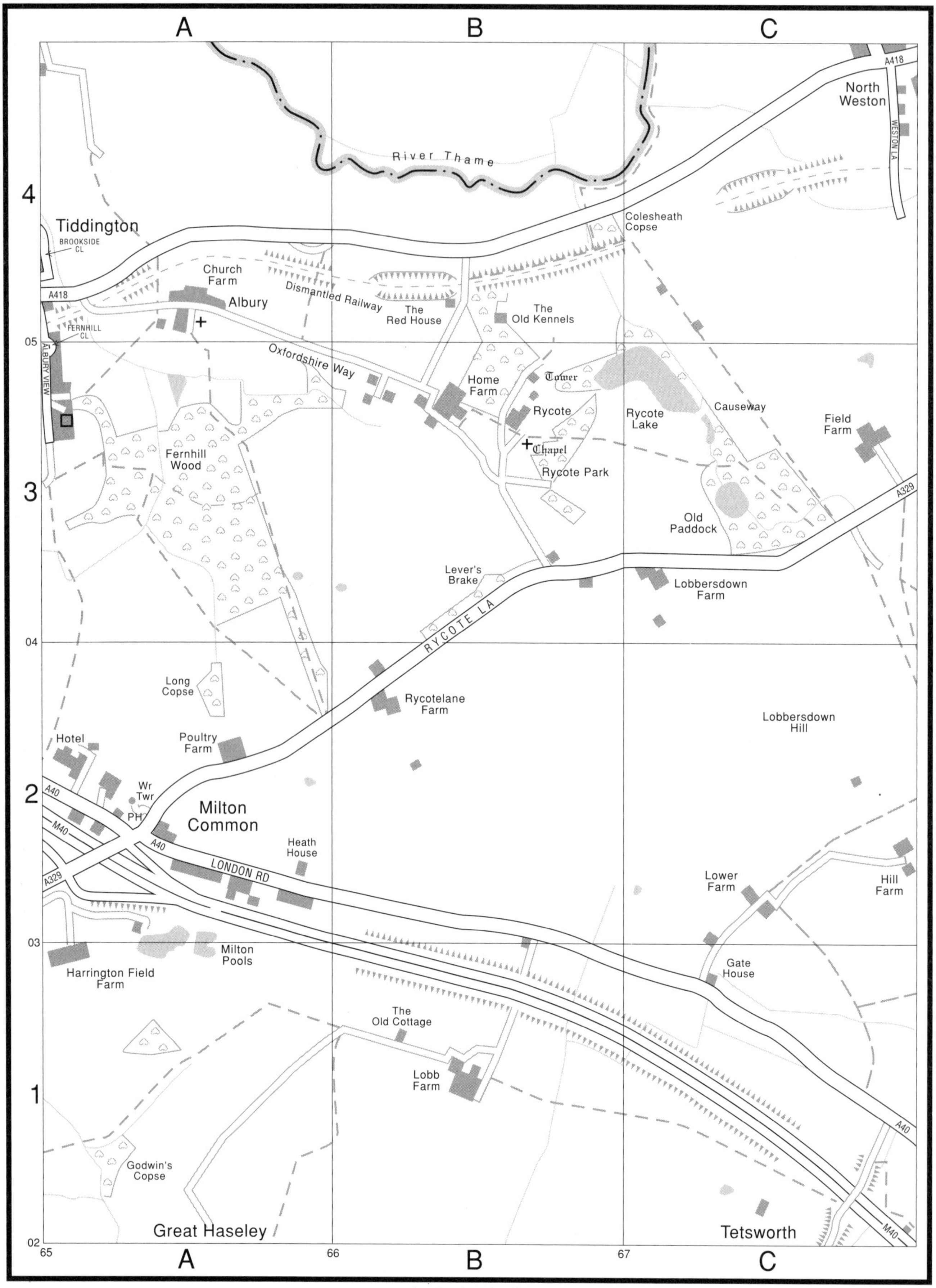

not continued, see key diagram

not continued, see key diagram

not continued, see key diagram

127

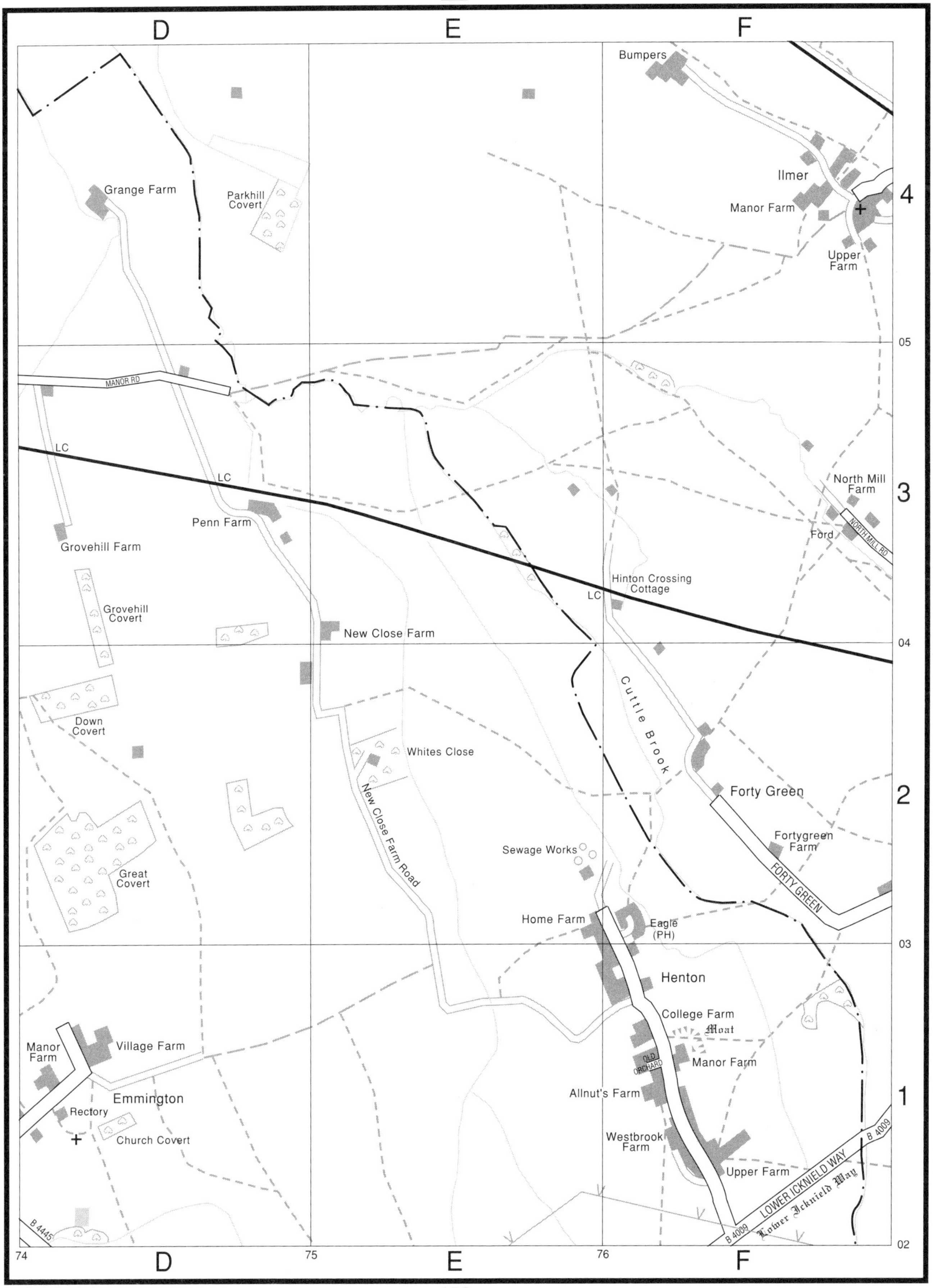
D
E
F
Bumpers
Ilmer
Manor Farm
Upper Farm
Grange Farm
Parkhill Covert
4
05
MANOR RD
LC
LC
Penn Farm
Grovehill Farm
North Mill Farm
3
Ford
NORTH MILL RD
Hinton Crossing Cottage
LC
Grovehill Covert
New Close Farm
04
Cuttle Brook
Down Covert
Whites Close
New Close Farm Road
Forty Green
2
Fortygreen Farm
FORTY GREEN
Sewage Works
Great Covert
Home Farm
Eagle (PH)
03
Henton
College Farm
Moat
Manor Farm
Village Farm
OLD ORCHARD
Manor Farm
Allnut's Farm
1
Emmington
Rectory
Church Covert
Westbrook Farm
Upper Farm
LOWER ICKNIELD WAY
B 4009
Lower Icknield Way
B 4009
B 4445
74
75
76
02
D
E
F

138

147

128

137

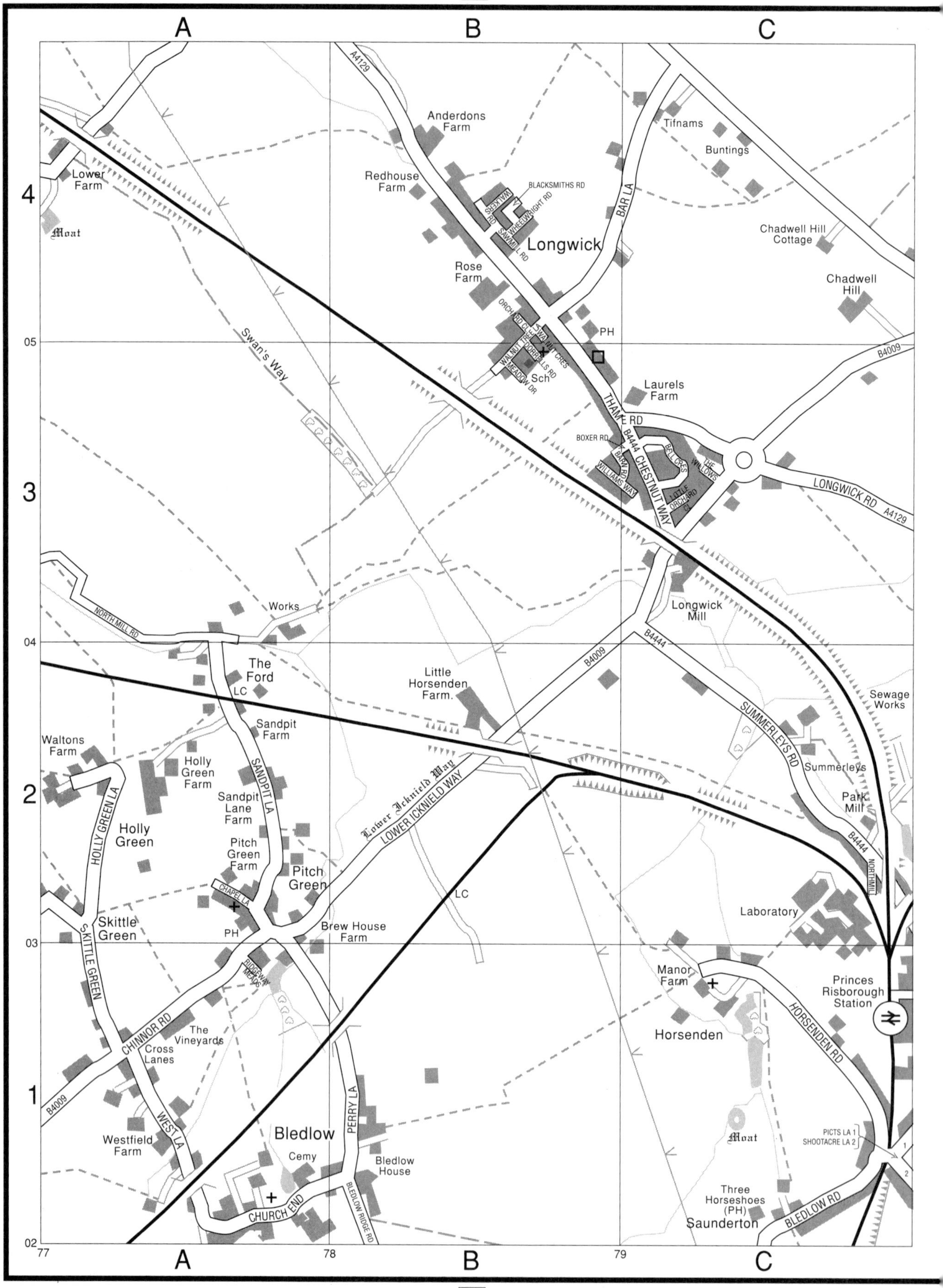
A
B
C
A4129
Anderdons Farm
Tifnams
Buntings
Lower Farm
Redhouse Farm
BLACKSMITHS RD
WALKERS RD
WHEELWRIGHT RD
SAWMILL RD
BAR LA
Moat
Longwick
Chadwell Hill Cottage
Rose Farm
Chadwell Hill
PH
Swan's Way
B4009
Sch
Laurels Farm
THAME RD
BOXER RD
B4444
CHESTNUT WAY
WILLIAMS WAY
BELL CRES
THE WILLOWS
LITTLE ORCHARD CL
LONGWICK RD
A4129
Works
Longwick Mill
NORTH MILL RD
B4444
B4009
The Ford
LC
Little Horsenden Farm
Sewage Works
SUMMERLEYS RD
Sandpit Farm
Waltons Farm
Holly Green Farm
SANDPIT LA
Lower Icknield Way
LOWER ICKNIELD WAY
Summerleys
Sandpit Lane Farm
HOLLY GREEN LA
Holly Green
Park Mill
Pitch Green Farm
Pitch Green
B4444
NORTHMILL
CHAPEL LA
LC
Laboratory
Skittle Green
PH
Brew House Farm
SKITTLE GREEN
RIDGEWAY MEADS
Manor Farm
Princes Risborough Station
CHINNOR RD
The Vineyards
Cross Lanes
HORSENDEN RD
Horsenden
B4009
WEST LA
PERRY LA
Westfield Farm
Bledlow
Moat
PICTS LA 1
SHOOTACRE LA 2
Cemy
Bledlow House
CHURCH END
BLEDLOW RIDGE RD
Three Horseshoes (PH)
Saunderton
BLEDLOW RD
4
05
3
04
2
03
1
02
77
78
79

148

129

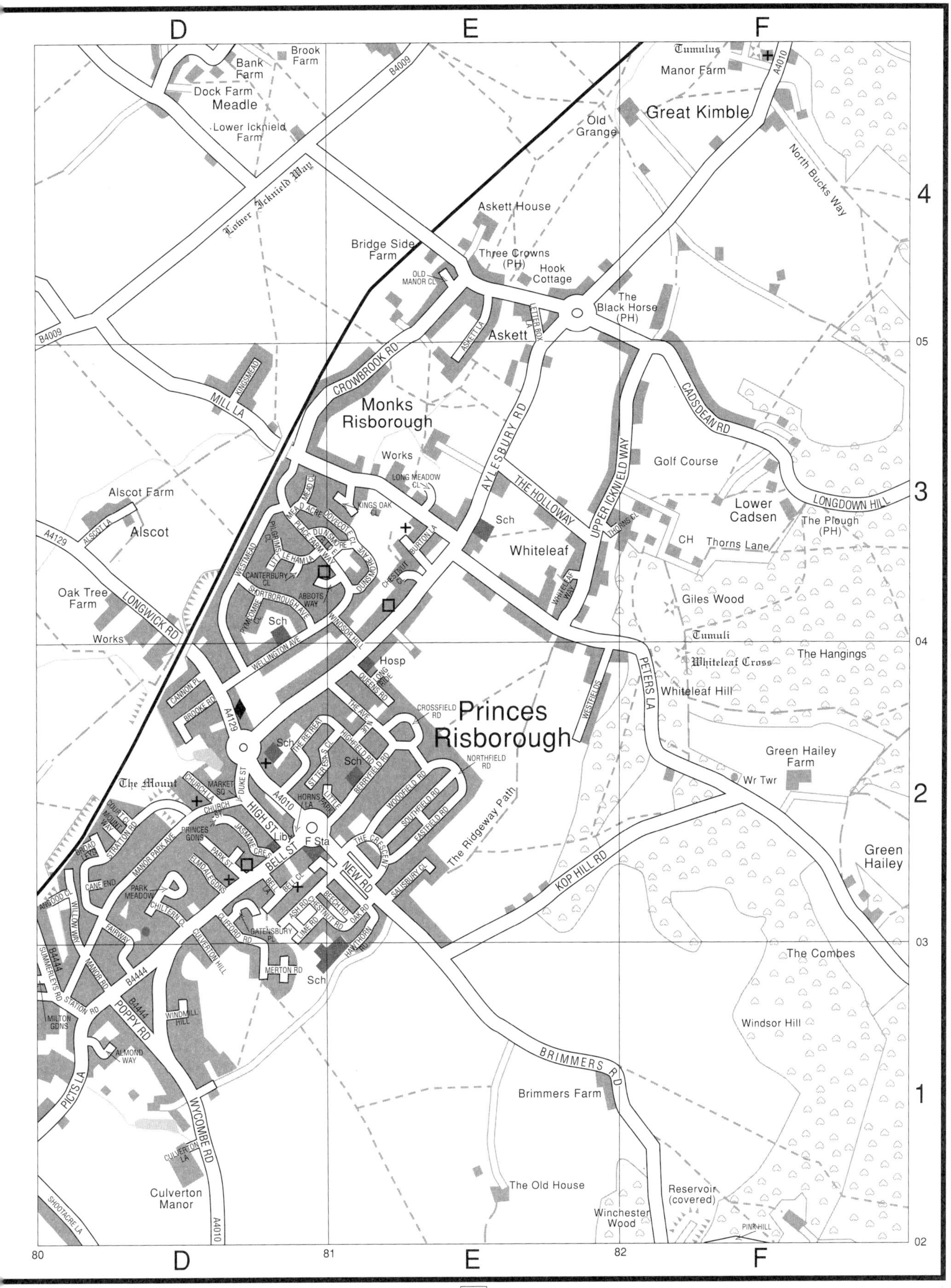

D
E
F
Tumulus
Brook Farm
Bank Farm
Dock Farm
Meadle
Manor Farm
A4010
B4009
Lower Icknield Farm
Old Grange
Great Kimble
North Bucks Way
Lower Icknield Way
Askett House
Bridge Side Farm
Three Crowns (PH)
Hook Cottage
OLD MANOR CL
The Black Horse (PH)
LETTER BOX LA
ASKETT LA
Askett
B4009
MILL LA
KINGSMEAD
CROWBROOK RD
Monks Risborough
CADSDEAN RD
AYLESBURY RD
UPPER ICKNIELD WAY
Works
LONG MEADOW CL
Golf Course
THE HOLLOWAY
Alscot Farm
KINGS OAK CL
LONGDOWN HILL
Lower Cadsen
ALSCOT LA
Alscot
A4129
Sch
THORNS CL
CH
Thorns Lane
The Plough (PH)
Whiteleaf
MEAD ACRE
DOVECOT CL
PLACE FARM WAY
DUNSMORE AVE
BURTON LA
CHESTNUT CL
PILGRIMS CL
LITTLEHAM LA
WESTMEAD
CANTERBURY CL
SHORTBOROUGH AVE
ABBOTS WAY
WHITELEAF WAY
Oak Tree Farm
LONGWICK RD
Giles Wood
PYMCOMBE CL
Sch
WINDSOR HILL
Works
WELLINGTON AVE
Tumuli
Whiteleaf Cross
The Hangings
Hosp
LONG RIDE
QUEENS RD
CANNON PL
BROOKE RD
Whiteleaf Hill
PETERS LA
WESTFIELDS
A4129
THE AVE
CROSSFIELD RD
Princes Risborough
THE RETREAT
HIGHFIELD RD
Sch
ST TERESA'S CL
BERRYFIELD RD
Sch
NORTHFIELD RD
Green Hailey Farm
Wr Twr
The Mount
CHURCH LA
MARKET SQ
DUKE ST
A4010
HORNS LA
LITTLE PARK
WOODFIELD RD
The Ridgeway Path
COURT CL
MOUNT WAY
CHURCH ST
HIGH ST
SOUTHFIELD RD
EASTFIELD RD
PRINCES GDNS
JASMINE CRES
Liby
F Sta
THE CRESCENT
KOP HILL RD
Green Hailey
BROAD LEYS
STRATTON RD
MANOR PARK AVE
PARK ST
BELL ST
ELMDALE GDNS
NEW RD
SALISBURY CL
CANE END
PARK MEADOW
BELL CL
BELL LA
BEECH RD
ASH RD
CHESTNUT RD
OAK RD
LIME RD
WILLOW WAY
CHILTERN CL
CLIFFORD RD
GATENSBURY PL
HAWTHORN RD
FAIRWAY
CULVERTON HILL
The Combes
B4444
SUMMERLEYS RD
MANOR RD
B4444
MERTON RD
Sch
STATION RD
POPPY RD
WINDMILL HILL
MILTON GDNS
Windsor Hill
ALMOND WAY
BRIMMERS RD
PICTS LA
Brimmers Farm
WYCOMBE RD
CULVERTON LA
The Old House
Reservoir (covered)
Culverton Manor
Winchester Wood
SHOOTACRE LA
A4010
PINK HILL
80
81
82
D
E
F
4
05
3
04
2
03
1
02

140

149

130

139

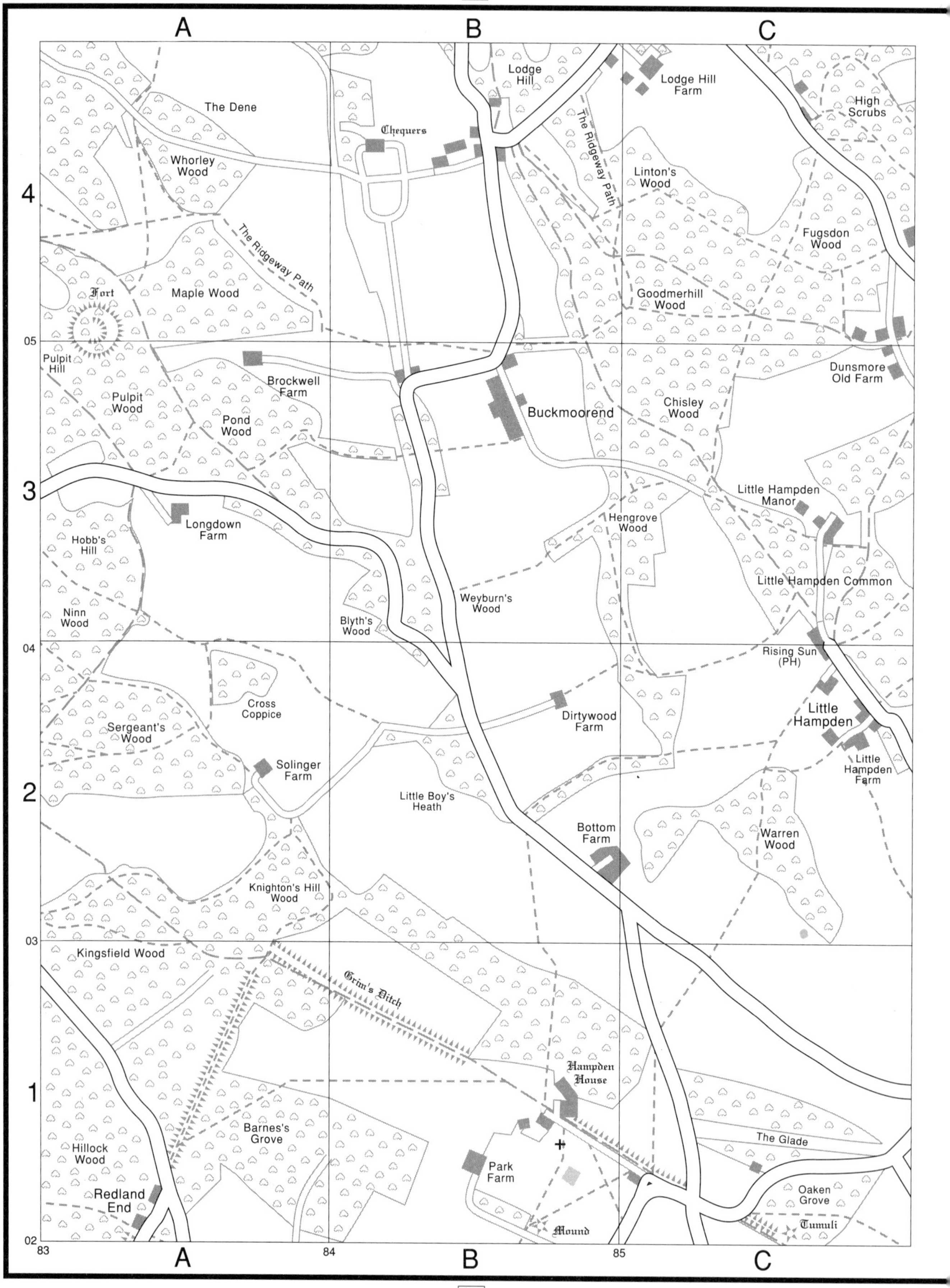
A
B
C
4
3
2
1
05
04
03
02
83
84
85
The Dene
Whorley Wood
Chequers
Lodge Hill
Lodge Hill Farm
High Scrubs
The Ridgeway Path
Linton's Wood
Fugsdon Wood
Fort
Maple Wood
Goodmerhill Wood
Pulpit Hill
Pulpit Wood
Brockwell Farm
Pond Wood
Buckmoorend
Chisley Wood
Dunsmore Old Farm
Little Hampden Manor
Longdown Farm
Hengrove Wood
Hobb's Hill
Little Hampden Common
Weyburn's Wood
Ninn Wood
Blyth's Wood
Rising Sun (PH)
Cross Coppice
Dirtywood Farm
Sergeant's Wood
Little Hampden
Little Hampden Farm
Solinger Farm
Little Boy's Heath
Bottom Farm
Warren Wood
Knighton's Hill Wood
Kingsfield Wood
Grim's Ditch
Hampden House
Barnes's Grove
The Glade
Hillock Wood
Park Farm
Oaken Grove
Redland End
Mound
Tumuli

150

131

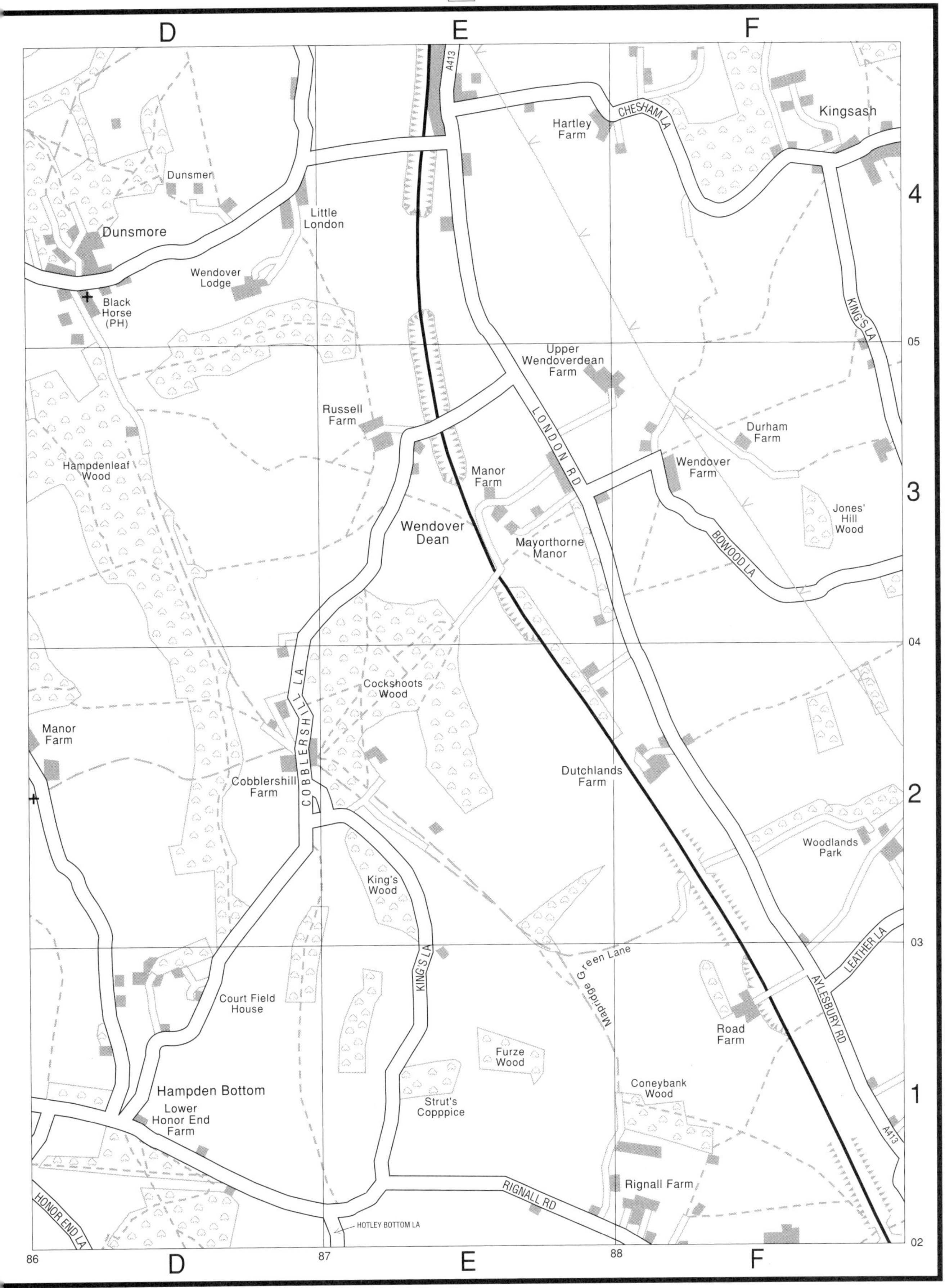
D
E
F
A413
CHESHAM LA
Hartley Farm
Kingsash
Dunsmer
Dunsmore
Little London
Wendover Lodge
Black Horse (PH)
4
KING'S LA
05
Upper Wendoverdean Farm
Russell Farm
LONDON RD
Durham Farm
Hampdenleaf Wood
Manor Farm
Wendover Farm
3
Jones' Hill Wood
Wendover Dean
Mayorthorne Manor
BOWOOD LA
04
Cockshoots Wood
Manor Farm
COBBLERSHILL LA
Cobblershill Farm
Dutchlands Farm
2
Woodlands Park
King's Wood
03
LEATHER LA
Mapridge Green Lane
KING'S LA
Court Field House
AYLESBURY RD
Road Farm
Furze Wood
Coneybank Wood
1
Hampden Bottom
Strut's Copppice
Lower Honor End Farm
A413
HONOR END LA
RIGNALL RD
Rignall Farm
HOTLEY BOTTOM LA
02
86
87
88
D
E
F

142

151

132

141

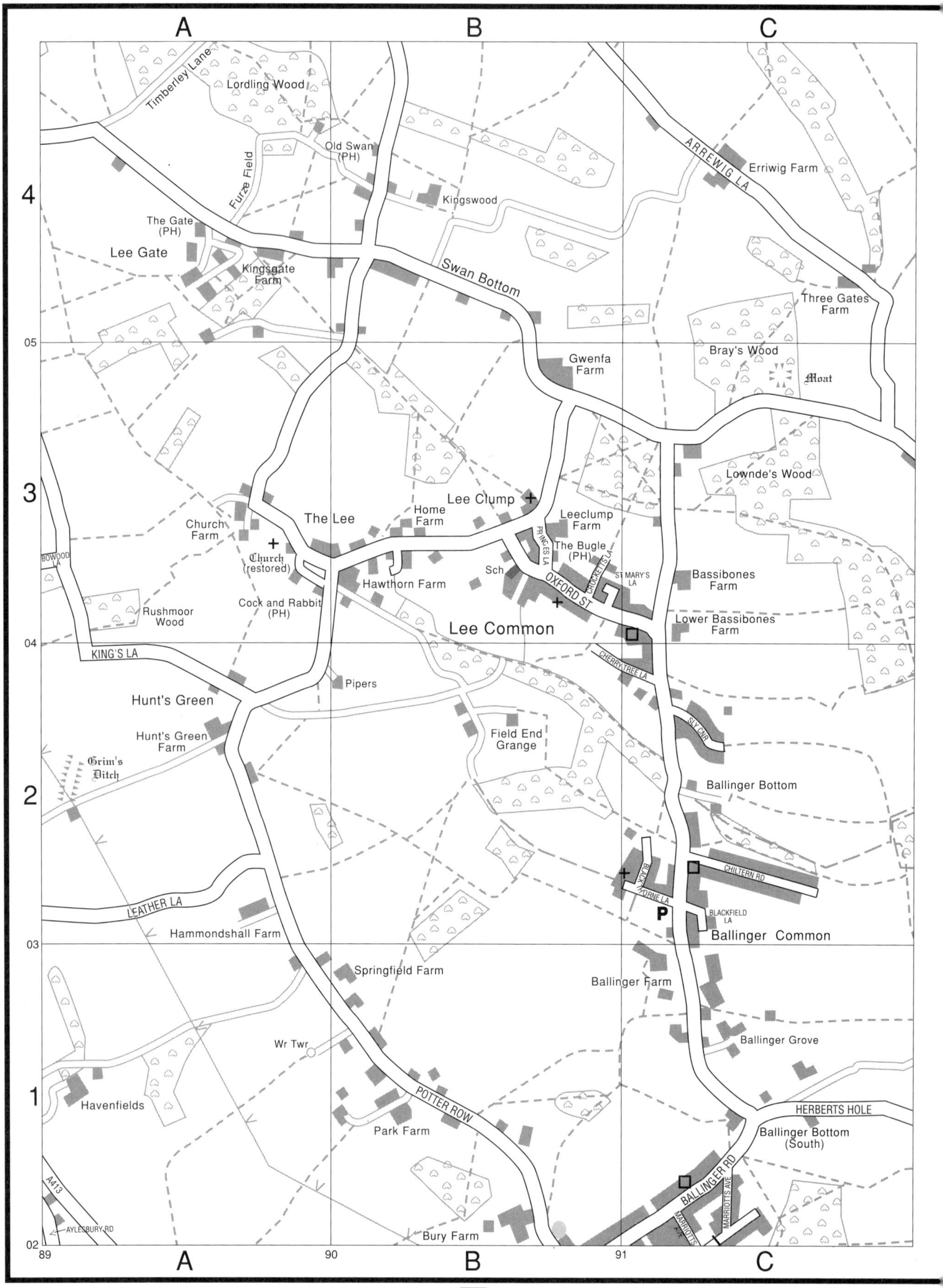
A
B
C
4
3
2
1
05
04
03
02
89
90
91
Timberley Lane
Lordling Wood
Furze Field
Old Swan
(PH)
Kingswood
The Gate
(PH)
Lee Gate
Kingsgate
Farm
Swan Bottom
ARREWIG LA
Erriwig Farm
Three Gates
Farm
Bray's Wood
Moat
Gwenfa
Farm
Lowndes's Wood
Lee Clump
Home
Farm
The Lee
Church
Farm
Church
(restored)
BOWOOD
LA
Leeclump
Farm
PRINCES LA
The Bugle
(PH)
CROCKETTS LA
ST MARY'S
LA
Bassibones
Farm
Sch
OXFORD ST
Hawthorn Farm
Cock and Rabbit
(PH)
Rushmoor
Wood
Lee Common
Lower Bassibones
Farm
CHERRY TREE LA
KING'S LA
Pipers
Hunt's Green
SLY CNR
Hunt's Green
Farm
Field End
Grange
Grim's
Ditch
Ballinger Bottom
BLACKTHORNE LA
CHILTERN RD
LEATHER LA
P
BLACKFIELD
LA
Hammondshall Farm
Ballinger Common
Springfield Farm
Ballinger Farm
Wr Twr
Ballinger Grove
Havenfields
POTTER ROW
HERBERTS HOLE
Ballinger Bottom
(South)
Park Farm
BALLINGER RD
A413
MARRIOTTS AVE
AYLESBURY RD
Bury Farm

152

133

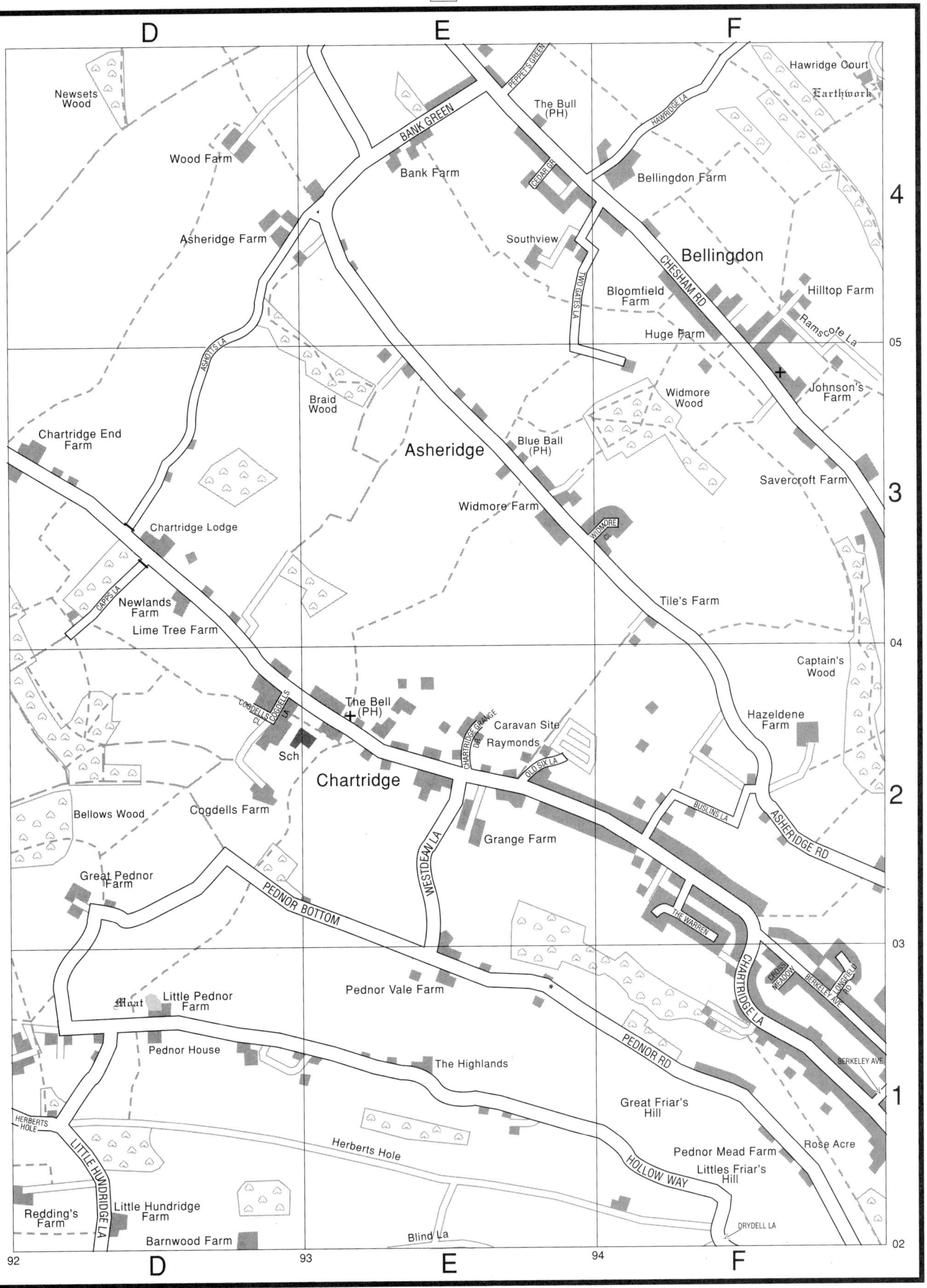

D
E
F
Newsets Wood
Wood Farm
Bank Green
Peppet's Green
The Bull (PH)
Hawridge La
Hawridge Court
Earthwork
Bank Farm
Cedar Gr
Bellingdon Farm
Asheridge Farm
Southview
Bellingdon
Chesham Rd
Two Gates La
Bloomfield Farm
Hilltop Farm
Ramscote La
Huge Farm
Ashotts La
Braid Wood
Widmore Wood
Johnson's Farm
Chartridge End Farm
Asheridge
Blue Ball (PH)
Savercroft Farm
Widmore Farm
Chartridge Lodge
Widmore Cl
Capps La
Newlands Farm
Lime Tree Farm
Tile's Farm
Captain's Wood
Cogdells Cl
Cogdells La
The Bell (PH)
Hazeldene Farm
Caravan Site
Chartridge Grange Dr
Raymonds
Sch
Old Six La
Chartridge
Buslins La
Asheridge Rd
Bellows Wood
Cogdells Farm
Grange Farm
Westdean La
Great Pednor Farm
Pednor Bottom
The Warren
Chartridge La
Cross Meadow
Berkeley Ave
Longfield Rd
Pednor Vale Farm
Moat
Little Pednor Farm
Pednor Rd
Pednor House
The Highlands
Berkeley Ave
Great Friar's Hill
Herberts Hole
Rose Acre
Pednor Mead Farm
Little Hundridge La
Hollow Way
Littles Friar's Hill
Redding's Farm
Little Hundridge Farm
Barnwood Farm
Blind La
Drydell La
4
05
3
04
2
03
1
02
92
93
94
D
E
F

144

153

134

143

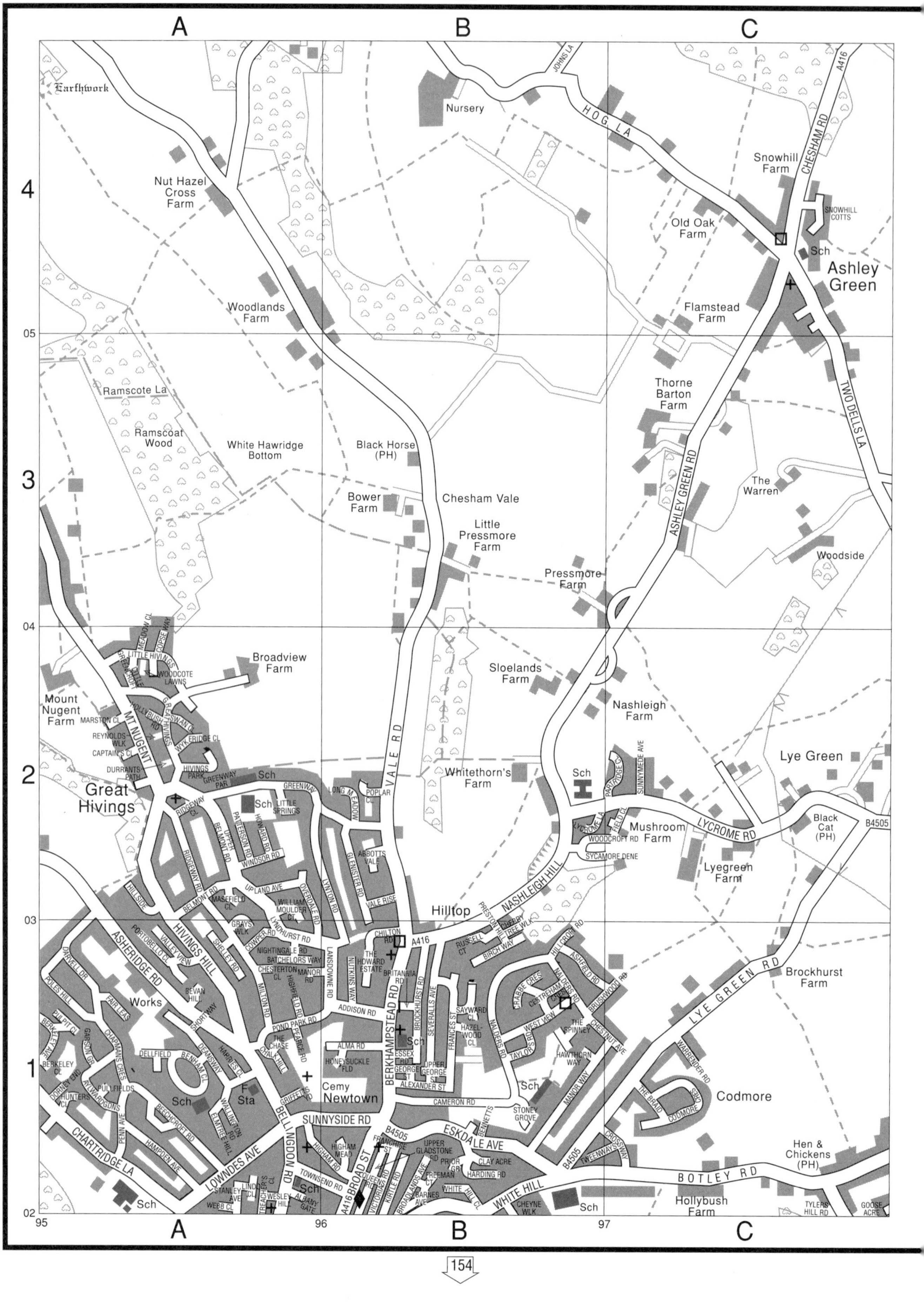
A
B
C
4
3
2
1
05
04
03
02
95
96
97
Earthwork
Nursery
HOG LA
JOHNS LA
CHESHAM RD
A416
Snowhill Farm
SNOWHILL COTTS
Sch
Ashley Green
Old Oak Farm
Nut Hazel Cross Farm
Woodlands Farm
Flamstead Farm
Ramscote La
Ramscoat Wood
White Hawridge Bottom
Black Horse (PH)
Thorne Barton Farm
TWO DELLS LA
The Warren
ASHLEY GREEN RD
Bower Farm
Chesham Vale
Little Pressmore Farm
Woodside
Pressmore Farm
Broadview Farm
Sloelands Farm
Mount Nugent Farm
Nashleigh Farm
VALE RD
Whitethorn's Farm
Lye Green
Great Hivings
MT NUGENT
Sch
Mushroom Farm
LYCROME RD
Black Cat (PH)
B4505
Lyegreen Farm
NASHLEIGH HILL
Hilltop
SYCAMORE DENE
WOODCROFT RD
SUNNYMEDE AVE
PARTRIDGE CL
HIVINGS HILL
ASHERIDGE RD
Works
LYE GREEN RD
Brockhurst Farm
BERKHAMPSTEAD RD
Codmore
F Sta
Sch
Cemy
Newtown
SUNNYSIDE RD
BELLINGDON RD
ESKDALE AVE
WHITE HILL
BOTLEY RD
Hen & Chickens (PH)
Hollybush Farm
CHARTRIDGE LA
LOWNDES AVE
BROAD ST
Sch
Sch
Sch
TYLERS HILL RD
GOOSE ACRE

154

135

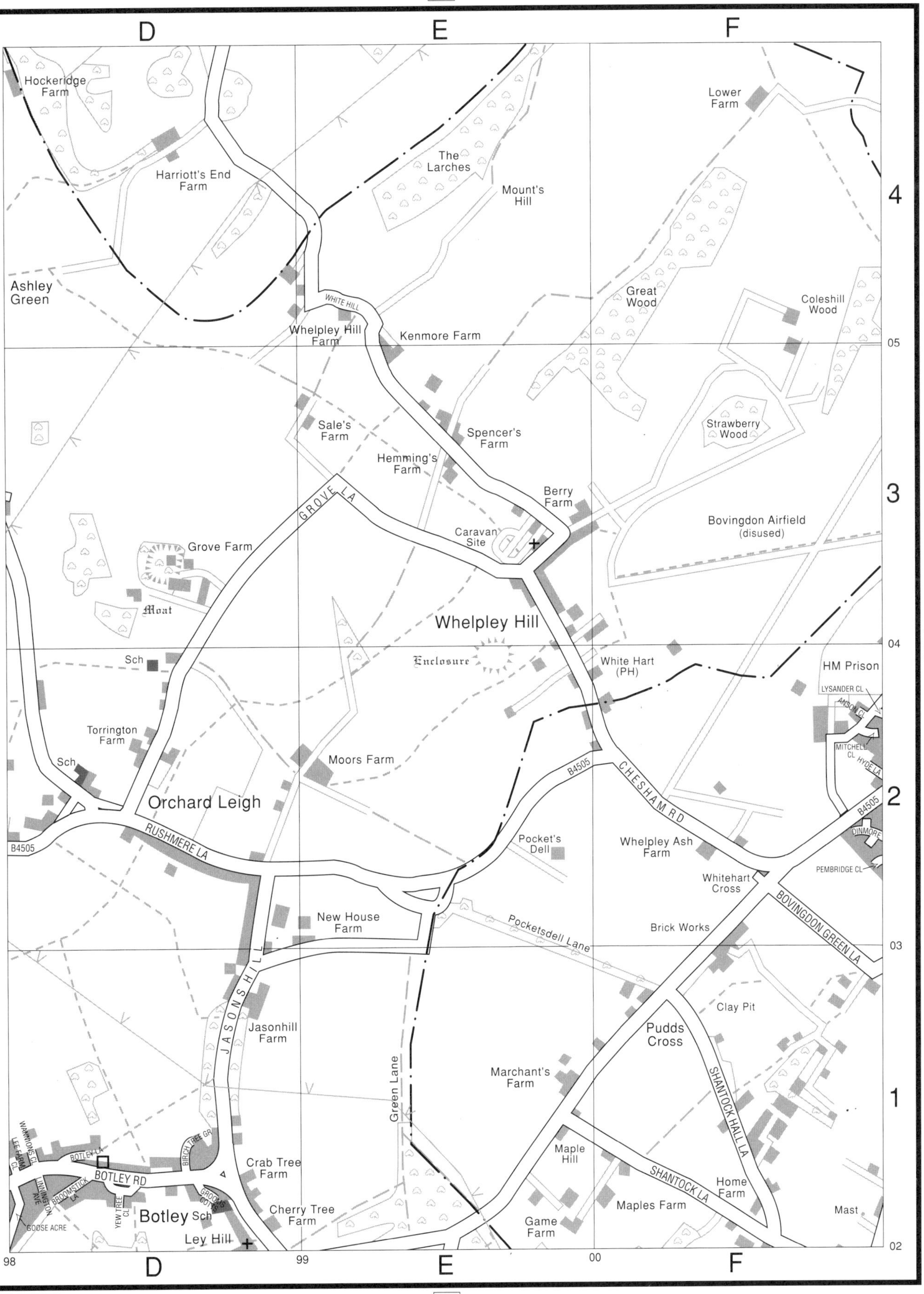
D
E
F
Hockeridge Farm
Harriott's End Farm
The Larches
Mount's Hill
Lower Farm
Ashley Green
WHITE HILL
Whelpley Hill Farm
Kenmore Farm
Great Wood
Coleshill Wood
Strawberry Wood
Sale's Farm
Spencer's Farm
Hemming's Farm
Berry Farm
GROVE LA
Caravan Site
Bovingdon Airfield (disused)
Grove Farm
Moat
Whelpley Hill
Enclosure
Sch
White Hart (PH)
HM Prison
LYSANDER CL
ANSON CL
MITCHELL CL
HYDE LA
Torrington Farm
Sch
Moors Farm
B4505
CHESHAM RD
Orchard Leigh
RUSHMERE LA
B4505
Pocket's Dell
Whelpley Ash Farm
B4505
DINMORE
PEMBRIDGE CL
Whitehart Cross
New House Farm
Pocketsdell Lane
Brick Works
BOVINGDON GREEN LA
JASONS HILL
Clay Pit
Pudds Cross
Jasonhill Farm
Marchant's Farm
SHANTOCK HALL LA
Green Lane
Maple Hill
WARMONS CL
LEE FARM CL
BOTLEY LA
BIRCH TREE GR
Crab Tree Farm
BOTLEY RD
LINNINGTON AVE
BROOMSTICK LA
YEW TREE CL
GROOMS COTTS
Botley
Sch
Cherry Tree Farm
SHANTOCK LA
Home Farm
Maples Farm
Game Farm
Mast
GOOSE ACRE
Ley Hill
4
05
3
04
2
03
1
02
98
99
00

146

155

not continued,see key diagram

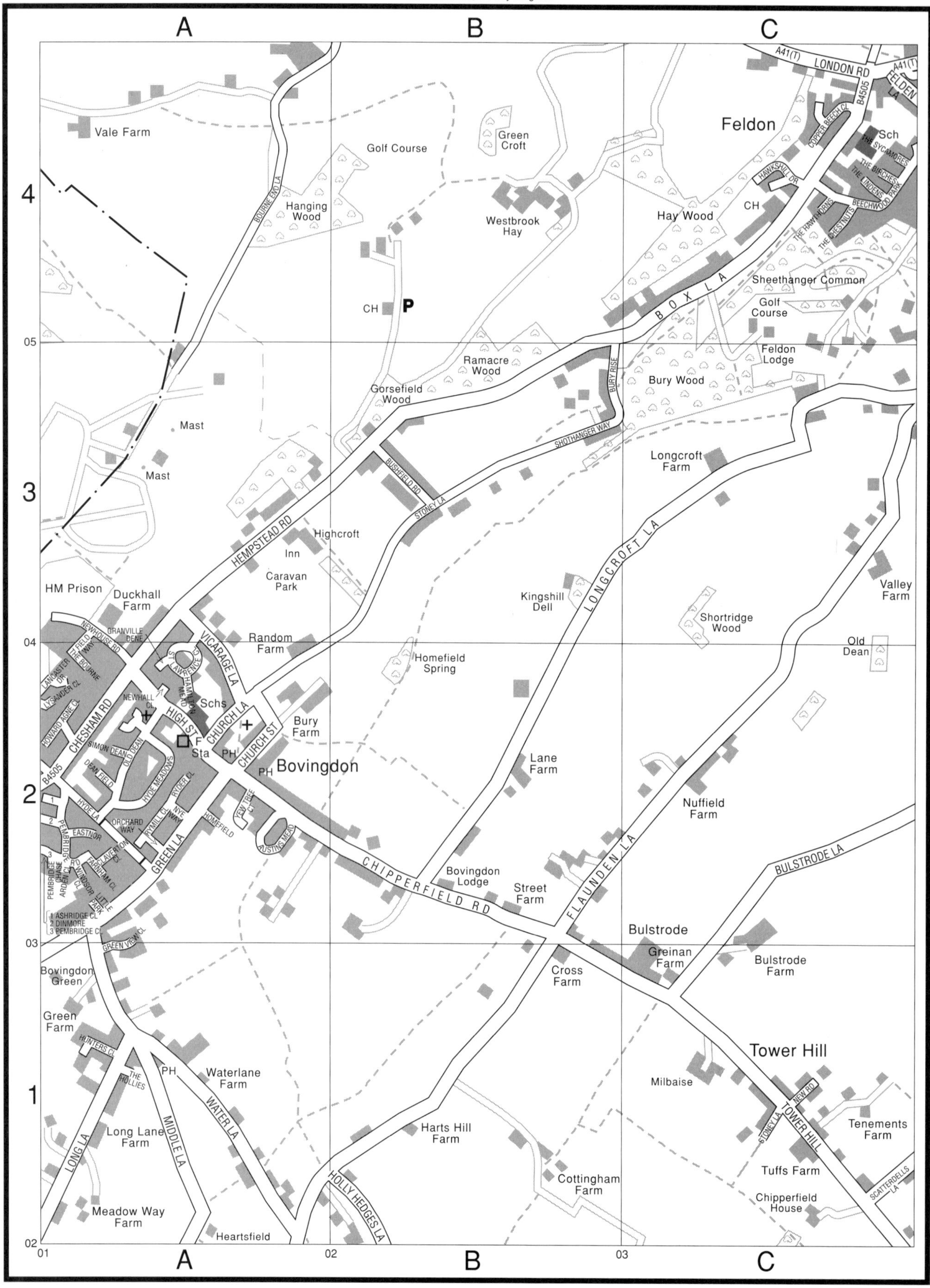

145

not continued,see key diagram

137

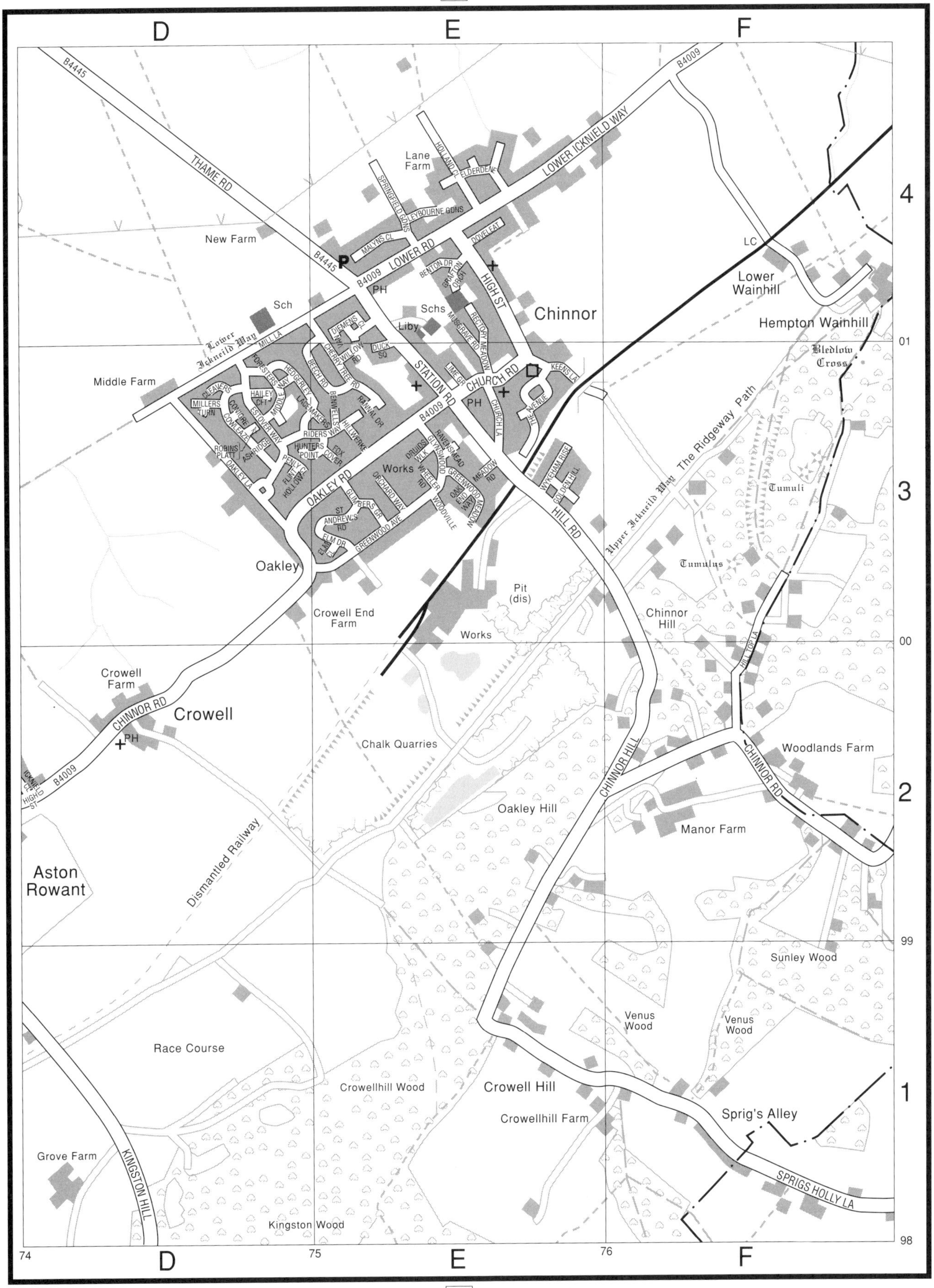

148

not continued, see key diagram

158

138

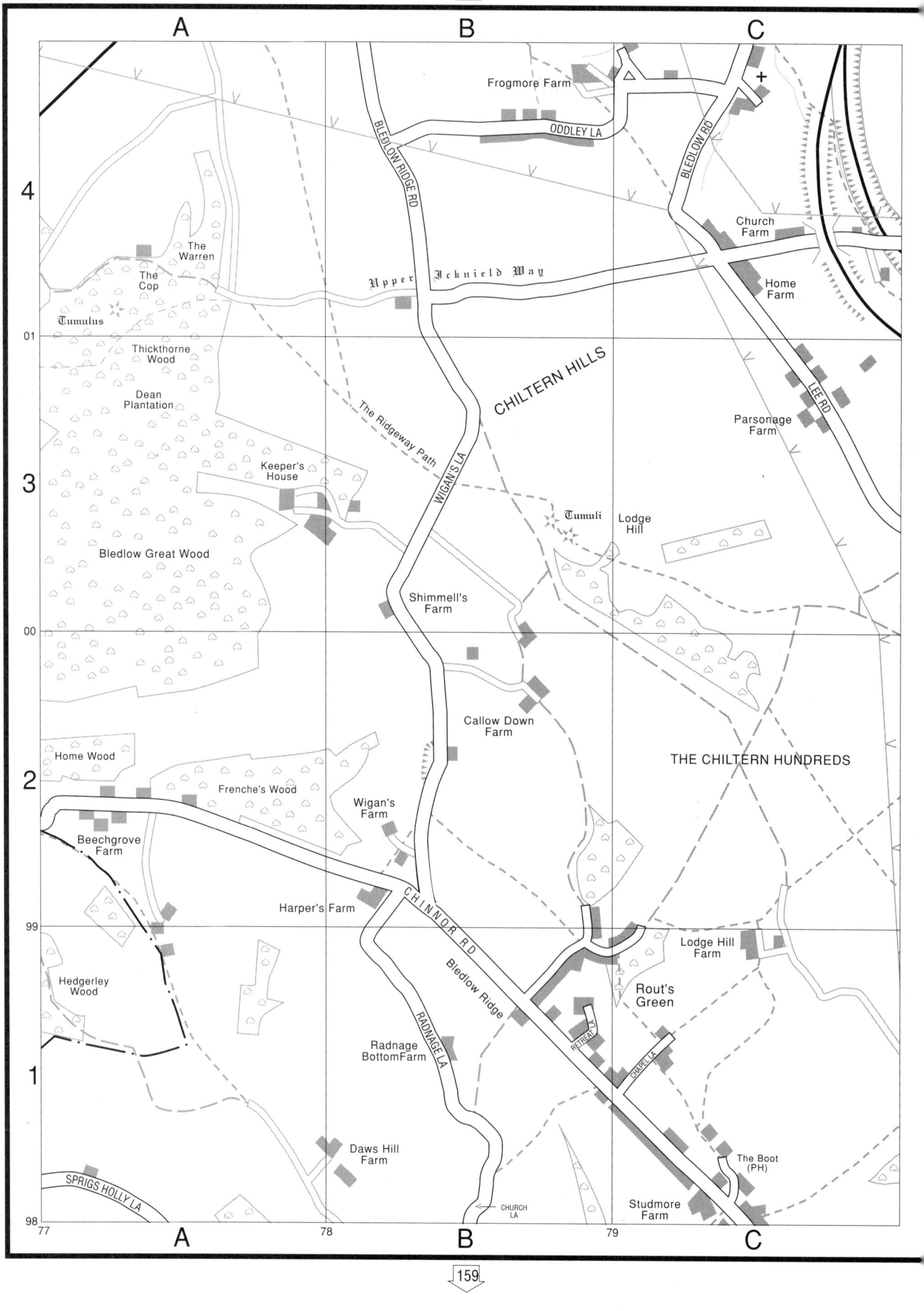
A
B
C
4
3
2
1
01
00
99
98
77
78
79
Frogmore Farm
ODDLEY LA
BLEDLOW RIDGE RD
BLEDLOW RD
Church Farm
Home Farm
The Warren
The Cop
Tumulus
Upper Icknield Way
Thickthorne Wood
Dean Plantation
CHILTERN HILLS
LEE RD
Parsonage Farm
The Ridgeway Path
WIGAN'S LA
Keeper's House
Tumuli
Lodge Hill
Bledlow Great Wood
Shimmell's Farm
Callow Down Farm
THE CHILTERN HUNDREDS
Home Wood
Frenche's Wood
Wigan's Farm
Beechgrove Farm
Harper's Farm
CHINNOR RD
Lodge Hill Farm
Hedgerley Wood
Bledlow Ridge
Rout's Green
RETREAT LA
CHAPEL LA
RADNAGE LA
Radnage Bottom Farm
Daws Hill Farm
The Boot (PH)
SPRIGS HOLLY LA
CHURCH LA
Studmore Farm

147

159

139

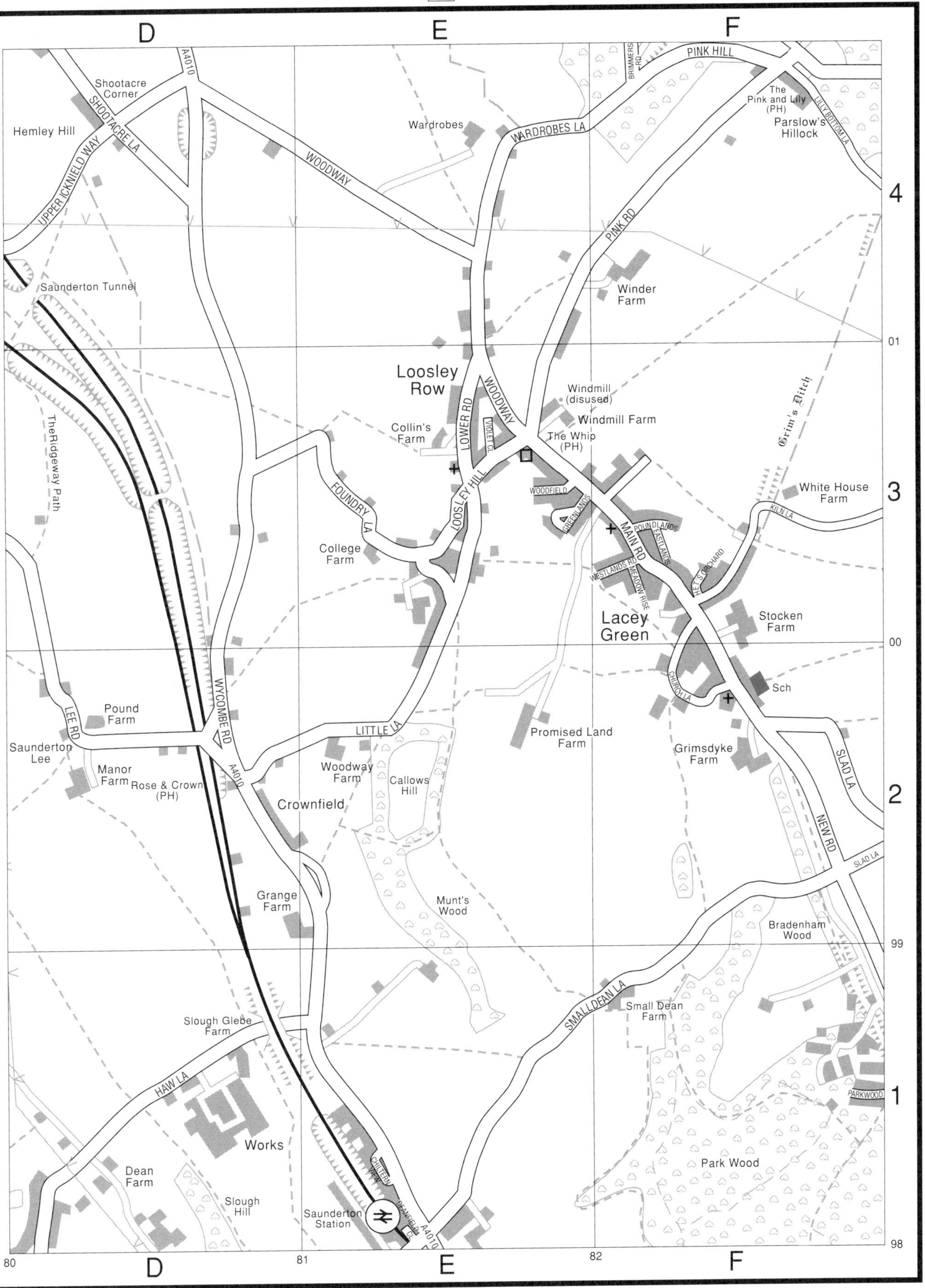
D
E
F
Shootacre Corner
Hemley Hill
SHOOTACRE LA
UPPER ICKNIELD WAY
A4010
WOODWAY
Wardrobes
WARDROBES LA
PINK HILL
BRIMMERS RD
The Pink and Lily (PH)
Parslow's Hillock
LILY BOTTOM LA
PINK RD
Saunderton Tunnel
Winder Farm
TheRidgeway Path
Loosley Row
LOWER RD
VIOLET CL
WOODWAY
Windmill (disused)
Windmill Farm
The Whip (PH)
Collin's Farm
Grim's Ditch
White House Farm
KILN LA
FOUNDRY LA
LOOSLEY HILL
WOODFIELD
GREENLANDS
POUNDLANDS
EASTLANDS
MAIN RD
WESTLANDS RD
MEADOW RISE
HETT'S ORCHARD
College Farm
Lacey Green
Stocken Farm
Sch
CHURCH LA
WYCOMBE RD
LEE RD
Pound Farm
Saunderton Lee
LITTLE LA
Promised Land Farm
Grimsdyke Farm
SLAD LA
Manor Farm
Rose & Crown (PH)
A4010
Woodway Farm
Callows Hill
Crownfield
NEW RD
SLAD LA
Grange Farm
Munt's Wood
Bradenham Wood
SMALLDEAN LA
Small Dean Farm
Slough Glebe Farm
HAW LA
PARKWOOD
Works
Park Wood
Dean Farm
Slough Hill
CHILTERN VIEW
DEANFIELD CL
Saunderton Station
A4010
4
3
2
1
01
00
99
98
80
81
82
D
E
F

150

160

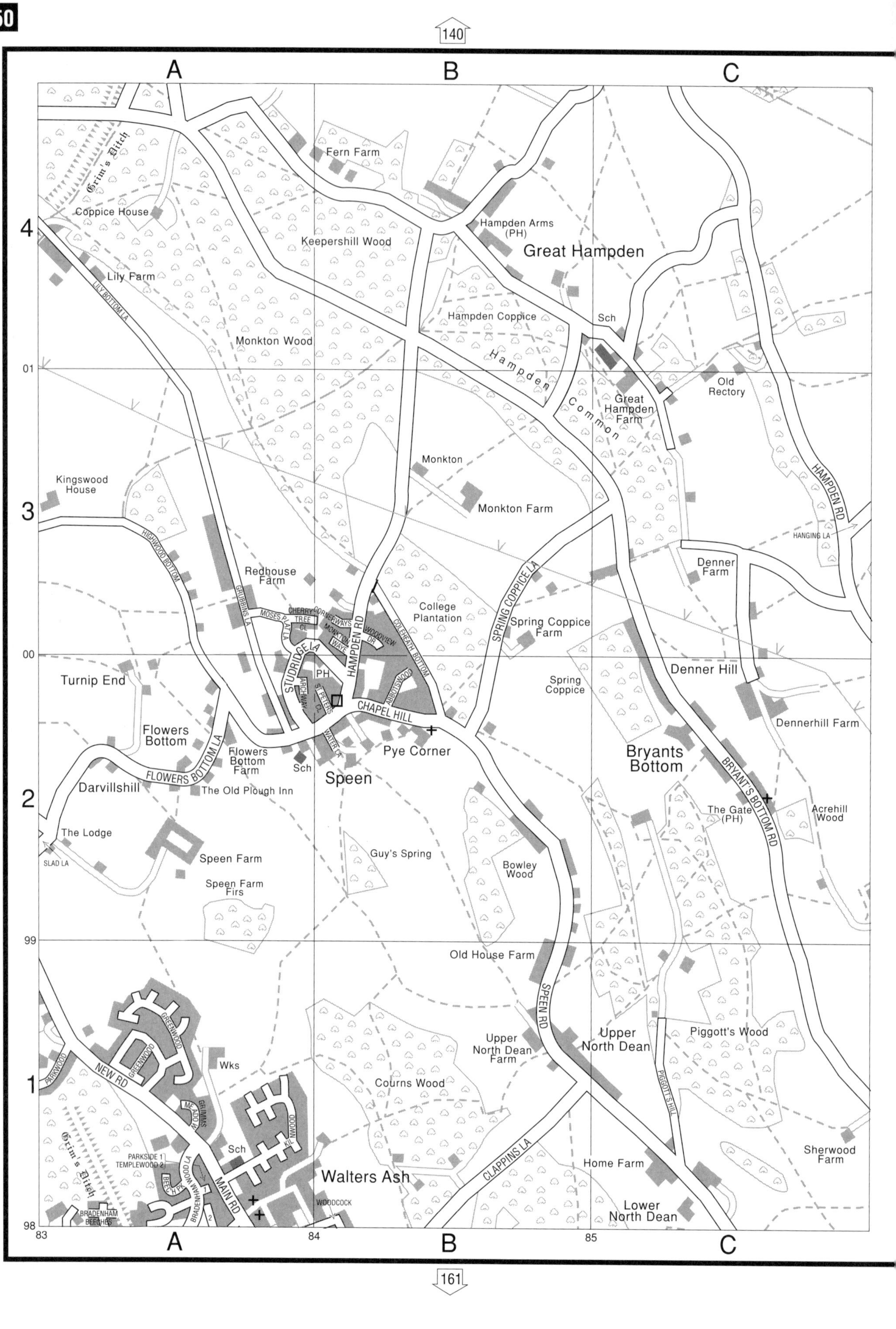
140
A
B
C
4
3
2
1
01
00
99
98
83
84
85
149
161
Grim's Ditch
Coppice House
Fern Farm
Keepershill Wood
Hampden Arms (PH)
Great Hampden
Lily Farm
LILY BOTTOM LA
Hampden Coppice
Sch
Monkton Wood
Hampden Common
Great Hampden Farm
Old Rectory
Monkton
Kingswood House
Monkton Farm
HAMPDEN RD
HANGING LA
HIGHWOOD BOTTOM
Redhouse Farm
Denner Farm
GRUBBINS LA
MOSES PLAT LA
CHERRY TREE CL
CORNERWAYS
MONKTON WAY
WOODVIEW DR
COLEHEATH BOTTOM
College Plantation
SPRING COPPICE LA
Spring Coppice Farm
STUDRIDGE LA
PH
Turnip End
ARCHWAY
ST PETERS CL
ABBOTSWOOD
CHAPEL HILL
Spring Coppice
Denner Hill
Dennerhill Farm
Flowers Bottom
FLOWERS BOTTOM LA
Flowers Bottom Farm
WATER CT
Sch
Pye Corner
Bryants Bottom
BRYANT'S BOTTOM RD
Darvillshill
The Old Plough Inn
Speen
The Gate (PH)
Acrehill Wood
The Lodge
SLAD LA
Speen Farm
Guy's Spring
Bowley Wood
Speen Farm Firs
Old House Farm
SPEEN RD
GREENWOOD
Upper North Dean Farm
Upper North Dean
Piggott's Wood
PARKWOOD
NEW RD
Wks
Courns Wood
PIGGOTT'S HILL
MEADOW
GRIMMS
KILNWOOD
Sherwood Farm
PARKSIDE 1
TEMPLEWOOD 2
Sch
CLAPPINS LA
Home Farm
BEECH PK
BRADENHAM WOOD LA
MAIN RD
Walters Ash
WOODCOCK
Lower North Dean
BRADENHAM BEECHES

141

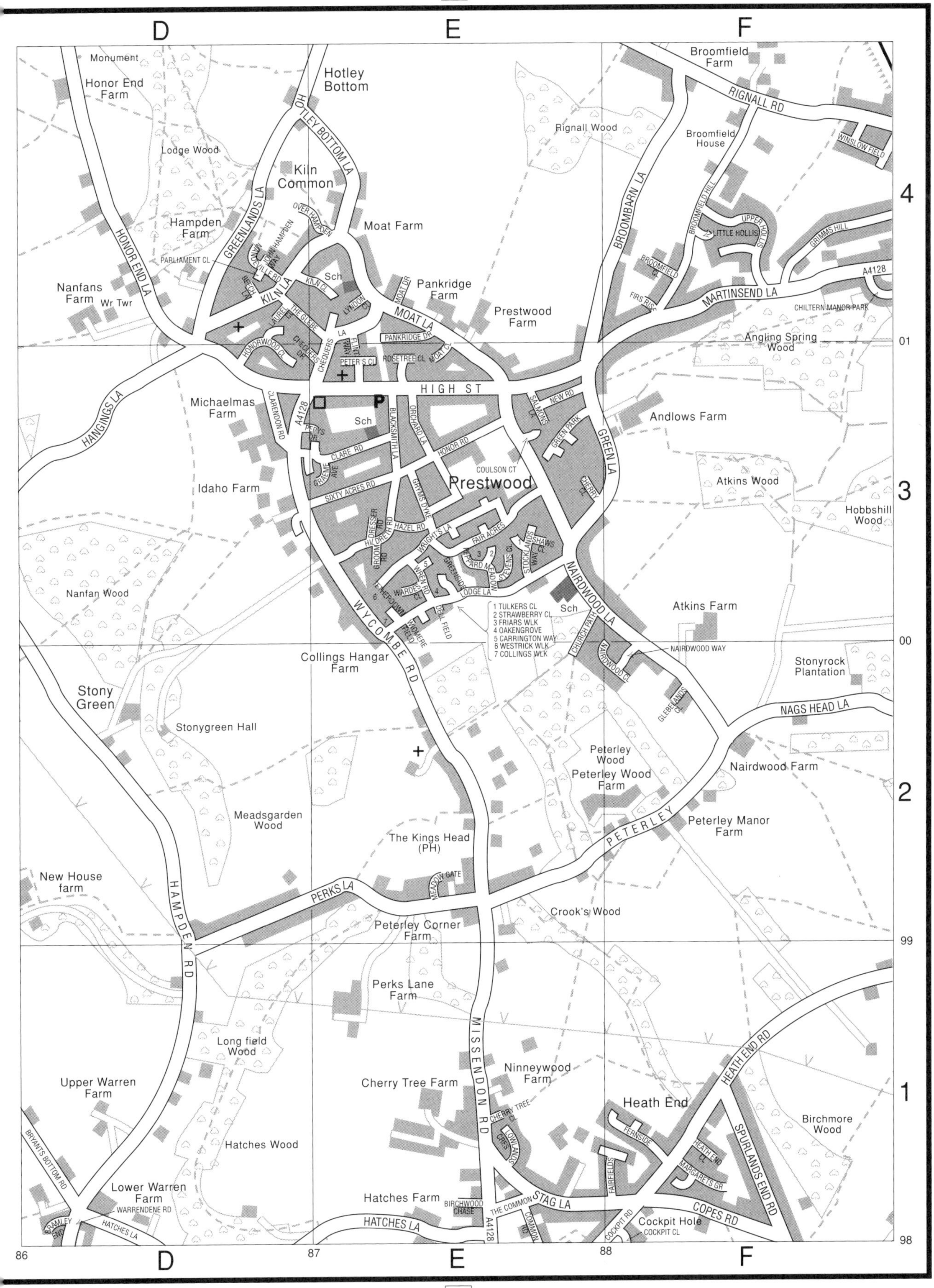

D
E
F
Monument
Honor End Farm
Hotley Bottom
Broomfield Farm
RIGNALL RD
Rignall Wood
Broomfield House
WINSLOW FIELD
Lodge Wood
Kiln Common
HOTLEY BOTTOM LA
BROOMBARN LA
BROOMFIELD HILL
UPPER HOLLIS
LITTLE HOLLIS
GRIMMS HILL
4
Hampden Farm
GREENLANDS LA
OVER HAMPDEN
Moat Farm
HONOR END LA
PARLIAMENT CL
Sch
BROOMFIELD CL
A4128
Nanfans Farm
Wr Twr
KILN LA
KILN CL
Pankridge Farm
MOAT DR
FIRS RISE
MARTINSEND LA
CHILTERN MANOR PARK
THE GLEBE
LYNDON CL
MOAT LA
Prestwood Farm
HONORWOOD CL
CHEQUERS DR
CHEQUERS LA
FLINT WAY
PANKRIDGE DR
Angling Spring Wood
01
PETER'S CL
ROSETREE CL
MOAT CL
HIGH ST
HANGINGS LA
Michaelmas Farm
CLARENDON RD
A4128
P
Sch
SALMONS LA
NEW RD
Andlows Farm
PEPYS DR
BLACKSMITH LA
ORCHARD LA
HONOR RD
GREEN PARK
GREEN LA
CLARE RD
COULSON CT
Idaho Farm
GREENE AVE
SIXTY ACRES RD
GRYMS DYKE
Prestwood
CHERRY CL
Atkins Wood
3
Hobbshill Wood
DRESSER RD
HAZEL RD
FAIR ACRES
WRIGHTS LA
SHAWS WAY
STOCKLANDS
STEVENS CL
MEADOW
GREENSIDE
NAIRDWOOD LA
Nanfan Wood
WARDES CL
LODGE LA
Sch
Atkins Farm
WYCOMBE RD
1 TULKERS CL
2 STRAWBERRY CL
3 FRIARS WLK
4 OAKENGROVE
5 CARRINGTON WAY
6 WESTRICK WLK
7 COLLINGS WLK
CHURCH PATH
00
NAIRDWOOD WAY
NAIRDWOOD CL
DELL FIELD
Collings Hangar Farm
Stonyrock Plantation
Stony Green
GLEBELANDS CL
NAGS HEAD LA
Stonygreen Hall
Peterley Wood
Peterley Wood Farm
Nairdwood Farm
2
Meadsgarden Wood
PETERLEY
Peterley Manor Farm
The Kings Head (PH)
New House farm
MEADOW GATE
HAMPDEN RD
PERKS LA
Crook's Wood
Peterley Corner Farm
99
Perks Lane Farm
MISSENDON RD
Long field Wood
HEATH END RD
Upper Warren Farm
Cherry Tree Farm
Ninneywood Farm
1
Heath End
CHERRY TREE CL
FERNSIDE
Birchmore Wood
SPURLANDS END RD
Hatches Wood
LOWLANDS CRES
HEATH END CL
MARGARETS GR
BRYANTS BOTTOM RD
FAIRFIELDS
Lower Warren Farm
Hatches Farm
BIRCHWOOD CHASE
THE COMMON
STAG LA
COPES RD
WARRENDENE RD
COMMON RD
COCKPIT RD
Cockpit Hole
COCKPIT CL
BRAMLEY END
HATCHES LA
HATCHES LA
A4128
98
86
87
88
D
E
F

152

162

142

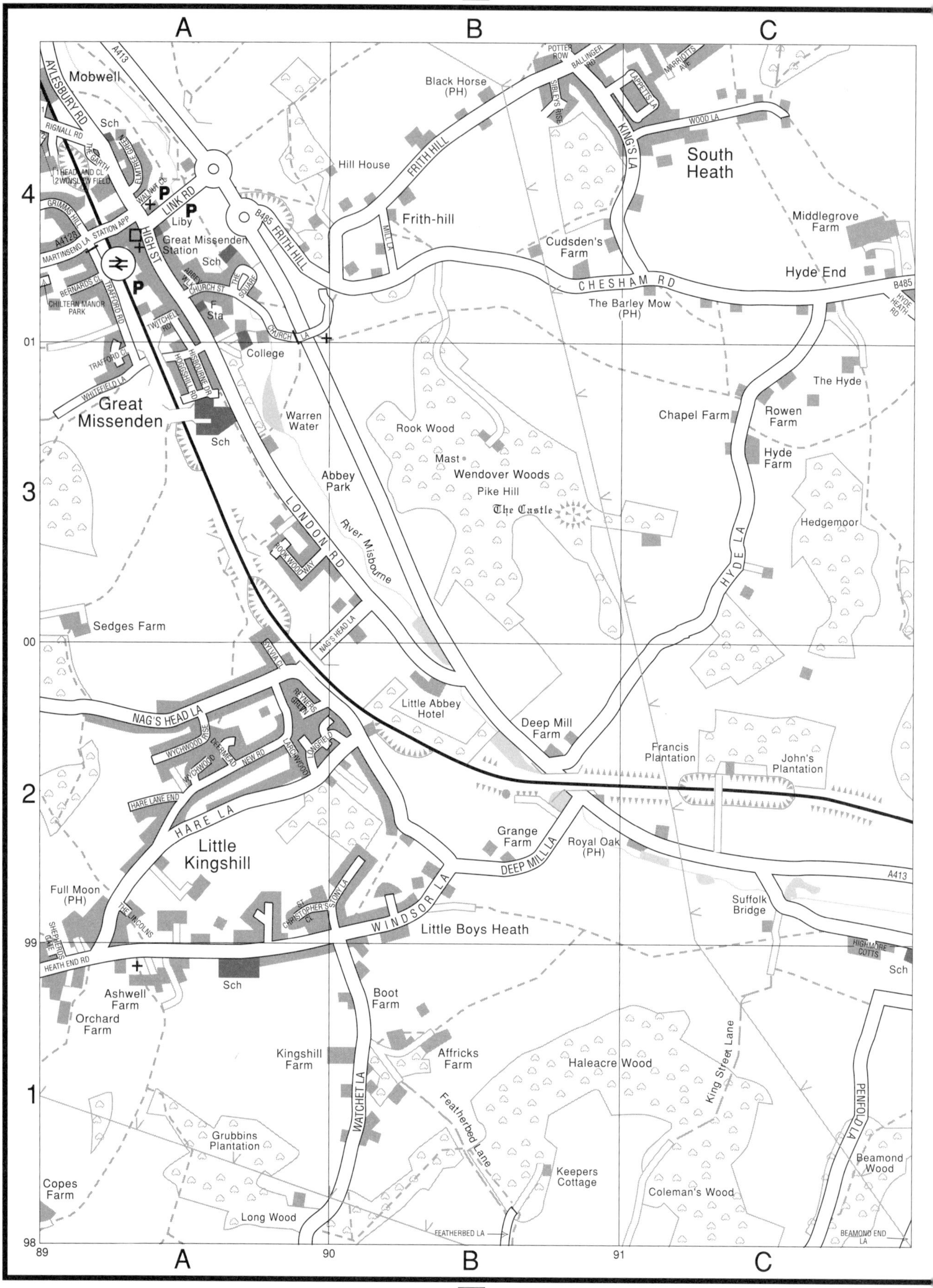
A
B
C
Mobwell
AYLESBURY RD
A413
Sch
RIGNALL RD
THE GARTH
ELMTREE GREEN
HEADLAND CL
WINSLOW FIELD
WALNUT CL
P
LINK RD
Liby
P
GRIMMS HILL
A4128
MARTINSEND LA
STATION APP
HIGH ST
Great Missenden Station
Sch
ABBEY WLK
CHURCH ST
THE SQUARE
P
BERNARDS CL
TRAFFORD RD
CHILTERN MANOR PARK
TWITCHELL RD
F Sta
CHURCH LA
College
TRAFFORD CL
HIGHBURN DR
HOGGSHILL RD
WHITEFIELD LA
Great Missenden
Warren Water
Sch
Black Horse (PH)
POTTER ROW
BALLINGER RD
SIBLEYS RISE
LAPPETTS LA
MARRIOTTS AVE
WOOD LA
FRITH HILL
KING'S LA
South Heath
Hill House
Frith-hill
MILL LA
B485 FRITH HILL
Cudsden's Farm
Middlegrove Farm
Hyde End
CHESHAM RD
B485
HYDE HEATH RD
The Barley Mow (PH)
The Hyde
Chapel Farm
Rowen Farm
Hyde Farm
Rook Wood
Mast
Wendover Woods
Pike Hill
The Castle
Abbey Park
LONDON RD
River Misbourne
ROCKWOOD WAY
Hedgemoor
HYDE LA
Sedges Farm
NAG'S HEAD LA
SYLVIA CL
REYNERS GREEN
Little Abbey Hotel
Deep Mill Farm
NAG'S HEAD LA
WYCHWOOD RISE
DEERMEAD
NEW RD
LARCHWOOD
LONGFIELD
WYCHWOOD
Francis Plantation
John's Plantation
HARE LANE END
HARE LA
Grange Farm
DEEP MILL LA
Royal Oak (PH)
Little Kingshill
A413
Full Moon (PH)
THE LINCOLNS
ST CHRISTOPHER'S CL
STONY LA
WINDSOR LA
Little Boys Heath
Suffolk Bridge
SHEPHERDS GATE
HEATH END RD
HIGHMORE COTTS
Sch
Sch
Ashwell Farm
Boot Farm
Orchard Farm
Kingshill Farm
Affricks Farm
Haleacre Wood
King Street Lane
PENFOLD LA
WATCHET LA
Featherbed Lane
Grubbins Plantation
Keepers Cottage
Beamond Wood
Copes Farm
Coleman's Wood
Long Wood
FEATHERBED LA
BEAMOND END LA
4
01
3
00
2
99
1
98
89
90
91
A
B
C

151

163

143

D
E
F
BLIND LA
Blind Lane
PEDNOR RD
DRYDELL LA
Willow Coppice
LITTLE HUNDRIDGE LA
The Plantation
Hundridge Manor
Chapel
Devil's Den
4
CHESHAM RD
Lower Hundridge Farm
B485
BROWNS RD
Hawthorn Farm
Halfway House Farm
MISSENDEN RD
B485
HALFWAY HOUSE LA
01
Hyde House
Halfway House Lane
HYDE HEATH RD
White's Wood
3
The Green
Monk's Wood
White House Farm
Sch
BULLBAITERS LA
Mantle's Wood
Hydeheath Common
The Plough (PH)
Hyde Heath
BRAYS LA
SAUNDERS END
HARVEST BANK
WESTFIELD
MEADOW WAY
BRAYS MEADOW
BRAYS CL
WALNUT WAY
00
Weedon Hill Farm
WEEDON HILL
COPPERKINS LA
Castle Tower
Motte & Bailey
BRAYS GREEN LA
Mantle's Farm
CHALK LA
Bray's Wood
KEEPERS LA
Weedonhill Farm
2
A413
The Vicarage
Lott's Wood
Ash Grove Plantation
Weedonhill Wood
Lime Farm
Mill End
99
Crown (PH)
High Spring
Sch
Keeper's Wood
Little Missendon
Ash Grove
Ostler's Wood
Toby's Farm
River Misbourne
Kennel Farm
BEAMOND END LA
New Sowed Wood
Toby's Lane
1
MOP END LA
Breaches Wood
Todd's Wood
Lower Park
SCHOOL LA
A413
98
92
93
94
D
E
F

154

164

144

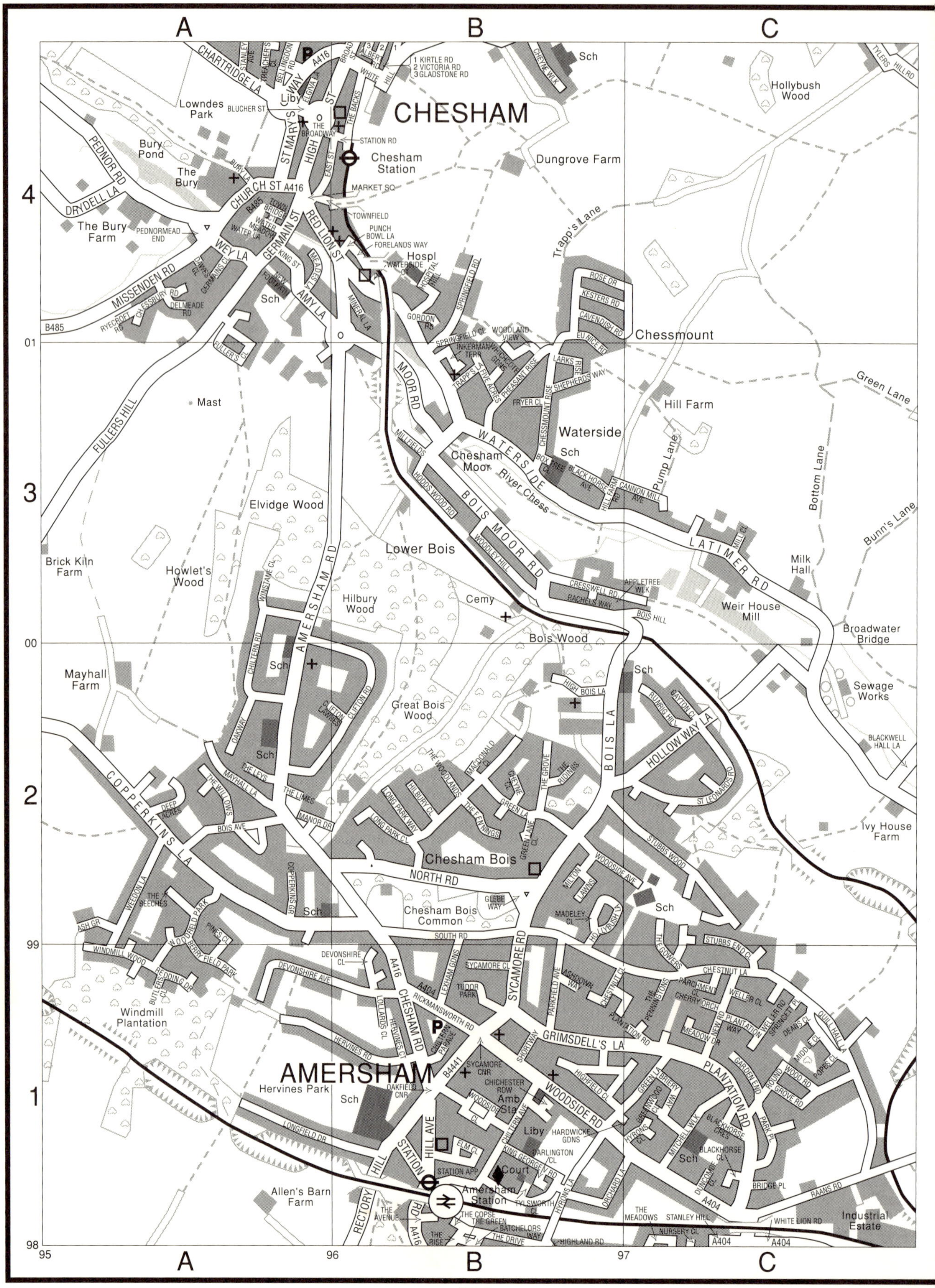
CHESHAM
AMERSHAM
Chesham Station
Amersham Station
Lowndes Park
Bury Pond
The Bury
The Bury Farm
Dungrove Farm
Hollybush Wood
Chessmount
Hill Farm
Waterside
Chesham Moor
River Chess
Elvidge Wood
Brick Kiln Farm
Howlet's Wood
Lower Bois
Hilbury Wood
Cemy
Bois Wood
Weir House Mill
Milk Hall
Broadwater Bridge
Mayhall Farm
Great Bois Wood
Sewage Works
Ivy House Farm
Chesham Bois
Chesham Bois Common
Windmill Plantation
Hervines Park
Allen's Barn Farm
Industrial Estate
Mast
Hospl
Sch
Liby
Court
Green Lane
Bottom Lane
Bunn's Lane
Pump Lane
Trapp's Lane
MISSENDEN RD
CHURCH ST
FULLERS HILL
AMERSHAM RD
MOOR RD
WATERSIDE
BOIS MOOR RD
LATIMER RD
BOIS LA
HOLLOW WAY LA
COPPERKINS LA
NORTH RD
SOUTH RD
SYCAMORE RD
CHESHAM RD
RICKMANSWORTH RD
GRIMSDELL'S LA
WOODSIDE RD
PLANTATION RD
STATION RD
HIGH ST
RED LION ST
A
B
C
4
3
2
1
95
96
97
01
00
99
98

153

165

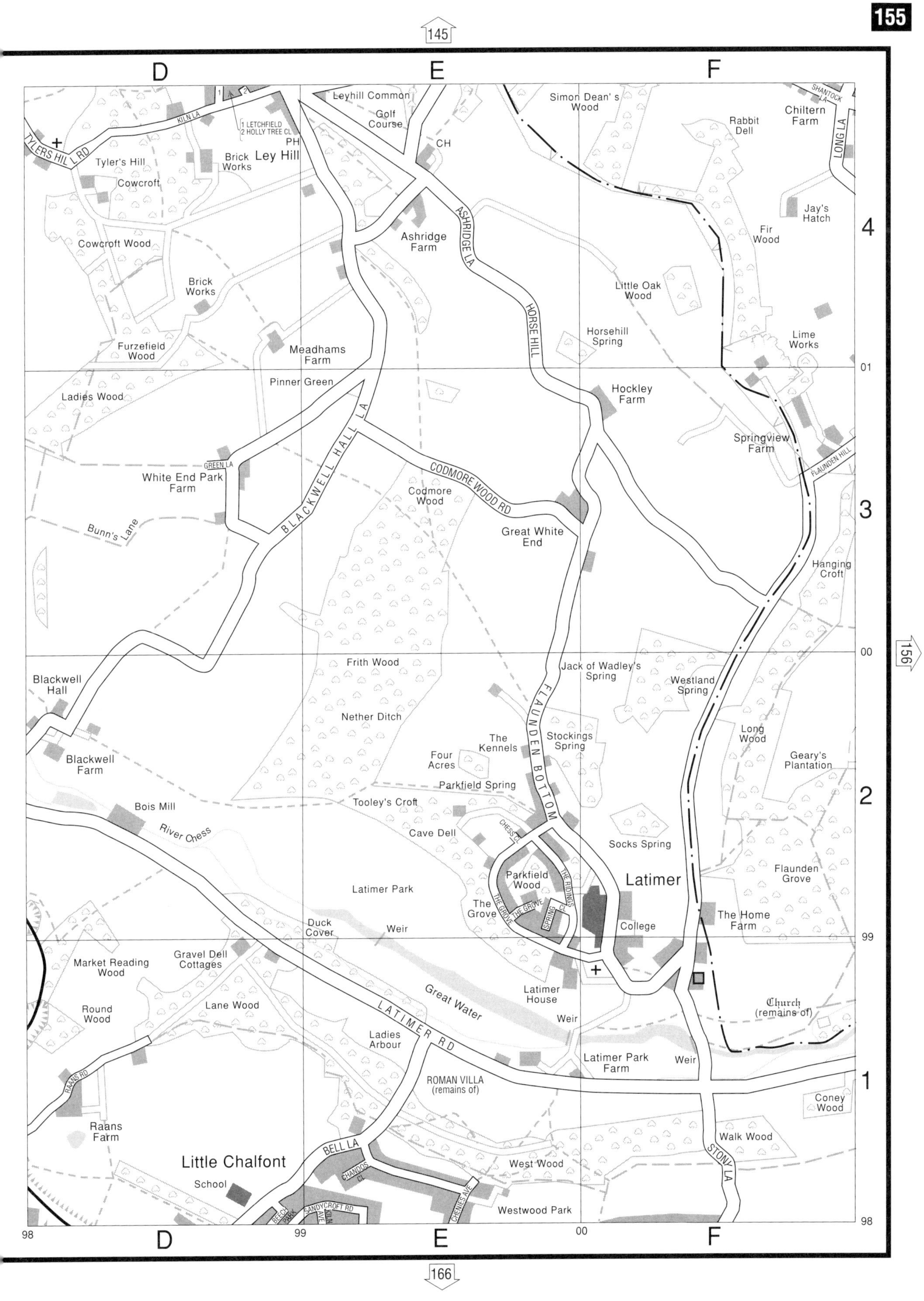
145
D
E
F
Leyhill Common
Golf Course
CH
Simon Dean's Wood
Chiltern Farm
Rabbit Dell
SHANTOCK LA
LONG LA
KILN LA
1 LETCHFIELD
2 HOLLY TREE CL
TYLERS HILL RD
Tyler's Hill
PH
Brick Works
Ley Hill
Cowcroft
Jay's Hatch
ASHRIDGE LA
Ashridge Farm
Fir Wood
Cowcroft Wood
4
Brick Works
Little Oak Wood
HORSE HILL
Horsehill Spring
Lime Works
Meadhams Farm
Furzefield Wood
01
Pinner Green
Hockley Farm
Ladies Wood
BLACKWELL HALL LA
Springview Farm
CODMORE WOOD RD
GREEN LA
FLAUNDEN HILL
White End Park Farm
Codmore Wood
3
Bunn's Lane
Great White End
Hanging Croft
00
156
Frith Wood
Jack of Wadley's Spring
Blackwell Hall
Westland Spring
FLAUNDEN BOTTOM
Nether Ditch
Long Wood
The Kennels
Stockings Spring
Blackwell Farm
Four Acres
Geary's Plantation
Parkfield Spring
2
Bois Mill
Tooley's Croft
River Chess
Cave Dell
CHESS CL
Socks Spring
Parkfield Wood
Latimer
Flaunden Grove
THE RIDINGS
Latimer Park
The Grove
THE GROVE
SPRING CL
The Home Farm
College
Duck Cover
Weir
99
Gravel Dell Cottages
Market Reading Wood
Great Water
Latimer House
Round Wood
Lane Wood
Church (remains of)
LATIMER RD
Weir
Ladies Arbour
Latimer Park Farm
Weir
RAANS RD
1
ROMAN VILLA (remains of)
Coney Wood
Raans Farm
Walk Wood
BELL LA
STONY LA
Little Chalfont
CHANDOS CL
West Wood
School
CHENIES AVE
SANDYCROFT RD
KILN AVE
BEECH PARK
Westwood Park
98
98
99
00
D
E
F
166

146

155

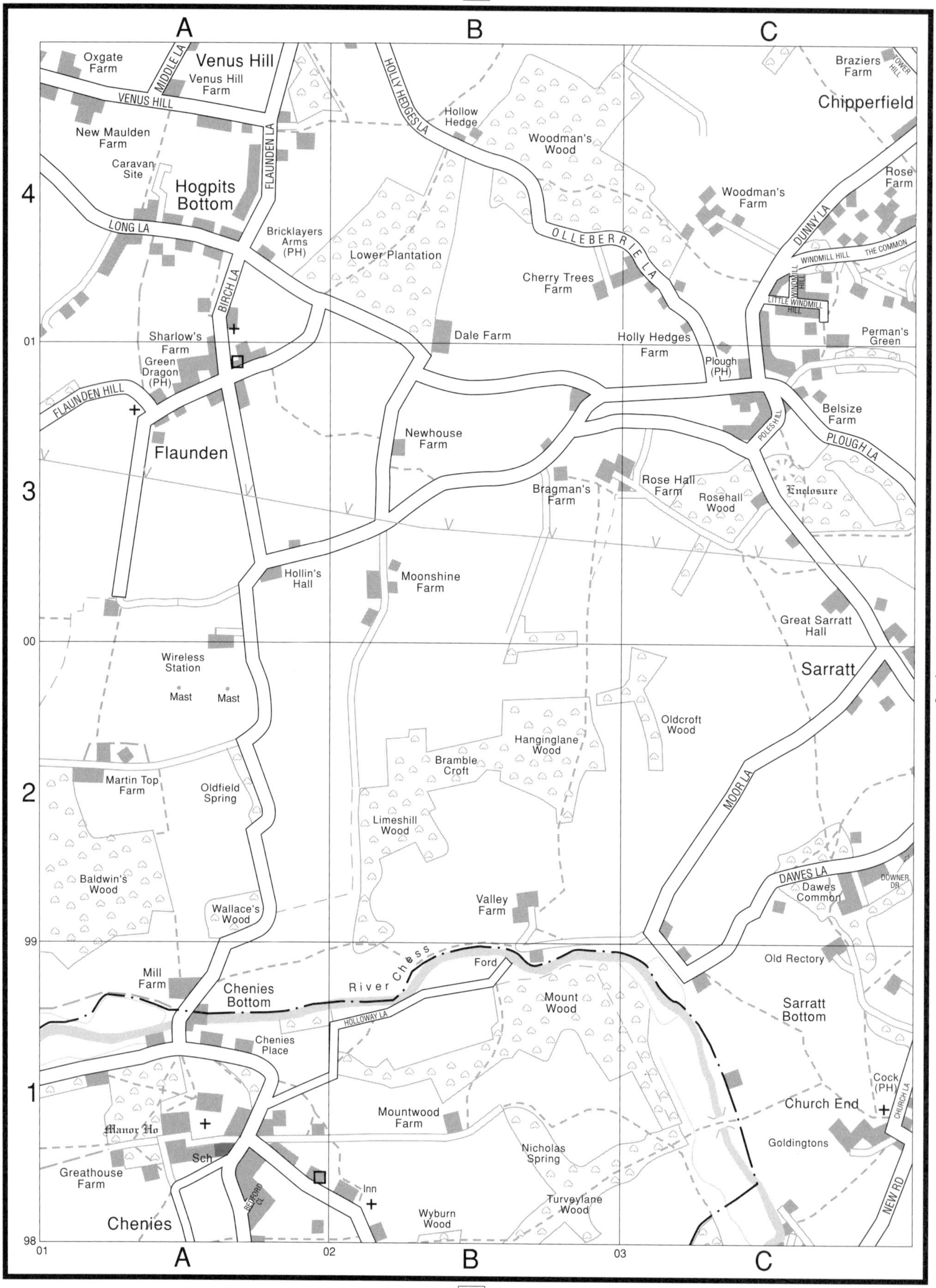

A
B
C
4
3
2
1
01
00
99
98
01
02
03
Oxgate Farm
MIDDLE LA
Venus Hill
Venus Hill Farm
VENUS HILL
New Maulden Farm
Caravan Site
Hogpits Bottom
FLAUNDEN LA
LONG LA
Bricklayers Arms (PH)
BIRCH LA
Sharlow's Farm
Green Dragon (PH)
FLAUNDEN HILL
Flaunden
HOLLY HEDGES LA
Hollow Hedge
Woodman's Wood
Lower Plantation
OLLEBERRIE LA
Cherry Trees Farm
Dale Farm
Holly Hedges Farm
Plough (PH)
Newhouse Farm
Bragman's Farm
Rose Hall Farm
Rosehall Wood
Hollin's Hall
Moonshine Farm
Braziers Farm
LOWER HILL
Chipperfield
Rose Farm
Woodman's Farm
DUNNY LA
WINDMILL HILL
THE COMMON
LITTLE WINDMILL HILL
Perman's Green
POLES HILL
Belsize Farm
PLOUGH LA
Enclosure
Great Sarratt Hall
Sarratt
Wireless Station
Mast
Mast
Oldcroft Wood
Hanginglane Wood
Bramble Croft
Martin Top Farm
Oldfield Spring
Limeshill Wood
MOOR LA
Baldwin's Wood
Wallace's Wood
Valley Farm
DAWES LA
Dawes Common
DOWNER DR
Old Rectory
Mill Farm
Chenies Bottom
River Chess
Ford
Mount Wood
Sarratt Bottom
HOLLOWAY LA
Chenies Place
Cock (PH)
CHURCH LA
Church End
Goldingtons
Mountwood Farm
Manor Ho
Sch
Greathouse Farm
Nicholas Spring
Inn
Turveylane Wood
Wyburn Wood
BEDFORD CL
Chenies
NEW RD

167

not continued, see key diagram

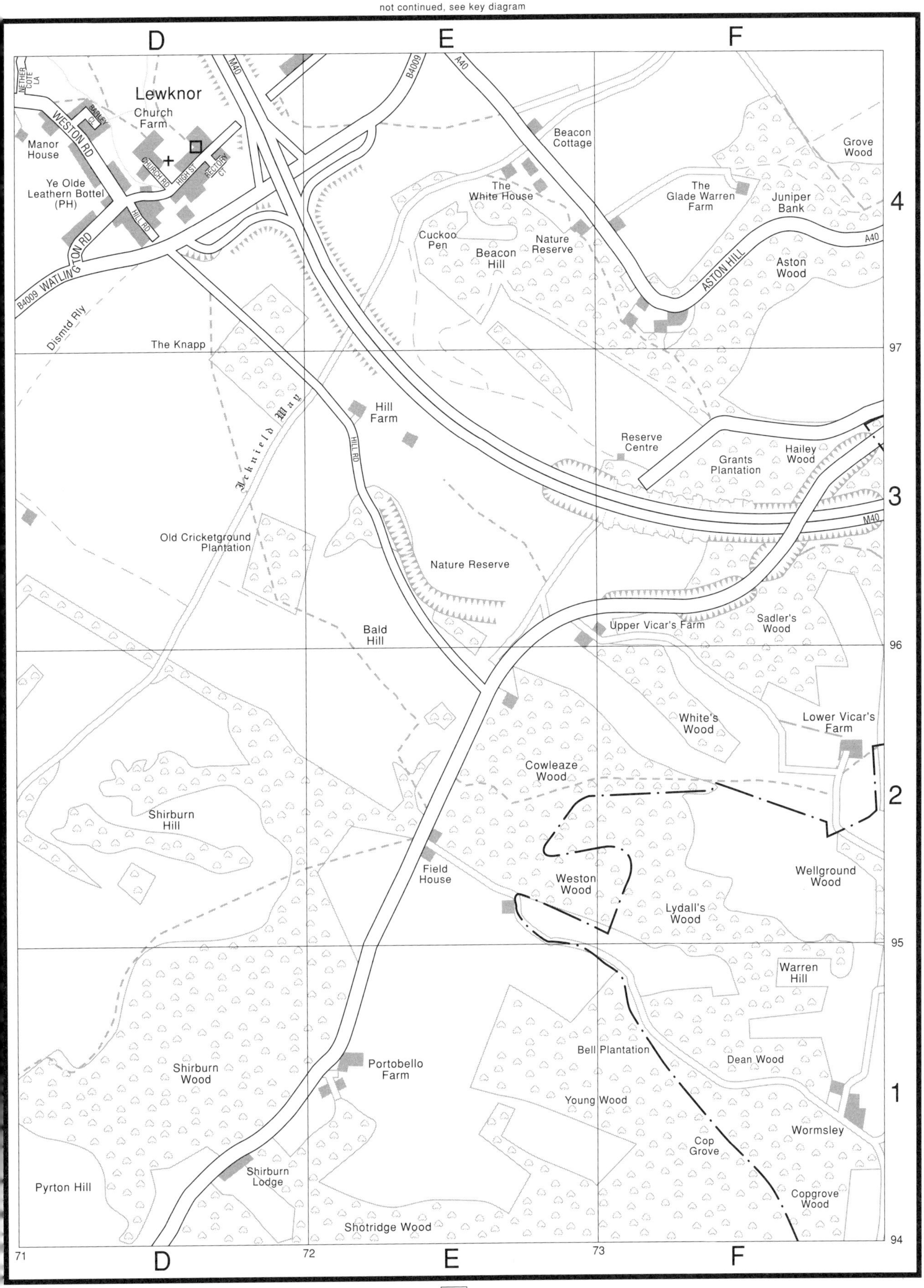

158

168

147

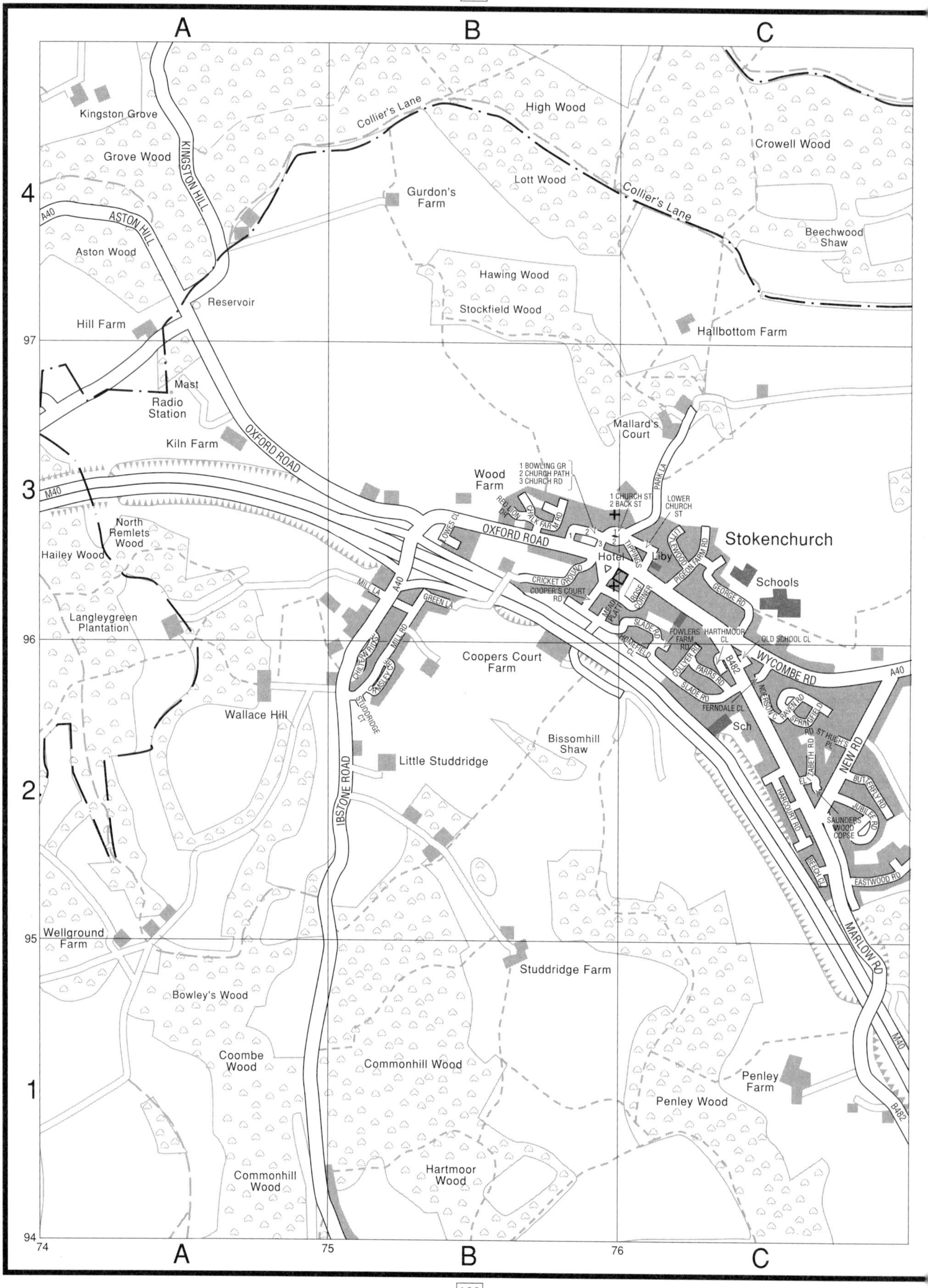
A
B
C
4
3
2
1
97
96
95
94
74
75
76
Kingston Grove
Grove Wood
KINGSTON HILL
Collier's Lane
High Wood
Crowell Wood
Lott Wood
Gurdon's Farm
A40
ASTON HILL
Aston Wood
Beechwood Shaw
Hawing Wood
Reservoir
Stockfield Wood
Hill Farm
Hallbottom Farm
Mast
Radio Station
Mallard's Court
Kiln Farm
OXFORD ROAD
PARK LA
1 BOWLING GR
2 CHURCH PATH
3 CHURCH RD
Wood Farm
1 CHURCH ST
2 BACK ST
LOWER CHURCH ST
M40
North Remlets Wood
Stokenchurch
Hailey Wood
Hotel
Liby
Schools
CRICKET GROUND
COOPER'S COURT RD
MILL LA
GREEN LA
GEORGE RD
Langleygreen Plantation
SLADE RD
FOWLERS FARM RD
HARTHMOOR CL
OLD SCHOOL CL
HOMEFIELD CL
CHILTERN RIDGE
MILL RD
Coopers Court Farm
WYCOMBE RD
B482
PARRS RD
Wallace Hill
STUDDRIDGE CT
FERNDALE CL
Sch
Bissomhill Shaw
Little Studdridge
NEW RD
IBSTONE ROAD
HARCOURT RD
BUTTERFLY RD
JUBILEE RD
SAUNDERS WOOD COPSE
BEECH CL
EASTWOOD RD
Wellground Farm
MARLOW RD
Studdridge Farm
Bowley's Wood
Coombe Wood
Commonhill Wood
Penley Farm
Penley Wood
Hartmoor Wood
Commonhill Wood

157

169

148

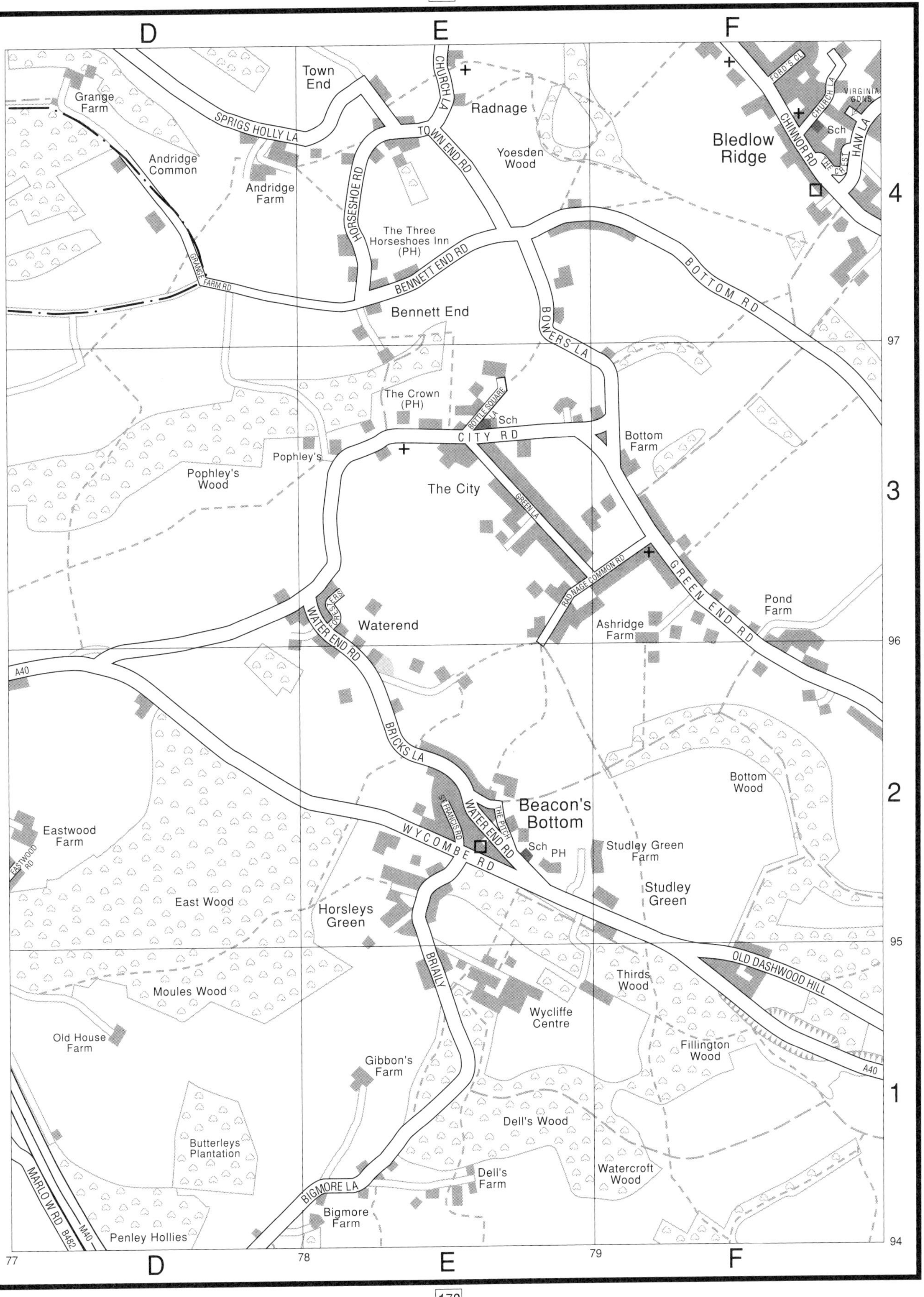
D
E
F
Town End
Grange Farm
Radnage
Bledlow Ridge
Andridge Common
Andridge Farm
Yoesden Wood
SPRIGS HOLLY LA
CHURCH LA
TOWN END RD
HORSESHOE RD
FORD'S CL
VIRGINIA GDNS
CHINNOR RD
HAW LA
THE CREST
Sch
The Three Horseshoes Inn (PH)
BENNETT END RD
GRANGE FARM RD
BOTTOM RD
Bennett End
BOWERS LA
The Crown (PH)
BOTTLE SQUARE LA
Sch
CITY RD
Bottom Farm
Pophley's
Pophley's Wood
The City
GREEN LA
RADNAGE COMMON RD
GREEN END RD
FORESTERS
Waterend
WATER END RD
Ashridge Farm
Pond Farm
A40
BRICKS LA
Bottom Wood
Beacon's Bottom
ST FRANCIS RD
WATER END RD
THE PITCH
Eastwood Farm
EASTWOOD RD
WYCOMBE RD
Sch
PH
Studley Green Farm
Studley Green
East Wood
Horsleys Green
BRIAILY
OLD DASHWOOD HILL
Thirds Wood
Moules Wood
Wycliffe Centre
Fillington Wood
A40
Old House Farm
Gibbon's Farm
Dell's Wood
Butterleys Plantation
Watercroft Wood
Dell's Farm
BIGMORE LA
MARLOW RD
B482
M40
Bigmore Farm
Penley Hollies
4
97
3
96
2
95
1
94
77
78
79
D
E
F
160

170

149

159

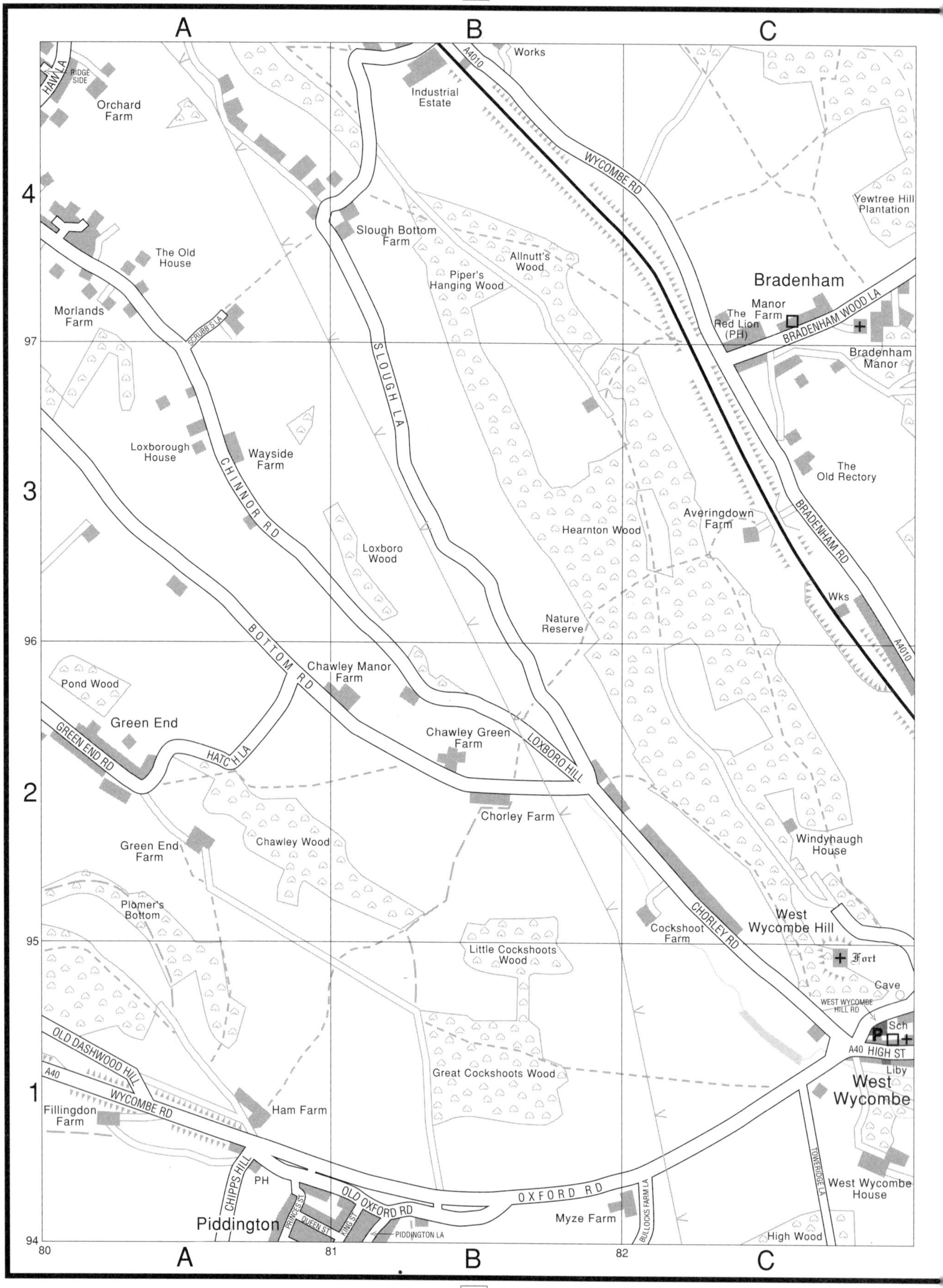
A
B
C
4
3
2
1
97
96
95
94
80
81
82
HAW LA
RIDGE SIDE
Orchard Farm
Industrial Estate
Works
A4010
WYCOMBE RD
Yewtree Hill Plantation
The Old House
Slough Bottom Farm
Allnutt's Wood
Piper's Hanging Wood
Bradenham
Manor Farm
The Red Lion (PH)
BRADENHAM WOOD LA
Bradenham Manor
Morlands Farm
SCRUBB'S LA
SLOUGH LA
Loxborough House
Wayside Farm
CHINNOR RD
The Old Rectory
Averingdown Farm
Hearnton Wood
BRADENHAM RD
Loxboro Wood
Wks
Nature Reserve
BOTTOM RD
Pond Wood
Chawley Manor Farm
Green End
GREEN END RD
HATCH LA
Chawley Green Farm
LOXBORO HILL
Chorley Farm
Windyhaugh House
Green End Farm
Chawley Wood
Plomer's Bottom
Cockshoot Farm
CHORLEY RD
West Wycombe Hill
Fort
Little Cockshoots Wood
Cave
WEST WYCOMBE HILL RD
Sch
A40 HIGH ST
Liby
OLD DASHWOOD HILL
A40
Great Cockshoots Wood
West Wycombe
Fillingdon Farm
WYCOMBE RD
Ham Farm
CHIPPS HILL
PH
TOWERIDGE LA
West Wycombe House
OLD OXFORD RD
OXFORD RD
PRINCES ST
QUEEN ST
KING ST
Piddington
PIDDINGTON LA
Myze Farm
BULLOCKS FARM LA
High Wood

171

150

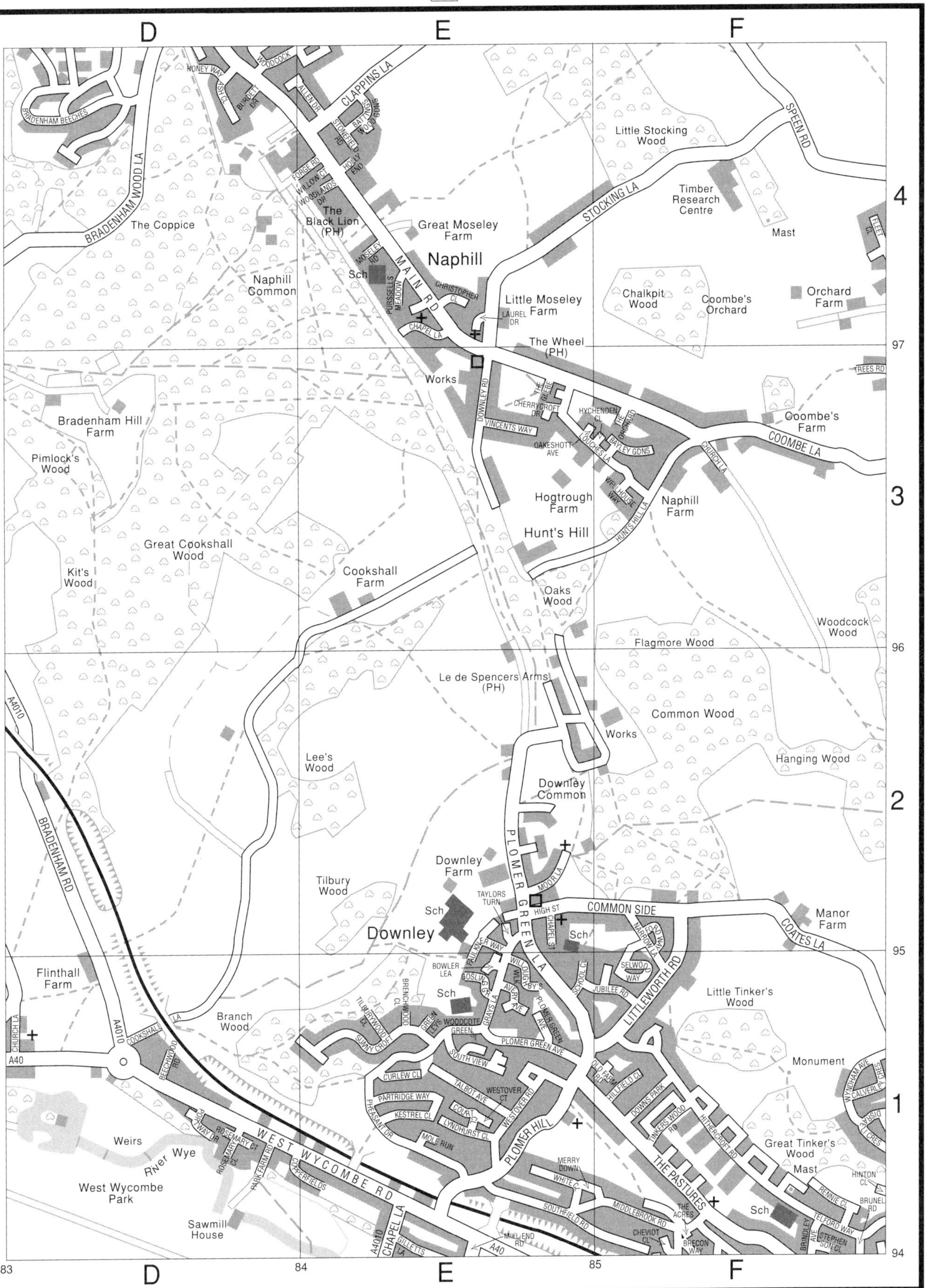
D
E
F
4
3
2
1
97
96
95
94
83
84
85
Naphill
Downley
Hunt's Hill
Bradenham Wood La
Bradenham Beeches
The Coppice
Naphill Common
The Black Lion (PH)
Great Moseley Farm
Main Rd
Clappins La
Stocking La
Little Stocking Wood
Timber Research Centre
Mast
Speen Rd
Little Moseley Farm
Chalkpit Wood
Coombe's Orchard
Orchard Farm
The Wheel (PH)
Works
Downley Rd
Vincents Way
Bradenham Hill Farm
Pimlock's Wood
Coombe's Farm
Coombe La
Church La
Hogtrough Farm
Naphill Farm
Hunts Hill La
Great Cookshall Wood
Kit's Wood
Cookshall Farm
Oaks Wood
Woodcock Wood
Flagmore Wood
Le de Spencers Arms (PH)
Common Wood
Works
Lee's Wood
Hanging Wood
Downley Common
Bradenham Rd
A4010
Plomer Green La
Downley Farm
Tilbury Wood
Sch
Common Side
Manor Farm
Coates La
High St
Littleworth Rd
Little Tinker's Wood
Flinthall Farm
Branch Wood
Monument
A40
West Wycombe Rd
Plomer Hill
The Pastures
Great Tinker's Wood
Weirs
River Wye
West Wycombe Park
Sawmill House
Chapel La

162

172

151

161

A
B
C
4
3
2
1
97
96
95
94
86
87
88
HATCHES LA
Longrove Plantations
WARRENDENE RD
CHERRY TREE CL
SOUTH MAUNDIN
FRIARS GDNS
Hughenden Valley
Sch
ORCHARD CL
TREES RD
TREES AVE
COOMBE LA
BURNHAM RD
WHITEFIELD RD
Lodge
BOSS LA
PIPERS LA
Gomms Wood
Boss Lane Farm
Provost Wood
A4128
VALLEY RD
Church Farm
Hughenden Manor
Hughenden Park
Sports Ground
Middle Lodge
WHITE HILL
COATES LA
HUGHENDEN RD
HUGHENDEN AVE
Wks
MANOR GDNS
CONINGSBY RD
Allot Gdns
GREEN HILL
RIDGE WAY
HAMILTON RD
Green Wood
Green Hill
Millfield Wood
NEW RD
HOMELANDS GDNS
MISSENDEN RD
COCKPIT RD
Springfields
White Lion (PH)
Sch
CRYERS HILL RD
SCHOOL CL
Cryers Hill
CRYERS HILL LA
Cemy
FOUR ASHES RD
Town Wood
Uplands
Four Ashes
CHURCH LA
Brands House
Cockshoot Wood
Masts
KINGSHILL RD
Sch
Terriers Farm
Terriers
AMERSHAM RD
GREEN RD
Sch
ARNISON AVE
A404
Great Kingshill
Hoppers Farm
Sladmore Farm
Industrial Estate
Hawbushes Farm
Primrose Farm
SPURLANDS END RD
WINDMILL LA
PRIMROSE HILL
Widmer End
Widmer End Farm
BRIMMERS HILL
Widmer Farm
NORTH RD
GRANGE RD
Royal Standard (PH)
Rec Gd
Schs
Grange Farm
BEAUMONT WAY
GREEN ST
Recreation Ground
PH
Sch
TOTTERIDGE LA
Sch
King's Wood
P

173

152

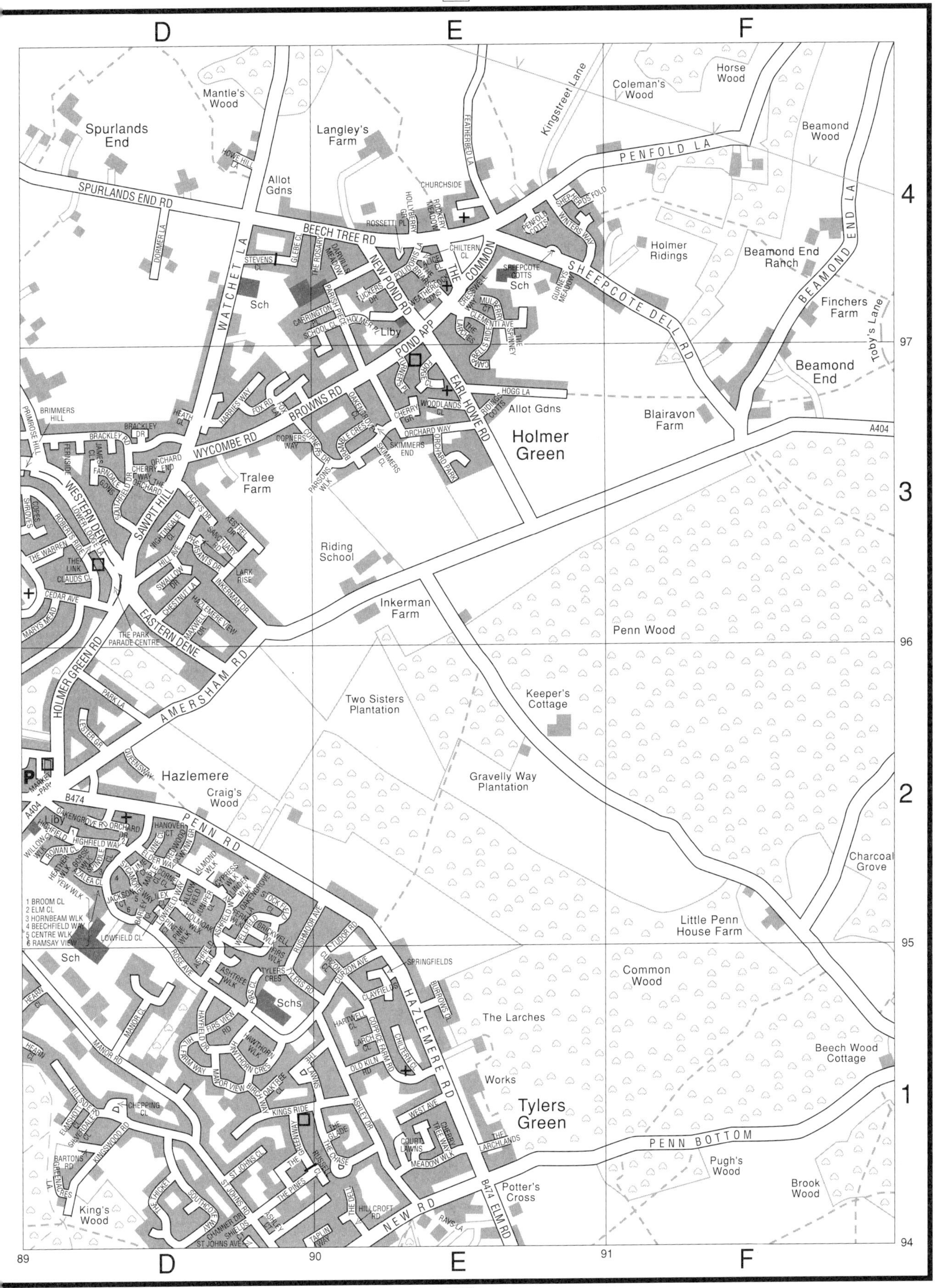
D
E
F
Mantle's Wood
Spurlands End
Langley's Farm
Coleman's Wood
Horse Wood
Kingstreet Lane
Beamond Wood
PENFOLD LA
SPURLANDS END RD
Allot Gdns
HOWE HILL LA
FEATHERBED LA
CHURCHSIDE
BEECH TREE RD
ROSSETTI PL
DORMER LA
STEVENS CL
WATCHET LA
Sch
THE COMMON
SHEEPCOTE COTTS
Sch
SHEEPCOTE DELL RD
Holmer Ridings
Beamond End Ranch
BEAMOND END LA
Finchers Farm
Toby's Lane
Beamond End
NEW POND RD
POND APP
Liby
EARL HOWE RD
HOGG LA
Allot Gdns
Blairavon Farm
Holmer Green
BROWNS RD
WYCOMBE RD
A404
Tralee Farm
WESTERN DENE
SAWPIT HILL
Riding School
Inkerman Farm
EASTERN DENE
THE PARK PARADE CENTRE
Penn Wood
HOLMER GREEN RD
AMERSHAM RD
Two Sisters Plantation
Keeper's Cottage
Hazlemere
Craig's Wood
Gravelly Way Plantation
B474
PENN RD
Charcoal Grove
1 BROOM CL
2 ELM CL
3 HORNBEAM WLK
4 BEECHFIELD WAY
5 CENTRE WLK
6 RAMSAY VIEW
Little Penn House Farm
Sch
Common Wood
Schs
HAZLEMERE RD
The Larches
Beech Wood Cottage
Works
Tylers Green
PENN BOTTOM
Pugh's Wood
Brook Wood
Potter's Cross
King's Wood
NEW RD
B474 ELM RD
4
3
2
1
97
96
95
94
89
90
91

164

174

153

A
B
C
4
3
2
1
97
96
95
94
92
93
94
High Wood
Shardeloes
Lower Park House
Lodges
SCHOOL LA
A413
MOP END LA
Toby's Lane
Upper Park
Summerville's Wood
Mop End Farm
Mop End
El Sub Sta
Wheatley Wood
The Rough Park
CHERRY LA
Model Farm
A404
Wycombe Lodge
Woodrow High House
Second Wood
Hundred Acres
Crematorium
Sch
Chancellors Corner
Woodrow
SCHOOL LA
Childs Farm
CHANCELLORS
Vicarage
WHIELDEN LA
Penn Street
Woodrow Farm
NEW RD
The Squirrel (PH)
Queen's Head (PH)
Factory
Priestlands Wood
Hit or Miss (PH)
Tragoe's Plantation
Picnic Area
HILL MEADOW
Coleshill
Pennstreet Farm
WHIELDEN LA
Coleshill Larches
West Wood
VILLAGE RD
MEADOW
COTT LA
Sch
NELSON CL
THE HILL
POND CL
Ferndale
Works
MANOR WAY
Red Lion (PH)
Charcoal Grove
Winchmore Hill
Penn House
BARRACKS HILL
Coleshill Common
The Potters Arms (PH)
COLESHILL LA
Pennhouse Grove
HORSEMOOR LA
Fagnall Farm
CHALK HILL
WINDMILL HILL
Glory Farm
FAGNALL LA
SAMPSONS HILL
MAGPIE LA
Lowlands
Luckings Farm
Hertfordshire House
Pennhouse Farm
Branches Wood
Penn Bottom
Lodge
Little Hertfordshire House

163

175

154

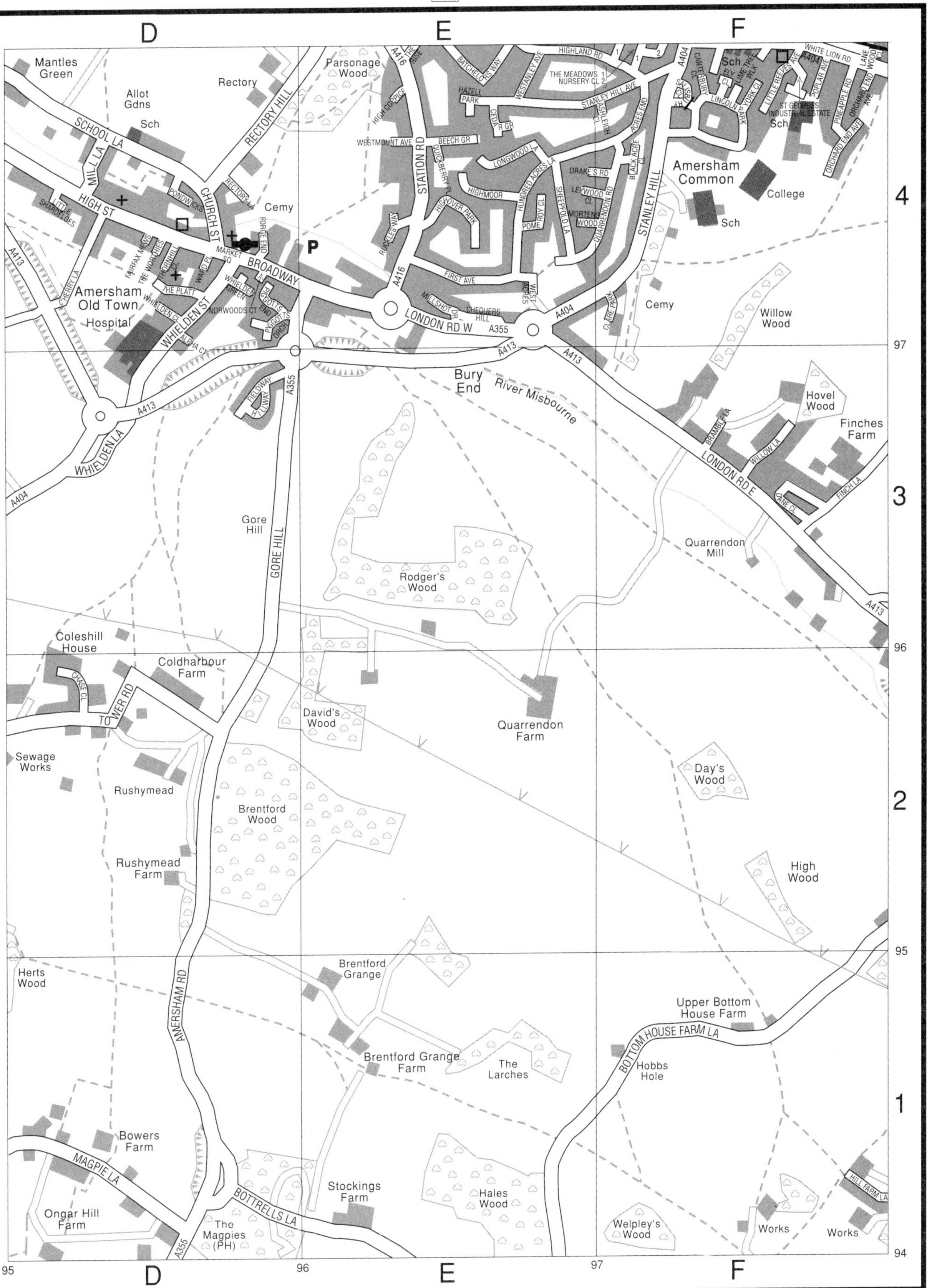

D
E
F
Mantles Green
Allot Gdns
Sch
Rectory
Parsonage Wood
SCHOOL LA
MILL LA
RECTORY HILL
HIGH ST
CHURCH ST
PONDWICKS
RECTORY LA
Cemy
FORGE END
MARKET SQ
BROADWAY
P
Amersham Old Town
Hospital
WHIELDEN ST
WHIELDEN LA
A413
A404
A416
A355
STATION RD
HIGHLAND RD
BATCHELORS WAY
WESTANLEY AVE
THE MEADOWS
NURSERY CL
STANLEY HILL AVE
HAZELL PARK
BEECH GR
WESTMOUNT AVE
HIGHMOOR
LONGWOOD LA
HUNDRED ACRES LA
DRAKE'S RD
LEYWOOD CL
MORTENS WOOD
QUARRENDON RD
SHEEPFOLD LA
BLACK ACRE CL
ACRES END
STANLEY HILL
FIRST AVE
RUCKLES WAY
MILLSHOT DR
CHEQUERS HILL
LONDON RD W
WEST ACRES
CLARE PARK
Amersham Common
College
Sch
Cemy
CANTERBURY CL
LINCOLN PARK
YORK CL
LITTLE REEVES AVE
POPLAR AVE
WHITE LION RD
PINEAPPLE RD
ORCHARD END AVE
ST GEORGES INDUSTRIAL ESTATE
Willow Wood
Bury End
River Misbourne
Hovel Wood
Finches Farm
BRAMBLE LA
WILLOW LA
LONDON RD E
FINCH LA
DANE CL
Gore Hill
GORE HILL
Rodger's Wood
Quarrendon Mill
Coleshill House
Coldharbour Farm
CHASE CL
TOWER RD
Sewage Works
Rushymead
David's Wood
Quarrendon Farm
Day's Wood
Brentford Wood
Rushymead Farm
High Wood
Herts Wood
AMERSHAM RD
Brentford Grange
Upper Bottom House Farm
BOTTOM HOUSE FARM LA
Brentford Grange Farm
The Larches
Hobbs Hole
Bowers Farm
MAGPIE LA
Stockings Farm
Hales Wood
BOTTRELLS LA
Ongar Hill Farm
The Magpies (PH)
Welpley's Wood
Works
Works
HILL FARM LA
4
3
2
1
97
96
95
94
95
96
97
166

176

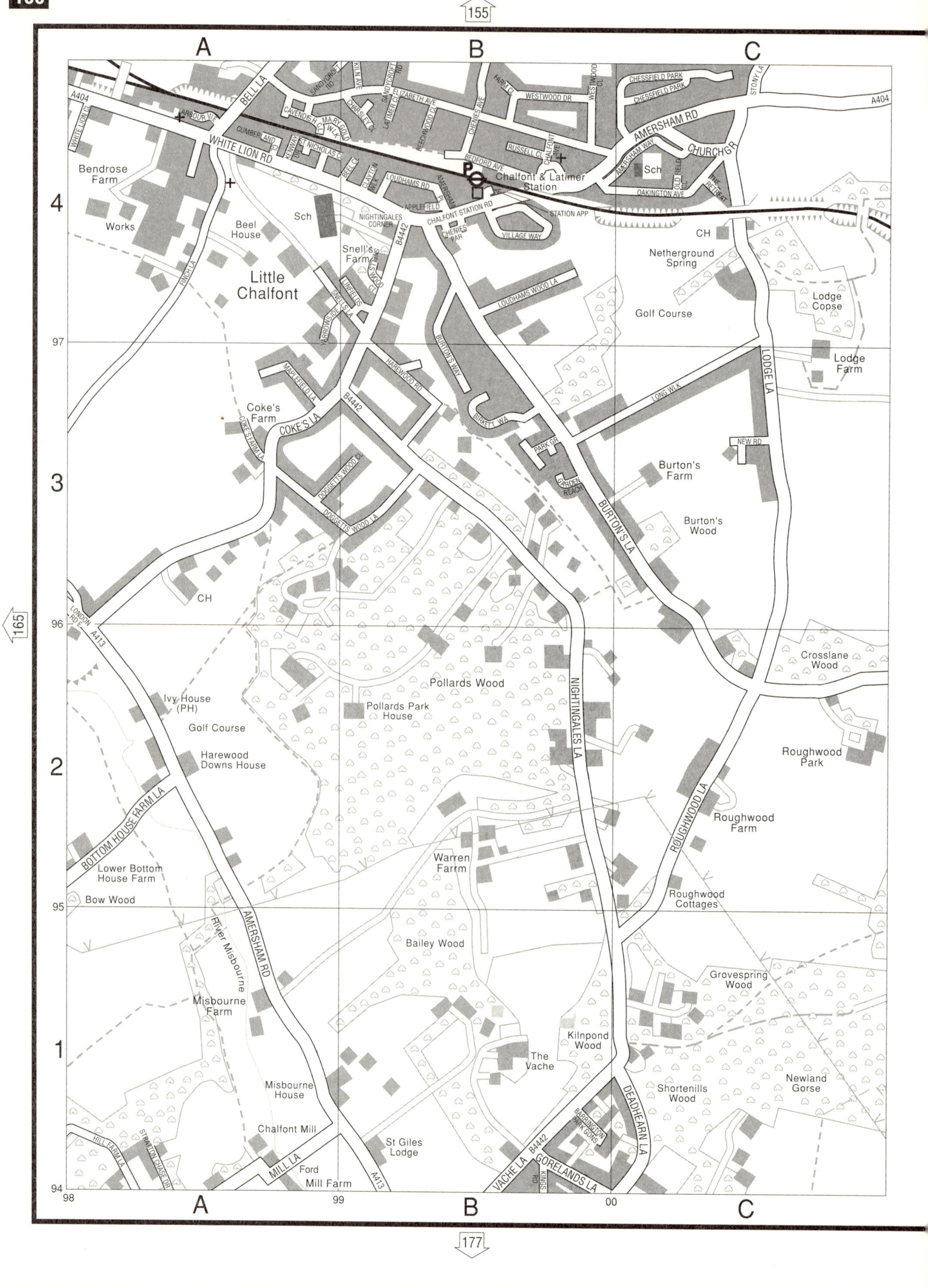
155
A
B
C
A404
WHITE LION RD
BELL LA
Bendrose Farm
Works
Beel House
Sch
Little Chalfont
Snell's Farm
NIGHTINGALES CORNER
B4442
Chalfont & Latimer Station
AMERSHAM RD
CHURCH GR
Sch
OAKINGTON AVE
STATION APP
VILLAGE WAY
CHALFONT STATION RD
CHENIES PAR
LOUDHAMS WOOD LA
BURTON'S WAY
HAREWOOD RD
Golf Course
Netherground Spring
CH
Lodge Copse
Lodge Farm
LODGE LA
LONG WLK
NEW RD
Burton's Farm
Burton's Wood
BURTON'S LA
BIRKETT WAY
PARK GR
GARDEN REACH
Coke's Farm
COKE'S LA
DOGGETTS WOOD CL
DOGGETTS WOOD LA
MAPLEFIELD LA
CH
LONDON RD
A413
Ivy House (PH)
Golf Course
Harewood Downs House
Pollards Wood
Pollards Park House
NIGHTINGALES LA
Crosslane Wood
Roughwood Park
Roughwood Farm
ROUGHWOOD LA
Roughwood Cottages
Warren Farrm
BOTTOM HOUSE FARM LA
Lower Bottom House Farm
Bow Wood
River Misbourne
AMERSHAM RD
Bailey Wood
Grovespring Wood
Misbourne Farm
Kilnpond Wood
The Vache
Shortenills Wood
Newland Gorse
DEADHEARN LA
Misbourne House
Chalfont Mill
St Giles Lodge
MILL LA
Ford
Mill Farm
VACHE LA
GORELANDS LA
HILL FARM LA
STRATTON CHASE DR
4
97
3
96
2
95
1
94
98
99
00
165
177

156

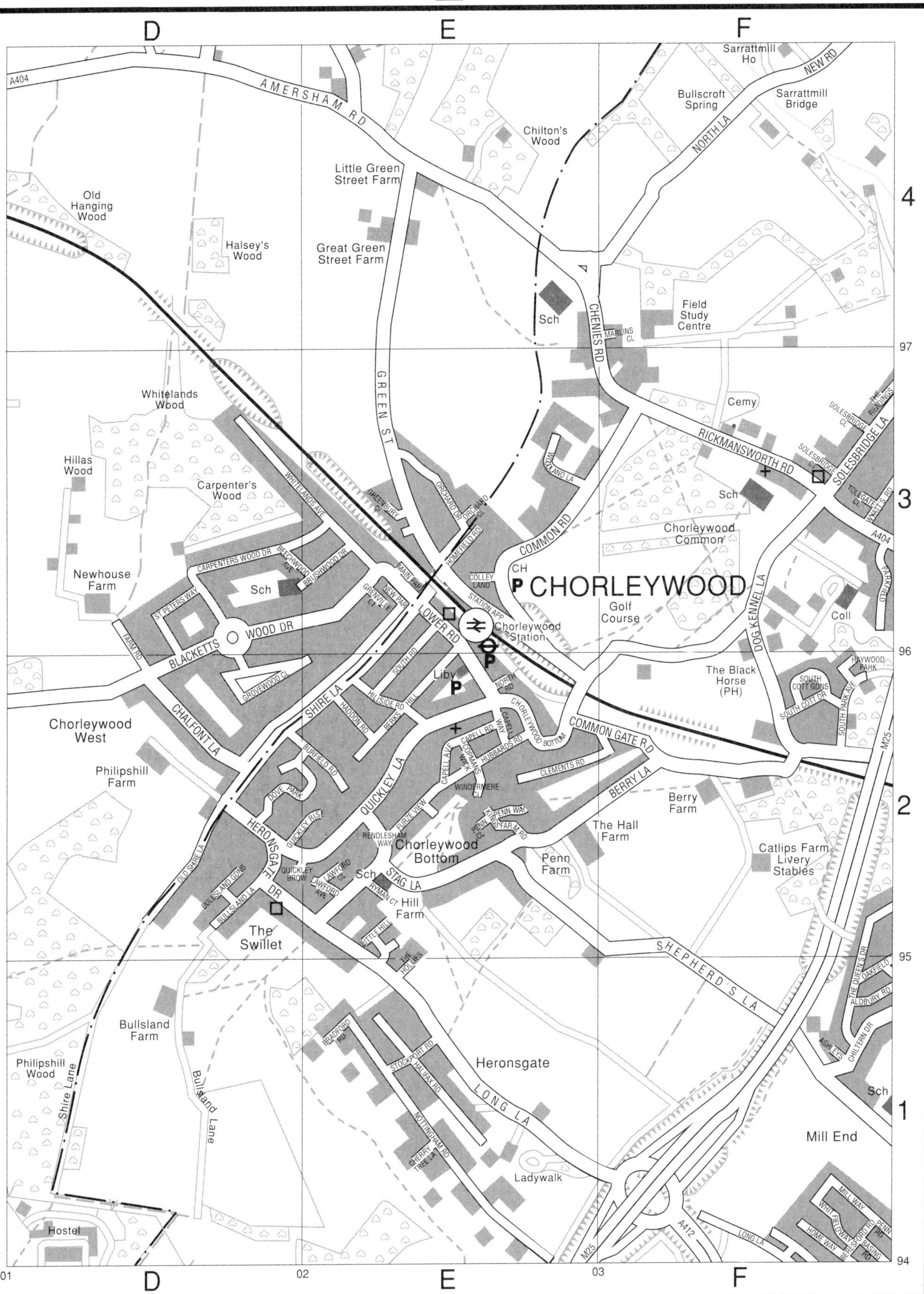

not continued, see key diagram

178

157

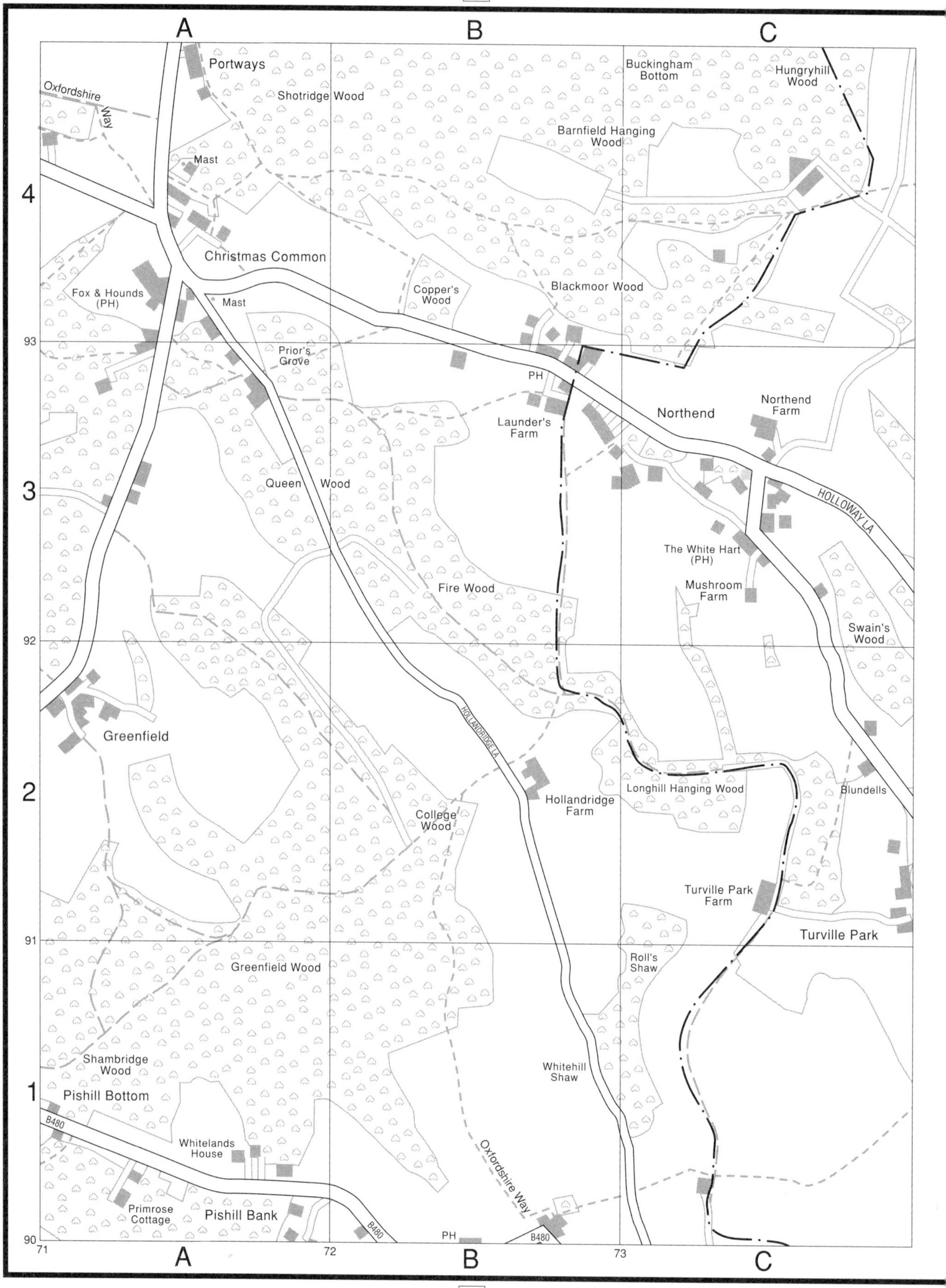

not continued, see key diagram

179

158

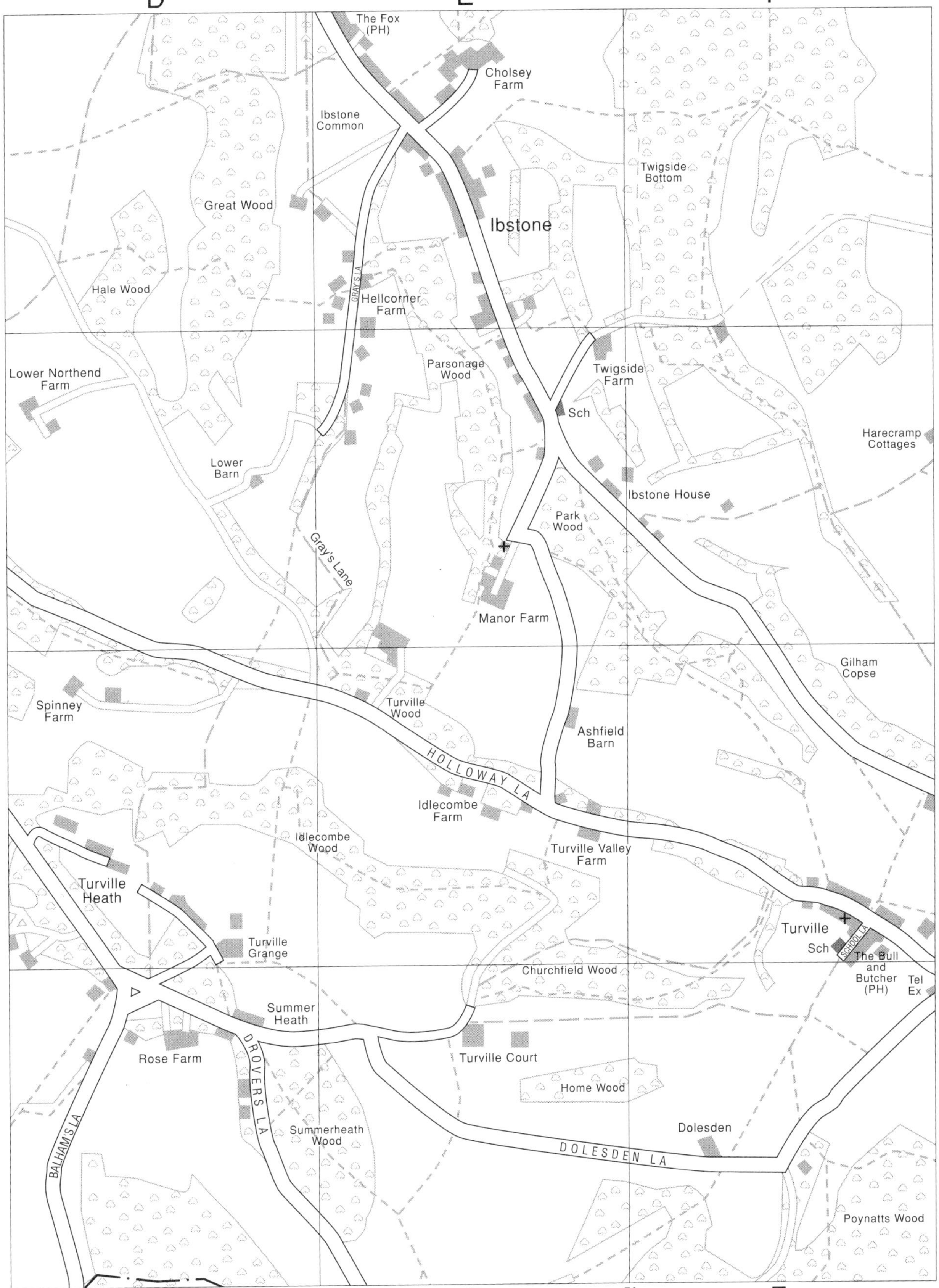
D
E
F
The Fox
(PH)
Cholsey
Farm
Ibstone
Common
Twigside
Bottom
Great Wood
Ibstone
GRAY'S LA
Hale Wood
Hellcorner
Farm
Lower Northend
Farm
Parsonage
Wood
Twigside
Farm
Sch
Harecramp
Cottages
Lower
Barn
Ibstone House
Park
Wood
Gray's Lane
Manor Farm
Gilham
Copse
Spinney
Farm
Turville
Wood
Ashfield
Barn
HOLLOWAY LA
Idlecombe
Farm
Idlecombe
Wood
Turville Valley
Farm
Turville
Heath
Turville
Sch
SCHOOL LA
The Bull
and
Butcher
(PH)
Tel
Ex
Turville
Grange
Churchfield Wood
Summer
Heath
Rose Farm
DROVERS LA
Turville Court
Home Wood
Summerheath
Wood
Dolesden
DOLESDEN LA
BALHAM'S LA
Poynatts Wood
4
3
2
1
93
92
91
90
74
75
76
D
E
F

170

180

159

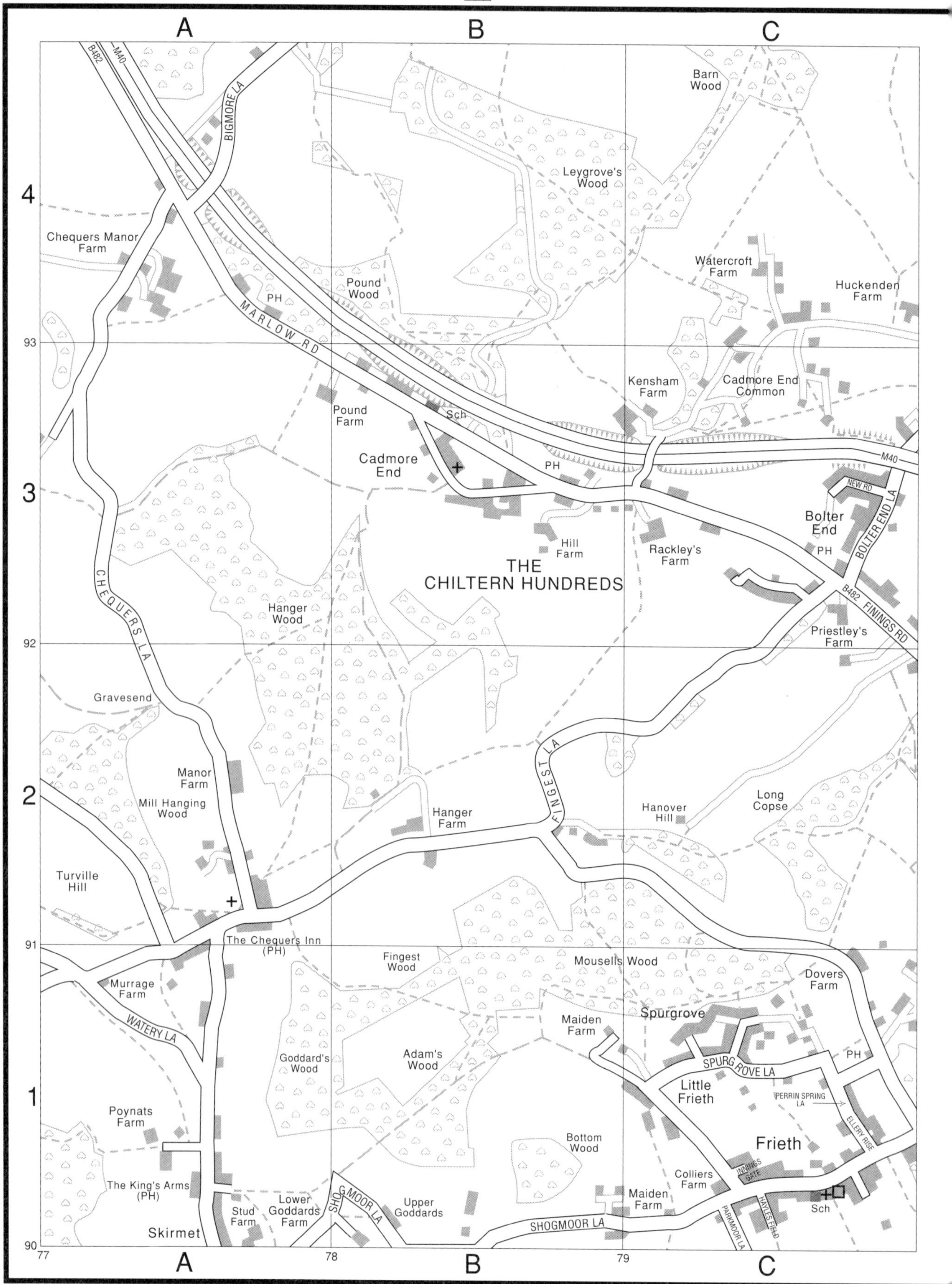
A
B
C
4
3
2
1
93
92
91
90
77
78
79
B482
M40
BIGMORE LA
Barn Wood
Leygrove's Wood
Chequers Manor Farm
Watercroft Farm
Huckenden Farm
Pound Wood
PH
MARLOW RD
Kensham Farm
Cadmore End Common
Pound Farm
Sch
Cadmore End
PH
M40
NEW RD
BOLTER END LA
Bolter End
PH
Hill Farm
Rackley's Farm
THE CHILTERN HUNDREDS
CHEQUERS LA
B482 FININGS RD
Hanger Wood
Priestley's Farm
Gravesend
FINGEST LA
Manor Farm
Mill Hanging Wood
Long Copse
Hanover Hill
Hanger Farm
Turville Hill
The Chequers Inn (PH)
Fingest Wood
Mousells Wood
Dovers Farm
Murrage Farm
Spurgrove
WATERY LA
Maiden Farm
PH
Goddard's Wood
Adam's Wood
SPURGROVE LA
Little Frieth
PERRIN SPRING LA
Poynats Farm
ELLERY RISE
Bottom Wood
Frieth
The King's Arms (PH)
Colliers Farm
INNINGS GATE
Lower Goddards Farm
Upper Goddards
Maiden Farm
Sch
Stud Farm
SHOGMOOR LA
SHOGMOOR LA
PARKMOOR LA
HAYLES FIELD
Skirmet

169

181

160

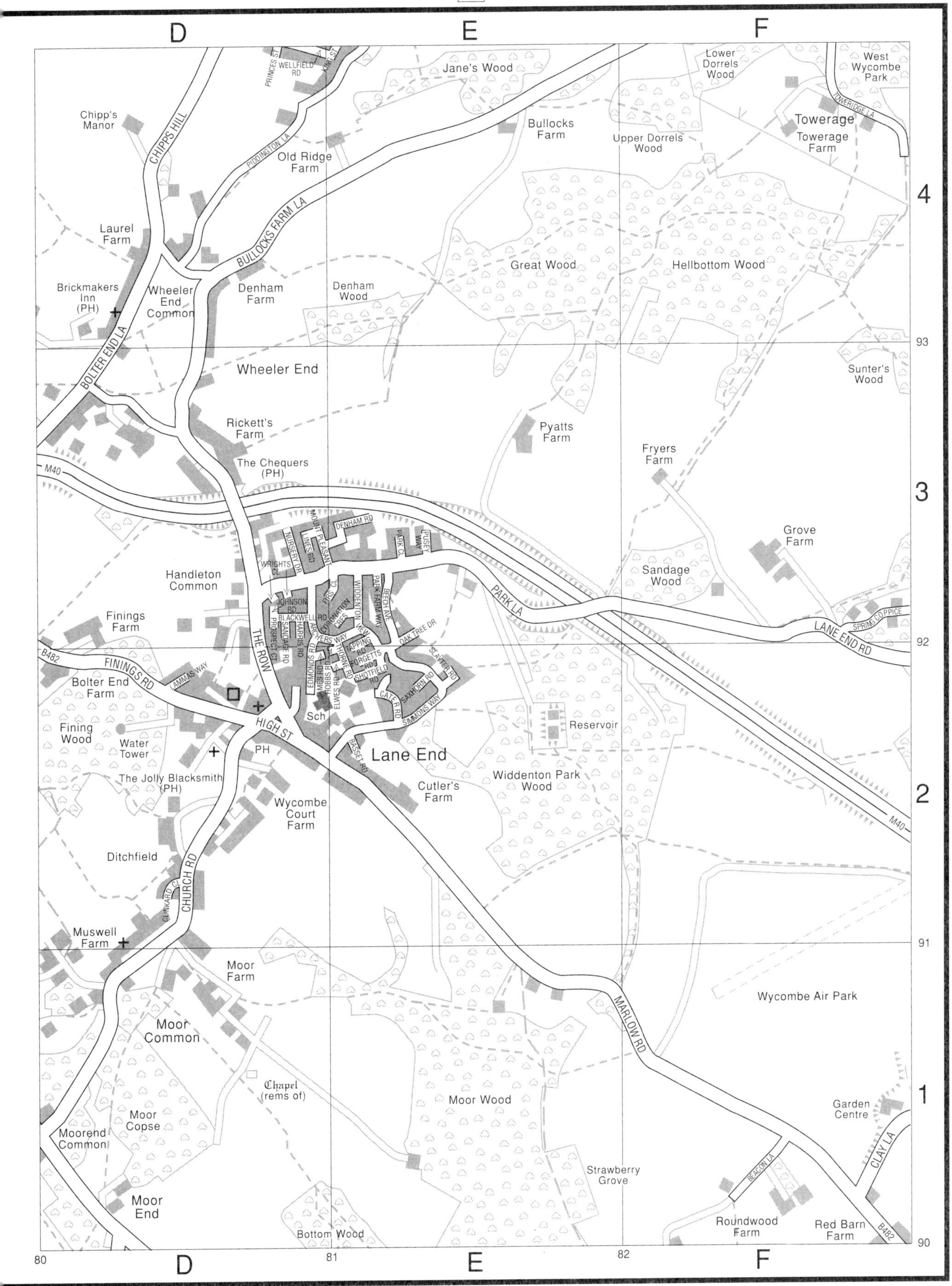
D
E
F
Jane's Wood
Lower Dorrels Wood
West Wycombe Park
WELLFIELD RD
PRINCES ST
KING ST
Chipp's Manor
CHIPPS HILL
Bullocks Farm
Upper Dorrels Wood
Towerage
Towerage Farm
TOWERIDGE LA
PIDDINGTON LA
Old Ridge Farm
4
Laurel Farm
BULLOCKS FARM LA
Great Wood
Hellbottom Wood
Brickmakers Inn (PH)
Wheeler End Common
Denham Farm
Denham Wood
BOLTER END LA
93
Wheeler End
Sunter's Wood
Rickett's Farm
Pyatts Farm
Fryers Farm
M40
The Chequers (PH)
3
MOUNT PLEASANT
DENHAM RD
NURSERY DR
LINES RD
PARK CL
PUSEY WAY
Grove Farm
WRIGHTS CL
Handleton Common
Sandage Wood
JOHNSON RD
FIRS CL
CORONATION CRES
WIDDENTON VIEW
PARK FARM WAY
BEECH AVE
PARK LA
Finings Farm
BLACKWELL RD
PROSPECT CT
SANDAGE RD
HARRIS RD
ARCHERS WAY
OAK TREE DR
SPRING COPPICE
LANE END RD
92
THE ROW
B482
FININGS RD
LAMMAS WAY
EDMONDS RD
JAMES RD
HOBBS RD
ELWES RD
THORNE RD
TAPPING RD
FORGETTS RD
SHOTFIELD RD
SLATTER RD
CATER RD
SAXHORN RD
SIMMONS WAY
Bolter End Farm
Fining Wood
Water Tower
HIGH ST
Sch
Reservoir
PH
BASSET RD
Lane End
The Jolly Blacksmith (PH)
Cutler's Farm
Widdenton Park Wood
2
Wycombe Court Farm
M40
Ditchfield
CHURCH RD
CLINKARD CL
Muswell Farm
91
Moor Farm
Wycombe Air Park
MARLOW RD
Moor Common
Chapel (rems of)
1
Moor Wood
Garden Centre
Moor Copse
Moorend Common
CLAY LA
Strawberry Grove
BEACON LA
Moor End
Roundwood Farm
Red Barn Farm
B482
Bottom Wood
90
80
81
82
D
E
F

172

182

161

171

A
B
C
Park Farm
Druid's Hutt
Toweridge Lane
Sands Wood
Sands
Works
Sunter's Wood
Round Wood
High Barber's Wood
Spring Coppice
Booker Common
Booker
Recreation Ground
Rowliff Wood
Liby
Schs
Sch
River Wye
Fords
Desborough Castle
Castlefield Wood
BRITANNIA INDUSTRIAL ESTATE
DESBOROUGH INDUSTRIAL PARK
WEST WYCOMBE RD
DASHWOOD AVE
DESBOROUGH RD
SUFFIELD RD
DESBOROUGH AVE
Amb Sta
Cressex
CORONATION RD
LANCASTER RD
CRESSEX RD
JOHN HALL WAY
HOLMERS FARM WAY
CREST RD
MARLOW RD
Holmer's Farm
Hospl
Hotel
Sports Centre
TA Centre
Clay Lane Farm
CLAY LA
HORNS LA
LANE END RD
NEW RD
CHAPEL LA
MILL END RD
A4010
A40
A404
M40
The Blacksmiths Arms (PH)
Handy Cross Farm
WINCHBOTTOM LA
Old House Farm
RAGMANS LA
Reading Shaw
Hill Green
Hillgreen Wood
Ragman's Castle
Hollyhill Wood
Redhouse Farm
Monkton Cottage
Refuse Destructor
1
2
3
4
90
91
92
93
83
84
85

162

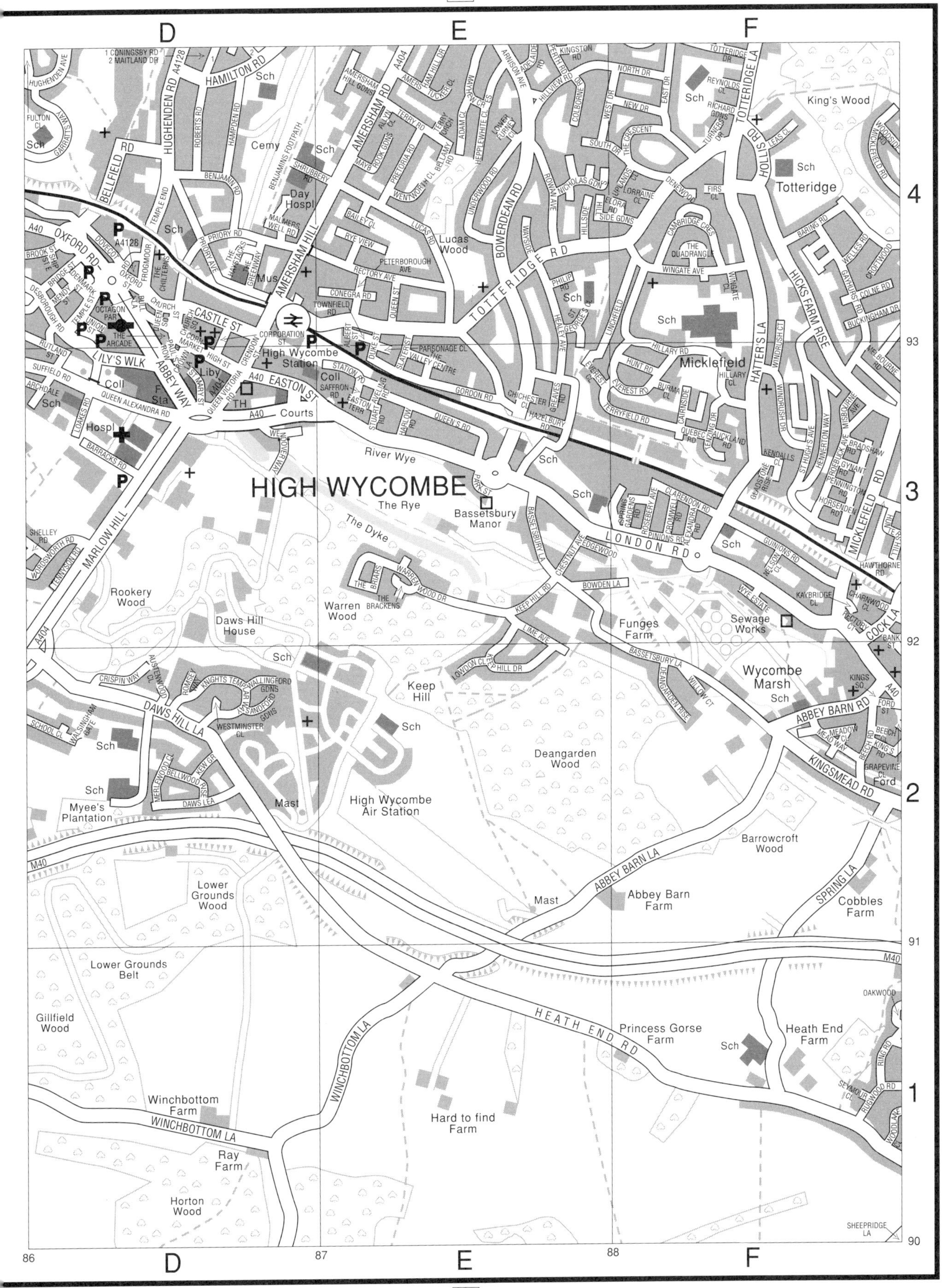
D
E
F
HIGH WYCOMBE
High Wycombe Station
River Wye
The Rye
The Dyke
Bassetsbury Manor
Micklefield
Totteridge
King's Wood
Lucas Wood
Rookery Wood
Warren Wood
Daws Hill House
Keep Hill
Funges Farm
Sewage Works
Wycombe Marsh
Deangarden Wood
High Wycombe Air Station
Myee's Plantation
Barrowcroft Wood
Lower Grounds Wood
Abbey Barn Farm
Cobbles Farm
Lower Grounds Belt
Gillfield Wood
Princess Gorse Farm
Heath End Farm
Winchbottom Farm
Hard to find Farm
Ray Farm
Horton Wood
Ford
Cemy
Day Hospl
Mus
Courts
Hospl
Liby
Coll
TH
Mast
Sch
OXFORD RD
CASTLE ST
EASTON ST
AMERSHAM HILL
HUGHENDEN RD
HAMILTON RD
BELLFIELD RD
TOTTERIDGE RD
TOTTERIDGE LA
HOLLIS RD
HATTER'S LA
MICKLEFIELD RD
LONDON RD
MARLOW HILL
DAWS HILL LA
ABBEY BARN LA
ABBEY BARN RD
KINGSMEAD RD
HEATH END RD
WINCHBOTTOM LA
SPRING LA
COCK LA
BASSETSBURY LA
QUEEN ALEXANDRA RD
LILY'S WLK
ABBEY WAY
QUEEN'S RD
GORDON RD
BOWERDEAN RD
HICKS FARM RISE
M40
A40
A404
A4128
86
87
88
90
91
92
93
1
2
3
4

174

184

163

King's Wood
Puttenham Place Farm
Twichels Wood
Red Lion (PH)
Penn
Vicarage Wood
The Crown (PH)
CHURCH RD
Stumpwell Lane
Cemy
The Knoll
Pastures Farm
Beacon Hill
Gomm's Wood
Little Gomm's Wood
Pond Wood
Bottom Farm
Town Farm
Gatemoor Wood
Coppice Hoop
Pimm's Grove
Parsonage Farm
Business Park
Riding School
Magpie Wood
Longfield Wood
Lude Farm
Sniggs Wood
Magpie Lodge
Caravan Park
King's Mead
River Wye
Back Stream
Factory
Upper Dearham's Farm
Loudwater
Fennell's Wood
White House Farm
Little Farm
Wooburn Moor
Industrial Estate
Ind Est
Cut-throat Wood
Golf Course
Highwayman's Farm
COCK LA
HAMMERSLEY LA
PAULS HILL
WHITEHOUSE LA
LONDON RD
STATION RD
BOUNDARY RD
KINGSMEAD RD
SWAINS LA
M40
A40
A4094
B474

185

173

164

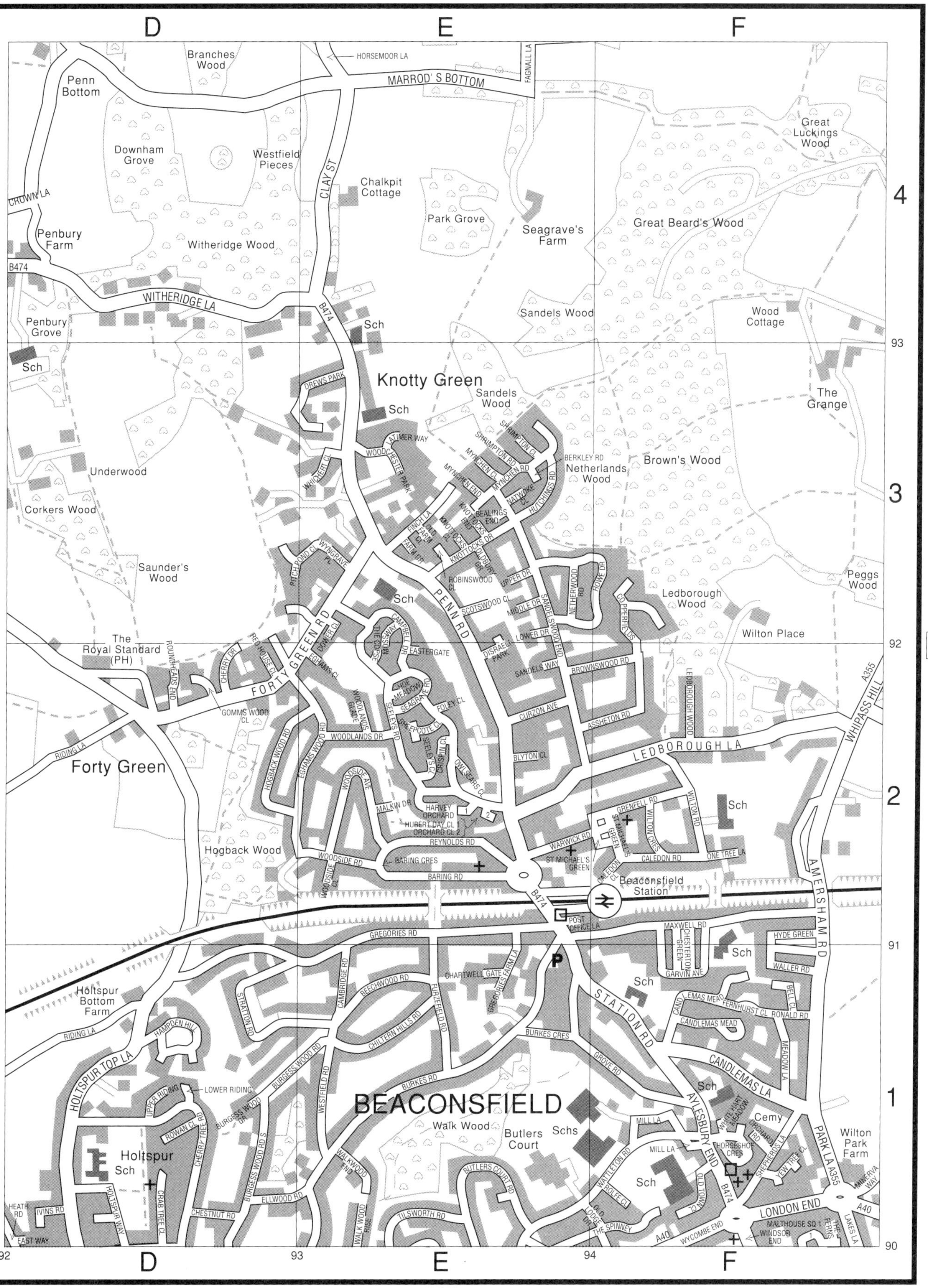
D
E
F
Branches Wood
Penn Bottom
HORSEMOOR LA
MARROD'S BOTTOM
FAGNALL LA
Downham Grove
Westfield Pieces
CLAY ST
Chalkpit Cottage
Great Luckings Wood
CROWN LA
Penbury Farm
Witheridge Wood
Park Grove
Seagrave's Farm
Great Beard's Wood
4
B474
WITHERIDGE LA
Penbury Grove
Sch
Sandels Wood
Wood Cottage
93
Knotty Green
DREWS PARK
Sandels Wood
The Grange
LATIMER WAY
WOODCHESTER PARK
WHICHERT CL
SHRIMPTON CL
SHRIMPTON RD
MYNCHEN RD
MYNCHEN CL
MYNCHEN END
BERKLEY RD
Netherlands Wood
Brown's Wood
Underwood
NATWOKE CL
HUTCHINGS RD
BEALINGS END
KNOTTOCKS END
KNOTTOCKS DR
FINCH LA
FARM GR
OLDBURY GR
3
Corkers Wood
WYNGRAVE PL
PITCH POND CL
ROBINSWOOD CL
UPPER DR
HOWE DR
NETHERWOOD RD
COPPERFIELDS
Saunder's Wood
PENN RD
Ledborough Wood
Peggs Wood
SCOTSWOOD CL
MIDDLE DR
SANDELSWOOD END
LOWER DR
Wilton Place
DISRAELI PARK
CAMPBELL DR
THE COPSE
DOWER CL
EASTERGATE
The Royal Standard (PH)
ROUNDHEAD END
CHERRY DR
RED HOUSE CL
FORTY GREEN RD
FORTY GREEN
ECHAMS CL
SANDELS WAY
BROWNSWOOD RD
92
LEDBOROUGH WOOD
A355
176
HOE MEADOW
SEAGRAVE RD
FOLEY CL
WOODLANDS GLADE
CURZON AVE
ASSHETON RD
WHIPASS HILL
GOMMS WOOD CL
RIDING LA
SEELEYS RD
SHEEPCOTE CL
WOODLANDS DR
SEELEYS CL
CRISPIN CL
Forty Green
HOGBACK WOOD RD
ECHAMS WOOD RD
BLYTON CL
LEDBOROUGH LA
WOODSIDE AVE
OWLSEARS CL
MALKIN DR
HARVEY ORCHARD
HUBERT DAY CL
ORCHARD CL
GRENFELL RD
WILTON RD
WILTON CRES
ST MICHAEL'S GREEN
2
Sch
REYNOLDS RD
Hogback Wood
WOODSIDE RD
BARING CRES
WARWICK RD
ST MICHAEL'S GREEN
CALEDON RD
ONE TREE LA
WOODSIDE CL
BARING RD
CALEDON CL
Beaconsfield Station
AMERSHAM RD
B474
POST OFFICE LA
GREGORIES RD
MAXWELL RD
CHESTERTON GREEN
HYDE GREEN
91
P
Sch
CHARTWELL GATE
GREGORIES FARM LA
GARVIN AVE
WALLER RD
Holtspur Bottom Farm
CAMBRIDGE RD
BEECHWOOD RD
Sch
STRATTON RD
FURZEFIELD RD
STATION RD
CANDLEMAS MEAD
FERNHURST CL
RONALD RD
BELL CL
RIDING LA
HAMPDEN HILL
CHILTERN HILLS RD
BURKES CRES
CANDLEMAS MEAD
MEADOW LA
HOLTSPUR TOP LA
GROVE RD
CANDLEMAS LA
BURGESS WOOD RD
LOWER RIDING
UPPER RIDING
WESTFIELD RD
BURKES RD
AYLESBURY END
Sch
1
BEACONSFIELD
WHITE HART MEADOW
Cemy
ROWAN CL
CHERRY TREE RD
BURGESS WOOD GR
Walk Wood
Butlers Court
Schs
MILL LA
ORCHARD RD
Wilton Park Farm
Holtspur Sch
WALKWOOD END
MILL LA
HORSESHOE CRES
SHEPHERDS LA
YEW TREE CL
PARK LA A355
BURGESS WOOD RD S
BUTLERS COURT RD
WATTLETON RD
MINERVA WAY
HOLTSPUR WAY
CRAB TREE CL
ELLWOOD RD
Sch
ROLFE CL
OLD TOWN CL
B474
HEATH RD
IVINS RD
CHESTNUT RD
WALK WOOD RISE
TILSWORTH RD
OLD LODGE DR
THE SPINNEY
LONDON END
A40
EAST WAY
WYCOMBE END
A40
MALTHOUSE SQ
WINDSOR END
THE FERNS
LAKES LA
90
92
93
94
D
E
F

186

165

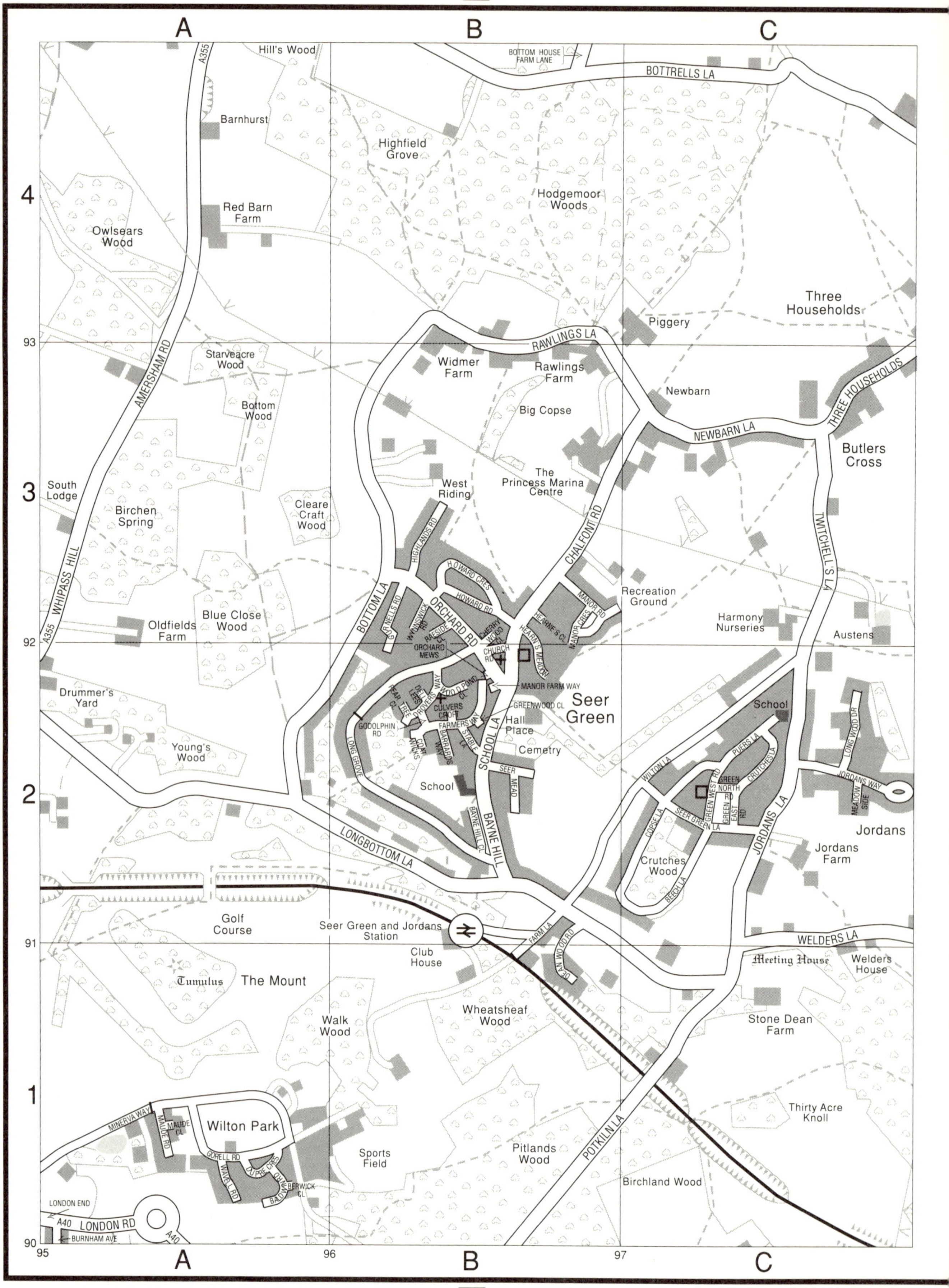
A
B
C
Hill's Wood
BOTTOM HOUSE FARM LANE
BOTTRELLS LA
A355
Barnhurst
Highfield Grove
Hodgemoor Woods
Red Barn Farm
Owlsears Wood
Three Households
Piggery
RAWLINGS LA
Starveacre Wood
Widmer Farm
Rawlings Farm
Newbarn
THREE HOUSEHOLDS
AMERSHAM RD
Bottom Wood
Big Copse
NEWBARN LA
Butlers Cross
South Lodge
West Riding
The Princess Marina Centre
Birchen Spring
Cleare Craft Wood
CHALFONT RD
TWITCHELL'S LA
WHIPASS HILL
HIGHLANDS RD
HOWARD CRES
Recreation Ground
BOTTOM LA
Blue Close Wood
Oldfields Farm
HOWARD RD
MANOR RD
Harmony Nurseries
Austens
ORCHARD RD
ORCHARD MEWS
CHURCH RD
HEARNE'S CL
HEARN'S MEADOW
MANOR CRES
Drummer's Yard
MANOR FARM WAY
Seer Green
GREENWOOD CL
School
GODOLPHIN RD
CULVERS CROFT
FARMERS WAY
Hall Place
LONG WOOD DR
Young's Wood
LONG GROVE
Cemetry
WILTON LA
PUERS LA
CRUTCHES LA
SCHOOL LA
SEER MEAD
GREEN WEST RD
GREEN NORTH RD
JORDANS WAY
School
BAYNE HILL CL
BAYNE HILL
SEER GREEN LA
MEADOW SIDE
Jordans
COPSE LA
JORDANS LA
LONGBOTTOM LA
Crutches Wood
Jordans Farm
BEECH LA
Golf Course
Seer Green and Jordans Station
FARM LA
Club House
DEAN WOOD RD
WELDERS LA
Meeting House
Welders House
Tumulus
The Mount
Wheatsheaf Wood
Walk Wood
Stone Dean Farm
Thirty Acre Knoll
MINERVA WAY
MAUDE CL
MAUDE RD
Wilton Park
GORELL RD
WAVELL RD
DUPRE CRES
BERWICK CL
Sports Field
Pitlands Wood
POTKILN LA
Birchland Wood
LONDON END
A40
LONDON RD
BURNHAM AVE
4
3
2
1
93
92
91
90
95
96
97

175

187

166

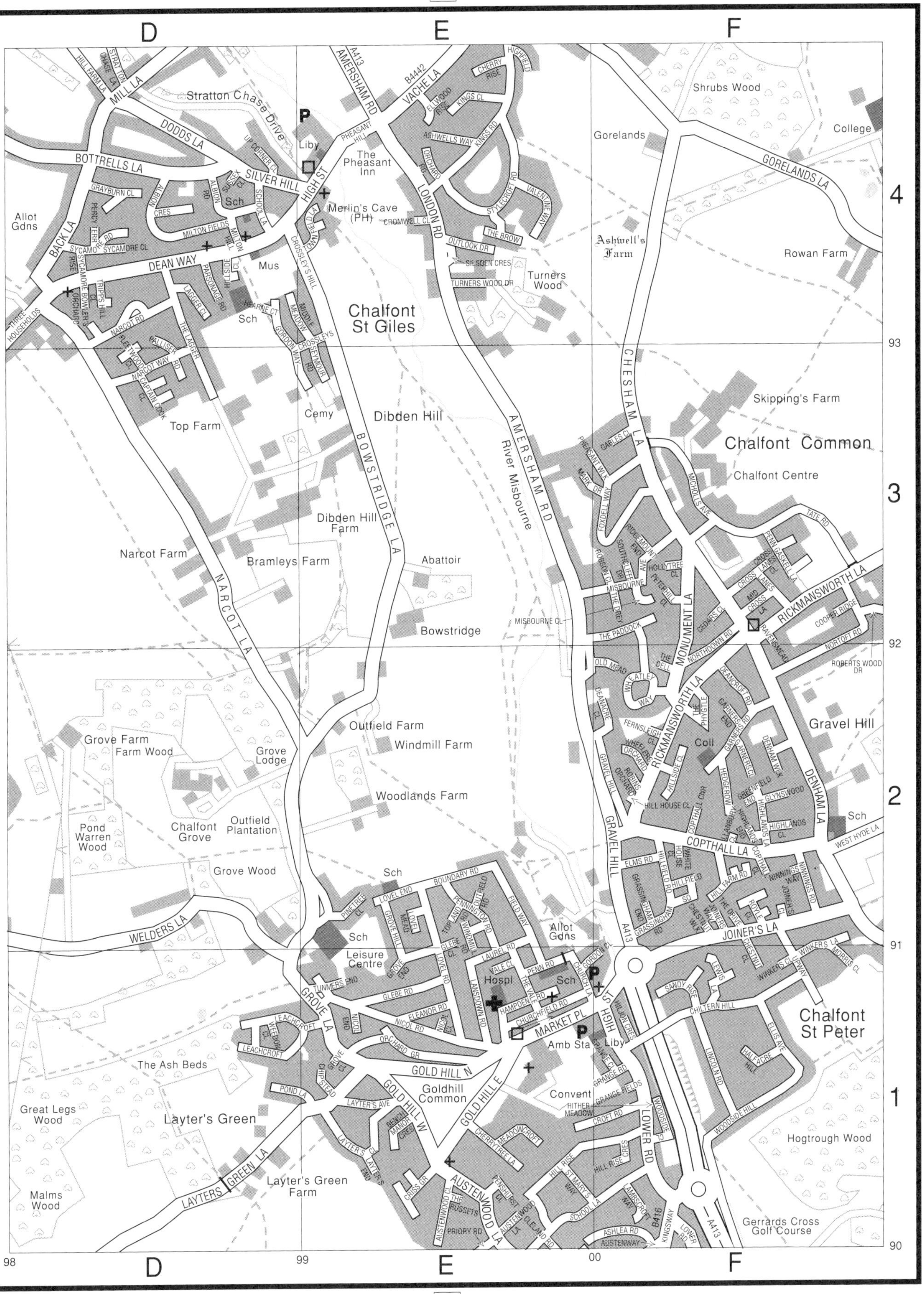

D
E
F
Stratton Chase Drive
DODDS LA
MILL LA
BOTTRELLS LA
SILVER HILL
HIGH ST
Liby
The Pheasant Inn
Merlin's Cave (PH)
AMERSHAM RD
VACHE LA
LONDON RD
CHERRY RISE
KINGS CL
ASHWELLS WAY
STYLECROFT RD
VALENTINE WAY
THE BROW
OUTLOOK DR
SILSDEN CRES
TURNERS WOOD DR
Turners Wood
Gorelands
Shrubs Wood
College
GORELANDS LA
Ashwell's Farm
Rowan Farm
Allot Gdns
BACK LA
DEAN WAY
Sch
Mus
Chalfont St Giles
THREE HOUSEHOLDS
NARCOT RD
NARCOT WAY
THE LAGGER
LAGGER CL
PARSONAGE RD
Top Farm
Cemy
Dibden Hill
BOWSTRIDGE LA
AMERSHAM RD
River Misbourne
CHESHAM LA
Skipping's Farm
Chalfont Common
Chalfont Centre
Dibden Hill Farm
Narcot Farm
Bramleys Farm
Abattoir
NARCOT LA
Bowstridge
MISBOURNE CL
MONUMENT LA
RICKMANSWORTH LA
NORTHDOWN RD
THE PADDOCK
OLD MEAD
WHEATLEY WAY
Gravel Hill
Outfield Farm
Windmill Farm
Grove Farm
Farm Wood
Grove Lodge
Coll
Woodlands Farm
Pond Warren Wood
Chalfont Grove
Outfield Plantation
GRAVEL HILL
HILL HOUSE CL
COPTHALL LA
DENHAM LA
Sch
WEST HYDE LA
Grove Wood
Sch
BOUNDARY RD
WELDERS LA
JOINER'S LA
Allot Gdns
Leisure Centre
Hospl
MARKET PL
Amb Sta
Liby
Chalfont St Peter
GROVE LA
The Ash Beds
GOLD HILL N
Goldhill Common
GOLD HILL W
GOLD HILL E
Convent
LOWER RD
CHILTERN HILL
LINCOLN RD
WOODSIDE HILL
Hogtrough Wood
Great Legs Wood
Layter's Green
LAYTERS GREEN LA
Layter's Green Farm
AUSTENWOOD LA
Malms Wood
A413
Gerrards Cross Golf Course
93
92
91
90
4
3
2
1
98
99
00
178

188

167

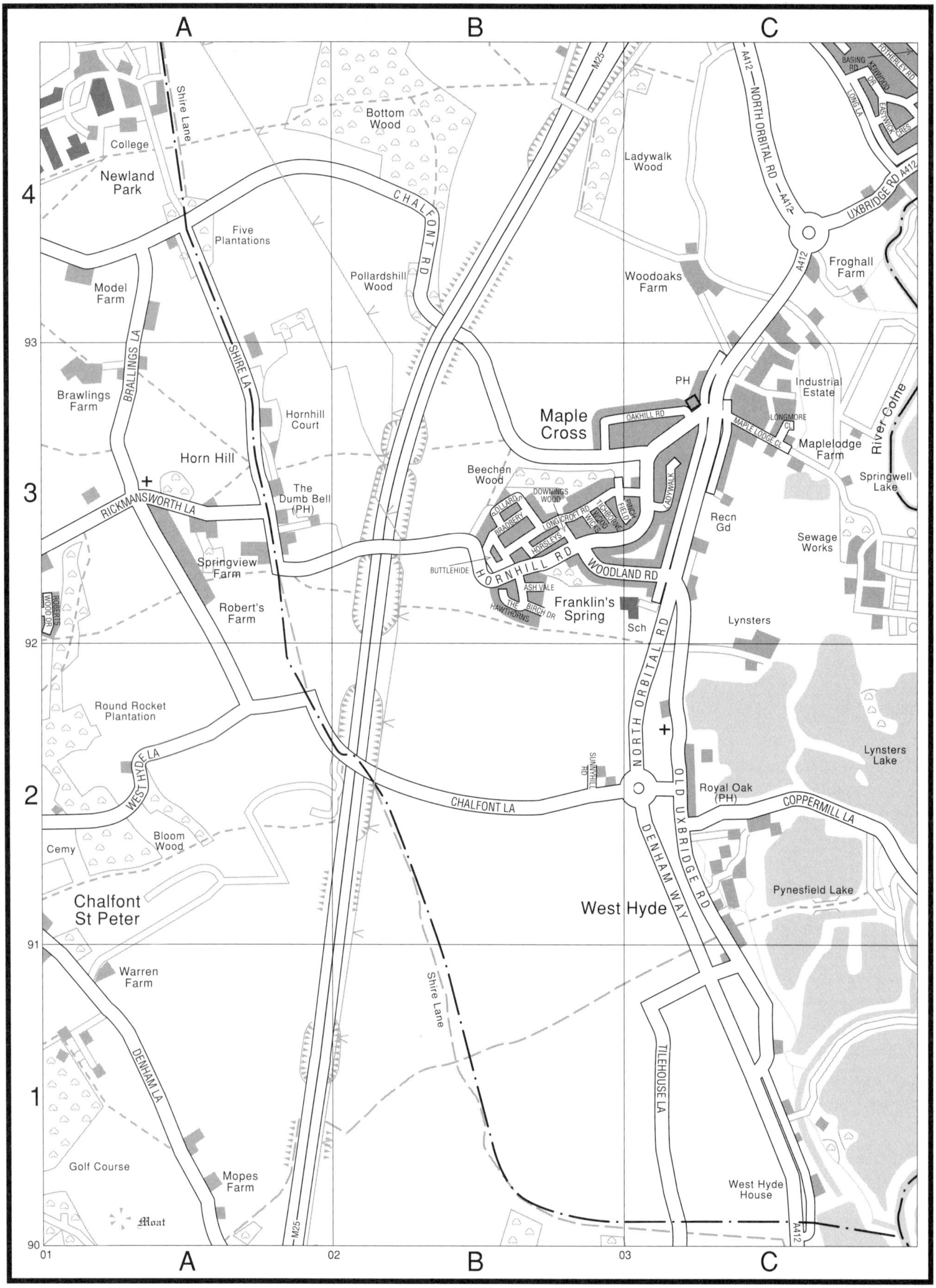

177

not continued, see key diagram

189

168
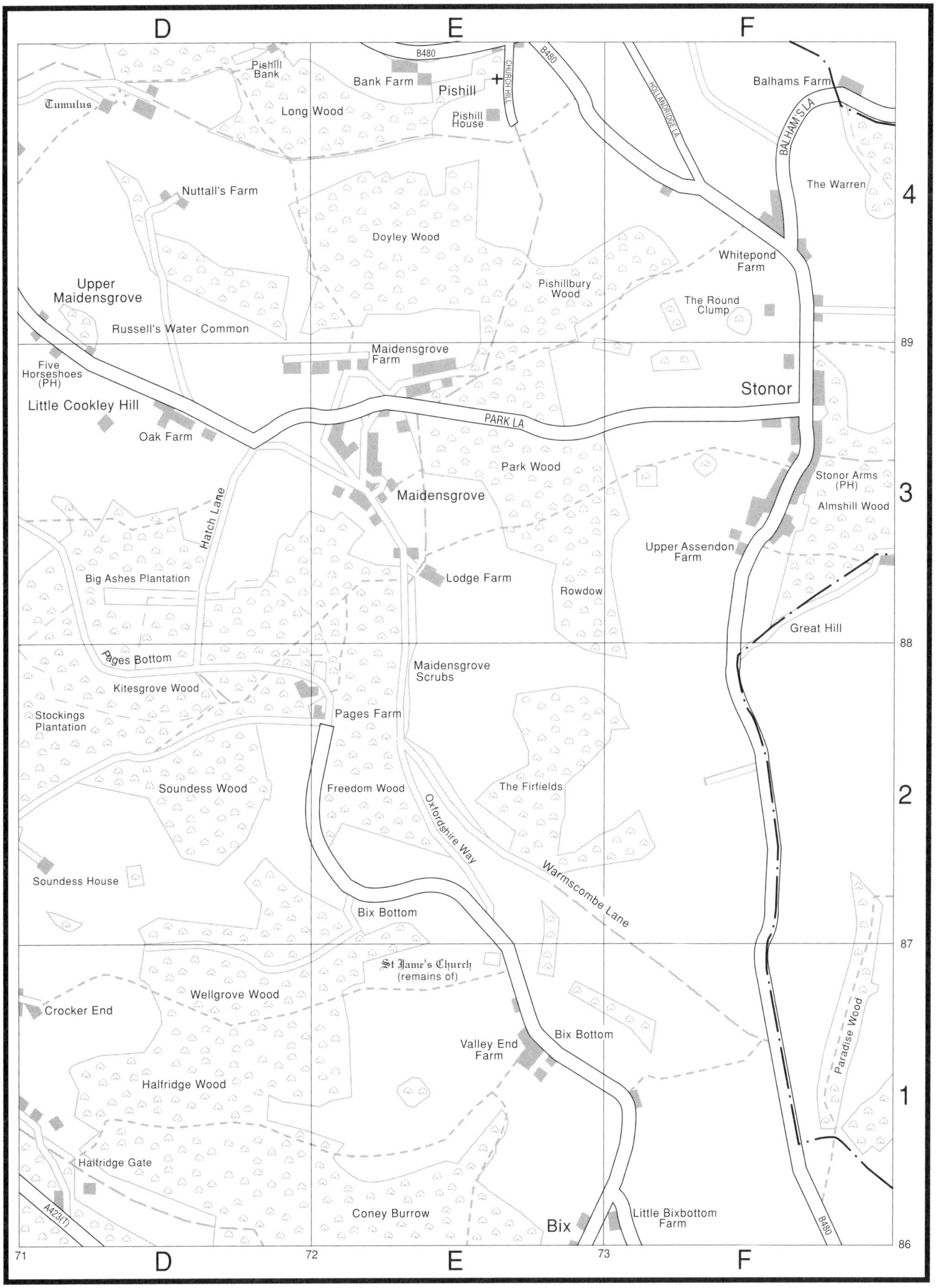

180
not continued, see key diagram
not continued, see key diagram

169

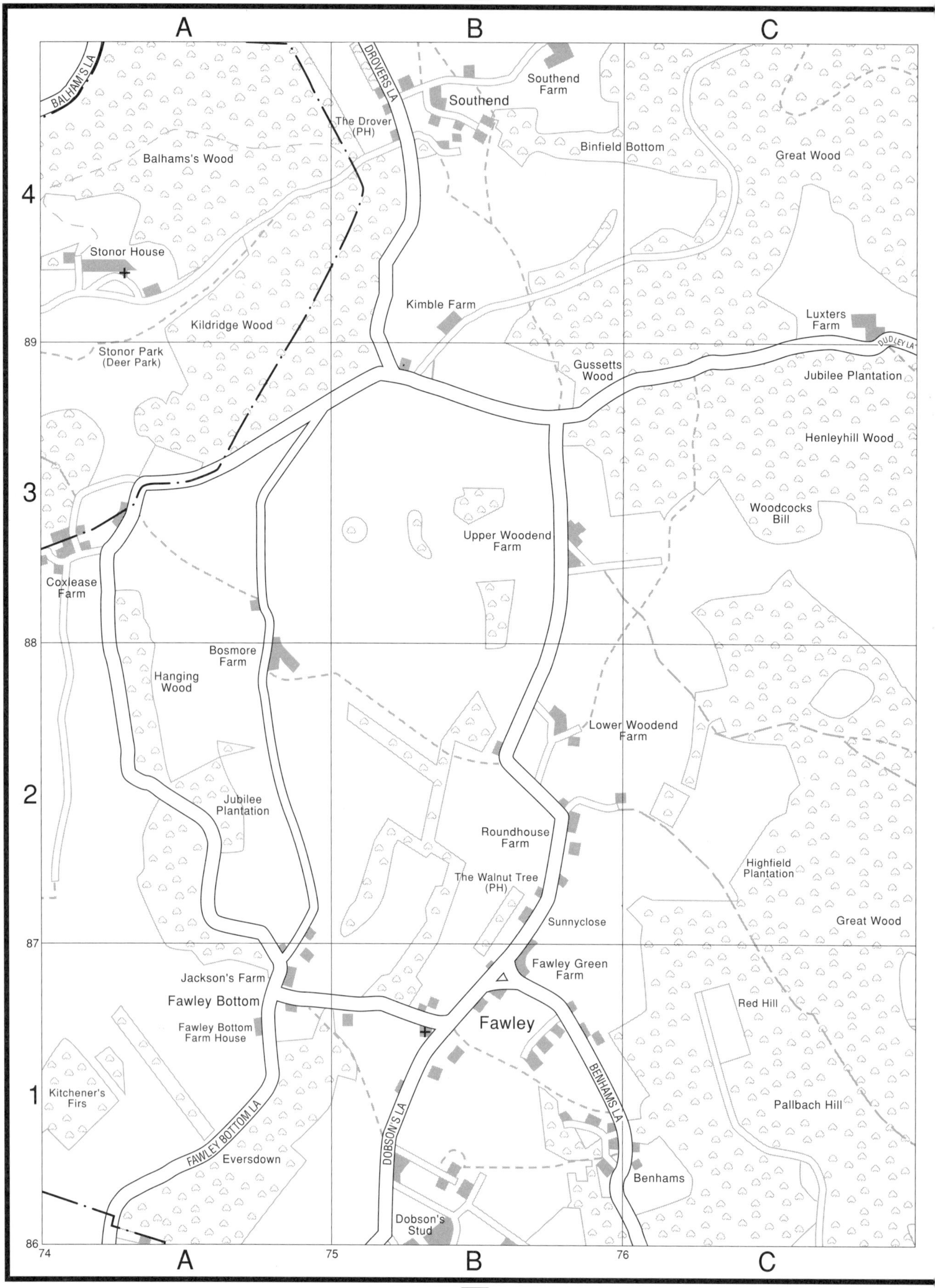

A
B
C
BALHAM'S LA
DROVERS LA
Southend
Southend Farm
The Drover (PH)
Binfield Bottom
Great Wood
Balhams's Wood
Stonor House
Kimble Farm
Luxters Farm
Kildridge Wood
DUDLEY LA
Stonor Park (Deer Park)
Gussetts Wood
Jubilee Plantation
Henleyhill Wood
Woodcocks Bill
Upper Woodend Farm
Coxlease Farm
Bosmore Farm
Hanging Wood
Lower Woodend Farm
Jubilee Plantation
Roundhouse Farm
Highfield Plantation
The Walnut Tree (PH)
Sunnyclose
Great Wood
Fawley Green Farm
Jackson's Farm
Fawley Bottom
Red Hill
Fawley
Fawley Bottom Farm House
Kitchener's Firs
BENHAMS LA
Pallbach Hill
DOBSON'S LA
FAWLEY BOTTOM LA
Eversdown
Benhams
Dobson's Stud
4
3
2
1
89
88
87
86
74
75
76
A
B
C

179

191

170

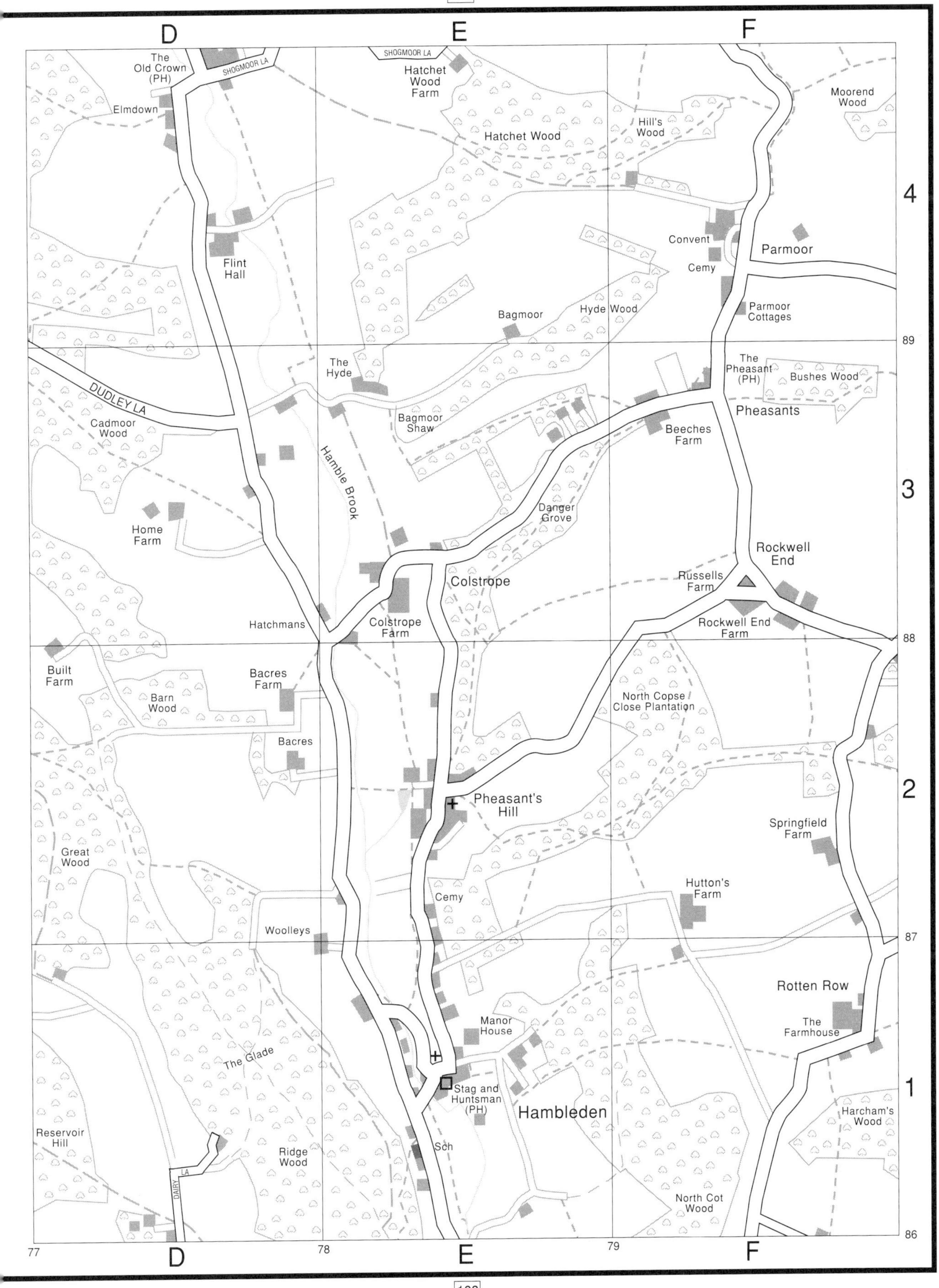
D
E
F
SHOGMOOR LA
The Old Crown (PH)
Elmdown
Hatchet Wood Farm
Moorend Wood
Hill's Wood
Hatchet Wood
4
Convent
Parmoor
Cemy
Flint Hall
Bagmoor
Hyde Wood
Parmoor Cottages
89
The Hyde
The Pheasant (PH)
Bushes Wood
DUDLEY LA
Cadmoor Wood
Bagmoor Shaw
Pheasants
Beeches Farm
Hamble Brook
3
Home Farm
Danger Grove
Rockwell End
Colstrope
Russells Farm
Hatchmans
Colstrope Farm
Rockwell End Farm
88
Built Farm
Bacres Farm
Barn Wood
North Copse Close Plantation
Bacres
2
Pheasant's Hill
Springfield Farm
Great Wood
Hutton's Farm
Cemy
Woolleys
87
Rotten Row
Manor House
The Farmhouse
The Glade
1
Stag and Huntsman (PH)
Hambleden
Harcham's Wood
Reservoir Hill
Sch
Ridge Wood
DAIRY LA
North Cot Wood
86
77
78
79

182

192

171

A
B
C
4
3
2
1
89
88
87
86
80
81
82
Moorend Wood
Bottom Wood
Finnamore Lane
Beacon Farm
B482
Beacon Lane
Young Offender Institution
Finnamore Wood
Bluey's Farm
The Roost
Chisbridge Cross
Chisbridge
Copy Green
Shillingridge Wood
Holme Wood Cottage
Holme Wood
Holme Wood
Woodlands
Denelands Farm
Oaklands Farm
Kent's Wood
Hawkins Farm
FRIETH RD
Mundaydean Bottom
MUNDAYDEAN LA
Bottom House
Woodend House
Fountain's
Woodend Farm
Holywick
Arbon
Lower Woodend
Walnut Tree Farm
Heath Wood
Lord's Wood
Marlow Common
MARLOW COMM
Homefield Wood
Rogues Plantation
Davenport Wood
Bockmer End Farm
Bockmer End
Pullingshill Wood
Bockmer House
Woodland Plain
BOCKMER LA
Widefield
Hook's Farm

181

193

172

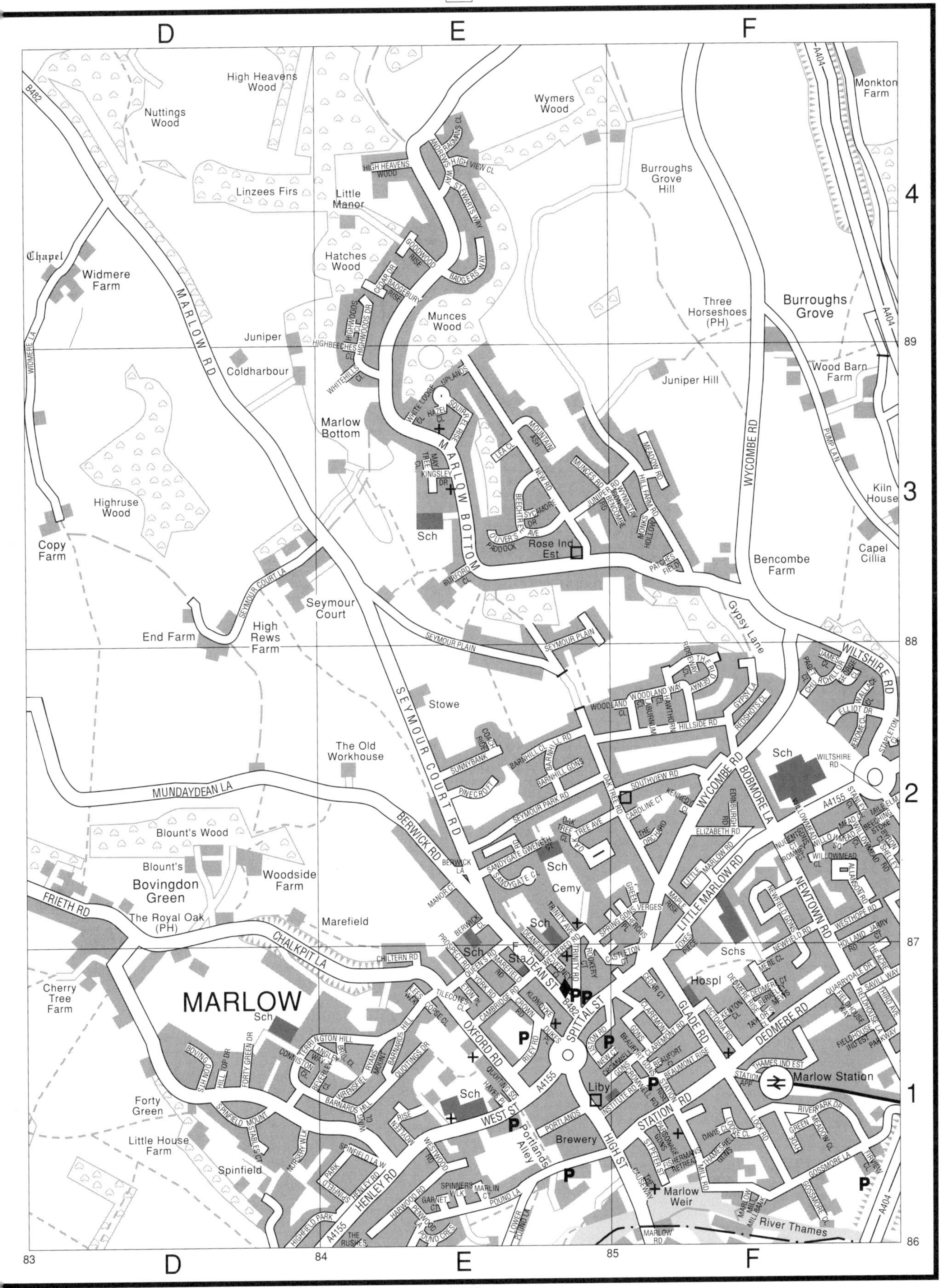
D
E
F
4
3
2
1
89
88
87
86
83
84
85
B482
High Heavens Wood
Nuttings Wood
Wymers Wood
Monkton Farm
A404
Linzees Firs
Little Manor
Burroughs Grove Hill
Chapel
Widmere Farm
Hatches Wood
MARLOW RD
Munces Wood
Three Horseshoes (PH)
Burroughs Grove
Juniper
WIDMERE LA
Coldharbour
Wood Barn Farm
Juniper Hill
Marlow Bottom
MARLOW BOTTOM
WYCOMBE RD
PUMP LA
Highruse Wood
Kiln House
Sch
Rose Ind Est
Copy Farm
Capel Cillia
Bencombe Farm
SEYMOUR COURT LA
Seymour Court
Gypsy Lane
End Farm
High Rews Farm
SEYMOUR PLAIN
WILTSHIRE RD
Stowe
SEYMOUR COURT RD
The Old Workhouse
MUNDAYDEAN LA
BERWICK RD
A4155
Blount's Wood
Blount's
Bovingdon Green
Woodside Farm
Cemy
FRIETH RD
The Royal Oak (PH)
Marefield
CHALKPIT LA
Cherry Tree Farm
MARLOW
Hospl
Schs
Sta
SPITTAL ST
GLADE RD
DEDMERE RD
Marlow Station
Forty Green
WEST ST
Portlands Alley
Brewery
HIGH ST
STATION RD
Little House Farm
Spinfield
HENLEY RD
Liby
Marlow Weir
River Thames
MARLOW RD

184

194

173

183

A
B
C
4
3
2
1
89
88
87
86
86
87
88
Horton Wood
Bloom Wood
Bloom Farm
WINCHBOTTOM LA
New Farm
PH
Sheepridge
SHEEPRIDGE LA
Merton's Hole Cottage
Pigeon House Farm
A404
Fern House
Cemy
Fern
Wilton Farm
Caravan Site
Coronach
Pump Farm
PUMP LA N
PUMP LA S
MARLOW RD
Sch
SCHOOL LA
CHURCH RD
The King's Head (PH)
Little Marlow
Well End
ELM LA
ABBEY RD
A4155
POUND LA
Manor House
THE AVENUE
FARM RD
The Abbey
THE DRIVE
STAPLETON CL
LITTLE MARLOW RD
MILL
ELM
GRATTAN CT
BUTLER CT
BRISTOW CT
DOUGLAS CT
THE CHASE
GUNTHORPE RD
HOBART CT
THE CROFT
PARKWAY
WILTSHIRE RD
COLDMOORHOLME LA
SPADE OAK MEADOW
The Spade Oak (PH)
P
Spade Oak Farm
Abbotsbrook
LC
Westhorpe House
Westhorpe Farm
Sewage Works
The Moor
River Thames
1 MARCHANT CT
2 WASHINGTON CT
SAVILL WAY
FOURTH AVE
FIRST AVE
Tumuli
Cock Marsh
Noah's House
Patches
Sewage Wks
Stone House
STONE HOUSE LA
Coney Copse
WINTER HILL
GIBRALTAR LA
Winter Hill
RIVERWOODS DR
RIVERWOODS AVE
BRADCUTTS LA
TERRY'S LA
Harvest Moon
Graythatch
Golf Course

195

174

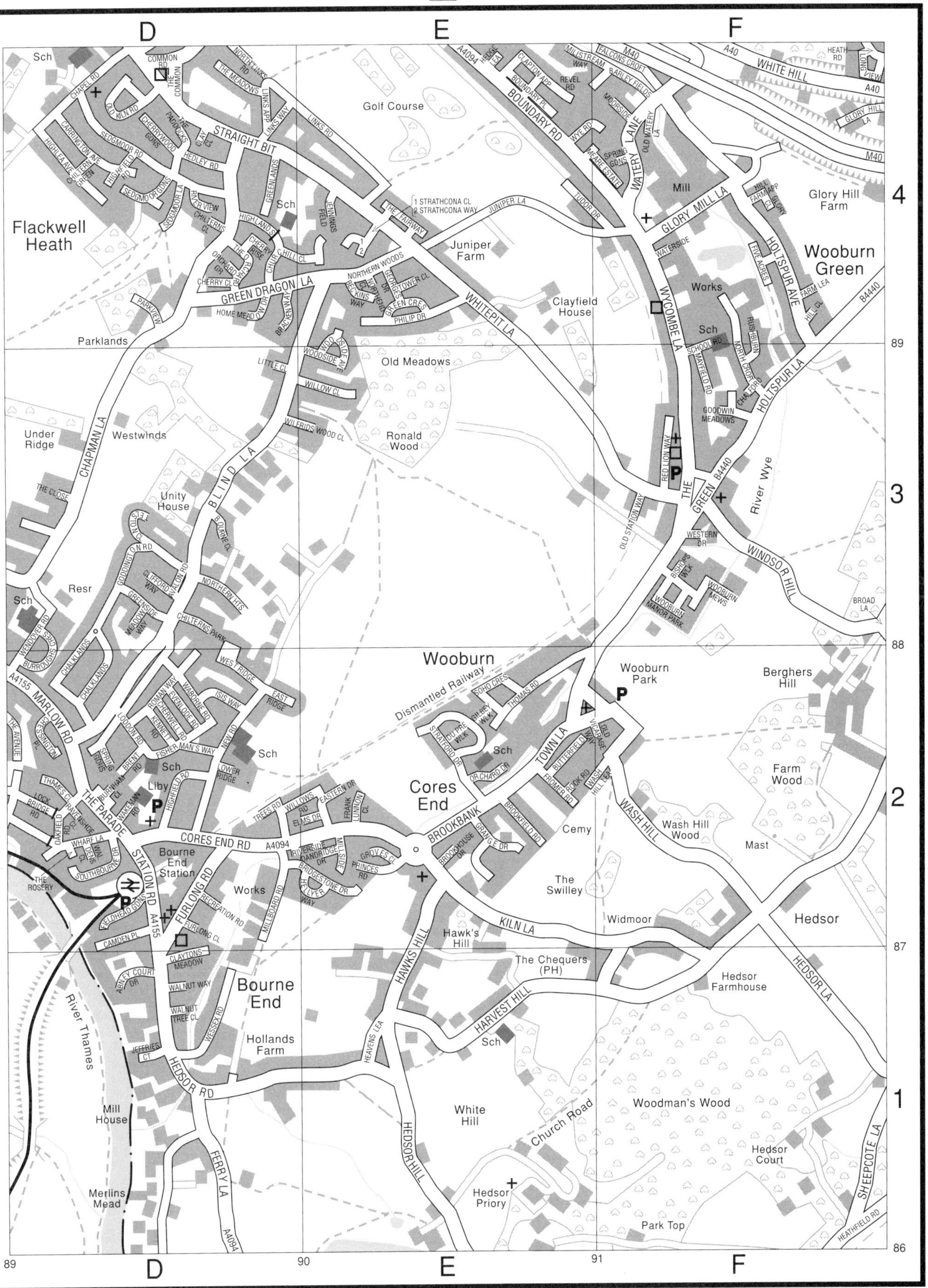

D
E
F
Flackwell Heath
Wooburn Green
Wooburn
Cores End
Bourne End
Hedsor
Sch
Golf Course
Juniper Farm
Clayfield House
Old Meadows
Ronald Wood
Parklands
Under Ridge
Westwinds
Unity House
Resr
Glory Hill Farm
Mill
Works
Wooburn Park
Berghers Hill
Farm Wood
Wash Hill Wood
Mast
Cemy
The Swilley
Widmoor
Hawk's Hill
The Chequers (PH)
Hedsor Farmhouse
Hollands Farm
Bourne End Station
Liby
Mill House
Merlins Mead
White Hill
Hedsor Priory
Woodman's Wood
Hedsor Court
Park Top
River Thames
River Wye
Dismantled Railway
STRAIGHT BIT
GREEN DRAGON LA
CHAPMAN LA
BLIND LA
WHITEPIT LA
JUNIPER LA
WYCOMBE LA
BOUNDARY RD
WATERY LANE
GLORY MILL LA
HOLTSPUR AVE
HOLTSPUR LA
WINDSOR HILL
WHITE HILL
M40
A40
A4094
A4155
B4440
MARLOW RD
CORES END RD
STATION RD
FURLONG RD
HEDSOR RD
FERRY LA
HAWKS HILL
HEDSORHILL
HARVEST HILL
KILN LA
WASH HILL
HEDSOR LA
BROOKBANK
TOWN LA
THE PARADE
Church Road
SHEEPCOTE LA
HEATHFIELD RD
1 STRATHCONA CL
2 STRATHCONA WAY
4
3
2
1
89
88
87
86
89
90
91

186

196

175

185

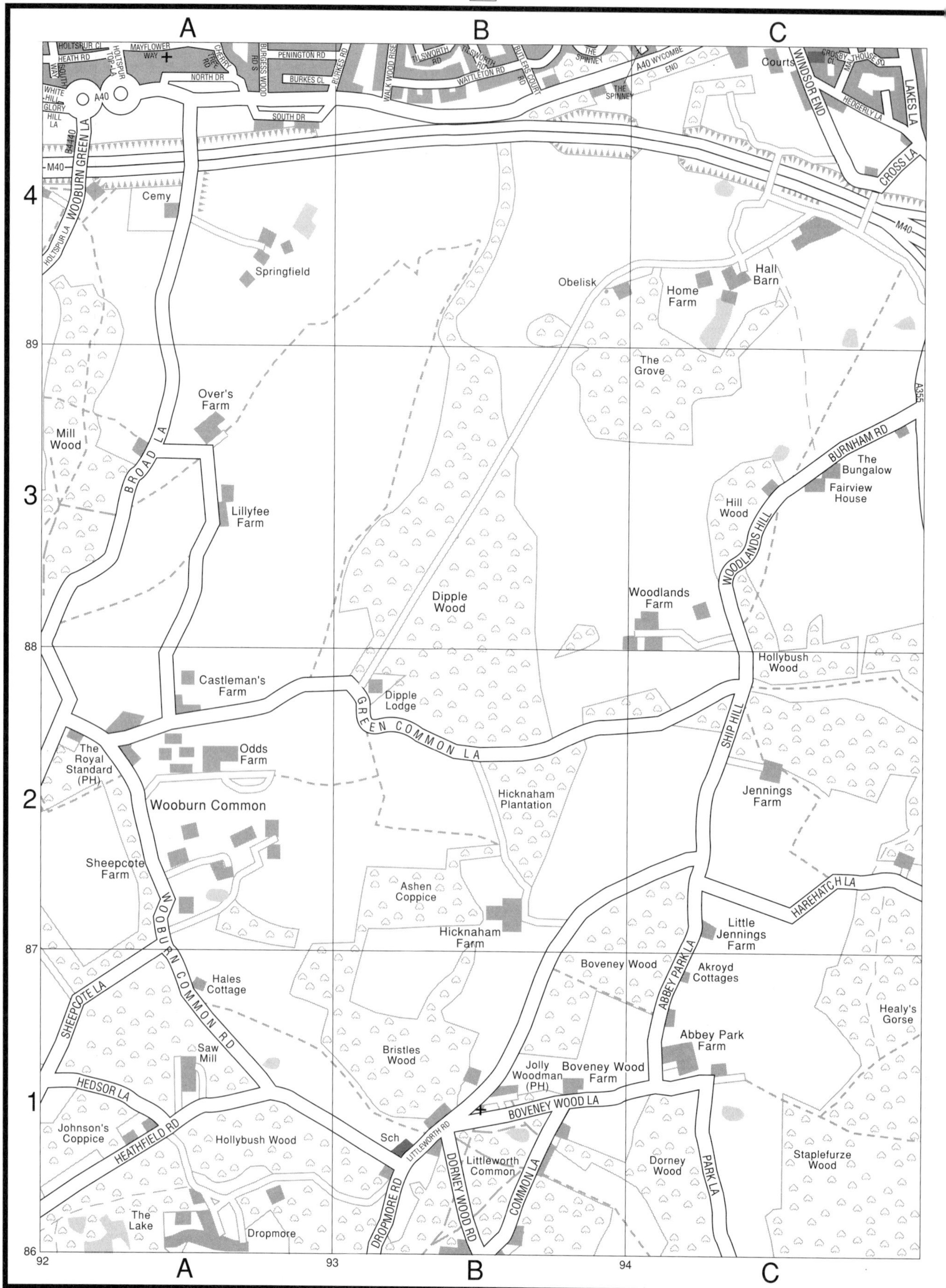
A
B
C
4
3
2
1
89
88
87
86
92
93
94
HOLTSPUR CL
HEATH RD
MAYFLOWER WAY
NORTH DR
PENINGTON RD
BURKES CL
BURKES RD
SOUTH DR
WALK WOOD RISE
TILSWORTH RD
WATTLETON RD
BUTLERS COURT RD
THE SPINNEY
A40 WYCOMBE END
Courts
WINDSOR END
LAKES LA
HEDGERLY LA
CROSS LA
A40
M40
B4440
WOOBURN GREEN LA
HOLTSPUR LA
Cemy
Springfield
Obelisk
Home Farm
Hall Barn
The Grove
A355
BURNHAM RD
The Bungalow
Fairview House
Hill Wood
WOODLANDS HILL
Over's Farm
Mill Wood
BROAD LA
Lillyfee Farm
Dipple Wood
Woodlands Farm
Castleman's Farm
Dipple Lodge
GREEN COMMON LA
Hollybush Wood
SHIP HILL
The Royal Standard (PH)
Odds Farm
Wooburn Common
Hicknaham Plantation
Jennings Farm
Sheepcote Farm
Ashen Coppice
HAREHATCH LA
Hicknaham Farm
Little Jennings Farm
WOOBURN COMMON RD
Boveney Wood
Akroyd Cottages
ABBEY PARK LA
SHEEPCOTE LA
Hales Cottage
Healy's Gorse
Saw Mill
Bristles Wood
Abbey Park Farm
Jolly Woodman (PH)
Boveney Wood Farm
HEDSOR LA
BOVENEY WOOD LA
Johnson's Coppice
HEATHFIELD RD
Hollybush Wood
Sch
LITTLEWORTH RD
Littleworth Common
Dorney Wood
Staplefurze Wood
PARK LA
COMMON LA
DROPMORE RD
DORNEY WOOD RD
The Lake
Dropmore

197

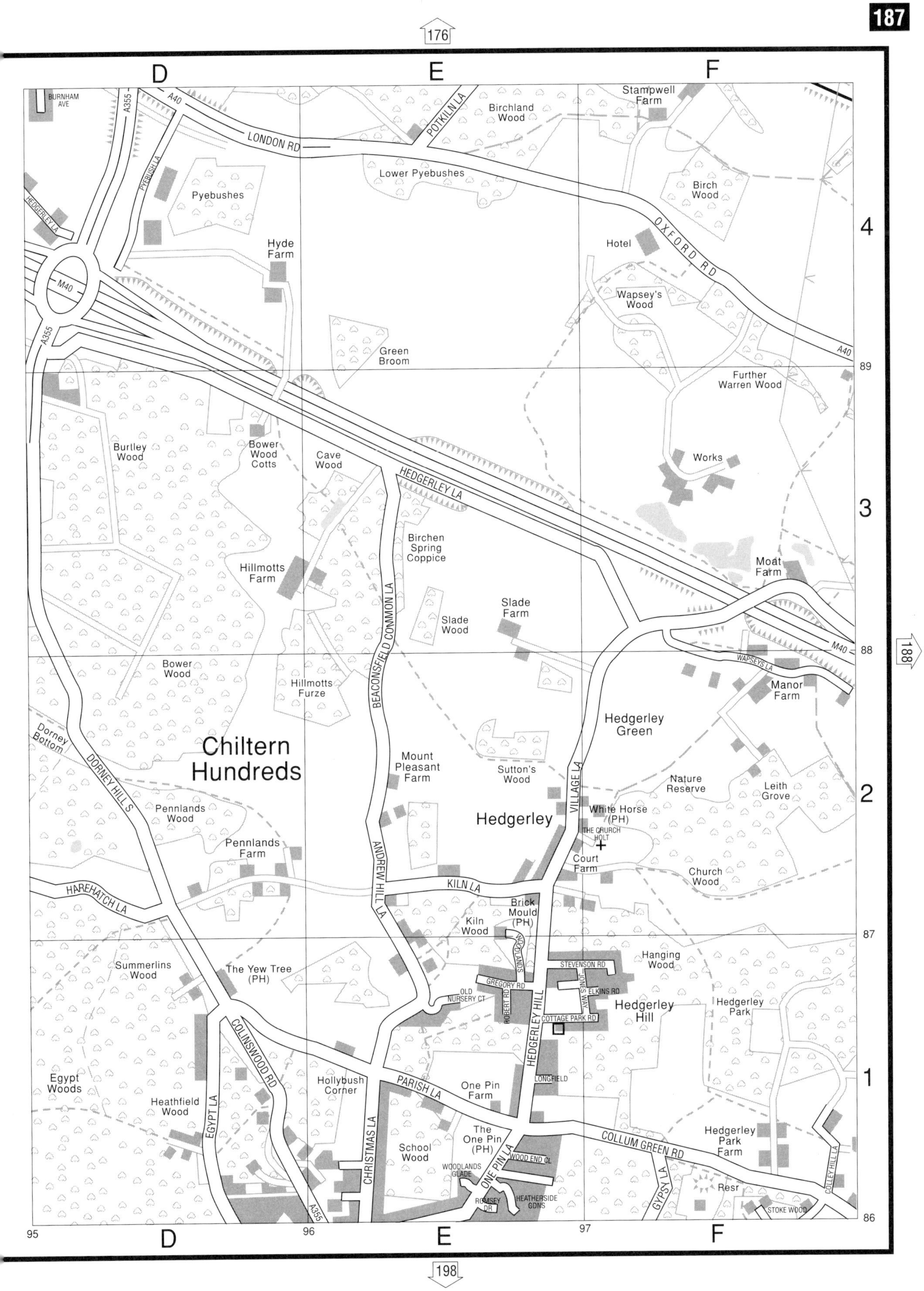
176
D
E
F
BURNHAM AVE
A355
A40
LONDON RD
POTKILN LA
Birchland Wood
Stampwell Farm
PYEBUSH LA
Pyebushes
Lower Pyebushes
Birch Wood
HEDGERLEY LA
OXFORD RD
Hyde Farm
Hotel
M40
Wapsey's Wood
A355
Green Broom
A40
Further Warren Wood
Burtley Wood
Bower Wood Cotts
Cave Wood
HEDGERLEY LA
Works
Birchen Spring Coppice
Hillmotts Farm
Moat Farm
BEACONSFIELD COMMON LA
Slade Wood
Slade Farm
M40
WAPSEYS LA
Manor Farm
Bower Wood
Hillmotts Furze
Hedgerley Green
Dorney Bottom
DORNEY HILL S
Chiltern Hundreds
Mount Pleasant Farm
Sutton's Wood
VILLAGE LA
Nature Reserve
Leith Grove
Pennlands Wood
Hedgerley
White Horse (PH)
THE CHURCH HOLT
Pennlands Farm
ANDREW HILL LA
Court Farm
Church Wood
HAREHATCH LA
KILN LA
Brick Mould (PH)
Kiln Wood
WOODLANDS
Summerlins Wood
The Yew Tree (PH)
STEVENSON RD
Hanging Wood
GREGORY RD
JONES WAY
ELKINS RD
OLD NURSERY CT
ROBERT RD
Hedgerley Hill
Hedgerley Park
COLINSWOOD RD
HEDGERLEY HILL
COTTAGE PARK RD
Egypt Woods
Hollybush Corner
PARISH LA
One Pin Farm
LONGFIELD
Heathfield Wood
EGYPT LA
CHRISTMAS LA
School Wood
The One Pin (PH)
COLLUM GREEN RD
Hedgerley Park Farm
WOODLANDS GLADE
ONE PIN LA
WOOD END CL
GYPSY LA
COLLEY HILL LA
Resr
ROMSEY DR
HEATHERSIDE GDNS
A355
STOKE WOOD
4
3
2
1
89
88
87
86
95
96
97
188
198

177

187

A
B
C
4
3
2
1
89
88
87
86
98
99
00
Austenwood
Sch's
Sch
PRIORY WAY
PRIORY RD
THE ROWANS
LEWINS RD
MALTMANS LA
1 SCHOOL LA
2 CLELAND RD
AUSTENWOOD LA
AUSTENWAY
THE RIDGEWAY
KINGSWAY B416
CLAYDON LA
CLAYDON END
LOWER RD
RUSSELL HILL
A413
CH
River Misbourne
Golf Course
Research Laboratory
LAYTERS GREEN LA
MUMFORDS LA
Siblet's Wood
MumfordsFarm
BULL LA
MILTON AVE
LATCHMOOR WAY
ACREFIELD RD
THE GREENWAY
THE QUEENSWAY
SOUTH SIDE
FIRS END
Schs
MAYFIELD AVE
LATCHMOOR AVE
LATCHMOOR GR
OVAL WAY
ORCHEHILL AVE
B416
NORTH PARK
Sch
PARK DR
SOUTH PARK VIEW
SOUTH PARK CRES
PARKSIDE
NORGROVE PARK
AMERSHAM RD
A40
SOUTH VIEW RD
LAYTERS WAY
RAYLANDS MEAD
BENTINCK CL
P
ORCHEHILL RISE
ETHORPE CRES
ETHORPE CL
PACKHORSE RD
SOUTH PARK
Gerrards Cross Station
STATION APP
BULSTRODE WAY
STATION RD
Liby
OAK END WAY
MARSHAM LA
WOODLANDS
Jarretts Hill
MAIN DR
WEST COMM
WEST COMMON
WEST COMMON CL
FULMER WAY
MARSHAM WAY
Bulstrode Park
TOP PARK
VALLEY WAY
WOODBANK AVE
DONNAY CL
OXFORD RD
Bulstrode
Gerrards Cross Common
GERRARDS CROSS
MARSHAM LODGE
EAST COMMON
VICARAGE WAY
WOODHILL AVE
MILL LA
HILLCREST WAYE
HILL WAYE
BULSTRODE CT
Fort
Crab Hill
B416
Grove Plantation
Sch
BEECH WAYE
MOREANDS DR
Ponders
HEDGERLEY LA
M40
CAMP RD
WAYSIDE GDNS
MANOR LA
DENMEAD
PINEWOOD CL
DUKES LA
NALLZEE
DUKES WOOD AVE
GAVIOTS WAY
Woodhill Farm
A40
GAVIOTS GREEN
HEUSDEN WAY
GAVIOTS CL
Upper Meadow
DUKES CL
COOMBE VALE
DUKES WOOD DR
CHEYNE CL
DUKES RIDE
The Rancho
St Huberts
High Meadows
WINDSOR RD
DUKES KILN DR
BIRCHDALE
UPLANDS CL
ELMWOOD PARK
MOUNT HILL LA
Hedgerley Park
Mount Hill Farm
HOWARDS THICKET
HIGH BEECHES
THE GLADE
DALE SIDE
THE UPLANDS
ST HUBERTS CL
FULMER RD
St Hubert's Home Farm
ST HUBERTS LA
Mounthill Wood
Park House
FULMER DR
HOWARDS WOOD DR
Fish Ponds
Fulmerfields
Cemy
Pickeridge Wood
Low Farm
The Oldhouse Farm
FULMER LA
Alderbrook
B416
M40

199

178

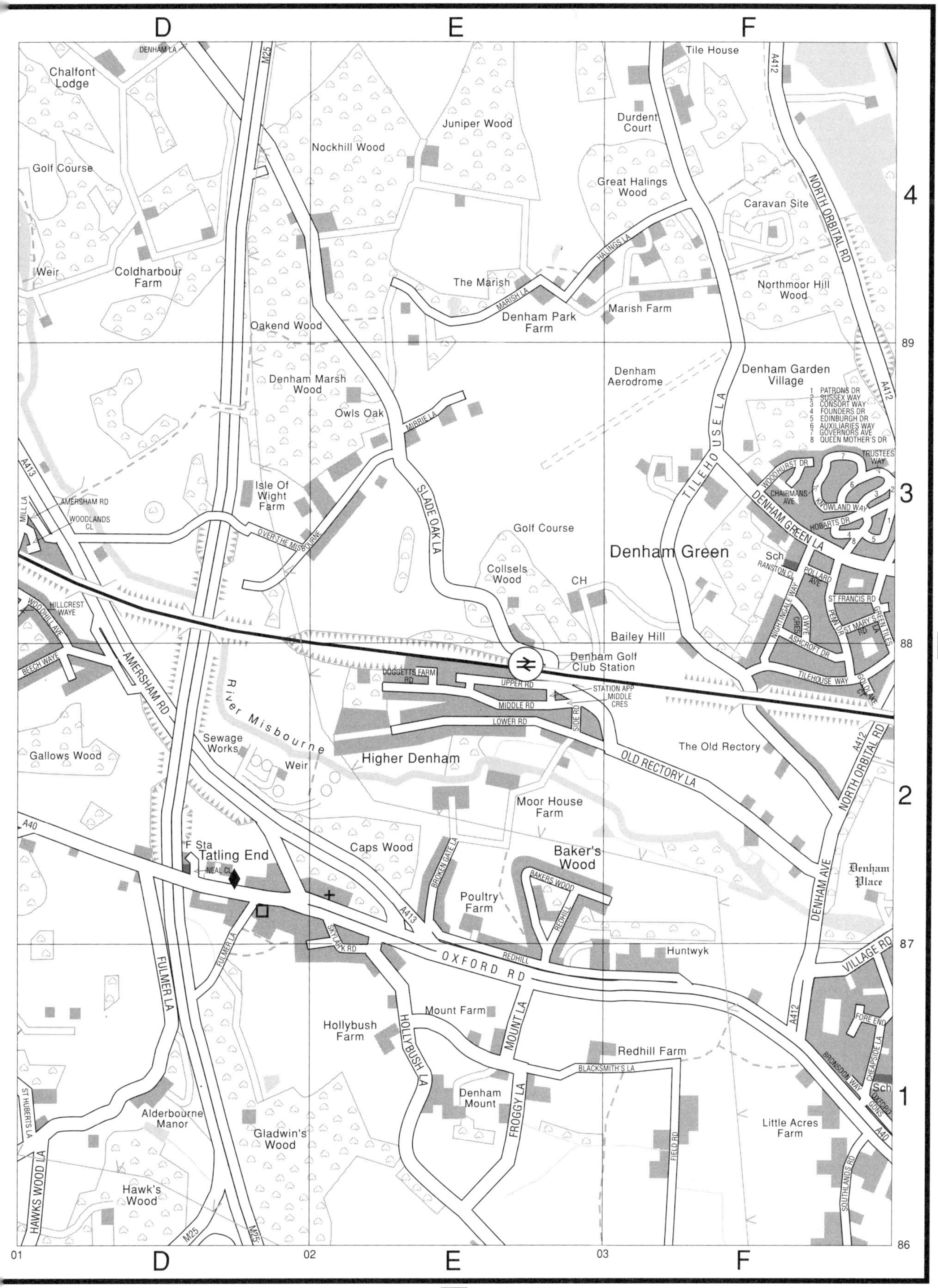

D
E
F
Chalfont Lodge
DENHAM LA
M25
Golf Course
Weir
Coldharbour Farm
Nockhill Wood
Juniper Wood
Durdent Court
Tile House
A412
Great Halings Wood
Caravan Site
NORTH ORBITAL RD
4
HALINGS LA
The Marish
MARISH LA
Denham Park Farm
Marish Farm
Northmoor Hill Wood
Oakend Wood
89
Denham Aerodrome
Denham Garden Village
Denham Marsh Wood
Owls Oak
MIRRIE LA
TILEHOUSE LA
1 PATRONS DR
2 SUSSEX WAY
3 CONSORT WAY
4 FOUNDERS DR
5 EDINBURGH DR
6 AUXILIARIES WAY
7 GOVERNORS AVE
8 QUEEN MOTHER'S DR
TRUSTEES WAY
WOODHURST DR
CHAIRMANS AVE
KNOWLAND WAY
DENHAM GREEN LA
HOBARTS DR
3
A413
MILL LA
AMERSHAM RD
WOODLANDS CL
Isle Of Wight Farm
OVER THE MISBOURNE
SLADE OAK LA
Golf Course
Denham Green
Sch
RANSTON CL
POLLARD AVE
Collsels Wood
CH
ST FRANCIS RD
NIGHTINGALE WAY
OWL CRES
PENN DR
ST MARY'S RD
GREEN TILES LA
ASHCROFT DR
HILLCREST WAYE
WOODHILL AVE
BEECH WAYE
AMERSHAM RD
Bailey Hill
Denham Golf Club Station
88
TILEHOUSE WAY
DOGGETTS FARM RD
UPPER RD
STATION APP
MIDDLE CRES
MIDDLE RD
LOWER RD
SIDE RD
River Misbourne
Sewage Works
Weir
Higher Denham
OLD RECTORY LA
The Old Rectory
A412
NORTH ORBITAL RD
Gallows Wood
2
Moor House Farm
A40
F Sta
Tatling End
NEAL CL
Caps Wood
BROKEN GATE LA
Baker's Wood
BAKERS WOOD
REDHILL
Poultry Farm
DENHAM AVE
Denham Place
A413
SKYLARK RD
REDHILL
OXFORD RD
Huntwyk
VILLAGE RD
87
FULMER LA
FULMER LA
Hollybush Farm
HOLLYBUSH LA
Mount Farm
MOUNT LA
Redhill Farm
BLACKSMITH'S LA
A412
FORE END
BRONSDON WAY
CHEAPSIDE LA
Sch
OXFORD GDNS
A40
1
ST HUBERTS LA
Alderbourne Manor
Denham Mount
FROGGY LA
Gladwin's Wood
FIELD RD
Little Acres Farm
SOUTHLANDS RD
HAWKS WOOD LA
Hawk's Wood
M25
M25
01
02
03
86
D
E
F

190

200

not continued, see key diagram

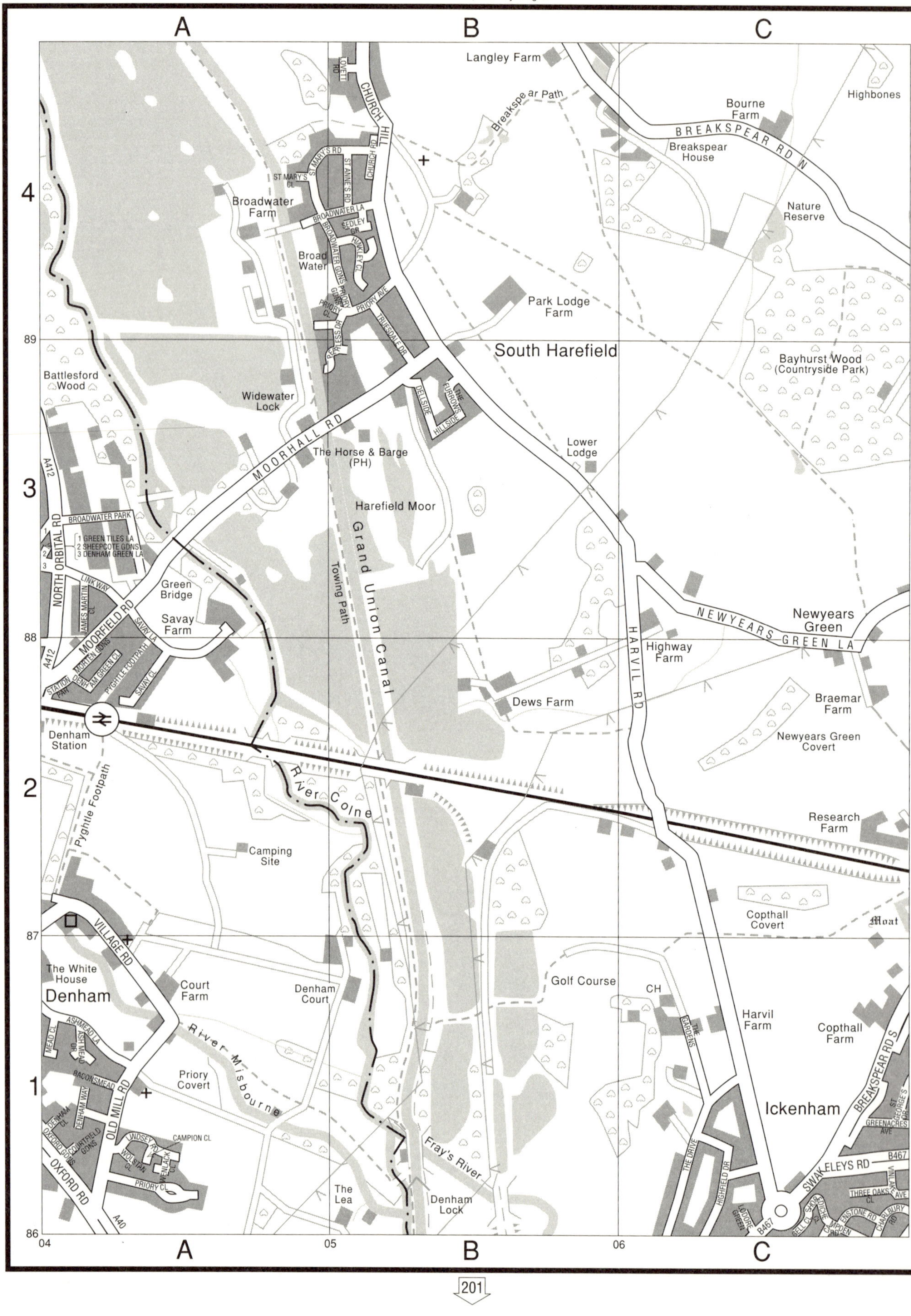

189

201

180

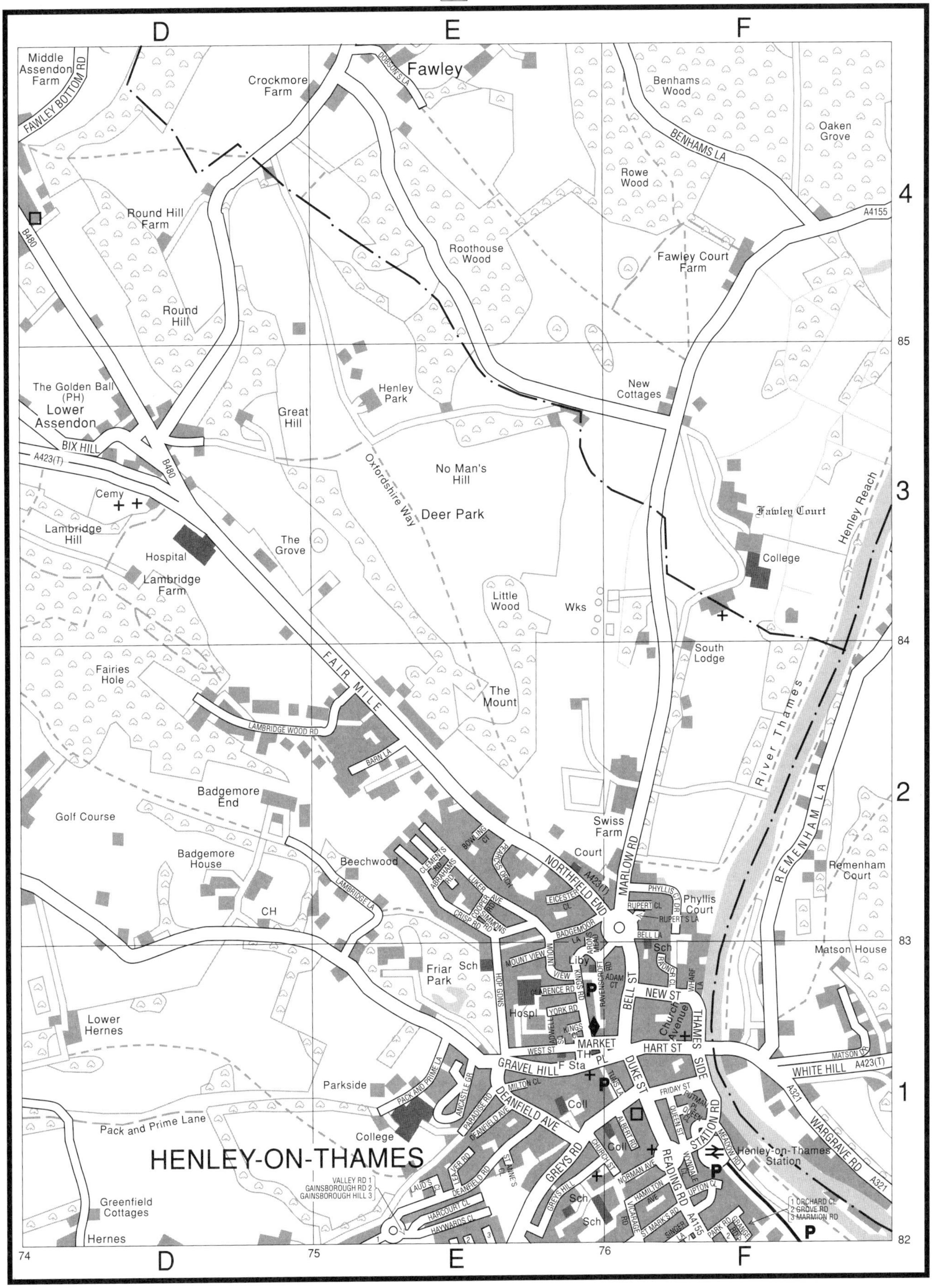
D
E
F
Middle Assendon Farm
FAWLEY BOTTOM RD
Crockmore Farm
Fawley
DOBSON'S LA
Benhams Wood
Oaken Grove
BENHAMS LA
Rowe Wood
Round Hill Farm
B480
Roothouse Wood
Fawley Court Farm
A4155
4
Round Hill
85
The Golden Ball (PH)
Lower Assendon
Henley Park
Great Hill
New Cottages
BIX HILL
A423(T)
B480
Oxfordshire Way
No Man's Hill
Cemy
Deer Park
Fawley Court
Henley Reach
3
Lambridge Hill
Hospital
The Grove
College
Lambridge Farm
Little Wood
Wks
84
South Lodge
Fairies Hole
FAIR MILE
The Mount
LAMBRIDGE WOOD RD
BARN LA
River Thames
Badgemore End
2
Golf Course
Swiss Farm
REMENHAM LA
Badgemore House
Beechwood
Court
NORTHFIELD END
A423(T)
MARLOW RD
Remenham Court
BOWLING CT
PEARCES ORCH
CLEMENTS RD
ABRAHAMS RD
LUKER AVE
COOPER RD
SIMMONS RD
CRISP RD
LAMBRIDGE LA
CH
LEICESTER CL
PHYLLIS CT DR
RUPERT CL
Phyllis Court
RUPERT'S LA
BADGEMOOR LA
BELL LA
83
Matson House
MOUNT VIEW
Sch
Liby
ARGYLE RD
MEAD
RIVERSIDE CL
WHARF LA
Friar Park
Sch
HOP GDNS
KINGS RD
RAVENSCROFT RD
ADAM CT
BELL ST
NEW ST
CLARENCE RD
YORK RD
Hospl
Church Avenue
THAMES SIDE
Lower Hernes
KINGS CT
MARKET PL
HART ST
TH
WEST ST
F Sta
GRAVEL HILL
DUKE ST
MATSON DR
WHITE HILL
A423(T)
MILTON CL
TUNS LA
FRIDAY ST
Parkside
PACK AND PRIME LA
ANCASTLE GR
DEANFIELD AVE
PUTMAN PL
QUEEN ST
STATION RD
A321
1
Coll
PARADISE RD
DEANFIELD AVE
ALBERT RD
WARGRAVE RD
MEADOW RD
Pack and Prime Lane
College
Coll
QUEEN ST
HENLEY-ON-THAMES
GREYS RD
CHURCH ST
READING RD
WYNDALE CL
Henley-on-Thames Station
VALLEY RD 1
GAINSBOROUGH RD 2
GAINSBOROUGH HILL 3
LEAVER RD
DEANFIELD RD
ST ANNE'S CL
NORMAN AVE
UPTON CL
A321
LAUD'S CL
GREYS HILL
HAMILTON AVE
1 ORCHARD CL
2 GROVE RD
3 MARMION RD
Greenfield Cottages
HARCOURT CL
Sch
VICARAGE RD
ST MARK'S RD
A4155
HAYWARDS CL
Sch
SINGER LA
PARK RD
GRANGE RD
Hernes
82
74
75
76
D
E
F

192

181

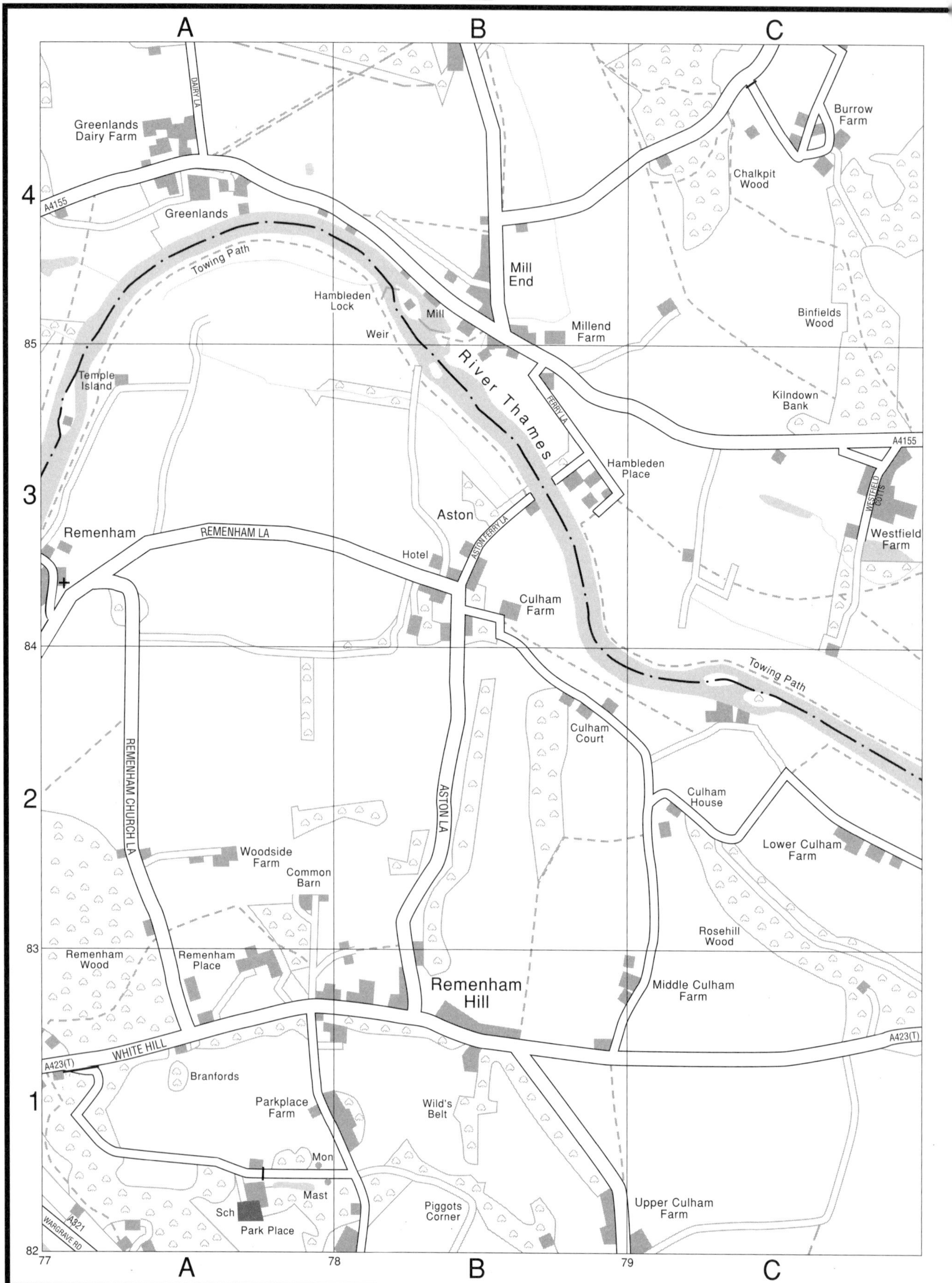

191

not continued,see key diagram

182

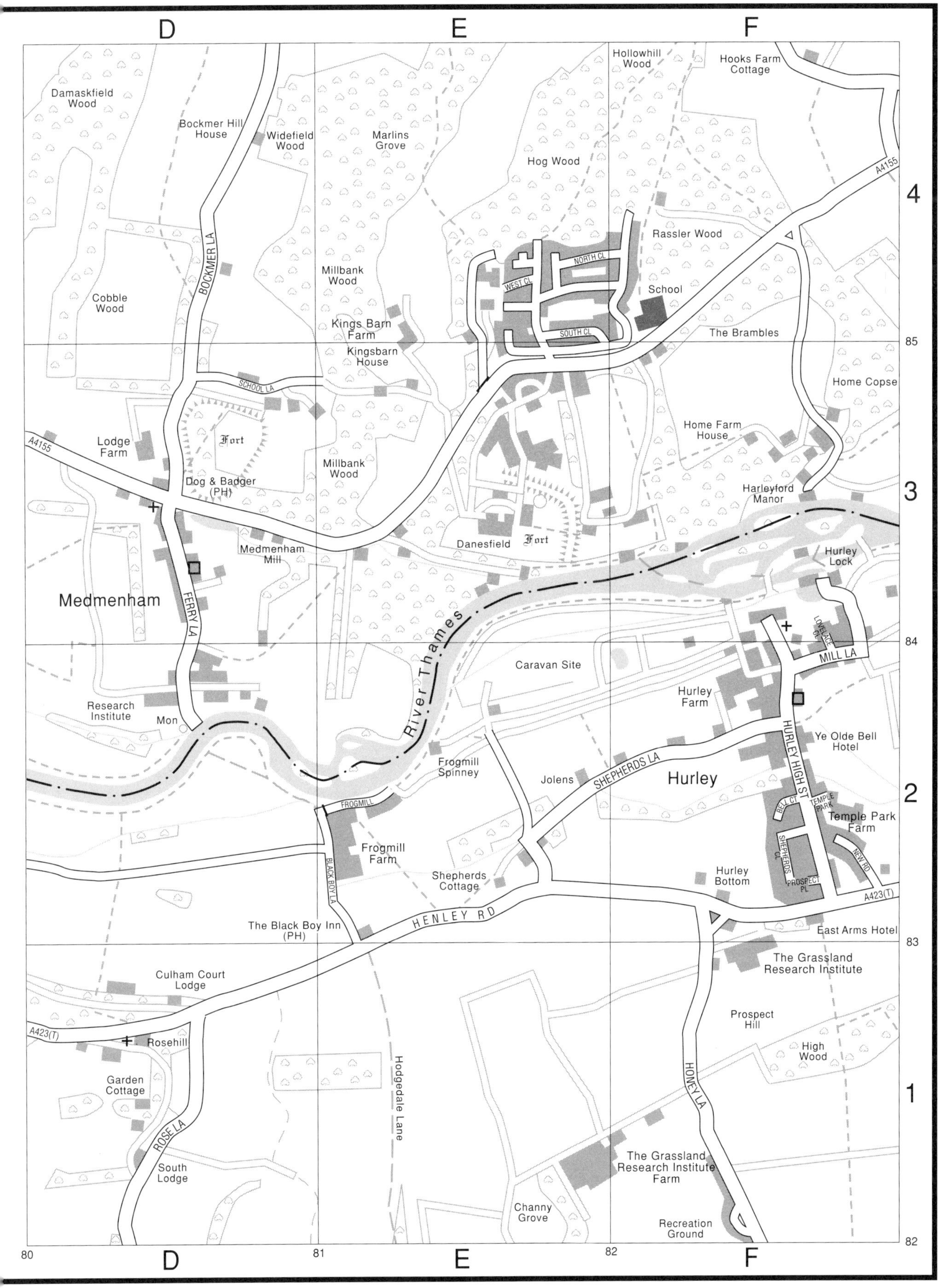

D
E
F
Damaskfield Wood
Bockmer Hill House
Widefield Wood
Marlins Grove
Hollowhill Wood
Hooks Farm Cottage
Hog Wood
A4155
4
BOCKMER LA
Rassler Wood
Millbank Wood
NORTH CL
WEST CL
School
Cobble Wood
Kings Barn Farm
SOUTH CL
The Brambles
Kingsbarn House
85
SCHOOL LA
Home Copse
Fort
Home Farm House
A4155
Lodge Farm
Millbank Wood
Dog & Badger (PH)
Harleyford Manor
3
Danesfield
Fort
Medmenham Mill
Hurley Lock
Medmenham
FERRY LA
River Thames
LOVELACE RD
84
MILL LA
Caravan Site
Hurley Farm
Research Institute
Mon
Ye Olde Bell Hotel
HURLEY HIGH ST
Frogmill Spinney
Jolens
SHEPHERDS LA
Hurley
2
FROGMILL
BELL CT
TEMPLE PARK
Temple Park Farm
Frogmill Farm
SHEPHERDS CL
NEW RD
BLACK BOY LA
Shepherds Cottage
Hurley Bottom
PROSPECT PL
A423(T)
HENLEY RD
The Black Boy Inn (PH)
East Arms Hotel
83
The Grassland Research Institute
Culham Court Lodge
Prospect Hill
A423(T)
Rosehill
High Wood
Garden Cottage
Hodgedale Lane
1
HONEY LA
ROSE LA
The Grassland Research Institute Farm
South Lodge
Channy Grove
Recreation Ground
82
80
81
82
D
E
F

194

183

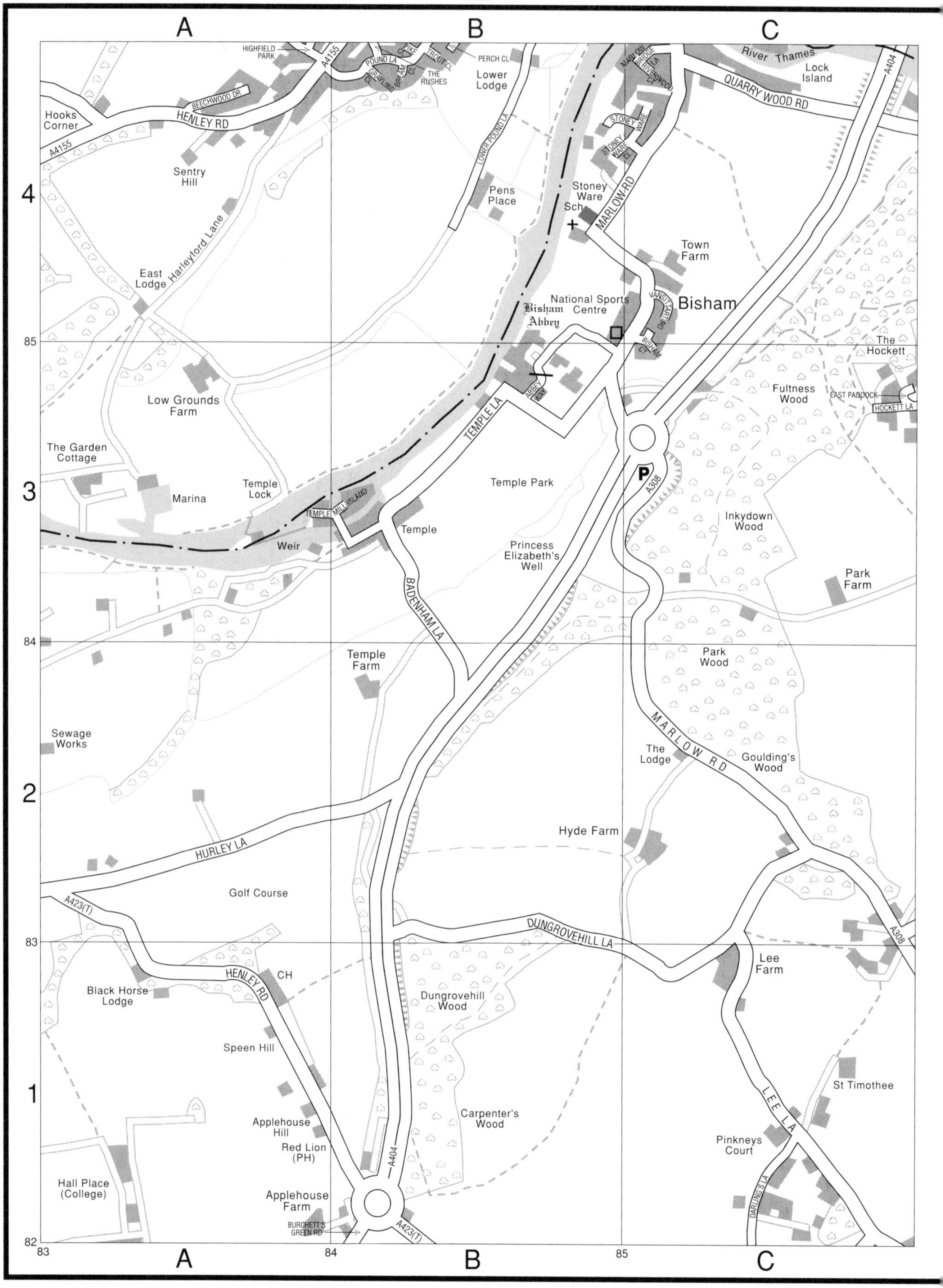
A
B
C
4
3
2
1
85
84
83
82
River Thames
Lock Island
QUARRY WOOD RD
A404
HIGHFIELD PARK
A4155
POUND LA
PERCH CL
THE RUSHES
Lower Lodge
Hooks Corner
BEECHWOOD DR
HENLEY RD
A4155
Sentry Hill
LOWER POUND LA
Pens Place
STONEY WARE
Stoney Ware Sch
MARLOW RD
Town Farm
Harleyford Lane
East Lodge
National Sports Centre
Bisham Abbey
Bisham
The Hockett
Low Grounds Farm
ABBEY WAY
TEMPLE LA
Fultness Wood
EAST PADDOCK
HOCKETT LA
The Garden Cottage
Temple Lock
Marina
Temple Park
P
A308
TEMPLE MILL ISLAND
Temple
Weir
Princess Elizabeth's Well
Inkydown Wood
Park Farm
BADENHAM LA
Temple Farm
Park Wood
Sewage Works
The Lodge
MARLOW RD
Goulding's Wood
HURLEY LA
Hyde Farm
Golf Course
A423(T)
DUNGROVEHILL LA
A308
Lee Farm
HENLEY RD
CH
Black Horse Lodge
Dungrovehill Wood
Speen Hill
St Timothee
LEE LA
Applehouse Hill
Carpenter's Wood
Red Lion (PH)
Pinkneys Court
A404
Hall Place (College)
Applehouse Farm
DARLINGS LA
BURCHETT'S GREEN RD
A423(T)
83
84
85

193

184

D E F

196

D E F

202

185

195

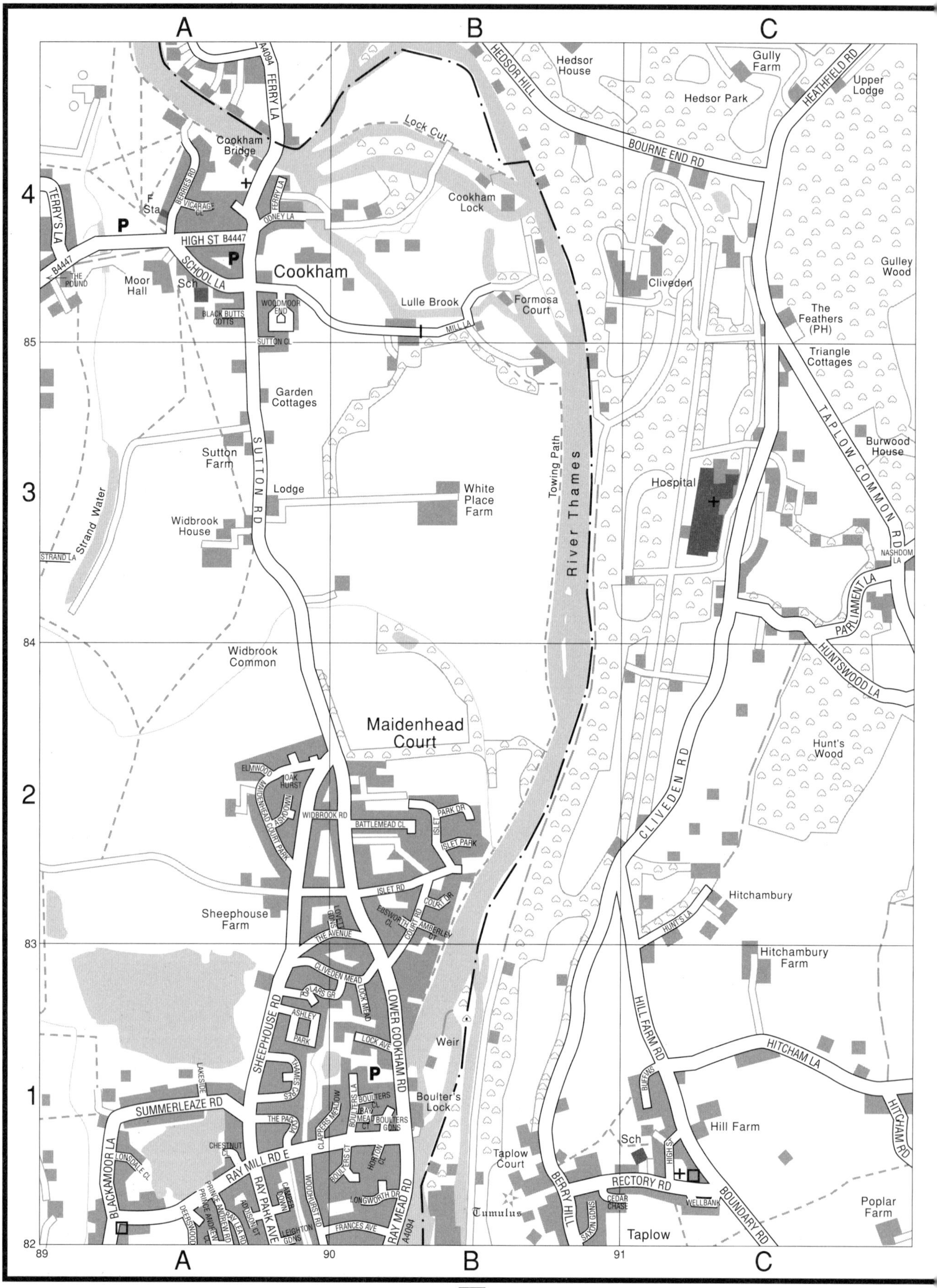

A
B
C
4
3
2
1
85
84
83
82
89
90
91
Cookham
Cookham Bridge
Sta
Moor Hall
Sch
THE POUND
TERRY'S LA
B4447
HIGH ST B4447
SCHOOL LA
BERRIES RD
VICARAGE CL
FERRY LA
A4094 FERRY LA
ODNEY LA
BLACK BUTTS COTTS
WOODMOOR END
SUTTON CL
Lock Cut
Cookham Lock
Lulle Brook
MILL LA
Formosa Court
Hedsor House
HEDSOR HILL
Gully Farm
Hedsor Park
Upper Lodge
HEATHFIELD RD
BOURNE END RD
Cliveden
Gulley Wood
The Feathers (PH)
Triangle Cottages
TAPLOW COMMON RD
Burwood House
Hospital
NASHDOM LA
PARLIAMENT LA
HUNTSWOOD LA
Hunt's Wood
Garden Cottages
Sutton Farm
SUTTON RD
Lodge
White Place Farm
Towing Path
River Thames
Widbrook House
Strand Water
STRAND LA
Widbrook Common
Maidenhead Court
ELMWOOD
OAK HURST
MAIDENHEAD COURT PARK
ASHDOWN
WIDBROOK RD
BATTLEMEAD CL
ISLET PARK DR
ISLET
ISLET PARK
ISLET RD
COURT DR
COURT RD
EBSWORTH CL
AMBERLEY CT
LOVETT GDNS
THE AVENUE
CLIVEDEN RD
Hitchambury
HUNT'S LA
Sheephouse Farm
Hitchambury Farm
CLIVEDEN MEAD
POPLARS GR
LOCK MEAD
ASHLEY PARK
SHEEPHOUSE RD
LOWER COOKHAM RD
LOCK AVE
Weir
THAMES CRES
LAKESIDE
HILL FARM RD
HITCHAM LA
BUFFINS
Boulter's Lock
BOULTERS LA
BOULTERS CL
BOULTERS GDNS
RAY MEAD CT
CLAPPERS MEADOW
THE PAGODA
SUMMERLEAZE RD
CHESTNUT CL
RAY MILL RD E
LONSDALE CL
BLACKAMOOR LA
DEERSWOOD
PRINCE ANDREW CL
PRINCE ANDREW RD
RAY LEA RD
ADDISON CT
RAY PARK AVE
CAMPER DOWN
LEIGHTON GDNS
WOODHURST RD
BOULTERS CT
HORTON CL
LONGWORTH DR
FRANCES AVE
RAY MEAD RD
A4094
Taplow Court
Tumulus
BERRY HILL
Sch
HIGH ST
RECTORY RD
CEDAR CHASE
SAXON GDNS
WELLBANK
BOUNDARY RD
Taplow
Hill Farm
HITCHAM RD
Poplar Farm

203

186

D
E
F
Root Mound
Abbey Wood
Brook End Farm
Lower Brook End
Littleworth Corner
Kilnwood
Dorney Wood
Whitespark Wood
Settlement
Cabrook
Tower Wood
Towerwood
Burnham Beeches
Little Barns Wood
Lambournes Wood
Wymers Wood
Juniper Grove
Settlement
Pumpkin Hill Cottage
Pumpkin Hill
Golf Course
Fox Den
Longmead
Snowball Farm
Poyle Cottages
Rose Hill
Rose Hill Farm
Westalls
Hunts Wood Farm
High Meadow
CH
Burnham
Cant's Hill
Burnham Grove
Bottom Waltons
Grove Wood
Hitcham Park
Court Farm
Convent
Hitcham House Farm
Hitcham House
New Cut
Sch
Sta
Liby
The Priory
Britwell
HORSESHOE HILL
DROPMORE RD
DORNEY WOOD RD
CURRIERS LA
PARK LA
PUMPKIN HILL
HAWTHORN LA
NIGHTINGALE PARK
THOMPKINS LA
NASHDOM LA
ROSE HILL
LONGMEAD LA
CHALK PIT LA
BRICKFIELD LA
HUNTSWOOD LA
TAPLOW COMMON RD
WYMERS WOOD RD
GREEN LA
GROVE RD
CROW PIECE LA
ALLERDS RD
WALTON LA
BOWMANS CL
REDWOOD
ASHCROFT CT
POYLE LA
PINK LA
WYMERS CL
GRENVILLE CL
CHEVELEY GDNS
HAZELHURST RD
BENTLEY PARK
LINKSWOOD RD
OXFORD AVE
CAMBRIDGE AVE
WYNDHAM CRES
NORTH BURNHAM CL
HALL MEADOW
NORTHLANDS DR
BALDWIN RD
PIPERS CL
THE FAIRWAY
KIMBERS DR
TOCKLEY WAY
CLONMEL WAY
BREDWARD CL
ALMOND RD
BAY TREE CT
FAIRFIELD RD
LONG DR
COURT LA
BRITWELL RD
FARNHAM LA
FARNHAM LA SAMPSONS GREEN
DOVE HOUSE CRES
MASCOLL PATH
ROKESBY RD
WAVELL GDNS
GORE RD
HITCHAM LA
HAMILTON GDNS
MINNIECROFT RD
BEECHES WAY
WILMOT RD
HIGH ST
THE GRANGE
GREEN LANE CT
JENNERY LA
BURN WLK
SUMMERS RD
DAWES EAST RD
HATCHGATE GDNS
HOGFAIR LA
CHURCH ST
LINCOLN HATCH LA
PARKGATE
SANDS FARM DR
THE PRECINCTS
EIGHT ACRES
LENT RISE RD
LENT GREEN LA
ALICE LA
ST PETER'S CL
STOMP RD
WINDSOR LA
SHENSTONE DR
ST MICHAEL'S CT
LOWER BRITWELL RD
HAYMILL RD
PORTLAND CL
PRIORY RD
BURNHAM AVE
ORCHARDVILLE
BURLINGTON RD
THE GREEN
HITCHAM RD
BLUMFIELD CT
BLUMFIELD CRES
STRATFORD CL
NEWPORT RD
LYNCH HILL LA
WORDSWORTH RD
BARTELOTTS RD
TENNYSON WAY
COVERDALE WAY
VAUGHAN WAY
KESTREL PATH
WHITTAKER RD
LITTLE BROOK AVE
EGERTON RD
BASSETT WAY
PEMBERTON RD
FOSTERS PATH
TOMLIN RD
FAIRVIEW RD
VERMONT RD
SCAFELL RD
NORTHMEAD RD
MARESCROFT RD
LONG FURLONG DR
DOWNING PATH
WINTOUN PATH
GARRARD RD
CECIL WAY
GAVESTON RD
CALBROKE RD
PENRYMAN WAY
TRAVIC RD
MARUNDEN GREEN
GOODWIN RD
CHILWICK RD
SKYDMORE PATH
NEWCHURCH RD
TEESDALE RD
4
3
2
1
85
84
83
82
92
93
94

198

204

187

197

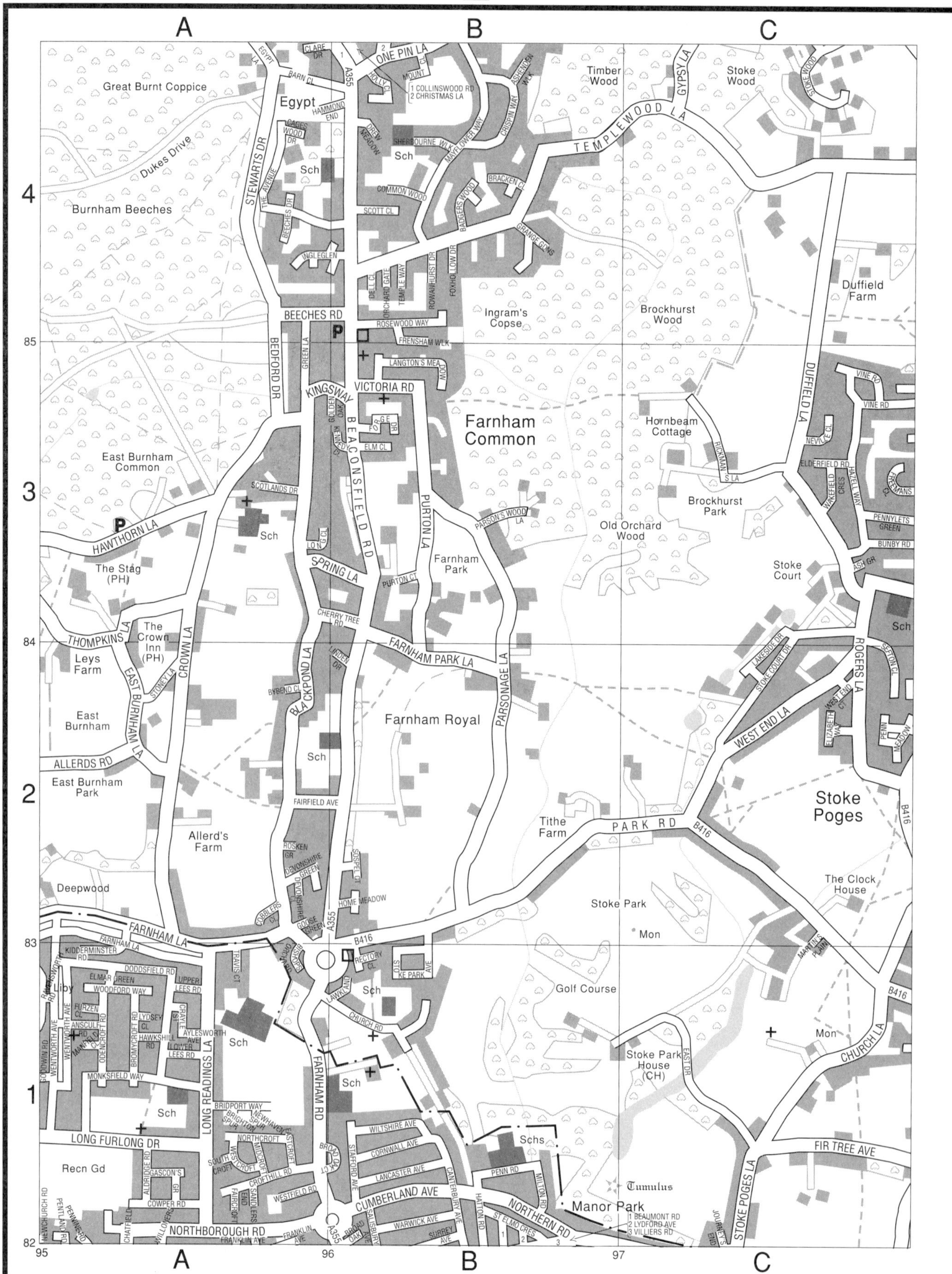

A
B
C
4
3
2
1
85
84
83
82
95
96
97
Great Burnt Coppice
Egypt
Dukes Drive
Burnham Beeches
East Burnham Common
Hawthorn La
The Stag (PH)
Thompkins La
The Crown Inn (PH)
Leys Farm
East Burnham
Allerds Rd
East Burnham Park
Allerd's Farm
Deepwood
Farnham La
Stewarts Dr
Bedford Dr
Crown La
East Burnham La
Stoney La
Long Readings La
Beeches Rd
Green La
Kingsway
Victoria Rd
Beaconsfield Rd
Scotlands Dr
Spring La
Cherry Tree Rd
Blackpond La
Linden Dr
Byrend Cl
Fairfield Ave
Rosken Gr
Devonshire Green
Cobblers Cl
Goose Green
Home Meadow
Gospel Ct
Purton La
Purton Ct
Farnham Park La
Farnham Park
Farnham Royal
Parsonage La
Parson's Wood La
Farnham Common
Ingram's Copse
One Pin La
1 Collinswood Rd
2 Christmas La
Sherbourne Wlk
Mayflower Way
Crispin Way
Ashenden Wlk
Templewood La
Gypsy La
Common Wood
Scott Cl
Badgers Wood
Bracken Cl
Grange Gdns
Ingleglen
Orchard Gate
Temple Way
Rowanhurst Dr
Foxhollow Dr
Rosewood Way
Frensham Wlk
Langton's Meadow
Elm Cl
Timber Wood
Stoke Wood
Brockhurst Wood
Hornbeam Cottage
Rickman's La
Brockhurst Park
Old Orchard Wood
Duffield Farm
Duffield La
Vine Rd
Neville Cl
Elderfield Rd
Wakefield Cres
Hazell Way
Freemans Cl
Pennylets Green
Bunby Rd
Ash Gr
Stoke Court
Sch
Rogers La
Sefton Cl
Lakeside Dr
Stoke Court Dr
West End La
West End Ct
Elizabeth Way
Penn Meadow
Stoke Poges
B416
Tithe Farm
Park Rd
Stoke Park
Mon
Golf Course
The Clock House
Martin's Plain
Church La
Stoke Park House (CH)
East Dr
Fir Tree Ave
Stoke Poges La
Journeys End
Tumulus
Manor Park
1 Beaumont Rd
2 Lydford Ave
3 Villiers Rd
Northern Rd
Penn Rd
Milton Rd
Hatton Ave
Canterbury Ave
St Elmo Cres
Surrey Ave
Warwick Ave
Cumberland Ave
Salisbury Ave
Lancaster Ave
Cornwall Ave
Wiltshire Ave
Stafford Ave
Broad Oak Ct
Broad Oak Ave
Farnham Rd
A355
Church Rd
Rectory Cl
Stoke Park Ave
Travis Ct
Schs
Kidderminster Rd
Doddsfield Rd
Elmar Green
Upper Lees Rd
Woodford Way
Liby
Furzen Cl
Ansculf Rd
Lydsey Cl
Crayle St
Aylesworth Ave
Hawkshill Rd
Lower Lees Rd
Odencroft Rd
Bromycroft Rd
Wentworth Ave
Goodwin Rd
Monksfield Way
Bridport Way
Brighton Spur
Newhaven Spur
Eastcroft
Northcroft
Midcroft
Southcroft
Westcroft
Crofthill Rd
Westfield Rd
Fairacres
Sanders End
Long Furlong Dr
Recn Gd
Gascon's Gr
Aldridge Rd
Cowper Rd
Chatfield
Willoners
Northborough Rd
Franklin Ave
Newchurch Rd
Pentland Rd
Pennine Rd

205

188

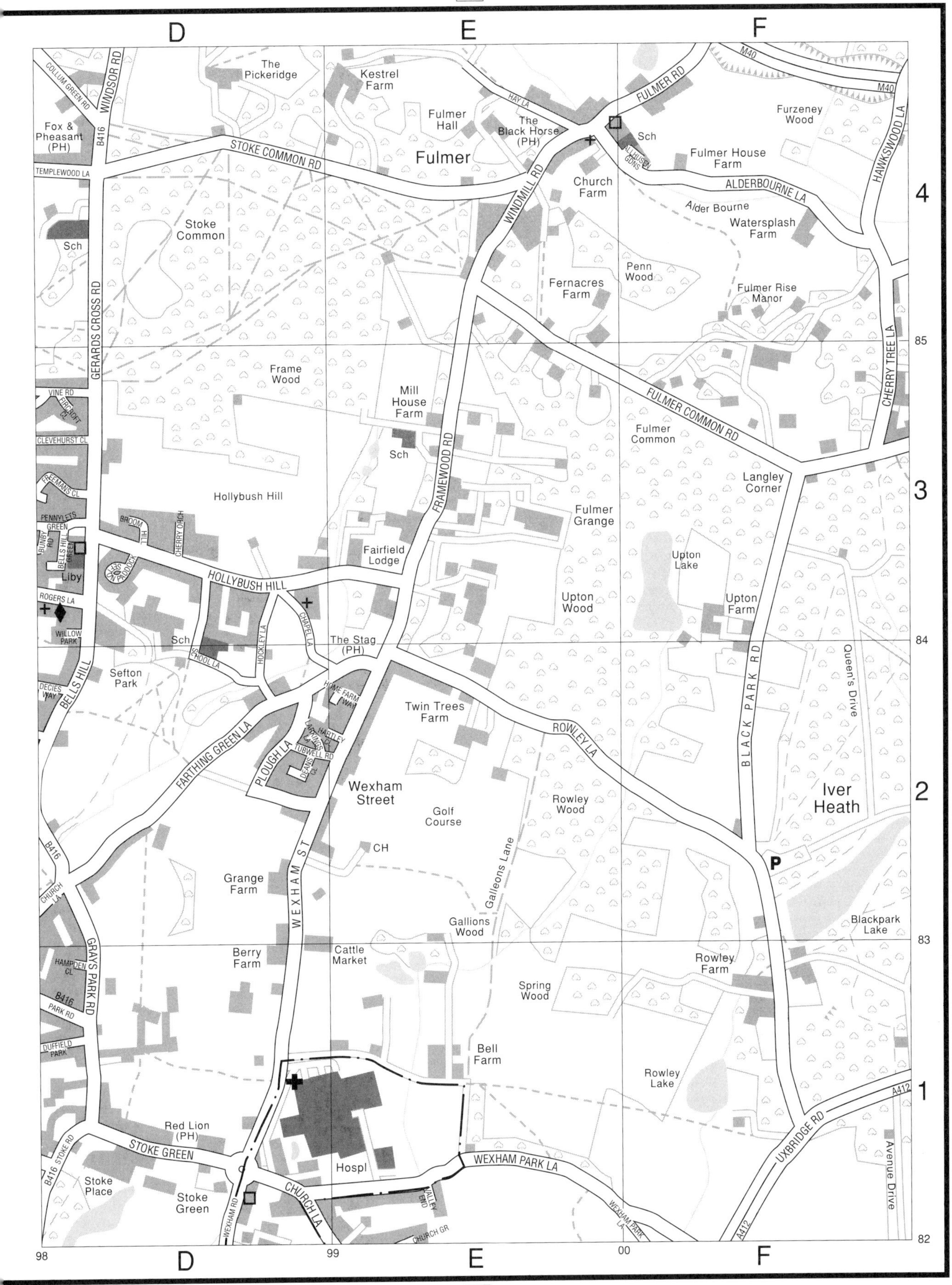
D
E
F
The Pickeridge
Kestrel Farm
Fulmer Hall
The Black Horse (PH)
Fulmer
HAY LA
FULMER RD
M40
Furzeney Wood
HAWKSWOOD LA
Fox & Pheasant (PH)
WINDSOR RD
COLLUM GREEN RD
B416
STOKE COMMON RD
TEMPLEWOOD LA
Sch
ALLHUSEN GDNS
Fulmer House Farm
Church Farm
ALDERBOURNE LA
Alder Bourne
Watersplash Farm
WINDMILL RD
Stoke Common
GERARDS CROSS RD
Penn Wood
Fernacres Farm
Fulmer Rise Manor
CHERRY TREE LA
Frame Wood
Mill House Farm
VINE RD
FIRCROFT CL
CLEVEHURST CL
FULMER COMMON RD
Fulmer Common
FRAMEWOOD RD
FREEMANS CL
Hollybush Hill
Langley Corner
Fulmer Grange
PENNYLETS GREEN
BROOM HILL
CHERRY ORCH
BUNBY RD
BELLS HILL GREEN
Liby
PADDOCK
Fairfield Lodge
Upton Lake
HOLLYBUSH HILL
ROGERS LA
WILLOW PARK
CHAPEL LA
Upton Wood
Upton Farm
Sch
SCHOOL LA
HOCKLEY LA
The Stag (PH)
Queen's Drive
Sefton Park
DECIES WAY
BELLS HILL
HOME FARM WAY
Twin Trees Farm
ROWLEY LA
BLACK PARK RD
HARTLEY CL
LARCHINGS
TUBWELL RD
DEANS CL
FARTHING GREEN LA
PLOUGH LA
Wexham Street
Golf Course
Rowley Wood
Iver Heath
B416
CH
Galleons Lane
P
CHURCH LA
Grange Farm
WEXHAM ST
Gallions Wood
Blackpark Lake
Berry Farm
Cattle Market
Rowley Farm
HAMPDEN CL
GRAYS PARK RD
Spring Wood
B416
PARK RD
DUFFIELD PARK
Bell Farm
Rowley Lake
A412
Red Lion (PH)
UXBRIDGE RD
Avenue Drive
STOKE GREEN
B416 STOKE RD
Hospl
WEXHAM PARK LA
Stoke Place
Stoke Green
CHURCH LA
VALLEY END
WEXHAM RD
CHURCH GR
WEXHAM PARK LA
A412
4
3
2
1
85
84
83
82
98
99
00
D
E
F

200

206

189

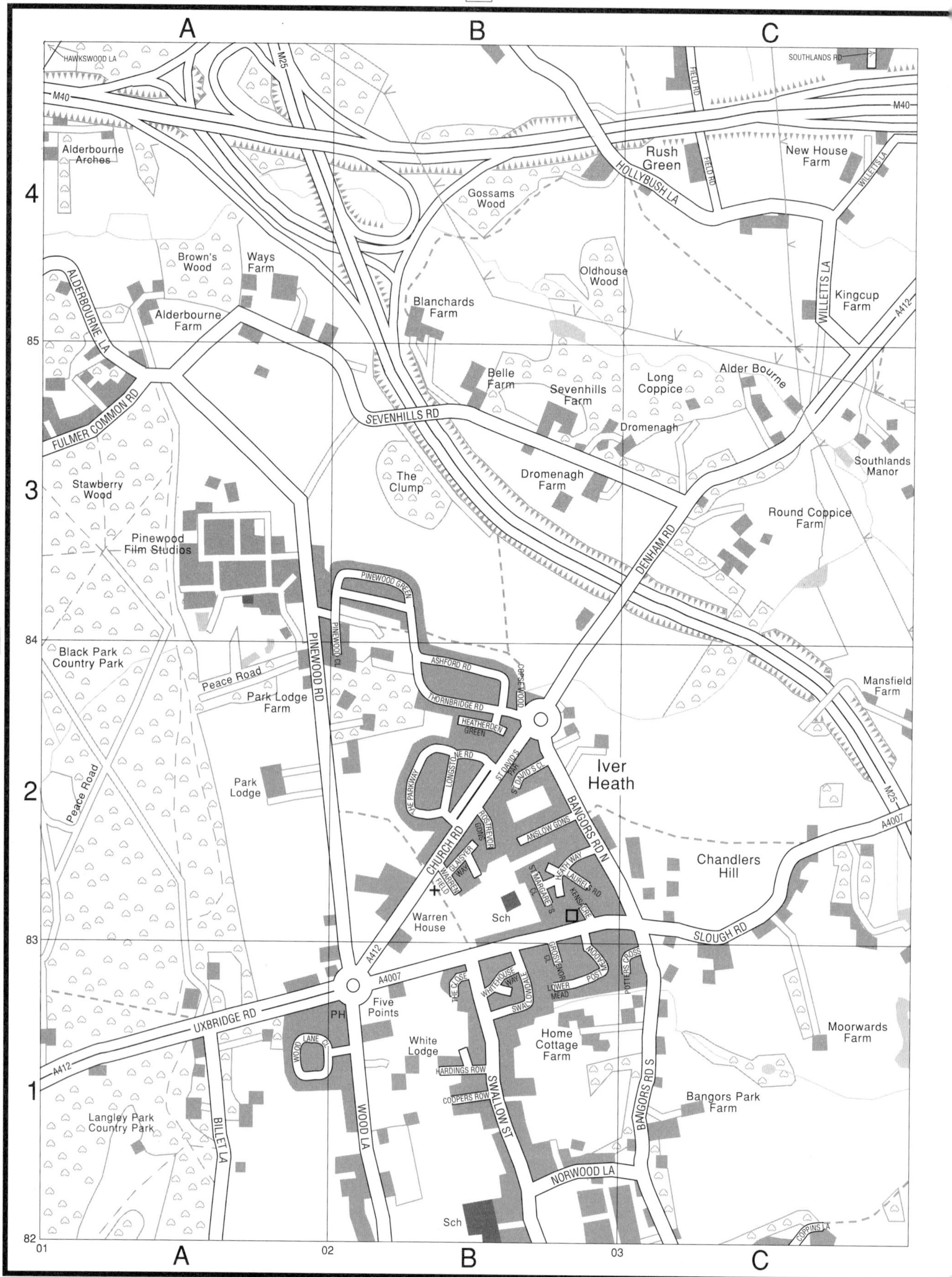
A
B
C
A
B
C
4
3
2
1
85
84
83
82
01
02
03
HAWKSWOOD LA
M40
M25
SOUTHLANDS RD
FIELD RD
Alderbourne Arches
Rush Green
New House Farm
HOLLYBUSH LA
WILLETTS LA
Gossams Wood
Brown's Wood
Ways Farm
Oldhouse Wood
Blanchards Farm
Kingcup Farm
A412
ALDERBOURNE LA
Alderbourne Farm
Belle Farm
Sevenhills Farm
Long Coppice
Alder Bourne
FULMER COMMON RD
SEVENHILLS RD
Dromenagh
Southlands Manor
Stawberry Wood
The Clump
Dromenagh Farm
Round Coppice Farm
Pinewood Film Studios
DENHAM RD
PINEWOOD GREEN
PINEWOOD CL
Black Park Country Park
PINEWOOD RD
ASHFORD RD
COPSE WOOD
Mansfield Farm
Peace Road
Park Lodge Farm
THORNBRIDGE RD
HEATHERDEN GREEN
Iver Heath
LONGSTONE RD
ST DAVID'S PAR
ST DAVID'S CL
Park Lodge
THE PARKWAY
Peace Road
BANGORS RD N
M25
ROSSTREVOR GDNS
ANSLOW GDNS
A4007
CHURCH RD
CLAISYER WAY
HEATH WAY
Chandlers Hill
WARREN FIELD
ST MARGARET'S CL
LAURELS RD
KENSACRE
Warren House
Sch
SLOUGH RD
A412
GROSVENOR CL
MOOR VIEW
POTTERS CROSS
A4007
THE CLOSE
WHITEHOUSE WAY
POST
LOWER MEAD
SWALLOWDALE
PH
Five Points
UXBRIDGE RD
Home Cottage Farm
Moorwards Farm
WOOD LANE CL
White Lodge
A412
HARDINGS ROW
COOPERS ROW
SWALLOW ST
BANGORS RD S
Bangors Park Farm
Langley Park Country Park
BILLET LA
WOOD LA
NORWOOD LA
Sch
COPPINS LA

199

207

190

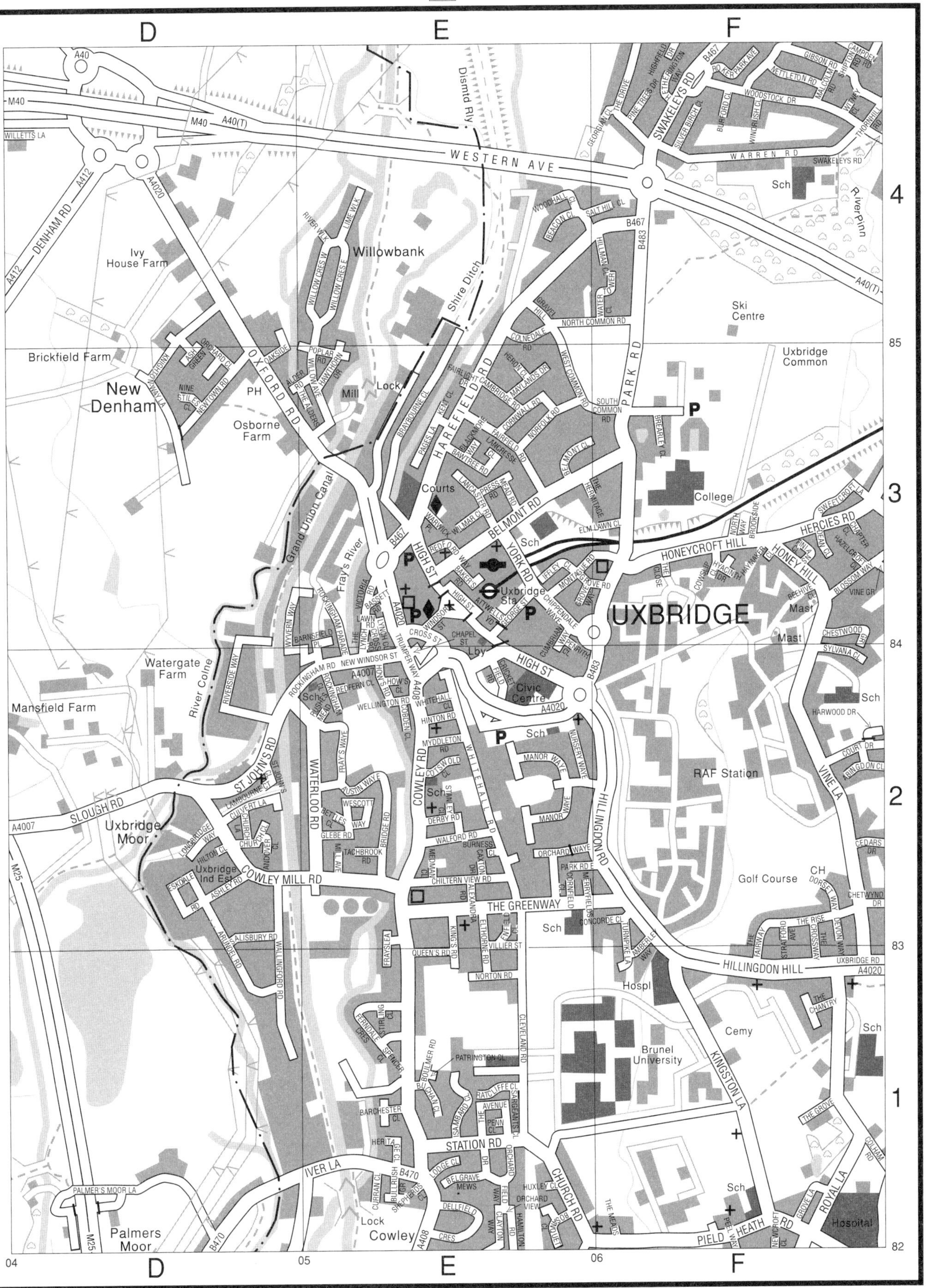

not continued, see key diagram

208

195

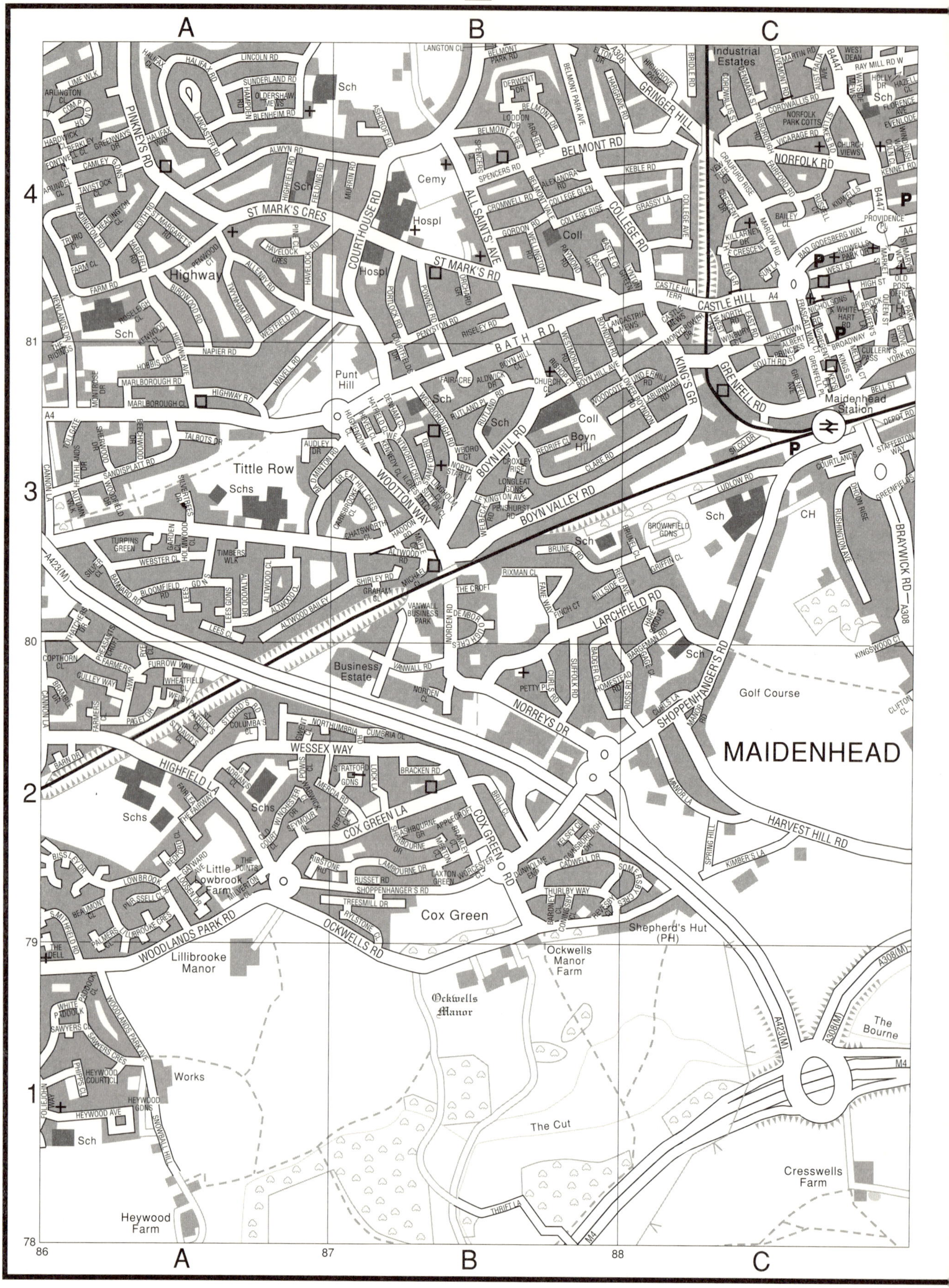

not continued, see key diagram

not continued, see key diagram

196

204

not continued, see key diagram

197

Lent Rise
Sch
Court
Schs
Burnham Station
Trading Estate
BUCKINGHAM AVE
BURNHAM LA
STATION RD
STOMP RD
EASTFIELD RD
PRIORY RD
HAYMILL RD
HITCHAM RD
LENT RISE RD
TAPLOW RD
HAG HILL LA
HUNTERCOMBE LA N
BATH RD
A4
M4
B3026
Pondleys Cottages
West Town Farm
Burnham Abbey
Huntercombe Manor
HUNTERCOMBE LA S
LAKE END RD
ST ANDREW'S WAY
ELMSHOTT LA
MERCIAN WAY
LOWER CIPPENHAM LA
CIPPENHAM LA
Liby
Schs
Moat
Cippenham
Recreation Ground
Lake End
Lake End Farm
Roundmoor Ditch
Sewage Works
MARSH LA
COURT LA
VILLAGE RD
The Palmer Arms (PH)
Dorney
Elm View Farm
Dorney Court
Court Farm
Manor Farm
Pigeonhouse Farm
COMMON RD
Riding School
Dorney Common
BOVENEY RD
Elm Farm Bungalow
Cress Brook
Roasthill Lane
River Thames
ETON WICK RD
Boveney Ditch
Eton Wick
Recn Gd
A
B
C
1
2
3
4
78
79
80
81
92
93
94

203

209

198

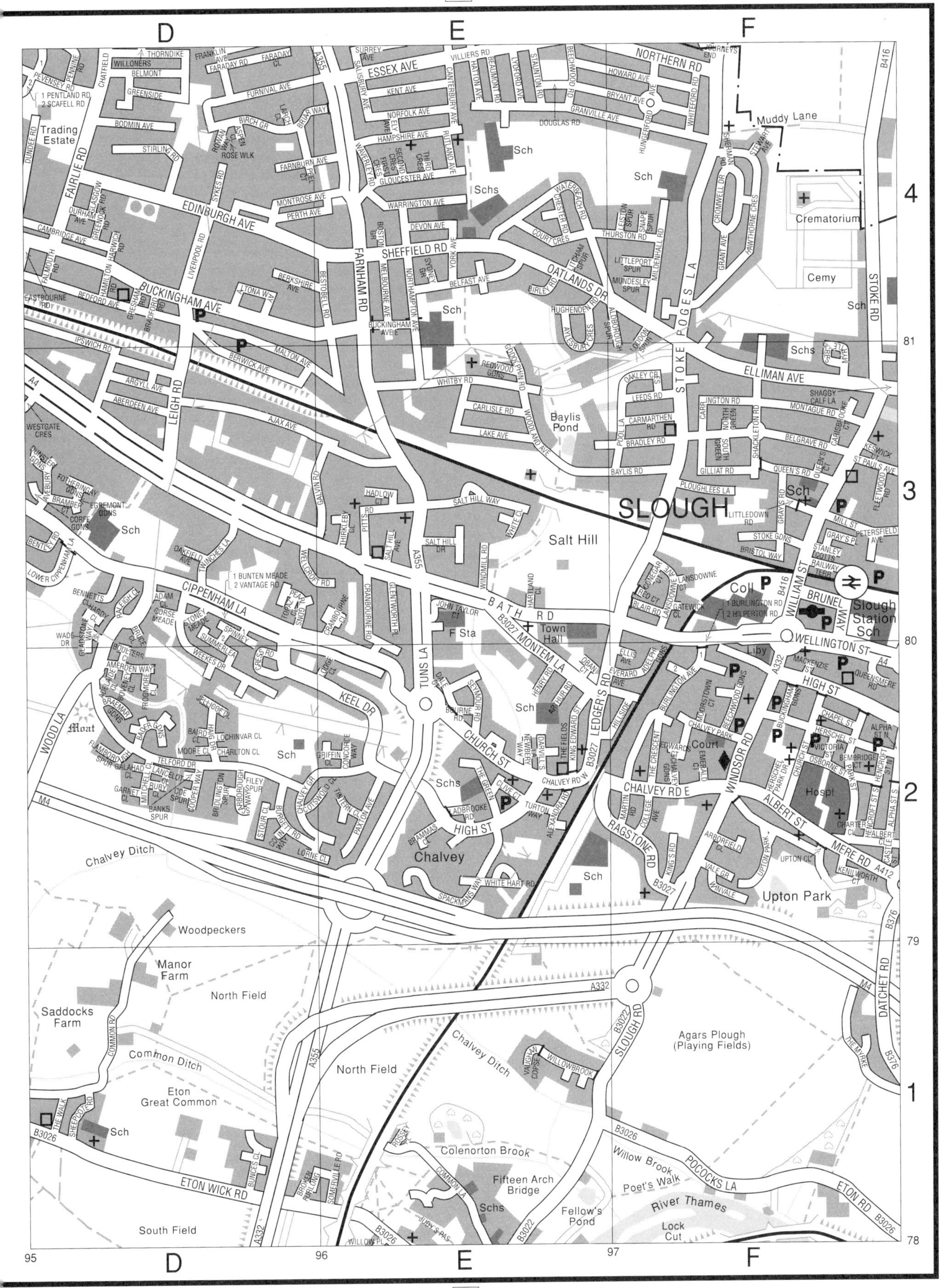
D
E
F
4
3
2
1
81
80
79
78
95
96
97
SLOUGH
Trading Estate
Sch
Schs
Crematorium
Cemy
Muddy Lane
Baylis Pond
Salt Hill
Coll
Slough Station
Town Hall
F Sta
Liby
Hospl
Court
Chalvey
Upton Park
Moat
Woodpeckers
Manor Farm
North Field
Saddocks Farm
Common Ditch
Eton Great Common
Chalvey Ditch
Agars Plough (Playing Fields)
Colenorton Brook
Fifteen Arch Bridge
Fellow's Pond
Willow Brook
Poet's Walk
River Thames
Lock Cut
South Field
ESSEX AVE
NORTHERN RD
EDINBURGH AVE
SHEFFIELD RD
OATLANDS DR
BUCKINGHAM AVE
FARNHAM RD
STOKE POGES LA
STOKE RD
ELLIMAN AVE
LEIGH RD
FAIRLIE RD
BATH RD
CIPPENHAM LA
WELLINGTON ST
HIGH ST
WINDSOR RD
CHALVEY RD E
ALBERT ST
MERE RD
CHURCH ST
TUNS LA
MONTEM LA
LEDGER'S RD
RAGSTONE RD
KEEL DR
WOOD LA
SLOUGH RD
DATCHET RD
ETON WICK RD
POCOCKS LA
ETON RD
COMMON RD
COMMON LA
WILLIAM ST
BRUNEL WAY
A4
A355
A332
A412
B3026
B3027
B3022
B416
B376
M4

206

210

199

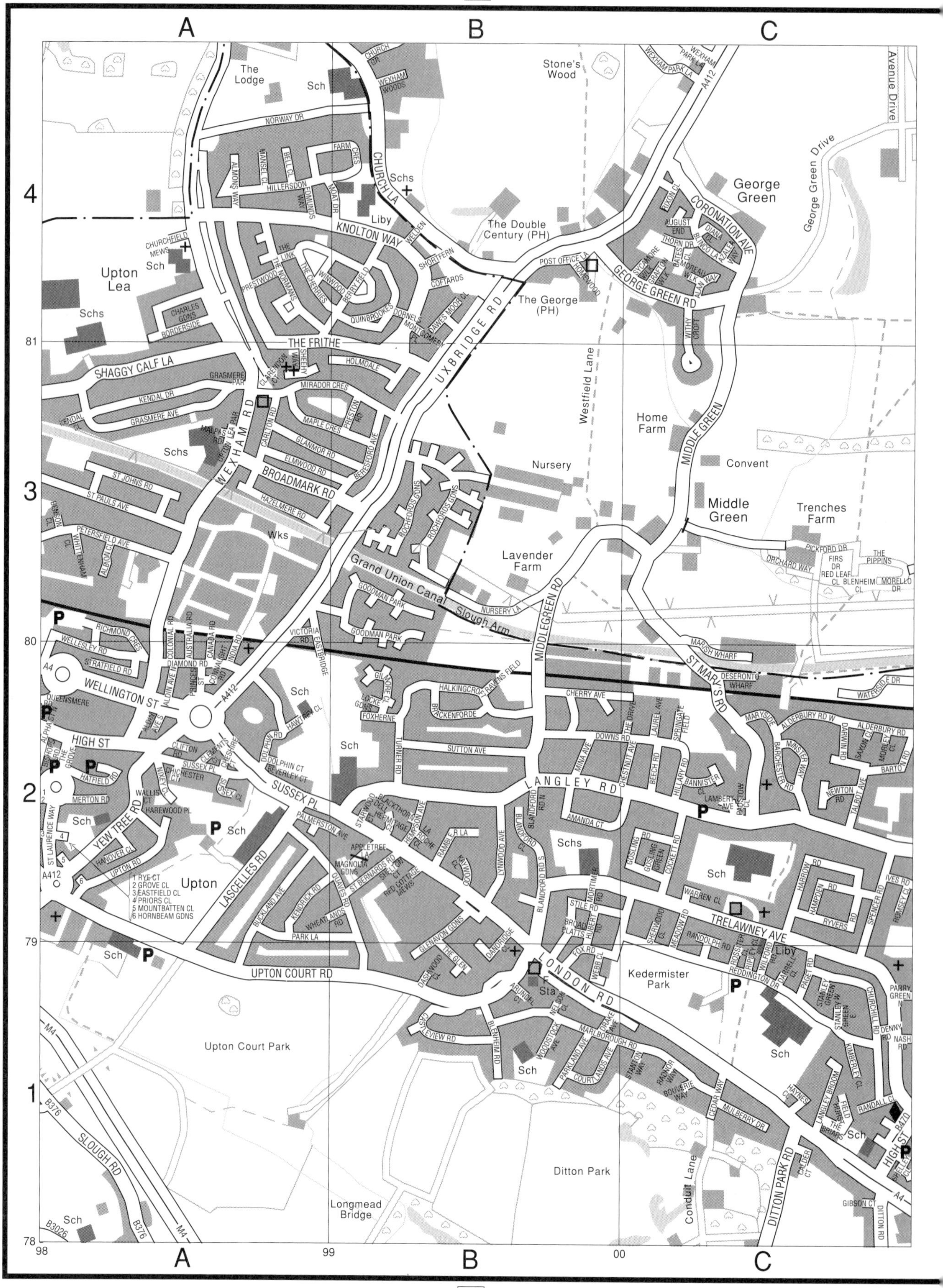
A
B
C
4
3
2
1
81
80
79
78
98
99
00
The Lodge
Sch
Stone's Wood
WEXHAM PARK LA
A412
Avenue Drive
NORWAY DR
CHURCH GR
WEXHAM WOODS
FARM CRES
ALMONS WAY
MANSEL CL
BELL CL
HILLERSDON
MOAT DR
CHURCH LA
Schs
Liby
KNOLTON WAY
George Green
George Green Drive
CORONATION AVE
DIXON CL
AUGUST END
THORN DR
The Double Century (PH)
POST OFFICE LA
HOLLYWOOD
GEORGE GREEN RD
WITHY CROFT
CHURCHFIELD MEWS
Upton Lea
Sch
Schs
CHARLES GDNS
BORDERSIDE
PRESTWOOD
THE NORMANS
THE CHERRIES
WINWOOD
BERRYFIELD
QUINBROOKES
SHORTFERN
COFTARDS
DORNELS
MONTGOMERY PL
DAWES MOOR CL
The George (PH)
THE FRITHE
SHAGGY CALF LA
GRASMERE PAR
KENDAL DR
GRASMERE AVE
KENDAL CL
HOLMDALE
MIRADOR CRES
UXBRIDGE RD
Westfield Lane
Home Farm
MIDDLE GREEN
MALPAS RD
UPTON LEA PAR
Schs
WEXHAM RD
CARLTON RD
MAPLE CRES
PRESTON RD
GLANMOR RD
ELMWOOD RD
BERESFORD AVE
BROADMARK RD
HAZELMERE RD
Nursery
Convent
Middle Green
Trenches Farm
ST JOHNS RD
ST PAULS AVE
BENSON CL
PETERSFIELD AVE
WHITTENHAM CL
ALBION CL
Wks
ROCHFORDS GDNS
Lavender Farm
PICKFORD DR
ORCHARD WAY
FIRS DR
RED LEAF CL
BLENHEIM CL
MORELLO DR
THE PIPPINS
Grand Union Canal
Slough Arm
GOODMAN PARK
NURSERY LA
MIDDLEGREEN RD
RICHMOND CRES
WELLESLEY RD
STRATFIELD RD
COLONIAL RD
AUSTRALIA RD
CANADA RD
INDIA RD
VICTORIA RD
EASTBRIDGE
A4
WELLINGTON ST
DIAMOND RD
CONNAUGHT RD
PRINCES ST
A412
Sch
GILMORE CL
LOCKE GDNS
FOXHERNE
HALKINGCROFT
HAVENSFIELD
BRACKENFORDE
CHERRY AVE
MARSH WHARF
ST MARY'S RD
DESERONTO WHARF
WATERSIDE DR
QUEENSMERE
HIGH ST
CLIFTON RD
SUSSEX PL
HAWTREY CL
DOLPHIN RD
DOLPHIN CT
BEVERLEY CT
SUTTON AVE
TURNER RD
DOWNS RD
MINA AVE
CHESTNUT AVE
THE DRIVE
LAUREL AVE
SPRINGATE FIELD
BEECH RD
HILLARY RD
BANNISTER CL
MARYSIDE
ALDERBURY RD W
ALDERBURY RD
MINSTER WAY
BARCHESTER RD
DARWIN RD
SAXON CL
MORLEY CL
BARTON RD
HATFIELD RD
MERTON RD
WALLIS CT
HAREWOOD PL
YEW TREE RD
ST LAURENCE WAY
HANOVER CL
UPTON RD
Sch
LASCELLES RD
SUSSEX PL
PALMERSTON AVE
BLACKTHORN DELL
HERMITAGE CL
RAMBLER LA
LANGLEY RD
BLANDFORD RD N
AMANDA CT
LAMBERT AVE
PADSTOW CL
NEWTON RD
TALBOT AVE
Schs
GOSLING RD
GOSLING GREEN
COCKETT RD
Sch
HARROW RD
HAMPDEN RD
IVES RD
1 RYE CT
2 GROVE CL
3 EASTFIELD CL
4 PRIORS CL
5 MOUNTBATTEN CL
6 HORNBEAM GDNS
Upton
A412
APPLETREE LA
MAGNOLIA GDNS
ST BERNARDS RD
BUCKLAND AVE
KENDRICK RD
WHEATLANDS RD
LYNWOOD AVE
BLANDFORD RD S
STILE RD
BROAD PLATTS
WARREN CL
TRELAWNEY AVE
SHERWOOD CL
MEADOW RD
RANDOLPH RD
RYVERS
SPENCER RD
UPTON COURT RD
PARK LA
GLENAVON GDNS
DANDRIDGE CL
DASHWOOD CL
THE GLEN
LONDON RD
F Sta
FOX RD
WEBB CL
Kedermister Park
ROSSITER CL
RIPLEY CL
WILFORD RD
DARRELL CL
Liby
REDDINGTON DR
PAGET RD
STANLEY GREEN E
STANLEY GREEN W
CHURCHILL RD
PARRY GREEN N
DENNY RD
NASH RD
ARUNDEL CT
WELBECK CT
CASTLEVIEW RD
BLENHEIM RD
WOODSTOCK AVE
DRAKE AVE
MARLBOROUGH RD
PARKLAND AVE
COURTLANDS AVE
STANTON WAY
RADNOR WAY
BOUVERIE WAY
CEDAR WAY
MULBERRY DR
Sch
Upton Court Park
Sch
KIMBERLEY CL
LANGLEY BROOM
THE BRIARS
HAYNES CL
RANDALL CL
B470
HIGH ST
M4
B376
SLOUGH RD
Ditton Park
Conduit Lane
DITTON PARK RD
CALDER CT
GIBSON CT
DITTON RD
A4
Longmead Bridge
Sch
B3026
B376
M4

205

211

200

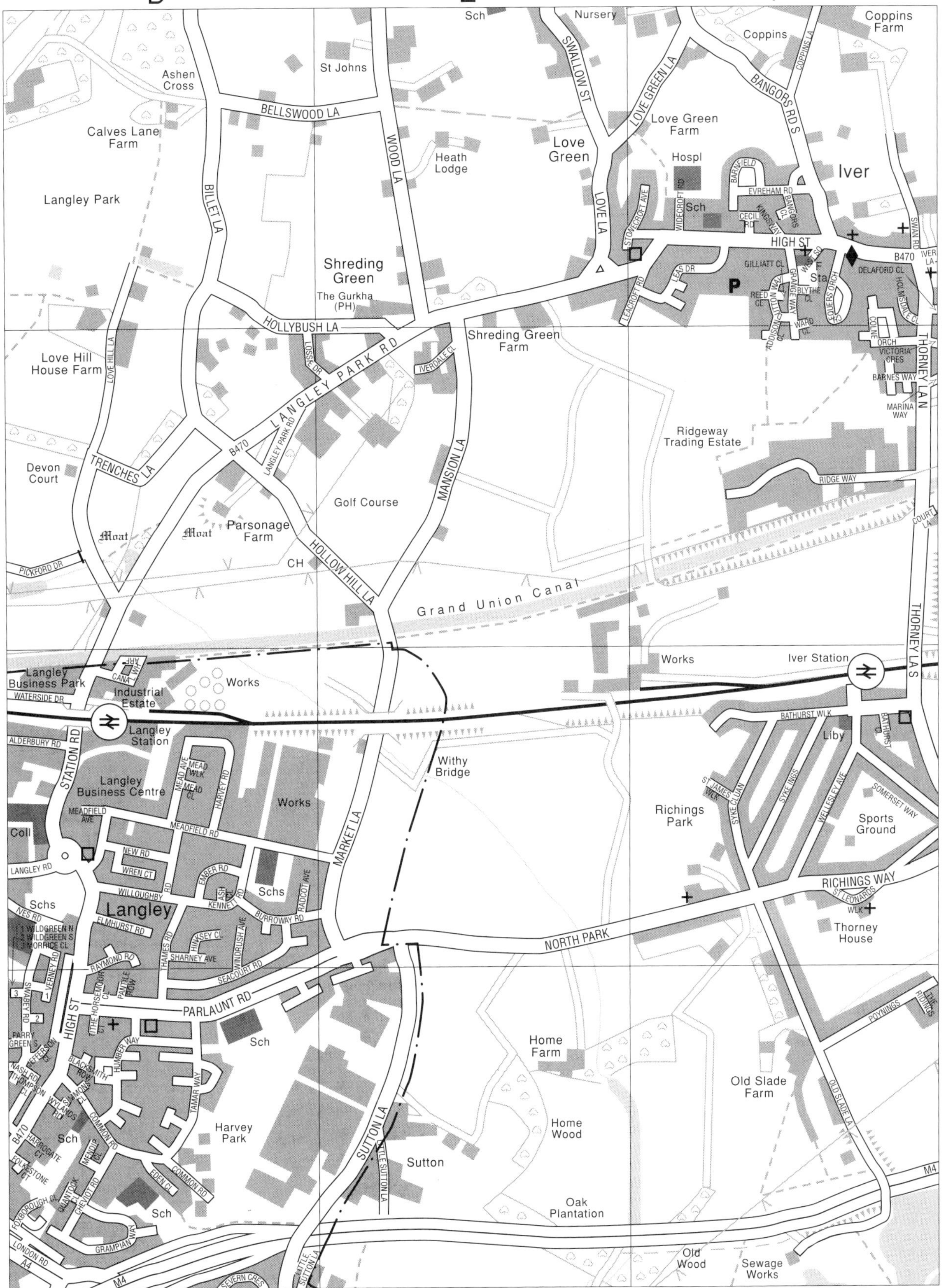

D
E
F
Sch
Nursery
Coppins
Coppins Farm
St Johns
Ashen Cross
BELLSWOOD LA
Calves Lane Farm
Langley Park
Heath Lodge
WOOD LA
Love Green
Love Green Farm
Hospl
Iver
Sch
HIGH ST
B470
Sta
P
Shreding Green
The Gurkha (PH)
HOLLYBUSH LA
LANGLEY PARK RD
Shreding Green Farm
Love Hill House Farm
Ridgeway Trading Estate
RIDGE WAY
Devon Court
TRENCHES LA
Golf Course
MANSION LA
Parsonage Farm
Moat
HOLLOW HILL LA
CH
Grand Union Canal
THORNEY LA N
THORNEY LA S
Works
Iver Station
Langley Business Park
Industrial Estate
Langley Station
Withy Bridge
Langley Business Centre
Works
Richings Park
Sports Ground
RICHINGS WAY
Coll
Schs
Langley
Schs
MARKET LA
NORTH PARK
Thorney House
PARLAUNT RD
HIGH ST
Sch
Home Farm
Old Slade Farm
Harvey Park
Home Wood
Sutton
SUTTON LA
Oak Plantation
Sch
M4
A4
Old Wood
Sewage Works
01
02
03
81
80
79
78
4
3
2
1

208

212

201

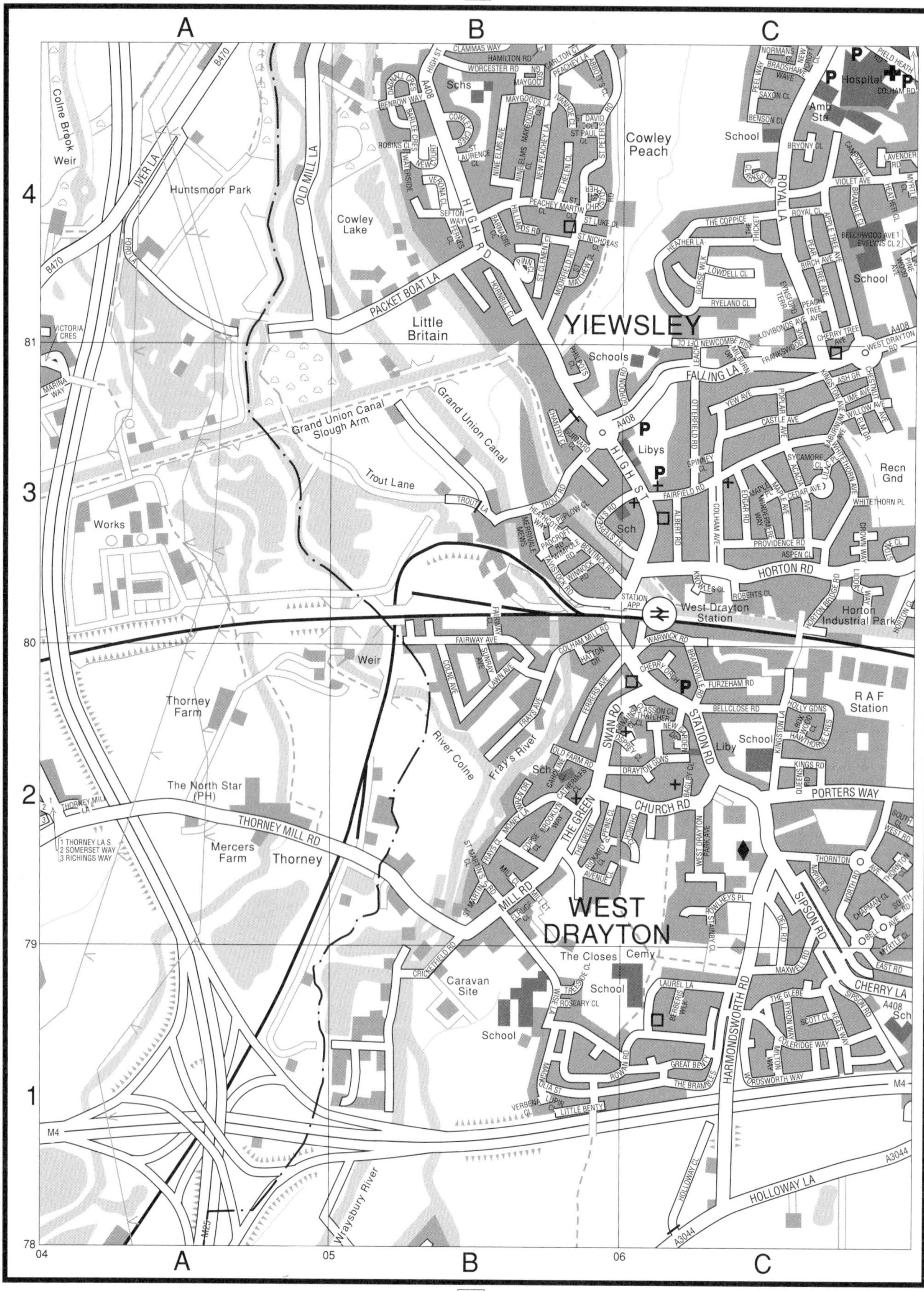

207

not continued, see key diagram

213

204

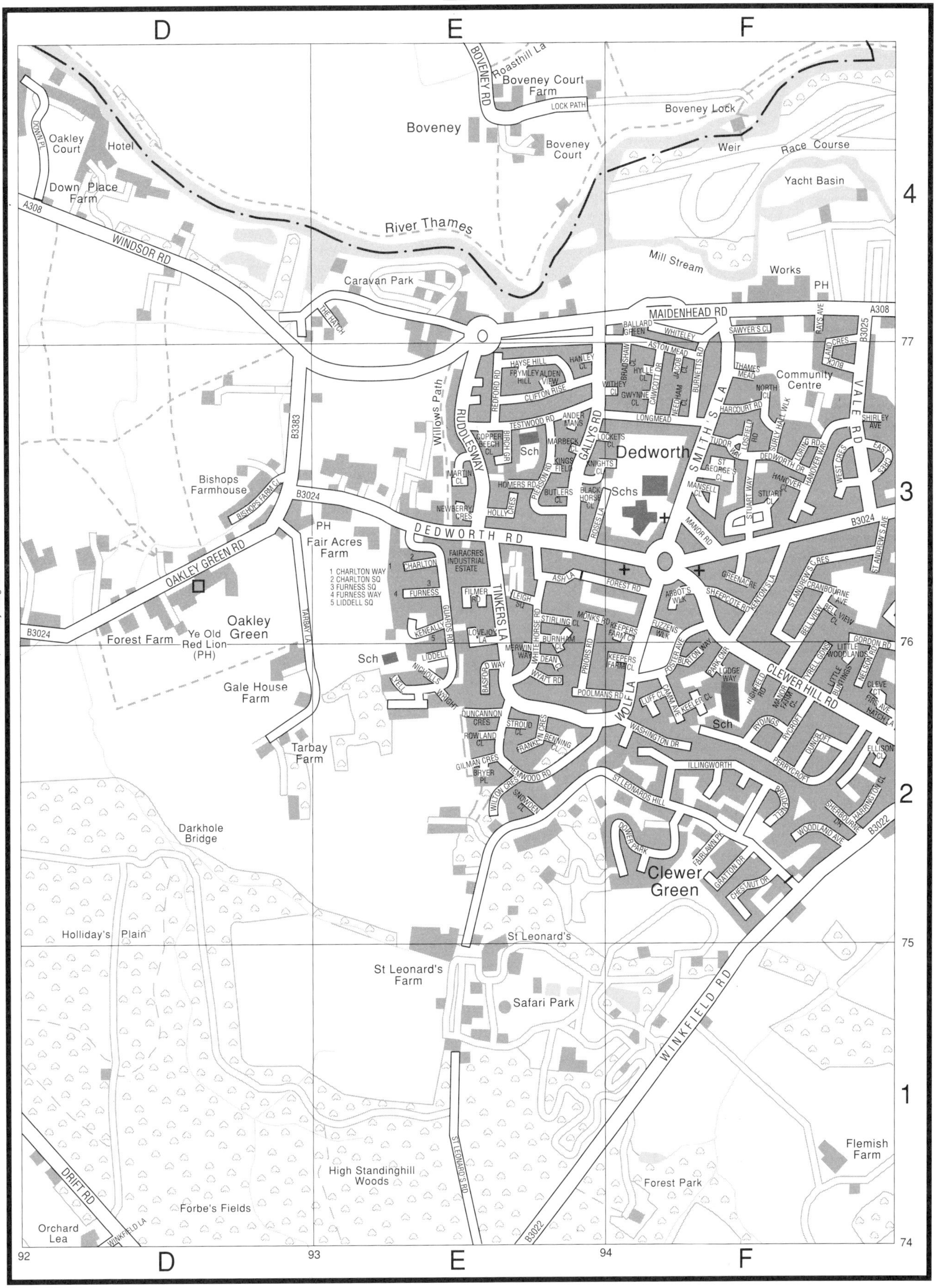

210

not continued, see key diagram

not continued, see key diagram

205

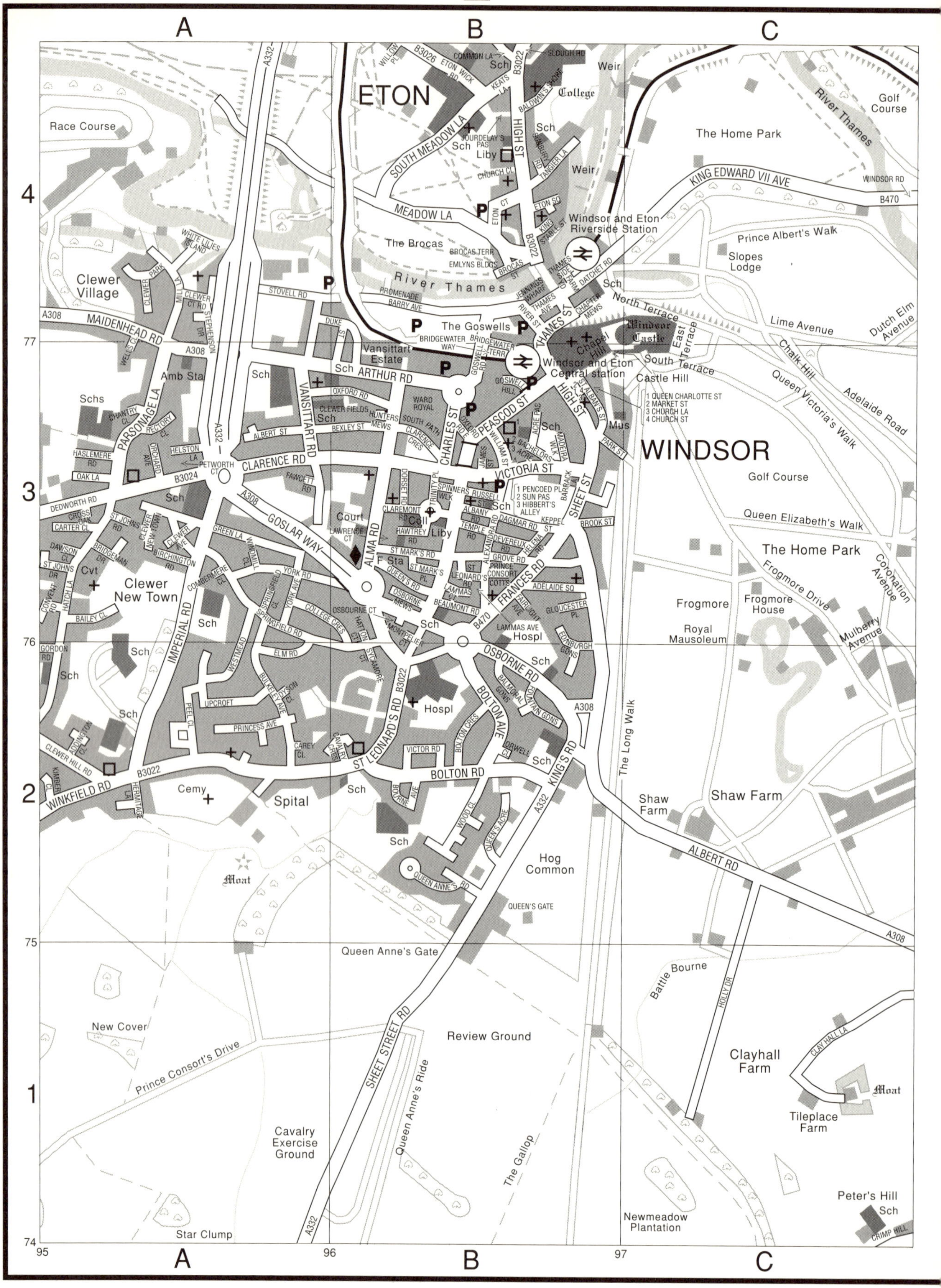

209

not continued, see key diagram

206

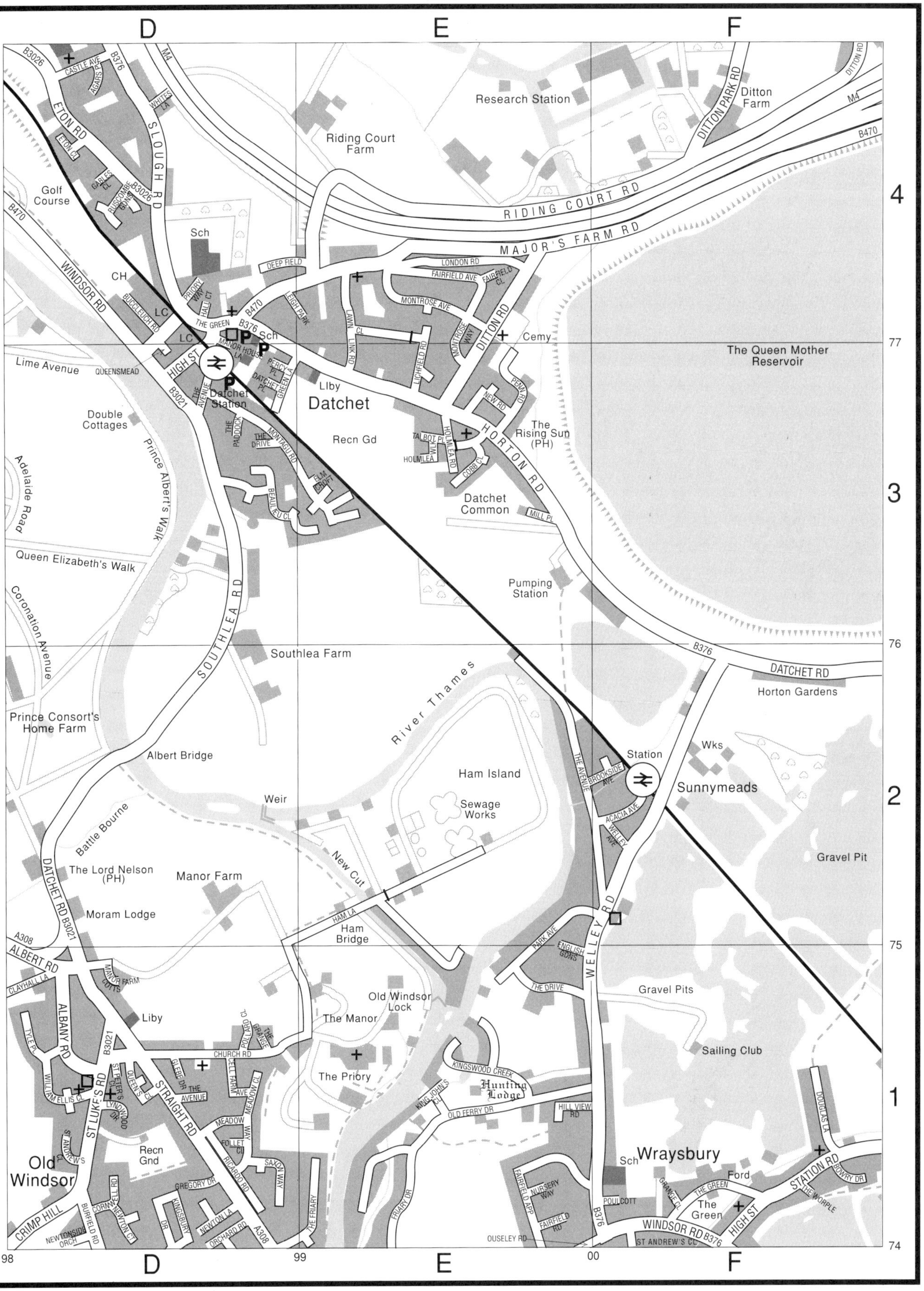
D
E
F
Research Station
Riding Court Farm
Ditton Farm
DITTON PARK RD
M4
B470
Golf Course
ETON RD
SLOUGH RD
B3026
B376
CASTLE AVE
AGARS PL
WHITES LA
RIDING COURT RD
MAJOR'S FARM RD
Sch
CH
LC
WINDSOR RD
DEEP FIELD
LONDON RD
FAIRFIELD AVE
MONTROSE AVE
DITTON RD
Cemy
THE GREEN
HIGH ST
Lime Avenue
QUEENSMEAD
Datchet Station
Datchet
Llby
Recn Gd
The Queen Mother Reservoir
The Rising Sun (PH)
HORTON RD
Double Cottages
Prince Albert's Walk
Adelaide Road
Datchet Common
MILL PL
Queen Elizabeth's Walk
Coronation Avenue
Pumping Station
SOUTHLEA RD
Southlea Farm
B376
DATCHET RD
Horton Gardens
River Thames
Prince Consort's Home Farm
Albert Bridge
Ham Island
Station
Wks
Sunnymeads
Weir
Sewage Works
Battle Bourne
Gravel Pit
The Lord Nelson (PH)
Manor Farm
New Cut
DATCHET RD B3021
Moram Lodge
HAM LA
Ham Bridge
WELLEY RD
A308
ALBERT RD
Gravel Pits
Liby
Old Windsor Lock
The Manor
ALBANY RD
Sailing Club
The Priory
CHURCH RD
KINGSWOOD CREEK
Hunting Lodge
OLD FERRY DR
HILL VIEW RD
STRAIGHT RD
ST LUKE'S RD
Recn Gnd
Sch
Wraysbury
Ford
Old Windsor
The Green
STATION RD
WINDSOR RD B376
HIGH ST
CRIMP HILL
THE FRIARY
FRIARY DR
77
76
75
74
4
3
2
1
98
99
00

212

207

211

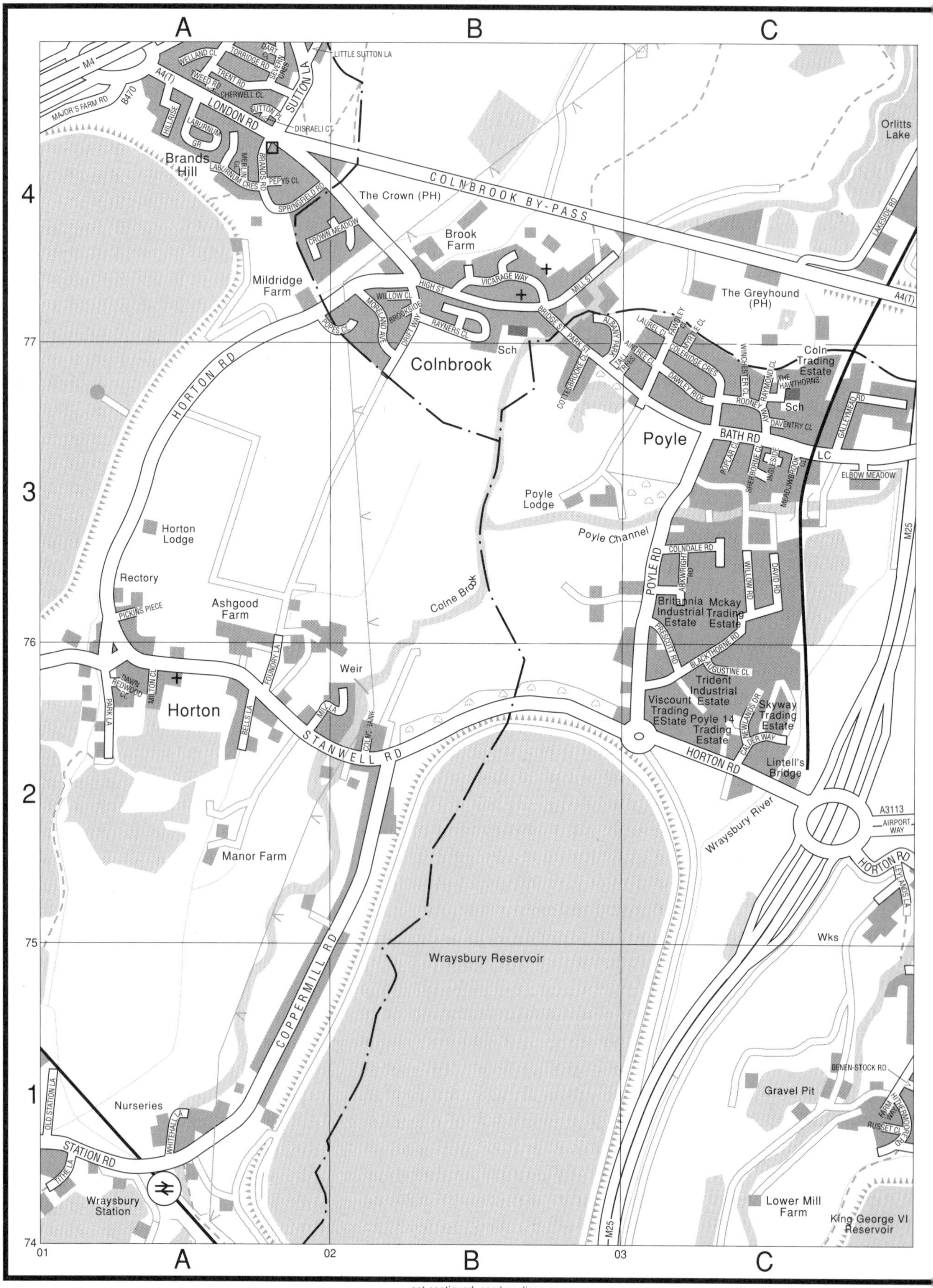

not continued, see key diagram

208

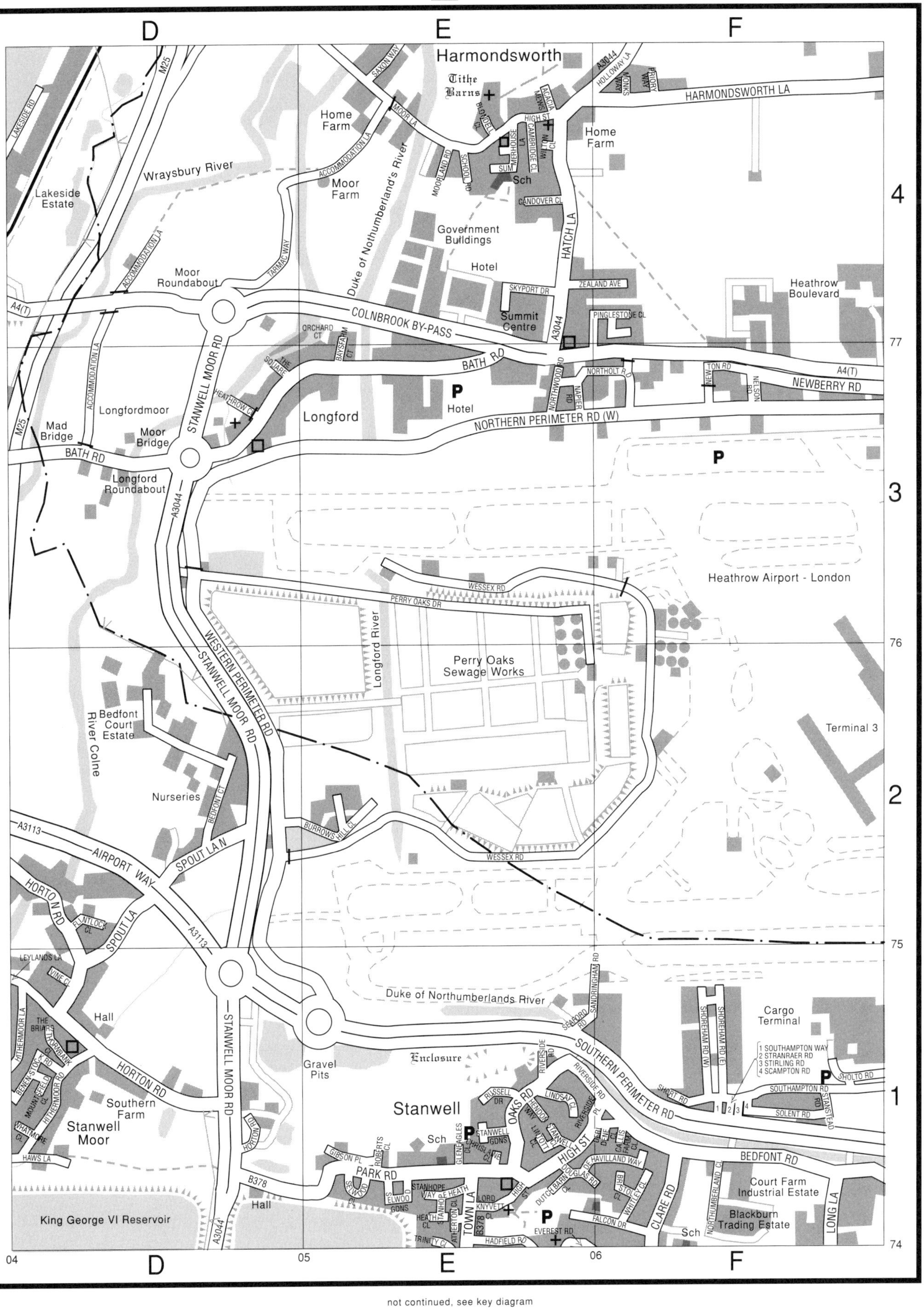

not continued, see key diagram

not continued, see key diagram

EXPLANATION OF THE STREET INDEX REFERENCE SYSTEM

Street names are listed alphabetically and show the locality, the map page number and a reference to the square in which the name falls on the map page.

Example:	Church La. Lud...96 B4
Church La	This is the full street name, which may have been abbreviated on the map.
Lud	This is the abbreviation for the town, village or locality in which the street falls.
96	This is the page number of the map on which the street name appears.
B4	The letter and figure indicate the square on the map in which the centre of the street falls. The square can be found at the junction of the vertical column carrying the appropriate letter and the horizontal row carrying the appropriate figure.

ABBREVIATIONS USED IN THE INDEX
Road Names

Approach	App	North	N
Avenue	Ave	Orchard	Orch
Broadway	Bwy	Parade	Par
By-Pass	By-Ps	Passage	Pas
Causeway	Cswy	Place	Pl
Common	Comm	Pleasant	Plea
Corner	Cnr	Precinct	Prec
Cottages	Cotts	Promenade	Prom
Court	Ct	Road	Rd
Crescent	Cres	South	S
Drive	Dri	Square	Sq
Drove	Dro	Street, Saint	St
East	E	Terrace	Terr
Gardens	Gdns	Walk	Wlk
Grove	Gr	West	W
Heights	Hts	Yard	Yd
Lane	La		

Towns, Villages and Rural Localities

Place	Abbreviation	Page	Grid
[illegible]	Adsk	53	F1
Akeley	Akel	42	A4
Aldbury	Ald	120	B3
Amersham	Ame	154	B1
Ashendon	Ash	97	F1
Ashley Green	Ash Gr	144	C4
Ashton	Ash	9	F4
Aspley Guise	Asp G	49	F2
Aspley Heath	Asp H	49	D1
Aston Abbots	A Abb	88	B3
Aston Clinton	Ast C	117	E3
Aston Rowant	Ast R	147	D2
Astwood	Ast	16	A2
Aylesbury	Ayl	116	B4
Beachampton	Beac	44	A3
Beacon's Bottom	B Bot	159	E2
Beaconsfield	Beac	175	E1
Beckley	Beck	108	A1
Berkhamsted	Berk	135	E3
Bierton	Bier	102	B2
Billington	Bill	91	E4
Bisham	Bish	194	C4
Blackthorn	Bktn	81	D3
Bledlow	Bled	138	A1
Bledlow Ridge	Bled R	159	F4
Botley	Bot	145	A1
Bourne End	Bou E	185	D1
Bovingdon	Bov	146	A2
Bow Brickhill	B Bkhl	48	B1
Bozeat	Boz	2	C4
Brackley	Brac	38	A4
Brill	Bri	69	A1
Buckingham	Buck	52	A4
Buckland Common	Buc Co	133	D2
Burnham	Burn	197	E2
Carlton	Carl	3	F2
Castlethorpe	Cast	19	F3
Chackmore	Chac	1	D2
Chalfont St Giles	C St G	177	E4
Chalfont St Peter	C St P	178	A2
Chartridge	Char	143	E2
Chearsley	Chea	112	A1
Cheddington	Ched	105	D4
Chenies	Chen	156	A1
Chesham	Ches	154	B4
Chicheley	Chic	23	E4
Chilton	Chil	111	D2
Chinnor	Chin	147	E3
Chipperfield	Chipf	156	C4
Cholesbury	Chol	133	E2
Chorleywood	Chor	167	B3
Clifton Reynes	C Rey	7	E2
Cold Brayfield	C Bray	8	A3
Coleshill	Cole	164	C2
Cookham	Cook	196	A4
Cosgrove	Cos	19	E1
Cranfield	Cran	25	E1
Cublington	Cub	78	A1
Cuddington	Cudd	113	D1
Dagnall	Dagn	107	E3
Datchet	Datch	211	E3
Deanshanger	Dean	31	E2
Denham	Den	190	A1
Denham Green	Den G	189	F3
Dinton	Dint	113	F1
Dorney	Dorn	204	B2
Dorton	Dor	96	C1
Drayton Beauchamp	Dra B	118	B3
Drayton Parslow	Dray P	68	B3
Dunstable	Dun	93	F4
East Claydon	E Clay	74	C4
Eaton Bray	Eat B	92	C3
Edgcott	Edgc	72	C1
Edlesborough	Edle	92	C2
Ellesborough	Elle	130	A1
Emberton	Emb	13	F4
Eton	Eton	210	B4
Farnham Common	Far C	198	B3
Fawley	Faw	180	B1
Feldon	Fel	146	C4
Finmere	Fin	50	B4
Flackwell Heath	Fla H	185	D4
Flaunden	Flau	156	A3
Frieth	Frie	170	C1
Fulmer	Fulm	199	E4
Gawcott	Gawt	51	F2
Gerrards Cross	Ger C	188	C3
Godington	Gdtn	61	F2
Grafton Regis	Graf R	9	E1
Granborough	Gran	75	F4
Great Brickhill	G Bhkl	58	E1
Great Haseley	G Has	136	A1
Great Horwood	G Hrwd	55	D1
Great Kimble	G Kim	139	F4
Great Kingshill	G Kin	162	C4
Great Missenden	G Mis	152	A3
Grendon Underwood	Gr Und	83	D4
Haddenham	Hadd	127	D3
Halton	Hal	117	E1
Hambledon	Hamb	181	E1
Hanslope	Hans	11	D2
Hardwick	Hdwk	87	D2
Harmondsworth	Harm	213	E4
Harrold	Harr	3	F4
Hartwell	Hart	10	B4
Hastoe	Has	132	C4
Haversham	Have	20	C1
Heath	Hth	60	A1
Hedgerley	Hedg	187	E2
Helmdon	Helm	26	A4
Henley-On-Thames	Hen-O-T	191	E1
High Wycombe	H Wyc	173	E3
Hoggeston	Hogg	77	D4
Holmer Green	Hol G	163	E3
Holton	Holt	122	B1
Horton	Hor	4	C4
Horton	Hort	212	A2
Horton-cum-Studley	Hor-c-S	108	A3
Hughenden Valley	Hgh V	162	A4
Hurley	Hurl	193	F2
Hyde Heath	H Hea	153	E3
Ibstone	Ibst	169	E4
Ickenham	Ick	190	C1
Ickford	Ick	124	A2
Iver	Iver	207	F4
Iver Heath	Iver H	200	B2
Ivinghoe	Ivin	105	F3
Lacey Green	Lac G	149	F3
Lane End	La En	171	E2
Lathbury	Lath	22	B4
Latimer	Lat	155	F2
Lavendon	Lave	7	F4
Leckhampstead	Leck	42	B4
Lee Common	Lee C	142	B3
Leighton Buzzard	L Buzz	80	C3
Lewknor	Lewk	157	D4
Lillingstone Lovell	Lill L	30	A3
Little Brickhill	L Bkhl	58	F3
Little Chalfont	L Chal	155	D1
Little Chalfont	L Chal	166	A4
Little Gaddesden	L Gad	121	E4
Little Horwood	L Hrwd	55	F1
Little Kingshall	L Kin	152	A2
Little Marlow	Lit M	184	B3
Long Crendon	L Cre	125	D3
Long Marston	Lon M	104	A2
Longwick	Lgwk	138	B4
Loudwater	Loud	174	B1
Ludgershall	Lud	96	B4
Maidenhead	Maid	202	C2
Maids Moreton	M Mor	41	F2
Maple Cross	Map Cr	178	B3
Marlow	Mar	183	D1
Marlow Bottom	Mar B	183	E3
Marsh Gibbon	M Gib	71	F2
Marsworth	Mars	105	D1
Medmenham	Medm	193	D3
Mentmore	Men	90	B2
Milton Keynes	M Keyn	46	B2
Milton Keynes Village	M K Vil	35	F2
Moulsoe	Moul	36	B4
Murcott	Mur	94	A2
Mursley	Mur	67	E3
Nash	Nash	44	B1
New Denham	N Den	201	D3
Newport Pagnell	N Pag	22	B3
Newton Blossomville	New B	8	A2
Newton Longville	Nwtn L	57	E2
Newton Purcell	Nwtn P	50	A1
North Crawley	N Craw	24	A3
North Marston	N Mar	76	A1
Northchurch	Nthch	134	C3
Oakley	Oak	109	E3
Oakley Green	Oak G	209	D3
Old Stratford	Old S	32	A4
Old Windsor	Old W	211	D1
Olney	Oln	6	C2
Oving	Oving	86	B4
Padbury	Pad	53	D1
Paulerspury	Paul	17	D4
Piddington (Bucks)	Pidd (B)	95	F4
Piddington (Northants)	Pid (N)	4	A4
Pitstone	Pit	105	E2
Potterspury	Pott	18	B1
Poundon	Pndn	71	F4
Preston Bissett	Pres B	62	A4
Prestwood	Pres	151	E3
Princes Risborough	P Ris	139	E2
Puttenham	Put	103	F1
Quainton	Qntn	85	D3
Ravenstone	Rav	5	E1
Remenham Hill	Rem H	192	B1
Ringshall	Rin	107	D1
Salford	Sal	37	E2
Sarratt	Sar	156	C2
Seer Green	Se Gr	176	B2
Shabbington	Shab	124	B2
Shalstone	Shal	39	F3
Shenley Brook End	She B E	46	A2
Shenley Church End	She C E	45	F4
Sherington	Sher	14	A1
Slapton	Slap	91	E3
Slough	Slough	205	F3
Soulbury	Soul	69	F2
South Harefield	S Har	190	B3
South Heath	S Hea	152	C4
St Leonard	St Le	132	C2
Stagsden	Stag	16	C3
Stanwell	Stan	213	E1
Steeple Claydon	Stp Cl	63	E2
Stewkley	Stew	68	C1
Stoke Bruerne	S Bru	9	D4
Stoke Goldington	S Gol	12	A3
Stoke Hammond	S Ham	69	F4
Stoke Mandeville	S Man	116	A1
Stoke Poges	Sto P	198	C2
Stokenchurch	Skch	158	C3
Stone	Sto	114	B3
Stoner	Ston	179	F3
Stratton Audley	S Adly	61	D1
Swanbourne	Swan	67	D2
Syresham	Syr	27	D4
Taplow	Tapl	196	C1
Tetsworth	Tet	136	A1
Thame	Tha	126	A1
Thornborough	Thrn	54	A4
Tiddington	Tidd	136	A4
Tingewick	Ting	51	D4
Totternhoe	Tott	93	D4
Tring	Tri	119	D2
Turvey	Turv	8	C3
Turweston	Turw	38	B4
Twyford	Twyf	62	B1
Tylers Green	Ty Gr	163	E1
Upper Arncott	U Arn	94	C4
Uxbridge	Uxb	201	E3
Waddesdon	Wadd	99	D4
Walter's Ash	Wal A	150	B1
Walton	Walt	48	A3
Warrington	Warr	7	D4
Water Stratford	W Str	40	A1
Waterperry	Wtpy	123	D1
Wavendon	Wave	48	C4
Weedon	Wedn	87	E1
Wendover	Wen	131	E2
West Drayton	W Dra	208	B2
Westbury	West	39	D2
Westcott	Wcot	98	B4
Weston Turville	W Tur	117	D1
Weston Underwood	W Und	6	A1
Whaddon	Whad	45	D1
Whitchurch	Whit	87	D3
Whitfield	Whit	26	B2
Wicker	Wick	31	D2
Wigginton	Wigg	119	E1
Wilstone	Wils	104	B1
Windsor	Wind	210	C3
Wing	Wing	79	F1
Wingrave	Win	89	E2
Winslow	Wins	66	A2
Woburn	Wbrn	60	C4
Woburn Sands	Wbn S	49	D3
Wooburn Green	Woo G	185	F4
Woodburn Green	Woo G	185	F4
Worminghall	Worm	123	F3
Wotton Underwood	W Und	97	E2
Wraysbury	Wray	211	F1
Yardley Gobion	Yard G	18	C3
Yardley Hastings	Y Has	1	A3

Abbey Barn La. H Wyc 173 F2
Abbey Barn La. Lit M 173 F2
Abbey Barn Rd. H Wyc 173 F2
Abbey Park. Burn 186 C2
Abbey Rd. Ayl 101 D1
Abbey Rd. Bou E 184 C3
Abbey Rd. M Keyn 34 A2
Abbey Rd. M Keyn 47 F3
Abbey Rd. Syr 27 E4
Abbey Terr. N Pag 22 B2
Abbey Way. Bish 194 B3
Abbey Way. H Wyc 173 D3
Abbey Way. M Keyn 34 A3
Abbey Way. Rav 5 F1
Abbey Wlk. S Hea 152 A4
Abbot Ridge. L Cre 125 E3
Abbot Wlk. L Cre 125 E3
Abbot's Wlk. Wind 209 F3
Abbots Cl. M Keyn 34 A3
Abbots Way. Lit M 172 B2
Abbots Way. P Ris 139 E3
Abbotsfield. M Keyn 47 D4
Abbotswood. Lac G 150 B2
Abbott's Cl. Uxb 208 B4
Abbotts Cl. Ayl 101 F1
Abbotts Rd. Ayl 101 F1
Abbotts Vale. Ches 144 B2
Abbotts Way. Win 89 D2
Abercromby Ave. H Wyc 172 C4
Aberdeen Ave. Slough 205 D3
Aberdeen Cl. M Keyn 46 C1
Abingdon Cl. Uxb 201 F2
Abingdon Wlk. Maid 195 F2
Abney Court Dr. Bou E 185 D1
Abraham Cl. M Keyn 35 E3
Abrahams Rd. Hen-O-T 191 E2
Abstacle Hill. Tri 118 C2
Acacia Ave. W Dra 208 C3
Acacia Ave. Wray 211 F2
Acacia Gr. Berk 135 D2
Acacia Mews. Harm 213 E4
Accommodation La. Harm 213 D4
Ackerman Cl. Buck 52 C4
Acorn Gdns. H Wyc 172 C2
Acorn Wlk. M Keyn 34 C1
Acre Pas. Wind 210 B3
Acre The. Mar 183 F1
Acrefield Rd. Ger C 188 B4
Acres End. Ame 165 F4
Acres The. H Wyc 161 F1
Adam Cl. Ayl 116 A2
Adam Cl. H Wyc 173 E4
Adam Cl. Slough 205 D3
Adams Ct. M Keyn 47 E4
Adams Way. Tri 119 D3
Addington Cl. Wind 210 A2
Addington Rd. Buck 41 E1
Addison Ct. Maid 196 A1
Addison Rd. Ches 144 B1
Addison Rd. Stp Cl 63 E1
Adelaide Cl. Slough 205 D2
Adelaide Rd. H Wyc 162 B1
Adelaide Sq. Wind 210 B3
Adelphi Gdns. Slough 205 F2
Adwell Sq. Hen-O-T 191 E1
Agars Pl. Datch 211 D4
Ailward Rd. Ayl 101 D1
Ainsdale Cl. M Keyn 46 B1
Aintree Cl. M Keyn 57 E3
Aintree Cl. Stan 212 C3
Airport Way. Stan 213 D2
Aiston Pl. Ayl 101 F1
Ajax Ave. Slough 205 D3
Akeman St. Tri 119 D2
Akerman Cl. M Keyn 33 D3
Akister Cl. Buck 52 C4
Alan Wlk. Slough 206 C4
Albany Gate. Ches 144 A1
Albany Park. Iver 212 B4
Albany Pl. Ayl 101 D1
Albany Rd. Old W 211 D1
Albany Rd. Wind 210 B3
Albert Cl. Slough 205 F2
Albert Rd. Ches 154 B4
Albert Rd. Hen-O-T 191 F1
Albert Rd. Old W 211 D1
Albert Rd. W Dra 208 C3
Albert Rd. Wind 210 C2
Albert St. Ayl 116 A4
Albert St. H Wyc 173 E4
Albert St. M Keyn 58 B4
Albert St. Maid 202 C4
Albert St. Slough 205 F2
Albert St. Tri 119 D2
Albert St. Wind 210 A3
Albion Cl. Slough 206 A3
Albion Cres. C St G 177 D4
Albion Rd. C St G 177 D4
Albion Rd. H Wyc 172 B3
Albion Rd. Pit 105 E3
Albion St. Ayl 115 F4
Albury Ct. M Keyn 33 F1
Albury View. Tidd 136 A3
Aldborough Spur. Slough 205 F4
Aldbourne Rd. Burn 204 A4
Aldbury Rd. Chor 167 F1
Aldebury Rd. Maid 195 F1
Alden View. Wind 209 E3
Aldene Rd. Hans 11 D2
Aldenham. M Keyn 47 E3
Alder Rd. N Den 201 E3
Alderbourne La. Fulm 200 A4
Alderbury Rd. Slough 206 C2
Alderbury Rd W. Slough 206 C2
Aldergill. M Keyn 34 B3
Aldermead. M Keyn 33 F3
Alderney Ct. Berk 135 E2
Alders The. N Den 201 E3
Alderson Cl. Ayl 101 D1
Alderton Dr. Rin 121 D4
Aldin Ave N. Slough 206 A2
Aldin Ave S. Slough 206 A2
Aldrich Dr. M Keyn 35 F4
Aldrich Pl. M Keyn 35 F4
Aldridge Rd. Slough 198 A1
Aldwick Dr. Maid 202 B3
Alexander Rd. Ayl 101 E1
Alexander St. Ches 144 B1
Alexandra Dr. N Pag 22 B1
Alexandra Rd. H Wyc 173 F3
Alexandra Rd. Maid 202 B4
Alexandra Rd. Slough 205 E2
Alexandra Rd. Uxb 201 E2
Alexandra Rd. Wind 210 B3
Alford Rd. H Wyc 172 B2
Alham Rd. Ayl 115 E3
Alice Cl. Hol G 163 E4
Alice La. Burn 197 D1
All Saints View. M Keyn 46 A4
All Saints' Ave. Maid 202 B4
Alladale Pl. M Keyn 33 E2
Allanson Rd. Mar 183 F2
Allen Cl. M Keyn 58 B3
Allen Dr. Wal A 161 E4
Allenby Rd. Maid 202 A4
Allerds Rd. Burn 198 A2
Alleyns La. Cook 195 E4
Allhusen Gdns. Fulm 199 F4
Allison Ct. M Keyn 35 E1
Allonby Way. Ayl 116 A4
Allyn Cl. H Wyc 173 E4
Alma Rd. Berk 134 C3
Alma Rd. Ches 144 B1
Alma Rd. Wind 210 B3
Almond Cl. N Pag 22 A2
Almond Rd. Burn 197 E1
Almond Way. P Ris 139 D1
Almond Wlk. Ty Gr 163 D2
Almons Way. Slough 206 A4
Alnwick Rd. Lon M 103 F4
Alpha Ct. Ame 165 D4
Alpha St N. Slough 206 A2
Alpha St S. Slough 205 F2
Alscot La. P Ris 139 D3
Alston Dr. M Keyn 33 F2
Althorpe Cres. M Keyn 34 A3
Altona Rd. Loud 174 B1
Altona Way. Slough 205 D4
Altwood Bailey. Maid 202 A3
Altwood Cl. Maid 202 A3
Altwood Dr. Maid 202 A3
Alverton. M Keyn 34 C4
Alvista Ave. Burn 204 A4
Alwin Cl. Ayl 115 E2
Alwyn Rd. Maid 202 A4
Alyngton. Berk 134 C4
Amanda Ct. Slough 206 B2
Amberley Ct. Maid 196 B2
Amberley Way. Uxb 201 F1
Amblers Way. Pad 53 D1
Ambleside. Ayl 116 A3
Ambrose Ct. M Keyn 35 E1
Amerden Cl. Tapl 203 E4
Amerden La. Tapl 203 E4
Amerden La. Tapl 203 F2
Amerden Way. Slough 205 D2
Amersham Hill. H Wyc 173 D4
Amersham Hill Dr. H Wyc 173 E4
Amersham Hill Gds. H Wyc 173 E4
Amersham Pl. L Chal 166 B4
Amersham Rd. Beac 176 A3
Amersham Rd. C St G 166 A1
Amersham Rd. C St P 177 E3
Amersham Rd. Char 154 A3
Amersham Rd. Ches 154 A3
Amersham Rd. Chor 166 C4
Amersham Rd. Den G 189 D2
Amersham Rd. Hol G 163 D2
Amersham Rd. L Chal 166 C4
Amersham Way. L Chal 166 C4
Amy La. Ches 154 A4
Ancastle Gr. Hen-O-T 191 E1
Anchor La. Ayl 115 F4
Andermans. Wind 209 E3
Anderson Cl. Skch 158 C2
Anding Way. Oln 6 C2
Andover Cl. Uxb 201 D2
Andrew Hill La. Hedg 187 E2
Andrews Cl. Soul 69 F2
Andrews Croft. M Keyn 34 C4
Andrews Way. Mar B 183 E4
Anershall. Win 89 D2
Angel Cl. M Keyn 35 D4
Angela Ct. Walt 48 A3
Angell Rd. M Keyn 32 C3
Angle Pl. Berk 135 D2
Anglefield Rd. Berk 135 D2
Anglesey Ct. M Keyn 46 A4
Angood Cl. P Ris 139 D2
Angstrom Cl. She B E 46 A3
Angus Dr. M Keyn 46 C1
Anne Cl. Maid 195 F1
Annes Gr. M Keyn 21 E1
Annesley Rd. N Pag 22 A2
Anns Cl. Ayl 116 A2
Anns Cl. Tri 118 C2
Ansculf Rd. Slough 198 A1
Anslow Gdns. Iver H 200 B2
Anslow Pl. Burn 204 B4
Anson Cl. Ayl 115 F2
Anson Cl. Bov 145 F2
Anson Rd. M Keyn 33 E3
Anstey Brook. W Tur 117 D2
Anstey Cl. Wadd 99 D3
Anton Way. S Man 115 E2
Aplin Rd. Ayl 116 B3
Apple Tree Ave. Uxb 208 C4
Apple Tree Ave. W Dra 208 C4
Appleacres. S Ham 69 E4
Applecroft. Berk 134 C3
Applecroft. Maid 202 B2
Applefield. L Chal 166 B4
Appletree La. Slough 206 B2
Appletree Wlk. Ches 154 B3
Appleyard Pl. M Keyn 34 C1
Approach Rd. Tapl 203 F4
Approach The. M Keyn 33 F1
Arborfield Cl. Slough 205 F2
Arbour View. L Chal 166 A4
Arbroath Cl. M Keyn 46 C2
Arbrook Ave. M Keyn 34 B2
Arcade The. H Wyc 173 D4
Archdale. H Wyc 173 D3
Archer Cl. Maid 202 B4
Archers Way. La En 171 D3
Archers Wells. M Keyn 47 D1
Archway. Lac G 150 A2
Arden Cl. Bov 146 A2
Ardenham La. Ayl 101 E1
Ardenham St. Ayl 101 E1
Ardwell La. M Keyn 33 D3
Argyle Ave. Ayl 101 D1
Argyll Ave. Slough 205 D3
Arkley Ct. Holy 203 E1
Arkwright Rd. Stan 212 C3
Arlington Ct. M Keyn 46 C2
Arlott Cres. M Keyn 46 C4
Armourer Dr. M Keyn 34 C3
Armstrong Cl. She C E 45 F3
Arncliffe Dr. M Keyn 34 A3
Arncott Rd. Pidd (B) 95 E4
Arncott Wood Rd. U Arn 94 C3
Arne La. Walt 48 B3
Arnison Ave. H Wyc 162 B1
Arnold Ct. Ayl 115 F3
Arons Mead. Hen-O-T 191 E1
Arrewig La. Dra B 132 B1
Arrewig La. St Le 142 C4
Arrow Pl. M Keyn 58 B2
Arthur Rd. Slough 205 E2
Arthur Rd. Wind 210 B3
Arundel Cl. Maid 202 A4
Arundel Ct. Slough 206 B1
Arundel Gr. M Keyn 57 F4
Arundel Rd. H Wyc 172 A3
Arundel Rd. Uxb 201 D1
Ascot Dr. L Buzz 80 B3
Ascot Rd. Holy 203 D1
Ascot Rd. Maid 203 D1
Ascott Ct. Ayl 101 F1
Ascott Rd. Ayl 101 F1
Ash Cl. Ayl 102 A1
Ash Cl. Wal A 161 D4
Ash Gr. Ame 154 A2
Ash Gr. Ayl 116 A4
Ash Gr. Sto P 198 C3
Ash Gr. W Dra 208 C3
Ash Green. N Den 201 D3
Ash Hill Rd. N Pag 22 A2
Ash La. Wind 209 E3
Ash Mead Dr. Den 190 A1
Ash Rd. H Wyc 172 B2
Ash Rd. P Ris 139 D2
Ash Rd. Tri 118 C2
Ash Vale. Map Cr 178 B3
Ashbourne End. Ayl 115 E2
Ashbourne Gr. Maid 202 B2
Ashburnham Cl. M Keyn 46 B1
Ashburnham Cres. L Buzz 80 C3
Ashby. M Keyn 47 D4
Ashby Rd. Berk 134 B4
Ashcroft Ct. Burn 197 D2
Ashcroft Dr. Den G 189 F2
Ashcroft Rd. Maid 202 B4
Ashcroft Terr. Tri 119 D3
Ashdown. Maid 196 A2
Ashdown Cl. M Keyn 35 D4
Ashdown Rd. H Wyc 174 A4
Ashdown Way. Ame 154 B1
Ashenden Wlk. Far C 198 B4
Ashendon Rd. Wcot 98 B3
Asheridge Rd. Ches 144 A1
Ashfield. M Keyn 34 B4
Ashfield Cl. Ty Gr 163 D1
Ashfield Gr. M Keyn 58 B4
Ashfield Rd. Ches 144 B1
Ashfield Way. Ty Gr 163 D2
Ashford Cl. Ayl 116 A3
Ashford Rd. Iver H 200 B2
Ashford Rise. Oak 109 E3
Ashgrove. Stp Cl 63 E1
Ashgrove Gdns. Oving 86 C4
Ashlea. Oln 6 C2
Ashlea Rd. Ger C 177 F1
Ashleigh Cl. Ame 165 F4
Ashley Cl. Ched 105 D4
Ashley Ct. Ty Gr 163 D1
Ashley Dr. Ty Gr 163 E1
Ashley Green Rd. Ash Gr 144 C3
Ashley Park. Maid 196 A1
Ashley Rd. Uxb 201 D2
Ashley Row. Ayl 102 A1
Ashleys. Chor 167 F1
Ashlyns Ct. Berk 135 D2
Ashlyns Rd. Berk 135 D2
Ashmead La. Den 190 A1
Ashotts La. Char 143 D3
Ashpole Furlong. M Keyn 46 A4
Ashridge. Chin 147 D3
Ashridge Cl. Bov 146 A2
Ashridge Cl. M Keyn 57 E4
Ashridge La. Bot 155 E4
Ashridge Rise. Berk 134 C3
Ashton Rd. S Bru 9 E4
Ashtree Wlk. Ty Gr 163 D1
Ashwell St. L Buzz 80 C4
Ashwells. Ty Gr 174 A4
Ashwells Manor Dr. Ty Gr 174 B4
Ashwells Way. C St G 177 E4
Ashwood. M Keyn 34 A4
Askett La. P Ris 139 E4
Aspen Cl. Ayl 102 A1
Aspen Cl. Slough 205 D4
Aspen Cl. W Dra 208 C3
Asplands Cl. Wbn S 49 D2
Aspley Hill. Asp G 49 E2
Aspley La. Asp G 49 F1
Aspreys. Oln 6 C3
Assheton Rd. Beac 175 F2
Astlethorpe. M Keyn 33 F1
Astley Rd. Tha 126 A1
Aston Abbotts Rd. Cub 78 B1
Aston Abbotts Rd. Wedn 87 F1
Aston Clinton Rd. W Tur 116 C4
Aston Ferry La. Rem H 192 B3
Aston Hill. Ast R 157 F4
Aston La. Rem H 192 B2
Aston Mead. Wind 209 F3
Aston Rd. Hadd 127 D3
Astrope La. Lon M 104 A2
Astwood Rd. Cran 25 E4
Atherstone Ct. M Keyn 33 E1
Atherton Cl. Stan 213 E1
Athlone Cl. Maid 195 F1
Atkins Cl. M Keyn 34 A2
Atterbrook. M Keyn 34 A2
Attingham Hill. M Keyn 34 A1
Attwells Yd. Uxb 201 E3
Auckland Cl. Maid 203 D4
Auckland Dr. H Wyc 173 F3
Auden Cl. N Pag 22 A3
Audley Mead. M Keyn 34 A2
August End. Slough 206 C4
Augustine Cl. Stan 212 C2
Augustus Rd. M Keyn 32 B2
Austen Ave. Oln 7 D2
Austen Ave. N Pag 7 D2
Austen Pl. Ayl 100 C1
Austenway. Ger C 188 C4
Austenwood Cl. Ger C 177 E1
Austenwood Cl. H Wyc 173 D2
Austenwood La. Ger C 188 B4
Austins Gate. Uxb 201 E2
Austins Mead. Bov 146 A2
Australia Ave. Maid 202 C4
Australia Rd. Slough 206 A2
Autumn Wlk. Maid 202 A3
Auxiliaries Way. Den G 189 F3
Avalon Rd. Bou E 185 D3
Avebury. Slough 205 D3
Avebury Bvd. M Keyn 34 C1
Avebury Bvd. M Keyn 35 D2
Avebury Bvd. M Keyn 46 B4
Aveling Rd. H Wyc 173 E3
Avenue Cl. W Dra 208 B2
Avenue Rd. M Mor 41 F2
Avenue Rd. Maid 203 D3
Avenue Rd. Wins 65 F2
Avenue The. Ame 154 B1
Avenue The. Bou E 185 D2
Avenue The. Chin 147 E3
Avenue The. Datch 211 D3
Avenue The. Dun 93 F4
Avenue The. Far C 198 A4
Avenue The. Maid 196 B2
Avenue The. Old W 211 D1
Avenue The. P Ris 139 D2
Avenue The. Uxb 201 E1
Avenue The. Whit 26 B2
Avenue The. Worm 123 F3
Avenue The. Wray 211 F2
Avery Ave. H Wyc 161 E1
Avington. M Keyn 33 F1
Avon Cl. N Pag 22 B2
Avon Gr. M Keyn 57 F4
Avon Pl. Ayl 115 E2
Avonbury Ct. Brac 38 A3
Avondale. Maid 195 E1
Awling Field. L Buzz 80 B4
Aylesbury Bsness Cen. Ayl 101 D1
Aylesbury Cres. Slough 205 E4
Aylesbury End. Beac 175 F1
Aylesbury Rd. Ast C 117 D3
Aylesbury Rd. Bier 102 A2
Aylesbury Rd. Chea 112 A1
Aylesbury Rd. Cudd 113 D2
Aylesbury Rd. Dra B 118 C1
Aylesbury Rd. Elle 129 F2
Aylesbury Rd. G Kim 129 F2
Aylesbury Rd. Hadd 126 B3
Aylesbury Rd. P Ris 139 E3
Aylesbury Rd. Tha 126 B3
Aylesbury Rd. Tri 118 C1
Aylesbury Rd. Wen 131 D3
Aylesbury Rd. Wing 79 F1
Aylesbury St. M Keyn 33 E3
Aylesbury St. M Keyn 58 C4
Aylesbury St W. M Keyn 33 E3
Aylesworth Ave. Slough 198 A1
Aylward Gdns. Ches 144 A1
Aynho Ct. M Keyn 45 F4
Ayr Way. M Keyn 46 C1
Aysgarth Park. Holy 203 D1
Azalea Cl. Ty Gr 163 D2
Azalea Way. Slough 206 C4

Babington Rd. Wen 131 E3
Baccara Gr. M Keyn 58 B4
Bachelors Acre. Wind 210 B3
Back Dr. Emb 12 C2
Back L. Gawt 51 F2
Back La. C St G 177 D4
Back St. Skch 158 C3
Back St. Thrn 54 A4
Back St. Wen 131 D2
Backs The. Ches 154 B4
Bacombe La. Wen 131 D2
Bacon Hill. Oln 6 C2
Baconsmead. Den 190 A1
Bad Godesberg Way. Maid 202 C4
Bader Gdns. Slough 205 D2
Badgebury Rise. Mar B 183 E4
Badgemoor La. Hen-O-T 191 E2
Badgemore Ct. M Keyn 33 E1
Badger Cl. Maid 202 B2
Badgers Way. Buck 52 C4
Badgers Way. Mar B 183 E4
Badgers Wood. Far C 198 B4
Badminton Rd. Maid 202 A3
Badminton View. M Keyn 34 A1
Bagley Cl. W Dra 208 C2
Bailey Cl. H Wyc 173 E4
Bailey Cl. Maid 202 C4
Bailey Cl. Wind 210 A3
Baird Cl. Slough 205 D2
Baker St. H Wyc 172 C4
Baker St. Wadd 99 D3
Baker's Rd. Uxb 201 E3
Bakers La. S Bru 9 D4
Bakers Walk. W Tur 116 C1
Bakers Wood. Den G 189 E2
Bakery Cl. Gr Und 83 D3
Bala Cl. M Keyn 58 B3
Bala Way. M Keyn 58 B3
Baldways Cl. Win 89 E2
Baldwin Cres. N Pag 22 A2
Baldwin Rd. Beac 176 A1
Baldwin Rd. Burn 197 E1
Baldwin's Shore. Eton 210 B4
Balham's La. Ibst 179 F4
Balham's La. Ston 179 F4
Ballard Cl. Ayl 116 A3
Ballard Green. Wind 209 F4
Ballinger Ct. Berk 135 D2
Ballinger Rd. S Hea 142 C1
Balmoral. Maid 195 D1
Balmoral Gdns. Wind 210 B2
Bamfords La. Turv 8 C3
Bamfords Yd. Turv 8 C3
Bampton Cl. M Keyn 46 C1
Banburies Cl. M Keyn 47 D1
Bangors Rd N. Iver H 200 B2
Bangors Rd S. Uxb 200 C1
Bank Green. Char 143 E4
Bank Mill. Berk 135 F2
Bank Mill La. Berk 135 F2
Bank Rd. Ty Gr 174 B4
Bank St. H Wyc 174 A2
Banks Rd. Hadd 127 D3
Banks Spur. Slough 205 D2
Bannard Rd. Maid 202 A3
Bannister Cl. Slough 206 C2
Bar La. Lgwk 138 C4
Barbers Mews. M Keyn 34 C3
Barbers Wk. Tri 118 C2
Barbers Wood Cl. H Wyc 172 A2
Barbers Wood Rd. H Wyc 172 A3
Barbury Ct. M Keyn 35 D4
Barchester Cl. Uxb 201 E1
Barchester Rd. Slough 206 C2
Bardney Cl. Maid 202 B2
Bardon Green. Ayl 101 F1
Bargeman Rd. Maid 202 C3
Baring Cres. Beac 175 E2
Baring Rd. Beac 175 E2

Baring Rd. H Wyc 173 F4
Barkers Croft. M Keyn 33 E2
Barkestone Cl. M Keyn 46 B1
Barkham Cl. Ched 104 C4
Barlee Cres. Uxb 208 B4
Barley Cl. Lewk 157 D4
Barley Cl. Ty Gr 163 D2
Barley Cl. W Tur 116 C1
Barley Fields. Woo G 185 F4
Barleycroft. M Keyn 46 C2
Barlow Rd. Wen 131 E3
Barn Cl. Far C 198 A4
Barn Cl. Maid 195 F1
Barn Ct. H Wyc 172 B4
Barn Dr. Maid 202 A2
Barn La. Hen-O-T 191 E2
Barn Rd. Lgwk 138 C3
Barnabas Rd. L Buzz 80 B3
Barnacre Cl. Uxb 208 B4
Barnard Cres. Ayl 115 F3
Barnards Hill. Mar 183 B1
Barncroft. Turv 8 C3
Barncroft Rd. Berk 134 C2
Barnes Ave. Ches 144 B1
Barnes Pl. M Keyn 46 C4
Barnett Way. Bier 102 A2
Barnfield Dr. M Keyn 47 E3
Barnhill Cl. Mar 183 E2
Barnhill Gdns. Mar 183 E2
Barnhill Rd. Mar 183 E2
Barnsbury Ave. Ayl 116 A4
Barnsfield Pl. Uxb 201 E3
Barons Cl. M Keyn 58 B4
Baronsmead Rd. H Wyc 172 C3
Barr's Rd. Burn 204 A4
Barrack Hill. Cudd 112 C3
Barrack La. Wind 210 B3
Barracks Hill. Cole 164 C1
Barracks Rd. H Wyc 173 D3
Barrards Way. Se Gr 176 B2
Barrie Cl. Ayl 100 C1
Barrington Park Gdns. C St G 166 B1
Barry Ave. Eton 210 B4
Barry Ave. M Keyn 34 B4
Barry Cl. H Wyc 172 B2
Bartelotts Rd. Slough 197 F1
Bartholomew Cl. Walt 48 A3
Bartlett Pl. Buck 41 F1
Barton Rd. M Keyn 58 B3
Barton Rd. Slough 206 C2
Bartons Rd. Ty Gr 163 D1
Bascote. M Keyn 47 E3
Base Cl. Ayl 101 F1
Basford Way. Wind 209 E2
Basildon Ct. M Keyn 45 F4
Basing Rd. Chor 167 F1
Baskerfield Gr. M Keyn 47 E4
Bass Mead. Cook 195 F3
Basset Rd. La En 171 E2
Bassetsbury La. H Wyc 173 F2
Bassett Rd. L Buzz 80 C4
Bassett Rd. Uxb 201 E3
Bassett Way. Slough 197 F1
Batchelor Cl. Ayl 101 F1
Batchelor Way. Ame 165 E4
Batchelors Way. Ches 144 A1
Bateman Dr. Ayl 115 F3
Bates Cl. Gran 75 F4
Bates Cl. M Keyn 35 E4
Bates Cl. Slough 206 C4
Bates Gdns. Dray P 68 B3
Bates La. W Tur 116 C1
Bath La. Buck 52 B4
Bath Rd. Harm 213 E3
Bath Rd. Stan 212 C3
Battersby Mews. Ayl 115 E4
Battings Wood Gdns. Wal A 161 E4
Battle Cl. Emb 13 F4
Battlemead Cl. Maid 196 B2
Baulk The. Ched 104 C4
Baulk The. Ivin 105 F3
Bawtree Rd. Uxb 201 E3
Bay La. Rav 5 E1
Bay Tree Cl. Loud 174 A1
Bay Tree Cl. Nwtn L 57 E2
Bayard Ave. M Keyn 34 C3
Bayley Cres. Burn 204 A4
Bayley Gdns. Wal A 161 F3
Baylis Rd. Slough 205 F3
Bayne Hill. Se Gr 176 B2
Bayne Hill Cl. Se Gr 176 B2
Baysfarm Ct. Harm 213 E3
Beacham Rd. H Wyc 172 B2
Beacon Ave. Dun 93 F4
Beacon Cl. Uxb 201 E4
Beacon Ct. M Keyn 46 B1
Beacon Hill. Ty Gr 174 B4
Beacon La. Mar B 171 F1
Beacon Rd. Ivin 106 C1
Beacon Rd. Rin 106 C1
Beacon Rd. Rin 107 D1
Beacon Way. Tri 119 E3
Beaconsfield Ave. H Wyc 162 A1
Beaconsfield Com La. Hedg 187 E3
Beaconsfield Pl. N Pag 22 B2
Beaconsfield Rd. Ast C 117 F2
Beaconsfield Rd. Ayl 115 F4
Beaconsfield Rd. Far C 198 B3
Beaconsfield Rd. Tri 118 C2
Beadlemead. M Keyn 47 E3
Beales La. Walt 48 A3
Bealings End. Beac 175 E3
Beamish Way. Wins 66 A3
Beamond End La. H Hea 163 F4
Beamond End La. Hol G 163 F4
Beanfare. M Keyn 47 D2
Beauchamp Cl. M Keyn 34 C3
Beaufort Cl. Ayl 116 B4
Beaufort Cl. Mar 183 F1
Beaufort Dr. M Keyn 35 E4
Beaufort Gdns. Mar 183 F1
Beaufort Pl. Maid 203 E2
Beaulieu Cl. Datch 211 D3
Beaumaris Gr. She C E 46 A3
Beaumont Cl. Maid 202 A2
Beaumont Rd. Slough 205 E4
Beaumont Rd. Wind 210 B3
Beaumont Rise. Mar 183 F1
Beaumont Way. Ty Gr 162 C2
Beaver Cl. Buck 52 C4
Beaverbrook Ct. M Keyn 46 C1
Bec La. M Keyn 35 D4
Beckets Sq. Berk 135 D3
Beckins Way. Fla H 185 E4
Beckinsale Gr. She C E 45 F4
Bedder Rd. H Wyc 172 B2
Bede Ct. L Gad 121 E4
Bedfont Ct. Stan 213 D2
Bedfont Rd. Stan 213 F1
Bedford Ave. L Chal 166 B4
Bedford Ave. Slough 205 D4
Bedford Cl. Chen 156 A1
Bedford Cl. Maid 202 A2
Bedford Dr. Far C 198 A3
Bedford Rd. Asp G 49 F3
Bedford Rd. C Bray 8 A3
Bedford Rd. Cran 25 E1
Bedford Rd. Sher 14 A1
Bedford Rd E. Y Has 1 B3
Bedford Rd W. Y Has 1 A3
Bedford St. Hth 60 C4
Bedford St. M Keyn 33 E3
Bedford St. M Keyn 58 B4
Bedgrove. Ayl 116 B3
Bedlam La. Chic 14 B1
Bedwins La. Cook 195 E3
Bedwyn Wlk. Ayl 115 E2
Beech Ave. La En 171 E3
Beech Ave. Oln 6 C2
Beech Cl. Bier 102 A2
Beech Cl. Buck 41 E1
Beech Cl. Fla H 174 A1
Beech Cl. H Wyc 173 F2
Beech Cl. Skch 158 C2
Beech Dr. Berk 135 E2
Beech Fern. Walt 48 A3
Beech Gr. Ame 165 E4
Beech Gr. Ayl 115 D3
Beech Gr. L Buzz 80 C4
Beech Green. Ayl 115 E3
Beech Hill Ct. Berk 135 E3
Beech House Dr. Pott 18 C2
Beech La. Pres 151 D4
Beech La. Se Gr 176 C2
Beech Leys. Stp Cl 63 F2
Beech Park. L Chal 155 D1
Beech Park. Wal A 150 A1
Beech Rd. Chin 147 E3
Beech Rd. H Wyc 173 F2
Beech Rd. N Pag 22 A2
Beech Rd. P Ris 139 E2
Beech Rd. Slough 206 C2
Beech Tree Rd. Hol G 163 E4
Beech Waye. Den G 189 D2
Beech Wlk. Tri 119 E2
Beechams The. Mur 67 E3
Beechcroft Rd. Ches 144 A1
Beechcroft Rd. M Keyn 57 F3
Beeches Dr. Far C 198 A4
Beeches Rd. Far C 198 A4
Beeches The. Ame 154 A2
Beeches The. Dean 31 F2
Beeches The. Tri 119 E2
Beeches Way. Burn 197 D1
Beechfield Way. Ty Gr 163 D2
Beechingstoke. Mar 183 C2
Beechtree Ave. Mar B 183 E3
Beechwood Ave. Chor 167 D3
Beechwood Ave. L Chal 155 E1
Beechwood Ave. Uxb 208 C4
Beechwood Cl. L Chal 166 B4
Beechwood Ct. Dun 93 F4
Beechwood Dr. Ald 120 B3
Beechwood Dr. Maid 202 A3
Beechwood Dr. Mar 194 A4
Beechwood Gdns. Slough 205 F2
Beechwood La. Wen 131 E3
Beechwood Park. Fel 146 C4
Beechwood Rd. Beac 175 E1
Beechwood Rd. H Wyc 161 D1
Beechwood Rd. Slough 205 E4
Beechwood Way. Ast C 117 F3
Beecroft Way. Dun 93 F4
Beehive Cl. Uxb 201 F3
Beel Cl. L Chal 166 B4
Beeward Cl. M Keyn 33 D3
Bekonscot Ct. M Keyn 21 F1
Belfast Ave. Slough 205 E4
Belgrave Mews. Uxb 201 E1
Belgrave Rd. Ayl 101 D2
Belgrave Rd. Slough 205 F3
Bell Alley. Wins 65 F2
Bell Ave. W Dra 208 C2
Bell Cl. Beac 175 F1
Bell Cl. Cub 78 A1
Bell Cl. Dray P 68 A3
Bell Cl. P Ris 139 D2
Bell Cl. Slough 206 A4
Bell Cl. Tha 125 F1
Bell Cres. Lgwk 138 C3
Bell Ct. Hurl 193 F2
Bell La. Berk 134 C3
Bell La. Hen-O-T 191 F2
Bell La. L Chal 155 E1
Bell La. P Ris 139 D2
Bell La. Syr 27 D4
Bell La. Tha 125 E1
Bell Leys. Win 89 D2
Bell St. Hen-O-T 191 F1
Bell St. Maid 202 C3
Bell St. P Ris 139 D2
Bell View. Wind 209 F3
Bell View Cl. Wind 209 F3
Bellamy Rd. H Wyc 173 E4
Bellclose Rd. W Dra 208 C2
Belle Vue. Sto 114 B3
Bellfield Rd. H Wyc 173 D4
Bellis Gr. M Keyn 47 E4
Bells Hill. Sto P 199 D2
Bells Hill Green. Sto P 199 D3
Bells La. Hort 212 A2
Bells Meadow. M Keyn 35 D4
Bellway. Wave 49 D3
Bellwether. M Keyn 33 D2
Bellwood Rise. H Wyc 173 D2
Belmers Rd. Wigg 119 E1
Belmont. Slough 205 D4
Belmont Cl. Uxb 201 E3
Belmont Cres. Maid 202 B4
Belmont Ct. M Keyn 33 E1
Belmont Dr. Maid 202 B4
Belmont Park Ave. Maid 202 B4
Belmont Park Rd. Maid 202 B4
Belmont Rd. Ches 144 A2
Belmont Rd. Maid 202 B4
Belmont Rd. Uxb 201 E3
Belmont Vale. Maid 202 B4
Belsize Ave. M Keyn 35 D1
Belton Rd. Berk 135 D3
Belvoir Ave. M Keyn 46 B1
Bembridge Ct. Slough 205 F2
Benbow Way. Uxb 208 B4
Bench Manor Cres. Ger C 177 E1
Bencombe Rd. Mar B 183 F3
Benen-stock Rd. Stan 213 D1
Benham Cl. Ches 144 A1
Benhams La. Faw 180 B1
Benjamin Rd. H Wyc 173 D4
Benjamins Footpath. H Wyc 173 D4
Bennet Cl. M Keyn 32 B2
Bennett End Rd. Bled R 159 E4
Bennett's Hill. Swan 76 B4
Bennetts. Ches 144 B1
Bennetts Cl. Slough 205 D3
Bennetts La. Wind 102 C4
Benning Ave. Dun 93 F4
Benning Cl. Wind 209 E2
Benson Cl. Slough 206 A3
Benson Cl. Uxb 208 C4
Bentall Cl. M Keyn 35 E4
Bentinck Cl. Ger C 188 B3
Bentinck Rd. W Dra 208 B3
Bentley Park. Burn 197 E2
Bentley Rd. Slough 205 D3
Benton Dr. Chin 147 E4
Benwell Cl. M Keyn 33 F3
Benwells. Chin 147 E3
Berakspear Rd N. S Har 190 C4
Berberis Cl. Walt 48 A3
Berberis Wlk. W Dra 208 C1
Bercham. M Keyn 33 F1
Beresford Ave. Ayl 101 E2
Beresford Ave. Slough 206 B3
Beresford Rd. Chor 167 F1
Beretun. M Keyn 33 F1
Berkeley Cl. Ches 144 A1
Berkeley Ave. Ches 143 F1
Berkeley Cl. S Gol 12 A3
Berkeley Mews. Mar 183 F1
Berkeley Rd. Loud 174 B1
Berkeley Rd. Tha 126 A1
Berkeley Rise. Ayl 101 D1
Berkhampstead Rd. Ches 144 B1
Berkley Cl. Maid 202 A4
Berkley Rd. Beac 175 E3
Berks Hill. Chor 167 E2
Berkshire Ave. Slough 205 D4
Berling Rd. M Keyn 33 F1
Bernard Cl. Cudd 112 C1
Bernard's Cl. Chea 112 A1
Bernards Cl. S Hea 152 A4
Bernards Way. Fla H 174 A1
Bernay Gdns. M Keyn 35 D4
Bernewood Cl. L Cre 125 E4
Berries Rd. Cook 196 A4
Berry Field. Slough 206 B4
Berry Field Park. Ame 154 A1
Berry Hill. Tapl 203 E4
Berry La. Asp G 49 F3
Berry La. Chor 167 F2
Berry Way. Nwtn L 57 E2
Berryfield. Ched 104 C4
Berryfield Rd. Ayl 101 D2
Berryfield Rd. P Ris 139 D2
Berwick Ave. Slough 205 D3
Berwick Cl. Beac 176 A1
Berwick Cl. Mar 183 E2
Berwick La. Mar 183 E2
Berwick Rd. Mar 183 E2
Bessemer Ct. M Keyn 22 A1
Bessimer Cres. Ayl 100 C1
Bestobell Rd. Slough 205 E4
Bettles Cl. Uxb 201 E2
Betty's Cl. Nwtn L 57 E2
Betty's La. Tri 119 D2
Bevan Hill. Ches 144 A1
Bevelwood Gdns. H Wyc 172 B4
Beverley Cl. Mar 183 B1
Beverley Ct. Slough 206 A2
Beverley Gdns. Maid 195 D1
Beverley Pl. M Keyn 35 D1
Bewdley Rd. L Buzz 80 B4
Bexley St. Wind 210 B3
Beyners Green. L Kin 152 A2
Bicester Rd. Ayl 101 D1
Bicester Rd. L Cre 125 E3
Bicester Rd. Lud 96 B4
Bicester Rd. M Gib 71 F2
Bicester Rd. Oak 109 E3
Bicester Rd. Twyf 62 B1
Bickleigh Cres. She B E 46 B2
Biddlesden Rd. West 39 D3
Bideford Green. L Buzz 80 B4
Bierton Rd. Ayl 101 F1
Bigfrith La. Cook 195 D3
Biggs La. Dint 113 F1
Bigmore La. B Bot 170 A1
Billet La. Berk 135 D3
Billingwell Pl. M Keyn 35 D1
Billwell. L Cre 125 E3
Bilton Rd. M Keyn 47 E1
Bingham Cl. M Keyn 46 B1
Bingham Rd. Burn 204 A4
Binghams The. Maid 203 D2
Birch Ave. W Dra 208 C4
Birch Ct. Ayl 115 E3
Birch Gr. Slough 205 D4
Birch Gr. Wind 209 E3
Birch La. Flau 156 A4
Birch Rd. Berk 134 B4
Birch Tree Gr. Bot 145 D1
Birch Way. Ches 144 B1
Birch Way. Ty Gr 163 D1
Birchdale. Ger C 188 B2
Birches Rise. H Wyc 172 C4
Birches The. Fel 146 C4
Birchfield Gr. M Keyn 58 B4
Birchington Rd. Wind 210 A3
Birchwood Chase. G Kin 151 E1
Birdlip. Walt 48 A3
Birds La. S Gol 12 A3
Birfield Rd. Loud 174 B1
Birinus Ct. H Wyc 172 B3
Birkdale Cl. M Keyn 57 E4
Birkett Way. L Chal 166 B3
Birley Rd. Slough 205 E4
Bisham Ct. Bish 194 C3
Bishop Ct. Maid 202 B3
Bishops Farm Cl. Oak G 209 D3
Bishops Orch. Far C 198 A1
Bishops Wlk. Ayl 115 F3
Bishops Wlk. Bou E 185 F3
Bishopstone. M Keyn 34 A3
Bishopstone. Sto 115 D1
Bishopstone Rd. Sto 114 B3
Bissley Dr. Maid 202 A2
Bit The. Wigg 119 E1
Bittenham Cl. Sto 114 C2
Bix Hill. Faw 191 D3
Black Acre Cl. Ame 165 F4
Black Boy La. Hurl 193 E2
Black Butts Cotts. Cook 196 A4
Black Horse Ave. Ches 154 B3
Black Horse Cl. Wind 209 E3
Black Park Rd. Fulm 199 F2
Black Park Rd. Iver H 199 F2
Blackdown. M Keyn 32 C2
Blacketts Wood Dr. Chor 167 D3
Blackfield La. S Hea 142 C2
Blackheath Cres. M Keyn 34 B2
Blackhorse Cl. Ame 154 C1
Blackhorse Cres. Ame 154 C1
Blackmoor Gate. M Keyn 46 B1
Blackmore Way. Uxb 201 E3
Blackpond La. Far C 198 A2
Blacksmith La. Pres 151 E3
Blacksmith's La. Den 189 E1
Blacksmiths Rd. Lgwk 138 B4
Blackthorn Cl. Bktn 81 D2
Blackthorn Dell. Slough 206 B2
Blackthorn Gr. Wbn S 49 D2
Blackthorne La. S Hea 142 C2
Blackthorne Rd. Stan 212 C2
Blackwater Dr. Ayl 115 E2
Blackwell End. Pott 18 B2
Blackwell Hall La. Bot 155 D3
Blackwell Hall La. Lat 155 D3
Blackwell Rd. La En 171 D3
Blackwood Cres. M Keyn 33 F3
Blair Rd. Slough 205 F3
Blake Way. Tha 126 A1
Blakedown Rd. L Buzz 80 B4
Blandford Cl. Slough 206 B2
Blandford Rd N. Slough 206 B2
Blandford Rd S. Slough 206 B2
Blatherwick Ct. She C E 45 F4
Blaydon Cl. M Keyn 57 E3
Bleasdale. M Keyn 34 B3
Bledlow Ridge Rd. Bled 148 B4
Blenheim Ave. M Keyn 32 C2
Blenheim Cl. Slough 206 C3
Blenheim Pl. Ayl 115 F3
Blenheim Pl. Syr 27 E4
Blenheim Rd. H Wyc 172 B2
Blenheim Rd. Maid 202 A4
Blenheim Rd. Slough 206 B1
Bletcham Way. B Bkhl 48 A2
Bletcham Way. M Keyn 47 F1
Bletcham Way. Walt 48 A2
Bletchley Rd. Nwtn L 57 E3
Bletchley Rd. She B E 46 A2
Bletchley Rd. Stew 68 B2
Blinco La. Slough 206 C4
Blind La. Bou E 185 D3
Blind La. Char 153 D4
Blind La. Fla H 185 D3
Bliss Ave. Cran 25 E1
Blisworth. M Keyn 47 E3
Blondell Cl. Harm 213 E4
Bloomfield Rd. Maid 202 A3
Bloomsbury Cl. Hth 60 C3
Blossom Way. Uxb 201 F3
Blucher St. Ches 154 A4
Blumfield Ct. Slough 197 E1
Blundells Rd. M Keyn 34 B3
Blyth Cl. Ayl 115 E3
Blythe Cl. N Pag 22 B2
Blyton Cl. Beac 175 E2
Bobmore La. Mar 183 F2
Bockmer La. Medm 193 D4
Boddington Rd. Wen 131 E2
Bodenham Cl. Buck 52 C4
Bodle Cl. M Keyn 35 D3
Bodmin Ave. Slough 205 D4
Bois Ave. Ame 154 A2
Bois Hill. Ches 154 C3
Bois La. Ame 154 B2
Bois Moor Rd. Ches 154 B3
Bolan Ct. She C E 45 F3
Bolter End La. La En 171 D3
Bolton Ave. Wind 210 B2
Bolton Cl. M Keyn 47 D1
Bolton Cres. Wind 210 B2
Bolton Rd. Wind 210 B2
Bond Ave. M Keyn 47 E2
Bonham Carter Rd. Hal 131 F4
Bonnards Rd. Nwtn L 57 E2
Bonnersfield. L Cre 125 E4
Booker La. H Wyc 172 B4
Booker Ave. M Keyn 34 B2
Bookerhill Rd. H Wyc 172 B3
Boot La. Dint 113 F1
Borderside. Slough 206 A4
Borough Rd. Brac 38 A3
Borough Wlk. M Keyn 34 C2
Bosanquet Cl. Uxb 201 E1
Boss La. Hgv V 162 A4
Bossiney Pl. M Keyn 34 C1
Bossington La. L Buzz 80 C4
Boston Gr. Slough 205 E4
Boswell Ct. Buck 41 F1
Boswell La. Dean 31 F2
Boswick La. Berk 134 B4
Bosworth Cl. M Keyn 46 C1
Botley La. Bot 145 D1
Botley Rd. Ches 144 C1
Bottesford Cl. M Keyn 46 B1
Bottle Square La. Bled R 159 E3
Bottom Ho Fm La. Ame 165 F1
Bottom House La. Wigg 120 A1
Bottom La. Se Gr 176 B3
Bottom Rd. Bled R 160 A3
Bottom Rd. Buc Co 133 D2
Bottom Rd. Dra B 132 C2
Bottrells La. Ame 176 C4
Bottrells La. C St G 176 C4
Bottrells La. Cole 176 B4
Botyl Rd. E Clay 74 C3
Boulmer Rd. Uxb 201 E1
Boulters Cl. Maid 196 B1
Boulters Cl. Slough 205 D2
Boulters Ct. Maid 196 B1
Boulters Gdns. Maid 196 B1
Boulters La. Maid 196 B1
Boundary Cres. M Keyn 32 C3
Boundary Pl. Woo G 185 E4
Boundary Rd. Brac 38 A3
Boundary Rd. Ger C 177 E2
Boundary Rd. Tapl 203 F4
Boundary Rd. Woo G 185 E4
Boundary The. M Keyn 46 C4
Bounds Croft. M Keyn 33 D2
Bounty St. M Keyn 33 F4
Bourbon St. Ayl 115 E4
Bourne Ave. Wind 210 B2

Bourne Cl. Bou E 185 D3
Bourne End La. Heml H 146 A4
Bourne End Rd. Bou E 196 C4
Bourne End Rd. Cran 25 E2
Bourne End Rd. Tapl 196 C4
Bourne Rd. Berk 134 C3
Bourne Rd. Slough 205 E2
Bourne The. Bov 146 A2
Bourton Rd. Buck 52 C4
Bourtonville. Buck 52 B4
Bouverie Way. Slough 206 C1
Boveney Cl. Slough 205 D2
Boveney Wood La. Burn 186 B1
Bovingdon Green La. Bov 145 F2
Bovingdon Hts. Mar 183 A1
Bow Brickhill Rd. Wbn S 48 C2
Bow Brickhill Rd. Wbn S 48 C2
Bowden La. H Wyc 173 E3
Bower Cl. Eat B 92 C3
Bower La. Eat B 92 C3
Bowerdean Rd. H Wyc 173 E4
Bowers La. Bled R 159 E4
Bowes Cl. N Pag 22 B2
Bowler Lea. H Wyc 161 E1
Bowler's Orch. C St G 177 D4
Bowles Pl. M Keyn 47 E4
Bowling Alley. Oving 86 B4
Bowling Ct. Hen-O-T 191 E2
Bowling Gr. Skch 158 B3
Bowling Green Rd. Cran 25 E1
Bowmans Cl. Burn 197 D2
Bowmont Dr. S Man 115 E2
Bowood Ct. M Keyn 33 F1
Bowry Dr. Wray 211 F1
Bowstridge La. C St G 177 E3
Bowyer Cres. Den G 189 F3
Bowyers Mews. M Keyn 34 C3
Box La. Fel 146 C4
Box Tree Cl. Ches 154 B3
Boxberry Gdns. Walt 48 A3
Boxer Rd. Lgwk 138 C3
Boxwell Rd. Berk 135 D2
Boxwood Cl. W Dra 208 C2
Boyce Cres. Walt 48 B3
Boycott Ave. M Keyn 34 C1
Boyn Hill Ave. Maid 202 B3
Boyn Hill Cl. Maid 202 B3
Boyn Hill Rd. Maid 202 B3
Boyn Valley Rd. Maid 202 B3
Boyndon Rd. Maid 202 B4
Bozenham Mill La. Ash 9 F3
Bozenham Mill La. Graf R 9 F2
Bracken Cl. Far C 198 B4
Bracken Rd. Maid 202 B2
Bracken Way. Fla H 185 D4
Brackenforde. Slough 206 B2
Brackens The. H Wyc 173 E3
Brackley Dr. Hol G 163 D3
Brackley La. Twyf 73 D3
Brackley Rd. Buck 41 D1
Brackley Rd. Chac 41 D1
Brackley Rd. Hol G 163 D3
Brackley Rd. West 39 D3
Bradbery. Map Cr 178 B3
Bradbourne Dr. B Bkhl 48 A2
Bradbury Cl. M Keyn 34 A2
Bradcutts La. Cook 195 F4
Braddenham Wlk. Ayl 115 F2
Braden Cl. Ayl 116 A3
Bradenham Beeches. Wal A 161 D4
Bradenham La. Bish 194 B3
Bradenham Rd. H Wyc 161 D2
Bradenham Wd La. Bled. R 161 D4
Bradfield Ave. Buck 41 E1
Bradford Rd. Chor 167 E1
Bradford Rd. Slough 205 D4
Bradley Cl. Oak 109 E3
Bradley Rd. Slough 205 F3
Bradshaw Cl. Wind 209 F3
Bradshaw Rd. H Wyc 173 F3
Bradshawe Waye. Uxb 208 C4
Bradvue Cres. M Keyn 34 A3
Bradwell Cmn Bvd. M Keyn 34 B2
Bradwell Rd. M Keyn 34 A1
Bradwell Rd. M Keyn 34 A3
Bradwell Rd. M Keyn 46 A4
Brae Hill. Bri 110 A4
Brae Hill Cl. Bri 110 A4
Braemar Gdns. Slough 205 D2
Bragenham La. L Buzz 70 B3
Bragenham La. Soul 70 B3
Bragenham Side. S Ham 69 F4
Braid The. Ches 144 C1
Brakynbery. Berk 134 C4
Brallings La. C St P 178 A3
Bramber Cl. M Keyn 57 F4
Bramber Ct. Slough 205 D3
Bramble Ave. M Keyn 34 C2
Bramble Cl. Uxb 208 C4
Bramble Cres. Hol G 163 E3
Bramble Dr. Maid 202 A2
Bramble La. Ame 165 F3
Brambles The. W Dra 208 C1
Bramcote Cl. Ayl 116 B4
Bramley Cl. Maid 202 B2
Bramley End. Hgh V 151 D1
Bramley Grange. M Keyn 58 B2
Bramley Rd. M Keyn 47 E2
Brammas Cl. Slough 205 E2
Brampton Ct. Maid 203 D4
Branch Rd. Loud 174 A1
Brandon Rd. H Wyc 172 A2
Brands Hill Ave. H Wyc 162 B1
Brands Rd. Slough 212 A4
Brandville Rd. W Dra 208 C2
Bransgill Ct. M Keyn 34 A2
Braunston. M Keyn 47 E3
Bravenfield. Pad 53 E1
Bray Cl. Maid 203 E2
Bray Ct. Holy 203 E1
Bray Rd. Maid 203 D3
Braybank. Maid 203 E2
Braybourne Cl. Uxb 201 B1
Braybrooke Dr. M Keyn 46 C2
Brayfield Rd. Maid 203 E2
Brays Cl. H Hea 153 E2
Brays Green La. H Hea 153 E2
Brays La. H Hea 153 E3
Brays Meadow. H Hea 153 E2
Brayton Ct. She B E 46 B3
Braywick Rd. Maid 203 D2
Braziers End. Buc Co 133 E1
Breachwell Pl. Men 91 D1
Breakspear Rd S. Ick 190 C1
Bream Cl. Mar 194 B4
Breamore Ct. M Keyn 45 F4
Brearley Ave. M Keyn 46 C4
Brearley Cl. Uxb 201 F3
Brecon Way. H Wyc 172 C4
Bredward Cl. Burn 197 D1
Brenchwood Cl. H Wyc 161 E1
Brendon Ct. M Keyn 46 B1
Brent. M Keyn 47 E3
Brent Rd. Bou E 185 D2
Brentwood Way. Ayl 116 A3
Breton. M Keyn 32 C3
Brewhouse La. Win 88 C1
Briaily. B Bot 159 E1
Briar Cl. Burn 204 A4
Briar Dene. Maid 195 E1
Briar Glen. Cook 195 F3
Briar Hill. M Keyn 33 F2
Briar Way. Berk 135 E2
Briar Way. Slough 205 D4
Briars The. H Wyc 173 E3
Briars The. Hol G 163 E4
Briars The. Slough 206 C1
Briars The. Stan 213 D1
Briary View. Whad 56 A4
Brick Cl. M Keyn 33 E1
Brick Hill. Ash 97 F1
Brick Kiln La. Bier 102 A2
Brickfield La. Burn 197 D2
Brickhill Manor Ct. L Bkhl 59 E3
Brickhill St. M Keyn 35 E3
Brickhill St. Walt 48 A3
Bricks La. Bled R 159 E2
Brickwell Wlk. Ty Gr 163 D2
Bricstock. A Abb 88 B2
Briden's Way. Hadd 126 C3
Bridge Ave. Cook 195 F3
Bridge Ave. Maid 203 D4
Bridge Bank Cl. Loud 174 A2
Bridge Pl. Ame 154 C1
Bridge Rd. Cast 19 F1
Bridge Rd. Ick 123 F1
Bridge Rd. Maid 203 D4
Bridge Rd. Uxb 201 E2
Bridge St. Berk 135 E2
Bridge St. Buck 52 B4
Bridge St. G Kim 129 E1
Bridge St. H Wyc 173 D4
Bridge St. Iver 212 B4
Bridge St. L Buzz 80 C4
Bridge St. M Keyn 33 F4
Bridge St. Maid 203 D4
Bridge St. Oln 6 C2
Bridge St. Thrn 54 A4
Bridge St. Turv 8 B3
Bridge Turn Ave. M Keyn 33 E4
Bridgeford Ct. M Keyn 46 C4
Bridgegate Bsnss Pk. Ayl 101 D1
Bridgeman Dr. Wind 210 A3
Bridgestone Dr. Bou E 185 E2
Bridgewater Rd. Berk 134 C4
Bridgewater Rd. Berk 135 D3
Bridgewater Terr. Wind 210 B3
Bridgewater Way. Wind 210 B3
Bridgeway. Cudd 112 C2
Bridgeway. M Keyn 34 A4
Bridle Cl. M Keyn 34 A3
Bridle Cl. Maid 195 F1
Bridle Gate. H Wyc 172 C3
Bridle Rd. Maid 195 F1
Bridle Way. Berk 135 D3
Bridleway. W Tur 116 C1
Bridlington Spur. Slough 205 D2
Bridport Way. Slough 198 A1
Briery Way. Ame 154 C1
Brighton Spur. Slough 198 A1
Brightwell Ave. Tott 93 E4
Brill Cl. Maid 202 B2
Brill Cl. Mar 183 B1
Brill Pl. M Keyn 34 B2
Brill Rd. Chl 111 D2
Brill Rd. Lud 96 A4
Brill Rd. Oak 109 F3
Brimmers Hill. Hol G 162 C3
Brimmers Rd. P Ris 139 E1
Brindlebrook. M Keyn 33 F1
Brindley Ave. H Wyc 161 F1
Bristle Hill. Buck 52 B4
Bristol Cl. Stan 213 F1
Bristol Way. Slough 205 F3
Bristow Cl. M Keyn 47 F1
Bristow Ct. Mar 184 A2
Britannia Ind Est. H Wyc 172 B4
Britannia Rd. Ches 144 B1
Britannia St. Ayl 115 F4
Britten Gr. Walt 48 B3
Brittons La. Sal 37 E2
Britwell Rd. Burn 197 E1
Broad Arrow Cl. M Keyn 34 C4
Broad Dean. M Keyn 47 D4
Broad La. Beac 186 A3
Broad Leys. P Ris 139 D2
Broad Oak. Slough 198 B1
Broad Oak Ct. Slough 198 B1
Broad Piece. M Keyn 35 D4
Broad Platts. Slough 206 B2
Broad St. Ches 144 B1
Broad St. N Pag 22 B2
Broad St. Syr 27 D4
Broadfields. Ayl 101 D1
Broadlands. M Keyn 47 D3
Broadlands Ave. Ches 144 B1
Broadmark Rd. Slough 206 A3
Broadwater. Berk 135 E3
Broadwater. M Keyn 47 E3
Broadwater Gdns. S Har 190 B4
Broadwater La. S Har 190 B4
Broadwater Park. Den G 190 A3
Broadwater Park. Holy 203 F1
Broadway. Ame 165 D4
Broadway. Maid 202 C4
Broadway Ave. M Keyn 21 F1
Broadway Cl. Ame 165 D4
Broadway The. Ches 154 A4
Brocas St. Eton 210 B4
Brocas Terr. Eton 210 B4
Brocas Way. Slap 91 D2
Brock La. Maid 202 C4
Brockhampton. M Keyn 35 D3
Brockhurst Rd. Ches 144 B1
Brockwell. N Pag 22 B2
Broken Furlong. Eton 205 D1
Broken Gate La. Den G 189 E2
Bromham Mill. M Keyn 21 F1
Bromley. Lon M 104 A2
Brompton Cl. Ayl 101 D1
Brompton Cres. Ayl 101 D1
Brompton Dr. Maid 195 E1
Bromycroft Rd. Slough 198 A1
Bronsdon Way. Den 189 F1
Bronte Cl. Ayl 100 C1
Brook Cl. Lud 96 B4
Brook Cl. M Keyn 57 F4
Brook End. N Craw 24 A3
Brook End. W Tur 117 D2
Brook La. Berk 135 D3
Brook La. Harr 3 F4
Brook La. New B 8 A2
Brook La. Tha 125 F1
Brook St. Ast C 117 E3
Brook St. Edle 92 C2
Brook St. H Wyc 173 D4
Brook St. Tri 119 D2
Brook St. Wind 210 B3
Brookbank. Bou E 185 E2
Brookdene Cl. Maid 195 F1
Brooke Rd. P Ris 139 D2
Brookfield Cl. Tri 119 D2
Brookfield Farm. Ast C 117 D2
Brookfield La. Buck 52 B4
Brookfield Rd. Bou E 185 E2
Brookfield Rd. Have 20 B1
Brookfield Rd. Have 20 B1
Brookfield Rd. Nwtn L 57 E2
Brookhouse Dr. Bou E 185 E2
Brooklands Rd. M Keyn 58 B4
Brooklyn Way. W Dra 208 B2
Brookside. Hal 117 E1
Brookside. Iver 212 B4
Brookside. Lill L 30 A3
Brookside. M Keyn 33 E2
Brookside. Oak 109 E3
Brookside. Tha 125 F1
Brookside. Uxb 201 F3
Brookside Ave. Wray 211 F2
Brookside Cl. Old S 32 A3
Brookside Cl. Tidd 136 A4
Brookway. Dean 31 F2
Broom Cl. Ty Gr 163 D2
Broom Hill. Cook 195 F3
Broom Hill. Sto P 199 D3
Broombarn La. G Mis 151 F4
Broomfield. M Keyn 33 E2
Broomfield Cl. G Mis 151 F4
Broomfield Hill. G Mis 151 F4
Broomlee. M Keyn 34 A3
Broomstick La. Bot 145 D1
Brora Cl. M Keyn 58 B3
Brotheridge Ct. Ayl 115 D3
Broughton Ave. Ayl 116 A4
Broughton Cl. Bier 102 A2
Broughton La. Ayl 116 B4
Broughton La. Bier 116 B4
Broughton Rd. Sal 37 E2
Brow The. C St G 177 E4
Brown Cl. N Pag 22 A2
Brown's Rise. Dra B 132 C2
Brownbaker Ct. M Keyn 34 C3
Browne Wills Cl. M Keyn 58 B4
Brownfield Gdns. Maid 202 C3
Browning Cres. M Keyn 58 A4
Brownlow Ave. Edle 92 C2
Brownlow La. Ched 105 D4
Brownlow Rd. Berk 135 E3
Brownlow Rise. Tott 93 D4
Browns Rd. Char 153 D4
Browns Rd. Hol G 163 E3
Browns Way. Asp G 49 F3
Brownsfield Rd. Yard G 18 C3
Brownswood Dr. Pott 18 B2
Brownswood Rd. Beac 175 F2
Broxbourne Cl. M Keyn 21 F1
Bruce Cl. Slough 205 D3
Brudenell. Wind 209 F2
Brudenell Dr. S Man 116 A1
Brunel Cl. Maid 202 C3
Brunel Rd. Ayl 100 C1
Brunel Rd. H Wyc 161 F1
Brunel Rd. Maid 202 B3
Brunel Way. Slough 205 F3
Brunleys. M Keyn 33 D2
Brunswick Cl. Ayl 101 D2
Brushwood Dr. Chor 167 E3
Brushwood Rd. Ches 144 B1
Bryans Cres. N Craw 24 A3
Bryanston Ave. Ayl 101 F1
Bryant Ave. Slough 205 F4
Bryant's Bottom Rd. Wal A 150 C2
Bryants Acre. Wen 131 D3
Bryer Pl. Wind 209 E2
Bryne La. Pad 53 D1
Bryony Cl. Uxb 208 C4
Bryony Pl. M Keyn 34 C3
Buccleuch Rd. Datch 211 D4
Buchan Cl. Uxb 201 E1
Buchanan Rd. U Arn 94 C4
Buckby. M Keyn 47 E3
Buckfast Ave. M Keyn 47 D1
Buckingham Ave. Slough 205 D4
Buckingham Ave E. Slough 205 E4
Buckingham Cl. H Wyc 174 A4
Buckingham Gate. M Keyn 35 D1
Buckingham Gdns. Slough 205 F2
Buckingham Rd. Brac 38 A3
Buckingham Rd. Dean 31 F1
Buckingham Rd. Edgc 72 C1
Buckingham Rd. Gawt 52 A3
Buckingham Rd. M Keyn 57 E4
Buckingham Rd. She B E 57 E4
Buckingham Rd. Stp Cl 63 F2
Buckingham Rd. Tri 118 C2
Buckingham Rd. Wick 31 D2
Buckingham Rd. Wick 31 F1
Buckingham Rd. Wins 65 F3
Buckingham St. Ayl 101 E1
Buckingham St. M Keyn 33 E4
Buckingham St. Ting 51 D3
Buckingham Way. Fla H 174 A1
Buckland Ave. Slough 206 A2
Buckland Cres. Wind 209 F3
Buckland Dr. M Keyn 47 E3
Buckland Rd. Dra B 118 A2
Bucklebury Cl. Holy 203 E1
Buckley Ct. M Keyn 32 C2
Buckman Cl. M Keyn 33 D3
Buckmaster Rd. H Wyc 172 B2
Buckthorn. M Keyn 33 F3
Budge Rd. Yard G 18 C3
Buffins. Tapl 196 C1
Bulbourne Cl. Berk 134 C3
Bulbourne Rd. Tri 119 E4
Bulkeley Ave. Wind 210 A2
Bull La. Ger C 188 B4
Bull La. H Wyc 173 D4
Bullbaiters La. H Hea 153 D3
Bullbeggars La. Berk 135 F2
Bullington End Rd. Cast 20 A3
Bullington End Rd. Cast 20 A3
Bullocks Farm La. H Wyc 171 F4
Bullocks Farm La. La En 171 D4
Bullrush Gr. Uxb 201 E1
Bulls La. Ick 124 A2
Bullsland Gdns. Chor 167 D2
Bullsland La. Chor 167 D2
Bulstrode Ct. Ger C 188 B3
Bulstrode La. Chipf 146 C2
Bulstrode Way. Ger C 188 B3
Bunby Rd. Sto P 198 C3
Bunces Cl. Eton 205 D1
Bunhill Cl. Dun 93 F4
Bunkers La. L Buzz 80 B3
Bunstrux. Tri 119 D2
Bunsty Ct. M Keyn 32 C2
Bunten Meade. Slough 205 D3
Bunyan Cl. Tri 119 D3
Burchard Cres. She C E 46 A3
Burchett's Green Rd. Bish 194 B1
Burcot Gdns. Maid 195 F2
Burcott Cl. Bier 102 A2
Burcott La. Bier 102 B2
Burdett Dr. Wal A 161 D4
Burewell. M Keyn 33 E1
Burfield Rd. Chor 167 E2
Burfield Rd. Old W 211 D1
Burford Cl. Ick 201 F4
Burford Cl. Mar B 183 E3
Burford Gdns. Burn 204 B4
Burgess Gdns. N Pag 22 A1
Burgess La. Dint 128 A4
Burgess Wood Gr. Beac 175 D1
Burgess Wood Rd. Beac 175 D1
Burgess Wood Rd S. Beac 175 D1
Burgett Rd. Slough 205 D2
Burghley Ct. M Keyn 45 F4
Burkes Cl. Beac 186 A4
Burkes Cres. Beac 175 E1
Burkes Rd. Beac 175 E1
Burleigh Piece. Buck 52 C4
Burleys Rd. Wins 65 F2
Burlington Ave. Slough 205 F2
Burlington Rd. Burn 197 D1
Burlington Rd. Slough 205 F2
Burma Cl. H Wyc 173 F3
Burn Wlk. Burn 197 D1
Burners La. M Keyn 33 D2
Burners La S. M Keyn 33 D2
Burness Cl. Uxb 201 E2
Burnetts Rd. Wind 209 F3
Burnham Ave. Beac 176 A1
Burnham Cl. Bou E 185 D2
Burnham Cl. H Wyc 172 B3
Burnham Cl. Wind 209 E3
Burnham Dr. M Keyn 34 B2
Burnham Field. W Tur 116 C4
Burnham Pl. Syr 27 D4
Burnham Rd. Beac 186 C3
Burnham Rd. Hgh V 162 A3
Burnham Rd. Wcot 98 A4
Burnhams The. Shab 124 B2
Burnmoor Cl. M Keyn 58 B2
Burns Cl. L Cre 125 E4
Burns Cl. N Pag 22 A2
Burns Rd. M Keyn 58 A4
Burnt Oak. Cook 195 F4
Burroughs Cres. Bou E 185 D2
Burrows Cl. Asp G 49 D3
Burrows Cl. Ty Gr 163 E1
Burrows Hill Cl. Stan 213 E2
Burt's La. L Cre 125 E3
Burton La. P Ris 139 E3
Burton Way. Wind 209 F2
Burton's La. L Chal 166 B3
Burton's Way. L Chal 166 B4
Burtree Cl. M Keyn 33 E3
Bury Ave. N Pag 22 B2
Bury Cl. N Pag 22 B2
Bury La. Ches 154 A4
Bury Rise. Fel 146 B3
Bury St. N Pag 22 B2
Buryhook Cnr. Holt 122 B1
Busby Cl. Buck 41 F1
Buscot Pl. M Keyn 45 F4
Bush The. Hadd 126 C3
Bushel Wharf. Tri 119 D3
Bushes La. Pres B 51 E1
Bushey Cl. Buck 41 F1
Bushey Cl. H Wyc 172 C4
Bushfield Rd. Bov 146 B3
Bushmead Rd. Whit 87 D3
Bushy Cl. M Keyn 47 D2
Buslins La. Char 143 F2
Bute Brae. M Keyn 46 C1
Butler Ct. Mar 184 A2
Butlers Cl. Ame 154 A1
Butlers Cl. Wind 209 E3
Butlers Court Rd. Beac 175 E1
Butlers Gr. M Keyn 34 B4
Butterfield. Bou E 185 E2
Butterfly Rd. Skch 158 C2
Buttermere. Ayl 116 A4
Buttermere Ave. Burn 204 B4
Buttermere Cl. M Keyn 58 B3
Buttfurlong. Hadd 127 D4
Buttlehide. Map Cr 178 B3
Bybend Cl. Far C 198 A2
Bycell Rd. M Mor 41 E3
Bye Green. W Tur 117 D2
Byerly Pl. M Keyn 34 C3
Byland Dr. Holy 203 D1
Byrd Cres. Walt 48 B3
Byron Cl. M Keyn 57 F4
Byron Cl. Mar 183 C2
Byron Dr. N Pag 22 A2
Byron Rd. Ayl 115 F3
Byron Way. W Dra 208 C1
Byward Cl. M Keyn 34 C4
Byways. Burn 204 A4

Cadman Gate. She B E 46 B3
Cadsdean Rd. P Ris 139 F3
Cadwell Dr. Maid 202 B2
Caernarvon Cres. M Keyn 57 F4
Caesars Cl. M Keyn 34 A3
Caesers Gate. Brac 38 A3
Cages Wood Dr. Far C 198 A4
Cairngorm Gate. M Keyn 46 B4
Cairnside. H Wyc 173 F3
Caithness Ct. M Keyn 46 C1
Calbroke Rd. Slough 197 F1
Caldecote La. N Pag 22 C1
Caldecote St. N Pag 22 B2

Calder Cl. Maid 195 F1
Calder Ct. Maid 195 E1
Calder Ct. Slough 206 C1
Calder Gdns. L Buzz 80 A4
Calder Vale. M Keyn 46 C1
Calder Way. Stan 212 C2
Caldewell. M Keyn 33 E1
Caldicot Cl. Ayl 116 A3
Caledon Cl. Beac 175 F2
Caledon Rd. Beac 175 F2
Caledonian Rd. M Keyn 33 F4
Calewen. M Keyn 33 F1
Callis Farm Cl. Stan 213 F1
Calluna Dr. M Keyn 47 D2
Calvards Croft. M Keyn 33 E2
Calverley Cres. H Wyc 161 F1
Calverton La. She C E 33 D1
Calverton Rd. M Keyn 32 B2
Cam Ct. M Keyn 57 F4
Cam Mead. Ayl 116 A3
Camberton Rd. L Buzz 80 C3
Camborne Ave. Ayl 116 A3
Cambridge Ave. Burn 197 D2
Cambridge Ave. Slough 205 D4
Cambridge Cl. Ayl 101 F1
Cambridge Cl. Harm 213 E4
Cambridge Cres. H Wyc 173 F4
Cambridge Pl. Ayl 101 E1
Cambridge Pl. Ayl 115 E4
Cambridge Rd. Beac 175 E1
Cambridge Rd. Mar 183 E1
Cambridge Rd. Uxb 201 E3
Cambridge St. Ayl 101 F1
Cambridge St. M Keyn 33 E3
Cambridge St. M Keyn 58 B4
Cambridge Terr. Berk 135 E2
Cambron. M Keyn 33 E1
Camden Pl. Bou E 185 D2
Camden Rd. Maid 195 E1
Cameron Rd. Ches 144 B1
Camley Gdns. Maid 202 A4
Camm Ave. Wind 209 F2
Camp Rd. Ger C 188 B2
Campbell Cl. Buck 52 C4
Campbell Cl. H Wyc 172 C4
Campbell Dr. Beac 175 E3
Campbells Ride. Hol G 163 E4
Campden Rd. Ick 190 C1
Camperdown. Maid 196 A1
Campion. M Keyn 21 F1
Campion Cl. Ayl 116 B4
Campion Cl. Den 190 A1
Campion Cl. Uxb 208 C4
Campion Rd. Hol G 162 C3
Campions Ct. Berk 135 D2
Canada Rd. Slough 206 A2
Candlemas La. Beac 175 F1
Candlemas Mead. Beac 175 F1
Candover Cl. Harm 213 E4
Candytuft Green. Hol G 162 C3
Cane End. P Ris 139 D2
Canford Ct. Ayl 115 F3
Cannock Cl. Maid 203 D3
Cannock Rd. Ayl 101 F2
Cannon Court Rd. Cook 195 E2
Cannon Court Rd. Maid 195 E2
Cannon Hill Cl. Maid 203 E1
Cannon La. Maid 202 A3
Cannon Mill Ave. Ches 154 C3
Cannon Pl. P Ris 139 D2
Cannon's Hill. Cudd 112 B3
Cannondown Rd. Cook 195 F3
Canon Hill Dr. Maid 203 D2
Canon Hill Way. Maid 203 D1
Canterbury Ave. Slough 198 B1
Canterbury Cl. Ame 165 F4
Canterbury Cl. P Ris 139 D3
Cantilupe Cl. Eat B 92 B3
Cantle Ave. M Keyn 35 D3
Cantley Cl. Ayl 101 F1
Capel Dr. M Keyn 34 C3
Capell Ave. Chor 167 E2
Capell Rd. Chor 167 E2
Capell Way. Chor 167 E2
Capps La. Char 143 D3
Capron. M Keyn 47 D3
Captain Cook Cl. C St G 177 D3
Captain's Cl. Ches 144 A2
Captains Wlk. Berk 135 E2
Caraway Cl. B Bkhl 48 A2
Cardigan Cl. M Keyn 46 C1
Carey Cl. Ayl 115 E2
Carey Cl. Wind 210 A2
Carey Way. Oln 7 D2
Careys Croft. Berk 135 D4
Carisbrooke Ave. H Wyc 172 A3
Carisbrooke Cl. Maid 202 B3
Carisbrooke Ct. Buck 41 F1
Carisbrooke Ct. Slough 205 F3
Carlina Pl. M Keyn 34 B2
Carlisle Rd. Slough 205 E3
Carlton Cl. Ayl 101 D1
Carlton Cl. N Pag 22 C2
Carlton Rd. Slough 206 A3
Carlton Rd. Turv 8 C4
Carlyle Ave. Ayl 115 F4
Carlyle Cl. N Pag 22 A2
Carmarthen Rd. Slough 205 F3
Carne The. M Keyn 32 C3
Carnoustie Cl. M Keyn 57 E4
Caroline Cl. W Dra 208 B2
Caroline Ct. Mar 183 F2
Carolus Creek. M Keyn 35 D4
Carpenter Ct. M Keyn 34 C3
Carpenters Wood Dr. Chor 167 D3
Carpenters Yard. Tri 119 D2
Carr Cl. Ayl 101 D1
Carrick Rd. M Keyn 34 C1
Carrington Ave. Fla H 185 D4
Carrington Cl. Hogg 77 F3
Carrington Cres. Wen 131 D4
Carrington Pl. Hol G 163 E4
Carrington Pl. Tri 119 D3
Carrington Rd. Ayl 115 E3
Carrington Rd. H Wyc 172 B3
Carrington Rd. N Pag 22 A2
Carrington Rd. Slough 205 F3
Carrington Way. Pres 151 E3
Carroll Cl. N Pag 22 A3
Carron Cl. L Buzz 80 A4
Carrs Dr. H Wyc 172 B4
Carter Cl. Wind 210 A3
Carter Wlk. Ty Gr 174 B4
Carter's La. N Mar 75 F1
Carters Cl. Sher 13 F1
Carters La. L Cre 125 D4
Carters La. M Keyn 33 D2
Carters La. Qntn 85 F3
Cartmel Cl. M Keyn 57 E3
Cartwright Pl. M Keyn 46 C4
Carver Hill Rd. H Wyc 172 C3
Carvers Mews. M Keyn 34 C3
Cascadia Cl. Loud 174 A1
Casterton Cl. M Keyn 34 B2
Castle Ashby Rd. Y Has 1 A4
Castle Ave. Datch 211 D4
Castle Ave. W Dra 208 C3
Castle Cl. Tott 93 D4
Castle Cl. Wing 79 F2
Castle Ct. Maid 202 B4
Castle Dr. Maid 202 B4
Castle Gate Way. Berk 135 E3
Castle Hill. Berk 135 E3
Castle Hill. Maid 202 C4
Castle Hill Ave. Berk 135 E3
Castle Hill Cl. Berk 135 E3
Castle Hill Rd. Tott 93 D4
Castle Hill Terr. Maid 202 C4
Castle La. Whit 86 C3
Castle Meadow Cl. N Pag 22 C2
Castle Mews. Berk 135 E2
Castle Mews. Maid 202 C4
Castle Park Rd. Wen 131 D3
Castle Rose. M Keyn 47 E3
Castle St. Ayl 115 E4
Castle St. Berk 135 E2
Castle St. Buck 52 B4
Castle St. H Wyc 173 D4
Castle St. M Gib 72 A2
Castle St. Slough 205 F2
Castle St. Win 89 D2
Castle View Gdns. H Wyc 172 B4
Castlesteads. M Keyn 33 F3
Castlethorpe Rd. Hans 11 D1
Castleton Ct. Mar 183 F1
Castleview Rd. Slough 206 B1
Caswell La. Hth 60 C4
Catchpole Cl. M Keyn 33 D3
Cater Rd. La En 171 E2
Catherine Ct. Buck 41 F1
Catherines Cl. W Dra 208 B2
Causeway The. Maid 203 E2
Causeway The. Mar 183 F1
Cautley Cl. Qntn 85 D3
Cavalier Rd. Tha 126 A1
Cavalry Cres. Wind 210 B2
Cavendish Cl. Burn 204 A4
Cavendish Cl. L Chal 166 A4
Cavendish Cl. Wen 131 D3
Cavendish Rd. Ches 154 B4
Cavendish Wlk. Tha 126 A1
Cavenham. M Keyn 33 F1
Caversham Green. Ayl 101 E1
Cawardon. M Keyn 34 B4
Cawcott Dr. Wind 209 F3
Caxton Dr. Uxb 201 E2
Caxton Rd. M Keyn 33 D4
Ceadr Rd. Berk 135 F2
Cecil Way. Slough 197 F1
Cedar Ave. Hol G 163 D3
Cedar Ave. W Dra 208 C3
Cedar Chase. Maid 196 B1
Cedar Cl. Ayl 102 A1
Cedar Ct. Mar 183 F1
Cedar Dr. Mar B 183 E4
Cedar Gr. Ame 165 E4
Cedar Gr. Char 143 E4
Cedar Lodge Dr. M Keyn 33 E4
Cedar Terr. H Wyc 172 C4
Cedar Way. Berk 135 E2
Cedar Way. Slough 206 C1
Cedars Cl. Akel 41 F4
Cedars Cl. C St P 177 F3
Cedars Dr. Uxb 201 F2
Cedars Rd. Maid 203 D4
Cedars The. Wen 131 D3
Cedars Way. L Buzz 80 C3
Cedars Way. N Pag 22 B2
Ceely Rd. Ayl 115 E3
Celina Cl. M Keyn 58 B4
Cell Farm Ave. Old W 211 D1
Central Ave. Cran 24 C1
Centre Wlk. Ty Gr 163 D2
Century Ave. M Keyn 46 C4
Cestreham Cres. Ches 144 B1
Chadbone Cl. Ayl 115 E4
Chadds La. M Keyn 47 E4
Chadwell Path. Ayl 116 B3
Chadwick Dr. M Keyn 47 D4
Chadwick St. H Wyc 162 B1
Chaffron Way. M Keyn 47 D4
Chaffron Way. She B E 46 B3
Chairborough Rd. H Wyc 172 B3
Chairmans Ave. Den G 189 F3
Chalcot Pl. M Keyn 45 F4
Chalet Cl. Berk 134 C2
Chalfont Ave. L Chal 166 B4
Chalfont Cl. M Keyn 34 A3
Chalfont La. Chor 167 D2
Chalfont La. Map Cr 178 B2
Chalfont Rd. Map Cr 178 B4
Chalfont Rd. Se Gr 176 B3
Chalfont Station Rd. L Chal 166 B4
Chalfont Way. Lit M 172 B2
Chalford. Woo G 185 F3
Chalgrove Cl. Maid 203 D3
Chalgrove End. S Man 116 A1
Chalgrove Rd. Tha 126 A1
Chalgrove Wlk. Ayl 115 E3
Chalk Farm Rd. Skch 158 B3
Chalk Hill. Ches 144 A1
Chalk Hill. Cole 164 C1
Chalk La. H Hea 153 D2
Chalk Pit La. Burn 197 D2
Chalklands. Bou E 185 D2
Chalkpit La. Mar 183 D2
Challacombe. M Keyn 46 B1
Challener Rd. H Wyc 172 B2
Challow Ct. Maid 195 E1
Chalmers Ave. Have 20 B1
Chalmers Ave. Have 20 B1
Chaloner Cl. Ayl 115 E3
Chaloner Rd. Ayl 115 E3
Chaloners Hill. Stp Cl 63 E2
Chalvey Gdns. Slough 205 F2
Chalvey Gr. Slough 205 D2
Chalvey Park. Slough 205 F2
Chalvey Rd E. Slough 205 F2
Chalvey Rd W. Slough 205 E2
Chamberlain Rd. Ayl 101 D1
Chancellors. Ty Gr 164 A3
Chancery Cl. M Keyn 34 A3
Chandlers Ct. M Keyn 47 F3
Chandos Cl. Buck 52 B4
Chandos Cl. L Chal 155 E1
Chandos Pl. M Keyn 58 B4
Chandos Rd. Buck 52 B4
Channer Dr. Ty Gr 174 A4
Chantry Cl. W Dra 208 B3
Chantry Cl. Wind 210 A3
Chantry Rd. Ayl 101 E2
Chantry The. Uxb 201 F1
Chapel Cl. Akel 41 F4
Chapel Cl. L Gad 121 E3
Chapel Dr. Ast C 117 F3
Chapel End La. Wils 118 B4
Chapel Hill. Soul 69 F2
Chapel La. Akel 41 F4
Chapel La. Bled 138 A2
Chapel La. Chil 111 D2
Chapel La. Dray P 68 A3
Chapel La. H Wyc 172 B4
Chapel La. Lon M 104 A2
Chapel La. S Bru 9 D4
Chapel La. S Man 116 A1
Chapel La. Sto P 199 D3
Chapel La. Thrn 54 A4
Chapel La. Tott 92 C4
Chapel La. Turw 38 A4
Chapel La. Wal A 161 E4
Chapel La. Wen 131 D2
Chapel La. Whit 26 B2
Chapel Rd. Dint 128 A4
Chapel Rd. Edle 92 A3
Chapel Rd. Fla H 185 D4
Chapel Sq. Stew 68 C1
Chapel St. Berk 135 E2
Chapel St. H Wyc 161 E2
Chapel St. Slough 205 F2
Chapel St. Tri 118 C2
Chapel St. Uxb 201 E2
Chapel St. Wbn S 49 D2
Chaplin Gr. She C E 45 E4
Chapman Ave. M Keyn 35 D3
Chapman Cl. W Dra 208 C2
Chapman La. Bou E 185 D3
Chapman La. Fla H 185 D3
Chapmans Cres. Ches 144 A1
Chapter. M Keyn 47 D3
Chapter Cl. Uxb 201 F3
Chardacre. M Keyn 33 F1
Charlbury Rd. Ick 190 C1
Charles Cl. Ayl 116 A2
Charles Dr. Tha 126 A1
Charles Gdns. Slough 206 A4
Charles St. Berk 135 D2
Charles St. Tri 119 D2
Charles St. Wind 210 B3
Charles Way. N Pag 22 B2
Charlton. Oak G 209 E3
Charlton Cl. Slough 205 D2
Charlton Cl. Swan 66 C2
Charlton Sq. Oak G 209 E3
Charlton Way. Oak G 209 E3
Charmfield Rd. Ayl 116 A3
Charnwood Cl. H Wyc 173 F3
Charsley Cl. L Chal 166 B4
Charter Cl. Slough 205 F2
Chartridge Grange Dr. Char 143 E2
Chartridge La. Char 143 F1
Chartridge La. Ches 143 F1
Chartridge La. Ches 154 A4
Chartwell Gate. Beac 175 E1
Chartwell Rd. N Pag 22 C2
Chase Ave. Walt 48 A2
Chase Cl. Cole 165 D2
Chase Park Rd. Y Has 1 A3
Chase The. Ches 144 A1
Chase The. Mar 184 A2
Chase The. Nwtn L 57 E2
Chase The. Ty Gr 163 E1
Chaseside Cl. Ched 105 D4
Chatfield. Slough 205 D4
Chatsworth. M Keyn 33 F1
Chatsworth Cl. Maid 202 B3
Chaucer Cl. Berk 134 C3
Chaucer Cl. N Pag 22 A2
Chaucer Dr. Ayl 115 F3
Chaucer Rd. M Keyn 58 A4
Chauntry Rd. Maid 203 D3
Chawton Cres. M Keyn 33 F1
Cheapside La. Den 189 F1
Chearsley Rd. L Cre 125 E4
Cheddington La. Lon M 104 B3
Cheddington La. Mars 104 B3
Cheddington Rd. Pit 105 E2
Chelsea Green. L Buzz 80 B3
Cheltenham Gdns. M Keyn 57 E3
Cheney Cl. Cub 78 A1
Cheney Way. Ayl 101 F1
Cheneys Wlk. M Keyn 47 D1
Chenies Ave. L Chal 166 B4
Chenies Par. L Chal 166 B4
Chenies Rd. Chor 167 E4
Chepping Cl. Ty Gr 163 D1
Chepstow Dr. M Keyn 57 E3
Chequers Cl. Pit 105 E2
Chequers Ct. Ayl 115 F2
Chequers End. Wins 66 A2
Chequers Hill. Ame 165 E4
Chequers La. Ibst 170 A3
Chequers La. La En 170 A2
Chequers La. N Craw 24 A3
Chequers La. Pit 105 E3
Chequers La. Pres 151 E3
Chequers The. Cast 19 F3
Cherington Gate. Maid 195 D1
Cheriton. M Keyn 46 C2
Cherleton. M Keyn 33 F1
Cherries The. Slough 206 A4
Cherry Ave. Slough 206 B2
Cherry Cl. Fla H 185 D4
Cherry Cl. Pres 151 E3
Cherry Dr. Beac 175 D2
Cherry Gdns. Tri 118 C2
Cherry Gr. Hol G 163 E3
Cherry La. Ame 164 B3
Cherry La. W Dra 208 C1
Cherry Leys. Stp Cl 63 F2
Cherry Orch. Ame 154 C1
Cherry Orch. Oln 6 C2
Cherry Orch. Sto P 199 D3
Cherry Orch. W Dra 208 C2
Cherry Rd. N Pag 22 A2
Cherry Rise. C St G 177 E4
Cherry Rise. Fla H 185 D4
Cherry St. H Wyc 174 A2
Cherry Tree Ave. W Dra 208 C4
Cherry Tree Cl. G Kin 151 E1
Cherry Tree Cl. Hgh V 162 A4
Cherry Tree Cl. Lac G 150 A3
Cherry Tree La. Buc Co 133 D2
Cherry Tree La. Chor 167 E1
Cherry Tree La. Fulm 199 F3
Cherry Tree La. Lee C 142 C2
Cherry Tree Rd. Chin 147 E3
Cherry Tree Rd. Far C 198 B3
Cherry Tree Way. Ty Gr 163 E1
Cherry Tree Wlk. Ches 144 B1
Cherry Tree Wlk. L Buzz 80 C4
Cherry Way. Hol G 163 D3
Cherrycroft Dr. Wal A 161 E3
Cherrytree La. Ger C 177 E1
Cherrywood Cl. Se Gr 176 B3
Cherrywood Gdns. Fla H 185 D4
Cherwell Cl. Maid 203 D4
Cherwell Cl. Slough 212 A4
Cherwell Rd. Ayl 115 E3
Cherwell Rd. Bou E 185 D2
Chesham Ave. M Keyn 34 B2
Chesham La. C St P 177 F3
Chesham Rd. Ame 154 B1
Chesham Rd. Ash Gr 135 D2
Chesham Rd. Berk 135 D2
Chesham Rd. Bov 145 F2
Chesham Rd. Char 143 F4
Chesham Rd. Char 153 E4
Chesham Rd. Wigg 133 E4
Cheshire Ct. Slough 206 A2
Cheslyn Gdns. M Keyn 35 D4
Chesney Wold. M Keyn 46 C3
Chess Cl. Lat 155 E2
Chess Cl. S Man 115 E2
Chessbury Rd. Ches 154 A4
Chessfield Park. L Chal 166 C4
Chessmount Rise. Ches 154 B3
Chester Cl. M Keyn 57 E4
Chester Rd. Slough 205 E4
Chesterfield Cres. Wing 79 F2
Chesterfield Pl. Ayl 115 D4
Chesterholm. M Keyn 33 F3
Chesterton Cl. Ches 144 A1
Chesterton Green. Beac 175 F2
Chestnut Ave. Ches 144 B1
Chestnut Ave. H Wyc 173 E3
Chestnut Ave. M Keyn 58 B4
Chestnut Ave. Slough 206 C2
Chestnut Ave. W Dra 208 C3
Chestnut Cl. Ame 154 B1
Chestnut Cl. Ast C 117 F3
Chestnut Cl. C St P 177 F1
Chestnut Cl. Dag 107 E3
Chestnut Cl. M Keyn 32 B3
Chestnut Cl. Maid 196 A1
Chestnut Cl. Nwtn L 57 E1
Chestnut Cl. P Ris 139 E3
Chestnut Cl. Wadd 99 D3
Chestnut Cres. Ayl 115 F3
Chestnut Cres. M Keyn 58 B4
Chestnut Dr. Berk 135 E2
Chestnut Dr. Wind 209 F2
Chestnut Hill. L Buzz 80 B4
Chestnut La. Ame 154 C1
Chestnut La. Hol G 163 D3
Chestnut Leys. Stp Cl 63 F2
Chestnut Rd. Beac 175 D1
Chestnut Rd. P Ris 139 E2
Chestnut Rd. Yard G 18 C3
Chestnut Rise. L Buzz 80 B4
Chestnut View. E Clay 74 C4
Chestnut Way. Hal 131 E4
Chestnut Way. Lgwk 138 C3
Chestnut Way. S Man 116 A1
Chestnut Wlk. C St P 177 F2
Chestnuts The. Fel 146 C4
Chestnuts The. Shab 124 B2
Chestwood Gr. Uxb 201 F3
Chetwode Cl. Buck 41 F1
Chetwynd Dr. Uxb 201 F2
Chevalier Gr. She C E 45 E4
Cheveley Gdns. Burn 197 E2
Cheviot Cl. H Wyc 161 F1
Cheviot Cl. L Buzz 80 B4
Cheviot Cl. Maid 203 D3
Cheyne Cl. Ame 154 B2
Cheyne Cl. Buck 41 F1
Cheyne Cl. Ger C 188 C2
Cheyne Cl. Pit 105 E2
Cheyne Wlk. Ches 154 B4
Chicheley Hill. Sher 23 D4
Chicheley Rd. Chic 23 F4
Chicheley Rd. N Craw 23 F4
Chicheley St. N Pag 22 C2
Chichester Cl. H Wyc 173 E3
Chichester Ct. Slough 206 A2
Chichester Row. Ame 154 B1
Chievely Ct. M Keyn 46 B1
Childs Way. M Keyn 35 E2
Childs Way. M Keyn 46 B4
Chiltern Ave. Ame 154 B1
Chiltern Ave. Edle 92 C2
Chiltern Ave. H Wyc 172 B3
Chiltern Ave. Sto 114 B3
Chiltern Cl. Berk 135 D3
Chiltern Cl. Hol G 163 E4
Chiltern Cl. P Ris 139 D2
Chiltern Cl. Sto 114 B3
Chiltern Cl. Ty Gr 163 E1
Chiltern Cl. Wen 131 D3
Chiltern Ct. Wins 65 F2
Chiltern Dr. Chor 167 F1
Chiltern Green. Fla H 185 D4
Chiltern Hill. C St P 177 F1
Chiltern Hills Rd. Beac 175 E1
Chiltern Manor Park. S Hea 152 A4
Chiltern Parade. Ame 154 B1
Chiltern Park Ave. Berk 135 D3
Chiltern Rd. Ame 154 A2
Chiltern Rd. Burn 204 A4
Chiltern Rd. Maid 203 D3
Chiltern Rd. Mar 183 B1
Chiltern Rd. S Hea 142 C2
Chiltern Rd. Wen 131 D3
Chiltern Rd. Win 89 D2
Chiltern Ridge. Skch 158 B2
Chiltern St. Ayl 115 F3
Chiltern View. Bled R 149 E1
Chiltern View Rd. Uxb 201 E2
Chiltern Way. Ast C 117 F1
Chiltern Way. Tri 119 E3
Chilterns Cl. Fla H 185 D4
Chilterns Park. Bou E 185 D3
Chilterns The. H Wyc 173 D4
Chilton Rd. Chea 112 A2
Chilton Rd. Ches 144 B1

Chilton Rd. L Cre 125 E4
Chilwick Rd. Slough 197 F1
Chinalls Cl. Fin 50 B3
Chinner Hill. Chin 147 F2
Chinner Rd. Chin 147 D3
Chinnor Rd. Bled 138 A1
Chinnor Rd. Bled R 160 A3
Chippendale Cl. H Wyc 162 B1
Chippendale Waye. Uxb 201 E3
Chipperfield Cl. M Keyn 34 A4
Chipperfield Rd. Bov 146 B2
Chipps Hill. La En 171 D4
Chipstead. Ger C 177 E1
Chislehampton. M Keyn 35 E2
Choke La. Cook 195 D2
Cholesbury La. Buc Co 133 D1
Chorley Rd. H Wyc 160 C2
Chorleywood Bottom. Chor 167 E2
Chrislaine Cl. Stan 213 E1
Christchurch Rd. Tri 118 C2
Christian Ct. M Keyn 35 E4
Christie Cl. N Pag 22 A3
Christmas La. Far C 187 E1
Christopher Cl. Wal A 161 E4
Church Green. L Cre 125 E4
Church Way. Sto 114 B3
Church Cl. Ast C 117 E3
Church Cl. Cudd 112 C2
Church Cl. Eton 210 B4
Church Cl. M Mor 41 F2
Church Cl. Maid 202 B3
Church Cl. Uxb 201 D2
Church Cl. W Dra 208 C2
Church Cl. Wick 31 D2
Church Croft. Edle 92 C2
Church Dr. Maid 203 E2
Church End. Adsk 53 F1
Church End. Bled 138 A1
Church End. Nwtn L 57 E2
Church End. Pott 18 C2
Church End. Sher 14 A1
Church End. Stp Cl 63 D3
Church End. Syr 27 E4
Church End. Wave 48 C4
Church End Rd. She B E 46 A2
Church Farm Cres. M Keyn 34 C4
Church Gr. L Chal 166 C4
Church Gr. Slough 206 B4
Church Green. Tott 93 D4
Church Green Rd. M Keyn 58 A4
Church Headland La. Whit 87 D3
Church Hill. Akel 41 F4
Church Hill. Asp G 49 F3
Church Hill. Ched 105 D4
Church Hill. Elle 130 A1
Church Hill. M Keyn 33 F1
Church Hill. S Har 190 B4
Church Hill. Ston 179 E4
Church Hill. Whad 45 D1
Church Holt The. Hedg 187 E2
Church La. Ast C 117 E2
Church La. Berk 135 E2
Church La. Bled R 159 E4
Church La. Bled R 159 F4
Church La. Bov 146 A2
Church La. Brac 38 B1
Church La. Chea 112 A1
Church La. Ched 105 D4
Church La. Chin 147 E3
Church La. Dean 31 F2
Church La. Eat B 92 C3
Church La. Edgc 72 C1
Church La. Emb 13 F4
Church La. G Hrwd 55 D2
Church La. Ger C 177 E1
Church La. Graf R 9 D1
Church La. Gran 75 F3
Church La. H Wyc 161 D1
Church La. Hol G 162 B2
Church La. Hor-c-S 108 A3
Church La. Lac G 149 F2
Church La. Lud 96 B4
Church La. M Keyn 34 A1
Church La. Maid 203 E2
Church La. Mars 104 C1
Church La. Mur 67 E3
Church La. N Pag 22 B4
Church La. Oving 86 B4
Church La. P Ris 139 D2
Church La. Pad 53 E1
Church La. Pott 18 C2
Church La. S Bru 9 D4
Church La. S Gol 12 A4
Church La. S Hea 152 A4
Church La. Slough 206 B4
Church La. Soul 69 F1
Church La. Sto P 198 C1
Church La. Ting 51 D3
Church La. Uxb 201 D2
Church La. W Tur 116 C1
Church La. Wal A 161 F3
Church La. Wen 131 E2
Church La. Whad 45 D1
Church La. Whit 87 D3
Church La. Wick 31 D2
Church La. Wind 210 B3
Church Lees. M Keyn 21 E1
Church Passage. N Pag 22 B2
Church Path. Maid 203 E2
Church Path. Pres 151 E3
Church Path. Skch 158 B3
Church Rd. B Bkhl 48 B1
Church Rd. Brac 38 A4
Church Rd. Chl 111 D2
Church Rd. Chin 147 E3
Church Rd. Cook 195 D3
Church Rd. Far C 198 B1
Church Rd. Graf R 9 E1
Church Rd. Ick 123 F2
Church Rd. Iver H 200 B2
Church Rd. Ivin 105 F3
Church Rd. L Buzz 80 C3
Church Rd. L Gad 121 E4
Church Rd. La En 171 D2
Church Rd. Lewk 157 D4
Church Rd. Lit M 184 B3
Church Rd. Maid 203 D3
Church Rd. Old W 211 D1
Church Rd. Pit 105 F2
Church Rd. S Ham 69 E4
Church Rd. S Har 190 B4
Church Rd. Se Gr 176 B2
Church Rd. Sher 13 F1
Church Rd. Skch 158 B3
Church Rd. Slap 91 E3
Church Rd. Tha 125 F1
Church Rd. Tott 93 D3
Church Rd. Ty Gr 174 C4
Church Rd. Uxb 201 E1
Church Rd. W Dra 208 C2
Church Sq. H Wyc 173 D4
Church Sq. L Buzz 80 C3
Church St. Ame 165 D4
Church St. Asp G 49 F3
Church St. Ayl 115 E4
Church St. Bov 146 A2
Church St. Bri 110 A4
Church St. Buck 52 B4
Church St. Burn 197 E1
Church St. Ches 154 A4
Church St. Gawt 52 A2
Church St. H Wyc 173 D4
Church St. Hen-O-T 191 E1
Church St. L Hrwd 55 F1
Church St. M Gib 71 F2
Church St. M Keyn 33 E4
Church St. M Keyn 33 F4
Church St. M Keyn 47 F1
Church St. M Mor 41 F2
Church St. N Mar 76 A1
Church St. Oln 7 D2
Church St. P Ris 139 D2
Church St. Qntn 85 D3
Church St. S Hea 152 A4
Church St. Skch 158 C3
Church St. Slough 205 E2
Church St. Slough 205 F2
Church St. Twyf 62 B1
Church St. Win 89 D1
Church St. Wind 210 B3
Church St. Wing 79 F1
Church St. Wins 65 F2
Church View. Hal 117 E1
Church View. Lon M 104 A2
Church View. Stp Cl 63 F1
Church Views. Maid 202 C4
Church Walk. W Tur 116 C1
Church Way. E Clay 74 C4
Church Wlk. M Keyn 57 F4
Church Wlk. N Craw 24 A3
Church Yard. Tri 119 D2
Churchfield Mews. Slough 206 A4
Churchfield Rd. Ger C 177 E1
Churchill Ave. Ayl 115 E3
Churchill Cl. Fla H 185 D4
Churchill Dr. Mar 183 F2
Churchill Rd. Slough 206 C1
Churchmere Wlk. Ayl 115 E3
Churchside. Hol G 163 E4
Churchway. Hadd 127 D4
Cinnamon Gr. Walt 48 A3
Cippenham La. Slough 205 D3
City Rd. Bled R 159 E3
Clailey Ct. M Keyn 32 C3
Clammas Way. Uxb 208 B4
Clapham Pl. M Keyn 34 B1
Clappers Meadow. Maid 196 B1
Clappins La. Wal A 161 E4
Clapton App. Woo G 185 E4
Clare Rd. Pres 151 E3
Clare Dr. Far C 198 A4
Clare Park. Ame 165 F4
Clare Rd. Maid 202 B3
Clare Rd. Stan 213 F1
Clarefield Dr. Maid 195 D1
Claremont Ave. M Keyn 32 C2
Claremont Cl. Ayl 115 F3
Claremont Gdns. Mar 183 F1
Claremont Rd. Mar 183 F1
Claremont Rd. Wind 210 B3
Clarence Cres. Wind 210 B3
Clarence Rd. Berk 135 E2
Clarence Rd. Hen-O-T 191 E1
Clarence Rd. M Keyn 32 C3
Clarence Rd. Wind 210 A3
Clarendon Ct. Slough 206 A3
Clarendon Dr. M Keyn 33 F1
Clarendon Dr. Tha 126 A1
Clarendon Rd. H Wyc 173 F3
Clarendon Rd. Pres 151 D3
Clarke Ct. Ayl 101 F1
Clarke Dr. H Wyc 174 A3
Clarke Rd. M Keyn 47 E2
Clarke's Spring. Tri 119 F3
Clarkes Dr. W Dra 208 C4
Clarkes Field Cl. Bri 110 A4
Classon Cl. W Dra 208 C2
Clauds Cl. Hol G 163 D3
Claverton Cl. Bov 146 A2
Clay Acre. Ches 144 B1
Clay Cl. Fla H 185 D4
Clay Hall La. Wind 210 C1
Clay Hill. M Keyn 33 F1
Clay La. Mar B 172 A1
Clay La. Wen 131 E3
Clay St. Cole 175 E4
Claydon Cl. Ayl 115 E3
Claydon Ct. H Wyc 172 C2
Claydon End. Ger C 188 C4
Claydon La. Ger C 188 C4
Claydon Path. Ayl 115 F2
Clayfield Rd. Hal 131 E4
Clayfields. Ty Gr 163 E1
Clayhill. Mar B 172 A1
Claymoor Park. Mar B 172 A1
Clays The. Hadd 127 D4
Clayton Gate. M Keyn 35 D4
Clayton Way. Uxb 201 E1
Clayton Wlk. L Chal 166 B4
Claytons Meadow. Bou E 185 D2
Clearbrook Cl. Loud 174 A2
Cleavers. Chin 147 D3
Cleavers Ave. M Keyn 34 C2
Cleeve Cres. M Keyn 47 D1
Clegg Sq. She B E 46 A3
Cleland Rd. Ger C 177 E1
Clementi Ave. Hol G 163 E4
Clements Cl. Slough 206 A2
Clements La. M Gib 71 F1
Clements Pl. Tri 119 D2
Clements Rd. Chor 167 E2
Clements Rd. Hen-O-T 191 E2
Clerkenwell Pl. M Keyn 35 D2
Cleve Ct. Wind 209 F2
Clevehurst Cl. Sto P 199 D3
Cleveland. M Keyn 34 A3
Cleveland Cl. Maid 203 D3
Cleveland Dr. L Buzz 80 B4
Cleveland Park.Ayl 101 F2
Cleveland Rd. Ayl 101 F2
Cleveland Rd. Uxb 201 E1
Clewer Ave. Wind 210 A3
Clewer Ct Rd. Wind 210 A4
Clewer Fields. Wind 210 B3
Clewer Hill Rd. Wind 209 F2
Clewer New Town. Wind 210 A3
Clewer Park. Wind 210 A4
Clifden Rd. Worm 123 E3
Clifford Ave. M Keyn 58 B4
Clifford Rd. P Ris 139 D2
Clifford Way. Bou E 185 D3
Clifton Cl. Maid 203 D2
Clifton Green. Ayl 101 D1
Clifton Lawnes. Ame 154 B2
Clifton Rd. Ame 154 B2
Clifton Rd. New B 7 F2
Clifton Rd. Slough 206 A2
Clifton Rise. Wind 209 E3
Clinkard Cl. La En 171 D2
Clinton Cres. Ayl 116 A4
Clive Ct. Slough 205 E2
Cliveden Mead. Maid 196 B1
Cliveden Rd. Tapl 196 C2
Clivemont Rd. Maid 202 C4
Cloister Garth. Berk 135 E2
Cloisters The. H Wyc 162 B1
Clonmel Way. Burn 197 D1
Close The. Ash 97 F1
Close The. Bier 102 A2
Close The. Bou E 185 D3
Close The. G Hrwd 55 D2
Close The. Iver H 200 B1
Close The. M Keyn 34 A2
Close The. M Keyn 47 E4
Close The. Oln 6 A1
Close The. Uxb 201 F3
Close The. Whit 87 D2
Closes The. Hadd 127 D4
Cloudberry. Walt 48 A3
Clover Cl. M Keyn 46 A4
Clover La. Ayl 115 F3
Clyde Pl. M Keyn 46 C1
Clydesdale Pl. M Keyn 34 C2
Coach Ride. Mar 183 E2
Coachmaker Ct. M Keyn 34 C3
Coat Wicks. Se Gr 176 B2
Coates La. H Wyc 162 A1
Coates Way. Wing 79 F2
Cobb Cl. Datch 211 E3
Cobb Hall. Nwtn L 57 E2
Cobb Rd. Berk 134 C2
Cobbetts Mount. Stp Cl 63 E1
Cobbetts Ride. Tri 118 C2
Cobblers Cl. Far C 198 A2
Cobblers Wick. Win 89 D2
Cobden Cl. Uxb 201 E2
Coberley Cl. M Keyn 35 D3
Cochran Cl. She C E 45 F4
Cock La. H Wyc 174 A3
Cockett Rd. Slough 206 C2
Cockpit Cl. G Kin 151 F1
Cockpit Rd. G Kin 162 B4
Coddimoor La. Whad 56 B4
Codmore Wood Rd. Lat 155 E3
Coe Spur. Slough 205 D2
Coftards. Slough 206 B4
Cogan Ct. She C E 45 F4
Cogdells Cl. Char 143 D2
Cogdells La. Char 143 D2
Coke's Farm La. L Chal 166 A3
Coke's La. Ame 166 A3
Coke's La. L Chal 166 A3
Colborne Rd. H Wyc 173 E4
Coldmoorholme La. Bou E 184 C2
Cole Rd. Ayl 115 E3
Coleheath Bottom. Lac G 150 B2
Coleridge Cl. M Keyn 58 A4
Coleridge Cl. N Pag 21 F2
Coleridge Cres. Stan 212 C3
Coleridge Way. W Dra 208 C1
Colesbourne Dr. M Keyn 35 D3
Coleshill La. Cole 164 B1
Coleshill Pl. M Keyn 34 B2
Colet Rd. Wen 131 E3
Coleville Rd. H Wyc 172 C3
Colham Ave. W Dra 208 C3
Colham Mill Rd. W Dra 208 B3
Colham Rd. Uxb 201 F1
Colin Way. Slough 205 D2
Colinswood Rd. Beac 187 D1
Colinswood Rd. Far C 187 D1
Colinswood Rd. Hedg 187 D1
College Ave. Maid 202 C4
College Ave. Slough 205 F2
College Cres. Oak 109 F2
College Cres. Wind 210 B3
College Glen. Maid 202 B4
College Rd. Ast C 117 E4
College Rd. Cran 24 C1
College Rd. Maid 202 C4
College Rise. Maid 202 B4
Colley Hill. M Keyn 34 A2
Colley Hill La. Hedg 187 F1
Colley Land. Chor 167 E3
Collier Cl. Maid 195 F1
Collings Walk. Pres 151 E3
Collingwood Cl. H Wyc 174 A3
Collins Wlk. N Pag 22 A2
Collum Green Rd. Far C 187 F1
Collum Green Rd. Sto P 187 F1
Collyer Rd. Skch 158 C2
Coln Cl. Maid 202 C4
Colnbrook By-Pass. Iver 212 B4
Colnbrook By-Pass. Slough 212 B4
Colndale Rd. Stan 212 C3
Colne. M Keyn 47 E3
Colne Ave. W Dra 208 B2
Colne Bank. Hort 212 B2
Colne Rd. H Wyc 173 F4
Colnedale Rd. Uxb 201 E4
Colonial Rd. Slough 206 A2
Colspie Croft. M Keyn 33 E2
Colston Bassett. M Keyn 46 B1
Coltman Ave. L Cre 125 E3
Colts Holm Rd. M Keyn 33 E4
Coltsfoot Pl. M Keyn 34 B2
Columbine Rd. Hol G 162 C3
Combe Rise. H Wyc 172 A4
Combermere Cl. Wind 210 A3
Common Field. Wigg 119 E1
Common Gate Rd. Chor 167 F2
Common La. Burn 186 B1
Common La. Eton 205 E1
Common La. M Keyn 34 A2
Common Rd. Chor 167 E3
Common Rd. Dag 107 F2
Common Rd. Eton 205 D1
Common Rd. Fla H 185 D4
Common Rd. G Kin 151 E1
Common Side. H Wyc 161 F2
Common St. Rav 5 E1
Common The. Berk 135 F3
Common The. Chipf 156 C4
Common The. Fla H 185 D4
Common The. G Kin 151 E1
Common The. Hol G 163 E4
Common Wood. Far C 198 B4
Como Rd. Ayl 116 A4
Comp The. Eat B 92 C3
Compton Dr. Maid 202 A4
Compton Rd. Wen 131 E3
Concorde Cl. Uxb 201 F2
Concorde Way. Slough 205 E2
Concourse The. M Keyn 58 B4
Concra Park. Asp G 49 E2
Condor Cl. M Keyn 47 D4
Conegar Ct. Slough 205 F3
Conegra Rd. H Wyc 173 E4
Congreve. M Keyn 47 E3
Conifer Rise. H Wyc 172 C3
Conigre. Chin 147 D3
Coningsby Cl. Maid 202 B2
Coningsby Rd. H Wyc 162 A1
Coniston Cres. Slough 204 B4
Coniston Green. Ayl 101 E2
Coniston Rd. L Buzz 80 B4
Coniston Way. M Keyn 58 B3
Connaught Cl. Maid 195 F1
Connaught Gdns. Berk 134 C4
Connaught Rd. Ayl 116 B4
Connaught Rd. Slough 206 A2
Conniburrow Bvd. M Keyn 34 C2
Conniston Cl. Mar 183 A1
Consort Way. Den G 189 F3
Constable Cl. M Keyn 34 C4
Constable Pl. Ayl 100 C1
Constable's Croft. U Arn 94 C4
Constantine Way. M Keyn 33 F3
Convent Rd. Wind 210 A3
Conway Cl. Ayl 115 F4
Conway Cl. Loud 174 B1
Conway Cl. M Keyn 57 F4
Conway Cres. M Keyn 57 F4
Conway Rd. Burn 204 A4
Conway Rd. Slough 204 A4
Cook's Meadow. Edle 92 C2
Cookerell Gr. She B E 46 B3
Cookfield Cl. Dun 93 F4
Cookham Dean Bm La. Cook 195 E4
Cookham Rd. Maid 195 F1
Cooks Cl. Ash 9 F4
Cooks La. Mur 67 F3
Coombe Ave. Wen 131 D2
Coombe Cl. S Man 116 B1
Coombe Dr. Dun 93 F4
Coombe Gdns. Berk 134 C3
Coombe Gdns. Hgh V 162 A3
Coombe La. Wal A 161 F3
Coombe Vale. Ger C 188 C2
Cooper Rd. Hen-O-T 191 E2
Cooper Ridge. C St P 177 F3
Cooper Way. Slough 205 D2
Cooper's Court Rd. Skch 158 B3
Cooper's Yd. Ayl 101 E1
Coopers Mews. M Keyn 34 C3
Coopers Row. Iver H 200 B1
Coots Cl. Buck 52 C4
Copes Rd. G Kin 151 F1
Copes Shroves. Hol G 162 C3
Copmans Wick. Chor 167 E2
Copners Dr. Hol G 163 E3
Copners Way. Hol G 163 D3
Copper Beech Cl. Fel 146 C4
Copper Beech Cl. Wind 209 E3
Copperfields. Beac 175 F3
Copperfields. H Wyc 161 D1
Copperkins Gr. Ame 154 A2
Copperkins La. Ame 154 A2
Coppermill La. Map Cr 178 C2
Coppermill Rd. Hort 212 A1
Coppermill Rd. Wray 212 A1
Coppice Cl. Ayl 102 A1
Coppice Farm Rd. Ty Gr 163 E1
Coppice The. H Wyc 172 A2
Coppice The. W Dra 208 C4
Coppice Way. Ayl 102 A1
Coppidwell Dr. Ayl 116 A3
Coppin La. M Keyn 34 A2
Coppins Cl. Berk 134 C2
Copse Cl. Mar 183 B1
Copse Cl. W Dra 208 B2
Copse Gate. Wins 66 A2
Copse La. Se Gr 176 C2
Copse The. Ame 154 B1
Copse The. Beac 175 E2
Copse Way. Ches 144 A2
Copse Wood. Iver H 200 B2
Copthall Cl. C St P 177 F2
Copthall Cnr. C St P 177 F2
Copthall La. C St P 177 F2
Copthorn Cl. Maid 202 A2
Copyground La. H Wyc 172 C4
Coram Cl. Berk 135 E2
Corbet Ride. L Buzz 80 B4
Corbett Cl. M Keyn 35 E4
Cordwainer Ct. M Keyn 34 C3
Cordwallis Rd. Maid 202 C4
Cordwallis St. Maid 202 C4
Cores End Rd. Bou E 185 D2
Corfe Cl. Ayl 116 A3
Corfe Cres. M Keyn 57 F4
Corfe Gdns. Slough 205 D3
Coriander Ct. Walt 48 A3
Corin Cl. M Keyn 58 B3
Corin Way. M Keyn 58 B3
Corn Hill. M Keyn 33 F1
Corn Market. H Wyc 173 D4
Cornbrook Rd. Ayl 115 E3
Cornbury Cres. M Keyn 35 D3
Cornel Cl. Ty Gr 163 D2
Cornelia Cl. M Keyn 58 B3
Cornerways. Lac G 150 B3
Cornfield Cl. Uxb 201 E2
Cornwall Ave. Slough 198 B1
Cornwall Cl. Maid 195 F1
Cornwall Gr. M Keyn 46 C1
Cornwall Rd. Uxb 201 E3
Cornwell Rd. Old W 211 D1
Coronation Cres. La En 171 E3
Coronation Ave. Slough 206 C4
Coronation Pl. Stp Cl 63 E1
Coronation Rd. Cran 25 D1
Coronation Rd. H Wyc 172 B2
Coronation Rd. M Keyn 32 C3
Coronation Villas. Ayl 115 F4

Corporation St. H Wyc 173 D4
Corrigan Cl. M Keyn 58 A4
Corsham Ct. M Keyn 33 F1
Cosgrove Rd. Old S 32 B4
Cotman Cl. M Keyn 33 D3
Cotswold Cl. L Buzz 80 B4
Cotswold Cl. Maid 203 D3
Cotswold Cl. Slough 205 E2
Cotswold Cl. Uxb 201 E2
Cotswold Green. Ayl 101 F1
Cotswold Way. H Wyc 172 C4
Cottage Grounds. Sto 114 B3
Cottage Park Rd. Hedg 187 E1
Cottesbrooke Cl. Stan 212 B3
Cottesloe Cl. Wing 79 F2
Cottesloe Ct. M Keyn 32 C3
Cottesloe Rd. Ayl 115 F3
Cottingham Gr. M Keyn 58 A4
Cottisford Cres. M Keyn 21 F1
Cottland Clay. Hadd 127 D4
Coulson Way. Burn 204 A4
Countisbury. M Keyn 46 B1
County Rd. Brac 38 A3
Cours La Ville Cl. Wins 65 F2
Court Cl. Ayl 115 F4
Court Cl. Holy 203 E1
Court Cl. P Ris 139 D2
Court Cnr. Oln 6 C2
Court Cres. Slough 205 E4
Court Dr. Maid 196 B2
Court Dr. Uxb 201 F2
Court La. Burn 197 E1
Court Lawns. Ty Gr 163 E1
Court Rd. Cran 25 D1
Court Rd. Maid 196 B2
Court The. Sal 37 E2
Courtfield Gdns. Den 190 A1
Courtfields Dr. Maid 202 B3
Courthouse Cl. Wins 65 F3
Courthouse Rd. Maid 202 B4
Courtlands. Maid 202 C3
Courtlands Ave. Slough 206 B1
Coventon Rd. Ayl 101 E1
Coverdale. M Keyn 46 B3
Coverdale Way. Slough 197 F1
Covert Cl. Berk 134 B3
Covert Rd. Berk 134 B3
Cow La. Edle 92 C2
Cow La. Gawt 51 F2
Cow La. Tri 119 E2
Cowdray Cl. M Keyn 35 E2
Cowleaze. Chin 147 D3
Cowley Cl. Bier 102 A2
Cowley Cres. Uxb 208 B4
Cowley Mill Rd. Uxb 201 D2
Cowley Rd. Uxb 201 E2
Cowper Cl. N Pag 22 A2
Cowper Rd. Berk 135 D2
Cowper Rd. Ches 144 A1
Cowper Rd. Oln 6 C2
Cowper Rd. Slough 198 A1
Cowper St. Oln 7 D3
Cowpers Orch. W Und 6 A1
Cowslip Cl. Uxb 201 F3
Cowslip Rd. Hol G 162 C4
Cox Green La. Maid 202 B2
Cox Green Rd. Maid 202 B2
Coxborrow Cl. Cook 195 F4
Coxwell Cl. Buck 41 F1
Crab Tree Cl. Beac 175 D1
Crab Tree Cl. Oln 6 C3
Crabbe Cres. Ches 144 B1
Crabtree Rd. Hadd 127 D3
Craddocks Cl. M Keyn 34 A2
Cradley Wlk. Ayl 101 F2
Craigmore Ave. M Keyn 57 F4
Craigwell Ave. Ayl 116 B4
Cranberry Cl. Walt 48 A3
Cranbourne Ave. Wind 209 F3
Cranbourne Cl. Slough 205 E3
Cranbourne Rd. Slough 205 E3
Cranbrook Dr. Maid 195 E1
Crane Way. Cran 25 E1
Cranes Cl. Turv 8 C3
Cranesbill Pl. M Keyn 34 C2
Cranfield Rd. Ast 16 A1
Cranfield Rd. Cran 25 F2
Cranfield Rd. Moul 36 C4
Cranfield Rd. Sal 37 E3
Cranfield Rd. Wave 49 D4
Craufurd Rise. Maid 202 C4
Craven The. M Keyn 34 B2
Crawley Rd. Cran 25 D2
Crawley Rd. Hth 60 C4
Crawley's La. Wigg 133 F4
Crayle St. Slough 198 A1
Creed St. M Keyn 33 E4
Creighton Rd. W Und 83 F1
Crendon Rd. Chea 112 A1
Crendon St. H Wyc 173 D3
Crescent Dr. Maid 202 C4
Crescent The. Cran 24 C1
Crescent The. H Wyc 173 F4
Crescent The. Have 20 C1
Crescent The. Have 20 C1
Crescent The. M Keyn 21 F1
Crescent The. M Keyn 47 E1
Crescent The. Maid 202 C4
Crescent The. Mars 105 D1
Crescent The. P Ris 139 E2
Crescent The. Pit 105 E2
Crescent The. Slough 205 F2
Creslow Ct. M Keyn 32 C3
Cress Rd. Slough 205 D2
Cressex Rd. H Wyc 172 B2
Cressington Pl. Bou E 185 D2
Cresswell Rd. Ches 154 B3
Cresswell Way. Hol G 163 E4
Cresswells Mead. Holy 203 E1
Crest Rd. Lit M 172 B2
Crest The. Bled R 159 F4
Creswick Meadow. Ayl 116 A3
Crew Curve. Berk 134 C4
Cricket Field Rd. Uxb 201 E2
Cricket Ground. Skch 158 B3
Cricketers Row. Wins 66 A2
Cricketfield Rd. W Dra 208 B1
Cricklebeck. M Keyn 34 A3
Crimp Hill. Old W 211 D1
Crisp Rd. Hen-O-T 191 E2
Crispen Rd. M Keyn 34 A4
Crispin Cl. Beac 175 E2
Crispin Field. Pit 105 E2
Crispin Way. Far C 198 B4
Crispin Way. H Wyc 173 D2
Criss Gr. Ger C 177 E1
Crocketts La. Lee C 142 B3
Crocus Dr. Ayl 115 D3
Croft Courtyard. Hadd 126 C3
Croft Green. Dun 93 F4
Croft Rd. Ayl 115 F4
Croft Rd. Ger C 177 F1
Croft The. Hadd 126 C3
Croft The. Maid 202 B3
Croft The. Mar 184 A2
Crofthill Rd. Slough 198 A1
Crofts End. Sher 14 A1
Crofts La. Nwtn L 57 F2
Croftwood. H Wyc 173 F4
Cromarty Ct. M Keyn 46 C2
Cromer Cl. L Gad 121 F2
Cromhamstone. Sto 114 B3
Cromwell Ave. Ayl 101 E1
Cromwell Ave. N Pag 22 A2
Cromwell Ave. Tha 126 A1
Cromwell Cl. C St G 177 E4
Cromwell Ct. Buck 41 F1
Cromwell Dr. Slough 205 F4
Cromwell Gdns. Mar 183 F1
Cromwell Rd. H Wyc 173 F3
Cromwell Rd. Maid 202 B4
Cromwell Rd. Mar 183 F1
Cropredy Ct. Buck 41 F1
Cropwell Bishop. M Keyn 46 B1
Crosby Cl. Beac 186 C4
Crosby Ct. She C E 45 F3
Crosland Rd. Ayl 116 A3
Cross End. Wave 48 C4
Cross La. Beac 186 C4
Cross La. Ting 51 D3
Cross La. W Und 6 A1
Cross Lanes. C St P 177 F3
Cross Lanes Cl. C St P 177 F3
Cross Meadow. Ches 143 F1
Cross Oak. Wind 210 A3
Cross Oak Rd. Berk 135 D2
Cross Rd. H Wyc 172 B3
Cross Rd. Uxb 201 E3
Cross St. N Pag 22 B2
Cross St. Uxb 201 E3
Cross Tree Rd. Wick 31 D2
Crossfield Cl. Berk 134 C2
Crossfield Rd. P Ris 139 D2
Crosshills. M Keyn 32 B2
Crosslands. M Keyn 34 C4
Crossley's Hill. C St G 177 E4
Crossleys. C St G 177 E4
Crossway. Ches 144 C1
Crossway The. Uxb 201 F2
Crossways. Berk 134 C2
Crow La. Wave 49 D4
Crow Piece La. Burn 197 F2
Crowbrook Rd. P Ris 139 E3
Crown La. Burn 198 A2
Crown La. H Wyc 173 D3
Crown La. Maid 203 D4
Crown La. Ty Gr 174 C4
Crown Meadow. Iver 212 A4
Crown Rd. Mar 183 E1
Crown Way. W Dra 208 C3
Crown Wlk. M Keyn 34 C2
Crowther Ct. She B E 46 B3
Croxley Rise. Maid 202 B3
Cruickshank Gr. She C E 45 F4
Crummock Pl. M Keyn 58 B3
Crutches La. Se Gr 176 C2
Cryers Hill La. G Kin 162 B3
Cubb Field. Ayl 115 D4
Cublington Rd. A Abb 88 B3
Cuddington Hill. Cudd 112 C2
Cuddington Rd. Dint 113 F2
Cuff La. G Bkhl 59 E1
Culbertson La. M Keyn 33 F3
Culham Dr. Maid 195 F1
Cullen Pl. M Keyn 58 B3
Cullern's Pass. Maid 202 C3
Culley Way. Maid 202 A2
Cullyn Rd. H Wyc 172 B2
Culmstock Cl. M Keyn 46 B1
Culrain Pl. M Keyn 33 E2
Culvers Croft. Se Gr 176 B2
Culvert La. Uxb 201 D2
Culverton Hill. P Ris 139 D2
Culverton La. P Ris 139 D1
Cumberland Ave. Slough 198 B1
Cumberland Cl. Ayl 116 A4
Cumberland Cl. L Chal 166 A4
Cumbria Cl. Maid 202 B2
Cumbrian Way. H Wyc 172 C4
Cumbrian Way. Uxb 201 E3
Curlew Cl. Berk 135 E2
Curlew Cl. H Wyc 161 E1
Curls La. Maid 202 C2
Curls Rd. Maid 202 B2
Curran Cl. Uxb 201 E1
Currier Dr. M Keyn 34 C3
Curriers La. Burn 197 E4
Curtis Way. Berk 135 E2
Curzon Ave. Beac 175 E2
Curzon Ave. Ty Gr 163 E1
Curzon Cl. Ty Gr 163 E1
Cutlers Mews. M Keyn 34 C3
Cuttlebrook Gdns. Tha 125 E1
Cypress. N Pag 22 A2
Cypress Wlk. Ty Gr 163 D2

D'ville Ct. She C E 46 A3
Dacre Rd. Hal 131 F4
Dadbrook. Cudd 112 C1
Dadbrook Cl. Cudd 112 C1
Dadfield Cl. Cudd 112 C1
Dag Lane. S Gol 12 A4
Dagmar Rd. Wind 210 B3
Dagnall Cres. Uxb 208 B4
Dagnall Rd. Eat B 93 E1
Dagnall Rd. Oln 6 C2
Dairy La. Hamb 192 A4
Dale Cl. Brac 38 A4
Dale Ct. Slough 205 E2
Dale Side. Ger C 188 C1
Dalesford Rd. Ayl 116 A2
Dalston Cl. Ayl 101 F1
Dalvina Pl. M Keyn 33 E2
Dancers End La. Dra B 118 B1
Dandridge Cl. Slough 206 B1
Dandridge Dr. Bou E 185 E2
Dane Cl. Ame 165 F3
Dane Ct. Ayl 115 E2
Dane Rd. M Keyn 47 F1
Daniels Welch. M Keyn 47 D3
Danstead Way. She C E 45 E4
Dansteed Way. M Keyn 34 B2
Danvers Croft. Tri 119 E3
Darin Ct. She C E 45 F4
Dark La. Chea 112 A1
Dark La. Oving 86 B4
Dark La. Win 89 E1
Darley Cl. Ayl 116 A3
Darley Gate. M Keyn 35 D3
Darley's Cl. Gr Und 83 D3
Darling's La. Bish 194 C1
Darlington Cl. Ame 154 B1
Darnel Cl. M Keyn 47 D3
Darr's La. Berk 134 B3
Darrell Cl. Slough 206 C1
Dart Cl. Ayl 115 E3
Dart Cl. N Pag 22 B2
Dart Cl. Slough 212 A4
Dartmouth Rd. Oln 6 C2
Darvell Dr. Ches 144 A1
Darvill Rd. Sto 114 A3
Darvill's La. Slough 205 E2
Darvills Meadow. Hol G 163 E4
Darwin Rd. Slough 206 C2
Dashfield Gr. Hol G 162 C3
Dashwood Ave. H Wyc 172 B4
Dashwood Cl. Slough 206 B1
Datchet Pl. Datch 211 D3
Datchet Rd. Datch 205 F1
Datchet Rd. Eton 205 F1
Datchet Rd. Hort 211 F2
Datchet Rd. Old W 211 D2
Datchet Rd. Wind 210 B4
Daubeney Gate. She C E 45 F3
Daventry Cl. Stan 212 C3
David Cl. Ayl 116 A2
David Rd. Stan 212 C3
Davies Cl. Ayl 115 E4
Davies Ct. H Wyc 172 B3
Davis Cl. Mar 183 F1
Davy Ave. M Keyn 46 B3
Dawes Cl. Ches 154 A4
Dawes East Rd. Burn 197 E1
Dawes La. Sar 156 C2
Dawes Moor Cl. Slough 206 B4
Dawley Ride. Stan 212 C3
Dawn Redwood Cl. Hort 212 A2
Daws Hill La. H Wyc 173 D2
Daws Lea. H Wyc 173 D2
Dawson Cl. Wind 210 A3
Dawson Rd. M Keyn 47 E2
Daylesford Ct. M Keyn 35 D3
De Clare Ct. Buck 41 F1
De Havilland Way. Stan 213 F1
Deacon Cl. H Wyc 172 A2
Deadhearn La. C St G 166 C1
Dean Cl. Ayl 116 A3
Dean Cl. H Wyc 172 C3
Dean Cl. Uxb 201 F3
Dean Cl. Wind 209 E2
Dean Farm La. Soul 69 F2
Dean Field. Bov 146 A2
Dean La. Cook 195 E4
Dean Rd. Stew 68 A1
Dean St. Mar 183 E1
Dean The. Win 89 D2
Dean Way. C St G 177 D4
Dean Wood Rd. Se Gr 176 B1
Dean's Rd. M Keyn 33 E4
Deanacre Cl. C St P 177 F2
Deancroft Rd. C St P 177 F2
Deanfield Ave. Hen-O-T 191 E1
Deanfield Cl. Bled R 149 E1
Deanfield Cl. Mar 183 E2
Deanfield Rd. Hen-O-T 191 E1
Deangarden Rise. H Wyc 173 F2
Deans Cl. Ame 154 C1
Deans Cl. Sto P 199 D2
Deans Cl. Tri 119 D2
Deans Furlong. Tri 119 D2
Deans Meadow. Dag 107 E3
Deanshanger Rd. Old S 32 A3
Deanshanger Rd. Wick 31 D2
Deansway. Ches 144 A1
Deben Cl. N Pag 22 C2
Decies Way. Sto P 199 D2
Dedmere Ct. Mar 183 F1
Dedmere Rd. Mar 183 F1
Dedmere Rise. Mar 183 F1
Dedworth Dr. Wind 209 F3
Dedworth Rd. Wind 209 E3
Deep Acres. Ame 154 A2
Deep Field. Datch 211 D4
Deep Mill La. L Kin 152 B2
Deepdale. M Keyn 34 B3
Deerfern Cl. M Keyn 21 F1
Deerfield Cl. Buck 52 C4
Deermead. L Kin 152 A2
Deerswood. Maid 196 A1
Deethe Cl. Wbn S 49 D3
Delahay Rise. Berk 135 D3
Delamere Cl. Ayl 101 F1
Delamere Gdns. L Buzz 80 B4
Delaware Dr. M Keyn 35 D4
Dell Cl. Far C 198 B4
Dell Field. Pres 151 E3
Dell Lees. Se Gr 176 B2
Dell Rd. Berk 134 B4
Dell Rd. W Dra 208 C2
Dell The. Ayl 102 A1
Dell The. C St P 177 F2
Dell The. Maid 202 A1
Dell The. Ty Gr 163 E1
Dellfield. Ches 144 A1
Dellfield Ave. Berk 135 D3
Dellfield Cl. Berk 135 D3
Dellfield Cres. Uxb 201 E1
Dells. Oln 6 C2
Dellside. S Har 190 B3
Delmeade Rd. Ches 154 A4
Deltic Ave. M Keyn 34 A1
Demoram Cl. Wins 65 F2
Denbigh Hall. M Keyn 46 C2
Denbigh Hall Dr. M Keyn 46 C2
Denbigh Rd. M Keyn 47 D1
Denbigh Rd. Tha 126 A1
Denbigh Way. M Keyn 47 E1
Denborough Cres. Maid 202 B3
Denby Walk. Ayl 116 A4
Dene Cl. Asp G 49 E2
Dene Cl. Wins 66 A2
Dene The. Stp Cl 63 E2
Denewood. H Wyc 173 F4
Denham Ave. Den G 189 F2
Denham Cl. Den 190 A1
Denham Cl. M Keyn 57 E4
Denham Cl. Maid 202 B3
Denham Green Cl. Den G 190 A2
Denham Green La. Den G 189 F3
Denham La. C St P 178 A1
Denham Rd. Iver H 200 C3
Denham Rd. La En 171 E3
Denham View. Gran 75 F3
Denham Way. Den 190 A1
Denham Way. Map Cr 178 C2
Denham Wlk. C St P 177 F2
Denmark St. H Wyc 173 D4
Denmark St. M Keyn 58 C4
Denmark St. Maid 202 C4
Denmead. M Keyn 33 F1
Denmead Cl. Ger C 188 C2
Denny Rd. Slough 206 C1
Depot Rd. Maid 203 D3
Derby Rd. Uxb 201 E2
Dere Pl. M Keyn 58 C2
Derehams Ave. Loud 174 B2
Derehams La. Loud 174 B2
Derek Rd. Maid 203 E4
Deri Dene Cl. Stan 213 F1
Derwent Cl. N Pag 22 B2
Derwent Dr. Burn 204 B4
Derwent Dr. M Keyn 57 F4
Derwent Dr. Maid 202 B4
Derwent Rd. L Buzz 80 A4
Desborough Ave. H Wyc 172 C3
Desborough Green. Ayl 101 E1
Desborough Ind Pk. H Wyc 172 C4
Desborough Park Rd. H Wyc 172 C4
Desborough Rd. H Wyc 172 C4
Desborough St. H Wyc 172 C4
Deseronto Wharf. Slough 206 C2
Develin Cl. M Keyn 34 C4
Devereux Pl. Ayl 101 D1
Devereux Rd. Wind 210 B3
Deverill Rd. S Man 115 E2
Devon Ave. Slough 205 E4
Devon Cl. M Keyn 46 C1
Devon Way. Uxb 201 F2
Devonshire Ave. Ame 154 A1
Devonshire Cl. Ame 154 B1
Devonshire Cl. Far C 198 A2
Devonshire Green. Far C 198 A2
Dexter Ave. M Keyn 46 C4
Dhoon Rise. Maid 202 C3
Diamond Rd. Slough 206 A2
Diana Cl. Slough 206 C4
Dickens Rd. M Keyn 33 E4
Dickens Way. Ayl 100 C1
Dicks Way. Ayl 100 C2
Dingle Dell. L Buzz 70 C1
Dinglederry. Oln 6 C2
Dinmore. Bov 145 F2
Disraeli Cres. H Wyc 161 F1
Disraeli Ct. Slough 212 A4
Disraeli Park. Beac 175 E2
Ditchingham Cl. Ayl 115 D4
Ditton Park Rd. Datch 211 F4
Ditton Rd. Datch 211 E3
Ditton Rd. Slough 211 F4
Dobbins La. Wen 131 D3
Dobson's La. Faw 191 E4
Doctors' Common Rd. Berk 135 D2
Dodkin. M Keyn 47 D3
Dodsfield Rd. Slough 198 A1
Dog Kennel La. Chor 167 F3
Doggett St. L Buzz 80 C4
Doggetts Farm Rd. Den G 189 E2
Doggetts Wood Cl. L Chal 166 B3
Doggetts Wood La. L Chal 166 B3
Dolben Ct. M Keyn 35 E4
Dolesden La. Ibst 169 E1
Dollicot. Hadd 126 C4
Dolphin Ct. Slough 206 A2
Dolphin Rd. Slough 206 A2
Dolphin Sq. Tri 119 D2
Don The. M Keyn 46 B1
Donnay Cl. Ger C 188 B3
Donnington. M Keyn 34 A3
Doon Way. M Keyn 58 B3
Dorchester Cl. S Man 116 A1
Dorchester Ave. M Keyn 47 D1
Dorchester Cl. Maid 195 D1
Doreen Cl. M Keyn 58 B4
Dormans Cl. M K Vil 36 A1
Dormer Ave. Wing 79 F2
Dormer Cl. Ayl 115 D3
Dormer Ct. Ayl 101 F1
Dormer La. Hol G 163 D4
Dornels. Slough 206 B4
Dorney End. Ches 144 A1
Dorney Hill S. Hedg 187 D2
Dorney Pl. M Keyn 34 B2
Dorney Reach Rd. Dorn 203 F2
Dorney Wood Rd. Burn 197 E3
Dorrells Rd. Lgwk 138 B3
Dorrien's Croft. Berk 134 C4
Dorset Cl. Berk 134 C3
Dorset Cl. M Keyn 46 C1
Dorset Pl. Ayl 116 B3
Dorset Rd. Wind 210 B3
Dorset Way. Uxb 201 F2
Dorton Cl. M Keyn 33 F1
Douglas Ct. Mar 184 A2
Douglas Gdns. Berk 135 D3
Douglas La. Wray 211 F1
Douglas Pl. M Keyn 46 C4
Douglas Rd. Ayl 102 A1
Douglas Rd. Slough 205 E4
Douglas Rd. Stan 213 E1
Dove Cl. Ayl 115 E3
Dove Cl. Buck 52 C4
Dove Cl. N Pag 22 B2
Dove House Cl. Edle 92 C2
Dove House Cl. Wins 66 A2
Dove House Cres. Slough 197 F1
Dove Park. Chor 167 D2
Dove St. Stew 78 C4
Dovecot Rd. H Wyc 173 D4
Dovecote. Hadd 126 C3
Dovecote. N Pag 22 B2
Dovecote Cl. Hadd 126 C3
Dovecote Cl. P Ris 139 E3
Doveleat. Chin 147 E4
Dover Gate. M Keyn 57 F4
Dover Hedge. Ayl 116 B4
Dower Cl. Beac 175 E3
Dower Park. Wind 209 F2
Down Pl. Oak G 209 D4
Downdean. M Keyn 47 D4
Downer Cl. Buck 52 C4
Downham Rd. Wbn S 49 E2
Downing Path. Burn 197 F1
Downings Wood. Map Cr 178 B3
Downland. M Keyn 33 F1
Downley Ave. M Keyn 34 B2

Downley Rd. Wal A 161 E3
Downs Park. H Wyc 161 F1
Downs Rd. Slough 206 B2
Downs View. B Bkhl 48 B1
Drake Ave. Slough 206 B1
Drake's Rd. Ame 165 F4
Drakeloe Cl. Hth 60 C4
Drakes Mews. She C E 45 F4
Drakewell Rd. B Bkhl 48 B1
Drayton Gdns. W Dra 208 C2
Drayton Rd. Ayl 101 E1
Drayton Rd. M Keyn 58 B3
Drayton Rd. Nwtn L 57 E1
Dresser Rd. Pres 151 E3
Drew Meadow. Far C 198 B4
Drews Park. Beac 175 E3
Drey The. C St P 177 F3
Drift Rd. Oak G 209 D1
Drift Way. Iver 212 B4
Drift Way. Oln 6 C3
Drive The. Ame 154 B1
Drive The. Bou E 184 C2
Drive The. C St P 177 F2
Drive The. Cran 24 B1
Drive The. Datch 211 D3
Drive The. Ick 190 C1
Drive The. Slough 206 C2
Drive The. Wray 211 E1
Dropmore Rd. Burn 197 E3
Drovers Croft. M Keyn 33 D2
Drovers La. Ibst 169 D1
Drovers Way. Dun 93 F4
Drovers Way. Se Gr 176 B2
Druids Wlk. Chin 147 E3
Drummond Ride. Tri 119 D3
Drydell La. Ches 153 F4
Dryden Cl. Ayl 101 F1
Dryden Cl. N Pag 22 A2
Du Pre Wlk. Bou E 185 E2
Duck End. G Bkhl 59 E1
Duck La. Hth 60 C4
Duck La. Lud 96 B4
Duck Sq. Chin 147 E3
Duckmore La. Tri 118 C1
Dudley La. Frie 181 D3
Dudswell La. Berk 134 B4
Duffield La. Sto P 198 C3
Duffield Park. Sto P 199 D1
Duke St. Asp G 49 E2
Duke St. Eton 210 B4
Duke St. H Wyc 173 E3
Duke St. Hen-O-T 191 F1
Duke St. P Ris 139 D2
Dukes Cl. Ger C 188 B2
Dukes Cl. Shab 124 B1
Dukes Dr. M Keyn 47 E1
Dukes La. Ger C 188 C2
Dukes Piece. Buck 52 C4
Dukes Pl. Mar 183 E1
Dukes Ride. Ger C 188 C2
Dukes Ride. L Buzz 70 C2
Dukes Way. Berk 135 D3
Dukes Wood Ave. Ger C 188 C2
Dukes Wood Dr. Ger C 188 B2
Dulverton Dr. She B E 46 B2
Dulwich Cl. N Pag 22 B1
Dumfries Cl. M Keyn 46 C2
Dunbar Cl. M Keyn 57 E4
Dunbar Dr. Tha 126 A1
Duncan Rd. Cran 24 C1
Duncannon Cres. Wind 209 E2
Dunchurch Dale. Walt 48 A3
Duncombe Cl. Ame 154 C1
Duncombe Rd. Berk 134 C3
Duncombe St. M Keyn 58 B4
Duncroft. Wind 209 F2
Dundale Rd. Tri 119 D2
Dundee Rd. Slough 205 D4
Dungrovehill La. Bish 194 B2
Dunholme End. Maid 202 B2
Dunny La. Chipf 156 C4
Dunsham La. Ayl 101 F1
Dunsley Pl. Tri 119 D2
Dunsmore Ave. P Ris 139 E3
Dunsmore Ride. P Ris 139 E3
Dunstable Rd. Dag 107 E4
Dunstable Rd. Eat B 93 D3
Dunstable Rd. Tott 93 E4
Dunster Ct. M Keyn 46 C2
Dunster Gdns. Slough 205 D3
Dunston Hill. Tri 119 D2
Dunton Rd. Stew 78 B3
Dunvedin Pl. M Keyn 33 E2
Dunvegan Cl. M Keyn 58 B2
Dupre Cres. Beac 176 A1
Durham Ave. Slough 205 D4
Durrans Ct. M Keyn 47 F1
Durrants La. Berk 134 C3
Durrants Path. Ches 144 A2
Durrants Rd. Berk 134 C3
Durrell Cl. L Buzz 80 C4
Dutch Barn Cl. Stan 213 E1
Dyers Mews. M Keyn 34 C3
Dyersdale. M Keyn 34 B3
Dyson Cl. Wind 210 A2

Eagle Wlk. M Keyn 34 C2
Eagles Rd. Ayl 116 A4
Eames Cl. Ayl 101 F2
Earl Cl. H Wyc 162 A1
Earl Howe Rd. Hol G 163 E3
Earls Cl. M Keyn 58 B4
Earls Willow. M Keyn 34 A4
Earlsfield. Holy 203 E1
Earlswood Cl. Ayl 116 A3
Easington La. Chil 111 D1
East Burnham La. Burn 198 A2
East Common. Ger C 188 C3
East Cres. Wind 209 F3
East Dales. M Keyn 34 B3
East Dr. H Wyc 173 F4
East Dr. Sto P 198 C1
East Hills. Cran 25 D1
East Paddock. Bish 194 C3
East Rd. Cran 24 C1
East Rd. Maid 202 C4
East Rd. W Dra 208 C1
East Ridge. Bou E 185 D2
East St. Adsk 53 F1
East St. Ches 154 A4
East St. Oln 6 C2
East Way. Beac 175 D1
Eastbourne Rd. Slough 205 D4
Eastbridge. Slough 206 A3
Eastbrook Cl. Pidd (B) 95 F4
Eastbury Ct. M Keyn 46 B1
Eastcote Rd. Ayl 116 A2
Eastcourt Dr. Hol G 162 C3
Eastcroft. Slough 198 A1
Eastergate. Beac 175 E2
Eastern Dene. Hol G 163 D3
Eastern Dr. Bou E 185 E2
Eastern St. Ayl 101 F1
Eastfield Cl. Slough 206 A2
Eastfield Cres. Yard G 18 C3
Eastfield Dr. Hans 11 D2
Eastfield Rd. Ayl 116 A4
Eastfield Rd. Burn 204 A4
Eastfield Rd. P Ris 139 E2
Eastlands. Lac G 149 F3
Eastnor. Bov 146 A2
Easton St. H Wyc 173 D3
Easton Terr. H Wyc 173 E3
Eastwick Cres. Chor 178 C4
Eastwood Rd. Skch 158 C2
Eaton Ave. H Wyc 172 B4
Eaton Ave. M Keyn 58 B4
Eaton Bray Rd. Edle 92 B3
Eaton Bray Rd. Tott 92 C4
Eaton Rd. Ayl 115 E4
Ebble Cl. Ayl 115 E2
Ebsworth Cl. Maid 196 B2
Eddington Ct. M Keyn 46 B1
Eddy St. Berk 135 D3
Eden Cl. S Man 115 E2
Eden Wlk. M Keyn 46 C1
Edgar Rd. W Dra 208 C3
Edge Hill Ct. Buck 41 F1
Edgecombe Rd. Ayl 116 A3
Edgecote. M Keyn 46 A4
Edgehill. Tha 125 F1
Edgewood. H Wyc 173 E3
Edinburgh Ave. Slough 205 D4
Edinburgh Dr. Den G 189 F3
Edinburgh Rd. Maid 195 F1
Edinburgh Rd. Mar 183 F2
Edison Sq. She B E 46 B3
Edith Rd. Maid 202 A4
Edlyn Cl. Berk 134 C3
Edmonds Cl. Buck 41 F1
Edmonds Rd. La En 171 D2
Edmund Ct. She C E 45 F4
Edmunds Cl. H Wyc 172 B3
Edmunds Gdns. H Wyc 172 B3
Edmunds Way. Slough 206 A4
Edrich Ave. M Keyn 46 C4
Edward Cl. Ayl 116 A2
Edward Walk. Ayl 116 A2
Edwards Ct. Slough 205 F2
Edwin Cl. B Bkhl 48 B1
Edy Ct. M Keyn 34 A1
Eeles Cl. Ayl 100 C2
Egerton Cl. Brac 38 A4
Egerton Rd. Berk 135 D3
Egerton Rd. Slough 197 F1
Eghams Cl. Beac 175 E2
Eghams Wood Rd. Beac 175 E2
Egmont Ave. M Keyn 32 C3
Egremont Gdns. Slough 205 D3
Egypt La. Burn 187 D1
Eight Acres. Burn 197 D1
Eight Acres. Tri 119 D2
Elbow Meadow. Stan 212 C3
Elder Cl. Loud 174 A2
Elder Gate. M Keyn 34 B1
Elder Way. Ty Gr 163 D2
Elderdene. Chin 147 E4
Elderfield Rd. Sto P 198 C3
Eleanor Cl. Hth 60 C4
Eleanor Gdns. Ayl 115 F3
Eleanor Rd. Ger C 177 E1
Eleanor Wlk. Hth 60 C4
Elfords. M Keyn 47 D3
Elgar Gr. Walt 48 B2
Elgiva La. Ches 154 A4
Elham Way. Ayl 116 A2
Eliot Cl. Ayl 100 C1
Eliot Cl. N Pag 21 F3
Elizabeth Cl. Ayl 116 A2
Elizabeth Dr. Tri 119 D3
Elizabeth Rd. Mar 183 F2
Elizabeth Rd. Skch 158 C2
Elizabeth Way. Sto P 198 C2
Elkins Rd. Hedg 187 F1
Ellen Pl. Ayl 115 E3
Ellen Rd. Ayl 115 E3
Ellenstow. M Keyn 34 A2
Ellery Rise. Frie 170 C1
Ellesborough Rd. Wen 131 D2
Ellesmere Cl. Tott 93 E3
Ellesmere Rd. Berk 135 E2
Elliman Ave. Slough 205 F3
Ellington Ct. Tapl 203 E4
Ellington Gdns. Tapl 203 E4
Ellington Park. Maid 195 F1
Ellington Rd. Tapl 203 E4
Elliot Dr. Mar 183 F2
Ellis Ave. C St P 177 F1
Ellis Ave. Slough 205 F2
Ellisgill Ct. M Keyn 34 A2
Ellison Cl. Wind 209 F2
Ellsworth Rd. H Wyc 172 C2
Ellwood Rd. Beac 175 D1
Ellwood Rise. C St G 177 E4
Elm Brook Cl. Chea 112 B1
Elm Cl. Ame 154 B1
Elm Cl. Chin 147 E3
Elm Cl. Elle 130 B2
Elm Cl. Far C 198 B3
Elm Cl. Nwtn L 57 E1
Elm Cl. Ty Gr 163 D2
Elm Cl. W Tur 116 C1
Elm Croft. Datch 211 E3
Elm Dr. Chin 147 E3
Elm Dr. Dean 31 E3
Elm Farm Rd. Ayl 116 A3
Elm Gr. Berk 135 E2
Elm Gr. Maid 202 C4
Elm Gr. W Dra 208 C3
Elm Gr. Wbn S 49 D2
Elm Green. Ayl 115 E4
Elm La. Bou E 184 C3
Elm Lawn Cl. Uxb 201 F3
Elm Rd. H Wyc 172 B2
Elm Rd. Ty Gr 174 B4
Elm Rd. Wind 210 A2
Elm St. Buck 52 B4
Elm Tree Wlk. Tri 119 D3
Elm Trees. L Cre 125 D4
Elmar Green. Slough 198 A1
Elmdale Gdns. P Ris 139 D2
Elmers Cl. Beac 44 A3
Elmers Park. M Keyn 58 A4
Elmfields Gate. Wins 66 A2
Elmhurst Cl. M Keyn 46 C2
Elmhurst Rd. Ayl 101 F1
Elmlea Dr. Oln 6 C2
Elms Dr. Bou E 185 E2
Elms Rd. C St P 177 F2
Elms The. M Keyn 57 F4
Elmshott Cl. Ty Gr 163 D1
Elmside. Wins 66 A2
Elmtree Green. S Hea 152 A4
Elmtree Hill. Ches 144 A1
Elmwood. Turv 8 C3
Elmwood Cl. Oak 109 E3
Elmwood Cl. Oak 109 E3
Elmwood Park. Ger C 188 C2
Elmwood Rd. Slough 206 A3
Elora Rd. H Wyc 173 F4
Elruge Cl. W Dra 208 B2
Elsmore Cl. Ayl 116 A2
Elthorne Rd. Uxb 201 E2
Elthorne Way. N Pag 22 B1
Elton. M Keyn 47 E4
Elton Dr. Maid 202 B4
Elwes Rd. La En 171 E2
Ely Ave. Slough 205 E4
Ely Cl. Ame 165 F4
Ember Path. Ayl 115 E2
Emberton Gdns. M Keyn 32 C3
Emerald Cl. E Clay 74 C4
Emerald Ct. Slough 205 F2
Emerton Ct. Berk 134 C4
Emerton Garth. Berk 134 C4
Emlyns Bldgs. Eton 210 B4
Emma Rothschild Cl. Tri 119 D3
Enborne Cl. S Man 115 E2
Enfield Cl. Uxb 201 E2
Engaine Dr. She C E 45 F4
English Gdns. Wray 211 E1
Enmore Gate. M Keyn 35 D2
Ennell Gr. M Keyn 58 B3
Ennerdale Cl. M Keyn 58 B3
Ennerdale Cres. Burn 204 B4
Enstone Rd. Ick 190 C1
Epsom Gr. M Keyn 57 E3
Eriboll Cl. L Buzz 80 A4
Erica Rd. M Keyn 33 F2
Esk Way. M Keyn 46 C1
Eskdale Ave. Ches 144 B1
Eskdale Gdns. Holy 203 D1
Eskdale Rd. S Man 116 A1
Eskdale Rd. Uxb 201 D2
Essendon Ct. M Keyn 32 C3
Essex Ave. Slough 205 E4
Essex Cl. M Keyn 46 C1
Essex Rd. Ches 144 B1
Eston Ct. M Keyn 34 A3
Estover Way. Chin 147 D3
Ethorpe. M Keyn 33 F1
Ethorpe Cl. Ger C 188 C3
Ethorpe Cres. Ger C 188 C3
Eton Cl. Datch 211 D4
Eton Cres. M Keyn 33 E3
Eton Ct. Eton 210 B4
Eton Pl. Mar 183 B1
Eton Rd. Datch 211 D4
Eton Sq. Eton 210 B4
Eton Wick Rd. Eton 205 D1
Eunice Rd. Ches 154 B4
Evans Cl. Ayl 116 A2
Evans Gate. M Keyn 46 C4
Evelyn Cl. Wing 79 F1
Evelyns Cl. Uxb 208 C4
Evenlode. Maid 202 C4
Evenlode Cl. Ayl 115 E3
Evenlode Rd. Bou E 185 D2
Everard Ave. Slough 205 F2
Everest Cl. H Wyc 173 E3
Everest Rd. H Wyc 173 F3
Everglade. M Keyn 47 D4
Exchange St. Ayl 115 F4
Exmoor Gate. M Keyn 46 C1
Eyethrope Rd. Sto 114 A3
Eynsford Terr. W Dra 208 C4
Eynsham Ct. M Keyn 35 E1

Fagnall La. Cole 164 B1
Fair Acres. Pres 151 E3
Fair Leas. Ches 144 A1
Fair Meadow. Wins 66 A2
Fair Mile. Ayl 116 A4
Fair Mile. Hen-O-T 191 E2
Fairacre. Maid 202 B3
Fairacres Ind Est. Wind 209 E3
Faircroft. Slough 198 A1
Fairfax. M Keyn 34 B3
Fairfax Cres. Ayl 101 F1
Fairfax Mews. Ame 165 D4
Fairfield App. Wray 211 E1
Fairfield Ave. Datch 211 E4
Fairfield Cl. Datch 211 E4
Fairfield Cl. Oln 7 D2
Fairfield La. Far C 198 A2
Fairfield Rd. Burn 197 E1
Fairfield Rd. Paul 17 D4
Fairfield Rd. Uxb 201 E3
Fairfield Rd. W Dra 208 C3
Fairfield Rd. Wray 211 E1
Fairfields. G Kin 151 F1
Fairford Cres. M Keyn 35 D3
Fairford Rd. Maid 202 C4
Fairlawn Pk. Wind 209 F2
Fairlea. Maid 202 A2
Fairlie Rd. Slough 205 D4
Fairlight Ave. Wind 210 B3
Fairlight Dr. Uxb 201 E3
Fairthorn Cl. Tri 118 C2
Fairview La. Fla H 174 A1
Fairview Rd. Burn 204 A4
Fairview Rd. Slough 197 F1
Fairway. P Ris 139 D1
Fairway Ave. W Dra 208 B3
Fairway Cl. W Dra 208 B3
Fairway The. Burn 197 E2
Fairway The. Fla H 185 E4
Fairway The. Maid 202 A2
Fairway The. Uxb 201 F2
Fairways. M Keyn 33 E1
Falcon Ave. M Keyn 35 D1
Falcon Dr. Stan 213 F1
Falcon Ridge. Berk 135 E2
Falcons Croft. Woo G 185 F4
Falling La. W Dra 208 C3
Fallow Field. Ty Gr 163 D2
Falmouth Pl. M Keyn 34 C1
Falmouth Rd. Slough 205 D4
Fane Way. Maid 202 B3
Fantail La. Tri 118 C2
Faraday Cl. Slough 205 D4
Faraday Dr. She B E 46 B3
Faraday Rd. Ayl 101 D1
Faraday Rd. Slough 205 D4
Farinton. M Keyn 33 F1
Farm Cl. H Wyc 174 A4
Farm Cl. L Chal 166 B4
Farm Cl. Holy 203 E1
Farm Cl. Maid 202 A4
Farm Cl. Stew 78 C4
Farm Cres. Slough 206 B4
Farm Gr. Beac 175 E3
Farm La. Beac 176 B2
Farm Lea. Woo G 185 F4
Farm Pl. Berk 134 C3
Farm Rd. Bou E 184 C2
Farm Rd. Brac 38 A3
Farm Rd. Chor 167 D3
Farm Rd. Maid 202 A4
Farm Way. Stan 212 C1
Farm Yd. Wind 210 B4
Farmborough. M Keyn 47 E3
Farmborough Cl. Ayl 102 A1
Farmers Cl. Maid 202 A2
Farmers Way. Maid 202 A2
Farmers Way. Se Gr 176 B2
Farnburn Ave. Slough 205 D4
Farndale Gdns. Hol G 163 D3
Farnham Cl. Bov 146 A2
Farnham Ct. M Keyn 33 F1
Farnham La. Slough 198 A2
Farnham Park La. Far C 198 B2
Farnham Rd. Slough 205 E4
Farnley Rd. Ayl 101 F1
Farrer Cl. Whit 26 B2
Farrier Pl. M Keyn 35 D3
Farthing Gr. M Keyn 47 E3
Farthing Green La. Sto P 199 D2
Farthingales The. Maid 203 D4
Fassets Rd. Loud 174 A1
Faulkner Way. H Wyc 161 E2
Faulkner's Way. L Buzz 80 C4
Favell Dr. M Keyn 46 C2
Faversham Cl. Tri 119 D2
Fawcett Rd. Wind 210 A3
Fawley Bottom La. Faw 180 A1
Fawley Cl. Maid 195 E1
Fawsley Cl. Iver 212 C4
Featherbed La. Hol G 163 E4
Featherstone Rd. M Keyn 33 D3
Felden La. Fel 146 C4
Fells Cl. L Cre 125 E3
Fences La. Emb 13 D1
Fennel Dr. M Keyn 34 C2
Fennels Farm Rd. Fla H 174 A1
Fennels Rd. H Wyc 174 A2
Fennels Way. Fla H 174 A1
Fennimore Cl. Oak 109 E2
Fennings The. Ame 154 B2
Fenny Rd. S Ham 69 F4
Fennymere. M Keyn 33 E1
Fenton Ct. M Keyn 45 F4
Fern Dr. Burn 204 A4
Fern Gr. M Keyn 58 B3
Fern La. Hadd 127 D3
Fern La. Hadd 127 D4
Fern Wlk. Ty Gr 163 D2
Ferndale. M Keyn 35 D1
Ferndale Cl. Skch 158 C2
Ferndale Cres. Uxb 201 E1
Fernes Cl. Uxb 208 B4
Fernhill Cl. Tidd 136 A4
Fernhurst Cl. Beac 175 F1
Fernie Fields. H Wyc 172 B2
Fernley Ct. Maid 195 E1
Ferns The. Beac 175 F1
Fernside. G Kin 151 F1
Fernside. Hol G 163 D3
Fernsleigh Cl. C St P 177 F2
Ferrers Ave. W Dra 208 B2
Ferry La. Bou E 185 D1
Ferry La. Hamb 192 B3
Ferry La. Medm 193 D3
Ferry Rd. Maid 203 E2
Field Rd. Mur 94 A3
Field Cl. Ayl 102 A1
Field Cl. Ches 144 C2
Field Cl. Ick 124 A2
Field Cl. Sher 14 A1
Field End. L Cre 125 F3
Field End. Tri 119 D3
Field Hurst. Slough 206 C1
Field La. M Keyn 33 D3
Field Rd. Den 189 F1
Field Rd. H Wyc 172 A3
Field Way. Ayl 102 A1
Field Way. Bov 146 A3
Field Way. Ger C 177 E2
Field Way. Uxb 201 E1
Field Wlk. M Keyn 34 C2
Fieldhead Gdns. Bou E 185 D2
Fieldhouse Ind Est. Mar 183 F1
Fieldhouse La. Mar 183 F1
Fieldhouse Way. Mar 183 F1
Fielding Rd. Maid 202 A4
Fields The. Slough 205 E2
Fieldway. Ame 165 D3
Fieldway. Berk 135 F1
Fieldway. Wigg 119 E1
Filey Spur. Slough 205 D2
Filmer Rd. Wind 209 E3
Finch Cl. M Keyn 35 F2
Finch Cres. L Buzz 80 C3
Finch Ct. Maid 202 B3
Finch End. Ty Gr 174 B4
Finch La. Ame 166 A4
Finch La. Beac 175 E3
Finch La. L Chal 166 A4
Finch Rd. Berk 135 D2
Findlay Way. M Keyn 58 B4
Fingest La. Frie 170 C2
Fingest La. La En 170 B2
Finians Cl. Uxb 201 F3
Finings Rd. La En 171 D2
Finmere Cres. Ayl 116 B3
Fir Tree Ave. Sto P 198 C1
Fircroft Cl. Sto P 199 D3
Fire La. Nwtn L 57 E2
Firs Ave. Wind 209 F2
Firs Cl. H Wyc 173 F4
Firs Cl. La En 171 E3
Firs Cl. Ty Gr 163 D1
Firs Cl. Whit 87 D3
Firs Ct. Bier 102 B2
Firs Dr. Slough 206 C3

Firs End. Ger C 188 B4
Firs Rise. G Mis 151 F4
Firs The. Bier 102 B2
Firs The. Bri 110 A4
Firs The. Wigg 119 E1
Firs View Rd. Ty Gr 163 D1
Firs Wlk. Ty Gr 163 D1
First Ave. Ame 165 E4
First Ave. M Keyn 47 E1
First Ave. Mar 184 A1
First Cres. Slough 205 E4
Firview Cl. Mar 183 F1
Fish Ponds La. Tha 125 E1
Fisherman's Way. Bou E 185 D2
Fishermans Cl. Oln 6 C2
Fishermans Retreat. Mar 183 F1
Fishermead Bvd. M Keyn 35 D1
Fishery Rd. Maid 203 D3
Fishweir. Stew 68 B1
Five Acre Wood. H Wyc 172 B3
Five Acres. Ches 154 B3
Five Acres. Woo G 185 F4
Flaggs Meadow. Oln 6 C2
Flambard Cl. M Keyn 35 D4
Flamborough Spur. Slough 205 D2
Flaunden Bottom. Lat 155 F2
Flaunden Hill. Flau 156 A3
Flaunden La. Bov 146 B2
Flavius Gate. Brac 38 A4
Fleet Cl. Buck 41 F1
Fleet Cl. Wal A 161 F4
Fleet St. Ayl 101 E1
Fleet The. M Keyn 35 D1
Fleetwood Cl. C St G 177 D3
Fleetwood Rd. Slough 205 F3
Fleetwood Way. Tha 125 F1
Fleming Dr. M Keyn 47 D3
Fletcher Cl. Ayl 100 C2
Fletchers Mews. M Keyn 34 C3
Flint Hollow. Chin 147 D3
Flint St. Hadd 127 D3
Flint Way. Pres 151 E4
Flintlock Cl. Stan 213 D2
Flitton Ct. M Keyn 32 C3
Flora Thompson Dr. N Pag 21 F3
Florence Ave. Maid 203 D4
Florin Cl. M Keyn 35 D4
Flowers Bottom La. Lac G 150 A2
Foley Cl. Beac 175 E2
Foliejohn Way. Maid 202 A1
Follet Cl. Old W 211 D1
Folley La. N Craw 24 A3
Folly La. Hart 10 B4
Folly Rd. Dean 31 E2
Fontwell Cl. Maid 202 A4
Fontwell Dr. M Keyn 57 E3
Forches Cl. M Keyn 46 B1
Ford La. Iver 208 A4
Ford St. Buck 52 B4
Ford St. H Wyc 173 F2
Ford Way. H Wyc 161 F2
Ford's Cl. Bled R 159 F4
Fore End. Den 189 F1
Forelands Way. Ches 154 B4
Forest Cl. Wen 131 D2
Forest Rd. Hans 10 C3
Forest Rd. Pid (N) 4 A4
Forest Rd. Wind 209 F3
Forest Rise. M Keyn 47 D4
Forest Way. H Wyc 174 A4
Foresters. B Bot 159 E3
Foresters. Chin 147 D3
Foresters. Oak 109 E3
Forfar Dr. M Keyn 46 C1
Forge Cl. Hol G 163 E3
Forge Cl. Hor-c-S 108 A3
Forge Cl. Stp Cl 63 F2
Forge Dr. Far C 198 B3
Forge End. Ame 165 D4
Forge Rd. Wal A 161 E4
Forge The. Emb 13 F4
Forgetts Rd. La En 171 E2
Forlease Cl. Maid 203 D3
Forlease Dr. Maid 203 D3
Forlease Rd. Maid 203 D3
Formby Cl. M Keyn 57 E4
Fortescue Dr. She C E 46 A3
Forty Green. Bled 137 F2
Forty Green Dr. Mar 183 A1
Forty Green Rd. Beac 175 E2
Foscote Rd. M Mor 41 F2
Foscott Way. Buck 41 F1
Foster Ave. Wind 209 F2
Foster Cl. Ayl 101 F1
Fosters La. M Keyn 34 A2
Fosters Path. Slough 197 F1
Fotherby Ct. Maid 203 D3
Fotheringay Gdns. Slough 205 D3
Fotherley Rd. Chor 178 C4
Founders Dr. Den G 189 F3
Founders Mews. M Keyn 34 C3
Foundry La. Hort 212 A2
Foundry La. Lac G 149 E3
Fountain Gdns. Wind 210 B2
Fountaine Cl. M Keyn 34 C4
Four Ashes Rd. G Kin 162 B3
Fourth Ave. Mar 184 A1
Fowler. M Keyn 34 B4
Fowler Rd. Ayl 115 D4
Fowlers Farm Rd. Skch 158 C2
Fox Cl. Wigg 119 E1
Fox Cover. Chin 147 E3
Fox Field. Hol G 162 C3
Fox Hill Cl. H Wyc 162 A1
Fox La. Hol G 163 D3
Fox Rd. Hol G 163 D3
Fox Rd. Slough 206 B1
Fox Rd. Wigg 119 E1
Fox Way. Buck 52 C4
Foxdell Way. C St P 177 F3
Foxes Piece. Mar 183 F2
Foxgate. N Pag 22 A2
Foxherne. Slough 206 B2
Foxhill. Oln 6 C3
Foxhollow Dr. Far C 198 B4
Foxton. M Keyn 47 E3
Framewood Rd. Sto P 199 E3
France Furlong. M Keyn 34 C4
Frances Ave. Maid 196 B1
Frances Rd. Wind 210 B3
Frances St. Ches 144 B1
Franchise St. Ches 144 B1
Frank Lunnon Cl. Bou E 185 E2
Franklin Ave. Slough 205 D4
Franklin Cl. Hadd 127 D4
Franklin Rd. Dun 93 F4
Franklin Rd. Hadd 127 D4
Franklins Croft. M Keyn 33 E3
Franklyn Cres. Wind 209 E2
Frankston Ave. M Keyn 32 C3
Frascati Way. Maid 202 C4
Fraser Rd. H Wyc 172 B3
Fray's Waye. Uxb 201 E2
Frays Ave. W Dra 208 B2
Frays Cl. W Dra 208 B2
Frayslea. Uxb 201 E2
Frederick St. Wadd 99 D4
Freeman Cl. M Keyn 33 D3
Freeman Ct. Ches 144 B1
Freemans Cl. Sto P 199 D3
Freemantle Rd. Ayl 115 F3
Fremantle Rd. H Wyc 162 C1
Frensham Dr. M Keyn 58 B4
Frensham Wlk. Far C 198 B3
Friarage Rd. Ayl 115 E4
Friars Field. Berk 134 C4
Friars Furlong. L Cre 125 E4
Friars Gdns. Hgh V 162 A4
Friars Walk. Pres 151 E3
Friars Wlk. Tri 119 D2
Friary Dr. Wray 211 E1
Friary Gdns. N Pag 22 B1
Friary The. Old W 211 E1
Friday St. Hen-O-T 191 F1
Friday St. L Buzz 80 C4
Frieth Rd. Mar 182 C3
Frieth Rd. Mar B 182 C3
Frith Hill. S Hea 152 A4
Frithe The. Slough 206 A4
Frithsden Copse. Berk 135 F4
Frog La. Cudd 112 C2
Froggy La. Den 189 E1
Frogmill. Hurl 193 E2
Frogmoor. H Wyc 173 D4
Frogmore Cl. Hgh V 162 A4
Frogmore Cl. Slough 205 D2
Frogmore St. Tri 119 D2
Frome Cl. Ayl 115 E3
Fromer Rd. Bou E 185 E2
Froxfield Ct. M Keyn 46 B1
Fryday St. M Keyn 46 C4
Fryer Cl. Ches 154 B3
Fryers La. H Wyc 172 B4
Frymley Hill. Wind 209 E3
Fullbrook Cl. Maid 203 D4
Fuller's Cl. Ches 154 A3
Fullers Hill. Char 154 A3
Fullers Hill. Ches 154 A3
Fullers Slade La. M Keyn 33 D2
Fulmer Common Rd. Fulm 199 F3
Fulmer Dr. Ger C 188 B1
Fulmer La. Ger C 189 D1
Fulmer Rd. Ger C 188 C1
Fulmer St. She B E 46 B2
Fulmer St. She C E 45 E3
Fulmer Way. Ger C 188 C3
Fulwell Rd. West 39 D2
Fulwoods Dr. M Keyn 47 D4
Furlong Cl. Bou E 185 D2
Furlong Cres. Sto 115 D1
Furlong La. Tott 93 E4
Furlong Rd. Bou E 185 D2
Furness. Oak G 209 E3
Furness Sq. Oak G 209 E3
Furness Way. Oak G 209 E3
Furnival Ave. Slough 205 D4
Furrow Way. Maid 202 A2
Furrows The. S Har 190 B3
Furtho La. Pott 18 C2
Fury Ct. She C E 45 F4
Furze La. Wins 65 F3
Furze Platt Rd. Maid 195 D1
Furze Rd. Maid 195 E1
Furze View. Chor 167 E2
Furze Way. M Keyn 33 E3
Furzefield Rd. Beac 175 E1
Furzeham Rd. W Dra 208 C2
Furzen Cl. Slough 198 A1
Fuzzens Wlk. Wind 209 F3
Fyfield Barrow. Walt 48 B3

Gables Cl. C St P 177 F3
Gables Cl. Datch 211 D4
Gables Cl. Maid 203 D4
Gables Cl. Wen 131 D2
Gables The. Hadd 127 D3
Gables The. L Buzz 80 C3
Gadge Cl. Tha 125 F1
Gadsden Ct. S Ham 69 F4
Gage Cl. Maid 202 C2
Gainsborough. Cook 195 F3
Gainsborough Dr. Maid 202 B2
Gainsborough Hill. Hen-O-T 191 E1
Gainsborough Pl. Ayl 100 C2
Gainsborough Rd. Ayl 115 F2
Gainsborough Rd. Hen-O-T 191 E1
Gairloch Ave. M Keyn 58 B3
Galahad Cl. Slough 205 D2
Galley Hill. M Keyn 32 C3
Galley La. G Bkhl 59 D2
Galley La. L Bkhl 59 D2
Galleymead Rd. Stan 212 C3
Galloway Cl. M Keyn 46 C1
Gallows La. H Wyc 172 B4
Gallys Rd. Wind 209 E3
Galsworthy Pl. Ayl 100 C1
Galvin Rd. Slough 205 E3
Gamnel Terr. Tri 119 D3
Ganton Cl. M Keyn 46 B1
Garamonde Dr. M Keyn 33 F1
Garbo Cl. She C E 45 E4
Garden Cl. Maid 202 A3
Garden Field La. Berk 135 F1
Garden Reach. L Chal 166 B3
Gardens The. Adsk 53 F1
Gardens The. Ick 190 C1
Gardiner Ct. M Keyn 33 F3
Gardner Rd. Maid 195 F1
Gardner's Cl. Dun 93 F4
Garland Way. Ast C 117 F3
Garners Cl. C St P 177 F2
Garners End. C St P 177 F2
Garners Rd. C St P 177 F2
Garnet Cl. Slough 205 D2
Garnet Ct. Mar 183 E1
Garrard Rd. Slough 197 F1
Garratts Way. H Wyc 173 D4
Garraways. M Keyn 47 D3
Garron Cl. S Man 115 E2
Garrowmore Gr. M Keyn 58 B3
Garry Cl. M Keyn 58 B3
Garson Gr. Ches 144 A1
Garston. M Keyn 33 F1
Garth The. S Hea 152 A4
Garvin Ave. Beac 175 F1
Gascon's Gr. Slough 198 A1
Gaskin Ct. M Keyn 35 D3
Gatcombe. M Keyn 33 F1
Gatehouse Cl. Ayl 101 E1
Gatehouse Rd. Ayl 101 E1
Gatehouse Way. Ayl 101 D1
Gatensbury Pl. P Ris 139 D2
Gatesdene Cl. L Gad 121 E4
Gatewick Cl. Slough 205 F3
Gatward Ave. Maid 202 A2
Gaveston Dr. Berk 135 D3
Gaveston Rd. Slough 197 F1
Gaviots Cl. Ger C 188 C2
Gaviots Green. Ger C 188 C2
Gaviots Way. Ger C 188 C2
Gawcott Rd. Buck 52 A3
Gayhurst Rd. H Wyc 173 F4
Gayton Cl. Ame 154 C2
Gell Cl. Ick 190 C1
George Cl. Mar 183 F2
George Green Rd. Slough 206 C4
George Rd. Skch 158 C3
George St. Ayl 115 E4
George St. Berk 135 E2
George St. Ches 144 B1
George St. H Wyc 172 C4
George St. Hth 60 C4
George St. M Keyn 47 F1
George St. Uxb 201 E3
George St. Wing 79 F1
Georges Dr. Fla H 185 E4
Georges Hill. Hol G 162 C3
Georgian Cl. Ick 201 F4
Geralds Rd. H Wyc 162 B1
Gerards Cross Rd. Sto P 199 D4
Germain St. Ches 154 A4
Germains Cl. Ches 154 A4
Germander Pl. M Keyn 34 B2
Gibbings Cl. N Mar 76 A2
Gibbs Cl. H Wyc 172 C4
Gibbwin. M Keyn 34 C4
Gibraltar La. Cook 184 B1
Gibson Ct. Slough 206 C1
Gibson La. Hadd 127 D3
Gibson Pl. Stan 213 E1
Gibson Rd. H Wyc 172 A2
Gibson Rd. Ick 201 F4
Gibsons Green. M Keyn 34 B2
Giffard Rd. M Keyn 58 B3
Giffard Way. L Cre 125 E4
Gifford Gate. M Keyn 34 C4
Gifford Pl. Buck 41 F1
Gilbert Cl. M Keyn 58 A4
Gilbert Scott Rd. Buck 41 E1
Gilbert Way. Berk 135 D2
Gilbert's Hill. Dra B 132 C2
Gilbey Wlk. Bou E 185 E2
Gilders Mews. M Keyn 34 C3
Gilletts La. H Wyc 161 E1
Gillfield Cl. H Wyc 172 C2
Gilliat Rd. Slough 205 F3
Gilman Cres. Wind 209 E2
Gilmore Cl. Slough 206 B2
Gilmore Rd. Ayl 101 F2
Gilpin Way. Oln 7 D2
Gilpin's Ride. Berk 135 F3
Gingers Cl. Ast C 117 F3
Gisburn Cl. M Keyn 34 A3
Glade Rd. Mar 183 F1
Glade The. Ger C 188 B1
Gladstone Cl. N Pag 22 B2
Gladstone Rise. H Wyc 173 F3
Gladstone Way. Slough 205 D3
Glaisyer Way. Iver H 200 B2
Glamorgan Cl. M Keyn 46 C1
Glanmor Rd. Slough 206 A3
Glasgow Rd. Slough 205 D4
Glastonbury Cl. M Keyn 47 D1
Glaven Rd. Ayl 115 E2
Glazier Dr. M Keyn 34 C3
Glebe Cl. Dorn 203 F2
Glebe Cl. Ger C 177 E2
Glebe Cl. Hol G 163 D4
Glebe Cl. M Mor 41 F2
Glebe Cl. Pit 105 E3
Glebe Dr. Brac 38 A4
Glebe Dr. Old W 211 D1
Glebe La. Hans 10 C3
Glebe Rd. Dean 31 F3
Glebe Rd. Ger C 177 E1
Glebe Rd. Maid 203 D3
Glebe Rd. Uxb 201 E2
Glebe The. Lave 7 F4
Glebe The. Pres 151 E4
Glebe The. Sto 114 B3
Glebe The. W Dra 208 C1
Glebe The. W Tur 116 C1
Glebe The. Wal A 161 E3
Glebe Way. Ame 154 B2
Glebelands Cl. Pres 151 F2
Gledfield Pl. M Keyn 33 E2
Gleeman Cl. M Keyn 33 D3
Glen The. Slough 206 B1
Glenavon Gdns. Slough 206 B2
Gleneagles Cl. M Keyn 57 E4
Gleneagles Cl. Stan 213 E1
Glenfield Cl. Ayl 116 A3
Glenham Rd. Tha 126 A1
Glenister Rd. Ches 144 B2
Glenister Rd. H Wyc 172 A2
Glenmore Cl. Fla H 174 A1
Glentworth Pl. Slough 205 E3
Glenwoods. N Pag 22 B2
Glimbers Gr. Chin 147 E3
Globe La. L Buzz 70 C1
Glory Hill La. Beac 185 F4
Glory Mill La. Woo G 185 F4
Glory Cl. Woo G 185 F4
Glory Hill La. Beac 186 A4
Gloucester Ave. Slough 205 E4
Gloucester Pl. Wind 210 B3
Gloucester Rd. M Keyn 33 E3
Gloucester Rd. Maid 195 F1
Glovers La. M Keyn 34 A2
Glyn Sq. M Keyn 33 E4
Glyn St. M Keyn 34 A4
Glynswood. C St P 177 F2
Glynswood. Chin 147 E3
Glynswood. H Wyc 162 A1
Glynswood Rd. Buck 41 E1
Goddards Croft. M Keyn 33 E3
Goddington Rd. Bou E 185 D3
Godolphin Rd. Se Gr 176 B2
Godolphin Rd. Slough 205 E3
Gogh Rd. Ayl 100 C1
Gold Hill E. Ger C 177 E1
Gold Hill N. Ger C 177 E1
Gold Hill W. Ger C 177 E1
Gold Oak Wlk. M Keyn 34 C2
Gold St. Hans 11 D1
Golden Ball La. Maid 195 D2
Golden Dr. M Keyn 47 D4
Golden Hill. Chin 147 E3
Golden Oak. Far C 198 B3
Golden Riddy. L Buzz 80 C4
Golder's Cl. Ick 123 F2
Goldfield Rd. Tri 118 C2
Goldilocks. Walt 48 A3
Goldlake Ct. Den G 189 F2
Goldsmith Dr. N Pag 21 F2
Gomm Rd. H Wyc 174 A2
Gomms Wood Cl. Beac 175 D2
Good Intent. Edle 92 C2
Goodman Gdns. M Keyn 47 E4
Goodman Park. Slough 206 B3
Goodwin Meadows. Woo G 185 F3
Goodwin Rd. Ayl 115 E4
Goodwin Rd. Slough 197 F1
Goodwins Mead. Ched 105 D4
Goodwood. M Keyn 45 F4
Goodwood Rise. Mar B 183 E4
Goose Acre. Bot 145 D1
Goose Acre. Ched 105 D4
Goose Green. Far C 198 A2
Goosen Green. Ayl 116 B3
Goran Ave. M Keyn 32 C2
Gordale. M Keyn 34 B3
Gordon Cl. Ger C 177 F1
Gordon Rd. Ches 154 B4
Gordon Rd. H Wyc 173 E3
Gordon Rd. Maid 202 B4
Gordon Rd. W Dra 208 C3
Gordon Rd. Wind 209 F3
Gordon Way. C St G 177 D4
Gore Hill. Ame 165 D3
Gore Rd. Burn 197 D1
Gorelands La. C St P 177 F4
Gorell Rd. Beac 176 A1
Goring. M Keyn 34 B4
Gorman Pl. M Keyn 58 C2
Gorrell Cl. Ting 51 D3
Gorricks. M Keyn 32 B2
Gorse Meade. Slough 205 D3
Gorse Rd. Cook 195 F3
Gorse Wlk. Ty Gr 163 D2
Gorse Wlk. W Dra 208 C4
Goslar Way. Wind 210 A3
Gosling Gr. H Wyc 161 E1
Gosling Green. Slough 206 C2
Gosling Rd. Slough 206 C2
Goss Ave. Wadd 99 D3
Gossmore Cl. Mar 183 F1
Gossmore La. Mar 183 F1
Gossom's End. Berk 135 D3
Gossoms Ryde. Berk 135 D3
Goswell Hill. Wind 210 B3
Goswell Rd. Wind 210 B3
Governors Ave. Den G 189 F3
Gowers The. Ame 154 C1
Goya Pl. Ayl 100 C1
Graces Maltings. Tri 119 D2
Graeme Ave. Pres 151 E3
Graemesdyke Rd. Berk 135 D2
Grafham Cl. M Keyn 35 D4
Grafton Cl. Maid 195 F1
Grafton Cl. Pott 18 C2
Grafton Cl. Slough 206 C4
Grafton Gate. M Keyn 34 B1
Grafton Orch. Chin 147 E4
Grafton Rd. Ayl 101 D1
Grafton Rd. Yard G 18 C4
Grafton St. H Wyc 172 B4
Grafton St. M Keyn 34 A2
Grafton St. M Keyn 46 C4
Graham Cl. Maid 202 B3
Graham Dr. H Wyc 172 A3
Graham Rd. Cook 195 F3
Grampian Gate. M Keyn 46 C4
Gramwell. She C E 45 F4
Granborough Rd. N Mar 76 A1
Granborough Rd. Wins 65 F1
Granes End. M Keyn 34 C4
Grange Cl. Ger C 177 F1
Grange Cl. L Buzz 80 B3
Grange Cl. M Mor 41 F2
Grange Cl. Wray 211 F1
Grange Dr. Bou E 185 E2
Grange Farm Rd. Bled R 159 D4
Grange Fields. Ger C 177 F1
Grange Gdns. Far C 198 B4
Grange Gdns. Wen 131 D3
Grange La. Cook 195 F4
Grange Rd. Cook 195 F4
Grange Rd. Ger C 177 F1
Grange Rd. Hen-O-T 191 F1
Grange Rd. Hol G 162 C3
Grange Rd. M Keyn 57 F4
Grange Rd. Pit 105 E3
Grange Rd. Tri 119 E2
Grange Rd. Ty Gr 162 C2
Grange Rd. Wils 104 B1
Grange The. Burn 197 E1
Grange The. Old W 211 D1
Grangers Croft. M Keyn 33 E2
Grant Ave. Slough 205 F4
Grantham Ct. She B E 46 B3
Granville Ave. Slough 205 E4
Granville Dene. Bov 146 A2
Granville Pl. Ayl 115 E4
Granville Rd. Berk 134 C3
Granville Sq. M Keyn 35 E4
Granville St. Ayl 115 E4
Grapevine Cl. H Wyc 173 F2
Grasmere. Ayl 116 A3
Grasmere Ave. Slough 206 A3
Grasmere Par. Slough 206 A3
Grasmere Way. L Buzz 80 B4
Grasmere Way. M Keyn 58 B3
Grass Hays. Ayl 116 B4
Grasscroft. M Keyn 46 C2
Grassingham End. C St P 177 F2
Grassingham Rd. C St P 177 F2
Grassington. M Keyn 34 A3
Grasslands. Ayl 102 A1
Grassy La. Maid 202 C4
Grattan Ct. Mar 184 A2
Gratton Dr. Wind 209 F2
Gravel Hill. C St P 177 F2
Gravel Hill. Hen-O-T 191 E1
Gravel Hill. Uxb 201 E4

Gravel Path. Berk 135 F3
Gravel Wlk. Emb 13 F4
Graveney Pl. M Keyn 35 D1
Gray's La. Ibst 169 E4
Gray's Pl. Slough 205 F3
Gray's Rd. Slough 205 F3
Grayburn Cl. C St G 177 D4
Grayling Cl. Mar 194 B4
Grays Cl. Paul 17 E4
Grays La. H Wyc 161 E1
Grays La. Paul 17 E4
Grays La. Yard G 18 C3
Grays Park Rd. Sto P 199 D1
Grays Wlk. Ches 144 A1
Great Benty. W Dra 208 C1
Great Brickhill La. L Bkhl 59 E3
Great Denson. M Keyn 47 D4
Great Ground. M Keyn 34 C4
Great Hill Cres. Maid 202 B3
Great Hivings. Ches 144 A2
Great Horwood Rd. G Hrwd 65 F4
Great La. Bier 102 A2
Great Monks St. M Keyn 33 E3
Great Stone. Cudd 112 C2
Greaves Rd. H Wyc 173 E3
Grecian St. Ayl 116 A4
Green Acre. Ayl 116 A4
Green Acres Cl. Whit 86 C4
Green Cl. Burn 204 A4
Green Cl. Maid 195 F1
Green Common La. Beac 186 B2
Green Cres. Fla H 185 E4
Green Dragon La. Fla H 185 D4
Green East Rd. Se Gr 176 C2
Green End. Gran 76 A4
Green End Rd. Bled R 159 F3
Green End St. Ast C 117 F3
Green Farm Rd. N Pag 22 B2
Green Hill. H Wyc 162 A1
Green Hill Cl. H Wyc 162 B1
Green La. Ame 154 C1
Green La. Asp G 49 F2
Green La. Bled R 159 E3
Green La. Bov 146 A2
Green La. Burn 197 E2
Green La. Datch 211 D3
Green La. Eat B 92 B4
Green La. Far C 198 A3
Green La. Ivin 105 F3
Green La. Lat 155 D3
Green La. Lgwk 128 A1
Green La. M Keyn 33 E3
Green La. Maid 203 D3
Green La. Pres 151 F3
Green La. Skch 158 B3
Green La. U Arn 94 C4
Green La. Wind 210 A3
Green Lane Cl. Ame 154 B2
Green Lane Ct. Burn 197 E1
Green Leys. H Wyc 161 E1
Green North Rd. Se Gr 176 C2
Green Park. Pres 151 E3
Green Park Dr. N Pag 22 B2
Green Rd. H Wyc 162 B1
Green St. Chor 167 E3
Green St. H Wyc 172 C4
Green St. Ty Gr 162 C2
Green The. A Abb 88 B3
Green The. Ame 154 B1
Green The. Burn 197 D1
Green The. Cast 19 F1
Green The. Chea 112 A1
Green The. Ched 105 D4
Green The. Cran 24 C1
Green The. Cudd 112 C2
Green The. Datch 211 D4
Green The. Dean 31 F2
Green The. Edle 92 C2
Green The. G Hrwd 55 D2
Green The. Hans 11 D1
Green The. Hor-c-S 108 A3
Green The. M Keyn 46 A4
Green The. M Keyn 47 E4
Green The. N Pag 22 B2
Green The. Paul 17 D4
Green The. Pit 105 E2
Green The. Qntn 85 D3
Green The. Slough 205 E2
Green The. Thrn 54 A4
Green The. Turv 8 C3
Green The. W Dra 208 B2
Green The. Woo G 185 F3
Green The. Wray 211 F1
Green Tiles La. Den G 189 F3
Green Verges. Mar 183 F2
Green View. Ayl 102 A1
Green View Cl. Bov 146 A1
Green Way. Nwtn L 57 E2
Green West Rd. Se Gr 176 C2
Greenacre. Wind 209 F3
Greenacres. Pit 105 E2
Greenacres Ave. Ick 190 C1
Greenacres La. Ty Gr 163 D1
Greenbury Cl. Chor 167 E3
Greene Field Rd. Berk 135 E2
Greene Wlk. Berk 135 E2
Greenfield End. C St P 177 F2
Greenfield Rd. N Pag 22 A2
Greenfields. Adsk 53 F1
Greenfields. Maid 203 D3
Greenfields. U Arn 94 C4
Greenhill Cl. M Keyn 46 A4
Greenlands. Fla H 185 D4
Greenlands. Lac G 149 E3
Greenlands Cl. N Pag 22 A2
Greenlands La. Pres 151 D4
Greenlaw Pl. M Keyn 47 D2
Greenleys La. M Keyn 33 E2
Greenock Rd. Slough 205 D4
Greenridge. Ty Gr 174 A4
Greenside. Bou E 185 D3
Greenside. Pres 151 E3
Greenside. Slough 205 D4
Greenway. Berk 135 D2
Greenway. Ches 144 A2
Greenway. G Hrwd 55 D1
Greenway. Hadd 126 C3
Greenway Par. Ches 144 A2
Greenway The. Ger C 188 B4
Greenway The. H Wyc 173 D4
Greenway The. Tri 118 C3
Greenway The. Ty Gr 163 D1
Greenway The. Uxb 201 E2
Greenway Wlk. Buck 41 F1
Greenways. B Bkhl 48 B1
Greenways. Eat B 92 B4
Greenways Dr. Maid 202 A4
Greenwich Gdns. N Pag 22 B1
Greenwood. Wal A 150 A1
Greenwood Ave. Chin 147 E3
Greenwood Cl. Ame 154 C1
Greenwood Cl. Se Gr 176 B2
Greenwood Meadow. Chin 147 E3
Greenwood Pl. Stp Cl 63 E2
Greenyard The. Y Has 1 A4
Greetham Rd. Ayl 116 B3
Gregories Dr. Walt 48 B3
Gregories Farm La. Beac 175 E1
Gregories Rd. Beac 175 E2
Gregory Dr. Old W 211 D1
Gregory Rd. Hedg 187 E1
Grenadine Way. Tri 119 D3
Grendon Rd. Edgc 72 C1
Grendon Rd. Gr Und 83 E2
Grendon Way. Bier 102 A2
Grenfell Ave. H Wyc 172 B4
Grenfell Ave. Maid 202 C3
Grenfell Pl. Maid 202 C3
Grenfell Rd. Beac 175 F2
Grenfell Rd. Maid 202 C3
Grenville Ave. Wen 131 D4
Grenville Cl. Burn 197 D2
Grenville Ct. Chor 167 E3
Grenville Green. Ayl 115 E2
Grenville Rd. Ayl 115 E3
Grenville Rd. Buck 41 E1
Grenville Way. Tha 126 A1
Gresham Ct. Berk 135 D2
Gresham Rd. Slough 205 D4
Greyhound La. Wins 66 A2
Greys Hill. Hen-O-T 191 E1
Greys Rd. Hen-O-T 191 E1
Greys The. M Keyn 47 E4
Greystoke Cl. Berk 135 D2
Griffetts Yd. Ches 144 A1
Griffin Cl. Maid 202 C3
Griffin Cl. Slough 205 E2
Griffin Industrial Mall. Ayl 101 D1
Griffin La. Ayl 101 D1
Griffon Cl. M Keyn 47 D4
Grimbald Ct. M Keyn 35 E4
Grimmer Cl. Ayl 100 C2
Grimms Hill. G Mis 151 F4
Grimms Meadow. Wal A 150 A1
Grimsdell's La. Ame 154 B1
Grimsdyke Rd. Wigg 119 E1
Gringer Hill. Maid 202 C4
Grizedale. M Keyn 34 A3
Groom Rd. Pres 151 E3
Grooms Cottages. Bot 145 D1
Groomsby Dr. Ivin 105 F3
Grosvenor Cl. Iver H 200 B1
Grosvenor Dr. Maid 203 E4
Grove Ash. M Keyn 47 E2
Grove Cl. Ger C 177 E1
Grove Cl. Slough 206 A2
Grove Ct. Bier 102 B3
Grove End. Ger C 177 E1
Grove Gdns. Tri 119 D3
Grove Hill. Ger C 177 E2
Grove La. Ash Gr 145 E3
Grove La. G Kim 129 F1
Grove La. Ger C 177 E1
Grove La. Uxb 201 F1
Grove Park. Tri 119 E3
Grove Rd. Ame 154 C1
Grove Rd. Beac 175 F1
Grove Rd. Burn 197 F2
Grove Rd. H Wyc 172 B4
Grove Rd. Hen-O-T 191 F1
Grove Rd. Maid 202 C4
Grove Rd. Tri 119 E3
Grove Rd. Turv 8 C3
Grove Rd. Ty Gr 162 C2
Grove Rd. Uxb 201 E3
Grove Rd. Wind 210 B3
Grove The. Ame 154 B2
Grove The. Lat 155 E2
Grove The. M Keyn 34 A2
Grove The. M Keyn 58 A4
Grove The. N Pag 22 A2
Grove The. Slough 206 A2
Grove The. Tri 119 E3
Grove The. Uxb 201 F1
Grove The. Wadd 99 D3
Grove The. Wbn S 49 D3
Grove Way. Uxb 201 E3
Grove Way. Wadd 99 D3
Groves Cl. Bou E 185 E2
Groves Rd. Hal 131 F4
Groves Way. Cook 195 F3
Groveway. M K Vil 47 E3
Groveway. M Keyn 47 E3
Groveway. Walt 47 E3
Grovewood Cl. Chor 167 D2
Grubbins La. Lac G 150 A3
Grubwood La. Cook 195 D4
Gryms Dyke. Pres 151 E3
Guards Club Rd. Maid 203 E4
Guards Rd. Oak G 209 E3
Guest Gdns. M Keyn 34 A4
Guinea Orch. Oln 6 C2
Guinions Rd. H Wyc 173 F3
Gun La. Sher 14 A1
Gunmaker Ct. M Keyn 34 C3
Gunthorpe Rd. Mar 184 A2
Gurnard Cl. W Dra 208 B3
Gurnards Ave. M Keyn 35 D1
Gurnells Rd. Se Gr 176 B3
Gurneys Meadow. Hol G 163 E4
Gwendale. Maid 195 E1
Gweneth Ct. Mar 183 E2
Gwent Cl. Maid 202 A2
Gwynne Cl. Tri 119 D3
Gwynne Cl. Wind 209 F3
Gynant Rd. H Wyc 173 F3
Gypsy La. Mar 183 F2
Gypsy La. Sto P 187 F1

Haberley Mead. M Keyn 34 A2
Habuchin La. Wins 66 A2
Hackett Pl. N Craw 24 A3
Haddington Cl. M Keyn 46 C1
Haddington Cl. Wen 131 E3
Haddington Way. Ayl 102 A1
Haddon. M Keyn 45 F4
Haddon Rd. Chor 167 E2
Haddon Rd. Maid 202 B3
Hadfield Rd. Stan 213 E1
Hadley Pl. M Keyn 34 B2
Hadlow Ct. Slough 205 E3
Hadrians Dr. M Keyn 34 A3
Hadrians Gate. Brac 38 A4
Hag Hill La. Burn 204 A4
Hag Hill Rise. Burn 204 A4
Haglis Dr. Wen 131 D3
Haig Dr. Slough 205 D2
Hailey Cft. Chin 147 D3
Hainault Ave. M Keyn 22 A1
Haines Cl. Ayl 100 C1
Haines Rd. Hol G 162 C3
Haithwaite. M Keyn 33 E1
Haldene. M Keyn 33 F1
Hale Ave. M Keyn 32 C3
Hale La. Wen 131 F2
Hale Rd. Wen 131 E2
Hale St. Ayl 115 F4
Hales Croft. Ayl 116 A2
Halfacre Hill. C St P 177 F1
Halfway House La. Ches 153 F4
Halifax Cl. Maid 202 A4
Halifax Rd. Chor 167 E1
Halifax Rd. H Wyc 172 B3
Halifax Rd. Maid 202 A4
Halifax Way. Maid 202 A4
Halings La. Den G 189 F4
Halkingcroft. Slough 206 B2
Hall Cl. M Mor 41 F2
Hall Ct. Datch 211 D4
Hall La. Chic 23 E4
Hall Meadow. Burn 197 D2
Hall Park. Berk 135 F2
Hall Park Gate. Berk 135 F2
Hall Park Hill. Berk 135 F2
Halldore Hill. Cook 195 F4
Halls Corner. Fla H 174 A1
Halton La. Hal 131 D4
Halton La. Wen 131 D4
Halton Wood Rd. Wen 131 E3
Haltonchesters. M Keyn 33 F3
Haly Cl. M Keyn 34 A2
Ham La. Old W 211 E2
Hamberlins La. Berk 134 A4
Hamble Dr. Ayl 115 E3
Hambling Pl. Dun 93 F4
Hamilton Ave. Hen-O-T 191 F1
Hamilton Gdns. Burn 197 D1
Hamilton La. M Keyn 57 E3
Hamilton Mead. Bov 146 A2
Hamilton Rd. Berk 135 D2
Hamilton Rd. H Wyc 162 B1
Hamilton Rd. Slough 205 D4
Hamilton Rd. Tha 126 A1
Hamilton Rd. Uxb 201 E1
Hamlins. M Keyn 47 D3
Hammersley La. Ty Gr 174 A3
Hammond Cres. M Keyn 35 D3
Hammond End. Far C 198 A4
Hampden Ave. Ches 144 A1
Hampden Cl. Ayl 115 E3
Hampden Cl. Sto P 199 D1
Hampden Gdns. Ayl 115 E3
Hampden Hill. Beac 175 D1
Hampden Rd. Ayl 115 E3
Hampden Rd. Ger C 177 E1
Hampden Rd. H Wyc 173 D4
Hampden Rd. Hgh V 151 D2
Hampden Rd. Lac G 150 B3
Hampden Rd. Maid 202 A4
Hampden Rd. Pres 151 D2
Hampden Rd. S Man 116 A1
Hampden Rd. Slough 206 C2
Hampden Rd. Wen 131 E3
Hampshire Ave. Slough 205 E4
Hampson Cl. M Keyn 34 A3
Hampstead Gate. M Keyn 34 B2
Hampton. M Keyn 46 A4
Hanbury Cl. Burn 204 A4
Handley Page Cl. Cran 24 C2
Hangings La. Pres 151 D3
Hanley Cl. Wind 160 E3
Hanmer Rd. M Keyn 47 F3
Hannon Rd. Ayl 115 E3
Hanover Cl. Slough 206 A2
Hanover Cl. Wind 209 F3
Hanover Ct. L Buzz 80 B4
Hanover Ct. Ty Gr 163 D2
Hanover Way. Wind 209 F3
Hanscomb Cl. M Keyn 35 E1
Hanslope Rd. Cast 19 F3
Hanson Way. Ayl 116 A2
Harborne Ct. M Keyn 33 E1
Harbourne Cl. S Man 115 E2
Harby Cl. M Keyn 46 B1
Harcourt. M Keyn 34 A2
Harcourt Cl. Dorn 203 F2
Harcourt Cl. Hen-O-T 191 E1
Harcourt Cl. L Buzz 80 C4
Harcourt Green. Ayl 101 D1
Harcourt Rd. Dorn 203 F2
Harcourt Rd. Skch 158 C2
Harcourt Rd. Tri 119 E2
Harcourt Rd. Wind 209 F3
Hardenwaye. H Wyc 162 C1
Harding Rd. Ches 144 B1
Hardings Row. Iver H 200 B1
Hardmead Rd. New B 8 A2
Hardwick Cl. Maid 202 A4
Hardwick Pl. Wbn S 49 D2
Hardwick Rd. Wbn S 49 D2
Hardwicke Gdns. Ame 154 C1
Hardy Cl. Ayl 115 F4
Hardy Cl. Slough 205 D3
Hare Cl. Buck 52 C4
Hare La. L Kin 152 A2
Hare Lane End. L Kin 152 A2
Hare Shoots. Maid 202 C3
Harebell Cl. Walt 48 A3
Harebell Wlk. Hol G 162 C3
Harefield Rd. Maid 202 A4
Harefield Rd. Uxb 201 E3
Harehatch La. Burn 186 C2
Harewood Pl. Slough 206 A2
Harewood Rd. L Chal 166 B3
Hargrave Rd. Maid 202 B4
Hargreaves Nook. M Keyn 22 A1
Harkness Cl. M Keyn 58 B3
Harkness Rd. Burn 204 A4
Harlans Cl. M Keyn 47 D4
Harlech Pl. M Keyn 57 F4
Harlestone Ct. M Keyn 22 A1
Harling Rd. Eat B 93 D2
Harlow Rd. H Wyc 173 E3
Harman Wlk. H Wyc 172 B2
Harmondsworth La. Harm 213 F4
Harmondsworth Rd. W Dra 208 C1
Harpers La. M Keyn 34 C4
Harrier Ct. M Keyn 47 D4
Harrier Dr. M Keyn 47 D4
Harries Cl. Ches 144 A1
Harries Way. Hol G 163 D3
Harrington Cl. Wind 209 F2
Harris Ct. Ayl 101 F1
Harris Rd. La En 171 D3
Harrison Pl. Tha 125 F1
Harroell. L Cre 125 E3
Harrold Rd. Lave 8 A4
Harrow Cl. Maid 195 F1
Harrow La. Maid 195 F1
Harrow Rd. Slough 206 C2
Harrow Yard. Tri 119 D2
Harrowden. M Keyn 34 A4
Hart St. Hen-O-T 191 F1
Harthmoor Cl. Skch 158 C2
Hartland Cl. Slough 205 E3
Hartley. M Keyn 34 C4
Hartley Cl. Sto P 199 E2
Harts Rd. Hadd 127 D3
Hartwell Cl. Ty Gr 163 E1
Hartwell End. Ayl 115 D4
Hartwell Rd. Ash 9 F4
Hartwell Rd. Hans 10 C3
Hartwort Cl. Walt 48 A3
Harvard Cl. M Keyn 21 F1
Harvest Bank. H Hea 153 E2
Harvest Hill. Bou E 185 E1
Harvest Hill Rd. Maid 202 C2
Harvester Cl. M Keyn 33 D3
Harvey Orch. Beac 175 E2
Harvey Rd. Ayl 115 F3
Harvey Rd. Dun 93 E4
Harvil Rd. Den G 190 C2
Harvil Rd. Ick 190 C2
Harwich Rd. Slough 205 D4
Harwood Dr. Uxb 201 F2
Harwood Rd. Mar 183 E1
Harwood St. M Keyn 34 A4
Hasgill Ct. M Keyn 34 A2
Haslemere Rd. Wind 210 A3
Haslow Ct. M Keyn 33 F2
Hasting Cl. Maid 203 E1
Hastings. M Keyn 32 C3
Hastoe Hill. Dra B 132 C4
Hastoe Hill. Has 119 D1
Hastoe La. Tri 119 D1
Hastoe Park. Ayl 101 F1
Hatch La. Bled R 160 A2
Hatch La. Harm 213 E4
Hatch La. Wind 210 A3
Hatch The. Oak G 209 E4
Hatches La. Hgh V 162 A4
Hatchgate Gdns. Burn 197 E1
Hatchlands. M Keyn 33 F1
Hatfield Cl. Maid 202 B3
Hatfield Rd. Slough 206 A2
Hatter's La. H Wyc 173 F4
Hatton. M Keyn 47 E3
Hatton Ave. Slough 198 B1
Hatton Ct. Wind 210 B3
Hatton Gr. W Dra 208 B2
Havelock Cres. Maid 202 A4
Havelock Rd. Maid 202 A4
Havelock St. Ayl 101 E1
Haven Shaw Cl. Ayl 116 A3
Havenfield Rd. H Wyc 172 B2
Haw La. Bled R 149 D1
Hawkins Cl. M Keyn 32 B3
Hawkmoor Cl. M Keyn 47 D4
Hawkridge. M Keyn 46 C2
Hawks Hill. Bou E 185 E1
Hawkshill Dr. Fel 146 C4
Hawkshill Rd. Slough 198 A1
Hawkswood. Oln 6 C3
Hawkswood La. Fulm 199 F4
Hawkwell Dr. Tri 119 E2
Hawkwell Estate. Old S 32 A4
Hawleys La. Whit 87 D3
Hawridge La. Char 143 F4
Hawridge La. Chol 143 F4
Hawridge Vale. Chol 133 F1
Haws La. Stan 213 D1
Hawthorn Ave. M Keyn 58 C4
Hawthorn Cl. Ayl 101 F1
Hawthorn Cl. Mar 183 F2
Hawthorn Cl. Turv 8 C3
Hawthorn Cres. Ty Gr 163 D1
Hawthorn Dr. N Den 201 E3
Hawthorn La. Burn 198 A3
Hawthorn Pl. Ty Gr 174 B4
Hawthorn Rd. P Ris 139 E2
Hawthorn Way. Ches 144 B1
Hawthorn Wlk. Ty Gr 163 D1
Hawthorne Cres. Slough 205 F4
Hawthorne Cres. W Dra 208 C2
Hawthorne Gdns. Fla H 174 A1
Hawthorne Rd. H Wyc 174 A3
Hawthorne Way. Wing 79 F2
Hawthorns The. Berk 135 D3
Hawthorns The. Fel 146 C4
Hawthorns The. Map Cr 178 B3
Hawthorns The. Stan 212 C3
Hawtrey Cl. Slough 206 A2
Hawtrey Rd. Wind 210 B3
Hay La. Fulm 199 E4
Haydock Cl. M Keyn 57 E3
Haydon Rd. Ayl 101 E1
Hayes Pl. Mar 183 E1
Hayes Rd. Dean 31 F3
Hayfield Dr. Ty Gr 163 D1
Hayles Field. Frie 170 C1
Haymaker Cl. Uxb 201 F3
Haymill Rd. Slough 197 E1
Haynes Cl. Slough 206 C1
Haynes Mead. Berk 135 D3
Haynes Way. B Bkhl 48 B1
Hayse Hill. Wind 209 E3
Haystacks The. H Wyc 173 D4
Haythorp Cl. M Keyn 35 D3
Haywards Cl. Hen-O-T 191 E1
Haywards Croft. M Keyn 33 D3
Haywood Park. Chor 167 F2
Haywood Park. Stew 68 B2
Haywood Way. Ayl 100 C2
Hazel Ave. Ayl 116 A4
Hazel Cl. Mar B 183 E3
Hazel Gr. M Keyn 58 B4
Hazel Rd. Berk 135 E2
Hazel Rd. Pres 151 E3
Hazelbury Rd. H Wyc 173 E3
Hazelcroft Cl. Uxb 201 F3
Hazelhurst Dr. Ayl 116 A3
Hazelhurst Rd. Burn 197 E2
Hazell Cl. Maid 203 D4
Hazell Park. Ame 165 E4
Hazell Way. Sto P 198 C3

Hazelmere Rd. Slough 206 A3
Hazelwood. M Keyn 34 C4
Hazelwood Cl. Ches 144 B1
Hazely. Tri 119 E2
Hazlemere Rd. Ty Gr 163 E1
Hazlemere View. Hol G 163 D3
Hazley Wlk. Buck 41 F1
Headington Cl. Maid 202 A4
Headington Rd. Maid 202 A4
Headland Cl. S Hea 152 A4
Healey Ave. H Wyc 173 E4
Heaney Cl. N Pag 22 A3
Hearn Cl. Ty Gr 162 C1
Hearn's Meadow. Se Gr 176 B2
Hearne Ct. C St G 177 D4
Hearne Dr. Holy 203 D1
Hearne's Cl. Se Gr 176 B3
Heath Cl. Ayl 116 A3
Heath Cl. Hol G 163 D3
Heath Cl. Stan 213 E1
Heath Ct. L Buzz 70 C2
Heath End Cl. G Kin 151 F1
Heath End Rd. Fla H 173 E1
Heath End Rd. G Kin 151 F1
Heath End Rd. L Kin 151 F1
Heath End Rd. Lit M 173 E1
Heath La. Asp H 49 D1
Heath Rd. Beac 185 F4
Heath Rd. G Bkhl 59 E1
Heath The. L Buzz 70 C2
Heath Way. Iver H 200 B2
Heathcote Way. W Dra 208 B3
Heathcroft. M Keyn 34 C4
Heather Cl. W Dra 208 C4
Heather La. W Dra 208 C4
Heather Mead. Eat B 92 C3
Heather Wlk. Ayl 115 D3
Heather Wlk. Ty Gr 163 D2
Heatherden Green. Iver H 200 B2
Heatherside Gdns. Far C 187 E1
Heathfield. M Keyn 33 F2
Heathfield Rd. H Wyc 172 A4
Heathfield Rd. Tapl 186 A1
Heathlands Dr. Maid 202 A3
Heathrow Cl. Harm 213 D3
Heavens Lea. Bou E 185 E1
Hedge Lea. Woo G 185 E4
Hedgerley. Chin 147 D3
Hedgerley Hill. Hedg 187 E1
Hedgerley La. Beac 187 E3
Hedgerley La. Ger C 187 E3
Hedgerows The. M Keyn 46 C2
Hedley Rd. Fla H 185 D4
Hedsor Hill. Bou E 185 E1
Hedsor La. Bou E 185 F1
Hedsor La. Tapl 186 A1
Hedsor Rd. Bou E 185 D1
Helena Rd. Wind 210 B3
Helford Cl. Ayl 115 E2
Helford Pl. M Keyn 35 D1
Hellyer Way. Bou E 185 E2
Helston La. Wind 210 A3
Helston Pl. M Keyn 34 C1
Hemel Hempstead Rd. Dag 107 F1
Hemingway Rd. Ayl 100 C1
Hemmings The. Berk 134 C2
Hemmingway Cl. N Pag 21 F3
Hemp La. Wigg 119 E1
Hempson Ave. Slough 206 B2
Hempstead Rd. Bov 146 A3
Hemwood Rd. Wind 209 E2
Hencroft St N. Slough 205 F2
Hencroft St S. Slough 205 F2
Henders. M Keyn 32 C3
Hendon Way. Stan 213 E1
Hendons Way. Holy 203 D1
Hendrix Dr. She C E 45 E4
Henley Rd. Bish 194 A1
Henley Rd. Bish 194 A1
Henley Rd. Hurl 193 E2
Henley Rd. Mar 183 E1
Henley Rd. Mar 194 A4
Hennerton Way. H Wyc 173 F3
Henrietta Rd. Tha 126 A1
Henry Rd. Ayl 116 A4
Henry Rd. Slough 205 E2
Henson Cl. Cran 24 C2
Hepleswell. M Keyn 33 F1
Hepplewhite Cl. H Wyc 173 E4
Herbert Rd. H Wyc 174 A4
Herberts Hole. S Hea 142 C1
Hercies Rd. Uxb 201 F3
Herd's Hill. Stp Cl 64 A2
Herdman Cl. M Keyn 33 D3
Heritage Cl. Uxb 201 E1
Hermitage Cl. Slough 206 B2
Hermitage La. Wind 210 A2
Hermitage The. Uxb 201 E3
Heron Cl. Ayl 116 B4
Heron Cl. Uxb 201 E3
Heron The. Ayl 101 F2
Herons Elm. Berk 134 C4
Herons Pl. Mar 183 F2
Heronsgate Dr. Chor 167 D2
Herriot Cl. N Pag 22 A3
Herschel Park Dr. Slough 205 F2
Herschel St. Slough 205 F2
Herston Cl. Ayl 116 A3
Hertford Pl. M Keyn 46 C1
Hervines Ct. Ame 154 B1
Hervines Rd. Ame 154 B1
Hesketh Rd. Yard G 18 C3
Het's Orch. Lac G 149 F3
Hetherington Cl. Slough 197 F1
Hetherington Way. Ick 201 F4
Hetton Cl. M Keyn 34 B2
Heusden Way. Ger C 188 C2
Hever Cl. Maid 202 B3
Hexham Gdns. M Keyn 57 E3
Heywood Ave. Maid 202 A1
Heywood Court Cl. Maid 202 A1
Heywood Gdns. Maid 202 A1
Hibbert Rd. Maid 203 D2
Hibbert's Alley. Wind 210 B3
Hicks Farm Rise. H Wyc 173 F4
Hide The. M Keyn 47 E3
Higgs Ct. M Keyn 46 A4
High Beeches. Ger C 188 B1
High Beeches. H Wyc 172 B3
High Bois La. Ame 154 B2
High Coppice. Ame 165 E4
High Heavens Wood. Mar B 183 E1
High Land Cl. Bri 96 A1
High Moors. Hal 131 D4
High Rd. Cook 195 F3
High Rd. Soul 69 F1
High Rd. Uxb 208 B4
High St. Ame 165 D4
High St. Ayl 115 F4
High St. Berk 134 C3
High St. Berk 135 E2
High St. Bov 146 A2
High St. Bri 110 A4
High St. Buck 41 E1
High St. Burn 197 E1
High St. C St G 177 E4
High St. Ched 105 D4
High St. Ches 154 A4
High St. Chin 147 E4
High St. Cook 196 A4
High St. Cran 25 D1
High St. Cub 78 A1
High St. Datch 211 D3
High St. Dean 31 F2
High St. Dint 113 F1
High St. Eat B 92 C3
High St. Edle 92 C2
High St. Emb 13 F4
High St. Eton 210 B4
High St. G Hrwd 55 D2
High St. Ger C 177 F1
High St. H Wyc 161 E2
High St. H Wyc 173 D3
High St. Hadd 126 C3
High St. Harm 213 E4
High St. Harr 3 F3
High St. Have 21 D2
High St. Hth 60 C4
High St. Iver 212 B4
High St. Ivin 105 F3
High St. L Buzz 80 C3
High St. L Cre 125 E3
High St. La En 171 D2
High St. Lave 7 F4
High St. Lewk 157 D4
High St. Lud 96 A4
High St. M Keyn 21 F1
High St. M Keyn 33 F4
High St. M Keyn 58 C4
High St. Maid 202 C4
High St. Maid 203 E2
High St. Mar 183 F1
High St. N Craw 24 A3
High St. N Mar 76 A1
High St. N Pag 22 B2
High St. Nash 44 B1
High St. Oln 6 C2
High St. P Ris 139 D2
High St. Paul 17 E4
High St. Pott 18 B2
High St. Pres 151 E3
High St. S Gol 12 A3
High St. S Hea 152 A4
High St. Sher 13 F1
High St. Slough 205 E2
High St. Slough 205 F2
High St. Stan 213 E1
High St. Syr 27 D4
High St. Tapl 196 C1
High St. Tha 125 E1
High St. Thrn 54 A4
High St. Tri 119 D2
High St. Turv 8 C3
High St. Uxb 201 E3
High St. W Dra 208 C3
High St. W Und 6 A1
High St. Wadd 99 D3
High St. Wbn S 49 D2
High St. Wcot 98 A4
High St. Wedn 87 E1
High St. Wen 131 D2
High St. Whad 45 D1
High St. Whit 87 D3
High St. Wind 210 B3
High St. Wing 79 E2
High St. Wing 79 F1
High St. Wins 65 F3
High St. Wray 211 F1
High St. Y Has 1 A3
High St. Yard G 18 C3
High St N. Stew 68 B1
High St S. Oln 6 C2
High St S. Stew 78 C4
High St The. M Keyn 33 E1
High Town Rd. Maid 202 C4
High Trees. M Keyn 47 E4
High View Cl. Mar B 183 E4
Higham Cross Rd. Hans 10 C2
Higham Mead. Ches 144 B1
Higham Rd. Ches 144 B1
Highbeeches Cl. Mar B 183 E4
Highbridge Rd. Ayl 115 F4
Highbridge Wlk. Ayl 115 F4
Highcroft Cl. Yard G 18 C3
Highfield. C St G 177 E4
Highfield. L Cre 125 E4
Highfield Ave. H Wyc 172 A3
Highfield Cl. Ame 154 B1
Highfield Cl. M Keyn 47 D1
Highfield Cl. N Pag 22 C2
Highfield Ct. Ty Gr 163 D2
Highfield Dr. Ick 190 C1
Highfield La. Maid 202 A2
Highfield Park. Mar 183 D1
Highfield Park. Mar 194 A4
Highfield Rd. Berk 135 E2
Highfield Rd. Bou E 185 D2
Highfield Rd. Ches 144 A1
Highfield Rd. Fla H 185 D4
Highfield Rd. Maid 202 A4
Highfield Rd. P Ris 139 D2
Highfield Rd. Tri 118 C2
Highfield Rd. Wigg 119 E1
Highfield Rd. Wind 209 F2
Highfield Rd. Wins 65 F3
Highfield Way. Ty Gr 163 D2
Highfield Way. Y Has 1 A3
Highgate Over. Walt 48 A3
Highgrove Hill. M Keyn 45 F4
Highgrove Park. Maid 202 C4
Highland Cl. M Keyn 46 C2
Highland Rd. Ame 165 E4
Highlands. Fla H 185 D4
Highlands Cl. C St P 177 F2
Highlands End. C St P 177 F2
Highlands La. C St P 177 F2
Highlands Rd. Buck 41 F1
Highlands Rd. Se Gr 176 B3
Highlea Ave. Fla H 185 D4
Highmoor. Ame 165 E4
Highmore Cotts. H Hea 152 C2
Highover Park. Ame 165 E4
Highview. Dean 31 F3
Highway. Dray P 68 B3
Highway Ave. Maid 202 A3
Highwood Ave. H Wyc 172 A3
Highwood Bottom. Lac G 150 A3
Highwood Cres. H Wyc 172 A3
Highwoods Cl. Mar B 183 E4
Highwoods Dr. Mar B 183 E4
Highworth Cl. H Wyc 162 C1
Hilbury Cl. Ame 154 B2
Hiljon Cres. Ger C 177 F1
Hill Ave. Ame 154 B1
Hill Ave. Hol G 163 D3
Hill Cl. Woo G 185 F4
Hill Farm App. Woo G 185 F4
Hill Farm La. C St G 166 A1
Hill Farm Rd. C St P 177 F2
Hill Farm Rd. Ches 154 B3
Hill Farm Rd. Mar B 183 F3
Hill Farm Rd. Tapl 196 C1
Hill Farm Way. Ty Gr 163 D1
Hill House Cl. C St P 177 F2
Hill Mead. Berk 135 D2
Hill Meadow. Cole 164 C2
Hill Rd. Chin 147 E3
Hill Rd. Lewk 157 D4
Hill Rd. Lewk 157 E3
Hill Rise. Ger C 177 E1
Hill Rise Cres. Ger C 177 F1
Hill Side. Ched 104 C4
Hill St. H Wyc 174 A3
Hill The. Cole 164 B2
Hill The. Syr 27 D4
Hill Top Dr. Mar 183 A1
Hill Top La. Chin 147 F2
Hill View. Berk 135 D3
Hill View. G Kim 129 E1
Hill View. Oak 109 E3
Hill View Rd. Wray 211 E1
Hill Waye. Ger C 188 C2
Hillary Cl. Ayl 116 A3
Hillary Cl. H Wyc 173 F3
Hillary Rd. H Wyc 173 F3
Hillary Rd. Slough 206 C2
Hillbottom Rd. H Wyc 172 A4
Hillcrest. Cran 25 E1
Hillcrest Ave. Cook 195 F3
Hillcrest Waye. Ger C 188 C2
Hillcroft Rd. Ches 144 B1
Hillcroft Rd. Ty Gr 163 E1
Hillersdon. Slough 206 A4
Hillersdon Chase. S Ham 69 E4
Hillesden Way. Buck 41 F1
Hillfield Cl. H Wyc 161 F1
Hillfield Rd. C St P 177 F2
Hillfield Sq. C St P 177 F2
Hilliard Dr. M Keyn 34 A2
Hilliards Rd. Uxb 208 B4
Hillier Rd. S Man 115 E2
Hillingdon Hill. Uxb 201 F1
Hillingdon Rd. Uxb 201 F2
Hillington Cl. Ayl 115 D4
Hillman Cl. Uxb 201 F4
Hillmead Ct. Tapl 203 F4
Hillrise. Slough 212 A4
Hills Cl. M Keyn 34 C4
Hills La. Cook 195 E4
Hillside. Ches 144 A2
Hillside. Gawt 51 F2
Hillside. H Wyc 173 E4
Hillside. Maid 202 B3
Hillside. S Har 190 B3
Hillside. Slough 205 F2
Hillside Cl. C St G 177 D4
Hillside Cl. C St P 177 F2
Hillside Cl. U Arn 94 C4
Hillside Gdns. Berk 135 E2
Hillside Gdns. H Wyc 173 E4
Hillside Rd. Chor 167 E2
Hillside Rd. Mar 183 F2
Hillside Rd. Ty Gr 163 D1
Hilltop. L Cre 125 E3
Hilltop Ave. Buck 41 F1
Hilltop Rd. Berk 135 E2
Hillview. Sher 14 A1
Hillview Rd. H Wyc 173 E4
Hillway. Ame 165 D3
Hillway. Wave 49 D3
Hillwerke. Chin 147 E3
Hilperton Rd. Slough 205 F2
Hilton Ave. Ayl 101 F1
Hilton Cl. Uxb 201 D2
Himley Green. L Buzz 80 B3
Hindhead Knoll. Walt 48 A3
Hinkley Cl. S Har 190 B4
Hinton Cl. H Wyc 162 A1
Hinton Rd. Uxb 201 E2
Hipwell Ct. Oln 6 C2
Hisbourne Dr. G Mis 152 A3
Hitcham La. Burn 197 D1
Hitcham La. Tapl 196 C1
Hitcham Rd. Burn 204 A4
Hither Meadow. Ger C 177 F1
Hithercroft Rd. H Wyc 161 F1
Hithermoor Rd. Stan 213 D1
Hivings Hill. Ches 144 A1
Hivings Park. Ches 144 A2
Hobart Cl. H Wyc 162 C1
Hobart Cres. M Keyn 35 D4
Hobart Ct. Mar 184 A2
Hobart Rd. H Wyc 162 B1
Hobarts Dr. Den G 189 F3
Hobbis Dr. Maid 202 A3
Hobbs Rd. La En 171 E2
Hobsons Wk. Tri 118 C3
Hockett La. Bish 195 D3
Hockett La. Cook 195 D3
Hockley La. Sto P 199 D3
Hockliffe Brae. Walt 48 A3
Hodds Wood Rd. Ches 154 B3
Hodge Lea La. M Keyn 33 E2
Hodgemore Ct. M Keyn 21 F1
Hoe Meadow. Beac 175 E2
Hog Hall La. Dag 107 D3
Hog La. Ash Gr 144 B4
Hog La. Berk 134 E1
Hogarths Ct. M Keyn 33 F1
Hogback Wood Rd. Beac 175 D2
Hogfair La. Burn 197 E1
Hogg La. Hol G 163 E3
Hoggshill Rd. G Mis 152 A3
Hogshaw Rd. Gran 75 F3
Hogtrough La. Wen 131 E1
Holdom Ave. M Keyn 47 E1
Holes La. Oln 6 C2
Holiday La. Hans 10 C2
Holland Cl. Chin 147 E4
Holland Cl. Wen 131 D2
Holland Rd. Ayl 101 D1
Holland Rd. Mar 183 F2
Holland Way. N Pag 22 B2
Hollandridge La. Ston 168 B2
Hollandridge La. Ston 179 F4
Holliday Cl. She C E 45 F4
Holliday St. Berk 135 E2
Hollies The. Bov 146 A1
Hollies The. Chor 167 E1
Hollies The. Tri 119 D2
Hollies The. Wigg 119 E1
Hollin La. M Keyn 33 F2
Hollingdon Rd. Soul 69 E2
Hollington. L Cre 125 D1
Hollinwell Cl. M Keyn 46 B1
Hollis Rd. H Wyc 173 F4
Hollow Hill End. Gran 75 F4
Hollow Rise. H Wyc 162 A1
Hollow Way. Ches 143 F1
Hollow Way La. Ame 154 C2
Hollow Way La. Ches 154 C2
Holloway Cl. W Dra 208 C1
Holloway La. Chen 156 B1
Holloway La. Ibst 169 E2
Holloway La. W Dra 208 C1
Holloway The. Dra B 118 B2
Holloway The. P Ris 139 E3
Holly Wlk. Asp H 49 D1
Holly Cl. Far C 198 B4
Holly Cl. She C E 45 F3
Holly Cres. Wind 209 E3
Holly Dr. Berk 135 E2
Holly Dr. Maid 202 C4
Holly Dr. Wind 210 C1
Holly End. Wal A 161 E4
Holly Gdns. W Dra 208 C2
Holly Green La. Bled 138 A2
Holly Hedges La. Bov 156 B4
Holly Tree Cl. Bot 155 D4
Holly Tree La. Cudd 112 C2
Hollyberry Gr. Hol G 163 E4
Hollybush Hill. Sto P 199 D3
Hollybush La. Ame 154 B2
Hollybush La. Cook 195 D3
Hollybush La. Den 200 C4
Hollybush Rd. Ches 144 A2
Hollyfield. Tri 119 E3
Hollyfield Cl. Tri 119 E3
Hollytree Cl. C St P 177 F3
Holm Gate. M Keyn 46 A4
Holman St. Ayl 101 E1
Holmanleaze. Maid 203 D4
Holmdale. Slough 206 B3
Holmer Green Rd. Ty Gr 163 D2
Holmer La. H Wyc 172 B2
Holmer Pl. Hol G 163 E4
Holmers Ct. H Wyc 172 A2
Holmers Farm Way. H Wyc 172 B2
Holmers Farm Way. Lit M 172 B2
Holmers Farm Way. Mar B 172 B2
Holmewood. M Keyn 46 C2
Holmlea Rd. Datch 211 E3
Holmlea Wlk. Datch 211 E3
Holmoak Wlk. Ty Gr 163 D2
Holmwood Cl. Maid 202 A3
Holst Cres. Walt 48 B2
Holt The. Buck 52 C4
Holton Rd. Buck 41 E1
Holts Green. G Bkhl 59 E1
Holtspur Ave. Woo G 185 F4
Holtspur Cl. Beac 186 A4
Holtspur La. Woo G 185 F3
Holtspur Top La. Beac 175 D1
Holtspur Way. Beac 175 D1
Holyport Rd. Holy 203 D1
Holyrood. M Keyn 45 F4
Holywell Pl. M Keyn 35 E1
Home Cl. M Keyn 47 D1
Home Cl. W Tur 116 C1
Home Farm. Nwtn L 57 E2
Home Farm La. G Bkhl 59 E1
Home Farm Rd. Berk 134 B4
Home Farm Way. Sto P 199 E2
Home Meadow. Far C 198 B2
Home Meadow Dr. Fla H 185 D4
Home Way. Chor 167 F1
Homefield. Bov 146 A2
Homefield Cl. Skch 158 C2
Homelands Gdns. G Kin 162 B4
Homeridings House. M Keyn 34 A2
Homers Rd. Wind 209 E3
Homestall Cl. M Keyn 46 A4
Homestead Farm. Dint 114 A2
Homestead Rd. Maid 202 B2
Homestead The. Lit M 172 B2
Homestead The. She C E 46 A3
Homestead Way. Pott 18 C2
Homeward Ct. M Keyn 46 A4
Homewood. Slough 206 B4
Hondur Cl. Bier 102 A1
Honey Hill. Uxb 201 F3
Honey La. Hurl 193 F1
Honey Way. Wal A 161 D4
Honeycroft Hill. Uxb 201 F3
Honeypot Cl. M Keyn 34 A2
Honeysuckle Fld. Ches 144 B1
Honeysuckle Rd. Hol G 162 C4
Honeywick La. Eat B 92 C4
Honor End La. Pres 151 D4
Honor Rd. Pres 151 E3
Honorwood Cl. Pres 151 D4
Hoods Farm Cl. Bier 102 B2
Hooper Gate. M Keyn 35 E4
Hop Gdns. Hen-O-T 191 E1
Hopcraft Cl. U Arn 94 C4
Hopkins Cl. M K Vil 36 A1
Hopkins Ct. Ayl 101 F1
Hoppers Meadow. M Keyn 46 A4
Hoppers Way. G Kin 162 B4
Hopton Rd. Tha 126 A1
Horn La. M Keyn 32 B3
Horn St. Wins 65 F2
Hornbeam. N Pag 22 A2
Hornbeam Cl. H Wyc 172 A2
Hornbeam Gdns. Slough 206 A2
Hornbeam Wlk. Ty Gr 163 D2
Hornbill Cl. Uxb 208 B4
Horners Croft. M Keyn 33 E3
Hornhill Rd. Map Cr 178 B3
Horns La. H Wyc 172 A2
Horns La. P Ris 139 D2
Horse Hill. Bot 155 E4
Horseguards Dr. Maid 203 D4
Horsemoor La. Cole 164 B1

Horsenden Rd. Bled 138 C1
Horsenden Rd. H Wyc 173 F3
Horseshoe Cl. Ched 105 D4
Horseshoe Cres. Beac 175 F1
Horseshoe Hill. Burn 197 D4
Horseshoe Rd. Bled R 159 E4
Horsleys. Map Cr 178 B3
Horton Bridge Rd. W Dra 208 C3
Horton Cl. Maid 196 B1
Horton Cl. W Dra 208 C3
Horton Gate. M Keyn 21 F1
Horton Rd. Datch 211 E3
Horton Rd. Hort 212 A3
Horton Rd. Ivin 91 D1
Horton Rd. Slap 91 E3
Horton Rd. Stan 213 D2
Horton Rd. W Dra 208 C3
Hortonsfield Rd. Yard G 18 C3
Horwood Ct. M Keyn 47 E1
Hospital Circular Rd. Wen 131 E3
Hospital Hill. Ches 154 B4
Hotch Croft. Cran 25 E2
Hotley Bottom La. Pres 151 E4
Houghton Ct. M Keyn 45 F4
Housman Cl. N Pag 22 A3
How's Cl. Uxb 201 E2
How's Rd. Uxb 201 E2
Howard Agne Cl. Bov 146 A2
Howard Ave. Ayl 116 A3
Howard Ave. Slough 205 F4
Howard Cres. Se Gr 176 B3
Howard Rd. Ches 144 A2
Howard Rd. Se Gr 176 B3
Howard Way. N Pag 23 D2
Howards Thicket. Ger C 188 B1
Howards Wood Dr. Ger C 188 B1
Howarth Rd. Maid 203 D3
Howe Dr. Beac 175 F3
Howe Hill La. Hol G 163 D4
Howland Pl. Hth 60 C4
Hoylake Cl. M Keyn 57 E4
Hubbard Cl. Buck 41 F1
Hubbards Rd. Chor 167 E2
Hubert Day Cl. Beac 175 E2
Hubert Rd. Slough 206 B2
Huckleberry Cl. Walt 48 A3
Hudnall La. L Gad 121 F4
Hudson La. She C E 45 E4
Hughenden Ave. H Wyc 173 D4
Hughenden Green. Ayl 115 F2
Hughenden Rd. H Wyc 162 A1
Hughenden Rd. Slough 205 E4
Hughendon Cl. Maid 202 B3
Hulbert End. Ayl 116 B3
Hulcombe Wlk. Ayl 101 F1
Hull Cl. Ayl 115 F3
Hulton Dr. Emb 13 F4
Humber Dr. Ayl 115 E3
Humber Way. M Keyn 46 C1
Hundred Acres La. Ame 165 E4
Hungerford Ave. Slough 205 F4
Hungerford Dr. Maid 195 F2
Hunstanton Way. M Keyn 57 E4
Hunt Rd. H Wyc 173 F3
Hunt's La. Tapl 196 C2
Hunter Dr. M Keyn 58 B3
Hunter St. Buck 52 B4
Hunters Cl. Bov 146 A1
Hunters Cl. Ches 144 A1
Hunters Cl. Tri 119 D3
Hunters Hill. H Wyc 173 F3
Hunters Mews. Wind 210 B3
Hunters Park. Berk 135 F3
Hunters Point. Chin 147 E3
Hunters Reach. M Keyn 34 A2
Huntingbrooke. M Keyn 45 F4
Huntingdon Cres. M Keyn 57 E3
Huntley Cl. H Wyc 162 B1
Hunts Hill La. Wal A 161 F3
Huntsman Gr. M Keyn 22 A1
Huntsmans. Dag 107 E3
Huntswood La. Burn 196 C2
Huntswood La. Tapl 196 C2
Hurley High St. Hurl 193 F2
Hurley La. Bish 194 A2
Hurley La. Hurl 194 A2
Hurstfield Dr. Burn 204 A4
Hutchings Cl. M Keyn 46 A4
Hutchings Rd. Beac 175 E3
Hutton Ave. M Keyn 34 C1
Hutton Way. Asp G 49 D3
Huxley Cl. N Pag 21 F2
Huxley Cl. Uxb 201 E1
Hyacinth Dr. Uxb 201 F3
Hychenden Cl. Wal A 161 F3
Hyde Cl. N Pag 22 B1
Hyde Green. Beac 175 F2
Hyde Green. Mar 183 F1
Hyde Heath Rd. S Hea 153 D3
Hyde La. Bov 146 A2
Hyde La. S Hea 152 C3
Hyde Meadows. Bov 146 A2
Hyde The. W Tur 116 C1
Hylle Cl. Wind 209 F3
Hylton Rd. H Wyc 172 B4
Hyrons Cl. Ame 154 C1
Hyrons La. Ame 154 B1

Ibstone Ave. M Keyn 34 B2
Ibstone Rd. Skch 158 B2
Ickford Rd. Shab 124 B1
Ickford Rd. Worm 123 F3
Icknield Cl. Chin 147 D2
Icknield Cl. Wen 131 E3
Icknield Cres. Tri 119 D3
Icknield Way. Eat B 93 E2
Icknield Way. Tri 118 C2
Iffley Cl. Uxb 201 E3
Ilchester Cl. Maid 202 B3
Ilex Cl. Ty Gr 163 D2
Illingworth. Wind 209 F2
Illingworth Pl. M Keyn 46 C4
Imperial Rd. Wind 210 A3
In The Ray. Maid 203 D4
India Rd. Slough 206 A2
Ingleglen. Far C 198 A4
Ingleside. Stan 212 C3
Ingleton Cl. M Keyn 34 B2
Ingram Ave. Ayl 116 B3
Inholder Ct. M Keyn 34 C3
Inkerman Dr. Hol G 163 D3
Inkerman Terr. Ches 154 B3
Inn Farm Ct. N Pag 22 B4
Innings Gate. Frie 170 C1
Institute Rd. Burn 203 F4
Institute Rd. Mar 183 F1
Institute Rd. Tapl 203 F4
Intalbury Ave. Ayl 101 D1
Inverness Cl. M Keyn 46 C1
Inwood Cl. Cook 195 D3
Ipswich Rd. Slough 205 D4
Ireton Ct. Tha 125 F1
Iris Cl. Ayl 115 D3
Ironmonger Ct. M Keyn 34 C3
Irvine Dr. S Man 116 A1
Irving Cres. Ched 105 D4
Isaacson Dr. Walt 48 B3
Isambard Cl. Uxb 201 E1
Isis Cl. S Man 115 E2
Isis Way. Bou E 185 D2
Isis Wlk. M Keyn 46 C1
Island The. Stp Cl 63 E1
Islet Park. Maid 196 B2
Islet Park Dr. Maid 196 B2
Islet Rd. Maid 196 B2
Ivanhoe Cl. Uxb 208 B4
Iver La. Iver 208 A4
Iver La. Uxb 201 E1
Iver La. Uxb 208 A4
Ivinghoe View. Ayl 102 A1
Ivinghoe Way. Edle 92 C1
Ivins Rd. Beac 175 D1
Ivy Cl. N Pag 22 C2
Ivy La. Bier 102 A1
Ivy La. G Bhkl 70 A4
Ivy La. Nwtn L 57 E2
Ivy La. Stew 68 C1
Ivy La. Wing 79 E2
Ivyhouse La. Berk 135 F3

Jack's La. Turv 8 C3
Jackson Ct. Ty Gr 163 D2
Jackson Rd. Ayl 101 D2
Jacksons Cl. Edle 92 C2
Jacob Cl. Wind 209 F3
Jamaica. M Keyn 47 D3
James Cl. Hol G 163 D3
James Cl. Mar 183 F2
James Martin Cl. Den G 190 A3
James Rd. La En 171 D2
James St. Wind 210 B3
James Way. M Keyn 47 D1
Jane Cl. Ayl 116 A2
Jansel Sq. Ayl 116 A3
Jarry Ct. Mar 183 F2
Jarvis Cl. Ayl 116 A3
Jasmine Cl. Ayl 116 A2
Jasmine Cres. P Ris 139 D2
Jasons Hill. Bot 145 D1
Jeeves Cl. M Keyn 47 E4
Jeffries Ct. Bou E 185 D1
Jellicoe Cl. Slough 205 D2
Jenkins La. Dra B 132 C2
Jenna Way. N Pag 23 D2
Jenner Rd. Ayl 115 F3
Jennery La. Burn 197 E1
Jennings. M Keyn 34 B4
Jennings Field. Fla H 185 E4
Jennings Wharf. Wind 210 B4
Jerome Cl. Mar 183 F2
Jersey Rd. M Keyn 33 E3
Jesse's La. L Cre 125 E3
Job's La. Cook 195 D4
John Hall Way. H Wyc 172 B2
John Hall Way. Lit M 172 B2
John Hampden Way. Pres 151 D4
John Taylor Ct. Slough 205 E3
Johns La. Ash Gr 134 C1
Johnson Rd. La En 171 D3
Joiner's Cl. C St P 177 F2
Joiner's La. C St P 177 F2
Joiners Way. C St P 177 F2
Joiners Way. Lave 7 F4
Jonathans. M Keyn 47 D3
Jones Way. Hedg 187 E1
Jordans La. Se Gr 176 C2
Jordans Way. Se Gr 176 C2
Joules Ct. She B E 46 B3
Jourdelay's Pas. Eton 210 B4
Journeys End. Slough 205 F4
Jubilee Rd. H Wyc 161 F1
Jubilee Rd. H Wyc 172 C4
Jubilee Rd. Skch 158 C2
Judge's La. L Buzz 80 C3
Judy's Pas. Eton 205 E1
Juniper Cl. Ty Gr 163 D2
Juniper Dr. H Wyc 172 B3
Juniper Dr. Maid 203 D4
Juniper La. Fla H 185 E4
Juniper Rd. Mar B 183 E3

Kaplan Cl. She B E 46 A3
Katherine Cl. Ty Gr 174 B4
Katrine Pl. M Keyn 58 B3
Kaybridge Cl. H Wyc 173 F3
Kaywoo Cl. Slough 206 B2
Keach Cl. Wins 66 A3
Keaton Cl. She C E 45 E4
Keats Cl. H Wyc 172 C3
Keats Cl. N Pag 22 A2
Keats La. Eton 210 B4
Keats Way. M Keyn 57 F4
Keats Way. W Dra 208 C1
Keble Cl. Ayl 115 D4
Keble Rd. Maid 202 C4
Keel Dr. Slough 205 E2
Keeler Cl. Wind 209 F2
Keen's Cl. H Wyc 162 C1
Keens La. Chin 147 E3
Keep Hill Dr. H Wyc 173 E2
Keep Hill Rd. H Wyc 173 E3
Keepers Farm Cl. Wind 209 F2
Keepers Farm Cl. Wind 209 F3
Keepers La. Ame 153 E2
Keinches La. Whit 87 D3
Kellan Dr. M Keyn 35 D1
Kelsey Cl. Maid 202 B2
Kelso Cl. M Keyn 57 E3
Kelvin Cl. H Wyc 172 C4
Kelvin Dr. She B E 46 B3
Kemble Ct. M Keyn 35 D3
Kempton Gdns. M Keyn 57 E3
Kenchester. M Keyn 33 F3
Kendal Cl. Ayl 116 A3
Kendal Cl. Slough 206 A3
Kendal Dr. Slough 206 A3
Kendal Gdns. L Buzz 80 B4
Kendalls Cl. H Wyc 173 F3
Kendrick Rd. Slough 206 A2
Keneally. Oak G 209 E3
Kenilworth Ct. Slough 205 F2
Kenilworth Dr. Ayl 101 E1
Kenilworth Dr. M Keyn 57 F4
Kennedy Cl. Far C 198 B3
Kennedy Cl. Maid 202 B3
Kennedy Cl. Mar 183 F2
Kennel La. Cook 195 E4
Kennet Cl. Ayl 115 E2
Kennet Cl. H Wyc 162 B1
Kennet Dr. M Keyn 57 F4
Kennet Pl. M Keyn 57 F4
Kennet Rd. Maid 202 C4
Kennett Rd. Bou E 185 D2
Kennington Cl. N Pag 22 B2
Kensacre. Iver H 200 B2
Kensington Dr. M Keyn 33 F1
Kent Ave. Slough 205 E4
Kent Cl. Uxb 201 E3
Kent Way. Maid 195 F1
Kentmere Rd. Ayl 116 A4
Kenton Cl. Mar 183 F1
Kenton's La. Wind 209 F3
Kents Rd. M Keyn 34 B4
Kenway Dr. L Chal 166 A4
Kenwell Ct. M Keyn 35 E2
Kenwood Gate. M Keyn 35 D1
Kenwood Cl. Maid 202 A4
Kenwood Dr. Chor 178 C4
Keppel Ave. Have 20 B1
Keppel Ave. Have 20 B1
Keppel St. Wind 210 B3
Kepwick. M Keyn 33 F1
Kercroft. M Keyn 33 F1
Kernow Cres. M Keyn 35 D1
Kerria Pl. M Keyn 47 D2
Kersey. M Keyn 34 B4
Kesters Rd. Ches 154 B4
Kestrel Cl. Berk 135 E2
Kestrel Cl. H Wyc 161 E1
Kestrel Dr. Hol G 163 D3
Kestrel Path. Slough 197 F1
Kestrel Way. Buck 52 C4
Keswick Ct. Slough 205 F3
Keswick Rd. Hans 11 D1
Ketchmere Cl. L Cre 125 E3
Ketton Cl. M Keyn 35 E4
Kew Ct. M Keyn 33 F1
Kew Gr. H Wyc 173 D2
Keyes Way. Buck 41 F1
Keynes Cl. N Pag 22 C2
Keys La. Maid 202 C3
Khasiaberry. Walt 48 A3
Kidd Cl. She C E 45 F3
Kidderminster Rd. Slough 198 A2
Kidwells Cl. Maid 202 C4
Kidwells Park Dr. Maid 202 C4
Kildonan Pl. M Keyn 33 E2
Kilfillan Gdns. Berk 135 D2
Killarney Dr. Maid 202 C4
Kiln Ave. L Chal 155 E1
Kiln Cl. Pres 151 E4
Kiln La. Bot 155 D4
Kiln La. Bou E 185 E2
Kiln La. Hedg 187 E2
Kiln La. Lac G 149 F3
Kiln La. Pres 151 D4
Kilner Rd. Ayl 115 F3
Kilnwood. Wal A 150 A1
Kilpin Green. N Craw 24 A3
Kimbells Cl. Shab 124 B1
Kimber Cl. Wind 210 A2
Kimber's La. Maid 202 C2
Kimberley Cl. Slough 206 C1
Kimbers Dr. Burn 197 E1
Kimblewick La. G Kim 129 E2
Kimbolton Ct. M Keyn 35 D4
Kincardine Dr. M Keyn 46 C2
Kindleton. M Keyn 34 C4
King Charles Cl. Buck 41 F1
King Edward Ave. Ayl 116 A4
King Edward St. M Keyn 33 F4
King Edward St. Slough 205 E2
King Edward VII Ave. Wind 210 C4
King George Cres. M Keyn 32 C3
King George V Rd. Ame 154 B1
King John's Cl. Wray 211 E1
King St. Ches 154 A4
King St. H Wyc 160 B1
King St. M Keyn 32 C3
King St. Tri 119 D2
King Stable St. Eton 210 B4
King's Gr. Maid 202 C3
King's La. Lee C 142 A2
King's La. S Hea 152 C4
King's Rd. Ayl 115 F4
King's Rd. H Wyc 173 F2
King's Rd. Slough 205 F2
King's Rd. Uxb 201 E2
King's Rd. Wind 210 B2
Kingfisher Rd. Buck 52 C4
Kinghorn Park. Maid 195 E2
Kings Cl. C St G 177 E4
Kings Cl. Hen-O-T 191 E1
Kings Cl. Worm 123 E3
Kings Ct. Berk 135 E3
Kings Farm Rd. Chor 167 E2
Kings Hall Par. Wen 131 D2
Kings La. Cook 195 D4
Kings Mead. Edle 92 C2
Kings Meadow. Bier 102 B2
Kings Oak Cl. P Ris 139 E3
Kings Rd. Berk 135 D2
Kings Rd. C St G 177 E4
Kings Rd. Hen-O-T 191 E1
Kings Rd. W Dra 208 C2
Kings Ride. Ty Gr 163 D1
Kings Sq. H Wyc 173 F2
Kings St. Maid 202 C3
Kingsbridge. M Keyn 46 B1
Kingsbury. Ayl 115 E4
Kingsbury Dr. Old W 211 D1
Kingsdale Rd. Berk 135 D2
Kingsey Rd. Tha 126 B1
Kingsfield. Wind 209 E3
Kingsfold. M Keyn 34 A4
Kingshill Rd. H Wyc 162 B1
Kingshill Rd. Hol G 162 B2
Kingshill Way. Berk 135 D1
Kingshorn La. Maid 195 E2
Kingsland Rd. Ayl 116 A2
Kingsley Cl. N Pag 21 F2
Kingsley Cres. H Wyc 172 C3
Kingsley Dr. Mar B 183 E3
Kingsley Wlk. Tri 119 D2
Kingsmead. P Ris 139 D3
Kingsmead Rd. H Wyc 173 F2
Kingsmead Rd. Loud 173 F2
Kingston Ave. M Keyn 32 C3
Kingston Ave. W Dra 208 C3
Kingston La. Uxb 201 F1
Kingston La. W Dra 208 C2
Kingston Rd. H Wyc 162 B1
Kingstone Hill. Ast R 158 A4
Kingsway. Far C 198 B3
Kingsway. Ger C 188 C4
Kingswood Ave. Ty Gr 174 A4
Kingswood Creek. Wray 211 E1
Kingswood Ct. Maid 202 C3
Kingswood La. W Und 96 C3
Kingswood Rd. Ty Gr 163 D1
Kinloch Pl. M Keyn 58 C3
Kinross Dr. M Keyn 46 C1
Kinson Green. Ayl 101 F2
Kipling Dr. N Pag 21 F2
Kipling Rd. M Keyn 58 A4
Kirkstall Pl. M Keyn 46 C4
Kirtle Rd. Ches 144 B1
Kirtlington. M Keyn 35 D3
Kitchener Rd. H Wyc 172 C4
Kite Field. Berk 134 C4
Kite Hill. M Keyn 47 D4
Kitsbury Rd. Berk 135 D2
Kitsbury Terr. Berk 135 D2
Klondyke. Mar 183 E1
Knapp Gate. She C E 45 F4
Knaves Beech. Loud 174 B1
Knaves Beech Way. Loud 174 B1
Knaves Hill. L Buzz 80 B4
Knaves Hollow. Woo G 174 B1
Knebworth Gate. N Pag 22 A1
Knighton Way La. N Den 201 D3
Knights Cl. Eat B 92 C3
Knights Cl. G Bkhl 59 E1
Knights Cl. Wind 209 E3
Knights Hill. H Wyc 172 C3
Knights Templar W. H Wyc 173 D2
Knolls Cl. Win 89 D2
Knolton Way. Slough 206 B4
Knottocks Cl. Beac 175 E3
Knottocks Dr. Beac 175 E3
Knottocks End. Beac 175 E3
Knowl Gate. M Keyn 46 B4
Knowland Way. Den G 189 F3
Knowles Cl. W Dra 208 C3
Knowles Green. M Keyn 58 B4
Knowsley Cl. Maid 195 D1
Kop Hill Rd. P Ris 139 E2
Kop Hill Rd. Pres 139 E2
Krohn Cl. Buck 52 C4
Krypton Cl. She B E 46 B3
Kynaston Ave. Ayl 115 F2

La Roche Cl. Slough 206 B2
Laburnham Rd. Maid 202 C3
Laburnum Ave. W Dra 208 C3
Laburnum Cl. Mar 183 F2
Laburnum Cres. Slough 212 A4
Laburnum Gr. M Keyn 58 C4
Laburnum Gr. Slough 212 A4
Laburnum Rd. H Wyc 172 B3
Lace Mews. Oln 7 D2
Lacemakers. Chin 147 E3
Lacemakers. L Cre 125 E4
Laceys Dr. Hol G 163 D3
Lacy Dr. M Keyn 35 D4
Ladbroke Cl. Ayl 101 F1
Ladbrooke Rd. Slough 205 E2
Ladymead Cl. Whad 56 A4
Ladysmith Rd. Ivin 105 F3
Ladywalk. Map Cr 178 B3
Laggan Rd. Maid 195 F1
Laggan Sq. Maid 195 F1
Laggen Ct. M Keyn 58 B2
Lagger Cl. C St G 177 D4
Lagger The. C St G 177 D4
Lagonda Cl. N Pag 22 C2
Laiden Cl. M Keyn 58 B2
Lake Ave. Slough 205 E3
Lake Cl. Wins 66 A3
Lakes La. Beac 186 C4
Lakes La. N Pag 22 A3
Lakeside. Maid 196 A1
Lakeside. Tri 119 D3
Lakeside Dr. Sto P 198 C2
Lakeside Rd. Iver 212 C4
Lamb Cl. N Pag 22 A2
Lambe Rd. Wen 131 E3
Lambert Ave. Slough 206 C2
Lambert Wlk. Tha 125 F1
Lamberts Croft. M Keyn 33 E3
Lambourn Ct. M Keyn 46 B1
Lambourne Ave. S Man 115 E2
Lambourne Ct. Uxb 201 D2
Lambourne Dr. Maid 202 B2
Lambridge La. Hen-O-T 191 E2
Lambridge La. Hen-O-T 191 E2
Lambridge Wd R. Hen-O-T 191 D2
Lambscroft Way. Ger C 177 F1
Lambtons Way. Wins 66 A3
Lammas. M Keyn 47 D3
Lammas Ave. Wind 210 B3
Lammas Ct. Wind 210 B3
Lammas Rd. Ched 105 D4
Lammas Way. La En 171 D2
Lammas Way. Loud 174 B1
Lampets Cross. M Keyn 47 D3
Lamport Ct. M Keyn 46 A4
Lamva Ct. M Keyn 32 C3
Lancaster Ave. Slough 198 B1
Lancaster Dr. Bov 146 A2
Lancaster Gate. M Keyn 57 F4
Lancaster Rd. Ayl 116 A3
Lancaster Rd. H Wyc 172 C2
Lancaster Rd. Maid 202 A4
Lancaster Rd. Uxb 201 E3
Lancaster Ride. Ty Gr 174 A4
Lancastria Mews. Maid 202 B4
Lance Way. H Wyc 174 A3
Lancelot Cl. Slough 205 D2
Lanchester Rd. Cran 24 B1
Lancot Ave. Dun 93 F4
Lancot Dr. Dun 93 F4
Lancotbury Cl. Tott 93 D4
Lancresse Cl. Uxb 201 E3
Lander Rd. Ayl 100 C2
Landsborough Gate. M Keyn 35 E4
Lane End Rd. H Wyc 172 A3
Lane The. Graf R 9 E1
Lane The. Mur 67 E3
Lane Wood Cl. Ame 165 F4
Lanfranc Gdns. M Keyn 35 D4
Langcliffe Dr. M Keyn 34 B3
Langdale Cl. M Keyn 58 B2
Langdale Cl. Maid 203 D3
Langdon Ave. Ayl 116 A3

Langdon St. Tri 119 D2
Langland Rd. M Keyn 47 E3
Langlands. Lave 7 F4
Langley Broom. Slough 206 C1
Langley Rd. Slough 206 B2
Langley Way. Mar 183 B1
Langston Dr. M Keyn 33 F2
Langstone Cl. Ayl 101 F2
Langton Cl. Maid 202 B4
Langton's Meadow. Far C 198 B3
Lanner Wlk. M Keyn 47 D4
Lansdell Ave. H Wyc 172 A2
Lansdown Rd. Ger C 177 E1
Lansdown Way. H Wyc 172 C2
Lansdowne Ave. Slough 205 F3
Lansdowne Ct. Slough 205 F3
Lansdowne Rd. Ayl 101 E1
Lansdowne Rd. Ches 144 B1
Lanthorn Cl. M Keyn 34 C3
Lappetts La. S Hea 152 C4
Larch Cl. Ayl 102 A1
Larch Cl. Slough 205 D4
Larch Cl. Ty Gr 163 E1
Larch Gr. M Keyn 58 C4
Larches The. Berk 134 B3
Larches The. Hol G 163 E4
Larchfield Rd. Maid 202 C3
Larchlands The. Ty Gr 163 E1
Larchwood. L Kin 152 A2
Lark Cl. Buck 52 C4
Lark Rise. Hol G 163 D3
Larkfield Cl. H Wyc 162 C1
Larkin Cl. N Pag 22 A3
Larkings La. Sto P 199 D2
Larks Rise. Ches 154 B3
Larkspur Way. Hol G 162 C3
Larvic Rd. Ayl 115 E3
Larwood Pl. M Keyn 34 C1
Lascelles Cl. M Keyn 35 D4
Lascelles Rd. Slough 206 A2
Laser Cl. She B E 46 B3
Lashlake Rd. Tha 125 F1
Lassell Gdns. Maid 203 D4
Latchmoor Ave. Ger C 188 B4
Latchmoor Gr. Ger C 188 B4
Latchmoor Way. Ger C 188 B4
Latimer. M Keyn 32 C2
Latimer Cl. L Chal 166 B4
Latimer Rd. Ches 155 E1
Latimer Rd. Lat 155 E1
Latimer Way. Beac 175 E3
Laud's Cl. Hen-O-T 191 E1
Launceston Ct. She C E 46 A3
Laurel Ave. Slough 206 C2
Laurel Cl. Iver 212 C4
Laurel Cl. Pres 151 D4
Laurel Cl. She C E 45 E4
Laurel Dr. Loud 174 A2
Laurel Dr. Wal A 161 E4
Laurel La. W Dra 208 C1
Laurel Rd. Ger C 177 E1
Laurels Rd. Iver H 200 B2
Laurels The. H Wyc 172 B2
Laurels The. M Keyn 47 E1
Lautrec Way. Ayl 100 C1
Lavender Gr. Walt 48 A3
Lavender Rd. Uxb 208 C4
Lavender Way. Hol G 162 C4
Lavender Wlk. Ayl 115 D3
Lavendon Rd. Oln 7 D3
Lawford Ave. Chor 167 E2
Lawford Cl. Chor 167 E2
Lawkland. Far C 198 B1
Lawn Ave. W Dra 208 B2
Lawn Cl. Datch 211 E4
Lawn Hill. Edgc 73 D1
Lawn Rd. Uxb 201 E3
Lawns The. Bri 96 A1
Lawns The. Ty Gr 163 D1
Lawrence Ct. Wind 210 B3
Laws Cl. Turv 8 C3
Lawsone Rise. H Wyc 162 A1
Laxton Green. Maid 202 B2
Lay Rd. Ayl 101 D1
Layter's Ave. Ger C 177 E1
Layter's Cl. Ger C 177 E1
Layter's End. Ger C 177 E1
Layters Green La. Ger C 177 D1
Layters Way. Ger C 188 B3
Lea Cl. Mar B 183 E3
Leach Rd. Ayl 115 E4
Leachcroft. Ger C 177 D1
Leacroft Cl. W Dra 208 C4
Leaders Cl. Win 89 D2
Leafield Rise. M Keyn 33 E1
Leapingwell La. Wins 66 A3
Leas Cl. H Wyc 173 F4
Leather La. G Mis 142 A2
Leaver Rd. Hen-O-T 191 E1
Leckhampstead Rd. Akel 42 A4
Leckhampstead Rd. Wick 31 D2
Ledborough La. Beac 175 F2
Ledborough Wood. Beac 175 F2
Ledbury. M Keyn 21 E1
Ledger's Rd. Slough 205 E2
Lee Cres. Sto 114 B3
Lee Farm Cl. Bot 145 D1
Lee La. Bish 194 C1
Lee La. Maid 194 C1
Lee Rd. Ayl 115 E3
Lee Rd. Qntn 85 D3
Leeches Way. Ched 105 D4
Leeds Rd. Slough 205 F3
Lees Cl. Maid 202 A3
Lees Gdns. Maid 202 A3
Lees Wlk. Mar 183 B1
Leicester Cl. Hen-O-T 191 E2
Leigh Hill. M Keyn 46 B1
Leigh Park. Datch 211 D4
Leigh Rd. Slough 205 D3
Leigh Sq. Wind 209 E3
Leigh St. H Wyc 172 C4
Leighton Gdns. Maid 196 A1
Leighton Rd. Edle 92 B2
Leighton Rd. L Buzz 80 C4
Leighton Rd. S Ham 69 F4
Leighton Rd. Soul 70 A1
Leighton Rd. Win 89 E2
Leighton Rd. Wing 80 A2
Leighton St. Hth 60 C3
Leiston Spur. Slough 205 F4
Lembrook Wlk. Ayl 115 E3
Lenborough Cl. Buck 52 B4
Lenborough Ct. M Keyn 35 E1
Lenborough Rd. Buck 52 B4
Lennon Dr. She C E 45 F4
Lennox Rd. M Keyn 58 B4
Lent Green La. Burn 197 D1
Lent Rise Rd. Burn 197 D1
Lenthall Cl. M Keyn 34 A2
Leon Ave. M Keyn 58 B4
Leonards Cl. Edgc 72 C1
Leopard Dr. M Keyn 35 D4
Leopold Rd. L Buzz 80 B4
Lester Gr. Ty Gr 163 D2
Lesters Rd. Cook 195 E3
Letchfield. Bot 155 D4
Letter Box La. P Ris 139 E4
Leven Cl. L Buzz 80 A4
Leven Cl. M Keyn 58 B3
Levings Cl. Ayl 101 D2
Lewins Rd. Ger C 188 B4
Lewis Cl. N Pag 21 F3
Lewis La. C St P 177 F1
Lexham Gdns. Ame 154 B1
Lexington Ave. Maid 202 B3
Leybourne Gdns. Chin 147 E4
Leyburne Cl. Men 90 B4
Leyfield Rd. Ayl 115 F3
Leylands La. Stan 212 C2
Leys Rd. M Keyn 46 A4
Leys The. Ame 154 A2
Leys The. Tri 119 D2
Leys The. Wbn S 49 D2
Leys View. Sher 13 F1
Leywood Cl. Ame 165 F4
Lichfield Down. Walt 48 A3
Lichfield Rd. Datch 211 E3
Liddall Way. W Dra 208 C3
Liddell. Oak G 209 E3
Liddell Sq. Oak G 209 E3
Lightlands La. Cook 195 F3
Ligo Ave. S Man 116 B1
Lilac Pl. W Dra 208 C3
Lillac Cl. Nwtn L 57 E2
Lillibrooke Cres. Maid 202 A2
Lilly Bottom La. Lac G 150 A4
Lily's Wlk. H Wyc 173 D3
Limbaud Cl. Walt 48 A3
Lime Ave. Buck 52 C4
Lime Ave. H Wyc 173 E3
Lime Ave. W Dra 208 C3
Lime Cl. N Pag 22 A2
Lime Cl. Ty Gr 163 D2
Lime Gr. Chin 147 E3
Lime Gr. L Buzz 80 C4
Lime Gr. Wbn S 49 D2
Lime Rd. P Ris 139 D2
Lime Rd. Yard G 18 C3
Lime St. Oln 6 C2
Lime Tree Cl. G Kin 162 B4
Lime Tree Wlk. Ame 165 F4
Lime Wlk. Maid 202 A4
Lime Wlk. N Den 201 E4
Limes Ave. Ayl 116 A4
Limes The. Ame 154 A2
Limes The. M Keyn 32 C3
Limes The. M Keyn 58 C4
Limmer La. H Wyc 172 A2
Limmers La. G Kin 162 B4
Linceslade Gr. M Keyn 46 A4
Linchfield. H Wyc 173 F4
Lincoln. M Keyn 34 B4
Lincoln Ct. Berk 135 D2
Lincoln Hatch La. Burn 197 E1
Lincoln Park. Ame 165 F4
Lincoln Park Bs Cntr. H Wyc 172 B3
Lincoln Rd. C St P 177 F1
Lincoln Rd. H Wyc 172 C3
Lincoln Rd. Maid 202 A4
Lincolns The. L Kin 152 A2
Linden Ave. Maid 195 E1
Linden Ct. H Wyc 172 B3
Linden Dr. Far C 198 B2
Linden End. Ayl 115 F3
Linden Gr. M Keyn 34 C4
Linden Way. Dint 128 A4
Linden Wlk. Ty Gr 163 D2
Lindens The. Fel 146 C4
Lindo Cl. Ches 144 A1
Lindsay Ave. H Wyc 172 C4
Lindsay Cl. Stan 213 E1
Lindsey Rd. Den 190 A1
Lines Hill. A Abb 88 A2
Lines Rd. La En 171 D3
Lines The. A Abb 88 B2
Linfields. L Chal 166 B4
Linford Ave. N Pag 22 A2
Linford La. M Keyn 35 E2
Linford La. M Keyn 35 E4
Lingfield. M Keyn 33 F2
Lingfield Cl. H Wyc 174 A3
Lingholm Cl. Maid 202 B3
Link Rd. Datch 211 E3
Link Rd. H Wyc 172 B3
Link Rd. S Hea 152 A4
Link The. Hol G 163 D3
Link The. Slough 206 A4
Link Way. Den G 190 A3
Links Rd. Fla H 185 E4
Links Way. Fla H 185 D4
Linkswood Rd. Burn 197 E2
Linnet Cl. H Wyc 172 A2
Linnet Dr. Wcot 98 B3
Linnington Ave. Bot 145 D1
Linslade Rd. L Buzz 70 C2
Lintlaw Pl. M Keyn 47 D2
Linton Cl. M Keyn 34 B2
Lintott Ct. Stan 213 E1
Linx The. M Keyn 47 D1
Lionel Ave. Wen 131 D3
Lionel Cl. Wen 131 D3
Lipscome Dr. Buck 41 F1
Lisle Rd. H Wyc 162 A1
Lisleys Field. G Kin 162 B4
Lissel Rd. M Keyn 47 F3
Lisset Rd. Maid 203 D3
Lister Green. Ayl 115 F3
Liston Rd. Mar 183 E1
Litcham Spur. Slough 205 E4
Little Benty. W Dra 208 B1
Little Bridge St. Berk 135 E2
Little Britain. Wadd 99 D4
Little Buntings. Wind 209 F2
Little Cl. Fla H 185 D3
Little Cl. H Wyc 172 C2
Little Greencroft. Ches 144 A2
Little Ham La. P Ris 139 D3
Little Hame. M Keyn 35 F2
Little Hampden Cl. Wen 131 D2
Little Hill. Chor 167 E2
Little Hivings. Ches 144 A2
Little Hollis. G Mis 151 F4
Little Hoo. Tri 118 C2
Little Horwood Rd. G Hrwd 55 E2
Little Horwood Rd. L Hrwd 55 E2
Little Hundridge La. Char 153 D4
Little Kimble Hill. G Kim 129 F1
Little La. Bled R 149 E2
Little La. Lac G 149 E2
Little La. Y Has 1 A4
Little Linford La. Have 21 E2
Little London. Dean 31 F2
Little London. Whit 87 D3
Little London Green. Oak 109 F3
Little Marlow Rd. Mar 183 F2
Little Meadow. M Keyn 46 B4
Little Mollards. Win 89 D2
Little Orchard Cl. Lgwk 138 C3
Little Park. Bov 146 A2
Little Park. P Ris 139 E2
Little Reeves Ave. Ame 165 F4
Little Shardeloes. Ame 165 D4
Little Spinney. Cran 25 E2
Little Springs. Ches 144 A2
Little St. Y Has 1 A3
Little Stanton. M Keyn 34 B4
Little Sutton La. Slough 212 A4
Little Tring Rd. Tri 118 C3
Little Twye Rd. Dra B 132 C2
Little Windmill Hill. Sar 156 C4
Little Woodlands. Wind 209 F2
Littlebrook Ave. Slough 197 F1
Littlecote. M Keyn 34 A1
Littledown Rd. Slough 205 F3
Littlemere. M Keyn 33 E1
Littleport Spur. Slough 205 F4
Littlewood. Skch 158 C3
Littleworth. Wing 79 F2
Littleworth Rd. Burn 186 B1
Littleworth Rd. H Wyc 161 F1
Liverpool Rd. Slough 205 D4
Livesey Hill. She B E 46 A3
Lloyds. M Keyn 47 D4
Loakes Rd. H Wyc 173 D3
Lochinvar Cl. Slough 205 D2
Lochnell Rd. Berk 134 C3
Lock Ave. Maid 196 B1
Lock Bridge Rd. Bou E 185 D2
Lock La. Maid 202 B2
Lock Mead. Maid 196 B1
Lock Path. Dorn 209 E4
Lock Rd. Mar 183 F1
Lock Rd. Mar 183 F1
Lock View La. M Keyn 47 F1
Locke Gdns. Slough 206 B2
Locke Rd. M Keyn 58 B4
Lockets Cl. Wind 209 E3
Lodden Cl. S Man 115 E2
Loddon Dr. Maid 202 B4
Loddon Rd. Bou E 185 D2
Loddon Spur. Slough 205 F4
Lodge Cl. Mar 183 F1
Lodge Cl. Pad 53 E1
Lodge Cl. Slough 205 E2
Lodge Cl. Uxb 201 E1
Lodge Gate. M Keyn 34 C4
Lodge La. L Chal 166 C3
Lodge La. Pres 151 E3
Lodge La. S Ham 69 F4
Lodge Park The. N Pag 22 B2
Lodge Way. Wind 209 F2
Lodore Green. Ick 190 C1
Lollards Cl. Ame 154 B1
Lombardy Dr. Berk 135 E2
Lomond Dr. L Buzz 80 B4
Lomond Dr. M Keyn 58 B2
London End. Beac 175 F1
London End. Hth 60 C3
London End. Nwtn L 57 E2
London End La. B Bkhl 48 B1
London Rd. Beac 187 D4
London Rd. Berk 135 F2
London Rd. Buck 52 C3
London Rd. C St G 177 E4
London Rd. Datch 211 E4
London Rd. Dra B 118 A2
London Rd. Fel 146 C4
London Rd. G Has 136 A2
London Rd. G Mis 152 A3
London Rd. H Wyc 173 F3
London Rd. Holt 122 A1
London Rd. L Kin 152 A3
London Rd. Loud 173 F3
London Rd. M K Vil 36 A3
London Rd. M Keyn 46 A4
London Rd. N Pag 22 C1
London Rd. Old S 32 B4
London Rd. Slough 206 C1
London Rd. Tri 119 E2
London Rd. Wen 131 E1
London Rd E. Ame 165 F3
London Rd W. Ame 165 E4
Londrina Terr. Berk 135 E2
Long Cl. Far C 198 A3
Long Crendon Rd. Shab 124 B2
Long Croft Rd. Map Cr 178 B3
Long Dr. Burn 197 E1
Long Furlong. Hadd 126 C3
Long Furlong. Sto 114 A3
Long Furlong Dr. Slough 197 F1
Long Grove. Se Gr 176 B2
Long La. Bov 155 F4
Long La. Chor 167 E1
Long La. Cook 195 E3
Long La. Flau 155 F4
Long La. Oln 6 C2
Long Ley. Ched 105 D4
Long Lional. Ayl 115 E4
Long Marston Rd. Mars 104 C1
Long Massey. Oln 6 C3
Long Meadow. Ayl 116 A3
Long Meadow. Ches 144 B2
Long Meadow Cl. P Ris 139 E3
Long Park Way. Ame 154 B2
Long Plough. Ast C 117 E3
Long Readings La. Slough 198 A1
Long Ride. P Ris 139 D2
Long Row. Leck 30 C1
Long Street Rd. Hans 11 D2
Long View. Berk 135 D3
Long Wlk. L Chal 166 C3
Long Wood Dr. Se Gr 176 C2
Longbottom La. Beac 176 A2
Longbottom La. Se Gr 176 B2
Longbridge Cl. Tri 119 D3
Longbridge Way. Uxb 201 D2
Longcroft. Ast C 117 F3
Longcroft Ave. Wen 131 E3
Longcroft La. Bov 146 B3
Longcross. M Keyn 35 D3
Longdown Hill. P Ris 139 F3
Longfellow Dr. N Pag 22 A2
Longfield. Hedg 187 E1
Longfield. L Kin 152 A2
Longfield Dr. Ame 154 A1
Longfield Gdns. Tri 118 C2
Longfield Rd. Ches 143 F1
Longfield Rd. Tri 118 C2
Longfoot La. Paul 17 E4
Longland Way. H Wyc 172 B3
Longlands Ct. Wins 66 A3
Longlands Wlk. Wins 66 A3
Longleat Ct. M Keyn 33 F1
Longleat Gdns. Maid 202 B3
Longmead. Wind 209 F3
Longmead La. Burn 197 E3
Longstone Rd. Iver H 200 B2
Longview. Beac 185 F4
Longville. M Keyn 33 D4
Longwick Rd. Lgwk 139 D3
Longwick Rd. P Ris 139 D3
Longwood La. Ame 165 E4
Longworth Dr. Maid 196 B1
Lonsdale Cl. Maid 196 A1
Lonsdale Way. Holy 203 E1
Loosen Dr. Maid 202 A2
Loosley Hill. Lac G 149 E3
Lord Knyvetts Cl. Stan 213 E1
Lords Cl. M Keyn 47 E1
Lordsmead. Cran 25 E1
Loriner Pl. M Keyn 35 D3
Loring Rd. Berk 135 E2
Loring Rd. Dun 93 F4
Loring Rd. Wind 209 F3
Lorne Cl. Slough 205 D2
Lorraine Cl. H Wyc 173 F4
Loseley Ct. M Keyn 33 F1
Losfield Rd. Wind 209 F3
Lothersdale. M Keyn 34 A3
Lothian Cl. M Keyn 46 C1
Louches La. Wal A 161 E3
Loudhams Rd. L Chal 166 B4
Loudhams Wood La. L Chal 166 B4
Loughton Rd. M Keyn 34 A2
Lovat St. N Pag 22 B2
Lovatt Dr. M Keyn 57 F4
Lovejoy La. Wind 209 E3
Lovel End. Ger C 177 E2
Lovel Mead. Ger C 177 E2
Lovel Rd. Ger C 177 E1
Lovelace Cl. Hurl 193 F3
Lovett Gdns. Maid 196 B2
Lovett Rd. S Har 190 B4
Lovibonds Ave. W Dra 208 C4
Lowbrook Cl. Ayl 116 A2
Lowbrook Dr. Maid 202 A2
Lowdell Cl. W Dra 208 C4
Lowdon Cl. H Wyc 173 E2
Lower Boyndon Rd. Maid 202 C3
Lower Britwell Rd. Slough 197 E1
Lower Church St. Cudd 112 C2
Lower Church St. Skch 158 C3
Lower Cl. Ayl 115 D4
Lower Cookham Rd. Maid 196 B1
Lower Dr. Beac 175 E3
Lower End. Ash 97 F1
Lower End. Pidd (B) 95 F4
Lower End. Thrn 53 F4
Lower End. Win 89 D1
Lower End Rd. Wave 49 D4
Lower Farm Cl. Shab 124 B2
Lower Farm Gate. Dint 114 A2
Lower Furney Cl. H Wyc 173 E4
Lower Green. Wcot 98 B4
Lower Green La. Chea 112 B1
Lower Icknield Way. Ast C 117 F2
Lower Icknield Way. Bled 38 B2
Lower Icknield Way. Chin 147 E4
Lower Icknield Way. Dra B 118 B4
Lower Icknield Way. G Kim 129 E1
Lower Icknield Way. Mars 118 B4
Lower Icknield Way. P Ris 138 B2
Lower Icknield Way. Wils 118 B4
Lower King's Rd. Berk 135 E3
Lower Lees Rd. Slough 198 A1
Lower Lodge La. Hol G 163 D3
Lower Mead. Iver H 200 B1
Lower Pound La. Mar 183 E1
Lower Rd. Bktn 81 D2
Lower Rd. Chin 147 E4
Lower Rd. Chor 167 E3
Lower Rd. Cook 195 F4
Lower Rd. Den G 189 E2
Lower Rd. Ger C 188 C4
Lower Rd. Lac G 149 E3
Lower Rd. S Man 115 F2
Lower Rd. Whit 87 D2
Lower Ridge. Bou E 185 D2
Lower Riding. Beac 175 D1
Lower St. Paul 17 D4
Lower St. Qntn 85 D3
Lower Stonehayes. M Keyn 34 C4
Lower Way. G Bkhl 59 E1
Lower Way. Pad 53 E1
Lower Wiggington. Wigg 133 F4
Lowes Cl. Skch 158 B3
Lowfield Cl. Ty Gr 163 D2
Lowfield Way. Ty Gr 163 D2
Lowlands Cres. G Kin 151 E1
Lowman Way. Ayl 115 E2
Lowndes Ave. Ches 144 A1
Lownes Gr. She C E 45 F4
Loxbeare Dr. She B E 46 B2
Loxboro Hill. Bled R 160 B2
Loxley Rd. Berk 134 C3
Lucas Pl. M Keyn 47 E4
Lucky La Or Cock La. Ayl 101 E1
Ludgate. Tri 118 C2
Ludgershall Rd. Pidd (B) 95 F4
Ludlow Cl. M Keyn 57 F4
Ludlow Mews. H Wyc 174 A2
Ludlow Pl. Ayl 116 B4
Ludlow Rd. Maid 202 C3
Luff Cl. Wind 209 F2
Lufford Park. M Keyn 34 C4
Luker Ave. Hen-O-T 191 E2
Lukes La. Lon M 104 B2
Lukes Lea. Mars 105 D1
Lullingston Dr. M Keyn 33 F3
Lumber La. Paul 17 D4
Lundholme. M Keyn 34 A3
Lupin Cl. W Dra 208 B1
Lutman La. Maid 195 F1
Lycrome La. Ches 144 B2

Lycrome Rd. Ches 144 C2
Lydford Ave. Slough 205 E4
Lydiard. M Keyn 33 F1
Lydiard Cl. Ayl 116 A2
Lydsey Cl. Slough 198 A1
Lye Green Rd. Ches 144 C1
Lyell. Oak G 209 E3
Lyme Ave. Berk 134 B4
Lynch Cl. Uxb 201 E3
Lynch Hill La. Slough 197 F1
Lynch The. Uxb 201 E3
Lyndhurst Ave. Cook 195 F3
Lyndhurst Cl. H Wyc 161 E1
Lyndhurst Rd. Ches 144 A1
Lyndon Cl. Pres 151 E4
Lyndwood Dr. Old W 211 D1
Lyneham Gdns. Maid 195 D1
Lynher Cl. Ayl 115 E2
Lynmouth Cres. She B E 46 B2
Lynott Cl. She C E 45 F3
Lynton Green. Maid 202 C4
Lynton Rd. Ches 144 B2
Lynwood Ave. Slough 206 B2
Lynwood Rd. Ayl 116 A3
Lyon Rd. M Keyn 47 D1
Lysander Cl. Bov 146 A2

Macdonald Cl. Ame 154 B2
Mackenzie St. Slough 205 F2
Maclaren Ct. M Keyn 46 C4
Madeira Wlk. Wind 210 B3
Madeley Cl. Ame 154 B2
Madeley Rd. Ayl 115 F3
Magdalen Cl. M Keyn 32 B3
Magenta Cl. M Keyn 58 B3
Magnolia Dene. Ty Gr 162 C1
Magnolia Gdns. Slough 206 B2
Magnolia St. W Dra 208 B1
Magpie Cl. Fla H 174 A1
Magpie La. Cole 165 D1
Magpie La. Fla H 174 A1
Magpie La. Loud 174 A2
Magpie Way. Slough 197 F1
Magpie Way. Wins 66 A3
Mahoney Ct. H Wyc 172 C4
Maidenhead Crt Pk. Maid 196 A2
Maidenhead Rd. Cook 195 F3
Maidenhead Rd. Oak G 209 F4
Maidenhead Rd. Wind 209 F4
Main Dr. Ger C 188 B3
Main Par. Chor 167 E3
Main Rd. Ast 16 A2
Main Rd. Dray P 68 A3
Main Rd. Gr Und 83 D3
Main Rd. Lac G 149 F3
Main Rd. Syr 27 E4
Main Rd. Wadd 99 D1
Main Rd. Wal A 161 E4
Main Rd N. Dag 107 D3
Main Rd S. Dag 107 E2
Main St. Adsk 53 F1
Main St. Ash 97 F1
Main St. Beac 44 A3
Main St. Cast 19 F1
Main St. Chac 41 D2
Main St. Gawt 51 F2
Main St. Mur 67 E3
Main St. Pad 53 D1
Main St. Pres B 62 A4
Main St. Shal 39 F3
Main St. Ting 51 D3
Main St. Turw 38 B4
Main St. Twyf 62 B1
Main St. Twyf 72 C3
Main St. W Tur 116 C1
Main St. West 39 D2
Maitland Dr. H Wyc 173 D4
Maitland Rd. Hal 131 E4
Major's Farm Rd. Datch 211 E4
Malborough Way. Yard G 18 C3
Malcolm Rd. Ick 201 F4
Malders La. Cook 195 E2
Malders La. Maid 195 E2
Malins Gate. M Keyn 34 C4
Malkin Dr. Beac 175 E2
Malletts Cl. M Keyn 32 C3
Mallow Gate. M Keyn 34 C2
Mallow Park. Maid 195 E1
Malmers Well Rd. H Wyc 173 D4
Malpas Rd. Slough 206 A3
Malting Cl. S Gol 12 A3
Malting La. Ald 120 B3
Malting La. Dag 107 E3
Maltings Cl. Cran 25 D1
Maltings The. Chac 41 D2
Maltings The. Oln 7 D2
Maltmans La. Ger C 188 B4
Malton Ave. Slough 205 D3
Malvern Cl. H Wyc 172 C4
Malvern Dr. L Buzz 80 B4
Malvern Dr. M Keyn 32 C2
Malvern Rd. Ayl 116 B4
Malvern Rd. Maid 195 E1
Malyns Cl. Chin 147 E4
Mandelyns. Berk 134 C4
Mandeville Rd. Ayl 115 F3
Mandeville Rd. Pres 151 D4
Manfield Cl. Slough 198 A1
Manor Cl. Berk 135 E2
Manor Cl. Cast 19 F1
Manor Cl. M Keyn 35 F2
Manor Cl. Sal 37 E2
Manor Cl. Ty Gr 163 D1
Manor Cres. Se Gr 176 B3
Manor Cres. Wen 131 E3
Manor Ct. Mar 183 E2
Manor Dr. Ame 154 A2
Manor Dr. Ayl 101 F1
Manor Dr. Have 20 C1
Manor Dr. Stew 78 C4
Manor Farm Cl. Sto 114 B3
Manor Farm Cl. W Tur 116 C1
Manor Farm Cl. Wind 209 F2
Manor Farm Cotts. Old W 211 D1
Manor Farm La. Men 90 B4
Manor Farm Way. Se Gr 176 B2
Manor Gdns. H Wyc 162 A1
Manor House Cl. Ayl 101 F1
Manor House La. Datch 211 D3
Manor La. Ger C 188 B2
Manor La. Maid 202 C2
Manor Park. M Mor 41 F2
Manor Park Ave. P Ris 139 D2
Manor Pound Rd. Ched 105 D4
Manor Rd. Akel 41 F4
Manor Rd. Ayl 101 F1
Manor Rd. Ched 104 C4
Manor Rd. Ches 144 A1
Manor Rd. Have 20 C1
Manor Rd. M Keyn 33 D4
Manor Rd. Maid 202 C2
Manor Rd. N Pag 22 A2
Manor Rd. Nwtn L 57 E2
Manor Rd. Oak 109 E3
Manor Rd. Oving 86 B4
Manor Rd. P Ris 139 D1
Manor Rd. Se Gr 176 B3
Manor Rd. Tow 137 D3
Manor Rd. Tri 119 D3
Manor Rd. Ty Gr 163 D1
Manor Rd. Wen 131 E3
Manor Rd. Wind 209 F3
Manor Rd. Wing 102 B4
Manor St. Berk 135 E2
Manor St. Buck 52 B4
Manor View. Ty Gr 163 D1
Manor Way. Ches 144 B1
Manor Way. Cole 164 C2
Manor Way. Yard G 18 C3
Manor Waye. Uxb 201 E2
Manorfields Rd. Old S 32 A3
Mansard Cl. Tri 119 D2
Manse Cl. M Keyn 32 B3
Mansel Cl. Cast 19 F1
Mansel Cl. Slough 206 A4
Mansell Cl. She C E 46 A3
Mansell Cl. Wind 209 F3
Manshead Ct. M Keyn 32 C3
Mansion Dr. Tri 119 D2
Mansion Hill. Hal 131 F4
Mansion La. Harr 3 F3
Maple Ave. W Dra 208 C3
Maple Cl. H Wyc 172 B3
Maple Cl. Maid 202 B3
Maple Cl. Ty Gr 163 D2
Maple Cres. Slough 206 A3
Maple Gr. M Keyn 58 C4
Maple Gr. Wbn S 49 D2
Maple Leys. Stp Cl 63 F2
Maple Lodge Cl. Map Cr 178 B2
Maple Pl. W Dra 208 C3
Maple Rise. Mar 183 F2
Mapledean. M Keyn 33 F2
Mapledurham Wlk. Maid 195 F2
Maplefield La. L Chal 166 A3
Marbeck Cl. Wind 209 E3
March Pl. Ayl 115 D4
Marchant Ct. Mar 184 A2
Mardle Rd. L Buzz 80 C3
Mare Leys. Buck 52 C4
Maree Cl. L Buzz 80 B4
Maree Cl. M Keyn 58 B3
Marefield Rd. Mar 183 B1
Marescroft Rd. Slough 197 F1
Margarets Gr. G Kin 151 F1
Marigold Pl. M Keyn 34 C2
Marigold Wlk. Hol G 162 C3
Marina Dr. Dun 93 F4
Marina Dr. M Keyn 33 E3
Marina Way. Iver 208 A3
Marish La. Den G 189 E4
Marish Wharf. Slough 206 C2
Marjoram Pl. M Keyn 34 C2
Mark Dr. C St P 177 E3
Market Hill. M Keyn 47 D4
Market Hill. Whit 86 C3
Market Par. Ty Gr 163 D2
Market Pl. Ger C 177 E1
Market Pl. Hen-O-T 191 E1
Market Pl. Hth 60 C4
Market Pl. Oln 6 C2
Market Sq. Ame 165 D4
Market Sq. Ayl 115 E4
Market Sq. Ches 154 A4
Market Sq. Hans 11 D1
Market Sq. P Ris 139 D2
Market Sq. Wins 65 F2
Market St. Ayl 115 E4
Market St. Maid 202 C4
Market St. Wind 210 B3
Marlborough Cl. Maid 202 A3
Marlborough Gate. M Keyn 34 C2
Marlborough Rd. Ayl 115 F2
Marlborough Rd. Maid 202 A3
Marlborough Rd. Slough 206 C1
Marlborough St. M Keyn 34 C3
Marlborough Tdng Es. H Wyc 172 C4
Marley Gr. She C E 45 F4
Marlin Cl. Berk 134 C3
Marlin Ct. Mar 183 E1
Marlin Hill. Has 133 D4
Marlins Cl. Chor 167 F4
Marlow Bottom. Mar B 183 E3
Marlow Bridge La. Bish 194 C4
Marlow Comm. Mar 182 C2
Marlow Dr. N Pag 22 A2
Marlow Hill. H Wyc 173 D3
Marlow Mill. Mar 183 F1
Marlow Rd. B Bot 170 A1
Marlow Rd. Bish 194 C2
Marlow Rd. Bou E 184 B3
Marlow Rd. H Wyc 172 C2
Marlow Rd. Hen-O-T 191 F2
Marlow Rd. La En 171 E1
Marlow Rd. Lit M 184 B3
Marlow Rd. Maid 202 C4
Marlow Rd. Mar B 171 F1
Marmion Rd. Hen-O-T 191 F1
Marquis Ct. Hth 60 C4
Marram Cl. M Keyn 47 D3
Marriotts Ave. S Hea 142 C1
Marriotts Cl. Hadd 126 C3
Marriotts La. Hadd 126 C3
Marriotts Way. Hadd 126 C3
Marrod's Bottom. Cole 175 E4
Marron La. M Keyn 33 E3
Marroway. S Man 116 B1
Marroway. W Tur 116 B1
Marsh Dr. M Keyn 21 F1
Marsh End Rd. N Pag 22 B2
Marsh La. Tapl 203 F3
Marsh Lane. S Man 129 F4
Marsh Rd. G Kim 129 E2
Marsh Rd. Shab 124 B2
Marshalls La. M Keyn 35 E1
Marshalls Lea. Bier 102 B2
Marsham Cl. Ayl 116 A2
Marsham La. Ger C 188 C3
Marsham Lodge. Ger C 188 C3
Marsham Way. Ger C 188 C3
Marshcroft La. Tri 119 E3
Marshworth. M Keyn 47 E3
Marston Cl. Ches 144 A2
Marston Ct. Lon M 104 A2
Marston Hill. Cran 25 F1
Marston Hill. Oving 86 B4
Marston Rd. Gran 75 F3
Marston Rd. Tha 126 A1
Marstonfields Rd. N Mar 76 A1
Marsworth Rd. Pit 105 E2
Martin Cl. Buck 52 C4
Martin Cl. M Keyn 34 C3
Martin Cl. Wind 209 E3
Martin Rd. Maid 202 C4
Martin Rd. Slough 205 F2
Martin's Plain. Sto P 198 C2
Martingale Pl. M Keyn 34 C3
Martins Dr The. L Buzz 80 C4
Martinsend La. G Mis 151 F4
Marunden Green. Slough 197 F1
Mary Macmanus Dr. Buck 41 E1
Marygold Wlk. L Chal 166 B4
Maryland Rd. M Keyn 35 D4
Marys Mead. Hol G 163 D3
Maryside. Slough 206 C2
Mascoll Path. Slough 197 F1
Masefield Cl. Ches 144 A2
Masefield Cl. N Pag 22 A2
Masefield Gr. M Keyn 58 A4
Maslin Dr. M Keyn 47 D3
Mason. M Keyn 34 B4
Mason's Ct. Ayl 115 D4
Massie Cl. M Keyn 35 D3
Matilda Gdns. She C E 46 A3
Matlock Rd. Ayl 101 F1
Matson Dr. Hen-O-T 191 F1
Matthew Ct. She C E 46 A3
Matthews Cl. Ayl 101 F1
Maud Jane's Cl. Ivin 105 F3
Maude Cl. Beac 176 A1
Maude Rd. Beac 176 A1
Maudsley Cl. She B E 46 B3
Mauduit Cl. Hans 11 D2
Maulden Gdns. M Keyn 35 D4
Maurice Mount. Hol G 162 C3
Maxwell Dr. Hol G 163 D3
Maxwell Rd. Beac 175 F2
Maxwell Rd. W Dra 208 C1
May Cl. Eat B 92 C3
May Rd. Turv 8 C3
May Tree Cl. Mar B 183 E3
Maybrook Gdns. H Wyc 173 E4
Maybush Wlk. Oln 6 C3
Mayditch Pl. M Keyn 34 B2
Mayfield Ave. Ger C 188 B4
Mayfield Rd. Woo G 185 F3
Mayflower Cl. Sto 114 C3
Mayflower Way. Beac 186 A4
Mayflower Way. Far C 198 B4
Maygoods Cl. Uxb 208 B4
Maygoods Green. Uxb 208 B4
Maygoods La. Uxb 208 B4
Mayhall La. Ame 154 A2
Mayhew Cres. H Wyc 173 E4
Maylands Dr. Uxb 201 E3
Maynard Cl. M Keyn 34 A2
Maypole Rd. Burn 204 A4
Mays Way. Pott 18 B2
Mcewen Ride. Hal 117 E1
Mckenzie Cl. Buck 52 B4
Mead Acre. P Ris 139 D3
Mead Cl. Den 190 A1
Mead Cl. Mar 183 F2
Mead Cl. P Ris 139 D3
Mead Platt. Skch 158 B3
Mead Rd. Uxb 201 E3
Mead St. H Wyc 174 A2
Mead The. Soul 69 F2
Mead Way. H Wyc 173 F2
Meades La. Ches 154 A4
Meadow Bank. S Man 116 B1
Meadow Cl. Ayl 102 A1
Meadow Cl. Berk 135 D1
Meadow Cl. Ches 144 A2
Meadow Cl. Cub 78 B1
Meadow Cl. H Wyc 173 F2
Meadow Cl. Mar 183 F1
Meadow Cl. Oak 109 E2
Meadow Cl. Old W 211 D1
Meadow Cott La. Cole 164 C2
Meadow Dr. Ame 154 C1
Meadow Dr. Lgwk 138 B3
Meadow Gate. Pad 53 D1
Meadow Gate. Pres 151 E2
Meadow Gdns. Buck 52 C3
Meadow La. Beac 175 F1
Meadow La. Eton 210 B4
Meadow La. M K Vil 36 A2
Meadow La. Pit 105 F2
Meadow Rd. Berk 135 D3
Meadow Rd. Chin 147 E3
Meadow Rd. Hen-O-T 191 F1
Meadow Rd. Mar B 183 F3
Meadow Rd. Slough 206 C2
Meadow Rise. Lac G 149 F3
Meadow Row. Buck 41 E1
Meadow Side. Se Gr 176 C2
Meadow View. L Cre 125 F2
Meadow View. Pott 18 B2
Meadow Way. Ayl 102 A1
Meadow Way. Dorn 203 F2
Meadow Way. H Hea 153 E2
Meadow Way. Old W 211 D1
Meadow Way. Tha 125 F1
Meadow Way. Wing 79 F2
Meadow Wlk. Buck 41 E1
Meadow Wlk. Ty Gr 163 E1
Meadoway. Sto 114 C3
Meadoway. Stp Cl 63 F2
Meadowbank Cl. L Cre 125 E4
Meadowbrook Cl. Stan 212 C3
Meadowcroft. Ayl 101 D2
Meadowcroft. Ger C 177 E1
Meadows The. Ame 154 C1
Meadows The. Fla H 185 D4
Meadowsweet. Walt 48 A3
Meads Cl. M Keyn 34 A4
Meads The. Berk 134 C3
Meads The. Tri 119 D2
Meads The. Uxb 201 F1
Meadway. Berk 135 F3
Meadway. Buck 52 C3
Meadway. Dun 93 F4
Meadway. Oving 76 C1
Meadway The. M Keyn 46 A4
Meare Estate. Woo G 185 F4
Meavy Cl. Loud 174 A2
Medale Rd. M Keyn 47 D3
Medallion Pl. Maid 203 D4
Medeswell. M Keyn 46 C2
Medhurst. M Keyn 33 F1
Medland. M Keyn 47 E4
Medley Cl. Eat B 92 C3
Medman Cl. Uxb 201 E2
Medway Cl. N Pag 22 C2
Meeting Oak La. Wins 66 A3
Megdale Pl. Ayl 101 E1
Melbourne Ave. Slough 205 E4
Melbourne Cl. Ayl 115 F3
Melbourne Rd. H Wyc 173 F3
Melford Green. Ayl 101 E2
Melfort Dr. L Buzz 80 A4
Melfort Dr. M Keyn 58 B2
Melick Rd. M Keyn 47 D2
Mellstock Rd. Ayl 115 F3
Melrose Ave. M Keyn 47 D1
Melrose Ct. H Wyc 162 A1
Melrose Wlk. Ayl 115 F3
Melton. M Keyn 34 B4
Melton Ct. Maid 202 C3
Mendip Way. H Wyc 172 C4
Mendy St. H Wyc 173 D4
Menmarsh Rd. Worm 123 F3
Menteith Cl. M Keyn 58 B3
Mentmore Cl. H Wyc 172 A3
Mentmore Ct. M Keyn 45 F4
Mentmore Gdns. L Buzz 80 C3
Mentmore Green. Ayl 115 F2
Mentmore Rd. Ched 104 C4
Mentmore Rd. H Wyc 172 A3
Mentmore Rd. L Buzz 80 C3
Mentmore View. Tri 118 C3
Mentone Ave. Asp G 49 E2
Mercers Dr. M Keyn 34 A3
Merchant La. Cran 24 C1
Merchant La. Cran 25 D1
Mercia Rd. Maid 202 B2
Mere Cl. Mar 183 F1
Mere Rd. Slough 205 F2
Meredith Dr. Ayl 100 C1
Merlewood Cl. H Wyc 173 D2
Merlin Cl. Slough 212 A4
Merlin Wlk. M Keyn 47 D4
Merling Croft. Berk 134 C4
Merrivale Mews. W Dra 208 B3
Merry Down. H Wyc 161 E1
Merryfields. Uxb 201 E2
Mersey Cl. M Keyn 46 C1
Mersey Way. M Keyn 46 C1
Merton Cl. Maid 202 B2
Merton Dr. M Keyn 47 D2
Merton Rd. P Ris 139 D1
Merton Rd. Slough 206 A2
Merwin Way. Wind 209 E2
Messenger Cl. Ayl 116 A3
Metcalfe Gr. M Keyn 22 A1
Michael Rd. Maid 202 B3
Michigan Dr. M Keyn 35 D4
Michigan Dr. N Pag 22 B1
Micholls Ave. C St P 177 F3
Micklefield Rd. Ty Gr 174 A4
Mickleton. M Keyn 35 D3
Mid Cross La. C St P 177 F3
Midcot Way. Berk 134 C3
Midcroft. Slough 198 A1
Middle Cl. Ame 154 C1
Middle Cres. Den G 189 E2
Middle Dr. Beac 175 E3
Middle Field. W Tur 116 C2
Middle Green. Slough 206 C3
Middle La. Bov 146 A1
Middle Meadow. C St G 177 E4
Middle Rd. Ayl 116 A4
Middle Rd. Berk 135 D2
Middle Rd. Den G 189 E2
Middle Walk. Burn 197 E1
Middle Way. Chin 147 D3
Middlebrook Rd. H Wyc 161 F1
Middlefield Cl. Buck 41 F1
Middlegreen Rd. Slough 206 B3
Middlesex Dr. M Keyn 46 C1
Middleton. M Keyn 34 C4
Middleway The. H Wyc 172 B3
Midhurst Cl. Ayl 116 A3
Midland Rd. Oln 7 D3
Midsummer Arc. M Keyn 34 C2
Midsummer Bvd. M Keyn 34 C1
Miersfield. Lit M 172 B2
Mikern Cl. M Keyn 58 B4
Milburn Ave. M Keyn 46 C4
Milburn Dr. W Dra 208 C3
Mildenhall Rd. Slough 205 F4
Mildun Way. H Wyc 172 B3
Mile Elm. Mar 184 A2
Milebush. L Buzz 80 B4
Milecastle. M Keyn 34 A3
Miles Cl. Ayl 116 A4
Miles Cl. M Keyn 22 A2
Milesmere. M Keyn 33 E1
Milfoil Ave. M Keyn 34 C2
Milford Ave. M Keyn 32 C2
Mill Ave. Uxb 201 E2
Mill Cl. Ches 154 C3
Mill Cl. W Dra 208 B2
Mill Cl. Win 89 D2
Mill Ct. W Dra 208 B2
Mill End Rd. H Wyc 172 B4
Mill Gdns. Tri 119 D2
Mill La. Ame 165 D4
Mill La. Asp G 49 E3
Mill La. Beac 175 F1
Mill La. Brac 38 A4
Mill La. Buck 52 B4
Mill La. C St G 177 D4
Mill La. Chin 147 D4
Mill La. Cook 196 B4
Mill La. Ger C 188 C3
Mill La. Hadd 126 A2
Mill La. Hor-c-S 108 A3
Mill La. Hort 212 A2
Mill La. Hurl 193 F2
Mill La. M Keyn 35 E2
Mill La. P Ris 139 D3
Mill La. S Hea 152 B4
Mill La. Sal 37 E2
Mill La. Skch 158 B3
Mill La. Tapl 203 E4
Mill La. Twyf 62 B1
Mill La. U Arn 94 C4
Mill La. W Tur 117 D1
Mill La. West 39 D2
Mill La. Win 89 E1
Mill La. Wind 210 A4
Mill Mead. Wen 131 D3
Mill Pl. Datch 211 E3

Mill Rd. Cran 25 E1
Mill Rd. L Buzz 80 C4
Mill Rd. M Keyn 58 C4
Mill Rd. Mar 183 F1
Mill Rd. Oak 109 E2
Mill Rd. Skch 158 B3
Mill Rd. Slap 91 E4
Mill Rd. W Dra 208 B2
Mill Rd. Whit 26 C2
Mill St. Ayl 101 F1
Mill St. Berk 135 E2
Mill St. H Wyc 172 C4
Mill St. Iver 212 B4
Mill St. N Pag 22 B3
Mill St. Slough 205 F3
Mill View Rd. Tri 118 C2
Mill Way. Asp G 49 E3
Mill Way. Ayl 115 E4
Mill Way. Chor 167 F1
Millards Cl. Cran 25 E1
Millbank. L Buzz 80 C4
Millbank. Mar 183 F1
Millboard Rd. Bou E 185 D2
Millers Turn. Chin 147 D3
Millers Way. M Keyn 33 E3
Millfield. Berk 135 E2
Millfield Ave. M Gib 71 F2
Millfield Cl. Cran 25 D1
Millfields. Ches 154 B3
Millhayes. M Keyn 34 C4
Millington Gate. M Keyn 35 E4
Mills Ct. M Keyn 33 D3
Millshot Dr. Ame 165 E4
Millside. Bou E 185 E2
Millstream Way. Woo G 185 F4
Milner Rd. Burn 204 A4
Milton Ave. Ger C 188 B4
Milton Cl. Hen-O-T 191 E1
Milton Cl. Hort 212 A2
Milton Dr. N Pag 22 C2
Milton Fields. C St G 177 D4
Milton Gdns. P Ris 139 D1
Milton Gr. M Keyn 57 F4
Milton Hill. C St G 177 D4
Milton Lawns. Ame 154 B2
Milton Rd. Ast C 117 F3
Milton Rd. Ayl 115 F3
Milton Rd. Ches 144 A1
Milton Rd. M Keyn 35 E4
Milton Rd. M Keyn 47 F4
Milton Rd. Slough 198 B1
Milton Way. W Dra 208 C1
Milverton Cl. Maid 202 A2
Mina Ave. Slough 206 B2
Mineral La. Ches 154 B4
Minerva Way. Beac 176 A1
Minniecroft Rd. Burn 197 D1
Minshull Cl. Buck 41 E1
Minster Way. Slough 206 C2
Minstrel Ct. M Keyn 34 A4
Minton Rise. Burn 204 A4
Mirador Cres. Slough 206 B3
Mirrie La. Den G 189 E3
Misbourne Ave. C St P 177 F3
Misbourne Ave. H Wyc 173 F3
Misbourne Cl. S Man 115 E2
Missenden Rd. Ches 154 A4
Missenden Rd. G Kin 151 E1
Missenden Rd. Wins 65 F2
Miswell La. Tri 118 C2
Mitcham Pl. M Keyn 34 B2
Mitcham Wlk. Ayl 101 D1
Mitchell Cl. Bov 145 F2
Mitchell Cl. Slough 205 D2
Mitchell Cl. Tha 125 F1
Mitchell Rd. Cran 24 C1
Mitchell Wlk. Ame 154 C1
Mitre St. Buck 52 B4
Moat Cl. Pres 151 E3
Moat Dr. Pres 151 E4
Moat Dr. Slough 206 B4
Moat End. Bier 102 A2
Moat La. A Abb 88 B2
Moat La. M Gib 71 F1
Moat La. Pres 151 E4
Moat La. Win 89 D1
Moffy Hill. Maid 195 F1
Mole Run. H Wyc 161 E1
Monet Pl. Ayl 100 C1
Money La. W Dra 208 B2
Monkey Island La. Holy 203 F1
Monks Hollow. Mar B 183 F3
Monks Rd. Wind 209 E3
Monks Way. Harm 213 F4
Monks Way. M Keyn 34 B3
Monksfield Way. Slough 198 A1
Monkton Waye. Lac G 150 B3
Monmouth Cl. Ayl 101 D1
Monro Ave. She C E 45 F4
Montabaur Rd. Brac 38 A4
Montagu Dr. M Keyn 47 D4
Montagu Rd. Datch 211 D3
Montague Rd. Ayl 115 E4
Montague Rd. Berk 135 D2
Montague Rd. Slough 205 F3
Montague Rd. Uxb 201 E3
Montem La. Slough 205 E2
Montgomerie Cl. Berk 135 D3
Montgomery Cres. M Keyn 35 D4
Montgomery Pl. Slough 206 B4
Montpelier Ct. Wind 210 B3
Montrose Ave. Datch 211 E4
Montrose Ave. Slough 205 D4
Montrose Dr. Maid 202 A3
Montrose Way. Datch 211 E4
Monument La. C St P 177 F3
Monycrower Dr. Maid 202 C4
Moon St. M Keyn 33 E3
Moor End. Eat B 92 C3
Moor End. Holy 203 E1
Moor End Cl. Eat B 92 C2
Moor End La. Eat B 92 C3
Moor La. H Wyc 161 E2
Moor La. Harm 213 E4
Moor La. Maid 195 F1
Moor La. Sar 156 C2
Moor Park. Hal 131 D4
Moor Park. M Keyn 57 E4
Moor Rd. Ches 154 B3
Moorbridge Rd. Maid 203 D4
Moore Cl. Slough 205 D2
Moore Rd. Berk 134 C3
Moorend La. Tha 125 F1
Moorend La. Tha 126 A1
Moorend Rd. Yard G 18 C3
Moores Hill. Oln 6 C3
Moorfield. Nwtn L 57 E2
Moorfield Rd. Den G 190 A3
Moorfield Rd. Uxb 208 B4
Moorfield Terr. Maid 203 D4
Moorfoot. M Keyn 33 D2
Moorgate. M Keyn 46 C4
Moorhall Rd. S Har 190 A3
Moorhills Cres. Wing 79 F2
Moorhills Rd. Wing 79 F2
Moorland Rd. Harm 213 E4
Moorlands. Wing 79 F2
Moorlands Rd. Wing 79 F2
Moorside. Woo G 185 F4
Moorside Cl. Maid 195 F1
Moorstown Ct. Slough 205 F2
Mop End La. H Hea 164 A4
Morar Cl. L Buzz 80 B4
Moray Pl. M Keyn 46 C1
Mordaunt Cl. Turv 8 C3
Mordaunts Cl. M Keyn 35 E1
More Ave. Ayl 115 E4
Moreau Wlk. Slough 206 C4
Morefields. Tri 119 D3
Moreland Ave. Iver 212 B4
Morelands Dr. Ger C 188 C2
Morello Dr. Slough 206 C3
Moreton Dr. Buck 41 F1
Moreton La. Sto 115 D1
Moreton Rd. Buck 41 E1
Morley Cl. Slough 206 C2
Morley Cres. Walt 48 B2
Morrel Cl. She C E 46 A3
Morris Cl. C St P 177 F1
Morris Wlk. N Pag 22 A2
Morrison Ct. She C E 45 F3
Mortain Dr. Berk 134 C3
Morten Gdns. Den G 190 A2
Mortens Wood. Ame 165 F4
Mortimer Hill. Tri 119 D2
Mortimer Rd. Slough 206 B2
Mortimer Rise. Tri 119 D2
Morton Cl. N Mar 76 A1
Morton Cl. Pit 105 E2
Mortons Fork. M Keyn 33 F3
Moseley Rd. Wal A 161 E4
Moses Plat La. Lac G 150 A3
Mossdale. M Keyn 34 A3
Mossway. Beac 175 E3
Mossy Vale. Maid 195 E1
Mount Ave. M Keyn 47 F2
Mount Cl. Ast C 117 F2
Mount Cl. Far C 198 B4
Mount Cl. H Wyc 172 C3
Mount Hill La. Hedg 188 A1
Mount La. Den 189 E1
Mount Pleasant. Asp G 49 F2
Mount Pleasant. Ayl 101 E1
Mount Pleasant. La En 171 D3
Mount Pleasant. M Keyn 47 E2
Mount Pleasant. S Gol 12 A4
Mount Pleasant. Soul 69 F2
Mount Pleasant. Stp Cl 63 F1
Mount Pleasant. Yard G 18 C3
Mount Pleasant Cl. Buck 52 B4
Mount St. Ayl 115 E4
Mount The. Asp G 49 E2
Mount The. M Keyn 47 F2
Mount View. Hen-O-T 191 E1
Mount Way. P Ris 139 D2
Mountain Ash. Mar B 183 E3
Mountbatten Cl. Slough 206 A2
Mounthill Ave. Old S 32 A4
Mountsfield Cl. N Pag 22 B2
Mountsfield Cl. Stan 213 D1
Mowbray Rd. Ayl 101 E1
Mowhills. Harr 3 F3
Moyleen Rise. Mar 183 B1
Mt Nugent. Ches 144 A2
Mt Pleasant. Whit 86 C4
Muirfield Dr. M Keyn 46 B1
Mulberry Cl. Tri 119 D3
Mulberry Ct. Hol G 163 E4
Mulberry Dr. Slough 206 C1
Mullen Ave. M Keyn 34 C2
Mullins Way. Ayl 100 C1
Mullion Pl. M Keyn 35 D1
Mumfords La. Ger C 188 A4
Munces Rd. Mar B 183 E3
Mundaydean La. Mar 183 D2
Mundesley Spur. Slough 205 F4
Murcott Rd. U Arn 94 B3
Murray Rd. Berk 135 E3
Murrey Cl. She B E 46 B3
Murrin Rd. Maid 202 B4
Mursley C. M Keyn 32 C3
Mursley Rd. L Hrwd 55 F1
Mursley Rd. Mur 67 D2
Musgrave Rd. Chin 147 E1
Myddleton Rd. Uxb 201 E2
Mylne Cl. H Wyc 172 C4
Mynchen Cl. Beac 175 E3
Mynchen End. Beac 175 E3
Mynchen Rd. Beac 175 E3
Myrke The. Datch 205 F1
Myrtle Bank. M Keyn 33 F3
Myrtle Cl. Stan 212 C3
Myrtle Cl. W Dra 208 C2
Myrtle Cl. W Dra 208 C4
Myrtle Cres. Slough 205 F3

Nag's Head La. G Kin 152 A2
Nag's Head La. L Kin 152 A2
Nailzee Cl. Ger C 188 C2
Nairdwood Cl. Pres 151 F2
Nairdwood La. Pres 151 E3
Nairdwood Way. Pres 151 F2
Nairn Ct. M Keyn 46 C1
Naisby Dr. G Bkhl 59 E1
Nalders Rd. Ches 144 B1
Nan Aires. Win 89 D2
Nancy Hall Ct. H Wyc 172 B2
Napier Cl. W Dra 208 C2
Napier Rd. Harm 213 E3
Napier St. M Keyn 58 B4
Nappin Cl. Ayl 101 D2
Nappins Cl. L Cre 125 E3
Narberth Dr. Ayl 116 A4
Narcot La. C St G 177 D3
Narcot La. Ger C 177 D3
Narcot Rd. C St G 177 D4
Narcot Way. C St G 177 D3
Narrow La. Asp H 49 D2
Narrow La. H Wyc 161 F2
Naseby Cl. N Pag 22 A2
Naseby Cl. Tha 126 A1
Naseby Ct. Buck 41 F1
Naseby Ct. M Keyn 34 A3
Nash Cl. Ayl 116 A2
Nash Cl. Qntn 85 D3
Nash Lee Rd. Elle 130 A3
Nash Rd. G Hrwd 55 D2
Nash Rd. Thrn 54 A4
Nash Rd. Whad 45 D1
Nashdom La. Burn 197 D3
Nashleigh Hill. Ches 144 B2
Nathaniel Wlk. Tri 119 D3
Natwoke Cl. Beac 175 E3
Neal Cl. Den G 189 D2
Neale Cl. Lit M 172 B2
Neapland. M Keyn 47 D3
Neath Cres. M Keyn 47 D1
Needham Cl. Wind 209 F3
Needlemakers. L Cre 125 E4
Nelson Cl. Cole 164 B2
Nelson Cl. H Wyc 173 F3
Nelson Cl. She C E 45 F3
Nelson Cl. Slough 206 B1
Nelson Rd. Dag 107 E3
Nelson Rd. Harm 213 F3
Nelson Rd. Wind 209 F2
Nelson St. Buck 52 B4
Nelson Terr. Ayl 115 E4
Nene Cl. Ayl 115 E2
Nene Cl. N Pag 22 B2
Nene Dr. M Keyn 57 F4
Ness Way. M Keyn 58 B3
Nether Cl. Brac 38 A4
Netherby Cl. Tri 119 E3
Nethercote La. Lewk 157 D4
Netherwood Rd. Beac 175 E3
Nettleden Rd. L Gad 121 F2
Nettleton Rd. Ick 201 F4
Nevill Cl. Hans 11 D1
Neville Cl. Sto P 198 C3
Nevis Cl. L Buzz 80 B4
Nevis Gr. M Keyn 58 C2
New Ct. Mar 183 E1
New Dr. H Wyc 173 F4
New Footpath. Ches 154 A4
New Garden Dr. W Dra 208 C2
New Inn La. Gawt 51 F2
New Par. Chor 167 E3
New Peachey La. Uxb 208 B4
New Pond Rd. Hol G 163 E4
New Rd. Ame 154 C1
New Rd. Ast C 117 F3
New Rd. Ayl 116 C3
New Rd. Berk 134 C4
New Rd. Berk 135 E3
New Rd. Bou E 185 D2
New Rd. Cast 19 F3
New Rd. Chipf 146 C1
New Rd. Cole 164 C2
New Rd. Cook 195 F4
New Rd. Datch 211 E3
New Rd. Dint 113 F1
New Rd. Dray P 68 B3
New Rd. G Kin 162 B4
New Rd. H Wyc 172 B3
New Rd. Harr 3 F3
New Rd. Hurl 193 F2
New Rd. L Buzz 80 C4
New Rd. L Chal 166 C3
New Rd. L Kin 152 A2
New Rd. La En 170 C3
New Rd. Lac G 149 F2
New Rd. Mar B 183 E3
New Rd. P Ris 139 E2
New Rd. Pres 151 E3
New Rd. Sar 156 C1
New Rd. Skch 158 C2
New Rd. Tri 119 D3
New Rd. Ty Gr 163 E1
New Rd. Wal A 150 A1
New Rd. Wedn 101 D4
New Rd. Wils 118 B4
New Road Cl. H Wyc 172 B3
New Road Gdns. H Wyc 172 B3
New St. Ayl 101 E1
New St. Berk 135 E2
New St. Ched 104 C4
New St. Hen-O-T 191 F1
New St. M Keyn 32 B3
New St. Ting 51 D3
New St. Wadd 99 D4
New Windsor St. Uxb 201 E2
Newbarn La. Se Gr 176 C3
Newberry Cres. Wind 209 E3
Newbery Way. Slough 205 E2
Newbolt Cl. Paul 17 D4
Newbury Ct. M Keyn 57 E3
Newbury Dr. Maid 203 D3
Newbury Rd. Harm 213 F3
Newcombe Rise. W Dra 208 C4
Newcourt. Uxb 208 B4
Newcroft Cl. Uxb 208 C4
Newell Cl. Ayl 116 A3
Newells Hedge. Pit 105 E3
Newfield Gdns. Mar 183 F2
Newfield Rd. Mar 183 F2
Newground Rd. Ald 120 A2
Newhall Cl. Bov 146 A2
Newhaven Spur. Slough 198 A1
Newhouse Rd. Bov 146 A3
Newlands Dr. Maid 202 A4
Newlands Dr. Stan 212 C2
Newlands Gdns. Wing 79 F1
Newlyn Pl. M Keyn 35 D1
Newmer Rd. H Wyc 172 A2
Newport Pagnell Rd. Stag 16 B2
Newport Rd. Ast 15 E1
Newport Rd. Emb 13 F4
Newport Rd. Hans 11 D1
Newport Rd. Hth 60 C4
Newport Rd. M Keyn 35 E1
Newport Rd. Moul 36 B4
Newport Rd. Slough 197 F1
Newport Rd. Wave 48 C4
Newton Cl. Slough 206 C2
Newton Ct. Old W 211 D1
Newton La. Old W 211 D1
Newton Rd. Dray P 68 B4
Newton Rd. Harm 213 F3
Newton Rd. M Keyn 57 F3
Newton Rd. Turv 8 C3
Newton St. Oln 7 D2
Newtonside Orch. Old W 211 D1
Newtown Rd. Mar 183 F2
Newtown Rd. N Den 201 D3
Newtown Rd. S Ham 69 E4
Newville. Wedn 87 E1
Newyears Green La. S Har 190 C3
Neyland Dr. Ayl 101 E2
Nicholas Gdns. H Wyc 173 E4
Nicholas Mead. M Keyn 34 C4
Nicholls. Oak G 209 E3
Nicholsons La. Maid 202 C4
Nicol Cl. Ger C 177 E1
Nicol End. Ger C 177 E1
Nicol Rd. Ger C 177 E1
Nightingale Cl. Hol G 163 D3
Nightingale Cl. Stp Cl 63 F1
Nightingale Park. Burn 197 F3
Nightingale Pl. Buck 41 F1
Nightingale Rd. Ayl 115 F3
Nightingale Rd. Ches 144 A1
Nightingale Rd. Wen 131 D3
Nightingale Way. Den G 189 F3
Nightingales Corner. L Chal 166 B4
Nightingales La. C St G 166 B2
Nightingales La. L Chal 166 B2
Nine Elms Ave. Uxb 208 B4
Nine Elms Cl. Uxb 208 B4
Nine Stiles Cl. N Den 201 D3
Ninnings Rd. C St P 177 F2
Ninnings Way. C St P 177 F2
Nixey Cl. Slough 206 A2
Noble Cl. M Keyn 35 D4
Nooke The. M Keyn 35 E4
Norbrek. M Keyn 33 F1
Norden Cl. Maid 202 B2
Norden Rd. Maid 202 B3
Norfolk Ave. Slough 205 E4
Norfolk Park Cotts. Maid 202 C4
Norfolk Rd. Maid 202 C4
Norfolk Rd. Turv 8 C3
Norfolk Rd. Uxb 201 E3
Norfolk Terr. Ayl 101 F1
Norgrove Park. Ger C 188 C4
Norman Ave. Hen-O-T 191 F1
Norman Way. Dun 93 F4
Normandy Dr. Berk 135 D3
Normandy Way. M Keyn 46 C1
Normans Cl. Uxb 208 C4
Normans The. Slough 206 A4
Normill Terr. Ast C 117 D3
Norreys Dr. Maid 202 B2
Norrington. M Keyn 33 F1
Norris Rd. U Arn 94 C4
North Bridge Rd. Berk 135 D3
North Burnham Cl. Burn 197 D2
North Cl. Dray P 68 B3
North Cl. Medm 193 E4
North Cl. Wind 209 F3
North Common Rd. Uxb 201 F4
North Crawley Rd. Moul 23 E2
North Crawley Rd. N Craw 23 E2
North Crawley Rd. N Pag 23 E2
North Croft. Wins 66 A2
North Croft. Woo G 185 F3
North Dr. Ayl 115 F3
North Dr. Beac 186 A4
North Dr. H Wyc 173 F4
North Eastern Rd. Ayl 101 E1
North Eighth St. M Keyn 34 C2
North Eleventh St. M Keyn 34 C2
North End Rd. Qntn 85 D3
North End Rd. Stp Cl 63 E2
North Fifth St. M Keyn 34 B1
North Gate. M Keyn 47 E1
North Green. Maid 195 F1
North Green. Slough 205 F3
North La. Chor 167 F4
North Lee La. S Man 129 F4
North Lines Rd. Fla H 174 A1
North Mill Rd. Bled 138 A3
North Ninth St. M Keyn 34 C2
North Orbital Rd. Den G 189 F4
North Orbital Rd. Map Cr 178 C2
North Park. Ger C 188 C4
North Rd. Ame 154 B2
North Rd. Berk 135 D2
North Rd. Chor 167 E2
North Rd. Hol G 162 B3
North Rd. Maid 202 C4
North Rd. W Dra 208 C2
North Ridge. M Keyn 35 D1
North Row. M Keyn 34 C2
North Seventh St. M Keyn 34 B1
North Sixth St. M Keyn 34 B1
North Sq. N Pag 22 B3
North St. Cast 19 F3
North St. M Keyn 34 A4
North St. M Keyn 47 E1
North St. Tha 125 E1
North Star La. Maid 202 B3
North Tenth St. M Keyn 34 C2
North Thirteenth St. M Keyn 34 C2
North Town Cl. Maid 195 F1
North Town Mead. Maid 195 F1
North Town Moor. Maid 195 F1
North Town Rd. Maid 195 F1
North Twelfth St. M Keyn 34 C2
North Way. Dean 31 F3
North Way. Pott 18 C1
North Way. Uxb 201 F3
Northall Cl. Eat B 92 B3
Northall Rd. Eat B 92 B3
Northampton Ave. Slough 205 E4
Northampton Rd. Brac 26 A1
Northampton Rd. Cast 19 E1
Northampton Rd. Graf R 9 E2
Northampton Rd. Lath 22 B3
Northampton Rd. Lave 7 F4
Northampton Rd. Y Has 1 A3
Northborough Rd. Slough 198 A1
Northcliffe. Eat B 92 C3
Northcroft. She B E 46 B3
Northcroft. Slough 198 A1
Northcroft. Wedn 87 E1
Northdean. Maid 195 F1
Northdown Rd. C St P 177 F2
Northend. Rav 5 F2
Northend Cl. Fla H 185 E4
Northend Sq. Buck 41 E1
Northern Hts. Bou E 185 D3
Northern Per R (W). Harm 213 F3
Northern Rd. Ayl 101 E1
Northern Rd. Slough 198 B1
Northern Woods. Fla H 185 E4
Northfield Dr. M Keyn 35 F3
Northfield End. Hen-O-T 191 E2
Northfield Rd. Ayl 116 A4
Northfield Rd. Maid 195 F1
Northfield Rd. P Ris 139 E2
Northlands Dr. Slough 197 E2
Northlands Rd. Adsk 53 F1
Northleigh. M Keyn 46 B1
Northmill. P Ris 138 C2

Northolt Rd. Harm 213 F3
Northumberland Ave. Ayl 116 A3
Northumberland Cl. Stan 213 F1
Northumbria Rd. Maid 202 A2
Northwich. M Keyn 47 E4
Northwood Rd. Harm 213 E3
Nortoft Rd. C St P 177 F3
Norton Rd. Uxb 201 E1
Norvic Rd. Mars 105 D1
Norway Dr. Slough 206 A4
Norwood La. Uxb 200 B1
Norwood Rd. Loud 174 A1
Norwoods Ct. Ame 165 D4
Nottingham Rd. Chor 167 E1
Nugent Cl. Mar 183 F2
Nup End Cl. Win 89 D2
Nup End La. Win 89 D2
Nurseries The. Eat B 92 C3
Nursery Cl. Ame 165 F4
Nursery Cl. Ty Gr 174 B4
Nursery Ct. H Wyc 172 B3
Nursery Dr. La En 171 D3
Nursery Gdns. M Keyn 34 A2
Nursery Gdns. Tri 119 D2
Nursery La. Slough 206 B3
Nursery La. Ty Gr 174 B4
Nursery Rd. Burn 204 A4
Nursery Way. Wray 211 E1
Nursery Waye. Uxb 201 E2
Nursery Wlk. Mar 183 A2
Nutfield La. H Wyc 172 C4
Nutkins Way. Ches 144 B1
Nutmeg Cl. Walt 48 A3
Nye Way. Bov 146 A2

O'Grady Way. Ayl 101 D2
Oadman Sq. She B E 46 B3
Oak Cres. H Wyc 172 B2
Oak Dr. Berk 135 E2
Oak End Way. Chin 147 E3
Oak End Way. Ger C 188 C3
Oak Green. Ayl 115 E4
Oak La. Buc Co 133 D1
Oak La. Wind 210 A3
Oak Rd. P Ris 139 E2
Oak Stubbs La. Dorn 203 F2
Oak Tree Ave. Mar 183 E2
Oak Tree Cl. Mar 183 E2
Oak Tree Dr. La En 171 E3
Oak Tree Rd. Mar 183 E2
Oak View. G Kin 162 B4
Oak Way. Wins 66 A2
Oak Wood. Berk 134 C2
Oakdown Cres. Oln 6 C2
Oaken Gr. Maid 195 E1
Oakengrove. Pres 151 E3
Oakengrove Cl. Hol G 163 E3
Oakengrove La. Ty Gr 163 D2
Oakengrove Rd. Ty Gr 163 D2
Oakeshott Ave. Wal A 161 E3
Oakfield. Chor 167 F1
Oakfield Ave. Slough 205 D3
Oakfield Cnr. Ame 154 B1
Oakfield Rd. Ayl 116 A4
Oakfield Rd. Bou E 185 D2
Oakhill Rd. Map Cr 178 B3
Oakhill Rd. She C E 45 F3
Oakhurst. Maid 196 A2
Oakington Ave. L Chal 166 C4
Oakland Way. Fla H 174 A1
Oakley Cres. Slough 205 F3
Oakley Gdns. M Keyn 35 D3
Oakley Green Rd. Oak G 209 D3
Oakley La. Chin 147 D3
Oakley Rd. Chin 147 E3
Oakridge. M Keyn 46 C2
Oakridge Ct. H Wyc 172 B3
Oakridge Rd. H Wyc 172 C4
Oaks Rd. Stan 213 E1
Oaks The. Berk 135 D2
Oakside. N Den 201 D3
Oaktree Cl. Ty Gr 163 D1
Oakway. Ame 154 A2
Oakwell Cl. Dun 93 F4
Oakwood. Fla H 174 A1
Oakwood Dr. M Keyn 58 C4
Oatlands Dr. Slough 205 E4
Oban Ct. Slough 205 E2
Ockwells Rd. Maid 202 B2
Octagon Par. H Wyc 173 D4
Octavian Dr. M Keyn 33 F3
Octavian Way. Brac 38 A4
Odell Cl. M Keyn 47 E4
Odencroft Rd. Slough 198 A1
Odney La. Cook 196 A4
Offas La. Wins 66 A3
Ogilvie Rd. H Wyc 172 C4
Okeford Dr. Tri 118 C2
Okeley La. Tri 118 C2
Old Barn Cl. Gawt 52 A2
Old Burrs. S Man 115 E2
Old Coach Dr. H Wyc 174 A2
Old Court Cl. Maid 202 A2
Old Dashwood Hill. La En 159 F1
Old Dean. Bov 146 A2
Old End. Pad 53 D1
Old Farm. Pit 105 E2
Old Farm Cl. Beac 175 E3
Old Farm Cl. Worm 123 E3
Old Farm Rd. H Wyc 161 F1
Old Farm Rd. W Dra 208 B2
Old Ferry Dr. Wray 211 E1
Old Field Cl. L Chal 166 C4
Old Forge Cl. Maid 203 D2
Old Forge Cl. Ting 51 D3
Old Forge Gdns. Bier 102 A2
Old Forge Rd. Loud 174 B1
Old Groveway. M Keyn 47 E3
Old Hardenwaye. H Wyc 162 C1
Old Horns La. Mar B 172 A2
Old Kiln Rd. Fla H 185 D4
Old Kiln Rd. Ty Gr 163 E1
Old Linslade Rd. L Buzz 70 C2
Old Lodge Dr. Beac 175 F1
Old Manor Cl. P Ris 139 E4
Old Manor Cl. Whad 45 D1
Old Marsh La. Dorn 203 F2
Old Marsh La. Tapl 203 F2
Old Mead. C St P 177 F2
Old Mill Cl. Hadd 127 D3
Old Mill Furlong. Wins 66 A3
Old Mill Gdns. Berk 135 E2
Old Mill La. Uxb 208 A4
Old Mill Rd. Den 190 A1
Old Nursery Ct. Hedg 187 E1
Old Orchard. Bier 102 A2
Old Orchard. Chin 137 F1
Old Orchard Mews. Berk 135 E2
Old Oxford Rd. La En 160 B1
Old Plough Cl. Chea 112 A1
Old Post Office La. Maid 202 C4
Old Rd. L Buzz 80 C4
Old Rectory La. Den G 189 F2
Old Risborough Rd. S Man 130 A4
Old School Cl. Hal 117 E1
Old School Cl. Skch 158 C2
Old School Yd. Stp Cl 63 E2
Old Six La. Char 143 E2
Old Station La. Wray 212 A1
Old Station Way. Bou E 185 F3
Old Stoke Rd. Ayl 115 E3
Old Town. Brac 38 A4
Old Town Cl. Beac 175 F1
Old Vicarage Way. Bou E 185 E2
Old Watery La. Woo G 185 F4
Old Windmill Way. L Cre 125 E4
Old Wolverton Rd. M Keyn 33 E4
Oldacres. Maid 203 D4
Oldbrook Bvd. M Keyn 46 C4
Oldbury Gr. Beac 175 E3
Olde Bell Cl. S Ham 69 F4
Olde Bell La. M Keyn 46 A4
Oldershaw Mews. Maid 202 A4
Oldfield Rd. Maid 203 D4
Oldhams Meadow. Bier 102 A1
Oldhouse Cl. H Wyc 172 C2
Oliffe Cl. Ayl 101 E2
Oliffe Way. Ayl 101 E2
Oline Ct. She C E 45 F3
Oliver Rd. M Keyn 58 B4
Oliver's Paddock. Mar B 183 E3
Olleberrie La. Sar 156 B4
Olney Rd. Emb 13 F4
Olney Rd. Lave 7 F4
One Pin La. Far C 187 E1
One Tree La. Beac 175 F2
Onslow Dr. Tha 126 A1
Opendale Rd. Burn 204 A4
Orchard Ave. Berk 135 D2
Orchard Ave. Wind 210 A3
Orchard Cl. Beac 175 E2
Orchard Cl. Chor 167 E3
Orchard Cl. Cran 25 D1
Orchard Cl. Hen-O-T 191 F1
Orchard Cl. Hgh V 162 A4
Orchard Cl. Lgwk 138 B4
Orchard Cl. M Keyn 57 F4
Orchard Cl. Maid 203 D2
Orchard Cl. N Den 201 D3
Orchard Cl. Oak 109 E2
Orchard Cl. S Man 116 A1
Orchard Cl. Wadd 99 D4
Orchard Cl. Wen 131 D3
Orchard Cl. Win 89 D2
Orchard Cl. Yard G 18 C3
Orchard Ct. Harm 213 E4
Orchard Dr. Ast C 117 F2
Orchard Dr. Bou E 185 E2
Orchard Dr. Chor 167 E3
Orchard Dr. L Buzz 80 B3
Orchard Dr. Ty Gr 163 D2
Orchard Dr. Uxb 201 E1
Orchard End. Edle 92 C2
Orchard End. Hol G 163 D3
Orchard End Ave. Ame 165 F4
Orchard Gate. Far C 198 B4
Orchard Gr. Fla H 185 D4
Orchard Gr. Ger C 177 E1
Orchard Gr. Maid 202 B4
Orchard La. Ame 154 B1
Orchard La. Harr 3 F4
Orchard La. Pres 151 E3
Orchard La. Stew 78 C4
Orchard Mews. Se Gr 176 B2
Orchard Park. Hol G 163 E3
Orchard Pl. West 39 D2
Orchard Rd. Beac 175 F1
Orchard Rd. C St G 177 E4
Orchard Rd. H Wyc 174 A2
Orchard Rd. Old W 211 D1
Orchard Rd. Se Gr 176 B3
Orchard Ri. Oln 6 C2
Orchard The. Ast C 117 F3
Orchard The. Fla H 185 D4
Orchard The. Hal 131 E4
Orchard The. Hol G 163 D3
Orchard The. Mar 183 F2
Orchard The. Pott 18 B2
Orchard The. Wal A 161 F3
Orchard View. Uxb 201 E1
Orchard Way. Ayl 101 F1
Orchard Way. Bov 146 A2
Orchard Way. Chin 147 E3
Orchard Way. Cran 25 D1
Orchard Way. E Clay 74 C3
Orchard Way. Eat B 92 C3
Orchard Way. Hol G 163 E3
Orchard Way. Ivin 105 F2
Orchard Way. N Craw 24 A3
Orchard Way. Slough 206 C3
Orchard Waye. Uxb 201 E2
Orchard Wlk. Lave 7 F4
Orchards The. Eat B 92 C4
Orchards The. Tri 118 C2
Orchardville. Burn 197 D1
Orchehill Ave. Ger C 188 B4
Orchehill Rise. Ger C 188 C3
Orkney Cl. M Keyn 46 C1
Orkney Cl. Stew 78 C4
Ormesby Cl. Ayl 116 A3
Ormond Rd. Tha 126 A1
Ormonde. M Keyn 34 B4
Ormsgill Ct. M Keyn 34 A3
Orne Gdns. M Keyn 35 D4
Orwell Cl. Ayl 115 E2
Orwell Cl. N Pag 21 F3
Orwell Cl. Wind 210 B2
Orwell Dr. Ayl 115 E2
Orwell Dr. S Man 115 E2
Osborn's Ct. Oln 6 C2
Osborne Mews. Wind 210 B3
Osborne Rd. Wind 210 B2
Osborne St. M Keyn 58 B4
Osborne St. Slough 205 F2
Osborne Way. Wigg 119 E1
Osbourne Ct. Wind 210 B3
Osbourne St. M Keyn 33 E3
Osier Way. Ayl 115 F4
Osmington Pl. Tri 118 C2
Osney Rd. Maid 195 F1
Osprey Cl. M Keyn 47 D4
Osprey Cl. W Dra 208 C2
Osprey Wlk. Ayl 101 F2
Osprey Wlk. Buck 52 C4
Ostler Gate. Maid 195 E1
Ostlers La. M Keyn 32 B3
Otter Cl. M Keyn 46 B1
Otterfield Rd. W Dra 208 C3
Otters Brook. Buck 52 C4
Oulton Cl. Ayl 116 A3
Ousebank St. N Pag 22 B3
Ousebank Way. M Keyn 32 B3
Ouseley Rd. Wray 211 E1
Outfield Rd. Ger C 177 E2
Outlook Dr. C St G 177 E4
Ouzel Cl. M Keyn 46 C1
Oval Way. Ger C 188 C4
Over Hampden. Pres 151 E4
Over The Misbourne. Den G 189 D3
Overdale Rd. Ches 144 A2
Overdales. Ty Gr 162 C2
Overend Cl. M Keyn 34 A2
Overn Ave. Buck 41 E1
Overn Cl. Buck 41 E1
Overn Cres. Buck 41 E1
Oversley Ct. M Keyn 22 A1
Overstrand. Ast C 117 F3
Overstreet. M Keyn 35 D4
Overton Dr. Tha 126 A1
Oving Rd. Oving 86 C4
Oving Rd. Whit 86 C4
Ovitts Cl. Wins 66 A3
Owlsears Cl. Beac 175 E2
Oxendon Ct. L Buzz 70 C1
Oxfield Cl. Berk 135 D2
Oxford Ave. Burn 197 D2
Oxford Gdns. Den 190 A1
Oxford Rd. Ayl 115 D4
Oxford Rd. Den 189 E1
Oxford Rd. Ger C 188 B3
Oxford Rd. H Wyc 173 D4
Oxford Rd. La En 160 B1
Oxford Rd. Mar 183 E1
Oxford Rd. N Den 201 D3
Oxford Rd. Oak 109 E3
Oxford Rd. Skch 158 B3
Oxford Rd. Sto 114 B3
Oxford Rd. Sto 115 D4
Oxford Rd. Tha 125 E1
Oxford Rd. Wind 210 B3
Oxford Rd E. Wind 210 B3
Oxford St. H Wyc 173 D4
Oxford St. Lee C 142 B3
Oxford St. M Keyn 32 B3
Oxford St. M Keyn 33 E3
Oxford St. M Keyn 58 B4
Oxleys. Oln 6 C2
Oxman La. M Keyn 33 D3

Pack & Prime L. Hen-O-T 191 E1
Packet Boat La. W Dra 208 B4
Packhorse Rd. Ger C 188 C3
Padcroft Rd. W Dra 208 B3
Paddock Cl. Maid 202 A1
Paddock The. Ayl 116 B4
Paddock The. C St P 177 F3
Paddock The. Datch 211 D3
Paddock The. Emb 13 F4
Paddock The. Maid 195 E1
Paddock Way. M Keyn 47 E1
Paddocks The. Fla H 185 D4
Paddocks The. H Wyc 172 A2
Paddocks The. Hadd 127 D3
Paddocks The. L Buzz 80 C4
Paddocks The. Stp Cl 63 F2
Paddocks The. Wen 131 D3
Padstow Ave. M Keyn 34 C1
Padstow Cl. Ayl 101 F1
Padstow Cl. Slough 206 C2
Page Hill Ave. Buck 41 F1
Pages Croft. Berk 135 D3
Pages La. Uxb 201 E3
Paget Cl. Mar 183 F2
Paget Dr. Maid 202 A2
Paget Rd. Slough 206 C1
Pagoda The. Maid 196 A1
Paines Orch. Ched 105 D4
Palliser Rd. C St G 177 D4
Palmer Ave. Ayl 115 E4
Palmer Ave. U Arn 94 C4
Palmer's Moor La. Uxb 201 D1
Palmers Cl. Maid 202 A2
Palmerston Ave. Slough 206 A2
Pankridge Dr. Pres 151 E4
Pannier Pl. M Keyn 35 D3
Parade The. Bou E 185 D2
Paradise. Nwtn L 57 E2
Paradise Rd. Hen-O-T 191 E1
Parchment Cl. Ame 154 C1
Parish La. Far C 187 E1
Parish Piece. Hol G 163 E4
Park Ave. N Pag 22 A2
Park Ave. Tott 93 D4
Park Ave. Wray 211 E2
Park Cl. Cast 19 F1
Park Cl. Hogg 77 F3
Park Cl. La En 171 E3
Park Cnr. Wind 209 F2
Park Farm Rd. H Wyc 161 D1
Park Farm Way. La En 171 E3
Park Gate. Wing 79 F1
Park Gdns. M Keyn 47 D1
Park Gr. L Chal 166 B3
Park Hill. Holt 122 A1
Park La. Beac 175 F1
Park La. Burn 197 F4
Park La. Eat B 92 B3
Park La. Hort 212 A2
Park La. La En 171 E3
Park La. Paul 17 D4
Park La. Skch 158 C3
Park La. Slough 206 A2
Park La. Ston 179 E3
Park La. Ty Gr 163 D2
Park Meadow. P Ris 139 D2
Park Par Cntr The. Hol G 163 D3
Park Pl. Ame 154 C1
Park Rd. Far C 198 B2
Park Rd. Gr Und 82 C4
Park Rd. Gran 75 F3
Park Rd. Hans 11 D1
Park Rd. Hart 10 B4
Park Rd. Hen-O-T 191 F1
Park Rd. M Keyn 32 B3
Park Rd. Sher 14 A1
Park Rd. Stan 213 E1
Park Rd. Sto P 198 B2
Park Rd. Tri 118 C1
Park Rd. Uxb 201 F3
Park Rd. Wins 65 F3
Park Rd E. Uxb 201 E2
Park Rd S. Wins 65 F2
Park Rise. Berk 134 C3
Park St. Ayl 115 F4
Park St. Berk 135 D3
Park St. H Wyc 173 E3
Park St. Hth 60 C4
Park St. Maid 202 C4
Park St. P Ris 139 D2
Park St. Slough 205 F2
Park St. Stan 212 B3
Park St. Tri 119 D2
Park St. Wind 210 B3
Park View. N Pag 22 B2
Park View Ct. H Wyc 172 B4
Park View Rd. Berk 135 D2
Parker Cl. M Keyn 34 A3
Parkfield. Chor 167 F3
Parkfield Ave. Ame 154 B1
Parkgate. Burn 197 E1
Parkland Ave. Slough 206 B1
Parklands. M Keyn 21 E1
Parkmoor La. Frie 170 C1
Parkside. Ger C 188 C4
Parkside. M Keyn 46 C2
Parkside. Maid 195 E1
Parkside. Wal A 150 A1
Parkview. Fla H 185 D4
Parkway. B Bkhl 48 B1
Parkway. Mar 184 A2
Parkway. Wave 49 D3
Parkway The. Iver H 200 B2
Parkwood. Wal A 150 A1
Parliament Cl. Pres 151 D4
Parliament La. Burn 196 C3
Parliament Rd. Tha 125 F1
Parneleys. M Keyn 35 F2
Parrock La. M K Vil 36 A1
Parrot Cl. Ayl 115 D3
Parrott's La. Buc Co 133 D2
Parrs Rd. Skch 158 C2
Parry Green N. Slough 206 C1
Parsley Cl. Walt 48 A3
Parslow Cl. S Man 115 E2
Parson's Fee. Ayl 115 E4
Parson's Wood La. Far C 198 B3
Parsonage Cl. H Wyc 173 E3
Parsonage Cl. Tri 119 D2
Parsonage Ct. Tri 119 D2
Parsonage Gdns. Mar 183 F1
Parsonage La. Far C 198 B2
Parsonage La. Wind 210 A3
Parsonage Pl. Tri 119 D2
Parsonage Rd. C St G 177 D4
Parsons Cl. Stew 78 C4
Parsons Cl. Wins 65 F2
Parsons Wlk. Hol G 163 E3
Parton Cl. Wen 131 D3
Parton Rd. Ayl 116 A4
Partridge Cl. Buck 52 C4
Partridge Cl. Ches 144 C2
Partridge Mead. Maid 195 F1
Partridge Piece. Cran 25 E2
Partridge Way. H Wyc 161 E1
Pascomb Rd. Dun 93 F4
Passalewe La. Walt 48 B4
Passmore. M Keyn 47 E3
Pastern Pl. M Keyn 35 D3
Pastures The. Ayl 102 A1
Pastures The. Edle 92 C2
Pastures The. H Wyc 161 F1
Patches Field. Mar B 183 F3
Paterson Rd. Ayl 115 E3
Patrick Haugh Rd. U Arn 94 C4
Patrick Way. Ayl 116 A2
Patrick's La. Dean 31 F2
Patrington Cl. Uxb 201 E1
Patriot Dr. M Keyn 34 A1
Patrons Dr. Den G 189 F3
Patterson Rd. Ches 144 A2
Pattison La. M Keyn 35 E2
Paul's Row. H Wyc 173 D3
Pauls Hill. Ty Gr 174 C3
Pavers Ct. S Man 115 E2
Paxton Ave. Slough 205 E2
Paxton Cl. Oln 6 C2
Paxton Cres. She B E 46 A3
Paxton Rd. Berk 135 E2
Paynes Dr. M Keyn 46 A4
Pea La. Berk 134 B4
Peach Meadow. Hal 131 D4
Peach Tree Ave. W Dra 208 C4
Peachey Cl. Uxb 208 B4
Peachey La. Uxb 208 B4
Peacock Rd. Mar 184 A2
Pear Tree Ave. W Dra 208 C4
Pear Tree Cl. Se Gr 176 B2
Pearce Cl. Ayl 115 F2
Pearce Cl. Maid 195 F1
Pearce Rd. Ches 144 A1
Pearce Rd. Maid 195 F1
Pearces Orch. Hen-O-T 191 E2
Pearl Gdns. Slough 205 D3
Pearse Gr. Walt 48 A2
Peascod St. Wind 210 B3
Peascroft. L Cre 125 E3
Pebble La. Ayl 115 E4
Pebblemoor. Edle 92 C2
Peckover Ct. M Keyn 33 F1
Pednor Bottom. Char 143 D2
Pednor Rd. Ches 143 F1
Pednormead End. Ches 154 A4
Peebles Pl. M Keyn 46 C2
Peel Cl. Wind 210 A2
Peel Ct. Slough 205 D4
Peel Rd. M Keyn 33 E3
Peel Way. Uxb 208 C4
Peerless Dr. S Har 190 B4
Peers Dr. Asp G 49 F2
Peers La. She C E 46 A3
Pelham Pl. M Keyn 34 C3
Pelham Rd. Tha 126 A1
Pelton Ct. She B E 46 B3
Pemberton Cl. Ayl 115 F3
Pemberton Rd. Slough 197 F1
Pembridge Chase. Bov 146 A2
Pembridge Cl. Bov 146 A2
Pembridge Rd. Bov 146 A2
Pembroke Rd. Ayl 101 F1
Pencarrow Pl. M Keyn 35 D1
Pencoed Pl. Wind 210 B3
Penfold. W Tur 116 C1
Penfold Cotts. Hol G 163 E4
Penfold La. H Hea 152 C1
Penfold La. Hol G 152 C1

Penington Rd. Beac ... 186 A4
Penling Cl. Cook ... 195 F3
Penly Cl. Chin ... 147 D3
Penmoor Cl. H Wyc ... 172 B4
Penn Ave. Ches ... 144 A1
Penn Bottom. Ty Gr ... 163 F1
Penn Cl. Chor ... 167 E2
Penn Cl. Uxb ... 201 E1
Penn Dr. Den G ... 189 F3
Penn Gaskell La. C St P ... 177 F3
Penn Meadow. Sto P ... 198 C2
Penn Rd. Ayl ... 115 E4
Penn Rd. Beac ... 175 E3
Penn Rd. Chor ... 167 F1
Penn Rd. Ger C ... 177 E1
Penn Rd. Slough ... 198 B1
Penn Rd. Ty Gr ... 163 D2
Penn Way. Chor ... 167 E2
Pennia Cl. M Keyn ... 46 B1
Pennine Rd. Slough ... 205 D4
Pennington Pl. Tha ... 126 A1
Pennington Rd. Ger C ... 177 E2
Pennington Rd. H Wyc ... 173 F3
Penningtons The. Ame ... 154 C1
Pennylets Green. Sto P ... 199 D3
Penrith Cl. Uxb ... 201 E3
Penrith Way. Ayl ... 116 A4
Penryn Ave. M Keyn ... 35 D1
Penshurst Cl. Ger C ... 177 E1
Penshurst Rd. Maid ... 202 B3
Pentewan Gate. M Keyn ... 34 C1
Pentland Rd. Ayl ... 115 F3
Pentland Rd. Slough ... 205 D4
Pentlands. M Keyn ... 32 C2
Pentlands The. H Wyc ... 174 A2
Penwood Ct. Maid ... 202 A4
Penwood La. Mar ... 183 E1
Penyston Rd. Maid ... 202 B4
Peplow Cl. W Dra ... 208 B3
Peppard Meadow. Pres ... 151 E3
Peppet's Green. Char ... 143 E4
Peppiatts The. Edle ... 92 A3
Pepys Cl. Slough ... 212 A4
Pepys Dr. Pres ... 151 E3
Perch Cl. Mar ... 194 B4
Percheron Pl. M Keyn ... 34 C3
Percy Pl. Datch ... 211 D3
Percy Terr. C St G ... 177 D4
Peregrine Cl. M Keyn ... 47 D4
Perks La. Pres ... 151 E2
Permayne. M Keyn ... 34 A4
Perracombe. M Keyn ... 46 C2
Perran Ave. M Keyn ... 35 D1
Perrin Spring La. Frie ... 170 C1
Perry Hill. Edgc ... 73 D1
Perry La. Bled ... 138 B1
Perry Oaks Dr. Harm ... 213 E3
Perry St. Wen ... 131 D3
Perrycroft. Wind ... 209 F2
Perryman Way. Slough ... 197 F1
Perth Ave. Slough ... 205 D4
Perth Cl. M Keyn ... 46 C1
Perth Rd. H Wyc ... 173 E4
Peter's Cl. Pres ... 151 E3
Peter's Pl. Berk ... 134 C3
Peterborough Ave. H Wyc ... 173 E4
Peterborough Gate. M Keyn ... 35 E3
Peterhill Cl. C St P ... 177 F3
Peterley. Pres ... 151 F2
Peters La. P Ris ... 139 F2
Peters La. Pres ... 139 F2
Petersfield Ave. Slough ... 206 A3
Petersham Cl. N Pag ... 22 B1
Pettifer Way. H Wyc ... 172 B3
Pettingrew Cl. Walt ... 48 A3
Petty Pl. Maid ... 202 B2
Petworth. M Keyn ... 33 F1
Petworth Ct. Wind ... 210 A3
Pevensey Cl. Ayl ... 116 A3
Pevensey Cl. M Keyn ... 57 F4
Pevensey Rd. Slough ... 205 D4
Peverel Dr. M Keyn ... 47 D2
Peveril Cl. Ayl ... 116 A3
Pevers La. W Und ... 6 A1
Pheasant Cl. Berk ... 135 E2
Pheasant Cl. Tri ... 119 D3
Pheasant Dr. H Wyc ... 161 E1
Pheasant Hill. C St G ... 177 E4
Pheasant Rise. Ches ... 154 B3
Pheasant Wlk. C St P ... 177 F3
Pheasants Croft. Maid ... 202 A3
Pheasants Dr. Hol G ... 163 D3
Philip Ct. She C E ... 46 A3
Philip Dr. Fla H ... 185 E4
Philip Rd. H Wyc ... 173 E4
Phillimore Cl. M Keyn ... 35 D4
Philpots Cl. W Dra ... 208 B3
Phipps Cl. Maid ... 202 A1
Phoebe La. Wave ... 48 C3
Phoenix Dr. M Keyn ... 46 C4
Phygtle The. C St P ... 177 F2
Phyllis Ct Dr. Hen-O-T ... 191 F2
Picasso Pl. Ayl ... 100 C1
Pickford Dr. Slough ... 206 C3
Picts La. P Ris ... 139 D1
Piddington La. La En ... 171 D4
Piddington Rd. Lud ... 96 A4
Pield Heath Rd. Uxb ... 201 F1
Pierson Rd. Wind ... 209 E3
Pigeon Farm Rd. Skch ... 158 C3
Piggott's Hill. Wal A ... 150 C1
Piggotts End. Ame ... 165 D4
Piggotts Orch. Ame ... 165 D4
Pightle Cres. Buck ... 41 E1
Pightle The. Buck ... 41 E1
Pightle The. M Mor ... 41 F2
Pightle The. Oving ... 86 B4
Pigott Dr. She C E ... 46 A3
Pigott Orch. Qntn ... 85 D3
Pike Cl. Mar ... 194 B4
Pike Corner. Ayl ... 116 B3
Pilch La. Adsk ... 54 B3
Pilch La. G Hrwd ... 54 B2
Pilch La. Thrn ... 54 B3
Pilgrims Cl. P Ris ... 139 D3
Pimms Cl. H Wyc ... 174 A3
Pimms Gr. H Wyc ... 174 A3
Pimpernel Gr. Walt ... 48 A3
Pinchfield. Map Cr ... 178 B3
Pinders Croft. M Keyn ... 33 D3
Pine Chase. H Wyc ... 172 A2
Pine Cl. Berk ... 135 D2
Pine Cl. Maid ... 202 A4
Pine Cl. Ty Gr ... 163 D2
Pine Crest Mews. L Buzz ... 80 C3
Pine Gr. Wbn S ... 49 D2
Pine Hill. Ty Gr ... 162 C2
Pine Road. Edle ... 106 C4
Pine Trees Dr. Ick ... 201 F4
Pine Wlk. Ty Gr ... 163 D2
Pineapple Rd. Ame ... 165 F4
Pinecroft. Mar ... 183 E2
Pinels Way. H Wyc ... 172 C2
Pines Cl. Ame ... 154 A1
Pines The. Ty Gr ... 163 D1
Pinetree Cl. Ger C ... 177 E2
Pinewood Ave. Uxb ... 208 C4
Pinewood Cl. Ger C ... 188 C2
Pinewood Cl. Iver H ... 200 B3
Pinewood Dr. M Keyn ... 58 C4
Pinewood Green. Iver H ... 200 B3
Pinewood Rd. H Wyc ... 172 B4
Pinewood Rd. Iver H ... 200 A2
Pinglestone Cl. Harm ... 213 F4
Pinions Rd. H Wyc ... 173 F3
Pink Hill. Lac G ... 149 F4
Pink La. Burn ... 197 D2
Pink Rd. Lac G ... 149 F4
Pinkard Ct. M Keyn ... 47 E4
Pinkneys Dr. Maid ... 195 D1
Pinkneys Rd. Maid ... 202 A4
Pinn Cl. Uxb ... 208 B4
Pipard. M Keyn ... 34 C4
Pipers Cl. Burn ... 197 E1
Pipers Croft. Dun ... 93 F4
Pipers La. G Kin ... 162 B4
Pippins Cl. W Dra ... 208 B2
Pippins The. Slough ... 206 C3
Pitch Pond Cl. Beac ... 175 E3
Pitch The. B Bot ... 159 E2
Pitchcott Rd. Oving ... 86 B4
Pitcher La. M Keyn ... 46 A4
Pitfield. M Keyn ... 33 D2
Pitt Green. Buck ... 41 F1
Pitts Rd. Slough ... 205 E3
Place Farm Way. P Ris ... 139 D3
Plaiters Cl. Tri ... 119 D2
Plantation Rd. Ame ... 154 C1
Plantation Rd. H Wyc ... 174 A4
Plantation Rd. L Buzz ... 70 C2
Platt The. Ame ... 165 D4
Pleasaunce The. Ast C ... 117 F3
Pleshey Cl. She C E ... 46 A3
Plomer Green Ave. H Wyc ... 161 E1
Plomer Green La. H Wyc ... 161 E2
Plomer Hill. H Wyc ... 161 E1
Plough La. Sar ... 156 C3
Plough La. Sto P ... 199 D2
Ploughlees La. Slough ... 205 F3
Ploughley Rd. U Arn ... 94 C4
Plover Cl. Buck ... 52 C4
Plover Cl. N Pag ... 22 C2
Plover The. Ayl ... 101 F2
Plover Wlk. Ayl ... 101 F2
Plowman Cl. M Keyn ... 33 D3
Plum Park La. Paul ... 17 E4
Plumer Rd. H Wyc ... 172 C4
Plumstead Ave. M Keyn ... 34 B2
Plym Cl. Ayl ... 115 E3
Pococks La. Eton ... 205 F1
Poets Chase. Ayl ... 115 F3
Points The. Maid ... 202 A2
Poles Hill. Ches ... 144 A1
Poles Hill. Sar ... 156 C3
Polidoris La. Hol G ... 163 E4
Polish Ave. Hal ... 131 F4
Pollard Ave. Den G ... 189 F3
Pollard Cl. Old W ... 211 D1
Pollards. Map Cr ... 178 B3
Pollywick Rd. Wigg ... 119 E1
Polruan Pl. M Keyn ... 35 D1
Pomeroy Cl. Ame ... 165 E4
Pond App. Hol G ... 163 E4
Pond Cl. Cole ... 164 B2
Pond Cl. Nwtn L ... 57 E1
Pond La. Ger C ... 177 D1
Pond Park Rd. Ches ... 144 A1
Pondwicks. Ame ... 165 D4
Pool La. Slough ... 205 F3
Poolmans Rd. Wind ... 209 E2
Popes Acre. Hadd ... 126 C3
Popes Cl. Ame ... 154 C1
Popes Cl. Iver ... 212 B4
Popes La. Cook ... 195 E4
Poplar Ave. Ame ... 165 F4
Poplar Ave. W Dra ... 208 C3
Poplar Cl. Ayl ... 102 A1
Poplar Cl. Stan ... 212 C3
Poplar Rd. Ayl ... 102 A1
Poplar Rd. Buck ... 52 B4
Poplar Rd. N Den ... 201 E3
Poplars Gr. Maid ... 196 A1
Poplars The. Wen ... 131 E3
Poppy Rd. P Ris ... 139 D1
Portal Rd. Wen ... 131 E3
Portchester Ct. M Keyn ... 33 F1
Porter's Cl. Dean ... 31 F2
Porters Way. W Dra ... 208 C2
Portfield Cl. Buck ... 52 C4
Portfield Way. Buck ... 52 C4
Portfields Rd. N Pag ... 22 A2
Porthleven Pl. M Keyn ... 35 D1
Portland Cl. Slough ... 197 E1
Portland Dr. M Keyn ... 35 E4
Portlands. Mar ... 183 E1
Portlock Rd. Maid ... 202 B4
Portmarnock Cl. M Keyn ... 57 E4
Portobello Cl. Ches ... 144 A1
Portrush Cl. M Keyn ... 57 E4
Portway. M K Vil ... 34 B2
Portway. M Keyn ... 35 E3
Portway. N Mar ... 76 A1
Portway. She C E ... 34 B2
Portway. Sto ... 114 C2
Portway Dr. H Wyc ... 161 D1
Portway Rd. Twyf ... 62 B1
Post Meadow. Iver H ... 200 B1
Post Office La. Beac ... 175 E2
Post Office La. Slough ... 206 B4
Post Office La. Whit ... 87 D3
Potash La. Lon M ... 104 A3
Potkiln La. Ger C ... 176 B1
Potter Row. S Hea ... 142 B1
Potters Cross. Iver H ... 200 C1
Potters La. M Keyn ... 33 D2
Poulcott. Wray ... 211 F1
Pound Cl. Stp Cl ... 63 E2
Pound Cl. Wick ... 31 D2
Pound Cres. Mar ... 183 E1
Pound Hill. G Bkhl ... 59 E1
Pound La. Lit M ... 184 B2
Pound La. Mar ... 183 E1
Pound La. N Craw ... 24 A4
Pound La. Pres B ... 62 A4
Pound St. Wen ... 131 D2
Pound The. Cook ... 195 F4
Pound The. Syr ... 27 D4
Poundfield La. Cook ... 195 F4
Poundfield Rd. Pott ... 18 C1
Poundlands. Lac G ... 149 F3
Powis Cl. Maid ... 202 A2
Powney Rd. Maid ... 202 B4
Poyle La. Burn ... 197 D2
Poyle Rd. Stan ... 212 C3
Prebendal Ave. Ayl ... 115 E4
Precedent Dr. M Keyn ... 34 A2
Precincts The. Burn ... 197 E1
Prescott Rd. Stan ... 212 C3
Presley Way. She C E ... 45 F4
Press Rd. Uxb ... 201 E3
Preston Ct. M Keyn ... 35 D4
Preston Hill. Ches ... 144 B1
Preston Rd. Slough ... 206 B3
Prestwick Cl. M Keyn ... 57 E4
Prestwood. Slough ... 206 A4
Prestwood Cl. H Wyc ... 172 B4
Pretoria Rd. H Wyc ... 173 E4
Primatt Cres. She C E ... 46 A3
Primrose Dr. Ayl ... 115 D3
Primrose Green. Hol G ... 162 C3
Primrose Hill. Hol G ... 162 C4
Prince Andrew Cl. Maid ... 196 A1
Prince Andrew Rd. Maid ... 196 A1
Prince Consort Cotts. Wind ... 210 B3
Prince Edward St. Berk ... 135 E2
Prince Philip Ave. Cran ... 24 B1
Prince's Rd. Ayl ... 115 F4
Princes Cl. Berk ... 135 D3
Princes Cl. Chil ... 111 D2
Princes Ct. L Buzz ... 80 C4
Princes Gdns. P Ris ... 139 D2
Princes La. Lee C ... 142 B3
Princes Rd. Bou E ... 185 E2
Princes Rd. La En ... 160 A1
Princes St. Slough ... 206 A2
Princes Way. M Keyn ... 58 B4
Princess Ave. Wind ... 210 A2
Princess St. Maid ... 202 C3
Printers End. Ayl ... 101 D1
Prior Gr. Ches ... 144 B1
Priors Cl. Maid ... 203 D1
Priors Cl. Slough ... 206 A2
Priors Park. M Keyn ... 46 B1
Priors Rd. Wind ... 209 E2
Priors Way. Maid ... 203 D1
Priory Ave. H Wyc ... 173 D4
Priory Ave. S Har ... 190 B4
Priory Cl. Ayl ... 101 E1
Priory Cl. Den ... 190 A1
Priory Cl. Hor-c-S ... 108 A3
Priory Cl. N Pag ... 22 C2
Priory Cl. S Har ... 190 B4
Priory Ct. Berk ... 135 E2
Priory Gdns. Berk ... 135 E2
Priory Gdns. S Har ... 190 B4
Priory Rd. Burn ... 204 B4
Priory Rd. Ger C ... 188 B4
Priory Rd. H Wyc ... 173 D4
Priory St. N Pag ... 22 C2
Priory Way. Datch ... 211 D4
Priory Way. Ger C ... 188 B4
Priory Way. Harm ... 213 F4
Pritchard Ct. M Keyn ... 34 C4
Progress Rd. H Wyc ... 172 A4
Promenade. Eton ... 210 B4
Prospect Cl. Dray P ... 68 B3
Prospect Ct. La En ... 171 D3
Prospect Pl. Cast ... 19 F3
Prospect Pl. Hurl ... 193 F2
Prospect Pl. Wing ... 79 F1
Prospect Rd. M Keyn ... 32 B3
Prospect Rd. Mar ... 183 B1
Providence Pl. Maid ... 202 C4
Providence Rd. W Dra ... 208 C3
Puers La. Se Gr ... 176 C2
Pulborough Cl. M Keyn ... 46 B1
Pulford Rd. L Buzz ... 80 C3
Pullfields. Ches ... 144 A1
Pulpit Cl. Ches ... 144 A1
Pulpit La. Oving ... 76 B1
Pulpit La. Oving ... 86 B4
Pump La N. Lit M ... 183 F3
Pump La S. Lit M ... 184 A2
Pumpkin Hill. Burn ... 197 F3
Pumpus Green. Wins ... 66 A2
Punch Bowl La. Ches ... 154 B4
Purbeck. M Keyn ... 34 B3
Purbeck Cl. Ayl ... 116 A3
Purcel Dr. N Pag ... 22 A2
Purssell Cl. Maid ... 202 A2
Purssells Meadow. Wal A ... 161 E4
Purton Ct. Far C ... 198 B3
Purton La. Far C ... 198 B3
Pury Rd. Graf R ... 9 D1
Pusey Way. La En ... 171 E3
Putman Pl. Hen-O-T ... 191 F1
Putnams Dr. Ast C ... 117 E3
Puxley Rd. Dean ... 31 E3
Pyebush La. Beac ... 187 D4
Pyghtle Footpath. Den G ... 190 A2
Pyghtle The. Oln ... 6 C2
Pyghtle The. Turv ... 8 C3
Pyghtles The. Qntn ... 85 D3
Pym Wlk. Tha ... 125 F1
Pymcombe Cl. P Ris ... 139 D3
Pyxe Ct. Walt ... 48 A2
Pyxe Ct. Walt ... 48 A2

Quadrangle The. H Wyc ... 173 F4
Quadrans Cl. M Keyn ... 35 D4
Quadrant The. H Wyc ... 162 C1
Quadrant The. Maid ... 203 D3
Quainton Rd. N Mar ... 76 A1
Quainton Rd. Wadd ... 99 D4
Quaker's Mead. W Tur ... 116 C2
Quaker's Mede. Hadd ... 127 D3
Quantock Cres. M Keyn ... 46 B1
Quarrendon Ave. Ayl ... 101 D1
Quarrendon Rd. Ame ... 165 F4
Quarry Cl. L Cre ... 125 E4
Quarrydale Dr. Mar ... 183 F1
Quaves Rd. Slough ... 206 B2
Quebec Rd. H Wyc ... 173 F3
Queen Alexandra R. H Wyc ... 173 D3
Queen Anne St. M Keyn ... 33 F4
Queen Anne's Rd. Wind ... 210 B2
Queen Catherine Rd. Stp Cl ... 63 F1
Queen Charlotte St. Wind ... 210 B3
Queen Cl. Hen-O-T ... 191 F1
Queen Eleanor St. M Keyn ... 32 B3
Queen Mother's Dr. Den G ... 189 F3
Queen Sq. H Wyc ... 173 D4
Queen St. Ayl ... 116 A4
Queen St. H Wyc ... 173 E4
Queen St. Hen-O-T ... 191 F1
Queen St. L Buzz ... 80 C4
Queen St. La En ... 160 A1
Queen St. M Keyn ... 32 C3
Queen St. Maid ... 202 C4
Queen St. Pit ... 105 E2
Queen St. Tri ... 119 D2
Queen St. Wcot ... 98 C3
Queen Victoria St. H Wyc ... 173 D3
Queen's Acre. Wind ... 210 B2
Queen's Cl. Old W ... 211 D1
Queen's Ct. Slough ... 205 F3
Queen's Dr The. Chor ... 167 F1
Queen's Gate. Wind ... 210 B2
Queen's La. Maid ... 202 C4
Queen's Pk. Ayl ... 115 F4
Queen's Rd. H Wyc ... 173 E3
Queen's Rd. Mar ... 183 B1
Queen's Rd. Slough ... 205 F3
Queen's Rd. Uxb ... 201 E1
Queen's Rd. Wind ... 210 B3
Queens Ave. N Pag ... 22 B2
Queens Cl. Tha ... 125 F1
Queens Mead. Ayl ... 116 B4
Queens Rd. Berk ... 135 D3
Queens Rd. Ches ... 144 B1
Queens Rd. P Ris ... 139 D2
Queens Rd. W Dra ... 208 C2
Queensmead. Datch ... 211 D3
Queensmead Rd. Loud ... 174 B1
Queensmere Rd. Slough ... 206 A2
Queensway. M Keyn ... 58 B4
Queensway. Maid ... 195 F1
Queensway. Ty Gr ... 163 D2
Queensway The. Ger C ... 188 B4
Quickberry Pl. Ame ... 165 E4
Quickley Brow. Chor ... 167 D2
Quickley La. Chor ... 167 E2
Quickley Rise. Chor ... 167 D2
Quill Hall La. Ame ... 154 C1
Quinbrookes. Slough ... 206 B4
Quince Cl. Walt ... 48 A3
Quinton Dr. M Keyn ... 34 A2
Quoiting Sq. Mar ... 183 E1
Quoitings Dr. Mar ... 183 B1

Raans Rd. Ame ... 154 C1
Rabans Cl. Ayl ... 100 C1
Rabans La. Ayl ... 100 C1
Rachels Way. Ches ... 154 B3
Radcliffe St. M Keyn ... 33 E3
Radclive Rd. Gawt ... 51 F3
Radcot Cl. Maid ... 195 F2
Radman Gr. M Keyn ... 33 D3
Radnage Com R. Bled R ... 159 E3
Radnor Cl. Hen-O-T ... 191 F1
Radnor End. Ayl ... 101 F1
Radnor Way. Slough ... 206 C1
Raeside Cl. Se Gr ... 176 B3
Ragmans Cl. Mar B ... 183 E4
Ragmans La. Mar B ... 172 B1
Ragnall's La. Hor-c-S ... 108 A3
Ragstone Rd. Slough ... 205 F2
Railway St. Ayl ... 115 F4
Railway Terr. Slough ... 205 F3
Rainbow Dr. M Keyn ... 46 C4
Rains Rd. L Chal ... 154 C1
Rainsborough. M Keyn ... 35 D4
Raleigh Cl. Slough ... 205 D3
Ralphs Retreat. Hol G ... 162 C2
Rambler Cl. Burn ... 204 A4
Rambler La. Slough ... 206 B2
Ramsay View. Ty Gr ... 163 D2
Ramsgill Ct. M Keyn ... 34 B3
Ramsons Ave. M Keyn ... 34 C2
Ramworth Way. Ayl ... 116 A3
Randall Cl. Slough ... 206 C1
Randolph Rd. Slough ... 206 C2
Ranelagh Gdns. N Pag ... 22 B1
Rangers Ct. M Keyn ... 33 F1
Rannal Dr. Chin ... 147 E3
Rannoch Cl. M Keyn ... 58 B3
Rannock Gdns. L Buzz ... 80 B4
Ranston Cl. Den G ... 189 F3
Ratcliffe Cl. Uxb ... 201 E1
Rathbone Cl. She C E ... 45 F4
Raven Cl. Ayl ... 101 F2
Raven Cres. Wcot ... 98 B3
Raven Rd. Skch ... 158 C2
Ravens Field. Slough ... 206 B2
Ravens La. Berk ... 135 E2
Ravens Wharf. Berk ... 135 E2
Ravensbourne Pl. M Keyn ... 35 D1
Ravenscroft Rd. Hen-O-T ... 191 E1
Ravenshoe Cl. Bou E ... 185 D2
Ravensmead. C St P ... 177 F3
Ravensmead. Chin ... 147 E3
Ravenstone Mill Rd. Rav ... 12 C4
Ravensworth Rd. Slough ... 198 A1
Ravigill P. M Keyn ... 33 E2
Rawling Rd. M Keyn ... 34 A2
Rawlings La. Se Gr ... 176 B4
Ray Dr. Maid ... 203 D4
Ray Lea Cl. Maid ... 203 D4
Ray Lea Rd. Maid ... 203 D4
Ray Lodge Mews. Maid ... 203 D4
Ray Mead Ct. Maid ... 196 B1
Ray Mead Rd. Maid ... 203 E4
Ray Mill Rd E. Maid ... 196 A1
Ray Mill Rd W. Maid ... 203 D4
Ray Park Ave. Maid ... 203 D4
Ray Park La. Maid ... 203 D4
Ray Park Rd. Maid ... 203 D4
Ray St. Maid ... 203 D4
Ray's Hill. Buc Co ... 133 E1
Ray's Hill. Chol ... 133 E1
Raylands Mead. Ger C ... 188 B3
Rayleigh Cl. She C E ... 46 A3
Raymond Cl. Stan ... 212 C3
Raymond Rd. Maid ... 202 B4
Rayners Ave. Loud ... 174 A2
Rayners Cl. Iver ... 212 B4
Rays Ave. Wind ... 209 F4
Rays La. Ty Gr ... 163 E1
Read Dr. Bier ... 102 B2
Reading Cl. Ayl ... 101 D2
Reading Rd. Hen-O-T ... 191 F1
Readings The. Chor ... 167 F3
Reads La. Cub ... 78 B1
Recreation Rd. Bou E ... 185 D2
Rectory Ave. H Wyc ... 173 E4

Rectory Cl. Far C ... 198 B1
Rectory Cl. Slap ... 91 E3
Rectory Cl. Wind ... 210 A3
Rectory Ct. H Wyc ... 173 F3
Rectory Ct. Lewk ... 157 D4
Rectory Dr. Wadd ... 99 D3
Rectory Fields. M Keyn ... 35 E2
Rectory Hill. Ame ... 165 E4
Rectory La. Ame ... 165 D4
Rectory La. Berk ... 135 E2
Rectory La. Y Has ... 1 A4
Rectory Meadow. Chin ... 147 E1
Rectory Orch. Lave ... 7 F4
Rectory Orch. Lave ... 7 F4
Rectory Rd. Tapl ... 196 C1
Red Cottage Mews. Slough .. 206 B2
Red Ct. Slough ... 205 F3
Red House Cl. Beac ... 175 D2
Red House Cl. Nwtn L ... 57 E2
Red Leaf Cl. Slough ... 206 C3
Red Lion Cl. Cran ... 25 D1
Red Lion Dr. Skch ... 158 B3
Red Lion St. Ches ... 154 B4
Red Lion Way. Woo G ... 185 F3
Red Lodge Gdns. Berk ... 135 D2
Redbourne Ct. M Keyn ... 32 C3
Redbridge. M Keyn ... 34 B4
Redcliffe Wlk. Ayl ... 101 D1
Redding Dr. Ame ... 154 A1
Redding Gr. She C E ... 45 F3
Reddington Dr. Slough ... 206 C1
Redfern Cl. Uxb ... 201 E2
Redfield Cl. Dun ... 93 F4
Redford Rd. Wind ... 209 E3
Redford Way. Uxb ... 201 E3
Redhill. Den G ... 189 E2
Redhouse Cl. H Wyc ... 172 C2
Redhuish Cl. She B E ... 46 B2
Redland Dr. M Keyn ... 46 B4
Redland Way. Ayl ... 116 A2
Redman Rd. H Wyc ... 172 A2
Redriff Cl. Maid ... 202 B3
Redshaw Cl. Buck ... 41 F1
Redshots Cl. Mar ... 183 F2
Redvers Gate. M Keyn ... 35 D4
Redwood. Burn ... 197 D2
Redwood Cl. Ty Gr ... 163 D2
Redwood Cl. Wing ... 79 F1
Redwood Dr. Wing ... 79 F1
Redwood Gate. She B E ... 46 B2
Redwood Gdns. Slough ... 205 E3
Redwood Glade. L Buzz ... 70 C2
Reeves Croft. M Keyn ... 33 E2
Reform Rd. Maid ... 203 D4
Regal Ct. Tri ... 119 D2
Regent Ct. Maid ... 202 C4
Regent Rd. Ayl ... 116 A4
Regent St. M Keyn ... 58 B4
Reid Ave. Maid ... 202 C3
Rembrandt End. Ayl ... 100 C1
Remenham Ch L. Rem H ... 192 A2
Remenham La. Rem H ... 191 F2
Remus Gate. Brac ... 38 A3
Rendlesham. M Keyn ... 35 E2
Rendlesham Way. Chor ... 167 E2
Renfrew Way. M Keyn ... 46 C2
Rennie Cl. H Wyc ... 161 F1
Repton Cl. Maid ... 202 B2
Retreat The. L Chal ... 166 C4
Retreat The. P Ris ... 139 D2
Revel Rd. Woo G ... 185 E4
Revesby Cl. Maid ... 202 B2
Reynold Dr. Bier ... 102 A1
Reynolds Cl. Cran ... 24 C2
Reynolds Cl. H Wyc ... 173 F4
Reynolds Rd. Beac ... 175 E2
Reynolds Wlk. Ches ... 144 A2
Rhondda Cl. M Keyn ... 47 F1
Rhuddlan Cl. She C E ... 45 F4
Rhymer Cl. Hans ... 10 C2
Ribble Cl. N Pag ... 22 C2
Ribble Cres. M Keyn ... 57 E4
Ribstone Rd. Maid ... 202 A2
Ricardo Rd. Old W ... 211 D1
Richard Gdns. H Wyc ... 173 F4
Richardson Pl. M Keyn ... 34 C1
Richardson St. H Wyc ... 172 C4
Richborough. M Keyn ... 34 A3
Richmond Cl. M Keyn ... 46 B1
Richmond Cres. Slough ... 206 A3
Richmond Rd. Ayl ... 116 B4
Richmond Way. N Pag ... 22 B2
Rickard Cl. S Man ... 115 E2
Rickard Cl. W Dra ... 208 B2
Rickford's Hill. Ayl ... 115 E4
Rickley La. M Keyn ... 58 A4
Rickman's La. Sto P ... 198 C3
Rickmansworth La. C St P ... 177 F2
Rickmansworth Rd. Ame ... 154 B1
Rickmansworth Rd. Chor ... 167 F3
Ride The. Tott ... 93 D3
Riders Way. Chin ... 147 E3
Ridge Side. Bled R ... 160 A4
Ridge View. Tri ... 119 E3
Ridge Way. H Wyc ... 162 B1
Ridgemount End. C St P ... 177 F3
Ridgeway. Berk ... 134 C2
Ridgeway. M Keyn ... 32 C2
Ridgeway. M Keyn ... 33 D3
Ridgeway. Wing ... 79 F2
Ridgeway Cl. Ches ... 144 A2
Ridgeway Cl. Mar ... 183 F2
Ridgeway Meads. Bled ... 138 A1
Ridgeway Rd. Ches ... 144 A2
Ridgeway The. Ger C ... 188 C4
Ridgeway The. Mar ... 183 F2
Ridgmont. Dean ... 31 F3
Ridgmont Cl. Dean ... 31 F3
Ridgway. Wbn S ... 49 D3
Riding Court Rd. Datch ... 211 E4
Riding La. Beac ... 174 C2
Riding The. Dean ... 31 F3
Ridings Cotts. Hol G ... 163 E3
Ridings The. Ame ... 154 B2
Ridings The. Lat ... 155 E2
Ridings The. Maid ... 202 A3
Ridings Way. Cub ... 78 A1
Rignall Rd. G Mis ... 151 F4
Riley Rd. Mar ... 183 E1
Rimsdale Ct. M Keyn ... 58 B2
Ring Rd. Fla H ... 173 E1
Ringshall Dr. L Gad ... 121 D4
Ringshall Rd. Dag ... 107 D2
Ringshall Rd. Rin ... 107 D1
Ringstead Way. Ayl ... 116 A3
Ripley Cl. Slough ... 206 C1
Ripon St. Ayl ... 101 E1
Risborough Rd. Elle ... 130 A4
Risborough Rd. Maid ... 202 C4
Risborough Rd. S Man ... 130 A4
Rise The. Ame ... 165 E4
Rise The. Gawt ... 51 F2
Rise The. Loud ... 174 A2
Rise The. Uxb ... 201 F2
Riseley Rd. Maid ... 202 B4
River Cl. N Pag ... 22 B2
River Gdns. Maid ... 203 E2
River Park Ind Est. Berk ... 135 D3
River Rd. Tapl ... 203 E4
River St. Wind ... 210 B4
River View. Fla H ... 185 D4
River Wlk. N Den ... 201 E4
Rivercrest Rd. Old S ... 32 A3
Riverpark Dr. Mar ... 183 F1
Riverside. N Pag ... 22 B2
Riverside Gdns. Berk ... 135 D3
Riverside Pl. Stan ... 213 F1
Riverside Rd. Stan ... 213 E1
Riverside Way. Uxb ... 201 D2
Riverwood Ct. Bish ... 194 C4
Riverwoods Ave. Mar ... 184 A1
Riverwoods Dr. Mar ... 184 A1
Rivetts Cl. Oln ... 6 C2
Rixband Cl. B Bkhl ... 48 A2
Rixman Cl. Maid ... 202 B3
Rixon Cl. Slough ... 206 C4
Roade Hill. Ash ... 9 F4
Robert Rd. Hedg ... 187 E1
Robert's Dr. Ayl ... 101 E1
Roberts Cl. Stan ... 213 E1
Roberts Cl. W Dra ... 208 C3
Roberts Rd. H Wyc ... 173 D4
Roberts Rd. Hadd ... 127 D3
Roberts Ride. Hol G ... 163 D3
Roberts Wood Dr. C St P ... 177 F3
Roberts Wood Dr. Map Cr ... 178 B2
Robertson Cl. She C E ... 45 F4
Robin Cl. Buck ... 52 C4
Robin Hill. Berk ... 135 E2
Robins Cl. Lit M ... 172 B2
Robins Cl. Uxb ... 208 B4
Robins Hill. M Keyn ... 47 D3
Robins Orchard. C St P ... 177 F2
Robins Platt. Chin ... 147 D3
Robinson Rd. Loud ... 174 A2
Robinswood Cl. Beac ... 175 E3
Robinswood Cl. L Buzz ... 70 C1
Roblin Cl. Ayl ... 115 F2
Robson Cl. C St P ... 177 F3
Roche Gdns. M Keyn ... 58 A4
Rochester Pl. Ayl ... 115 D4
Rochford Way. Burn ... 204 A4
Rochfords. M Keyn ... 46 C3
Rochfords Gdns. Slough ... 206 B3
Rock Cl. L Buzz ... 80 B3
Rock La. L Buzz ... 80 B4
Rockingham Cl. Uxb ... 201 E2
Rockingham Dr. M Keyn ... 34 C3
Rockingham Parade. Uxb ... 201 E3
Rockingham Rd. Uxb ... 201 E2
Rockspray Gr. Walt ... 48 A3
Rodney Way. Stan ... 212 C3
Roebuck Ave. H Wyc ... 173 F3
Rogers Croft. M Keyn ... 47 E4
Rogers La. Sto P ... 198 C2
Roker Park Ave. Ick ... 201 F4
Rokesby Rd. Slough ... 197 F1
Rolfe Cl. Beac ... 175 F1
Roman Lea. Cook ... 195 F4
Roman Way. Bou E ... 185 D2
Roman Way. Brac ... 38 A4
Romar Ct. M Keyn ... 47 E1
Romney Ct. Mar ... 183 F2
Romney Rd. Ayl ... 115 F2
Romsey Cl. Slough ... 206 C2
Romsey Dr. Far C ... 187 E1
Romsey Way. H Wyc ... 173 D2
Romulus Way. Brac ... 38 A3
Ronald Rd. Beac ... 175 F1
Rook Rd. Bou E ... 185 E2
Rook Wood Way. L Kin ... 152 A3
Rookery Ct. Mar ... 183 E1
Rookery La. Edgc ... 72 C1
Rookery Meadow. Hol G ... 163 E4
Rookery Way. Stp Cl ... 63 F2
Rosary The. Hol G ... 163 E4
Rose Ave. Ayl ... 101 E1
Rose Ave. Ty Gr ... 163 D1
Rose Corner. Skch ... 158 C3
Rose Dr. Ches ... 154 B4
Rose Hill. Burn ... 197 D3
Rose La. Know H ... 193 D1
Rose Wlk. Slough ... 205 D4
Roseary Cl. W Dra ... 208 B1
Rosebank Cl. Cook ... 195 F4
Rosebay Cl. Walt ... 48 A3
Rosebery Ave. H Wyc ... 173 F3
Rosebery Ave. L Buzz ... 80 C4
Rosebery Rd. Ast C ... 117 F3
Rosebery Way. Tri ... 119 D3
Rosehill. Berk ... 135 D2
Rosehill Cl. Twyf ... 62 B1
Roseleigh Cl. Maid ... 202 A4
Rosemary Cl. H Wyc ... 161 D1
Rosemary Ct. Walt ... 48 A3
Rosemary La. Hadd ... 127 D4
Rosemead. Ast C ... 117 F1
Rosery The. Bou E ... 185 D2
Roses Cl. Cub ... 78 A1
Roses La. Wind ... 209 E3
Rosetree Cl. Pres ... 151 E3
Rosewood Way. Far C ... 198 B4
Rosken Gr. Far C ... 198 A2
Roslyn Ct. M Keyn ... 35 E4
Ross Rd. A Abb ... 88 B3
Ross Rd. Maid ... 202 C2
Ross Way. M Keyn ... 46 C1
Rossal Pl. M Keyn ... 33 E2
Rossetti Pl. Hol G ... 163 E4
Rossey Pl. Eton ... 205 E1
Rossiter Cl. Slough ... 206 C1
Rossway La. Berk ... 134 A4
Rostrevor Gdns. Iver H ... 200 B2
Rothersthorpe. M Keyn ... 35 D4
Rothesay Cl. Ayl ... 101 F1
Rothschild Ave. Ast C ... 117 F3
Rothschild Rd. L Buzz ... 80 C4
Rothschild Rd. Wing ... 79 F1
Rotten Row. G Bkhl ... 59 E1
Roughwood La. C St G ... 166 C2
Round Hill. Sto ... 114 B3
Round Wood Rd. Ame ... 154 C1
Roundhead Dr. Tha ... 125 F1
Roundheads End. Beac ... 175 D2
Roundwood Rd. H Wyc ... 172 B4
Rovelley Ct. M Keyn ... 32 C3
Row The. La En ... 171 D2
Rowan Ave. H Wyc ... 173 E4
Rowan Cl. Beac ... 175 D1
Rowan Cl. Ty Gr ... 163 D2
Rowan Dr. Have ... 20 B1
Rowan Dr. Have ... 20 B1
Rowan Rd. W Dra ... 208 B1
Rowan Way. Slough ... 205 D4
Rowanhurst Dr. Far C ... 198 B4
Rowans The. Ger C ... 188 B4
Rowborough Rd. Hal ... 131 E4
Rowland Cl. Wind ... 209 E2
Rowland Way. Ayl ... 115 D4
Rowlands Cl. M Keyn ... 58 C4
Rowle Cl. M Keyn ... 34 C4
Rowley Furrows. L Buzz ... 80 B4
Rowley La. Iver H ... 199 E2
Rowley La. Sto P ... 199 E2
Rowlheys Pl. W Dra ... 208 C2
Rowliff Rd. H Wyc ... 172 B3
Rowsham Dell. M Keyn ... 21 F1
Rowsham Rd. Bier ... 102 B3
Roxburgh Way. M Keyn ... 46 C2
Royal Cl. W Dra ... 208 C4
Royal Ct. Tri ... 120 A3
Royal La. Uxb ... 208 C4
Royal La. W Dra ... 208 C4
Royce Cl. Dun ... 93 F4
Royce Rd. Cran ... 24 B2
Royle Cl. C St P ... 177 F2
Rubens Cl. Ayl ... 100 C1
Ruby Cl. Slough ... 205 D2
Ruckles Way. Ame ... 165 E4
Rudchesters. M Keyn ... 33 F3
Rudd's La. Hadd ... 127 D4
Ruddlesway. Wind ... 209 E3
Rugwood Rd. Fla H ... 173 E1
Run Furrow. Hadd ... 127 D4
Runford Ct. She B E ... 46 B3
Runnymead. M Keyn ... 21 F1
Runrig Hill. Ame ... 154 C2
Rupert Ave. H Wyc ... 172 C2
Rupert Cl. Hen-O-T ... 191 F2
Rupert Way. Tha ... 126 A1
Rupert's La. Hen-O-T ... 191 F2
Ruscombe Gdns. Datch ... 211 D4
Rushall Rd. Tha ... 126 A1
Rushbrooke Cl. H Wyc ... 162 C1
Rushburn. Woo G ... 185 F3
Rushendon Furlong. Ivin ... 105 E3
Rushes Mead. Uxb ... 201 E2
Rushes The. Maid ... 203 D3
Rushington Ave. Maid ... 202 C3
Rushmere Cl. B Bkhl ... 48 B1
Rushmere La. Ash Gr ... 145 D2
Rushmoor Ave. Ty Gr ... 163 D2
Rushton Ct. M Keyn ... 45 F4
Ruskin Ct. N Pag ... 22 B1
Ruskin Way. Ayl ... 101 E1
Russell Ave. Ayl ... 115 E3
Russell Cl. L Chal ... 166 B4
Russell Cl. Ty Gr ... 163 D1
Russell Ct. Ches ... 144 B1
Russell Ct. Maid ... 202 C4
Russell Dr. Stan ... 213 E1
Russell St. M Keyn ... 32 B3
Russell St. Wbn S ... 49 D2
Russell St. Wind ... 210 B3
Russet Cl. Stan ... 212 C1
Russet Rd. Maid ... 202 B2
Russets The. Ger C ... 177 E1
Russett Hill. Ger C ... 188 C4
Rutherford Rd. Ayl ... 115 F2
Ruthven Cl. M Keyn ... 58 B2
Rutland Ave. H Wyc ... 172 B3
Rutland Ave. Slough ... 205 E4
Rutland Pl. Maid ... 202 B3
Rutland Rd. Maid ... 202 B3
Rutland St. H Wyc ... 173 D3
Ryans Mount. Mar ... 183 B1
Rycote La. G Has ... 136 B3
Rycroft. M Keyn ... 46 C2
Rycroft. Wind ... 209 F2
Rydal Way. H Wyc ... 172 A3
Rydal Way. M Keyn ... 58 B3
Ryder Cl. Bov ... 146 A2
Rydings. Wind ... 209 F2
Rye Cl. Maid ... 202 A2
Rye Ct. Slough ... 206 A2
Rye The. Eat B ... 92 A4
Rye View. H Wyc ... 173 E4
Ryecroft Rd. Ches ... 154 A4
Ryeland. M Keyn ... 32 C3
Ryeland Cl. W Dra ... 208 C4
Rylstone Cl. M Keyn ... 34 A2
Rylstone Cl. Maid ... 202 B2
Ryman Ct. Chor ... 167 E2
Rymill Cl. Bov ... 146 A2
Ryvers Rd. Slough ... 206 C2

Sabina Cl. H Wyc ... 172 C3
Saddlers Green. Asp G ... 49 D3
Saddlers Pl. M Keyn ... 35 D3
Saffron Rd. H Wyc ... 173 E3
Saffron St. M Keyn ... 58 B4
Saham Croft Cl. Wins ... 65 F2
St Adrian's Cl. Maid ... 202 A2
St Aidan's Cl. M Keyn ... 57 F3
St Alban's Rd. Wins ... 65 F2
St Alban's St. Wind ... 210 B3
St Andrew's Ave. Wind ... 209 F3
St Andrew's Cl. H Wyc ... 162 C1
St Andrew's Cl. Old W ... 211 D1
St Andrew's Cl. Wray ... 211 F1
St Andrew's Cres. Wind ... 209 F3
St Andrew's Rd. Chin ... 147 E3
St Andrew's Rd. M Keyn ... 57 F4
St Andrews Way In Es. Ayl ... 101 E1
St Anne's Cl. Hen-O-T ... 191 E1
St Anne's Cl. Wen ... 131 D3
St Anne's Rd. Ayl ... 115 D4
St Anne's Rd. S Har ... 190 B4
St Anthony's Cl. Ayl ... 115 D4
St Bernards Rd. Slough ... 206 B2
St Birinus. Fla H ... 174 A1
St Catherine's Ave. M Keyn ... 57 E3
St Catherine's Ct. Ayl ... 115 D4
St Chad's Rd. Maid ... 202 A2
St Christopher Rd. Uxb ... 208 B4
St Christopher's Cl. L Kin ... 152 A2
St Clement Cl. Uxb ... 208 B4
St Clement's Dr. M Keyn ... 57 F3
St-cloud Way. Maid ... 203 D4
St Columba's Cl. Maid ... 202 A2
St David Cl. Uxb ... 208 B4
St David's Cl. Iver H ... 200 B2
St David's Cl. Maid ... 202 A2
St David's Par. Iver H ... 200 B2
St David's Rd. M Keyn ... 57 F3
St Dunstans. M Keyn ... 47 D3
St Edmund's Cl. Ayl ... 115 D4
St Edmunds. Berk ... 135 E2
St Edwards Ct. M Keyn ... 34 C4
St Elmo Cres. Slough ... 198 B1
St Faith's Cl. Nwtn L ... 57 E2
St Francis Rd. B Bot ... 159 E2
St Francis Rd. Den G ... 189 F3
St George's Cl. H Wyc ... 173 E4
St George's Cl. Wind ... 209 F3
St George's Dr. Ick ... 190 C1
St George's Rd. M Keyn ... 57 F3
St Georges Ind Est. Ame ... 165 F4
St Georges Way. M Keyn ... 33 E4
St Giles Mews. M Keyn ... 32 B3
St Giles St. M Keyn ... 33 F4
St Helen Cl. Uxb ... 208 B4
St Hilda's Ct. Ayl ... 115 D4
St Hilda's Way. Fla H ... 174 A1
St Huberts Cl. Ger C ... 188 C1
St Huberts La. Ger C ... 188 C1
St Hugh's Ave. H Wyc ... 173 F3
St Hugh's Pl. Skch ... 158 C2
St Ives Rd. Maid ... 203 D4
St James Cl. Hans ... 11 D1
St James St. M Keyn ... 33 F4
St James Way. Bier ... 102 A2
St John Cres. M Keyn ... 33 E3
St John St. N Pag ... 22 B2
St John's Ave. Ty Gr ... 174 A4
St John's Cl. Uxb ... 201 D2
St John's La. Wick ... 31 D2
St John's Rd. Ayl ... 101 F1
St John's Rd. M Keyn ... 57 F3
St John's Rd. Ty Gr ... 162 C1
St John's Rd. Uxb ... 201 D2
St John's St. Ayl ... 101 F1
St John's Terr. N Pag ... 22 B2
St John's Well Ct. Berk ... 135 D3
St John's Well La. Berk ... 135 D3
St Johns Cl. Ty Gr ... 163 D1
St Johns Dr. Wind ... 210 A3
St Johns Rd. Slough ... 206 A3
St Johns Rd. Ty Gr ... 163 D1
St Johns Rd. Wind ... 210 A3
St Josephs Cl. Oln ... 6 C2
St Katherine's Way. Berk ... 134 C4
St Laurence Cl. Uxb ... 208 B4
St Laurence Rd. Wins ... 65 F2
St Laurence Way. Slough ... 206 A2
St Lawrence Cl. Bov ... 146 A2
St Lawrence View. M Keyn ... 34 A2
St Leger Dr. M Keyn ... 34 C4
St Leonard's Rd. Oak G ... 209 E1
St Leonard's Rd. Wind ... 210 B2
St Leonard's Way. Edle ... 92 C1
St Leonards Hill. Wind ... 209 F2
St Leonards Rd. Ame ... 154 C2
St Luke Cl. Uxb ... 208 B4
St Luke's Rd. Maid ... 202 C4
St Luke's Rd. Old W ... 211 D1
St Margaret Ct. M Keyn ... 58 C4
St Margaret's Cl. Berk ... 135 E2
St Margaret's Cl. Iver H ... 200 B2
St Margaret's Rd. Maid ... 202 A4
St Margarets Cl. N Pag ... 22 C2
St Mark's Cres. Maid ... 202 A4
St Mark's Pl. Wind ... 210 B3
St Mark's Rd. Ayl ... 115 E4
St Mark's Rd. Hen-O-T ... 191 F1
St Mark's Rd. Maid ... 202 B4
St Mark's Rd. Wind ... 210 B3
St Martin Cl. Uxb ... 208 B4
St Martin's Cl. W Dra ... 208 B2
St Martin's Rd. W Dra ... 208 B2
St Martin's St. M Keyn ... 58 B4
St Mary St. H Wyc ... 173 D3
St Mary St. M Keyn ... 33 F4
St Mary's Ave. Berk ... 134 B3
St Mary's Ave. M Keyn ... 32 C3
St Mary's Ave. M Keyn ... 57 F4
St Mary's Cl. Maid ... 203 D4
St Mary's Cl. S Har ... 190 A4
St Mary's Cl. Wave ... 48 C4
St Mary's Glebe. Edle ... 92 C2
St Mary's La. Lee C ... 142 B3
St Mary's Rd. Den G ... 189 F3
St Mary's Rd. S Har ... 190 A4
St Mary's Rd. Slough ... 206 C2
St Mary's Sq. Ayl ... 115 E4
St Mary's Way. Ches ... 154 A4
St Mary's Way. Ger C ... 177 E1
St Mary's Way. L Buzz ... 80 C4
St Mary's Wlk. Maid ... 202 C4
St Marys Rd. E Clay ... 74 C4
St Matthew Cl. Uxb ... 208 B4
St Michael's Cl. Hal ... 117 E1
St Michael's Ct. Slough ... 197 E1
St Michael's Green. Beac ... 175 F2
St Michael's Way. Stp Cl ... 63 F2
St Michaels Cl. Stew ... 68 C1
St Nicholas Cl. Cub ... 78 A1
St Nicholas Cl. L Chal ... 166 A4
St Nicholas Cl. Uxb ... 208 B4
St Patrick's Cl. Maid ... 202 A2
St Patrick's Way. M Keyn ... 57 F3
St Paul Cl. Uxb ... 208 B4
St Paul's Rd. M Keyn ... 57 F3
St Pauls Ave. Slough ... 206 A3
St Pauls Ct. M Keyn ... 32 B3
St Peter St. Mar ... 183 F1
St Peter's Ave. Ayl ... 101 E2
St Peter's Cl. Burn ... 197 D1
St Peter's Cl. Old W ... 211 D1
St Peter's Hill. Tri ... 119 D2
St Peter's Rd. Brac ... 38 A4
St Peter's Rd. Maid ... 195 E1
St Peter's Rd. Uxb ... 208 B4
St Peters Cl. Lac G ... 150 B2
St Peters Cl. Loud ... 174 A1
St Peters Gate. Brac ... 38 A4
St Peters Way. Chor ... 167 D3
St Peters Way. M Keyn ... 34 A4
St Rumbolds La. Buck ... 52 B4
St Stephen's Rd. W Dra ... 208 B3
St Stephens Dr. M Keyn ... 35 D4
St Teresas Cl. P Ris ... 139 D2
St Vincents. Asp G ... 49 E2
Salden Cl. Dray P ... 68 B3
Salden Cl. She C E ... 46 A3

Salford Rd. Asp G 49 E4
Salisbury Ave. Slough 205 E4
Salisbury Cl. Ame 165 F4
Salisbury Cl. P Ris 139 E2
Salisbury Gr. M Keyn 21 F1
Salisbury Rd. H Wyc 162 B1
Salisbury Rd. Uxb 201 D2
Salmons La. Pres 151 E3
Salt Hill Ave. Slough 205 E3
Salt Hill Cl. Uxb 201 F4
Salt Hill Dr. Slough 205 E3
Salt Hill Way. Slough 205 E3
Saltash Cl. Loud 174 A2
Salter's Cl. Berk 134 C3
Salters Cl. Maid 203 D4
Salters La. Lud 96 B4
Salters Mews. M Keyn 34 C3
Salters Rd. Maid 203 D4
Sampsons Green. Slough 197 F1
Sampsons Hill. Cole 164 C1
San Remo Rd. Asp G 49 F2
Sanctuary Rd. Hol G 163 D3
Sandage Rd. La En 171 D3
Sandbrier Cl. Walt 48 A3
Sandbrook La. Wils 104 B1
Sandels Way. Beac 175 E2
Sandelswood End. Beac 175 E3
Sanders La. Pott 18 B2
Sandford Gdns. H Wyc 173 D2
Sandhill Rd. E Clay 74 C4
Sandholme. Stp Cl 63 F2
Sandhurst Dr. Buck 52 B4
Sandisplatt Rd. Maid 202 A3
Sandlers End. Slough 198 A1
Sandon Cl. Tri 118 C2
Sandown Ct. M Keyn 57 E3
Sandpit Hill. Ting 50 C3
Sandpit La. Bled 138 A2
Sandpits La. Ty Gr 174 B4
Sandringham Pl. M Keyn 58 B4
Sandringham Rd. Maid 195 F1
Sandringham Rd. Stan 213 F1
Sands Farm Dr. Burn 197 E1
Sandwell Ct. M Keyn 33 E1
Sandy Cl. Buck 52 C4
Sandy Cl. M Keyn 34 B4
Sandy La. Asp H 49 D1
Sandy La. L Buzz 70 C2
Sandy La. L Cre 125 D3
Sandy Mead. Holy 203 E1
Sandy Rise. C St P 177 F1
Sandycroft Rd. L Chal 155 E1
Sandygate Cl. Mar 183 E2
Sandygate Rd. Mar 183 E2
Sandywell Dr. M Keyn 35 D3
Santen Gr. M Keyn 58 B2
Sargeants Cl. Uxb 201 B1
Saunders End. H Hea 153 E3
Saunders Wd Cps. Skch 158 C2
Savay Cl. Den G 190 A2
Savay La. Den G 190 A3
Savernake Rd. Ayl 101 E2
Savill Way. Mar 183 F1
Sawmill Rd. Lgwk 138 B4
Sawpit Hill. Hol G 163 D3
Sawyer's Cl. Wind 209 F4
Sawyers Cl. Maid 202 A1
Sawyers Cres. Maid 202 A1
Saxhorn Rd. La En 171 E2
Saxon Cl. Dun 93 F4
Saxon Cl. Slough 206 C2
Saxon Cl. Uxb 208 C4
Saxon Gdns. Maid 196 B1
Saxon St. M Keyn 34 B3
Saxon St. M Keyn 47 E2
Saxon Way. Harm 213 E4
Saxon Way. Old W 211 D1
Saye & Sele Cl. Gr Und 82 C3
Sayers Gdns. Berk 135 D3
Sayward Cl. Ches 144 B1
Scampton Rd. Stan 213 F1
Scarborough Way. Slough 205 D2
Scarlett Ave. Wen 131 E3
Scars The. Edle 92 A3
Scatterdells La. Chipf 146 C1
Scatterill Cl. M Keyn 34 A2
School Cl. G Kin 162 B3
School Cl. H Wyc 161 E1
School Cl. H Wyc 173 D2
School Cl. Hol G 163 E4
School Cl. Ick 124 A2
School Dr. Nwtn L 57 E2
School End. G Hrwd 54 C2
School Hill. N Mar 76 A1
School Hill. Twyf 73 D3
School La. Ame 165 D4
School La. Buck 52 B4
School La. C St G 177 D4
School La. Cast 19 F3
School La. Chea 112 A1
School La. Cook 196 A4
School La. Eat B 92 C3
School La. Ger C 177 E1
School La. Ibst 169 F2
School La. Lit M 184 B3
School La. M Keyn 46 A4
School La. Maid 195 F1
School La. Medm 193 D3
School La. Oak 109 E3
School La. Pres B 62 A4
School La. S Ham 69 F4
School La. Se Gr 176 B2
School La. Sher 14 A1
School La. Sto P 199 D2
School La. Twyf 62 B1
School La. Ty Gr 164 A3
School La. W Tur 116 C1
School La. Wadd 99 D1
School La. Wadd 99 D3
School La. Yard G 18 C3
School Rd. Harm 213 E4
School Rd. Ty Gr 174 B4
School Rd. Woo G 185 F3
School St. M Keyn 33 F4
School Way. Loud 174 A1
Schorne La. N Mar 76 A1
Scotlands Dr. Far C 198 A3
Scotswood Cl. Beac 175 E3
Scott Cl. Far C 198 B4
Scott Cl. W Dra 208 C1
Scott Dr. N Pag 22 A3
Scott End. Ayl 100 C1
Scott Evans Ct. Wins 66 A3
Scotts Cl. M Gib 72 A2
Scotts La. Adsk 53 F1
Scriveners La. Paul 17 D4
Scrubb's La. Bled R 160 A4
Seaford Rd. Stan 213 E1
Seagrave Ct. Walt 48 A2
Seagrave Rd. Beac 175 E2
Seaton Dr. Ayl 115 E2
Secklow Gate. M Keyn 34 C2
Second Ave. M Keyn 47 E1
Second Cres. Slough 205 E4
Sedgemere. M Keyn 33 E1
Sedgemoor Dr. Tha 126 A1
Sedgmoor Gdns. Fla H 185 D4
Sedgmoor La. Fla H 185 D4
Sedgmoor Rd. Fla H 185 D4
Sedley Gr. S Har 190 B4
Sedrup La. Sto 114 C2
Seeleys Cl. Beac 175 E2
Seeleys Rd. Beac 175 E2
Seer Green La. Se Gr 176 C2
Seer Mead. Se Gr 176 B2
Sefton Paddock. Sto P 199 D3
Sefton Way. Uxb 208 B4
Selbourne Ave. M Keyn 57 F4
Selby Gr. She C E 46 A3
Selkirk Ave. Ayl 101 E1
Selkirk Gr. M Keyn 46 C1
Selwood Cl. Stan 213 E1
Selwood Gdns. Stan 213 E1
Selwood Way. H Wyc 161 F1
Selworthy. She B E 46 B2
Serjeants Green. M Keyn 34 C3
Serles Cl. M Keyn 47 D3
Seven Acres. L Cre 125 D4
Sevenhills Rd. Iver H 200 B3
Severalls Ave. Ches 144 B1
Severn Cres. Slough 212 A4
Severn Dr. N Pag 22 C2
Severn Way. M Keyn 46 C1
Severn Way. M Keyn 57 E4
Sewell Cl. Ayl 100 C1
Seymour Cl. Fla H 173 E1
Seymour Cl. Maid 202 A2
Seymour Court La. Mar B 183 D3
Seymour Court Rd. Mar 183 E2
Seymour Court Rd. Mar B 183 E2
Seymour Park Rd. Mar 183 E2
Seymour Plain. Mar 183 E3
Seymour Plain. Mar B 183 E3
Seymour Rd. Berk 134 C3
Seymour Rd. Slough 205 E2
Shackleton Pl. M Keyn 34 C1
Shackleton Rd. H Wyc 172 C3
Shackleton Rd. Slough 205 F3
Shaftesbury Cres. M Keyn 47 D1
Shaftesbury St. H Wyc 172 C4
Shaggy Calf La. Slough 206 A3
Shakespear Cl. N Pag 22 A3
Shannon Ct. M Keyn 35 D3
Shantock Hall La. Bov 145 F1
Shantock La. Bov 145 F1
Sharman Wlk. M Keyn 34 A2
Sharp Cl. Ayl 115 F3
Sharp's Cl. Wadd 99 D3
Sharrow Vale. H Wyc 172 C4
Shaw Cl. N Pag 22 A3
Shaw The. Cook 195 F3
Shaws Cl. Pres 151 E3
Shearmans. M Keyn 33 D2
Sheehy Way. Slough 206 A3
Sheep St. Wins 66 A2
Sheepcote Cl. Beac 175 E2
Sheepcote Cotts. Hol G 163 E4
Sheepcote Dell Rd. Hol G 163 F4
Sheepcote Gdns. Den G 190 A3
Sheepcote La. Tapl 186 A1
Sheepcote Rd. Eton 205 D1
Sheepcote Rd. Wind 209 F3
Sheepfold La. Ame 165 E4
Sheephouse Rd. Maid 196 A1
Sheepridge La. Bou E 184 C4
Sheepridge La. Fla H 184 C4
Sheerstock. Hadd 126 C3
Sheet St. Wind 210 B3
Sheet Street Rd. Wind 210 B1
Sheffield Dr. Ayl 115 F3
Sheffield Rd. Slough 205 E4
Shelburne Ct. H Wyc 172 C2
Shelburne Rd. H Wyc 172 C2
Sheldon Ct. M Keyn 33 F1
Sheldon Rd. Ick 124 A2
Shelley Cl. N Pag 22 A2
Shelley Cl. Slough 206 C1
Shelley Dr. M Keyn 57 F4
Shelley Rd. Ches 144 A1
Shelley Rd. H Wyc 172 C3
Shelley Rd. Mar 183 C2
Shellin Gr. M Keyn 58 B2
Shelsmore. M Keyn 35 D4
Shelton Ct. Slough 206 B2
Sheney Rd. M Keyn 57 F4
Shenley Rd. M Keyn 46 C1
Shenley Rd. She C E 46 A3
Shenley Rd. Whad 56 A4
Shenstone Dr. Slough 197 E1
Shenstone Hill. Berk 135 F3
Shepherd's La. Chor 167 F1
Shepherds. M Keyn 33 D2
Shepherds Cl. Hurl 193 F2
Shepherds Cl. Uxb 201 E1
Shepherds Fold. Hol G 163 E4
Shepherds Gate. L Kin 152 A1
Shepherds La. Beac 175 F1
Shepherds La. Hol G 162 C3
Shepherds La. Hurl 193 F2
Shepherds Row. Wins 66 A2
Shepherds Way. Ches 154 B3
Shepperds Cl. N Mar 76 A1
Shepperton Cl. Cast 19 F3
Sheraton Dr. H Wyc 162 B1
Sherborne Cl. Stan 212 C3
Sherbourne Dr. B Bkhl 48 A2
Sherbourne Dr. Maid 202 B2
Sherbourne Dr. Wind 209 F2
Sherbourne Wlk. Far C 198 B4
Shergold Way. Cook 195 F3
Sheriff Cl. Ayl 115 D4
Sherington Rd. Lath 22 C4
Sherington Rd. Sher 22 C4
Sherman Rd. Slough 205 F4
Sherwood Cl. Slough 206 C2
Sherwood Dr. M Keyn 47 D1
Sherwood Dr. Maid 202 A3
Shields Ct. Ty Gr 163 D1
Shifford Cres. Maid 195 F2
Shilling Cl. M Keyn 35 D4
Ship Hill. Burn 186 C2
Ship Rd. L Buzz 80 C3
Ship St E. H Wyc 173 D4
Shipley Rd. N Pag 22 A2
Shipman Ct. M Keyn 35 D4
Shipton Hill. M Keyn 34 A3
Shipton Rd. Ick 201 F4
Shire Ct. M Keyn 35 D3
Shire La. C St P 178 A3
Shire La. Chol 133 D2
Shire La. Chor 167 E2
Shire La. Has 133 D2
Shire La. N Craw 24 C2
Shires Rd. Brac 38 A3
Shirley Ave. Wind 209 F3
Shirley Rd. Maid 202 B3
Shogmoor La. Frie 170 B1
Sholto Rd. Stan 213 F1
Shootacre La. Lac G 149 D4
Shootacre La. P Ris 149 D4
Shootersway. Berk 134 C2
Shootersway La. Berk 134 C2
Shootersway Park. Berk 134 C2
Shop La. Y Has 1 A3
Shoppenhanger's Rd. Maid 202 C2
Shorediche Cl. Ick 190 C1
Shoreham Rd (E). Stan 213 F1
Shoreham Rd (W). Stan 213 F1
Shorham Rise. M Keyn 33 F1
Short Massey. Oln 6 C3
Short Rd. Stan 213 F1
Short St. H Wyc 172 C4
Shortborough Ave. P Ris 139 D3
Shortfern. Slough 206 B4
Shortway. Ame 154 B1
Shortway. Ches 144 A1
Shotfield Rd. La En 171 E2
Shothanger Way. Fel 146 B3
Shouler Cl. She C E 46 A3
Shrimpton Cl. Beac 175 E3
Shrimpton Rd. Beac 175 E3
Shrimpton Rd. H Wyc 172 A2
Shrubbery Rd. H Wyc 173 D4
Shrublands Ave. Berk 135 D2
Shrublands Rd. Berk 135 D3
Shugars Green. Tri 119 D3
Shutlanger Rd. S Bru 9 D4
Sibleys Rise. S Hea 152 B4
Side Rd. Den G 189 E2
Sidney Terr. Wen 131 D3
Silbury Arc. M Keyn 34 C2
Silbury Bvd. M Keyn 34 B1
Silco Dr. Maid 202 C3
Silicon Ct. She B E 46 B3
Silk Mill Way. Tri 119 D3
Silk St. Wadd 99 D3
Sillswood. Oln 6 C2
Silsden Cres. C St G 177 E4
Silver Birch Cl. Ick 201 F4
Silver Cl. Maid 202 A3
Silver Hill. C St G 177 D4
Silver St. Ayl 115 E4
Silver St. Cub 78 A1
Silver St. N Pag 22 B2
Silverbirches La. Asp H 49 D1
Silverdale Cl. Ayl 101 E1
Silverdale Cl. Ty Gr 163 D1
Silvermead. Worm 123 E3
Silvertrees Dr. Maid 202 A3
Silverweed Ct. Walt 48 A3
Simdims. Cran 25 D1
Simmons Rd. Hen-O-T 191 E2
Simmons Way. La En 171 E2
Simmons Way. Tha 125 F1
Simnel. M Keyn 47 D3
Simon Dean. Bov 146 A2
Simons Lea. M Keyn 34 A2
Simonsbath. M Keyn 46 B1
Simpson Cl. Maid 203 D4
Simpson Dr. M Keyn 47 F3
Simpson Pl. Ayl 115 F3
Simpson Rd. M Keyn 47 F2
Simpson Rd. Walt 47 F2
Simpson Rd. Walt 48 A3
Sinclair Ct. M Keyn 47 D2
Singer La. Hen-O-T 191 F1
Sipson Rd. W Dra 208 C1
Sipson Rd. W Dra 208 C2
Sitwell. N Pag 21 F3
Sixty Acres Rd. Pres 151 E3
Skeats Wharf. M Keyn 35 D4
Skeldon Gate. M Keyn 35 D2
Skene Cl. M Keyn 58 B2
Skimmers Cl. Hol G 163 E3
Skimmers End. Hol G 163 E3
Skimmers Field. Hol G 163 E3
Skippon Way. Tha 125 F1
Skipton Cl. M Keyn 35 E3
Skittle Green. Bled 138 A1
Skydmore Path. Slough 197 F1
Skylark Rd. Den G 189 E2
Skyport Dr. Harm 213 E4
Slad La. Lac G 149 F2
Slade La. M Keyn 33 D2
Slade Oak La. Den G 189 E3
Slade Rd. Skch 158 C2
Slade The. Nwtn L 57 E2
Slapton La. Edle 91 F3
Slated Row. M Keyn 33 D4
Slater St. H Wyc 173 E3
Slattenham Cl. Ayl 115 D4
Slave Hill. Hadd 126 C3
Slayter Rd. La En 171 E2
Slickett's La. Edle 92 C2
Slipe The. Ched 105 D4
Slough Rd. Datch 211 D4
Slough Rd. Eton 205 F1
Slough Rd. Iver H 200 C2
Slough Rd. Slough 205 F1
Sly Cnr. Lee C 142 C2
Smabridge Wlk. M Keyn 35 E4
Small Cres. Buck 52 C4
Smalldean La. Bled R 149 D1
Smeaton Cl. Ayl 100 C1
Smeaton Cl. M Keyn 22 A1
Smith's La. Wind 209 F3
Smithergill Ct. M Keyn 34 B3
Smithfield End. Swan 66 C2
Smithfield Rd. Maid 202 A2
Snaith Cres. M Keyn 46 A4
Snakeley Cl. Loud 174 B1
Snape Spur. Slough 205 F4
Snells Wood Ct. L Chal 166 B4
Snowball Hill. Maid 202 A1
Snowberry Cl. M Keyn 33 E3
Snowden Cl. Wind 209 E2
Snowdon Dr. M Keyn 46 B4
Snowdrop Way. Hol G 162 C4
Snowhill Cotts. Ash Gr 144 C4
Snowshill Ct. M Keyn 21 F1
Soardale. M Keyn 34 B3
Soho Cres. Bou E 185 E2
Sokeman Cl. M Keyn 33 D3
Solar Ct. M Keyn 21 F1
Solent Rd. Stan 213 F1
Solesbridge Cl. Chor 167 F3
Solesbridge Ct. Chor 167 F3
Solesbridge La. Chor 167 F3
Solters Cl. Lud 96 B4
Somerford Cl. Maid 203 D4
Somersby Cres. Maid 202 C2
Somerset Cl. M Keyn 46 C1
Somerville Rd. Eton 205 E1
Somerville Way. Ayl 115 D4
Soskin Dr. M Keyn 34 B3
Sospel Ct. Far C 198 B2
Soulbury Rd. L Buzz 80 B4
Soulbury Rd. Stew 68 C1
Soulbury Rd. Wing 79 E2
South Bank Rd. Berk 134 C3
South Cl. Medm 193 E4
South Cl. W Dra 208 C2
South Common Rd. Uxb 201 F3
South Cott Dr. Chor 167 F2
South Cott Gdns. Chor 167 F2
South Dr. Beac 186 A4
South Dr. H Wyc 173 E4
South Eighth St. M Keyn 34 C1
South End. Hadd 126 C3
South End La. Edle 92 A2
South Green. Slough 205 F3
South Lawne. M Keyn 57 F4
South Maundin. Hgh V 162 A4
South Meadow La. Eton 210 B4
South Ninth St. M Keyn 34 C1
South Park. Ger C 188 C3
South Park Ave. Chor 167 F2
South Park Cres. Ger C 188 C4
South Park Dr. Ger C 188 C4
South Park Gdns. Berk 135 D3
South Park View. Ger C 188 C4
South Path. Wind 210 B3
South Rd. Ame 154 B2
South Rd. Chor 167 E2
South Rd. Maid 202 C3
South Rd. W Dra 208 C2
South Row. M Keyn 34 C1
South Seventh St. M Keyn 34 C1
South Side. Ger C 188 B4
South St. Cast 19 F3
South St. Wen 131 D2
South Tenth St. M Keyn 34 C1
South Terr. M Keyn 58 B4
South Vale. Y Has 1 A3
South View. H Wyc 161 E1
South View Rd. Ger C 188 B4
South Way. Beac 186 A4
Southampton Rd. Stan 213 F1
Southampton Way. Stan 213 F1
Southbourne Dr. Bou E 185 D2
Southcliffe Dr. C St P 177 F3
Southcote Way. Ty Gr 163 D1
Southcott Village. L Buzz 80 B3
Southcourt Ave. L Buzz 80 B3
Southcourt Rd. L Buzz 80 B4
Southcroft. Slough 198 A1
Southern Per Rd. Stan 213 E1
Southern Rd. Ayl 101 E1
Southern Rd. Tha 125 F1
Southern Way. M Keyn 33 E3
Southfield Cl. M Keyn 35 F4
Southfield Dr. Hol G 163 D3
Southfield Gdns. Burn 204 A4
Southfield Rd. Ayl 116 A4
Southfield Rd. Fla H 174 A1
Southfield Rd. H Wyc 161 E1
Southfield Rd. P Ris 139 E2
Southlea Rd. Datch 211 D3
Southview Rd. Mar 183 F2
Southwick Ct. M Keyn 45 F4
Southwold Cl. Ayl 116 A3
Southwood Gdns. Cook 195 F3
Southwood Rd. Cook 195 F3
Sovereign Dr. M Keyn 35 D4
Spackmans Way. Slough 205 E2
Spade Oak Meadow. Bou E 184 C2
Spark Way. N Pag 21 F3
Spearing Rd. H Wyc 172 B3
Spearmint Cl. Walt 48 A3
Specklands. M Keyn 46 A4
Speedwell Pl. M Keyn 34 C2
Speen Rd. Wal A 150 B1
Speen Rd. Wal A 161 F4
Spencer. M Keyn 34 B4
Spencer Cl. Uxb 201 E1
Spencer Rd. Slough 206 C2
Spencer St. M Keyn 33 F4
Spencers Cl. Maid 202 B4
Spencers La. Cook 195 F3
Spencers Rd. Maid 202 B4
Spenlows Rd. M Keyn 47 D2
Spenser Rd. Ayl 115 F3
Sperling Rd. Maid 195 F1
Spickett's La. Cudd 113 D2
Spier's La. M Gib 71 F1
Spiert The. Sto 114 B3
Spindle Cl. Ty Gr 163 D2
Spinfield La W. Mar 183 E1
Spinfield Mount. Mar 183 A1
Spinfield Park. Mar 183 E1
Spinners Wlk. Mar 183 E1
Spinners Wlk. Wind 210 B3
Spinney. Slough 205 D3
Spinney Cl. Stp Cl 63 F1
Spinney Cl. W Dra 208 C3
Spinney Cres. Dun 93 F4
Spinney Hill Rd. Oln 6 C2
Spinney La. Asp G 49 F2
Spinney The. Beac 175 F1
Spinney The. Ches 144 B1
Spinney The. Hol G 163 E4
Spinney The. M Keyn 34 A2
Spinney The. Wins 66 A3
Spinneys The. Ty Gr 174 A4
Spittal St. Mar 183 E1
Spoondell. Dun 93 F4
Spoonley Wood. M Keyn 33 F3
Sportsman Cl. Stp Cl 63 E2
Spout La. Stan 213 D2
Spout Rd N. Stan 213 D2
Sprigs Holly La. Bled R 159 D4
Spring Cl. Lat 155 E2
Spring Cl. Maid 195 F1
Spring Coppice. H Wyc 171 F3
Spring Coppice La. Pres 150 B3

Spring Coppice La. Wal A 150 B3
Spring Field Rd. Berk 135 D3
Spring Gardens Rd. H Wyc 173 F3
Spring Gdns. Bou E 185 D2
Spring Gdns. Mar 183 F2
Spring Gdns. N Pag 22 B2
Spring Gdns. Woo G 185 F4
Spring Hill. Maid 202 C2
Spring La. Cook 195 E3
Spring La. Emb 7 E2
Spring La. Far C 198 B3
Spring La. Fla H 173 F2
Spring La. G Hrwd 55 D1
Spring La. Graf R 9 D1
Spring La. Oln 6 C2
Spring Meadow. Dor 97 D1
Spring Valley Dr. Hgh V 162 A4
Springate Field. Slough 206 C2
Springett Pl. Ame 154 C1
Springfield. Oln 6 C2
Springfield Bvd. M Keyn 35 D1
Springfield Cl. Ches 154 B4
Springfield Cl. Wind 210 A3
Springfield Gdns. Chin 147 E4
Springfield Gdns. Dean 31 F2
Springfield Park. Holy 203 E1
Springfield Rd. L Buzz 80 C4
Springfield Rd. Skch 158 C2
Springfield Rd. Slough 212 A4
Springfield Rd. Wind 210 A3
Springfields. Pad 53 E1
Springfields. Ty Gr 163 E1
Springfields Cl. Pad 53 E1
Springfields Ct. Pad 53 E1
Springfields Way. Cran 25 E1
Springhill Rd. Gr Und 83 D4
Springs La. Elle 130 A2
Spruce Dene. Ty Gr 162 C1
Spurgrove La. Frie 170 C1
Spurlands End Rd. G Kin 162 C4
Spurt La. Cudd 112 C2
Square The. Asp G 49 F2
Square The. Harm 213 D3
Square The. L Cre 125 E3
Square The. M Keyn 33 E3
Square The. Pres B 62 A4
Square The. S Hea 152 A4
Squires Cl. M Keyn 47 D3
Squirrel La. H Wyc 172 B3
Squirrel Rise. Mar B 183 E3
Squirrels Way. Buck 52 C4
Stable La. Se Gr 176 B2
Stable Rd. Hal 131 F4
Stablebridge Rd. Ast C 117 F2
Stables Ct. Mar 183 A1
Stacey Ave. M Keyn 33 E3
Stafferton Way. Maid 203 D3
Stafford Ave. Slough 198 B1
Stafford Cl. Burn 204 A4
Stafford Gr. She C E 46 A3
Stag La. Chor 167 E2
Stag La. G Kin 151 E1
Stainby Cl. W Dra 208 C2
Stainton Dr. M Keyn 34 B2
Stamford Ave. M Keyn 35 D1
Stamford Rd. Maid 202 B3
Stanbridge Cl. Hadd 127 D4
Stanbridge Ct. M Keyn 32 C3
Stanbridge Rd. Hadd 127 D3
Standing Way. M Keyn 47 E4
Standing Way. She B E 47 E4
Stanhope Cl. Wen 131 D4
Stanhope Heath. Stan 213 E1
Stanhope Rd. Ayl 116 A4
Stanhope Way. Stan 213 E1
Stanier Rise. Berk 134 C4
Stanley Ave. Ches 154 A4
Stanley Cl. Mar 183 F2
Stanley Cl. Uxb 201 E2
Stanley Cotts. Slough 205 F3
Stanley Ct. Oln 6 C2
Stanley Gdns. Tri 118 C2
Stanley Green E. Slough 206 C1
Stanley Green W. Slough 206 C1
Stanley Hill. Ame 165 F4
Stanley Hill Ave. Ame 165 F4
Stanley Rd. H Wyc 172 B4
Stanmore Gdns. M Keyn 22 A1
Stanton Ave. M Keyn 34 A3
Stanton Gate. M Keyn 34 B4
Stanton Way. Slough 206 C1
Stanway Cl. M Keyn 35 D3
Stanwell Cl. Stan 213 E1
Stanwell Gdns. Stan 213 E1
Stanwell Moor Rd. Harm 213 D2
Stanwell Moor Rd. Stan 213 D2
Stanwell Rd. Hort 212 B2
Stanwell Rd. Stan 212 B2
Staple Hall Rd. M Keyn 47 F1
Stapleton Cl. Mar 183 F2
Stars La. Dint 113 F1
Startins La. Cook 195 E4
Starwood Ct. Slough 206 B2
Staters Pound. M Keyn 35 D4
Statham Pl. M Keyn 46 C4
Station App. Ame 154 B1
Station App. Chor 167 E3
Station App. Den G 189 E2
Station App. Ger C 188 C3
Station App. L Chal 166 B4
Station App. Mar 183 F1
Station App. S Hea 152 A4
Station App. W Dra 208 C3
Station App. Wen 131 D2
Station Hill. Cook 195 F4
Station Par. Den G 190 A2
Station Rd. Ald 120 A3
Station Rd. Ame 165 E4
Station Rd. B Bkhl 48 B1
Station Rd. Beac 175 F1
Station Rd. Berk 135 E2
Station Rd. Bktn 81 D2
Station Rd. Bou E 185 D2
Station Rd. Buck 52 B4
Station Rd. Cast 19 F3
Station Rd. Ches 154 B4
Station Rd. Chin 147 E3
Station Rd. Cook 195 F4
Station Rd. Ger C 188 C3
Station Rd. H Wyc 173 E3
Station Rd. Hadd 126 C3
Station Rd. Hen-O-T 191 F1
Station Rd. Ivin 105 F3
Station Rd. L Buzz 80 C4
Station Rd. Lon M 104 A2
Station Rd. Loud 174 B1
Station Rd. M Gib 71 F2
Station Rd. Mar 183 F1
Station Rd. Men 91 D1
Station Rd. Mur 67 D4
Station Rd. N Pag 22 B2
Station Rd. P Ris 139 D1
Station Rd. Pad 53 D1
Station Rd. Qntn 85 D2
Station Rd. S Man 116 A1
Station Rd. Tapl 203 F4
Station Rd. Tri 119 E2
Station Rd. Tri 120 A3
Station Rd. Uxb 201 E1
Station Rd. W Dra 208 C2
Station Rd. Wbn S 49 D3
Station Rd. Wins 66 A3
Station Rd. Wray 212 A1
Station Rise. Mar 183 F1
Station St. Ayl 115 F4
Station Terrace. M Keyn 21 F1
Station Way. Ayl 115 E4
Staunton Rd. Slough 205 E4
Staveley Cl. Ayl 116 B3
Staying La. M Keyn 34 C3
Stephenson Cl. Ayl 115 D4
Stephenson Cl. H Wyc 161 F1
Stephenson Dr. Wind 210 A4
Stepnells. Mars 105 D1
Stevens Cl. Hol G 163 D4
Stevens Cl. Pres 151 E3
Stevenson Rd. Hedg 187 E1
Stewart Ave. Slough 205 F4
Stewarts Dr. Far C 198 A4
Stewarts Way. Mar B 183 E4
Stewkley La. Mur 67 F2
Stewkley Rd. Cub 78 B1
Stewkley Rd. Soul 69 E1
Stewkley Rd. Wing 79 D2
Stile Rd. Slough 206 B2
Stilebrook Rd. Oln 6 C3
Stirling Ave. Ayl 101 F1
Stirling Cl. M Keyn 35 D3
Stirling Cl. Uxb 201 E1
Stirling Cl. Wind 209 E3
Stirling Rd. Slough 205 D4
Stirling Rd. Stan 213 F1
Stock Field Cl. Ty Gr 163 D2
Stock La. Whad 45 D1
Stockdale. M Keyn 34 B3
Stocken Cl. Oln 6 C2
Stockhall Cres. Stew 68 B1
Stocking Green Cl. Hans 11 D2
Stocking La. Wal A 161 F4
Stocklake. Ayl 101 F1
Stocklake. Bier 101 F1
Stocklands Way. Pres 151 E3
Stockleys La. Ting 51 D3
Stockport Rd. Chor 167 E1
Stocks Rd. Ald 120 B4
Stocks The. Cast 19 F1
Stockway. Wedn 87 E1
Stockwell Furlong. Hadd 127 D3
Stockwell La. Wave 48 B4
Stoke Common Rd. Fulm 199 D4
Stoke Common Rd. Sto P 199 D4
Stoke Court Dr. Sto P 198 C2
Stoke Farm La. Ayl 115 F2
Stoke Gdns. Slough 205 F3
Stoke Green. Sto P 199 D1
Stoke La. G Bkhl 59 E1
Stoke Park Ave. Far C 198 B1
Stoke Poges La. Slough 205 F4
Stoke Rd. Ash 9 F4
Stoke Rd. Ayl 115 F3
Stoke Rd. L Buzz 70 C1
Stoke Rd. M Keyn 58 C3
Stoke Rd. Nwtn L 57 F2
Stoke Rd. Slough 205 F4
Stoke Wood. Sto P 198 C4
Stokenchurch Pl. M Keyn 34 B2
Stokes Croft. Hadd 127 D4
Stokes End. Hadd 127 D4
Stokes La. Hadd 127 D4
Stomp Rd. Burn 204 A4
Stompits Rd. Holy 203 E1
Stone Cl. W Dra 208 C3
Stone Croft. Sto 114 B3
Stone Ct. Emb 13 F4
Stone Hill. M Keyn 33 E1
Stone House La. Cook 184 B1
Stone View. Oving 86 B4
Stonebridge Rd. Ayl 101 D2
Stonecrop Pl. M Keyn 34 C2
Stonefield Rd. Wal A 161 E4
Stonegate. M Keyn 34 A3
Stonehaven Rd. Ayl 101 D1
Stoney Croft. Ald 120 B3
Stoney Grove. Ches 144 B1
Stoney La. Bov 146 B3
Stoney La. Burn 198 A2
Stoney La. Chipf 146 C1
Stoney Meade. Slough 205 D3
Stoney Ware. Bish 194 C4
Stoney Ware Cl. Bish 194 C4
Stonor Ct. M Keyn 45 F4
Stony La. Chen 155 F1
Stony La. L Chal 166 C4
Stony La. L Kin 152 B2
Stookslade. Win 89 D2
Stotfold Ct. M Keyn 32 C2
Stour Cl. M Keyn 57 F4
Stour Cl. N Pag 22 C2
Stour Cl. Slough 205 D2
Stovell Rd. Wind 210 A4
Stowe Ave. Chac 41 D2
Stowe Cl. Buck 41 E1
Stowe Ct. M Keyn 34 B4
Stowe Rise. Buck 41 E1
Stowe View. Ting 51 D4
Straight Bit. Fla H 185 D4
Straight Rd. Old W 211 D1
Strand La. Cook 195 F3
Strand The. Qntn 85 D3
Strangers La. Ting 51 D3
Strangford Dr. M Keyn 58 B2
Stranraer Rd. Stan 213 F1
Stratfield Ct. M Keyn 33 F1
Stratfield Rd. Slough 206 A2
Stratford Ave. Uxb 201 F2
Stratford Cl. Slough 197 E1
Stratford Dr. Ayl 115 D3
Stratford Dr. Bou E 185 E2
Stratford Gdns. Maid 202 B2
Stratford Rd. Buck 41 F1
Stratford Rd. Cast 19 E1
Stratford Rd. M Keyn 33 E4
Stratford Rd. M Mor 42 B1
Stratford Rd. Nash 44 B1
Stratford Rd. Whad 45 D1
Strathcona Cl. Fla H 185 E4
Strathcona Way. Fla H 185 E4
Strathnaver Pl. M Keyn 33 E2
Stratton Chase Dr. C St G 166 A1
Stratton Green. Ayl 116 A3
Stratton Rd. Beac 175 D1
Stratton Rd. P Ris 139 D2
Strawberry Cl. Pres 151 E3
Streamside Wlk. Ayl 115 E3
Streatham Pl. M Keyn 34 B1
Stretton Cl. Ty Gr 174 B4
Stringfellow Cl. Cran 24 C1
Stroud Cl. Wind 209 E2
Strudwick Dr. M Keyn 46 C4
Stuart Cl. M Keyn 47 E1
Stuart Cl. Wind 209 F3
Stuart Rd. H Wyc 173 E3
Stuart Way. Tha 126 A1
Stuart Way. Wind 209 F3
Stubbles La. Cook 195 D3
Stubbs End Cl. Ame 154 C1
Stubbs Wood. Ame 154 C2
Studdridge Ct. Skch 158 B2
Studham La. Dag 107 E2
Studland Cl. Ayl 116 A3
Studley Knapp. Walt 48 A3
Studridge La. Lac G 150 A3
Sturges Cl. Walt 48 A3
Stylecroft Rd. C St G 177 E4
Suffield Rd. H Wyc 172 C4
Suffolk Cl. M Keyn 46 C1
Suffolk Rd. Maid 202 B2
Sulby Cl. Ayl 115 E3
Sulgrave Cres. Tri 119 E3
Sulgrave Ct. M Keyn 45 F4
Sullivan Cres. Walt 48 B3
Summergill Ct. M Keyn 34 B3
Summerhayes. M Keyn 34 C4
Summerhouse La. Harm 213 E4
Summerlea. Slough 205 D3
Summerleaze Rd. Maid 196 A1
Summerleys. Eat B 92 C2
Summerleys Rd. Lgwk 138 C2
Summerleys Rd. P Ris 138 C2
Summers Rd. Burn 197 E1
Summerson Rd. M Keyn 46 C3
Sun Cres. Oak 109 E3
Sun La. Maid 202 C4
Sun Pas. Wind 210 B3
Sunbury Cl. M Keyn 34 A3
Sunbury Rd. Eton 210 B4
Sunderland Rd. Maid 202 A4
Sunningdale Cl. H Wyc 172 A3
Sunningdale Way. M Keyn 57 E4
Sunny Bank. Ched 104 C4
Sunny Bank. Hol G 162 C3
Sunny Croft. H Wyc 161 E1
Sunnybank. Mar 183 E2
Sunnybrook Cl. Ast C 117 E3
Sunnyhill Rd. Map Cr 178 B2
Sunnymede Ave. Ches 144 C2
Sunnyside Rd. Ches 144 B1
Sunray Ave. W Dra 208 B2
Sunridge Cl. N Pag 22 B2
Sunrise Parkway. M Keyn 34 C3
Sunset Cl. M Keyn 58 B4
Sunters Wood Cl. H Wyc 172 A3
Surly Hall Wlk. Wind 209 F3
Surrey Ave. Slough 198 B1
Surrey Pl. M Keyn 46 C1
Surrey Pl. Tri 119 D2
Surrey Rd. M Keyn 46 C1
Sussex Cl. C St G 177 D4
Sussex Cl. H Wyc 162 B1
Sussex Cl. Slough 206 A2
Sussex Pl. Slough 206 A2
Sussex Rd. M Keyn 46 C1
Sussex Way. Den G 189 F3
Sutcliffe Ave. M Keyn 34 C1
Sutherland Gr. M Keyn 46 C2
Sutherland Wlk. Ayl 115 F3
Sutton Ave. Slough 206 B2
Sutton Cl. Cook 196 A4
Sutton Cl. Maid 202 B3
Sutton Cl. Tri 119 D3
Sutton Ct. M Keyn 46 B1
Sutton Pl. Slough 212 A4
Sutton Rd. Cook 196 A3
Swains Cl. W Dra 208 C2
Swains La. Fla H 174 A1
Swakeleys Rd. Ick 201 F4
Swale Cl. Ayl 101 F2
Swale Rd. Ayl 115 E3
Swallow Cl. Buck 52 C4
Swallow Dr. Hol G 163 D3
Swallow La. S Man 116 A1
Swallow St. Iver H 200 B1
Swallowdale. Iver H 200 B1
Swallowfield. M Keyn 33 F1
Swan Cl. Buck 52 C4
Swan Cl. Ches 144 A2
Swan Cl. Ivin 92 A1
Swan Cl. Whit 87 D3
Swan Ct. Oln 7 D2
Swan La. M Gib 72 A2
Swan Rd. W Dra 208 B2
Swan Yd. M Keyn 32 B3
Swan's Way. N Mar 75 E1
Swanbourne Rd. Mur 67 E2
Swann Rd. Hal 131 E4
Swansons. Edle 92 C2
Sweetcroft La. Uxb 201 F3
Swift Cl. N Pag 22 A3
Swinden Ct. M Keyn 34 A2
Swing Gate La. Berk 135 E1
Switchback Cl. Maid 195 E1
Switchback Rd. Cook 195 F2
Switchback Rd N. Cook 195 F2
Switchback Rd N. Maid 195 F2
Switchback Rd S. Maid 195 E1
Switchback The. Maid 195 E1
Sycamore Ave. M Keyn 58 C4
Sycamore Cl. Ame 154 B1
Sycamore Cl. Buck 52 C4
Sycamore Cl. C St G 177 D4
Sycamore Cl. L Cre 125 E3
Sycamore Cl. Stew 68 B1
Sycamore Cl. W Dra 208 C3
Sycamore Cnr. Ame 154 B1
Sycamore Ct. H Wyc 172 B2
Sycamore Ct. Wind 210 B2
Sycamore Dene. Ches 144 B2
Sycamore Dr. Mar B 183 E3
Sycamore Dr. Tri 119 D2
Sycamore Leys. Stp Cl 63 F2
Sycamore Rd. Ame 154 B1
Sycamore Rd. C St G 177 D4
Sycamore Rd. H Wyc 172 B2
Sycamore Rise. Berk 135 E2
Sycamore Rise. C St G 177 D4
Sycamore Way. Ty Gr 163 D2
Sycamore Wlk. Slough 206 C4
Sycamores The. Fel 146 C4
Sydney Gr. Slough 205 E4
Sykes Rd. Slough 205 D4
Sylvana Cl. Uxb 201 F2
Sylvester Rd. Maid 195 F1
Sylvia Cl. L Kin 152 A2
Symington Ct. She B E 46 A3
Syon Gdns. N Pag 22 B1
Tabard Gdns. N Pag 22 B1
Tachbrook Rd. Uxb 201 E2
Tadmarton. M Keyn 35 D3
Tadmere. M Keyn 33 E1
Talbot Ave. H Wyc 161 E1
Talbot Ave. Slough 206 C2
Talbot Pl. Datch 211 E3
Talbot Rd. Ast C 117 F3
Talbots Dr. Maid 202 A3
Talbots Hyde. Oln 6 C2
Tall Trees. Stan 212 C3
Talland Ave. M Keyn 34 C1
Tamar Cl. Ayl 115 E2
Tamar Cl. Loud 174 A2
Tamworth Stubb. Walt 48 A3
Tancred Rd. H Wyc 162 A1
Tandra. M Keyn 47 D3
Tandys Cl. Turv 8 C3
Tangier La. Eton 210 B4
Tank House Rd. Wins 66 A3
Tanners Dr. M Keyn 22 A1
Tannery Rd. H Wyc 174 A2
Taplin Way. Ty Gr 163 E1
Taplow Common Rd. Burn 197 D3
Taplow Common Rd. Tapl 197 D3
Taplow Rd. Burn 204 A4
Tapping Rd. La En 171 E3
Tarbay La. Oak G 209 D3
Tarbert Cl. M Keyn 58 B3
Tarmac Way. Harm 213 D4
Task The. Oln 7 D2
Taskers Row. Edle 92 C2
Tatchbrook Cl. Maid 203 D4
Tate Rd. C St P 177 F3
Tathams La. Mur 67 D2
Tatling Gr. Walt 48 A3
Tattenhoe La. M Keyn 57 E4
Tattenhoe La. M Keyn 57 F4
Tattlers Hill. Win 89 D2
Taunton Deane. M Keyn 46 B1
Taurus Cl. Stp Cl 63 E1
Tavelhurst. M Keyn 33 F1
Tavistock Cl. Maid 202 A4
Tavistock Cl. Wbn S 49 D3
Tavistock Rd. W Dra 208 B3
Tavistock St. M Keyn 47 E1
Tay Rd. M Keyn 46 C1
Taylor Rd. Ayl 115 E3
Taylor's Cl. Mar 183 F1
Taylor's Ride. L Buzz 70 C1
Taylors Mews. M Keyn 34 C3
Taylors Rd. Ches 144 B1
Taylors Turn. H Wyc 161 E2
Teale Cl. U Arn 94 C4
Teasel Ave. M Keyn 34 C3
Tedder Rd. Wen 131 E3
Tees Way. M Keyn 46 B1
Teign Cl. N Pag 22 B2
Telford Cl. Ayl 100 C1
Telford Dr. Slough 205 D2
Telford Way. H Wyc 162 A1
Telford Way. M Keyn 22 A1
Telston Cl. Bou E 185 D3
Temperance Terr. M Keyn 32 B3
Temple. M Keyn 34 B4
Temple Cl. Buck 41 F1
Temple Cl. M Keyn 57 E4
Temple End. H Wyc 173 D4
Temple La. Bish 194 B3
Temple Mill Island. Bish 194 B3
Temple Park. Hurl 193 F2
Temple Rd. Wind 210 B3
Temple Sq. Ayl 115 E4
Temple St. Ayl 115 E4
Temple St. Bri 96 A1
Temple St. H Wyc 173 D4
Temple Way. Far C 198 B4
Templewood. Wal A 150 A1
Templewood La. Far C 198 B4
Tennyson Dr. N Pag 22 A2
Tennyson Gr. M Keyn 57 F4
Tennyson Rd. H Wyc 173 D3
Tennyson Way. Slough 197 F1
Tenzing Dr. H Wyc 173 F3
Terrace The. Asp G 49 F3
Terrace The. Maid 203 E2
Terrace The. Tri 119 D2
Terrington Hill. Mar 183 A1
Terry Dr. Ayl 101 E2
Terry Orch. H Wyc 173 E4
Terry Rd. H Wyc 173 E4
Terry's La. Cook 195 F4
Terryfield Rd. H Wyc 173 F3
Tess Rd. Ayl 115 E3
Testwood Rd. Wind 209 E3
Tetherdown. Pres 151 E3
Tews End La. Paul 17 E4
Thackeray End. Ayl 100 C1
Thame Rd. Ayl 115 E4
Thame Rd. Bktn 81 D2
Thame Rd. Bri 110 A4
Thame Rd. Chil 111 D2
Thame Rd. Chin 147 D4
Thame Rd. Hadd 126 B3
Thame Rd. L Cre 125 E2
Thame Rd. Lgwk 138 C3
Thame Rd. Pidd (B) 95 E3
Thames Ave. Wind 210 B4
Thames Cl. Bou E 185 D2
Thames Cl. M Keyn 57 F4
Thames Cres. Maid 196 A1
Thames Dr. N Pag 22 C2
Thames Ind Est. Mar 183 F1
Thames Mead. Wind 209 F3
Thames Side. Hen-O-T 191 F1
Thames Side. Wind 210 B4
Thames St. Wind 210 B4
Thamesfield Gdns. Mar 183 F1
Thane Ct. M Keyn 34 B4

Thatcher Cl. W Dra 208 C2
Thatchers Dr. Maid 202 A3
Theydon Ave. Wbn S 49 D2
Thicket The. Ty Gr 163 D1
Thicket The. W Dra 208 C4
Third Ave. M Keyn 47 D1
Third Ave. Mar 183 F1
Third Cres. Slough 205 E4
Thirkleby Cl. Slough 205 E3
Thirlby La. She C E 46 A3
Thirlmere Ave. Burn 204 B4
Thirlmere Ave. M Keyn 58 B3
Thirsk Gdns. M Keyn 57 E3
Thomas Dr. N Pag 22 A3
Thomas Rd. Bou E 185 E2
Thompkins La. Burn 198 A3
Thompson St. M Keyn 34 A4
Thomson Cl. Ayl 115 D3
Thomson Wlk. Ayl 115 D3
Thorn Dr. Slough 206 C4
Thorn Tree Dr. Tri 118 C2
Thornbank Cl. Stan 213 D1
Thornborough Rd. Nash 55 D4
Thornborough Rd. Nash 55 D4
Thornbridge Rd. Iver H 200 B2
Thorncliffe. M Keyn 33 E1
Thorndike. Slough 205 D4
Thorne Rd. La En 171 E2
Thorne Way. Ayl 101 F1
Thorney Mill La. Iver 208 A2
Thorney Mill Rd. W Dra 208 A2
Thorneycroft La. M Keyn 35 D3
Thornhill. Thrn 54 A4
Thornhill Cl. Ame 165 D4
Thornhill Rd. Ick 201 F4
Thornlea Croft. Oln 6 C2
Thorns Cl. P Ris 139 E3
Thornton Ave. W Dra 208 C2
Thornton Cl. W Dra 208 C2
Thornton Cres. Wen 131 D3
Thornton Rd. Nash 44 A1
Thorpe Cl. Ayl 116 A2
Thrasher Rd. Ayl 115 E3
Three Close La. Berk 135 E2
Three Households. C St G 176 C3
Three Oaks Cl. Ick 190 C1
Three Points La. Stp Cl 74 A3
Thresher Gr. M Keyn 33 D3
Thrift La. Maid 202 B1
Thrush Cl. H Wyc 172 B2
Thurlby Way. Maid 202 B2
Thurne Cl. N Pag 22 C2
Thursby Cl. M Keyn 35 E4
Thurston Rd. Slough 205 F4
Tibbys La. Cudd 112 C2
Tichborne. Map Cr 178 B3
Tickford St. N Pag 22 C2
Tidbury Cl. Wbn S 49 D2
Tiffany Cl. M Keyn 58 B3
Tilburywood Cl. H Wyc 161 E1
Tilecotes Cl. Mar 183 B1
Tilehouse Way. Den G 189 F2
Tilehouse La. Den G 189 F3
Tilers Rd. M Keyn 33 D1
Tilling Cres. H Wyc 174 A4
Tilman Cl. M Keyn 33 E3
Tilsworth Rd. Beac 175 E1
Timber La. Hth 60 C4
Tindal Rd. Ayl 101 F1
Tingewick Rd. Buck 52 A4
Tingewick Rd. Chac 51 F4
Tinkers La. Berk 134 A3
Tinkers La. Wind 209 E3
Tinkers Wood Rd. H Wyc 161 F1
Tintagel Ct. M Keyn 47 D4
Tintern Cl. Slough 205 E2
Tinterne Cl. Ayl 116 B3
Tippings. Skch 158 C3
Tithe Barn Dr. Holy 203 E1
Tithe Barn Dr. Holy 203 F1
Tithe Cl. Holy 203 E1
Tithe La. Wray 212 A1
Titmus Rd. Hal 131 F4
Tiverton Cres. Ayl 101 E2
Tockley Way. Burn 197 D1
Todd Cl. Ayl 115 D3
Tolcarne Ave. M Keyn 35 D1
Tollgate. Maid 202 A3
Tollgate Cl. Chor 167 F3
Tomlin Rd. Slough 197 F1
Tompion Rd. Ayl 100 C1
Tompkins La. M Gib 71 F1
Toms Hill Rd. Ald 120 B3
Toms Turn. Hol G 162 C3
Tongwell La. N Pag 22 B1
Tongwell St. M Keyn 35 F3
Tongwell St. M Keyn 35 F4
Tongwell St. Walt 48 B3
Top Park. Ger C 188 B3
Topaz Cl. Slough 205 D3
Topland Rd. Ger C 177 E2
Torre Cl. M Keyn 47 D1
Torridge Rd. Ayl 115 E2
Torridge Rd. Slough 212 A4
Torrington Rd. Berk 135 D2
Torwood Cl. Berk 134 C2
Totteridge Dr. H Wyc 162 C1
Totteridge La. H Wyc 162 C1
Totteridge Rd. H Wyc 173 E4
Totternhoe Rd. Dun 93 F4
Totternhoe Rd. Eat B 92 B4
Towan Ave. M Keyn 35 D1
Towcester Dr. Pott 18 A2
Towcester Rd. Old S 32 A4
Tower Cl. Berk 135 D2
Tower Cl. Fla H 185 E4
Tower Cotts. Mur 67 E4
Tower Cres. M Keyn 34 C3
Tower Dr. M Keyn 34 C4
Tower Hill. Chipf 146 C1
Tower Rd. Cole 165 D2
Tower St. H Wyc 162 B1
Toweridge La. H Wyc 160 C1
Toweridge La. H Wyc 172 B4
Towersey Way. Ayl 115 D4
Town Bridge Ct. Ches 154 A4
Town Cl. Fin 50 B3
Town End Cres. S Gol 12 A3
Town End Rd. Bled R 159 E4
Town Field La. C St G 177 E4
Town La. Bou E 185 E2
Town La. Stan 213 E1
Townfield. Ches 154 B4
Townfield Rd. H Wyc 173 E4
Townsend. M Gib 71 F1
Townsend Cotts. G Hrwd 55 D2
Townsend Piece. Ayl 101 E1
Townsend Rd. Ches 144 B1
Townside. Edle 92 C2
Townside. Hadd 126 C3
Trafalgar Ave. M Keyn 46 C1
Trafford Cl. G Mis 152 A3
Trafford Rd. S Hea 152 A4
Tramhill. Bri 96 A1
Tranlands Brigg. M Keyn 34 A2
Trapp's La. Ches 154 B3
Travell Ct. M Keyn 34 A2
Travic Rd. Slough 197 F1
Travis Ct. Slough 198 A1
Treacher's Cl. Ches 154 A4
Treadaway Hill. Fla H 174 A1
Treadaway Hill. Loud 174 A1
Treadaway Rd. Fla H 174 A1
Treehanger Cl. Tri 119 D2
Trees Ave. Hgh V 162 A3
Trees Rd. Bou E 185 D2
Trees Rd. Hgh V 162 A3
Treeside Cl. W Dra 208 B1
Treesmill Dr. Maid 202 B2
Trelawney Ave. Slough 206 C2
Tremayne Ct. M Keyn 47 D4
Trenchard Ave. Wen 131 E3
Trent Dr. N Pag 22 B2
Trent Rd. M Keyn 46 C1
Trent Rd. Slough 212 A4
Tresco Rd. Berk 134 C3
Trevelyan Way. Berk 135 D3
Treves Green. Ayl 115 F3
Trevithick La. She B E 46 A3
Trevone Ct. M Keyn 47 D4
Tring Ford Rd. Tri 119 D4
Tring Hill. Dra B 118 B2
Tring Rd. Ayl 116 A4
Tring Rd. Berk 134 B4
Tring Rd. Dun 93 F4
Tring Rd. Edle 106 C4
Tring Rd. Lon M 104 A2
Tring Rd. Wen 131 E3
Tring Rd. Win 89 E1
Trinity Ave. Mar 183 E2
Trinity Cl. Stan 213 E1
Trinity Pl. Wind 210 B3
Trinity Rd. M Keyn 33 D4
Trinity Rd. Mar 183 E1
Trinity Rd. Ty Gr 162 C2
Tripps Hill Cl. C St G 177 D4
Trispen Ct. M Keyn 47 D4
Trooper Rd. Ald 120 B3
Trout Cl. Mar 194 B4
Trout La. W Dra 208 B3
Trout Rd. W Dra 208 B3
Troutbeck. M Keyn 47 E4
Trubys Gdn. M Keyn 47 D4
Trueman Pl. M Keyn 46 C4
Truesdale Dr. S Har 190 B4
Trumper Way. Uxb 201 E2
Trunk Furlong Estate. Asp G 49 E3
Truro Cl. Maid 202 A4
Trustees Way. Den G 189 F3
Tubwell Rd. Sto P 199 D2
Tucker Cl. H Wyc 173 E4
Tuckers Dr. Hol G 163 E4
Tudor Dr. Woo G 185 E4
Tudor Gdns. Burn 204 B4
Tudor Gdns. M Keyn 32 C2
Tudor Park. Ame 154 B1
Tudor Rd. Ty Gr 163 E2
Tudor Way. Wind 209 F3
Tuffnell Cl. M Keyn 35 F4
Tulkers Cl. Pres 151 E3
Tulla Ct. M Keyn 58 B2
Tummell Way. M Keyn 58 B3
Tunmers End. Ger C 177 E1
Tuns La. Hen-O-T 191 F1
Tuns La. Slough 205 E2
Turnberry Cl. M Keyn 57 E4
Turner Cl. Ayl 101 F2
Turner Rd. Slough 206 B2
Turners Dr. H Wyc 173 F4
Turners Mews. M Keyn 34 C3
Turners Pl. Hol G 163 E3
Turners Wood Dr. C St G 177 E4
Turnfields. Ick 124 A2
Turnfurlong. Ayl 115 F4
Turnfurlong La. Ayl 116 A3
Turnip Cl. Chea 112 A1
Turnmill Ave. M Keyn 35 D1
Turnpike La. Uxb 201 F1
Turnpike Rd. H Wyc 172 B2
Turnpike The. Oak 109 E3
Turnpike Way. H Wyc 172 B2
Turpins Green. Maid 202 A3
Turton Way. Slough 205 E2
Turvey Cl. Ast C 117 F3
Turvey Rd. Ast 15 F3
Turvey Rd. Carl 3 F1
Turville Rd. Ayl 116 B3
Turweston Rd. Brac 26 A1
Tweed Cl. Berk 135 D3
Tweed Dr. M Keyn 46 B1
Tweed Rd. Slough 212 A4
Tweenways. Ches 144 C1
Twelve Leys. Win 89 D2
Twinches La. Slough 205 D3
Twist The. Wigg 119 E1
Twitchell La. Ast C 117 F3
Twitchell Rd. S Hea 152 A4
Twitchell's La. C St G 176 C3
Twitchen La. She B E 46 B2
Two Dells La. Ash Gr 145 D2
Two Gates La. Char 143 E4
Twyford La. Walt 48 B3
Twynham Rd. Maid 202 A4
Tyburn Ave. M Keyn 35 D1
Tyle Pl. Old W 211 D1
Tylers Cres. Ty Gr 163 D1
Tylers Green. M Keyn 34 B2
Tylers Hill Rd. Bot 154 C4
Tylers Rd. Ty Gr 163 D1
Tylsworth Cl. Ame 154 B1
Tyne Rd. Ayl 115 E2
Tyne Sq. M Keyn 46 B1
Tyneham Cl. Ayl 116 A2
Tyrell Cl. Buck 52 B4
Tyrell Gdns. Wind 209 F2
Tyrells Gdns. S Ham 69 F4
Tyrells Rd. S Ham 69 F4
Tyrill. M Keyn 34 B4
Tyson Pl. M Keyn 46 C4
Tythe Cl. Stew 78 C4
Tythe Gdns. Stew 78 C4
Tythe Mews. Edle 92 C2
Tyzack Rd. H Wyc 162 C1

Ullswater Cl. Burn 204 B4
Ullswater Dr. L Buzz 80 B4
Ulyett Pl. M Keyn 46 C4
Umberville Way. Slough 197 F1
Underhill Cl. Maid 202 C3
Underwood Pl. M Keyn 46 C4
Underwood Rd. H Wyc 173 E4
Union St. H Wyc 173 D4
Union St. N Pag 22 B3
Up Corner Cl. C St G 177 D4
Upcroft. Wind 210 A2
Upland Ave. Ches 144 A2
Uplands. Mar B 183 E3
Uplands Cl. Ger C 188 C2
Uplands Cl. H Wyc 173 F4
Uplands The. Ger C 188 C1
Upper Abbotts Hill. Ayl 115 D4
Upper Ashlyns Rd. Berk 135 D2
Upper Belmont Rd. Ches 144 A2
Upper Bray Rd. Maid 203 E2
Upper Church St. Cudd 112 C2
Upper Coombe. L Buzz 80 C4
Upper Dr. Beac 175 E3
Upper Fifth St. M Keyn 34 B1
Upper Fourth St. M Keyn 34 B1
Upper George St. Ches 144 B1
Upper Gladstone Rd. Ches 144 B1
Upper Hall Park. Berk 135 F1
Upper Hollis. G Mis 151 F4
Upper Hundreds. Ayl 115 F4
Upper Ickenfield Way. P Ris 149 D4
Upper Icknield Way. Ast C 117 F1
Upper Icknield Way. Bled 149 D4
Upper Icknield Way. Dra B 117 F1
Upper Icknield Way. Hal 117 F1
Upper Icknield Way. P Ris 139 E3
Upper Icknield Way. Pit 105 F1
Upper Icknield Way. Pris 149 D4
Upper Lees Rd. Slough 198 A1
Upper Lodge La. Hol G 162 C3
Upper Rd. Den G 189 E2
Upper Riding. Beac 175 D1
Upper Second St. M Keyn 34 B1
Upper St. Qntn 85 D3
Upper St. Ting 51 D3
Upper Stonehayes. M Keyn 34 C4
Upper Way. G Bkhl 59 E1
Upton Cl. Hen-O-T 191 F1
Upton Cl. Slough 205 F2
Upton Court Rd. Slough 206 A1
Upton Gr. She B E 46 B2
Upton Lea Par. Slough 206 A3
Upton Park. Slough 205 F2
Upton Rd. Dint 114 A2
Upton Rd. Slough 206 A2
Upway. C St P 177 F1
Uxbridge R. Uxb 201 F1
Uxbridge Rd. Slough 206 B3

Vache La. C St G 177 E4
Vache La. She C E 45 F3
Vale Cl. Ger C 177 E1
Vale Gr. Slough 205 F2
Vale Ind Centre The. Ayl 101 E1
Vale Rd. Ayl 101 F1
Vale Rd. Ches 144 B2
Vale Rd. Wind 209 F3
Vale Rise. Ches 144 B2
Vale The. Ger C 177 E1
Valens Cl. She C E 45 F4
Valentine Way. C St G 177 E4
Valley Centre The. H Wyc 173 E3
Valley Cl. Brac 38 A4
Valley Cres. Brac 38 A4
Valley End. Iver H 199 E1
Valley Rd. Berk 134 C3
Valley Rd. Brac 38 A4
Valley Rd. Buck 52 C4
Valley Rd. Fin 50 B3
Valley Rd. Hen-O-T 191 E1
Valley Rd. Hgh V 162 A3
Valley Rise. Brac 38 A4
Valley View. Ches 144 A1
Valley Way. Ger C 188 B3
Van Der Bilt Ct. M Keyn 33 F3
Van Diemens Cl. Chin 147 E4
Vandyke Cl. Wbn S 49 D3
Vane Rd. Tha 126 A1
Vansittart Rd. Bish 194 C4
Vansittart Rd. Wind 210 A3
Vantage Rd. Slough 205 D3
Vanwall Bsns Pk. Maid 202 B3
Vanwall Rd. Maid 202 B2
Vaughan Copse. Slough 205 E1
Vaughan Way. Slough 197 F1
Vauxhall. M Keyn 34 A3
Vellan Ave. M Keyn 35 D1
Venables La. M Keyn 35 D4
Ventfield Cl. Hor-c-S 108 A3
Venus Hill. Bov 156 A4
Verbena Cl. W Dra 208 B1
Verdon Dr. M Keyn 35 D4
Verity Pl. M Keyn 34 C1
Verley Cl. M Keyn 47 E4
Vermont Rd. Slough 197 F1
Verney Ave. H Wyc 172 B2
Verney Cl. Berk 134 C3
Verney Cl. Buck 41 E1
Verney Cl. Mar 183 E1
Verney Cl. Tri 119 E3
Verney Farm Cl. E Clay 74 C4
Verney Rd. Wins 65 F2
Verney Wlk. Ayl 115 E3
Verona Cl. Uxb 208 B4
Verwood Rd. Ayl 101 F1
Veryan Pl. M Keyn 35 D1
Vicarage Cl. Cook 196 A4
Vicarage Cl. Stp Cl 63 E1
Vicarage Cl. Wen 131 D3
Vicarage Cl. Yard G 18 C3
Vicarage Dr. Maid 203 E2
Vicarage Gdns. L Buzz 80 C3
Vicarage Gdns. M Keyn 34 A2
Vicarage Gdns. Mars 105 D1
Vicarage La. Bov 146 A2
Vicarage La. Ivin 105 F3
Vicarage La. Pidd (B) 95 F3
Vicarage La. Stp Cl 63 E1
Vicarage La. Wing 79 F1
Vicarage Rd. Ayl 115 E3
Vicarage Rd. Hen-O-T 191 F1
Vicarage Rd. L Buzz 80 C3
Vicarage Rd. M Keyn 32 B3
Vicarage Rd. M Keyn 34 A2
Vicarage Rd. M Keyn 58 C4
Vicarage Rd. Maid 202 C4
Vicarage Rd. Mars 105 D1
Vicarage Rd. Pit 105 E2
Vicarage Rd. Whad 56 A4
Vicarage Rd. Wigg 119 E1
Vicarage Rd. Wins 65 F2
Vicarage St. Wbn S 49 E2
Vicarage Way. Ger C 188 C3
Vicarage Way. Iver 212 B4
Vicarage Wlk. M Keyn 32 B3
Vicarage Wlk. Maid 203 E2
Vickery Way. Ayl 115 F3
Victor Rd. Wind 210 B2
Victoria Cres. Iver 208 A3
Victoria Rd. Berk 135 E2
Victoria Rd. Ches 144 B1
Victoria Rd. Far C 198 B3
Victoria Rd. L Buzz 80 C3
Victoria Rd. M Keyn 47 F1
Victoria Rd. Mar 183 F1
Victoria Rd. Slough 206 A3
Victoria Rd. Uxb 201 E3
Victoria St. Ayl 115 F4
Victoria St. H Wyc 172 C4
Victoria St. M Keyn 33 E3
Victoria St. Slough 205 F2
Victoria St. Wind 210 B3
Victory Rd. Berk 135 D3
Victory Rd. Stp Cl 63 E1
Victory Rd. Wen 131 D3
Vienna Gr. M Keyn 33 F3
Village Cl. Sher 13 F1
Village La. Hedg 187 E2
Village Rd. Cole 164 C2
Village Rd. Den 190 A2
Village Way. L Chal 166 B4
Villier St. Uxb 201 E2
Villiers Cl. Buck 41 F1
Villiers Rd. Slough 205 E4
Vincent Ave. She C E 45 F4
Vincent Cl. Ayl 101 D2
Vincents Way. Wal A 161 E3
Vine Cl. Stan 213 D1
Vine Cl. Ty Gr 163 D2
Vine Gr. Uxb 201 F3
Vine Rd. Sto P 198 C3
Vine The. Shab 124 B2
Vinetrees. Wen 131 D2
Vinlake Ave. Ick 190 C1
Vintners Mews. M Keyn 34 C3
Violet Ave. Uxb 208 C4
Violet Ave. W Dra 208 C4
Violet Cl. Lac G 149 E3
Virginia. M Keyn 47 D4
Virginia Gdns. Bled R 159 F4
Viscount Way. M Keyn 47 E1
Vivien Cl. Cook 195 F3
Vyne Cres. M Keyn 33 F1

Waborne Rd. Bou E 185 D2
Waddesdon Hill. Wadd 99 E2
Wade Dr. Slough 205 D3
Wadesmill La. Walt 48 A2
Wainers Croft. M Keyn 33 D2
Wainwrights. L Cre 125 E3
Waits Green. Chea 112 A1
Waivers Way. Ayl 116 A3
Wakefield Cl. M Keyn 34 C4
Wakefield Cres. Sto P 198 C3
Wakelins End. Cook 195 F4
Wakeman Rd. Bou E 185 D2
Walbrook Ave. M Keyn 35 D2
Waldeck Rd. Maid 203 D4
Waldens Cl. Bou E 185 D2
Walducks Cl. Stew 78 C4
Walford Rd. Uxb 201 E2
Walgrave Dr. M Keyn 34 A2
Walk House Cl. Cran 25 D1
Walk The. Eton 205 D1
Walk The. Wins 65 F2
Walk Wood Rise. Beac 186 B4
Walker Rd. Maid 203 D2
Walkers Rd. Lgwk 138 B4
Walkham Cl. Loud 174 A2
Walkwood End. Beac 175 E1
Wallace Cl. Mar 183 F2
Wallace Dr. Eat B 92 C3
Wallace End. Ayl 116 A3
Wallace St. M Keyn 33 F4
Wallbridge Cl. Ayl 115 D4
Waller Rd. Beac 175 F1
Wallingford. M Keyn 34 A3
Wallingford Gdns. H Wyc 173 D2
Wallingford Rd. Uxb 201 D1
Wallington Rd. Ches 144 A1
Wallis Ct. Slough 206 A2
Wallmead Gdns. M Keyn 46 A4
Walnut Cl. N Pag 22 A2
Walnut Cl. S Hea 152 A4
Walnut Cl. S Man 116 B1
Walnut Cres. Lgwk 138 B4
Walnut Dr. M Keyn 58 C4
Walnut Dr. M Mor 41 F2
Walnut Tree Cl. Bou E 185 D1
Walnut Tree Cl. H Wyc 172 B4
Walnut Tree La. Lgwk 138 B3
Walnut Way. Bou E 185 D1
Walnut Way. H Hea 153 E2
Walsh's Manor. M Keyn 34 B4
Walsingham Gate. H Wyc 173 D2
Walton Cl. H Wyc 162 C1
Walton Dene. Ayl 115 F4
Walton Dr. H Wyc 162 C1
Walton End. Walt 48 B3
Walton Gr. Ayl 115 F4
Walton Green. Ayl 115 F4
Walton Heath. M Keyn 57 E4
Walton La. Burn 197 F2
Walton Pl. W Tur 116 C2
Walton Rd. Ayl 115 F4
Walton Rd. B Bkhl 48 A2
Walton Rd. Walt 48 A3
Walton Rd. Walt 48 B4
Walton Rd. Wave 48 B4
Walton St. Ayl 115 F4
Walton Way. Ayl 116 A4
Wandlebury. M Keyn 35 D4
Wandsworth Pl. M Keyn 34 B2
Wannions Cl. Bot 145 D1
Wantage Cl. Wing 79 F2
Wantage Cres. Wing 79 F2
Wappenham Rd. Syr 27 D4
Wapping. L Cre 125 E3
Wapseys La. Hedg 187 F2
Ward Pl. Ame 165 D4
Ward Rd. Brac 38 A3

Ward Rd. M Keyn 47 F2
Ward Royal. Wind 210 B3
Wardes Cl. Pres 151 E3
Wardrobes La. Lac G 149 E4
Wargrave Rd. Rem H 191 F1
Warmstone Cl. Wadd 99 D3
Warmstone La. Wadd 99 D3
Warneford Ave. Wen 131 E3
Warners Cl. G Bkhl 59 E1
Warners Hill. Cook 195 E4
Warners Rd. Nwtn L 57 E2
Warren Bank. M Keyn 47 F3
Warren Cl. Buck 52 C4
Warren Cl. Slough 206 C2
Warren Field. Iver H 200 B2
Warren Rd. Ick 201 F4
Warren Rd. Yard G 18 C3
Warren The. Char 143 F2
Warren The. Hol G 163 D3
Warren Wood Dr. H Wyc 173 E3
Warrendene Rd. Hgh V 162 A4
Warrender Rd. Ches 144 C1
Warrington Ave. Slough 205 E4
Warrington Rd. Oln 7 D4
Warrington Rd. Warr 7 D4
Warwick Ave. H Wyc 172 A3
Warwick Ave. Slough 198 B1
Warwick Cl. Ast C 117 F3
Warwick Cl. Maid 202 A2
Warwick Dr. Wing 79 F1
Warwick Pl. M Keyn 57 F4
Warwick Pl. Uxb 201 E3
Warwick Rd. Beac 175 E2
Warwick Rd. Hans 11 D2
Warwick Rd. M Keyn 57 F4
Warwick Rd. W Dra 208 C3
Wash Hill. Bou E 185 F2
Wash Hill Lea. Bou E 185 F2
Washingleys. Cran 25 E1
Washington Ct. Mar 184 A2
Washington Dr. Wind 209 F2
Wastel. M Keyn 47 D3
Watchet La. Hol G 152 A2
Watchet La. L Kin 152 A2
Water Eaton Rd. M Keyn 58 B4
Water End Rd. Bled R 159 E2
Water La. Berk 135 E2
Water La. Bov 146 A1
Water La. Brac 38 A4
Water La. Ches 154 A4
Water La. Dint 128 A4
Water La. L Buzz 80 C4
Water La. Lac G 150 B2
Water La. Sher 13 F1
Water Meadow. Ches 154 A4
Water Tower Cl. Uxb 201 F4
Waterbeach Rd. Slough 205 E4
Waterloo Ct. M Keyn 46 C1
Waterloo Rd. L Buzz 80 C3
Waterloo Rd. Uxb 201 E2
Waterlow Cl. N Pag 22 B1
Watermill Way. W Tur 116 C1
Waterperry Rd. Worm 123 E3
Waterside. Berk 135 E2
Waterside. Ches 154 B3
Waterside. M Keyn 47 E4
Waterside. Uxb 208 B4
Waterside. Woo G 185 F4
Waterside Ct. Ches 154 B4
Watery La. Beac 44 A3
Watery La. Brac 38 A4
Watery La. Frie 170 A1
Watery La. Mars 104 C1
Watery La. Woo G 185 F4
Watling St. M Keyn 33 E1
Watling St. Pott 18 B2
Watling Terr. M Keyn 47 F1
Watlington Rd. Lewk 157 D4
Wattleton Rd. Beac 175 F1
Watts Cl. Hans 11 D2
Wavell Ct. M Keyn 35 D4
Wavell Gdns. Slough 197 F1
Wavell Rd. Beac 176 A1
Wavendon House Dr. Wave 49 D4
Wavendon Rd. Sal 37 E1
Waveney Cl. N Pag 22 C2
Waverley Rd. Slough 205 E4
Wayside. H Wyc 173 E4
Wayside Gdns. Ger C 188 B2
Wayside Mews. Maid 202 C4
Wealdstone Pl. M Keyn 35 D1
Weasel La. Nwtn L 57 E3
Weatherby. Dun 93 F4
Weathercock Cl. Asp G 49 D3
Weathercock Gdns. Hol G 163 E4
Weathercock La. Asp G 49 E2
Weathercock La. Wbn S 49 E2
Weavers End. Hans 11 D1
Weavers Hill. M Keyn 33 D2
Weavers Rd. Tri 118 C2
Webb Cl. Slough 206 B1
Webster Cl. Maid 202 A3
Webster Cl. Tha 125 F1
Webster Rd. Ayl 116 A3
Wedgewood Ave. M Keyn 22 A1
Wedgewood Dr. Hgh V 162 A3
Weedon Cl. Ger C 177 D1
Weedon Hill. Char 153 E3
Weedon La. Ame 154 A2
Weedon Rd. Ayl 101 E1
Weekes Dr. Slough 205 D2
Weill Rd. Ayl 116 A2
Weir La. Bktn 81 D2
Weir La. E Clay 74 C3
Weir La. Whit 86 C3
Welbeck Ave. Ayl 116 B3
Welbeck Rd. Maid 202 B3
Welby Cl. Maid 202 A2
Welden. Slough 206 B4
Welders La. C St G 177 D2
Welders La. Ger C 177 D2
Welders La. Se Gr 177 D2
Welford Way. Cudd 112 C2
Well Head Rd. Tott 93 E3
Well La. Wing 79 F1
Well St. Buck 52 B4
Welland Cl. Slough 212 A4
Welland Dr. N Pag 22 C2
Welland Rd. Ayl 115 E3
Wellbank. Tapl 196 C1
Wellbrook Mews. Tri 119 D2
Wellcroft. Ivin 105 F3
Wellcroft Rd. Slough 205 D3
Weller Cl. Ame 154 C1
Welles Rd. H Wyc 173 F4
Wellesbourne Gdns. H Wyc 162 B1
Wellesley Rd. Slough 206 A2
Welley Ave. Wray 211 F2
Welley Rd. Hort 211 F1
Welley Rd. Wray 211 F1
Wellfield. Ty Gr 163 D2
Wellfield Ct. M Keyn 35 E4
Wellfield Rd. La En 171 D4
Wellhouse Rd. Maid 195 F1
Wellhouse Way. Wal A 161 F3
Wellingborough Rd. Oln 6 C3
Wellington Ave. P Ris 139 D2
Wellington Pl. Ayl 115 F2
Wellington Pl. M Keyn 58 A4
Wellington Rd. Ayl 115 F2
Wellington Rd. H Wyc 172 C3
Wellington Rd. Maid 202 B4
Wellington Rd. Uxb 201 E2
Wellington St. Slough 206 A2
Wells Cl. Wind 210 A4
Welsh La. Chac 40 B3
Welton Rd. Ayl 116 A4
Wendover Rd. Ayl 116 B2
Wendover Rd. Bou E 185 D3
Wendover Rd. Burn 204 A4
Wendover Rd. S Man 116 B2
Wendover Rd. Slough 204 A4
Wendover Rd. Wen 116 B2
Wendover St. H Wyc 172 C4
Wendover Way. Ayl 115 F3
Wendover Way. H Wyc 173 D3
Wenlack Cl. Den 190 A1
Wentworth Ave. Slough 198 A1
Wentworth Cl. H Wyc 173 E4
Wentworth Cres. Maid 202 B3
Wentworth Way. M Keyn 57 E4
Wenwell Cl. Dra B 118 A2
Werth Dr. Asp H 49 D1
Wescott Way. Uxb 201 E2
Wesley Hill. Ches 144 A1
Wessex Rd. Bou E 185 D1
Wessex Rd. Harm 213 E2
Wessex Way. Maid 202 A2
Wessons Hill. Cook 195 E4
West Acres. Ame 165 E4
West Ave. Ty Gr 163 E1
West Cl. Medm 193 E4
West Comm. Ger C 188 B3
West Common Cl. Ger C 188 C3
West Common Rd. Uxb 201 E3
West Cres. Wind 209 F3
West Dales. M Keyn 34 B3
West Dean. Maid 202 C4
West Dr. H Wyc 173 E4
West Drayton Pk A. W Dra 208 C2
West Drayton Rd. Uxb 208 C4
West Edge. M Gib 71 F1
West End. W Tur 116 C1
West End Ct. Sto P 198 C2
West End La. Sto P 198 C2
West End Rd. Ched 104 C4
West End Rd. H Wyc 172 C4
West End St. H Wyc 172 C4
West Furlong. Pad 53 D1
West Hill. Asp G 49 E2
West Hyde La. C St P 178 A2
West La. Bled 138 A1
West La. Emb 13 F4
West Leith. Has 118 C1
West Rd. Berk 135 D3
West Rd. Cran 24 B1
West Rd. Maid 202 C4
West Rd. W Dra 208 C2
West Rd. Wbn S 49 D3
West Ridge. Bou E 185 D2
West Side Rise. Oln 6 C2
West St. Adsk 53 F1
West St. Ayl 101 E1
West St. Buck 41 E1
West St. Dun 93 F4
West St. Hen-O-T 191 E1
West St. L Buzz 80 C4
West St. Maid 202 C4
West St. Mar 183 E1
West St. Oln 6 C2
West St. Stp Cl 63 E1
West View. Ches 144 B1
West Way. Beac 174 C1
West Waye. H Wyc 162 B1
West Well Cl. Ting 51 D3
West Well La. Ting 51 D3
West Wycmb Hl R. H Wyc 160 C1
West Wycombe Rd. H Wyc 161 E1
Westanley Ave. Ame 165 E4
Westborough Ct. Maid 202 B3
Westborough Rd. Maid 202 B3
Westbourne St. H Wyc 172 C4
Westbrook. Holy 203 F1
Westbrook End. Nwtn L 57 E2
Westbury Cl. N Pag 22 A2
Westbury La. N Pag 22 A3
Westcliffe. M Keyn 33 E1
Westcroft. Slough 198 A1
Westdean La. Char 143 E2
Western Ave. Buck 41 E1
Western Ave. N Den 201 E4
Western Ave. Uxb 201 E4
Western Dene. Hol G 163 D3
Western Dr. Bou E 185 F3
Western Dr. Hans 11 D2
Western La. Wins 65 F2
Western Perimeter Rd. Harm 213 D2
Western Perimeter Rd. Stan 213 D2
Western Rd. G Hrwd 55 D2
Western Rd. M Keyn 33 E3
Western Rd. M Keyn 47 E1
Western Rd. Tri 118 C2
Westfield. H Hea 153 E2
Westfield. Slough 198 A1
Westfield Ave. Dean 31 E3
Westfield Cotts. Medm 192 C3
Westfield Rd. Beac 175 E1
Westfield Rd. Berk 134 C3
Westfield Rd. Dun 93 F4
Westfield Rd. M Keyn 58 B4
Westfield Rd. Maid 202 A4
Westfield Wlk. H Wyc 172 B3
Westfields. Buck 52 A4
Westfields. P Ris 139 E2
Westgate Ct. H Wyc 174 A2
Westhill. M Keyn 34 B4
Westhope Rd. Mar 183 F2
Westland Cl. Stan 213 F1
Westlands Rd. Lac G 149 F3
Westmead. P Ris 139 D3
Westmead. Wind 210 A2
Westminster Cl. Brac 38 A4
Westminster Cl. H Wyc 173 D2
Westminster Cres. Brac 38 A4
Westminster Dr. Ayl 115 F3
Westminster Dr. M Keyn 47 D1
Westmorland Ave. Ayl 116 A3
Westmorland Rd. Maid 202 B3
Westmount Ave. Ame 165 E4
Weston Ct. Ast C 117 E3
Weston La. G Has 136 C4
Weston Rd. Ast C 117 E3
Weston Rd. Lewk 157 D4
Weston Rd. Oln 6 C2
Weston Rd. Rav 5 C1
Weston Rd. Rav 5 F1
Weston Rd. W Und 6 C2
Westover Ct. H Wyc 161 E1
Westover Rd. H Wyc 161 E1
Westpits. Emb 13 F4
Westrick Walk. Pres 151 E3
Westwood. H Wyc 172 A2
Westwood Cl. L Chal 166 B4
Westwood Cl. M Keyn 45 F4
Westwood Dr. L Chal 166 B4
Westwood Rd. Mar 183 E1
Wetherby Gdns. M Keyn 57 E3
Wethered Dr. Burn 204 A4
Wethered Rd. Mar 183 E1
Wexham Park La. Iver H 199 E1
Wexham Park La. Sto P 199 E1
Wexham Rd. Slough 206 A3
Wexham St. Sto P 199 D2
Wexham Woods. Slough 206 B4
Wey La. Ches 154 A4
Whaddon Chase. Ayl 101 E1
Whaddon Rd. Mur 67 E4
Whaddon Rd. N Pag 22 A2
Whaddon Rd. Nash 44 A1
Whaddon Rd. Nwtn L 57 E2
Whaddon Rd. She B E 46 A2
Whaddon Way. M Keyn 46 C1
Whales La. M Gib 71 F1
Whalley Dr. M Keyn 47 D1
Wharf Cl. Wen 131 D3
Wharf La. Berk 134 B4
Wharf La. Hen-O-T 191 F1
Wharf La. Old S 32 B4
Wharf Rd. Wen 131 D3
Wharf View. Buck 41 F1
Wharfside. M Keyn 47 F1
Whatmore Cl. Stan 213 D1
Wheatfield Cl. Maid 202 A2
Wheatlands Rd. Slough 206 B2
Wheatley Way. C St P 177 F2
Wheeler Ave. Ty Gr 174 B4
Wheeler Rd. Chin 147 E3
Wheelers La. M Keyn 34 A3
Wheelers Orchard. C St P 177 F2
Wheelwright Mews. M Keyn 34 C3
Wheelwright Rd. Lgwk 138 B4
Wheelwrights. W Tur 116 C1
Whetstone Cl. M Keyn 34 A2
Whichcote Gdns. Ches 154 B3
Whichert Cl. Beac 175 E3
Whichford. M Keyn 22 A1
Whielden Cl. Ame 165 D4
Whielden Green. Ame 165 D4
Whielden La. Ame 165 D3
Whielden La. Cole 164 C3
Whielden St. Ame 165 D4
Whincup Cl. H Wyc 172 C2
Whinneys Rd. Loud 174 B2
Whipass Hill. Beac 176 A3
Whipsnade Rd. Dun 93 F3
Whitby Cl. M Keyn 47 D1
Whitby Rd. Slough 205 E3
Whitchurch Cl. Maid 195 F2
Whitchurch Cl. Wcot 98 A4
Whitchurch La. Oving 86 C4
Whitchurch Rd. Cub 78 A1
White Alder. M Keyn 33 F3
White Cl. H Wyc 161 E1
White Cl. Slough 205 E3
White Cres. Hal 131 E4
White Hart. Lud 96 A4
White Hart La. Hadd 127 D3
White Hart Meadow. Beac 175 F1
White Hart Rd. Maid 202 C4
White Hart Rd. Slough 205 E2
White Hill. Ash Gr 145 E4
White Hill. Beac 185 F4
White Hill. Ches 144 B1
White Hill. H Wyc 162 A1
White Hill. Rem H 192 A1
White Hill. Woo G 185 F4
White Hill Cl. Ches 144 B1
White Horse Dr. M Keyn 46 B1
White Horse La. Whit 87 D3
White Horse Rd. Wind 209 E3
White House Cl. C St P 177 F2
White Lilies Island. Wind 210 A4
White Lion Cl. Ame 166 A4
White Lion Rd. Ame 166 A4
White Lion Rd. L Chal 166 A4
White Lodge Cl. Mar B 183 E3
White Paddock. Maid 202 A1
Whitebaker Ct. M Keyn 34 C3
Whitecross Rd. Hadd 126 C3
Whitefield La. G Mis 152 A3
Whiteford Rd. Slough 205 F4
Whitegate Cross. M Keyn 47 D3
Whitehall Cl. Uxb 201 E2
Whitehall La. Wray 212 A1
Whitehall Rd. Uxb 201 E2
Whitehall St. Ayl 101 E1
Whitehill. Berk 135 E3
Whitehill. Oln 6 C3
Whitehill Ct. Berk 135 E3
Whitehills Cl. Mar B 183 E3
Whitehorns. N Pag 22 A2
Whitehouse Cl. Woo G 174 C1
Whitehouse La. Woo G 174 C1
Whitehouse Way. Iver H 200 B1
Whitelands Ave. Chor 167 D3
Whitelands Rd. H Wyc 172 B4
Whitelands Way. H Wyc 172 B4
Whiteleaf Way. P Ris 139 E3
Whiteley. Wind 209 F4
Whiteley Cres. M Keyn 57 F3
Whitepit La. Fla H 185 E4
Whites La. Datch 211 D4
Whitethorn Ave. W Dra 208 C3
Whitethorn Pl. W Dra 208 C3
Whitewood Rd. Berk 135 D2
Whitfield Rd. Hgh V 162 A3
Whitfield Way. Chor 167 F1
Whitley Cl. Stan 213 F1
Whitsun Pasture. M Keyn 35 D4
Whittaker Rd. Slough 197 F1
Whittenham Cl. Slough 206 A3
Whitworth La. M Keyn 46 A4
Whurley Way. Maid 195 F1
Whyteladyes La. Cook 195 F3
Whytingham Rd. Tri 119 E2
Wick Rd. Wigg 133 E4
Wicken Rd. Leck 30 C1
Widbrook Rd. Maid 196 A2
Widdenton View. La En 171 E3
Widmere Field. Pres 151 E3
Widmere La. Mar B 183 D1
Widmore Cl. Char 143 F3
Widnell La. Pidd (B) 95 E4
Wigmore Rd. Ayl 101 D1
Wilderness The. Berk 135 E2
Wilford Rd. Slough 206 C1
Wilfrids Wood Cl. Bou E 185 D3
Willen La. M Keyn 34 C4
Willen Park Ave. M Keyn 35 D4
Willen Rd. M Keyn 35 F2
Willen Rd. N Pag 22 B2
Willetts La. Den 200 C4
Willey Ct. M Keyn 32 C2
William Burt Cl. W Tur 116 C1
William Ellis Cl. Old W 211 D1
William Hill Dr. Bier 102 B2
William Moulder Ct. Ches 144 A2
William St. Berk 135 E2
William St. Slough 205 F3
William St. Wind 210 B3
Williams Circ. Walt 48 A2
Williams Cl. Ayl 101 E1
Williams Cl. Hans 10 C2
Williams Way. Lgwk 138 B3
Williiam Smith Cl. M Keyn 35 E2
Willis Rd. Hadd 127 D3
Willoners. Slough 205 D4
Willoughby's Wlk. H Wyc 161 E1
Willow Ave. H Wyc 172 A2
Willow Ave. N Den 201 E3
Willow Ave. W Dra 208 C3
Willow Chase. Ty Gr 162 C2
Willow Cl. Fla H 185 E3
Willow Cl. Iver 212 B4
Willow Cres E. N Den 201 E4
Willow Cres W. N Den 201 E4
Willow Ct. H Wyc 173 F2
Willow Ct. Wal A 161 E4
Willow Dr. Buck 52 C4
Willow Dr. Maid 203 D1
Willow Gr. Old S 32 A3
Willow La. Ame 165 F3
Willow Park. Sto P 199 D3
Willow Pl. Eton 210 B4
Willow Rd. Ayl 101 E1
Willow Rd. Brac 38 A3
Willow Rd. Chin 147 E3
Willow Rd. G Hrwd 55 D2
Willow Rd. Stan 212 C3
Willow Rd. Tha 125 F1
Willow Rise. Hadd 127 D4
Willow Way. Loud 174 A1
Willow Way. M Keyn 58 B4
Willow Way. P Ris 139 D2
Willow Way. Wing 79 F2
Willow Wlk. Ty Gr 163 D2
Willowbrook. Slough 205 E1
Willowford. M Keyn 33 F3
Willowmead. Sto 114 C3
Willowmead Sq. Mar 183 C2
Willowmead Cl. Mar 183 C2
Willowmead Cl. Mar 183 F2
Willowmead Gdns. Mar 183 C2
Willows Rd. Bou E 185 D2
Willows The. Ame 154 A2
Willows The. Lgwk 138 C3
Wilmar Cl. Uxb 201 E3
Wilmot Rd. Burn 197 D1
Wilson Ct. She C E 45 F4
Wilton Ave. M Keyn 58 A4
Wilton Cl. Harm 213 E4
Wilton Cres. Beac 175 F2
Wilton Cres. Wind 209 E2
Wilton La. Se Gr 176 C2
Wilton Rd. Beac 175 F2
Wiltshire Ave. Slough 198 B1
Wiltshire Rd. Mar 183 F2
Wimbledon Pl. M Keyn 34 B2
Wimpole Rd. W Dra 208 B3
Winbury Ct. Maid 202 C4
Wincanton Hill. M Keyn 57 E3
Winchbottom La. Lit M 184 A3
Winchendon Rd. Chea 112 A1
Winchester Cl. Stan 212 C3
Winchester Ct. Loud 174 A2
Winchester Dr. Maid 202 A2
Windemere Dr. M Keyn 58 B3
Windermere Cl. Ayl 116 A3
Windermere Cl. Chor 167 E2
Windermere Gdns. L Buzz 80 B4
Windermere Way. W Dra 208 C3
Windmill Cl. Buck 41 F1
Windmill Cl. Ivin 105 F3
Windmill Cl. Wind 210 A3
Windmill Dr. Hol G 162 C3
Windmill Hill. Chipf 156 C4
Windmill Hill. Cole 164 C1
Windmill Hill. P Ris 139 D1
Windmill Hill Dr. M Keyn 57 E4
Windmill La. Hol G 162 C4
Windmill Rd. Cook 195 F3
Windmill Rd. Fulm 199 E4
Windmill Rd. Ger C 177 E2
Windmill Rd. Hadd 126 C3
Windmill Rd. Slough 205 E3
Windmill Rd. Tha 126 C1
Windmill St. Bri 96 A1
Windmill Way. Cran 25 E2
Windmill Way. Tri 118 C2
Windmill Wood. Ame 154 A1
Windrush Cl. Ick 201 F4
Windrush Ct. H Wyc 173 F4
Windrush Dr. H Wyc 173 F3
Windrush Way. Maid 202 C4
Windsor Ave. L Buzz 80 C4
Windsor Ave. N Pag 22 B2
Windsor Cl. Bov 146 A2
Windsor Cres. Loud 174 B1
Windsor Dr. H Wyc 162 B1
Windsor End. Beac 186 C4
Windsor Hill. Bou E 185 F3
Windsor Hill. P Ris 139 E3
Windsor La. Burn 197 E1
Windsor La. L Kin 152 B2
Windsor Rd. Ayl 116 A4

Windsor Rd. Ches ... 144 A2
Windsor Rd. Datch ... 211 D4
Windsor Rd. Ger C ... 188 B2
Windsor Rd. Holy ... 203 E1
Windsor Rd. Maid ... 203 E1
Windsor Rd. Oak G ... 203 E1
Windsor Rd. Slough ... 205 F2
Windsor Rd. Wray ... 211 F1
Windsor St. M Keyn ... 33 E3
Windsor St. M Keyn ... 58 B4
Windsor St. Uxb ... 201 E3
Winemar Cl. Hans ... 11 D2
Wing Cl. Mar ... 183 B1
Wing Rd. Cub ... 78 B1
Wing Rd. L Buzz ... 80 B3
Wing Rd. Stew ... 78 C3
Wingate Ave. H Wyc ... 173 F4
Wingate Circ. Walt ... 48 A2
Wingate Cl. H Wyc ... 173 F4
Wingate Walk. Ayl ... 116 A4
Wingrave Rd. A Abb ... 88 C2
Wingrave Rd. Lon M ... 104 B1
Wingrave Rd. Tri ... 119 D3
Winkers Cl. C St P ... 177 F1
Winkers La. C St P ... 177 F2
Winkfield La. Oak G ... 209 D1
Winkfield Rd. Oak G ... 209 F1
Winnock Rd. W Dra ... 208 B3
Winsford Hill. M Keyn ... 46 C2
Winslow Field. G Mis ... 151 F4
Winslow Gdns. H Wyc ... 174 A4
Winslow Rd. G Hrwd ... 54 C1
Winslow Rd. Gran ... 75 F4
Winslow Rd. L Hrwd ... 55 E1
Winslow Rd. Mur ... 67 D2
Winslow Rd. Nash ... 55 E4
Winslow Rd. Swan ... 66 C2
Winslow Rd. Win ... 89 D2
Winstane Cl. Ame ... 154 A3
Winstanley La. She B E ... 46 B2
Winston Gdns. Berk ... 134 C2
Winter Hill. Cook ... 184 B1
Winter Hill Rd. Cook ... 195 D2
Winter Hill Rd. Maid ... 195 D2
Winterburn. M Keyn ... 34 A3
Winters Way. Hol G ... 163 E4
Winterton Dr. Ayl ... 115 F2
Wintoun Path. Slough ... 197 F1
Winvale. Slough ... 205 F2
Winwood. Slough ... 206 B4
Winwood Dr. Qntn ... 85 D3
Wise La. W Dra ... 208 B1
Wisley Ave. M Keyn ... 34 B2
Witan Gate. M Keyn ... 34 B1
Witchell. Wen ... 131 D2
Witham Way. Ayl ... 115 E2
Witheridge La. Ty Gr ... 175 D4
Withey Cl. Wind ... 209 F3
Withington. M Keyn ... 34 A3
Withy Croft. Slough ... 206 C4
Withycombe. M Keyn ... 46 C2
Witney Cl. Ick ... 201 F4
Wittmills Oak. Buck ... 41 F1
Woad La. M Keyn ... 34 C4
Woburn Ave. M Keyn ... 33 E3
Woburn La. Asp G ... 49 F2
Woburn Rd. Asp H ... 49 E1
Woburn Rd. Hth ... 60 B1
Woburn Sands Rd. B Bkhl ... 48 B2
Wodehouse Wlk. N Pag ... 22 A3
Wolf La. Wind ... 209 C2
Wolsey Gdns. M Keyn ... 34 A2
Wolstan Cl. Den ... 190 A1
Wolverton Rd. Have ... 20 B1
Wolverton Rd. Have ... 20 B1
Wolverton Rd. M Keyn ... 21 F1
Wooburn Common La. Tapl ... 186 A2
Wooburn Green La. Beac ... 186 A4
Wooburn Mnr Pk. Bou E ... 185 F3
Wooburn Mews. Bou E ... 185 F3
Wood Cl. Wind ... 210 B2
Wood End. L Hrwd ... 55 F1
Wood End. Nash ... 55 E4
Wood End Cl. Far C ... 187 E1
Wood End La. Moul ... 23 F1
Wood La. Asp G ... 49 E2
Wood La. M Keyn ... 34 C4
Wood La. Pott ... 18 C2
Wood La. S Hea ... 152 C4
Wood La. Slough ... 205 D2
Wood La. W Und ... 6 A1
Wood Lane Cl. Iver H ... 200 A1
Wood Pond Cl. Se Gr ... 176 B2
Wood Rd. Harr ... 3 F4
Wood St. M Keyn ... 33 F4
Wood St. Wadd ... 99 D4
Wood St. Wbn S ... 49 D2
Wood Way. Beac ... 174 C1
Woodbank Ave. Ger C ... 188 B3
Woodchester Park. Beac ... 175 E3
Woodcock. Wal A ... 161 D4
Woodcote. Maid ... 202 B3
Woodcote Green. H Wyc ... 161 E1
Woodcote Lawns. Ches ... 144 A2
Woodcroft Rd. Ches ... 144 B2
Woodfield. Lac G ... 149 E3
Woodfield Rd. P Ris ... 139 E2
Woodfield Dr. Maid ... 202 A3
Woodfield Park. Ame ... 154 A2
Woodford Way. Slough ... 198 A1
Woodhall Cl. Uxb ... 201 E4
Woodhill Ave. Ger C ... 189 D3
Woodhurst Dr. Den G ... 189 F3
Woodhurst Rd. Maid ... 196 A1
Woodland Ave. L Buzz ... 70 C1
Woodland Ave. Slough ... 205 E3
Woodland Ave. Wind ... 209 F2
Woodland Cl. H Wyc ... 172 B3
Woodland Cl. Mar ... 183 F2
Woodland Cl. Tri ... 118 C1
Woodland La. Chor ... 167 E3
Woodland Rd. Map Cr ... 178 B3
Woodland View. Ches ... 154 B3
Woodland View. M Keyn ... 33 E3
Woodland Way. Mar ... 183 F2
Woodlands. Ger C ... 188 C3
Woodlands. Hedg ... 187 E1
Woodlands Ave. Berk ... 135 E2
Woodlands Cl. Ger C ... 189 D3
Woodlands Cl. Hol G ... 163 E3
Woodlands Cres. Buck ... 41 E1
Woodlands Dr. Beac ... 175 E2
Woodlands Dr. Wal A ... 161 E4
Woodlands Glade. Beac ... 175 E2
Woodlands Glade. Far C ... 187 E1
Woodlands Hill. Beac ... 186 C3
Woodlands Park Ave. Maid ... 202 A1
Woodlands Park Rd. Maid ... 202 A2
Woodlands Pk R. Whi Wa ... 202 A2
Woodlands The. Ame ... 154 B2
Woodlands The. Ty Gr ... 162 C2
Woodlane Cl. Fla H ... 173 E1
Woodley Headland. M Keyn ... 47 E4
Woodley Hill. Ches ... 154 B3
Woodman Cl. Wing ... 79 F2
Woodmoor End. Cook ... 196 A4
Woodpiece Rd. U Arn ... 94 C4
Woodruff Ave. M Keyn ... 34 C2
Woodrush Cl. M Keyn ... 47 D2
Woods Pl. Wen ... 131 D2
Woodside. Asp G ... 49 E2
Woodside. Eat B ... 92 C3
Woodside. Fla H ... 185 E3
Woodside. M Keyn ... 32 C3
Woodside Ave. Ame ... 154 B2
Woodside Ave. Beac ... 175 E2
Woodside Ave. Fla H ... 185 E4
Woodside Cl. Beac ... 175 E2
Woodside Cl. Ger C ... 177 F1
Woodside Cl. Loud ... 174 A1
Woodside Hill. C St P ... 177 F1
Woodside Rd. Ame ... 154 B1
Woodside Rd. Beac ... 175 E2
Woodside Rd. H Wyc ... 174 A4
Woodside Way. L Buzz ... 80 B3
Woodside Way. Ty Gr ... 174 B4
Woodstock Ave. Slough ... 206 B1
Woodstock Cl. Ayl ... 116 A3
Woodstock Cl. Maid ... 195 F1
Woodstock Ct. M Keyn ... 34 A4
Woodstock Dr. Ick ... 201 F4
Woodview Dr. Lac G ... 150 B3
Woodville. Chin ... 147 E3
Woodville Cres. Yard G ... 18 C3
Woodway. Lac G ... 149 E3
Woodway. Lac G ... 149 E4
Woodways. Hadd ... 127 D3
Woollerton Cres. Wen ... 131 E3
Woolmans. M Keyn ... 33 D2
Wooton. Ash ... 97 F1
Wootton Way. Maid ... 202 B3
Worcester Cl. Maid ... 202 B2
Worcester Cl. N Pag ... 22 A2
Worcester Rd. Uxb ... 208 B4
Wordsworth Ave. N Pag ... 22 A2
Wordsworth Dr. M Keyn ... 58 A4
Wordsworth Rd. H Wyc ... 173 D3
Wordsworth Rd. Slough ... 197 E1
Wordsworth Way. W Dra ... 208 C1
Worlds End La. Wen ... 130 C4
Worminghall Rd. Ick ... 123 F2
Worminghall Rd. Oak ... 109 E2
Wormsley Cres. Skch ... 158 B2
Worple The. Wray ... 211 F1
Worster Rd. Cook ... 195 F3
Worthies The. Ame ... 165 D4
Worthington Rd. Dun ... 93 F4
Wotton End. Lud ... 96 B4
Wotton Path. Ayl ... 115 F2
Wotton Rd. Ash ... 97 F1
Wren Cl. Buck ... 52 C4
Wren Dr. W Dra ... 208 B2
Wren Rd. Pres ... 151 E3
Wren Wlk. Edle ... 92 C2
Wrensfield. Mar ... 183 B1
Wright. Oak G ... 209 E3
Wright's La. Pres ... 151 E3
Wrights Cl. La En ... 171 D3
Wyatt Cl. H Wyc ... 172 C4
Wyatt Rd. Wind ... 209 E2
Wyatt's Rd. Chor ... 167 F3
Wychwood. L Kin ... 152 A2
Wychwood Gdns. H Wyc ... 172 B3
Wychwood Rise. L Kin ... 152 A2
Wycombe End. Beac ... 175 F1
Wycombe Ind Mall. H Wyc ... 172 C4
Wycombe La. Woo G ... 185 F4
Wycombe Rd. B Bot ... 159 E2
Wycombe Rd. Bled R ... 149 D2
Wycombe Rd. Hol G ... 163 D3
Wycombe Rd. La En ... 159 F1
Wycombe Rd. Lac G ... 149 D2
Wycombe Rd. Mar ... 183 F2
Wycombe Rd. Mar B ... 183 F3
Wycombe Rd. P Ris ... 149 D2
Wycombe Rd. Pres ... 151 E3
Wycombe Rd. Skch ... 159 D2
Wycombe View. Fla H ... 174 A1
Wye Cl. Ayl ... 115 E3
Wye Cl. M Keyn ... 46 C1
Wye Estate. H Wyc ... 173 F3
Wye Rd. Woo G ... 185 E4
Wykeham Gate. Hadd ... 126 C3
Wykeham Rise. Chin ... 147 E3
Wykeham Way. Hadd ... 126 C3
Wykeridge Cl. Ches ... 144 A2
Wymering Rd. Ayl ... 116 B3
Wymers Cl. Burn ... 197 D2
Wymers Wood Rd. Tapl ... 197 D2
Wynbury Dr. H Wyc ... 162 C1
Wyndale Cl. Hen-O-T ... 191 F1
Wyndham Ave. H Wyc ... 161 F1
Wyndham Cres. Burn ... 197 D2
Wyness Ave. L Bkhl ... 59 F3
Wynford Green. Ayl ... 115 F3
Wyngates. L Buzz ... 80 C3
Wyngrave Pl. Beac ... 175 E3
Wynn Gr. Ty Gr ... 163 D2
Wynnstay Gdns. Mar B ... 183 F3
Wynnswick Rd. Se Gr ... 176 B3
Wyre Cl. Hadd ... 127 D3
Wyvern Way. Uxb ... 201 D3

Yardley Ave. Pit ... 105 E2
Yardley Green. Ayl ... 101 F1
Yardley Rd. Cast ... 19 E1
Yardley Rd. Oln ... 6 C3
Yardley Rd. Pott ... 18 C2
Yarrow Pl. M Keyn ... 34 C2
Yarrowside. L Chal ... 166 A4
Ye Meads. Tapl ... 203 F3
Yeates Cl. N Pag ... 21 F3
Yeates Cl. Tha ... 125 F1
Yeomans Dr. M Keyn ... 22 A1
Yew Ave. W Dra ... 208 C3
Yew Tree Cl. Beac ... 175 F1
Yew Tree Cl. Bot ... 145 D1
Yew Tree Cl. Eat B ... 92 C3
Yew Tree Cl. Ivin ... 105 F2
Yew Tree Cl. Maid ... 202 C4
Yew Tree Cl. Nwtn L ... 57 E2
Yew Tree Cl. S Man ... 116 A1
Yew Tree Ct. Bov ... 146 A2
Yew Tree Dr. Hol G ... 162 C3
Yew Tree Rd. Slough ... 206 A2
Yew Wlk. Ty Gr ... 163 D2
Yolsum Cl. Hadd ... 126 C3
York Ave. Slough ... 205 E4
York Ave. Wind ... 210 A3
York Cl. Ame ... 165 F4
York Pl. Ayl ... 115 F4
York Rd. H Wyc ... 172 C2
York Rd. Hen-O-T ... 191 E1
York Rd. M Keyn ... 32 B3
York Rd. Maid ... 203 D4
York Rd. Mar ... 183 B1
York Rd. Uxb ... 201 E3
York Rd. Wind ... 210 A3
Yorke Cl. Ast C ... 117 F3
Youens Rd. H Wyc ... 172 B3
Young Cl. Ayl ... 116 A3

Zealand Ave. Harm ... 213 F4